ASCENT®

CENTER FOR TECHNICAL KNOWLEDGE

CATIA V5-6R2017:
Introduction to Modeling

Learning Guide
1st Edition

ASCENT - Center for Technical Knowledge®
CATIA V5-6R2017: Introduction to Modeling
1st Edition

Prepared and produced by:

ASCENT Center for Technical Knowledge
630 Peter Jefferson Parkway, Suite 175
Charlottesville, VA 22911

866-527-2368
www.ASCENTed.com

Lead Contributor: Scott Hendren

ASCENT - Center for Technical Knowledge is a division of Rand Worldwide, Inc., providing custom developed knowledge products and services for leading engineering software applications. ASCENT is focused on specializing in the creation of education programs that incorporate the best of classroom learning and technology-based training offerings.

We welcome any comments you may have regarding this learning guide, or any of our products. To contact us please email: feedback@ASCENTed.com.

Contents

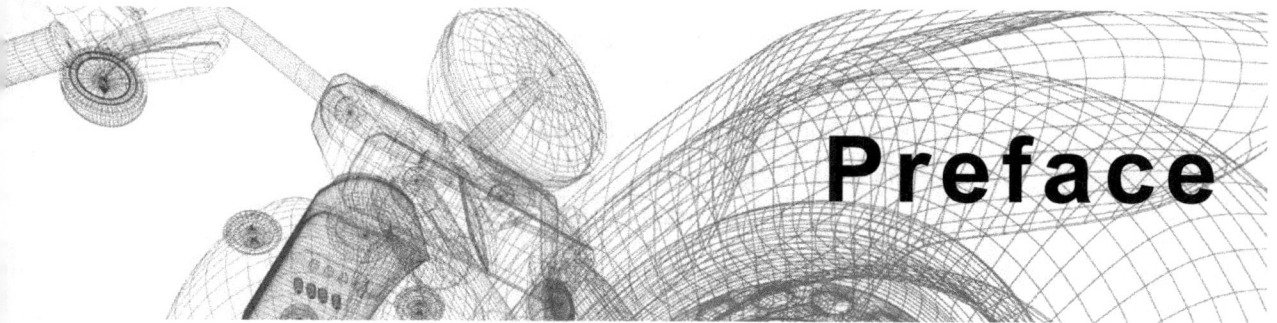

Preface

Using the *CATIA V5-6R2017: Introduction to Modeling* learning guide, you learn the process of designing models with CATIA V5 from conceptual sketching, through to solid modeling, assembly design, and drawing production. Upon completion of this learning guide, you will have acquired the skills to confidently work with CATIA V5. Gain an understanding of the parametric design philosophy of CATIA V5 in this extensive hands-on learning guide. It is expected that all new users of CATIA V5 need to complete this learning guide.

Topics Covered:

- Overview of Parametric Design Process

- Customization of CATIA V5 Environment

- Creating and Constraining Sketch Geometry

- Sketched Feature Techniques and Formulas

- Adding Material with Pad and Shaft Features

- Removing Material with Pocket and Groove Features

- Creating Reference Elements for construction and measurement

- Fillet, Chamfer, Hole, Draft, and Shell Dress-Up Features

- Pattern, Copy, and Mirror Duplication Features

- Thin Features, Stiffeners

- Obtaining Part Information

- Generative Drafting View Creation

- Generative Drafting Dimensioning and Annotation

- Rib and Slot Features

- Multi-sections Solid Features

- Feature Management Using the Hide / Show, Activate / Deactivate Functions

- Parent/Child Relationships and Feature Failure Resolution

- Assembly Design Workbench
- Constraint creation, assembly management, and PDM considerations
- Obtaining Assembly Information (Measure, Clash, and Bill of Materials)
- Standard Parts from Catalogs and Save Management
- Working with Multi-Body Models
- Effective Modeling Tips and Techniques

Note on Software Setup

This learning guide assumes a standard installation of the software using the default preferences during installation. Lectures and practices use the standard software templates and default options for the Content Libraries.

This guide was developed against CATIA V5-6R2017, Service Pack 1.

Lead Contributor: Scott Hendren

Scott Hendren has been a trainer and curriculum developer in the PLM industry for over 20 years, with experience on multiple CAD systems, including Pro/ENGINEER, Creo Parametric, and CATIA. Trained in Instructional Design, Scott uses his skills to develop instructor-led and web-based training products.

Scott has held training and development positions with several high profile PLM companies, and has been with the Ascent team since 2013.

Scott holds a Bachelor of Mechanical Engineering Degree as well as a Bachelor of Science in Mathematics from Dalhousie University, Nova Scotia, Canada.

Scott Hendren has been the Lead Contributor for *CATIA: Introduction to Modeling* since 2013.

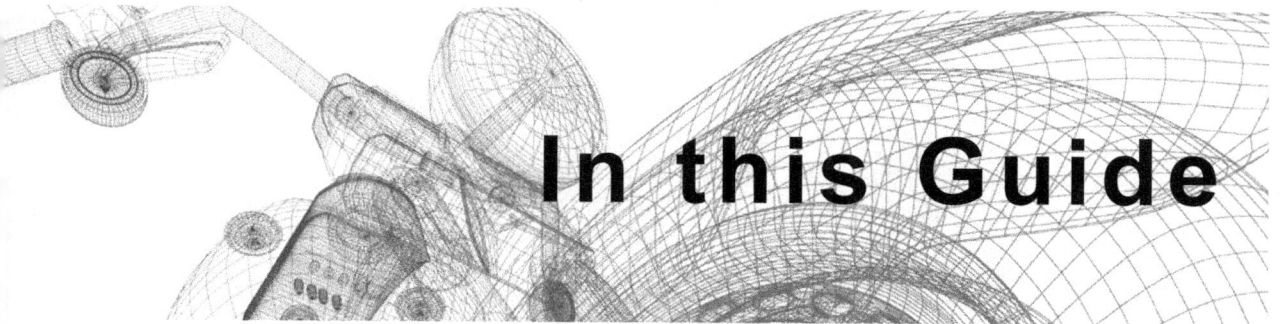

In this Guide

The following images highlight some of the features that can be found in this Learning Guide.

Practice Files

To download the practice files for this student guide, use the following steps:

1. Type the URL shown below into the address bar of your internet browser. The URL must be typed **exactly as shown**. If you are using an ASCENT ebook, you can click on the link to download the file.

   http://www.ASCENTed.com/getfile?id=xxxxxxxx   Address bar
   File   Edit   View   Favorites   Tools   Help

2. Press <Enter> to download the .ZIP file that contains the Practice Files

3. Once the download is complete, unzip the file to a local folder. The unzipped file contains an .EXE file.

4. Double-click on the .EXE file and follow the instructions to automatically install the Practice Files on the C:\ drive of your computer.

   Do not change the location in which the Practice Files folder is installed. Doing so can cause errors when completing the practices in this student guide.

   http://www.ASCENTed.com/getfile?id=xxxxxxxx

FTP link for practice files

Practice Files

The Practice Files page tells you how to download and install the practice files that are provided with this learning guide.

Chapter 1

Getting Started

In this chapter you learn how to start the AutoCAD® software, become familiar with the basic layout of the AutoCAD screen, how to access commands, use your pointing device, and understand the AutoCAD Cartesian workspace. You also learn how to open an existing drawing, view a drawing by zooming and panning, and save your work in the AutoCAD software.

Learning Objectives in this Chapter

- Launch the AutoCAD software and complete a basic initial setup of the drawing environment.
- Identify the basic layout and features of AutoCAD interface including the Ribbon, Drawing Window, and Application Menu.
- Locate commands and launch them using the Ribbon, shortcut menus, Application Menu, and Quick Access Toolbar.
- Locate points in the AutoCAD Cartesian workspace.
- Open and close existing drawings and navigate to the locations.
- Move around a drawing using the mouse, the **Zoom** and **Pan** commands, and the Navigation Bar.
- Save drawings in various formats and set the automatic save options using the **Save** commands.

Learning Objectives for the chapter

Chapters

Each chapter begins with a brief introduction and a list of the chapter's Learning Objectives.

Instructional Content

Each chapter is split into a series of sections of instructional content on specific topics. These lectures include the descriptions, step-by-step procedures, figures, hints, and information you need to achieve the chapter's Learning Objectives.

Side notes

Side notes are hints or additional information for the current topic.

Practice Objectives

Practices

Practices enable you to use the software to perform a hands-on review of a topic.

Some practices require you to use prepared practice files, which can be downloaded from the link found on the Practice Files page.

Chapter Review Questions

Chapter review questions, located at the end of each chapter, enable you to review the key concepts and learning objectives of the chapter.

Practice Files

To download the practice files for this learning guide, use the following steps:

1. Type the URL shown below into the address bar of your Internet browser. The URL must be typed **exactly as shown**. If you are using an ASCENT ebook, you can click on the link to download the file.

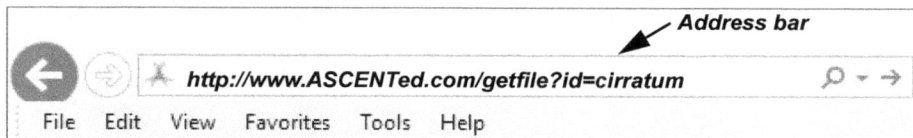

   Address bar

   http://www.ASCENTed.com/getfile?id=cirratum

   File   Edit   View   Favorites   Tools   Help

2. Press <Enter> to download the .ZIP file that contains the Practice Files.

3. Once the download is complete, unzip the file to a local folder. The unzipped file contains an .EXE file.

4. Double-click on the .EXE file and follow the instructions to automatically install the Practice Files on the C:\ drive of your computer.

   Do not change the location in which the Practice Files folder is installed. Doing so can cause errors when completing the practices in this learning guide.

http://www.ASCENTed.com/getfile?id=cirratum

Stay Informed!

Interested in receiving information about upcoming promotional offers, educational events, invitations to complimentary webcasts, and discounts? If so, please visit:

www.ASCENTed.com/updates/

Help us improve our product by completing the following survey:

www.ASCENTed.com/feedback

You can also contact us at: feedback@ASCENTed.com

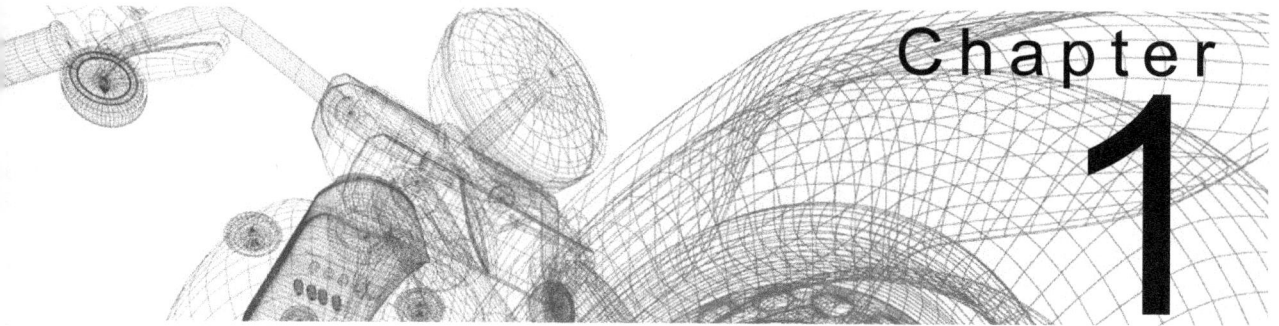

Overview

This chapter provides an overview of solid modeling, where you will use features and parameters to build a model. The relationships created with these features and parameters can be used to establish the design intent on the model. You will learn how CATIA maintains associativity between the model, assemblies, and drawings. You will become familiar with the CATIA user interface and will learn how to customize it, making it more efficient to work with.

Learning Objectives in this Chapter

- Understand the basics of solid modeling.
- Understand feature-based modeling.
- Understand the parametric and associative nature of CATIA.
- Understand how and why you capture a model's design intent during modeling.
- Become familiar with the CATIA user interface.
- Learn how to work with a model by opening it, customizing the display settings, and selecting entities.
- Learn how to access the online help system.

1.1 Fundamentals

Solid Modeling

CATIA is used to create three-dimensional (3D) solid models. The software *understands* that the model is *filled* with material. With a solid model, you can perform the following:

- Obtain the mass properties of a part.

- Determine if components in an assembly interfere with one another.

- Create cross-sections of an assembly or display part cross-sections in a drawing. Instead of manually *drawing* the views on the drawing, you can reference the part model to generate views and show the dimensions from the 3D geometry, as shown in Figure 1–1.

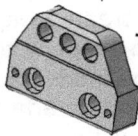

Part model is referenced to create drawing views

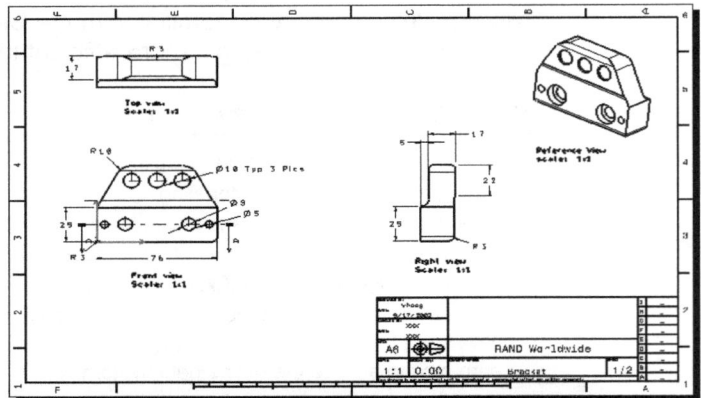

Figure 1–1

This process also applies to assemblies, as shown in Figure 1–2. You can locate existing part and assembly models relative to one another.

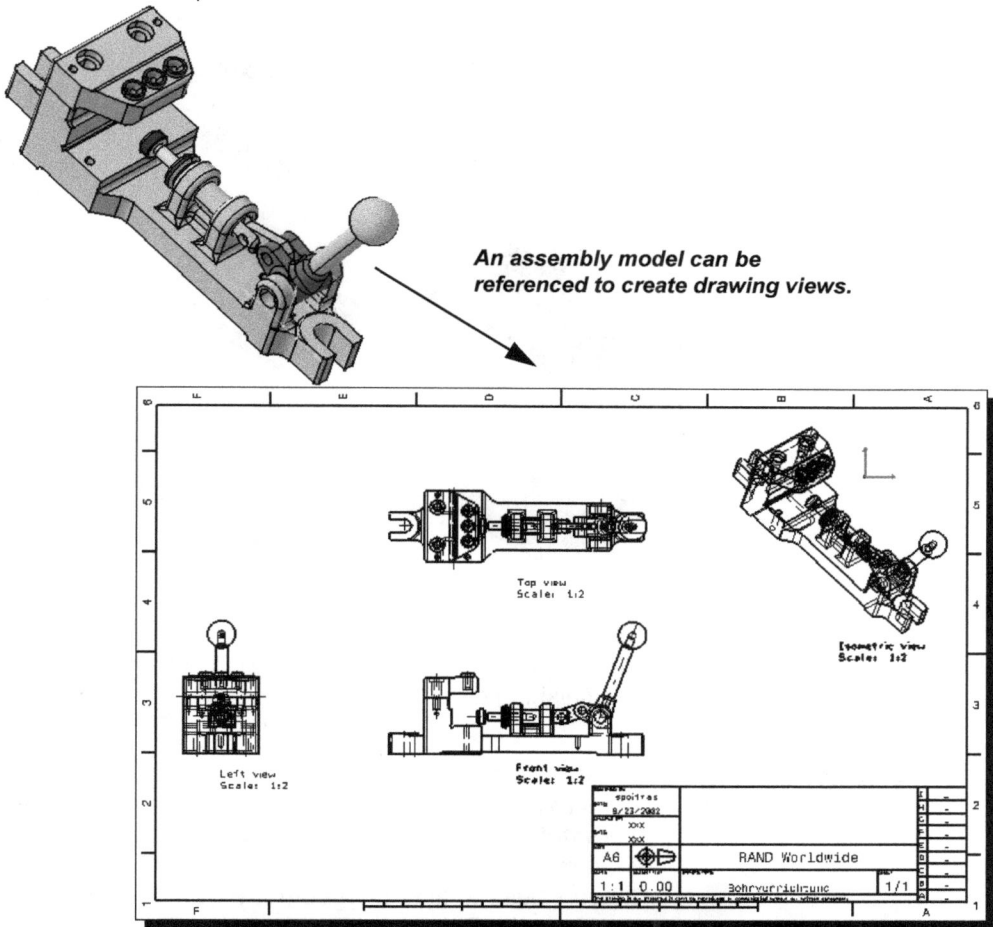

An assembly model can be referenced to create drawing views.

Figure 1–2

Feature-Based

The solid model evolves by creating features, one by one, until the geometry is complete. The part model (shown in Figure 1–3) is constructed by consecutively creating the following features:

1. Create a sketch.
2. Create a Pad feature.
3. Draft several walls of the part using a Draft feature.
4. Remove sharp edges of the geometry by creating a Fillet feature.
5. Create a Shell feature to hollow out the part.

6. Create another Pad feature to act as a cylindrical boss.
7. Center a Hole feature on the cylindrical Pad.
8. Duplicate the boss and hole to create the second boss, as shown in Figure 1–3.

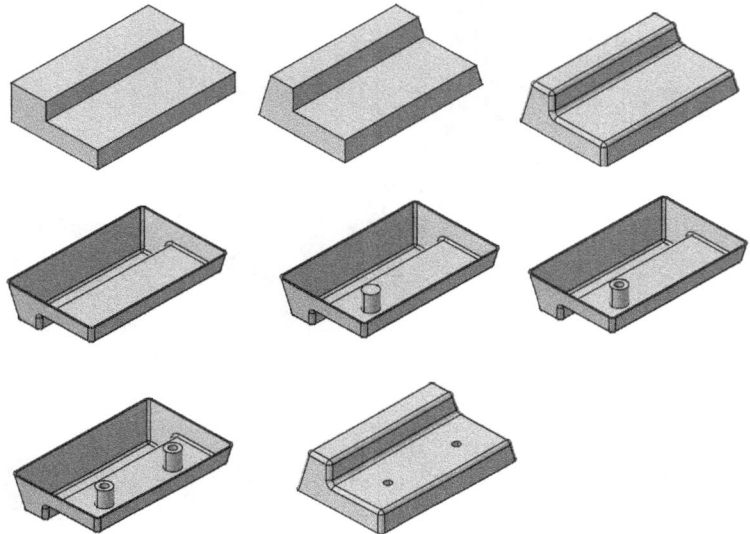

Figure 1–3

You can organize features based on the design intent by initially defining the overall size, major geometric shapes, and then later the finishing details.

Parametric

Features created in CATIA are parametric. All of the dimensional constraints used to define a feature's shape are considered *parameters*, and are accessible at any time. Double-click on a feature to display its dimensional constraints and change any of those values to alter the geometry. The dimensional value that positions the Pocket feature (shown in Figure 1–4) has changed. The position of the feature updates to reflect the design change.

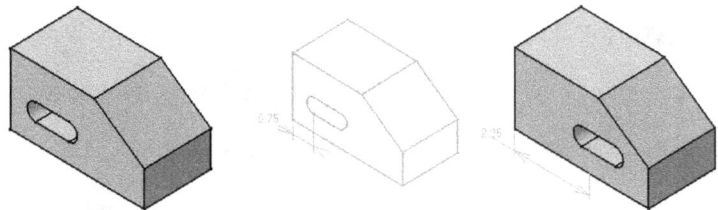

Figure 1–4

Associative

Drawings are created by referencing a model. When the model is changed, any drawings of that model are automatically updated the next time they are opened. Similarly, changing a part model automatically reflects in the assembly. Also, changes made in the assembly update in all other modes in CATIA, as shown in Figure 1–5.

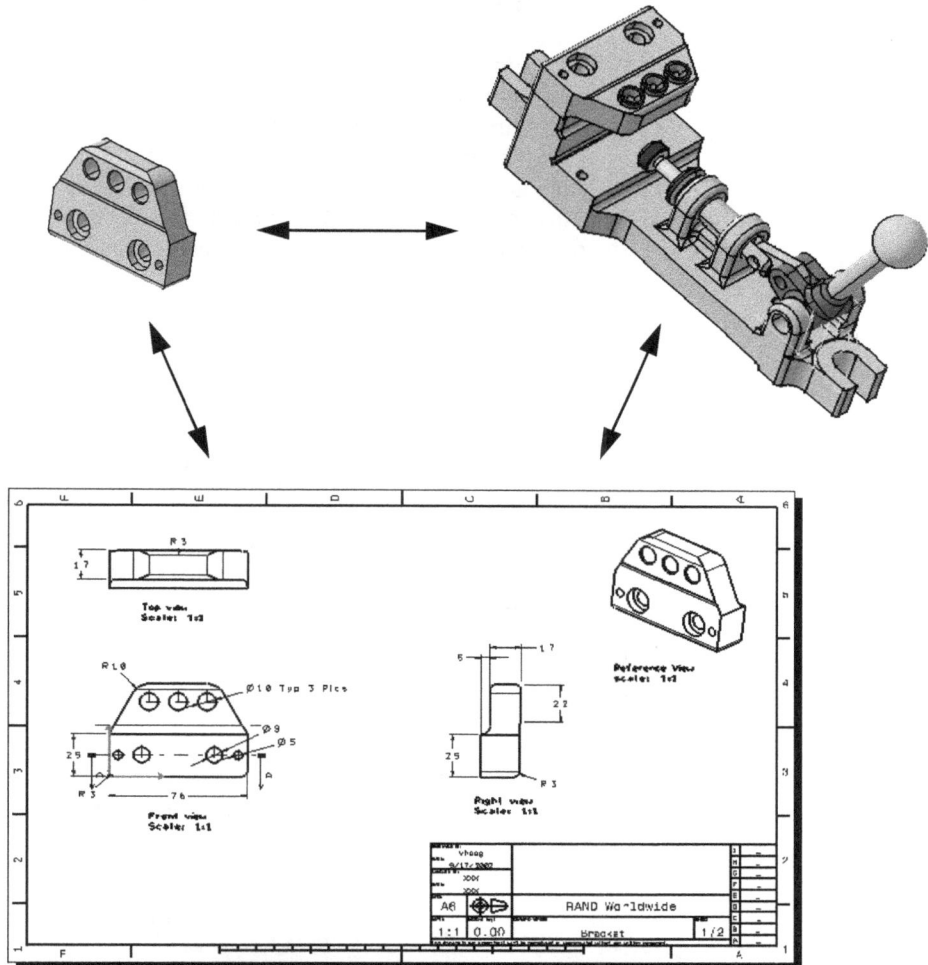

Figure 1–5

Associativity creates a dependency between models. The part models referenced by an assembly and/or drawing must be retrievable to work with the assembly and/or drawing.

1.2 Design Intent

The key to building parametric, feature-based, solid models is to ensure that they have a flexible and predictable behavior. This process is known as capturing *design intent*.

Method 1

One method of capturing design intent is to determine the feature's dimensioning scheme. Figure 1–6 shows an example of a part with a hole. When the Pad feature increases in length, the design intent of the hole determines how it behaves. If the hole is dimensioned to the end of the Pad, the hole moves to remain a distance of 3.00 from that end. If the hole is dimensioned to the face, it remains a distance of 6.00 from that face.

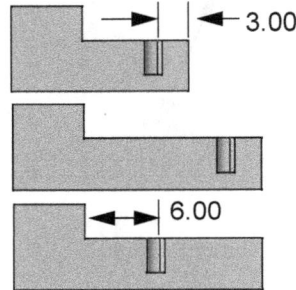

3.00

6.00

Figure 1–6

Method 2

A second method of capturing design intent is to select an option to limit your feature. A part with a hole is shown in Figure 1–7.

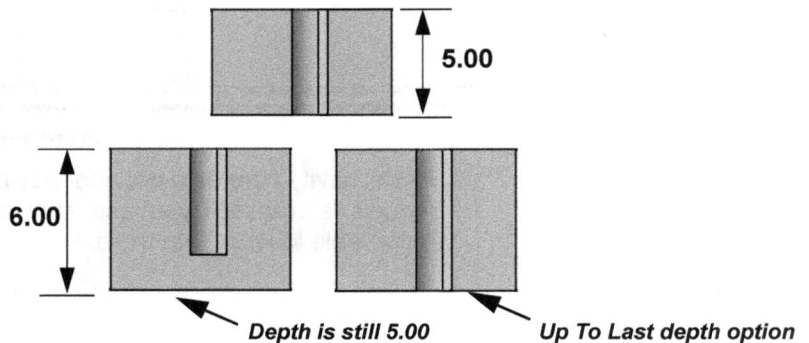

5.00

6.00

Depth is still 5.00   *Up To Last depth option*

Figure 1–7

The design intent is for the hole to pass through the entire model. When the Pad changes from 5.00 to 6.00, the resulting geometry displays differently depending on how the hole is limited. If the hole was created with a depth of 5.00, it no longer passes though the entire part. It must be changed to maintain the design intent. A better solution is to limit the hole using the **Up To Last** option and ensure that it always passes through the part, regardless of the height of the Pad feature.

Method 3

A third method of capturing design intent is to create symmetrical geometry. The design intent for the part (shown in Figure 1–8) is to have the Pocket remain at the center of the part.

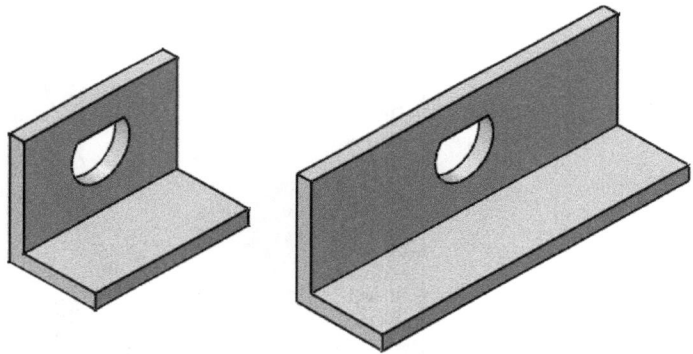

Figure 1–8

Constraining the Pocket from either end of the Pad feature does not capture the design intent. Constructing the Pad and Pocket relative to a center datum reference is preferable.

1.3 User Interface

Screen Layout

When you open a model in CATIA, the screen displays as shown in Figure 1–9. The major areas of the interface that are labeled are discussed in the following topics.

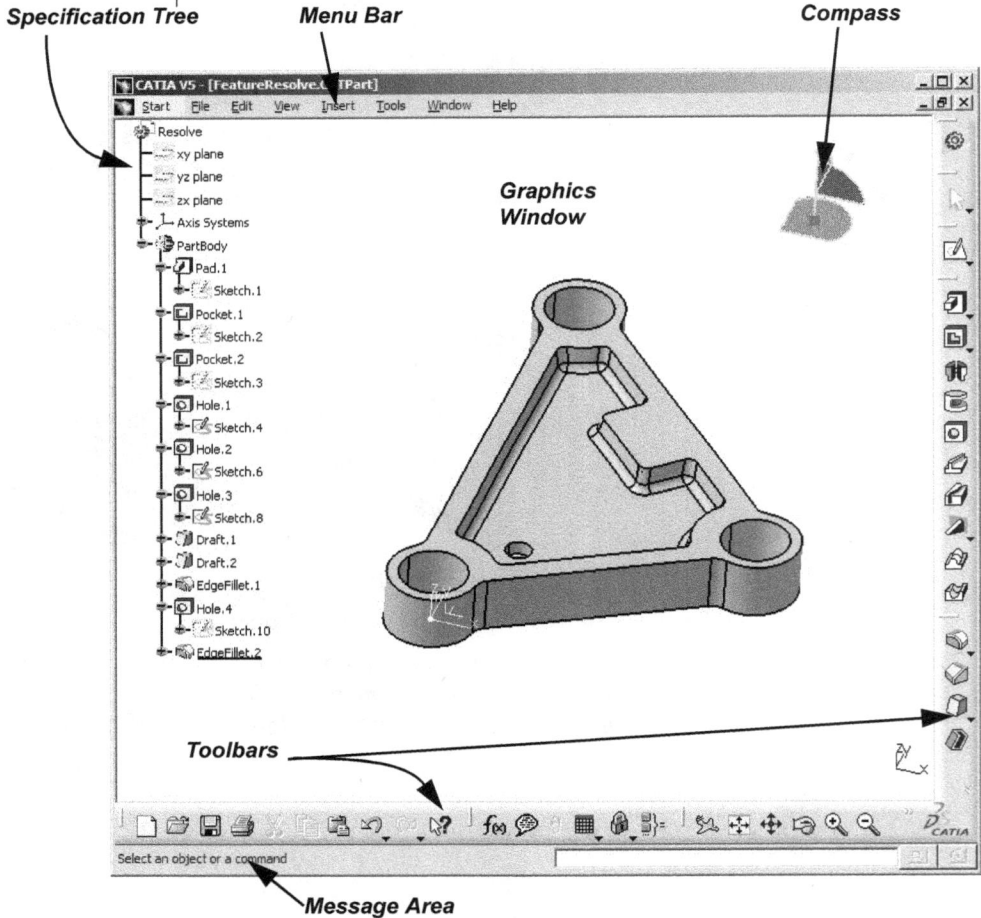

Figure 1–9

Toolbars and Menus

The primary way of interacting with the software is to select icons in the toolbars or commands in the menu bar. You can customize the interface by arranging the location of the toolbars and selecting the icons to display.

Message Area

In many cases, the software displays a single line prompt in the *Message* area, intended to help you perform a certain task. The following are the four messages that correspond to creating the keyhole sketch shown in Figure 1–10.

1. Define the center of the large radius.
2. Define the center of the small radius.
3. Select a point on the key hole profile to define the small radius.
4. Select a point on the key hole profile to define the large radius.

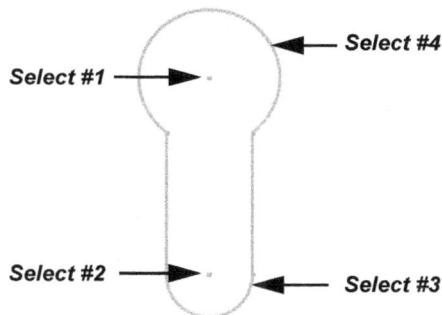

Figure 1–10

Specification Tree

The specification tree is available when working with parts, assemblies, and drawings. It displays a variety of information about the model and displays the features of the part in the order in which they were created, as shown in Figure 1–11. This provides quick access to parameters, functions, materials, and commonly used measurements.

The specification tree can be quickly toggled on and off by pressing <F3>.

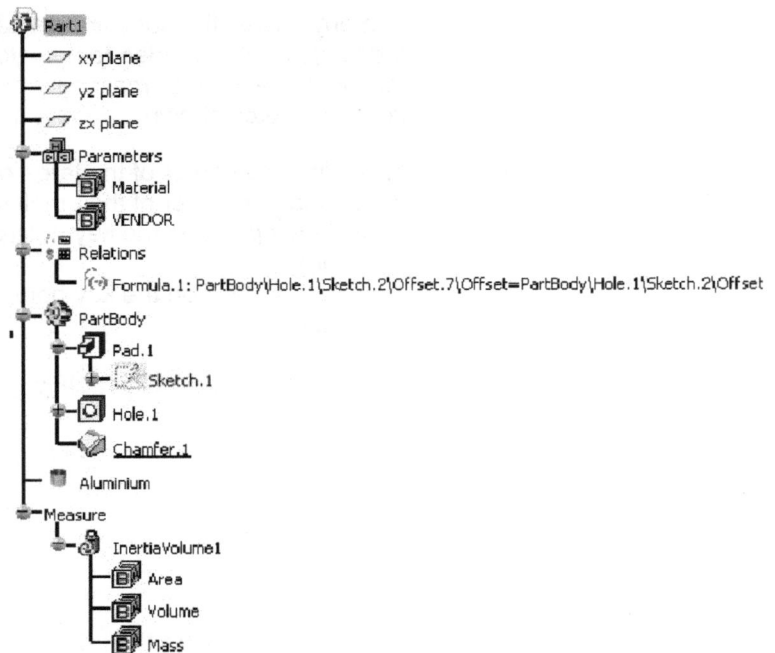

Figure 1–11

Compass

The compass is available for part and assembly models. It displays in the upper right corner of the model window and can perform various functions, as shown in Figure 1–12. The compass is used to:

- Freely rotate the model in all three directions.

- Rotate the model in a plane.

- Pan along one direction.

- Pan in a plane.

- View down an axis direction by selecting the X, Y, or Z letter. Selecting again flips the view in the opposite direction.

Click and drag the ball to rotate the model in all three directions.

Click and drag the arc to rotate the model in the YZ plane only.

Select X, Y, or Z to view down the axis.

Click and drag on the plane to pan the model in the YZ plane only.

Click and drag the straight axis to pan the model along the XY direction.

Figure 1–12

Workbenches

A workbench is a set of tools used to complete certain tasks. The workbenches used in this course are described as follows:

Icon	Workbench
	Sketcher
	Part Design
	Drafting
	Assembly Design

Other workbenches can be used for Analysis, Manufacturing, Digital Mock Up, and other advanced tasks. The active workbench is indicated by an icon in the toolbar, usually in the upper right corner of the screen, as shown in Figure 1–13.

Toolbars for Part Design tasks

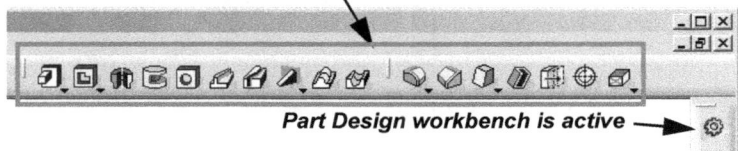

Part Design workbench is active

Figure 1–13

1.4 Working With Models

Opening a Model

Each time you save an object, it overwrites the file with the new information.

Models can be opened by clicking 📁 (Open) and selecting the model from a location on your computer. The file formats you will be working with are listed as follows:

Object	File Extension	Example
Part	.CATPart	**bracket.CATPart**
Drawing	.CATDrawing	**N12345.CATDrawing**
Assembly	.CATProduct	**AXLE.CATProduct**

Rendering a Model

Although you are working with a solid model, you can change how the geometry displays. These options can be accessed through the View Mode toolbar, as shown in Figure 1–14.

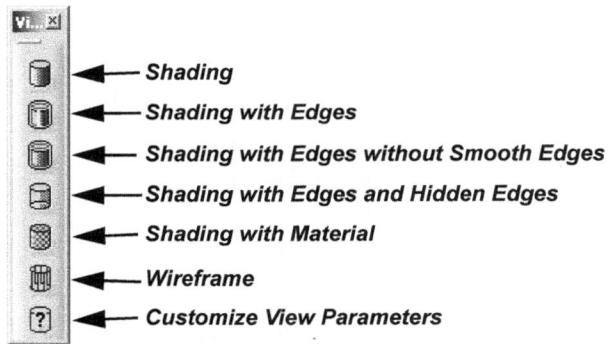

- *Shading*
- *Shading with Edges*
- *Shading with Edges without Smooth Edges*
- *Shading with Edges and Hidden Edges*
- *Shading with Material*
- *Wireframe*
- *Customize View Parameters*

Figure 1–14

To make all icons visible, drag the handle of the flyout menu to the toolbar.

This toolbar is an example of a modal menu. The icon changes to indicate your current View Mode. Each icon contains a flyout menu that expands when you click the down arrow.

Figure 1–15 shows an example of each icon listed in the View Mode toolbar. The **Customized View** option enables you to configure the display to suit your preferences, such as with hidden edges shown, with the material shown, or with faceted faces.

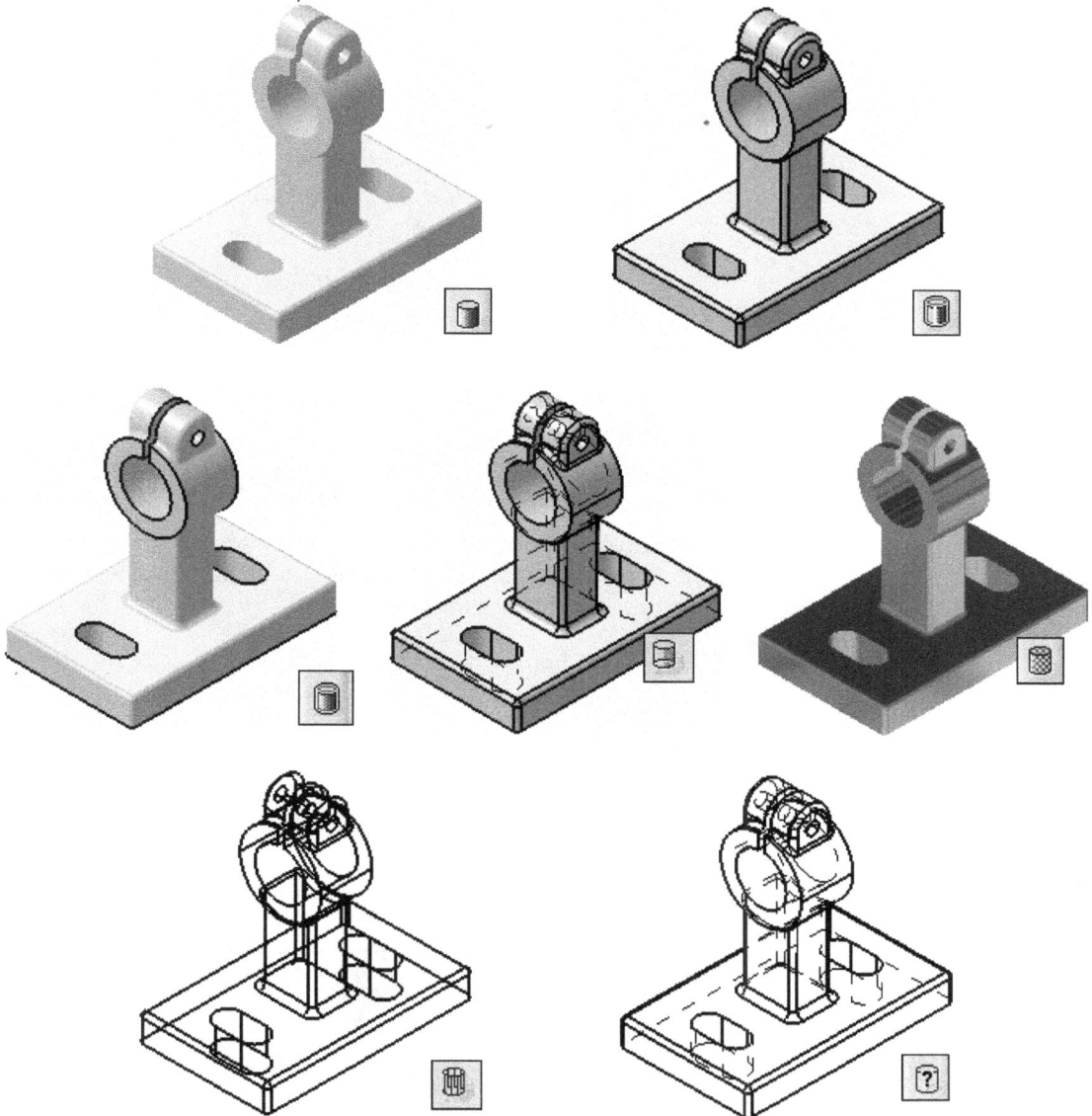

Figure 1–15

Model Navigation

*This toolbar is another example of a modal menu, where the icon changes each time you click a different **Quick View** icon.*

To thoroughly inspect your models, you must learn how to reorient the model, zoom in and out, and pan. There are several methods to navigate a model.

- The Quick Views toolbar contains predefined model orientations enabling you to view the model from commonly used orientations. Figure 1–16 shows the available Quick Views.

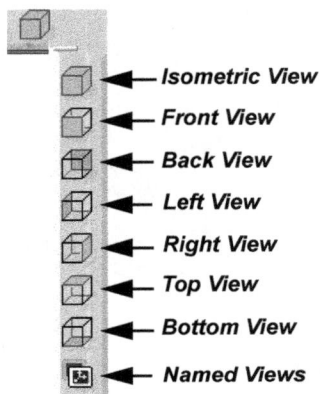

← *Isometric View*
← *Front View*
← *Back View*
← *Left View*
← *Right View*
← *Top View*
← *Bottom View*
← *Named Views*

Figure 1–16

To dynamically navigate the model, you can use specific toolbar icons, menu commands, or mouse shortcuts. The navigation functions are listed as follows:

Icon	Function	Mouse	Menu
	Pan	Hold Middle	**View>Pan**
	Rotate	Hold Middle + Hold Right or Hold Middle + Hold Left	**View>Rotate**
	Zoom	Hold Middle + Click Right or Hold Middle + Click Left	**View>Zoom In Out**
N/A	**Zoom Area**	N/A	**View>Zoom Area**
	Fit All In	N/A	**View>Fit All In**

	Create Multi-view	N/A	**N/A**
N/A	**Re-center on Geometry**	Click Middle on required geometry	**N/A**

Use the **Re-center on Geometry** function to rotate the model around a specific location on the model or geometry. Click the middle mouse button on the required geometry or model location to re-center the model. Then, use the **Rotate** function to spin the model around the centered geometry.

Preselect Navigator

The **Preselect Navigator** tool enables you to select geometric entities that are hidden or difficult to select on a model. The software lists all entities that exist beneath the current cursor position and enables you to scroll through this list to select the required entity.

How To: Use the Preselect Navigator

1. Position the cursor over the geometry that you want to select.
2. Press the <Up Arrow> or <Down Arrow>. The software lists all entities that are beneath the current cursor position, as shown in Figure 1–17. A display window opens, indicating the currently highlighted entity.

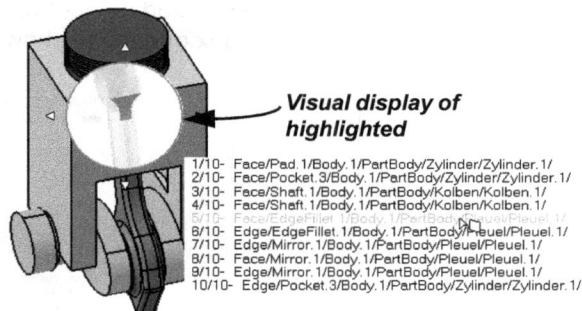

Visual display of highlighted

```
1/10-   Face/Pad.1/Body.1/PartBody/Zylinder/Zylinder.1/
2/10-   Face/Pocket.3/Body.1/PartBody/Zylinder/Zylinder.1/
3/10-   Face/Shaft.1/Body.1/PartBody/Kolben/Kolben.1/
4/10-   Face/Shaft.1/Body.1/PartBody/Kolben/Kolben.1/
5/10-   Face/EdgeFillet.1/Body.1/PartBody/Pleuel/Pleuel.1/
6/10-   Edge/EdgeFillet.1/Body.1/PartBody/Pleuel/Pleuel.1/
7/10-   Edge/Mirror.1/Body.1/PartBody/Pleuel/Pleuel.1/
8/10-   Face/Mirror.1/Body.1/PartBody/Pleuel/Pleuel.1/
9/10-   Edge/Mirror.1/Body.1/PartBody/Pleuel/Pleuel.1/
10/10-  Edge/Pocket.3/Body.1/PartBody/Zylinder/Zylinder.1/
```

Figure 1–17

3. To scroll through the list, continue pressing the <Up Arrow> or <Down Arrow>. Press the <Left Arrow> and <Right Arrow> to navigate the possible selections for the active component only. You can also navigate the list using the cursor.
4. To select an entity for further operation, select it from the list using the cursor or press <Enter>.

An alternative method is as follows:

1. Position the cursor over the geometry that you want to select.
2. Press and hold <Alt> and then select the model. The software lists all of the entities that are beneath the selection point.
3. Right-click to navigate through the possible selections, or move the cursor to make the appropriate selection, as shown in Figure 1–18.

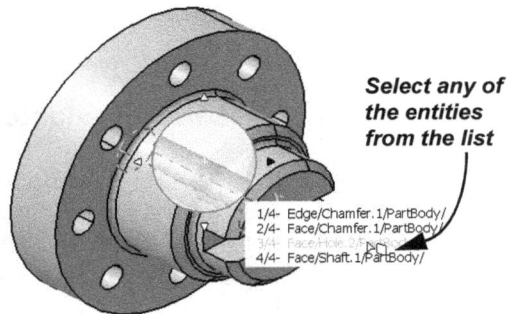

Select any of the entities from the list

1/4- Edge/Chamfer.1/PartBody/
2/4- Face/Chamfer.1/PartBody/
3/4- Face/Hole.2/PartBody/
4/4- Face/Shaft.1/PartBody/

Figure 1–18

This option is controlled through the **Preselect in geometry view** option (**Tools>Options>General>Display>***Navigation* tab).

User-Defined Views

To create a user-defined view, orient the model to the required orientation and select **View>Named Views.** The Named Views dialog box opens, as shown in Figure 1–19.

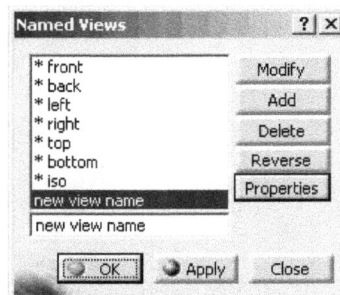

Figure 1–19

• Click **Add**. The name defaults to **Camera 1**. Enter the required name and click **Apply**.

1.5 Online Documentation

Online documentation is very useful and easily accessible. To learn about any function, press <F1> when working with that function. Your Internet browser opens the page where the topic is described, as shown in Figure 1–20.

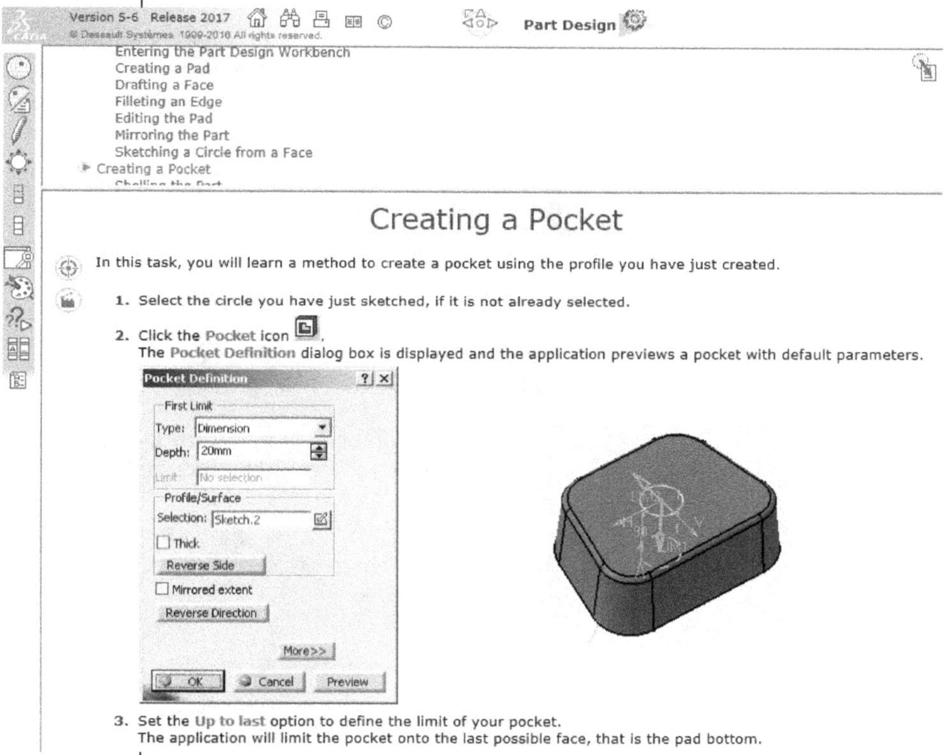

Figure 1–20

Online documentation usually includes structured practices that you can follow to gain hands-on experience with a particular function. At the top of the practice, the name of the component used in the practice displays as a blue hyperlink.

Practice 1a | Viewing a Part

Practice Objectives

- Open a part model and view it from different orientations.
- Change the display settings for the model.
- Investigate associativity between parts, drawings and assemblies.

In this practice, you will open an existing model and work with various visualization tools. You will also change the geometry of a model by editing parameters and deleting features, and note how these changes update in drawings and assemblies.

Task 1 - Open a part and change the display of the model.

1. Click (Open) in the toolbar to open a part.

2. In the File Selection dialog box, select **Flange_Lock.CATPart** and click **Open**.

3. Change the display to **Shading** by selecting the **Shading** icon in the flyout menu, as shown in Figure 1–21.

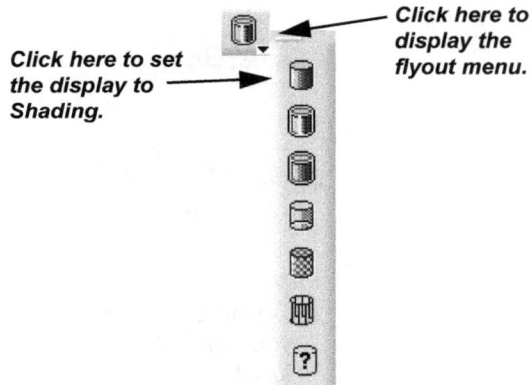

Click here to set the display to Shading.

Click here to display the flyout menu.

Figure 1–21

4. Repeat Step 1 to set the display to 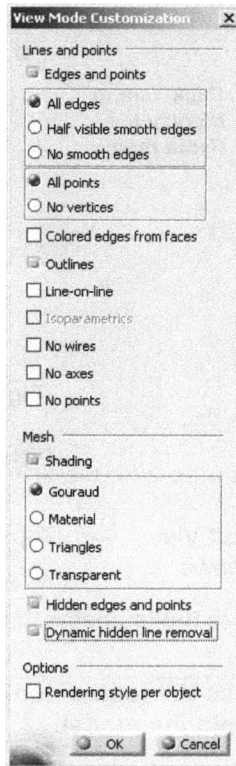 (Shading with
   Edges), (Shading with Material), and (Shading
   With Edges and Hidden Edges).

5. Set the display to (Custom View Parameters).

6. Set the options, as shown in Figure 1–22. Click **OK**. The
   model displays as shown in Figure 1–23.

Figure 1–22

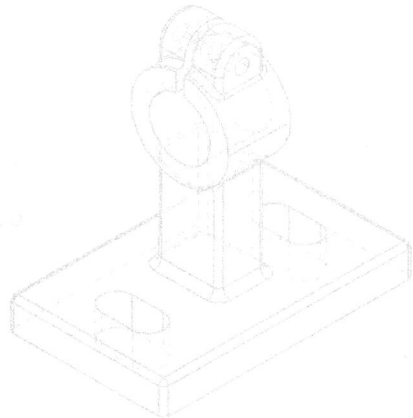

Figure 1–23

Task 2 - Use the Quick Views toolbar to change the model orientation.

1. Click (Shading with Edges) to set the display to **Shading With Edges**.

2. Change the display to **Front** by clicking (Front View) in the flyout menu, as shown in Figure 1–24.

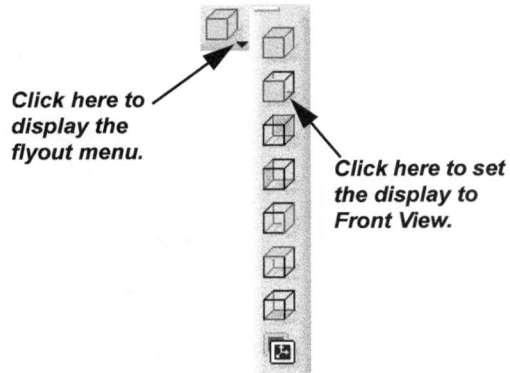

Click here to display the flyout menu.

Click here to set the display to Front View.

Figure 1–24

3. Repeat Step 2 for the (Back View), (Right View), (Left View), (Top View), and (Bottom View) quick views.

4. Return to the Isometric quick view.

Task 3 - Use the toolbar icons and menus to zoom, pan, and spin the model.

1. Click (Zoom In) several times to zoom in.

2. Click (Fit All In) to fit the model in the window.

*In some cases, the
zoom area box does not
display on the screen,
although the
functionality works
correctly.*

3. Click [Q] (Zoom Out) several times to zoom out.

4. In the menu bar, select **View>Zoom Area**. Use the left
    mouse button to draw a box around the area you want to
    zoom in to, as shown in Figure 1–25.

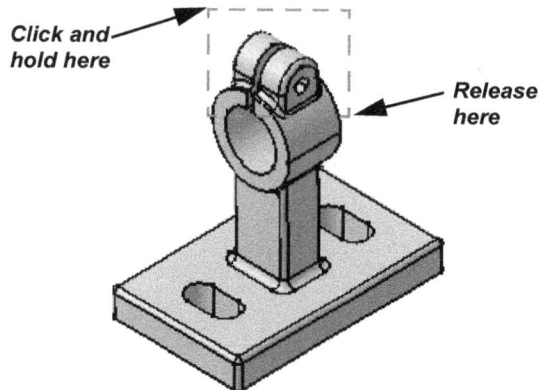

**Click and
hold here**

**Release
here**

Figure 1–25

5. Click [✛] (Pan) to pan the model. The icon turns orange to
    indicate that it is active.

6. Place the cursor near the bottom of the graphics window,
    hold the left mouse button, and drag the cursor to the top of
    the screen. You have panned down on the model.

*You learn additional
ways of panning and
zooming later in the
practice.*

7. [✛] (Pan) is longer orange. This means you must click the
    icon each time you want to pan.

8. Click [✛] (Fit All In) to fit the model in the window.

9. Click [↻] (Rotate) to rotate the model. Hold the left mouse
    button and move the cursor to rotate the model. The **Rotate**
    icon behaves in the same manner as the **Pan** icon, where
    you must click the icon each time you want to rotate the
    model.

Task 4 - Use the compass to dynamically rotate and pan the model.

1. Click ⬚ (Isometric View) to return to the Isometric quick view.

2. Click and drag the ball on top of the compass to rotate the model, as shown in Figure 1–26.

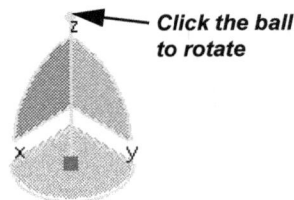

Click the ball to rotate

Figure 1–26

3. Return to the Isometric quick view.

4. Click and drag the curved edge of the XY plane to rotate the model about the Z-axis only, as shown in Figure 1–27.

Click here to rotate about the Z-axis.

Figure 1–27

5. Repeat Step 4 for the other two curved edges.

6. Return to the Isometric quick view.

7. Click and drag the X-, Y-, and Z-axes of the compass to translate the model along that direction, as shown in Figure 1–28.

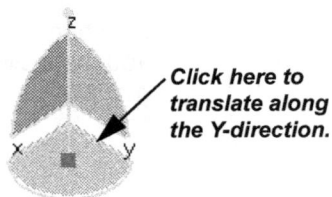

Click here to translate along the Y-direction.

Figure 1–28

Task 5 - Use the mouse to dynamically rotate, pan, and zoom the model.

1. Return to the Isometric quick view and fit the entire model in the window.

2. Hold the middle mouse button and move the cursor to pan the model.

3. Hold the middle mouse button and then left-click (or right-click) once. Move the cursor up and down to zoom in and out.

4. Press and hold the middle mouse button and then press and hold the left mouse button (or right mouse button), and move the cursor to rotate the model.

Task 6 - Use the specification tree to review the model geometry.

1. In the specification tree, select **Multipad.1** (you might need to expand PartBody by clicking the **+** symbol). The feature highlights in orange in the tree and on the model, as shown in Figure 1–29.

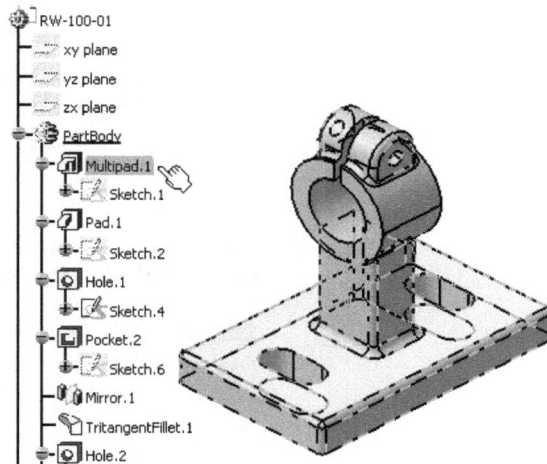

Figure 1–29

2. Repeat Step 1 for each feature under the PartBody branch (i.e., Pad.1, Hole.1, Pocket.2, Mirror.1, etc.). The selected feature is highlighted on the model and in the specification tree.

If you accidentally change the focus to the specification tree, you must understand how to activate the model.

3. Select the coordinate system in the lower right corner of the screen, as shown in Figure 1–30. The model turns gray, indicating that it is inactive. Select it again to make it active.

Figure 1–30

You can also change the focus to the specification tree by selecting any of the tree branches.

4. Press <F3> several times to hide and display the specification tree.

Task 7 - Change the size of several features.

1. Place the cursor over the large fillet at the base of the neck to highlight it, as shown in Figure 1–31. Double-click on it to display the radius dimension.

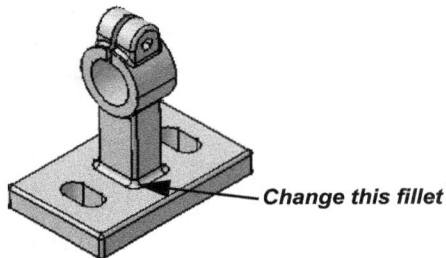

Change this fillet

Figure 1–31

2. In the Edge Fillet Definition dialog box, change *Radius* to **6.00 mm (0.236 in)**, as shown in Figure 1–32. Click **OK**.

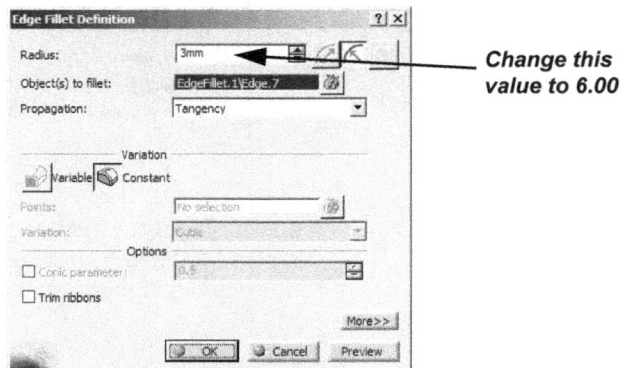

Change this value to 6.00

Figure 1–32

3. In the specification tree, double-click on ⊙ Hole.1 .

4. In the Hole Definition dialog box, change the *Diameter* to **13.00 mm (0.512 in)**, and click **OK**. The updated model is shown in Figure 1–33.

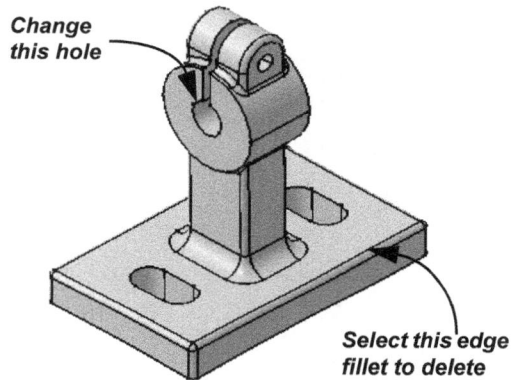

Change this hole

Select this edge fillet to delete

Figure 1–33

Task 8 - Delete features.

1. Select the edge fillet shown in Figure 1–33.

2. Right-click and select **Delete**.

3. Delete **Sketch.6** from the specification tree, as shown in Figure 1–34.

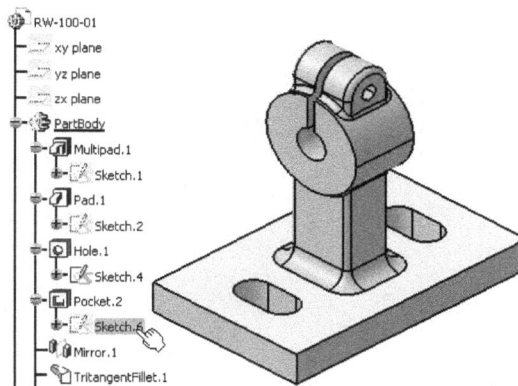

Figure 1–34

4. The Delete dialog box opens, as shown in Figure 1–35. It prompts you that the sketch is a parent feature and when deleted, its children are also deleted.

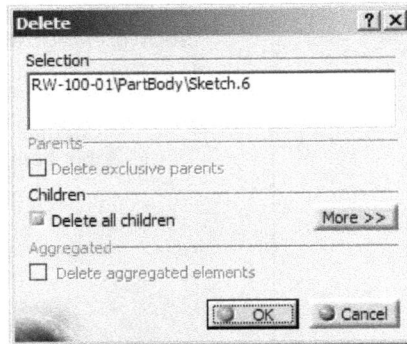

Figure 1–35

5. Click **OK**. The model displays as shown in Figure 1–36.

6. Click 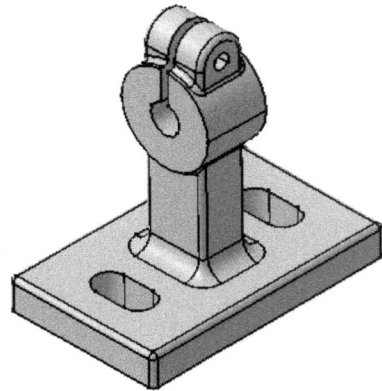 (Undo) to undo the deleting operations. The model displays as shown in Figure 1–37.

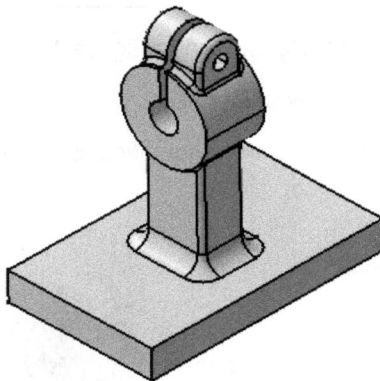

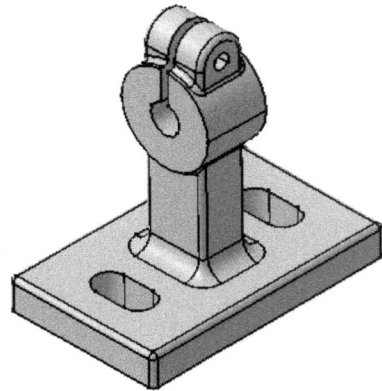

Figure 1–36   **Figure 1–37**

Task 9 - Cause a feature to fail.

1. In the specification tree, double-click on EdgeFillet.5 .

2. Modify the radius of the fillet to **30.00 mm (1.181 in)** and click **OK**.

   The radius of the fillet is too large and causes the **EdgeFillet.5** feature to fail. An Update Diagnosis dialog box opens, as shown in Figure 1–38.

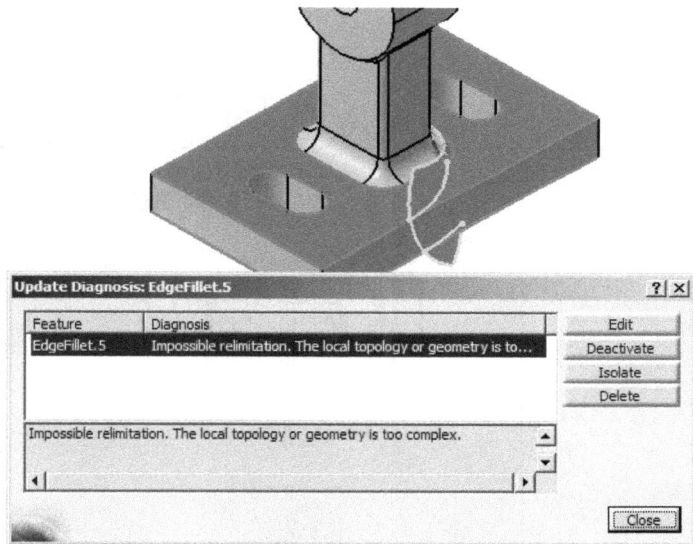

Figure 1–38

3. Undo the changes made to the Fillet feature and resolve the failure by clicking (Undo).

Task 10 - Open a drawing of the part to verify it has been updated.

1. In the toolbar, click (Open) to open the drawing.

2. In the File Selection dialog box, select **Flange_Lock.CATDrawing**.

3. Click **Open**.

4. The specification tree for the drawing displays ⟳ (Update current sheet), as shown in Figure 1–39. This indicates that the drawing is not up-to-date.

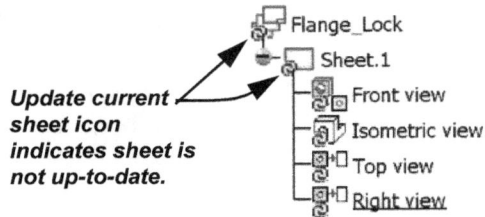

Update current sheet icon indicates sheet is not up-to-date.

Figure 1–39

5. Click ⟳ (Update current sheet) to update the views. The updated drawing is shown in Figure 1–40. Note that if set to inches, it will display with different dimensions.

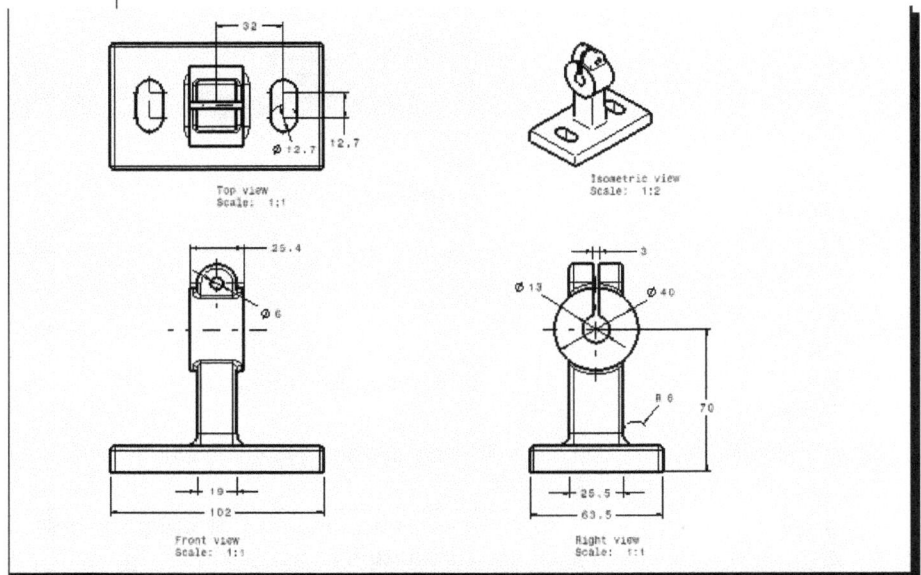

Figure 1–40

6. Select **Window>Tile Vertically** to display the model and drawing windows side-by-side.

7. Select **Window>Cascade** to arrange the windows with the window titles displaying.

Task 11 - Close the models to clear the screen.

1. With the drawing active, click 🖫 (Save) to save the drawing. A message displays, informing you that saving the modified drawing does not save the modified part, as shown in Figure 1–41.

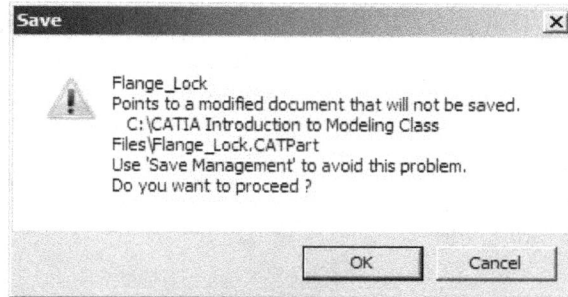

Save

⚠ Flange_Lock
Points to a modified document that will not be saved.
   C:\CATIA Introduction to Modeling Class
Files\Flange_Lock.CATPart
Use 'Save Management' to avoid this problem.
Do you want to proceed ?

[OK]   [Cancel]

Figure 1–41

2. Click **OK**.

3. Select **File>Close** to close the drawing window. The Close dialog box opens as shown in Figure 1–42. The software is warning you that the model is going to be closed without saving.

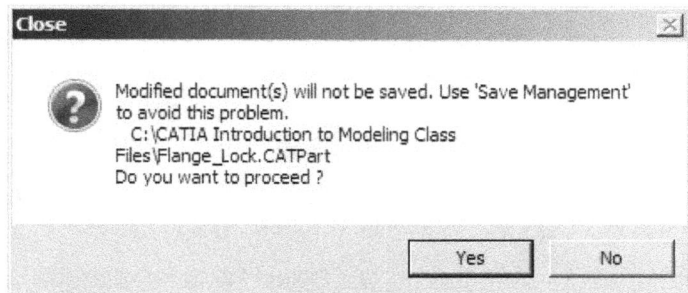

Close

❓ Modified document(s) will not be saved. Use 'Save Management'
to avoid this problem.
   C:\CATIA Introduction to Modeling Class
Files\Flange_Lock.CATPart
Do you want to proceed ?

[Yes]   [No]

Figure 1–42

4. Click **Yes** to close the drawing without saving the changes to the model.

Task 12 - Open the assembly model Flange_Lock.CATProduct.

1. Click ⬚ (Open) in the toolbar to open the assembly.

2. Select **Flange_Lock.CATProduct** in the File Selection dialog box.

3. Click **Open**. The assembly opens as shown in Figure 1–43. The assembly contains **Flange_Lock.CATPart** as one of its components.

You might have to collapse the constraints entry in the specification tree by selecting the - symbol.

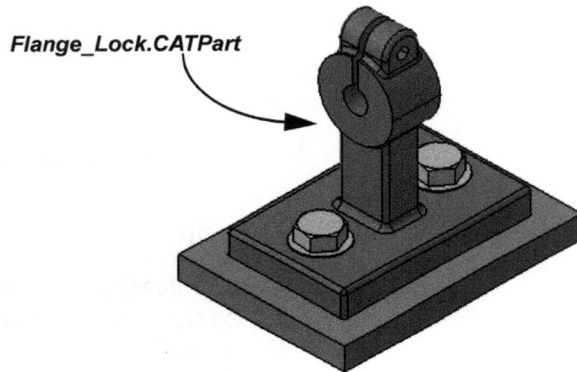

Flange_Lock.CATPart

Figure 1–43

4. Select **Window>Flange_Lock.CATPart** to activate the part model.

5. In the specification tree, double-click on ⬚ Hole.1 .

6. In the Hole Definition dialog box, change the *Diameter* to **25.0 (0.984 in)** and click **OK**.

7. Select **Window>Flange_Lock.CATProduct** to activate the assembly model. The change in the diameter of **Hole.1** has updated in the assembly model, as shown in Figure 1–44.

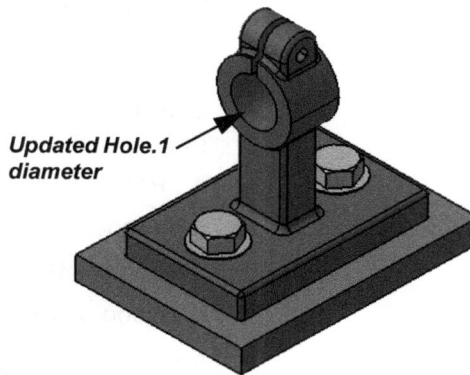

Updated Hole.1 diameter

Figure 1–44

8. With the assembly active, click 🖫 (Save) to save the model.

9. With the assembly active, select **File>Close**.

Design Considerations

By closing the assembly, the software detects that the modified component **Flange_Lock.CATPart**, must also be saved, as shown in the dialog box in Figure 1–45. It is recommended that you check modified assembly components to ensure that no changes are lost. Using **Save Management** ensures that all modified documents are saved.

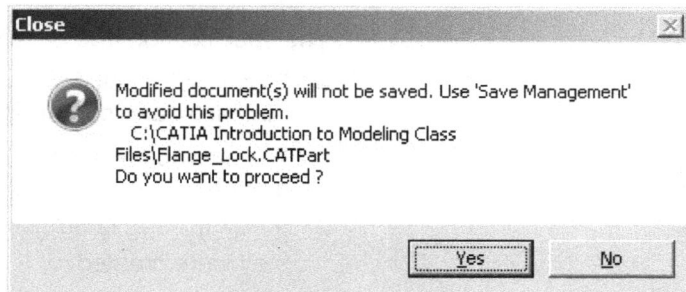

Figure 1–45

10. Click **Yes** to close the assembly file.

11. Save **Flange_Lock.CATPart** and close the window.

Chapter Review Questions

1. *Solid modeling evolves by creating features one by one until geometry is complete* best describes which attribute?

    a. Parametric

    b. Associative

    c. Feature Based

    d. None of the above.

2. Parametric can best be described as:

    a. Changes made in one mode of CATIA update throughout the other modes of CATIA.

    b. Solid modeling evolves by creating features, one by one, until the geometry is complete.

    c. Three-dimensional solid models.

    d. Dimensional constraints define a feature's shape, are considered *parameters*, and are accessible at any time.

3. After editing the dimensions of a part model, you must open all drawings referencing that part and make the same dimensional changes.

    a. True

    b. False

4. The specification tree is useful because:

    a. It provides quick access to parameters, functions, materials, and commonly used measurements.

    b. It is available when working with parts, assemblies, and drawings.

    c. It displays the features of the part in the order in which they were created.

    d. All of the above.

5. CATIA part files have a _____ filename extension.

    a. .PRT

    b. .Part

    c. .CATPart

    d. .CATProduct

6. enables you to view the Isometric view of the model.

   a. True

   b. False

7. To pan the model using the mouse, you press and hold which mouse button?

   a. Left

   b. Right

   c. Middle

8. To zoom the model using the mouse, you must press and hold the middle mouse button and click either the left or right mouse button.

   a. True

   b. False

9. Which tool can be used to zoom in or out on the shown geometry so that it fills all the available space?

   a.

   b.

   c.

   d.

10. You can open multiple windows in a CATIA session.

   a. True

   b. False

Answers: 1.c, 2.d, 3.b, 4.d, 5.c, 6.b, 7.c, 8.a, 9.a, 10.a

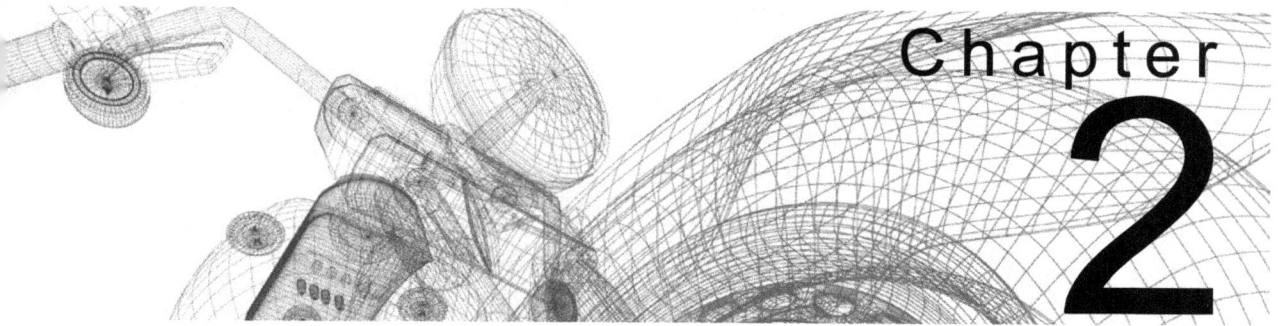

Customizing CATIA V5

In this chapter, you learn how to effectively manage files in the CATSetting folders, and how to customize the Options dialog box, toolbars, and workbenches to suit your preferences and requirements, and to help you work more efficiently.

Learning Objectives in this Chapter

- Understand where settings used to customize CATIA are stored.
- Review the settings in the Options dialog box.
- Review the recommended settings for completing this training.
- Learn how to manipulate toolbars to customize the interface and streamline your working environment.
- Customize CATIA to display your preferred Workbenches.

2.1 Managing CATSetting Files

Changes to the CATIA settings on Windows systems are automatically written to files in the *CATSettings* folder, located at *C:\Users\<user_name>\AppData\Roaming\DassaultSystemes\ CATSettings.*

- If CATIA is closed and re-opened, it opens using the same options that were set the last time it was customized.

- If the *Application Data* folder is not displayed on your Windows system, you might need to modify the folder properties to view it.

- The default files listed in the *CATSettings* folder vary, depending on the license of CATIA used. As customizations are made in the CATIA software, the list of files in the *CATSettings* folder increases. To return CATIA to its default settings, delete the files in this folder. The default files are written to the same folder the next time CATIA is started.

2.2 Options Dialog Box

When first started, CATIA uses a default set of configurations. These configurations include interface color scheme, model units, sketcher grid, spaceball configuration, and so on.

The Options dialog box opens by selecting **Tools>Options** in the menu bar, and is used to customize these options, shown in Figure 2–1.

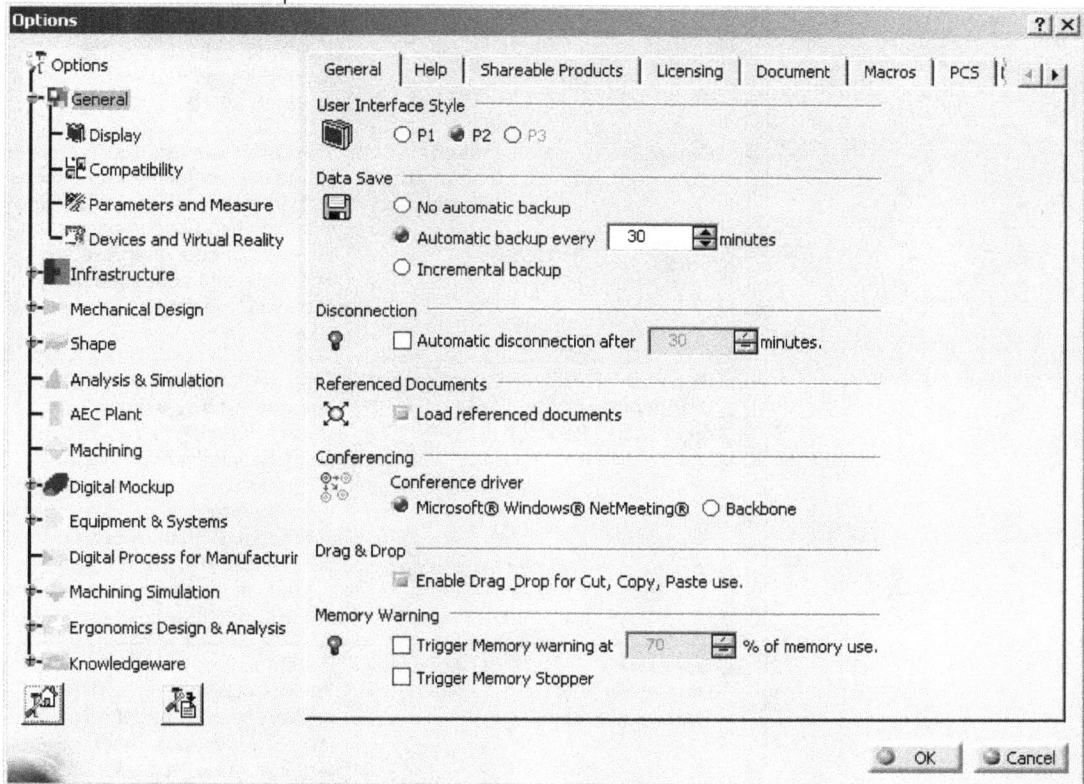

Figure 2–1

When setting the required options, the changes made are written to the files in the *CATSettings* folder. To customize the options outside CATIA, click or **Start** in the Windows task bar, and select **All Programs>CATIA>Tools>Settings Management V5-6R2017**.

Recommended Options

You should become familiar with the option menus to maximize efficiency within the CATIA environment. These options impact the results obtained when completing the practices available in this guide. The option menus are described as follows:

Path	Option	Value
General>*PCS* tab	**Undo**	The **Stack Size** option controls the number of undo operations that can be performed. Increasing this value also decreases CATIA performance, as the software must store more operation information. The maximum value is 99. It is recommended that you set this option to 15-20.
General> *Document* tab	**Linked Document Localization**	The **Other folders** option enables you to specify multiple directories that are searched by CATIA when locating linked documents, such as the components of an assembly. The more directories that are specified, the longer the search can take.
General> **Display>***Tree Manipulation* tab	**Zoom on Tree**	Disabling the **Tree zoom after clicking on any branch** option helps in working in the CATIA interface. Users often become confused when selecting a branch in the tree, which takes their focus off the model. With this option disabled, the tree can be zoomed by selecting the axis in the lower right corner of the window.
General> **Display>** *Performance* tab	**3D Accuracy**	These options control the quality of the model display in CATIA. A higher accuracy might result in an increase in system resource requirements. Proportional accuracy varies display quality relative to model size, while fixed accuracy does not. It is recommended that you set a *Proportional value* of **0.04**.
General> **Parameters and Measure>** *Knowledge* tab	**Parameter Tree View**	These options control the display of parameter values and formulae in the tree. It is recommended that you select **With value**.

General> Parameters and Measure> *Measure Tools* tab	Update	These options control the automatic update of measurements in a part and product model. It is recommended that you enable all options in this area.
General> Parameters and Measure> *Measure Tools* tab	Graphic Properties	These options control the display properties for measurements that display on the model. Since the default green color is difficult to read against the background, it is recommended that you change the *Color* option to **White**. The **Box Display** option can also be enabled to further highlight the measurement.
Infrastructure> Part Infrastructure> *Display* tab	Display In Specification Tree	These options control the display of model information in the tree. They include: • External References • Constraints • Parameters • Relations • Bodies under operations • Expand sketch-based feature nodes at creation It is recommended that you enable all of the options in this area.
Infrastructure> Part Infrastructure> *Part Document* tab	Hybrid design	Unless your company has standardized on the use of Hybrid Design, clear the **Enable hybrid design inside part bodies and bodies** option. Hybrid Design changes the way wireframe and surface elements are stored in a part model and should not be enabled unless instructed by your CAD Administrator.
Mechanical Design> Sketcher> *Sketcher* tab	Update	Select **Generate update errors when the sketch is under-constrained** to have the software open an Update Diagnosis dialog box when exiting Sketcher with an under-constrained profile.

2.3 Toolbar Customization

There are many toolbars available in CATIA, and depending on monitor size and screen resolution, your screen might not be able to display all of them. To work around this issue, you can learn to customize the toolbars.

Moving Toolbars

You can reposition toolbars on the screen using separators or double arrows.

Separators

Each toolbar contains a separator, as shown in Figure 2–2. To move the toolbar, select and drag the separator to a new position.

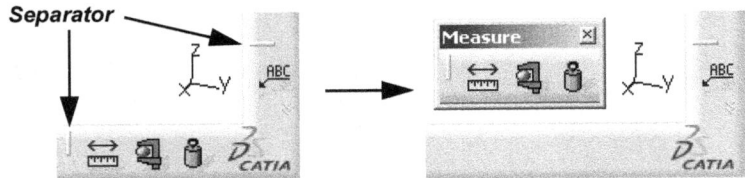

Figure 2–2

Double Arrows

If more toolbars display than can be shown in the window, double arrows display at the corner of the screen, indicating that additional icons are available, but not visible. The Annotations toolbar is shown in Figure 2–3. Either the double arrows or the separators can be used to move the toolbar.

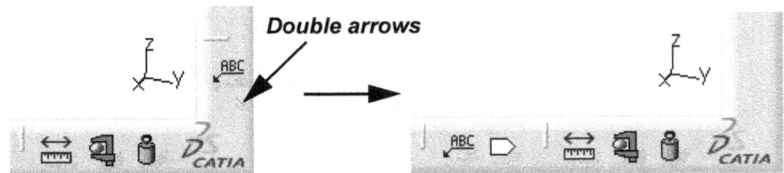

Figure 2–3

Toolbar Placement

Figure 2–4 shows only a few examples of the many toolbar placement methods that can be used.

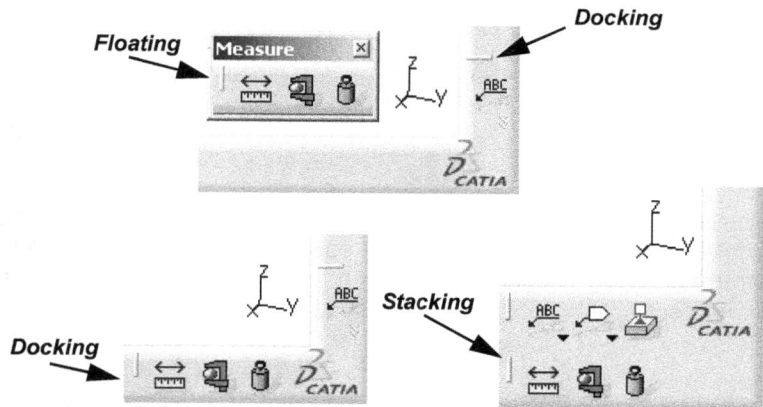

Figure 2–4

Add/Remove Toolbars

Toolbars can be customized to display task-specific icons using one of the following methods:

- Select **View>Toolbars** and toggle the toolbar name on and off by clicking ☑.

- Right-click on an area of the toolbar and toggle the toolbar name on and off by clicking ☑.

An example of the **Toolbar Selection option** menu is shown in Figure 2–5.

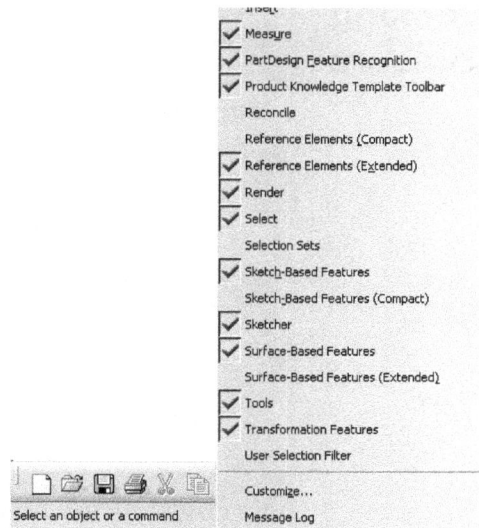

Figure 2–5

Expanding Flyouts

Flyout options are grouped by type.

Creating a new toolbar from a flyout does not remove the original flyout icon.

Some toolbar icons contain flyouts, which display additional icons when selected. For example, the **Pad** and **Pocket** feature icons contain flyouts, as shown in Figure 2–6.

- Clicking the flyout (the down arrow) displays the additional icons, as shown in Figure 2–7.

- You can reposition the icons displayed in the flyout as a separate toolbar by dragging the separator to a new position on the screen, as shown in Figure 2–8. You can position the flyout as a floating, docked, or stacked toolbar.

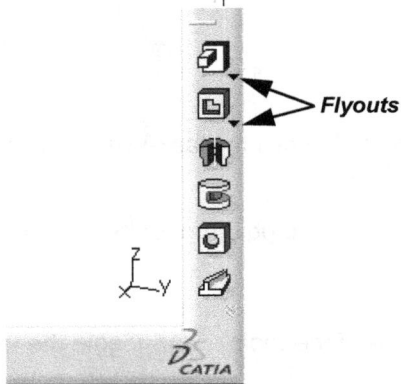

Figure 2–6

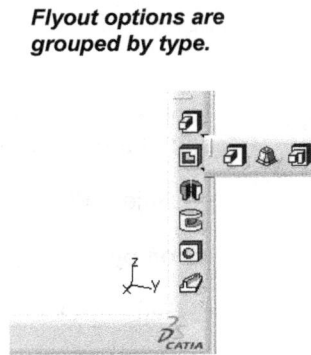

Flyout options are grouped by type.

Figure 2–7

Figure 2–8

Locking Toolbars

Toolbars can be locked into position. This prevents repositioning of docked toolbars until they are unlocked.

How To: Lock Toolbars

1. Select **Tools>Customize**.
2. In the Customize dialog box, select the *Options* tab.
3. Select **Lock Toolbar Position**.

Locking toolbars has the following results:

- Docked and stacked toolbars cannot be repositioned or changed to a floating toolbar.

- Floating toolbars can be repositioned, but not docked or stacked.

- Flyouts cannot be expanded to a toolbar.

2.4 Favorite Workbenches

By default, when CATAIA is started, the Workbench toolbar displays in the upper right side of the screen. The Part Design workbench is shown in Figure 2–9.

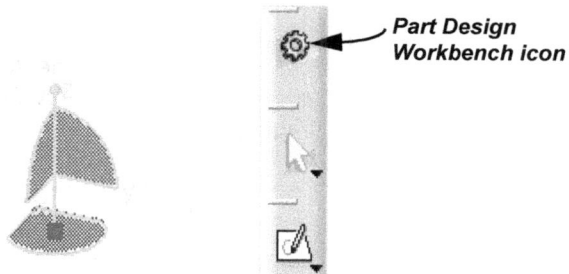

Part Design Workbench icon

Figure 2–9

CATIA can be customized to display the most commonly used workbenches by clicking the **Workbench** icon. The Welcome to CATIA V5 dialog box opens when you first click this icon, as shown in Figure 2–10.

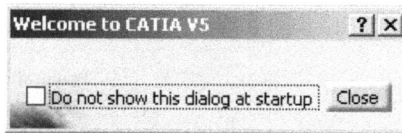

Figure 2–10

To change the **Workbench** icon to display the preferred **Workbench** icons, select **Tools>Customize** in the menu bar. The Customize dialog box opens, as shown in Figure 2–11.

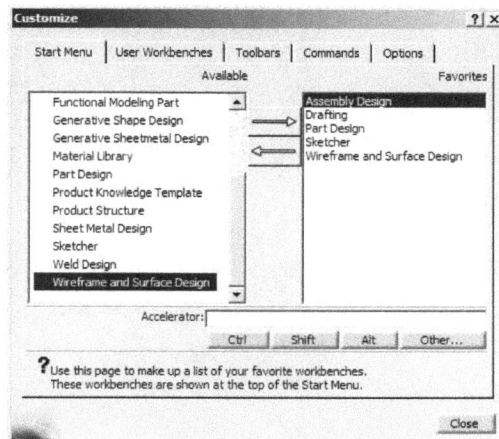

Figure 2–11

- Select the required workbenches in the left column of the *Start Menu* tab.

- Click ➡ to add them to the *Favorites* column in the right column.

Once you finish selecting your workbenches, click

⚙ (Workbench). The Welcome to CATIA V5 dialog box opens, displaying the list of favorite workbenches, as shown in Figure 2–12.

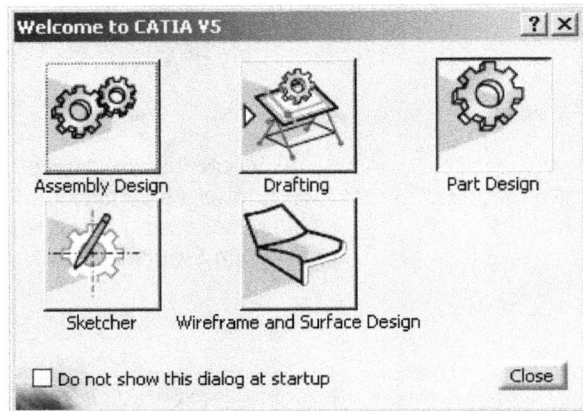

Welcome to CATIA V5

Assembly Design   Drafting   Part Design

Sketcher   Wireframe and Surface Design

☐ Do not show this dialog at startup   Close

Figure 2–12

Select one of the workbench icons to switch workbench modes. All toolbars update for functions specific to the selected workbench.

To toggle between favorite workbenches more quickly, you can display the Workbenches toolbar, as shown in Figure 2–13.

Workbenches

Figure 2–13

The list of favorites is also available for quick selection in the **Start** menu, as shown in Figure 2–14.

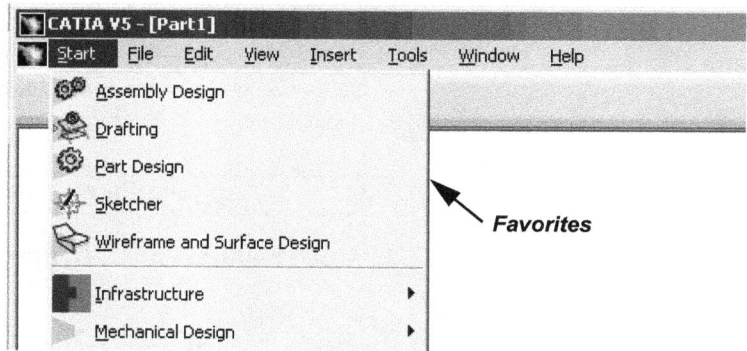

Figure 2–14

Practice 2a

Customization

Practice Objectives

- Set up favorite workbenches.
- Customize the on-screen toolbar display.
- Customize the CATIA configuration.

Task 1 - Set up favorite workbenches.

1. Open **Flange_Lock.CATPart**.

2. Click ⚙ (Workbench). The Welcome to CATIA V5 dialog box opens.

3. Close the dialog box. If ⚙ (Workbench) is not present, select **View>Toolbars** and ensure that ☑ displays next to the Workbench toolbar.

4. Add your favorite workbench icons to the dialog box. In the menu bar, select **Tools>Customize**.

5. In the *Start Menu* tab, add the five workbenches (shown in Figure 2–15) from the left column to the right column using ⟹.

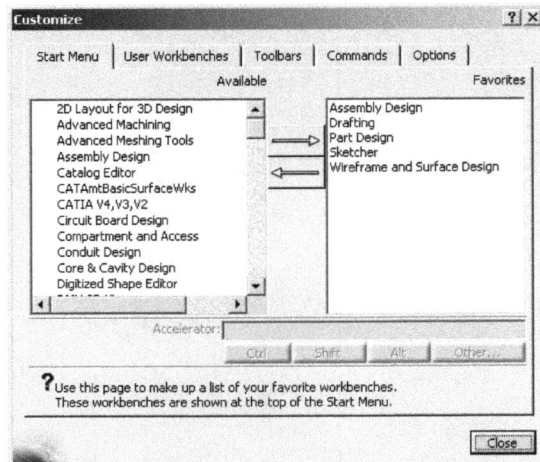

Figure 2–15

6. Close the Customize dialog box.

7. Click ⚙ (Workbench) again.

8. In the Welcome to CATIA V5 dialog box that opens, click

   (Drafting) to activate Drafting workbench.

9. Click **OK**. All of the toolbar icons update to drafting functions.

10. In the menu bar, select **Start**. Note that the five selected workbenches are now listed at the top of the **Start** menu.

11. In the menu bar, select **Window.** Select **Flange_Lock.CATPart** to switch windows back to the **Flange_Lock** part. Note that all of the toolbar icons update to part design functions.

Task 2 - Add a new toolbar to the interface.

---

1. Right-click on the message window, as shown in Figure 2–16. The list of available toolbars displays.

Figure 2–16

You might need to toggle ☑ off and then on again for the toolbar to display.

2. Toggle the **Graphic Properties** option so that ☑ displays.

3. The toolbar displays at the top of the CATIA window, as shown in Figure 2–17.

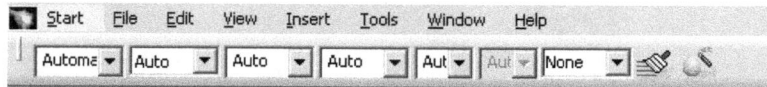

Figure 2–17

Task 3 - Customize toolbar positioning.

1. If the Part Design workbench is not currently active, click

   (Part Design Workbench) in the Workbench toolbar.

2. Move the Standard toolbar from the lower left corner of the screen to the left side of the screen by dragging the separator, as shown in Figure 2–18.

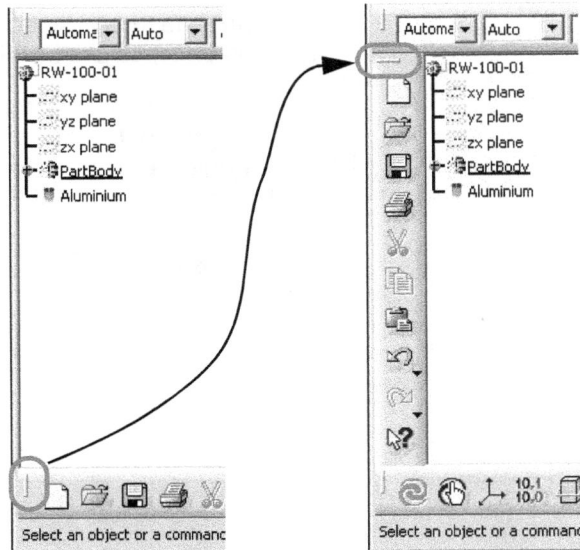

Figure 2–18

3. Click the down arrow on ⬇ (Select) to expand the flyout.

4. Drag the flyout to a new position on the screen to display the entire Select toolbar, as shown in Figure 2–19.

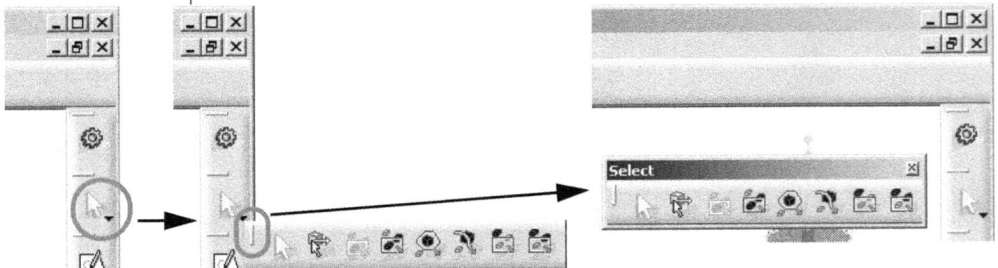

Figure 2–19

5. If any double arrows ( ) are present in the corners of the screen, drag them to expand the hidden icons.

6. Spend a few minutes familiarizing yourself with moving the toolbars and flyouts.

Task 4 - Lock the toolbar positions.

1. Select **Tools>Customize**. In the Customize dialog box, select the *Options* tab.

2. Select **Lock Toolbar Position**.

3. Close the Customize dialog box.

4. Try to move the docked toolbars, flyouts, and floating toolbars. Note what moves and what is locked.

5. Select **Tools>Customize** and select the *Options* tab.

6. Clear the **Lock Toolbar Position** option.

7. Close the Customize dialog box. The toolbar positions can be modified again.

Task 5 - Restore the position of the toolbars.

1. Restore the toolbars to their default positions. Select **Tools>Customize** and select the *Toolbars* tab.

2. Click **Restore Position**.

3. You are prompted to confirm that you want to restore all toolbars to their default positions. Click **OK** if you want to restore the positions or **Cancel** if you want to keep the new positioning.

4. Close the Customize dialog box.

Task 6 - Begin modifying your CATIA settings.

In this task, you will begin modifying the options in CATIA to the recommended settings for your training session.

1. Modify the display performance of CATIA. Select **Tools> Options**.

2. Select **General>Display** from the left side and select the *Performance* tab. Set the *3D Accuracy* to **Proportional**, with a value of **0.04**, as shown in Figure 2–20.

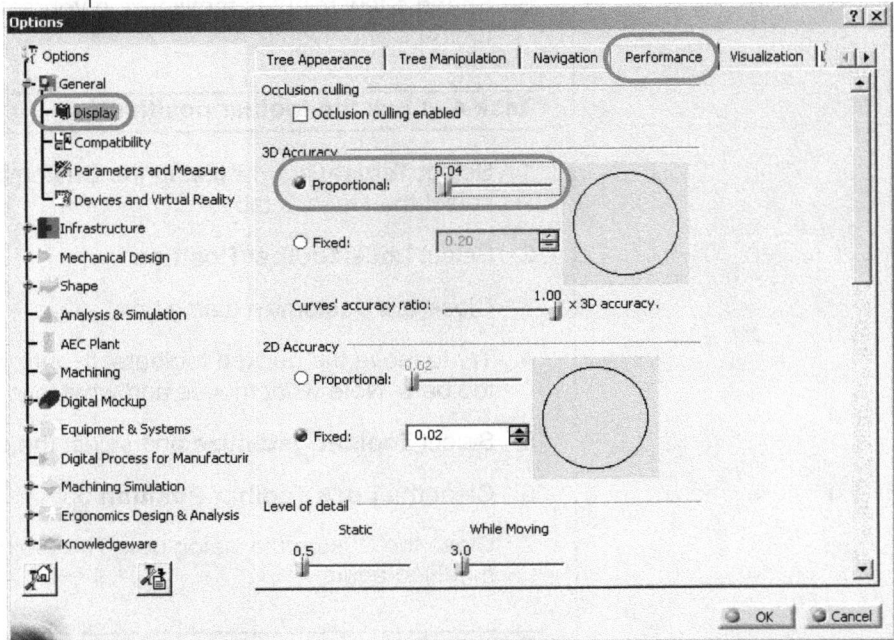

Figure 2–20

Task 7 - Complete the CATIA settings modification.

1. Use the following information as a guide to complete the remaining configurations. All of the configurations are done under **Tools>Options**.

Path	Option	Value
General>*PCS* tab	**Undo**	Set the *Stack Size* option to **15**.
General>*Document* tab	**Linked Document Localization**	Select **Other folders** in the *Linked Document Localization* field and click **Configure**. Add the path to the training files to the Other Folders dialog box.
General>Display> *Tree Manipulation* tab	**Zoom on Tree**	Clear the **Tree zoom after clicking on any branch** option.
General>Parameters and Measure> *Knowledge* tab	**Parameter Tree View**	Select **With value**.

General>Parameters and Measure> *Measure Tools* tab	Update	Select the **Automatic update in part** and **Automatic update in product** options.
Infrastructure>Part Infrastructure> *Display* tab	**Display In Specification Tree**	Select all options in this area.
Infrastructure>Part Infrastructure>*Part Document* tab	**Hybrid design**	Clear the **Enable hybrid design inside part bodies and bodies** option.

Chapter Review Questions

1. Changes made to the default configuration for CATIA are saved in the _____ folder.

   a. Settings

   b. CATSettings

   c. Config

   d. Properties

2. To open the Options dialog box:

   a. Select **File>Options**.

   b. Select **Edit>Settings**.

   c. Select **Tools>Options**.

   d. Click the **Open** icon.

3. What do the double arrows shown in Figure 2–21 indicate?

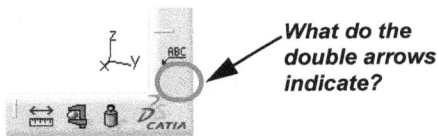

Figure 2–21

   a. Additional icons are present but not currently visible.

   b. The toolbar is currently docked.

   c. The toolbar has been customized.

   d. The toolbar is currently locked.

4. The _____ option prevents repositioning of docked toolbars.

   a. Lock Position of Toolbars.

   b. Fixed

   c. Config

   d. Properties

5. Once configured, you can switch between your favorite workbenches using what tools?

   a. Clicking the **Workbench** icon.

   b. From the Workbench toolbar.

   c. From the **Start** menu.

   d. All of the above.

6. You can stack multiple levels of toolbars on the top, bottom, right, or left side of the screen.

   a. True

   b. False

7. What does the small black arrow on an icon (shown in Figure 2–22) indicate?

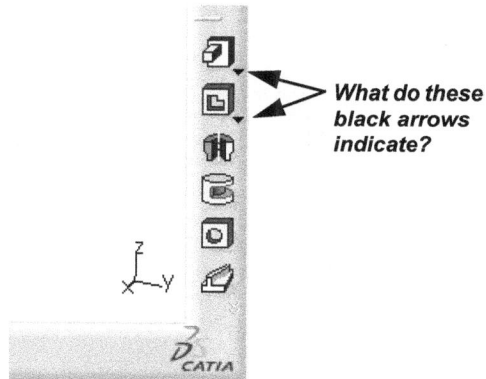

What do these black arrows indicate?

Figure 2–22

   a. The icon contains a flyout.

   b. The icon has been locked.

   c. The icon is not part of the default icons for this workbench.

   d. The black arrow is used to move the icon.

8. When CATIA is closed and re-opened, it opens using the same options that were set the last time it was customized.

   a. True

   b. False

Answers: 1.b, 2.c, 3.a, 4.a, 5.d, 6.a, 7.a, 8.a

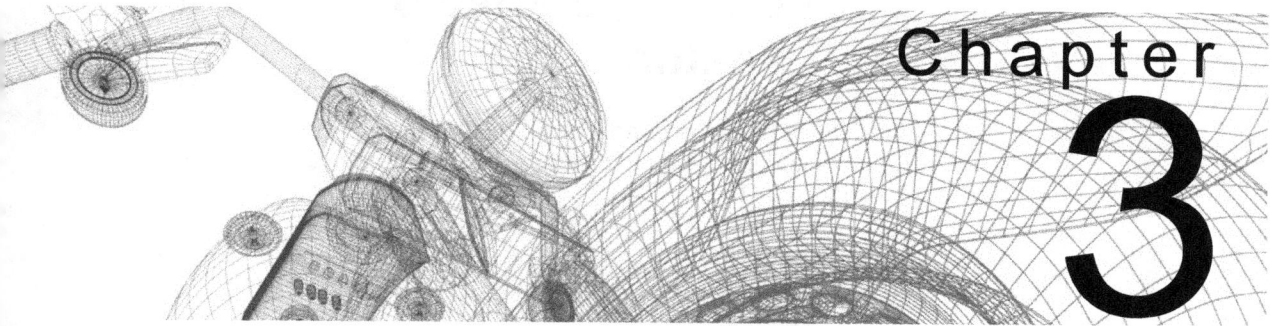

Creating Sketches

In this chapter you will learn how sketches are used to create features. You will learn some of the basic capabilities of the Sketcher Workbench, which enables you to create sketch-based features. You will use reference planes and surfaces to orient and sketch the profile of your first feature.

Learning Objectives in this Chapter

- Understand the basics of sketched features.
- Review the general steps for creating a new part.
- Understand the use of default and reference planes for sketching.
- Review the basic tools that you can use to create entities in sketches.
- Create a sketch for the model profile.
- Understand several operations for editing sketches.
- Learn various tips and techniques for working with sketches.
- Understand how features and sketches display in the specification tree.

3.1 Getting Started on Sketching Features

2D sketches are used to create 3D features. A sketching plane is selected and used to create a sketched feature, as shown in Figure 3–1.

Sketching plane

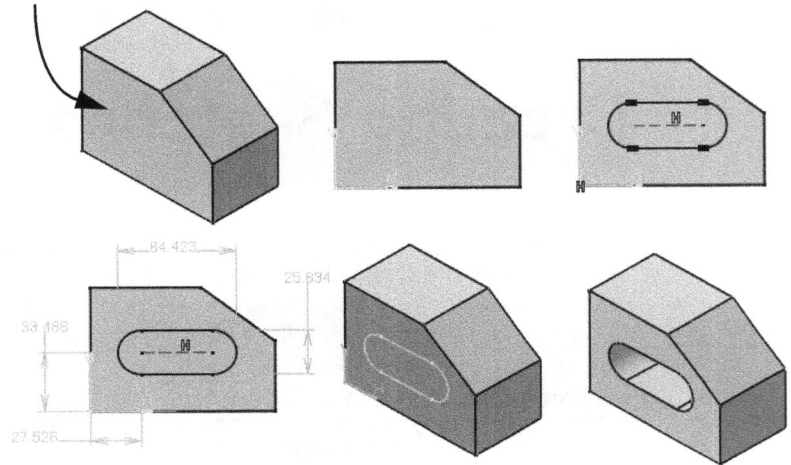

Figure 3–1

How To: Create a Sketched Feature

1. Select a sketching plane and enter the Sketcher workbench. The plane you select is initially oriented parallel to the screen. The Y-axis faces the top of the screen and the X-axis faces the right side of the screen.
2. Sketch the required profile or cross-section.
3. Create constraints/dimensions to define the size and location of the sketch.
4. Exit the Sketcher workbench.
5. Use the sketch to create a solid feature, such as a Pad or Pocket.

3.2 Creating a New Part

Sketches are an integral part of creating solid features in a CATPart file. To create a sketch, open an existing model (**File>Open**), or create a new part file.

How To: Create a New Part

1. Select **File>New**. The New dialog box opens, which enables you to define the type of file that is created.
2. Select **Part** in the List of Types drop-down list (shown in Figure 3–2), and then click **OK**. The New Part dialog box opens as shown in Figure 3–3.

*All part models created and opened have been created with the **Enable Hybrid Design** option cleared.*

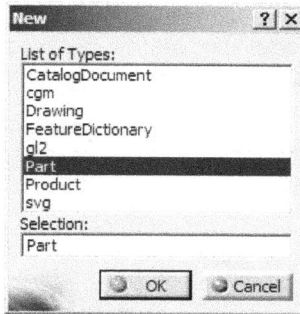

Figure 3–2

Figure 3–3

The following parameters can be configured for the new part:

Parameter	Description
Enter part name field	Enter a name for the part model. This name is automatically assigned to the Part Number of the new file.
Enable hybrid design option	Hybrid design uses a special type of body, called a hybrid body. It can contain both wireframe/surface and solid features. This enables direct integration of the surface and part design environments into a single body. For current purposes, the hybrid design environment is disabled.
Create a geometrical set option	When the hybrid design environment is disabled, a geometrical set is used to store wireframe and surface elements, as well as sketched elements. A geometrical set is automatically added to the new part file when this option is selected.

Create an ordered geometrical set option	When the hybrid design environment is enabled, an ordered geometrical set can be used to group together wireframe or surface geometry with order preserved.
Do not show this dialog box at startup option	The software does not open the dialog box when creating a new part file when this option is selected. Instead, the software automatically names the new part *Part#*, where # increments to the next available number, starting at 1.
	If this option is selected, the Part name dialog box can be restored by selecting **Tools>Options> Infrastructure>Part Infrastructure**, selecting the *Part Document* tab, and selecting the **'Display the New Part' dialog box** option.

3. Click **OK** when the part parameters have been specified. The model is created with three default reference planes that can be used as sketching planes, as shown in Figure 3–4.

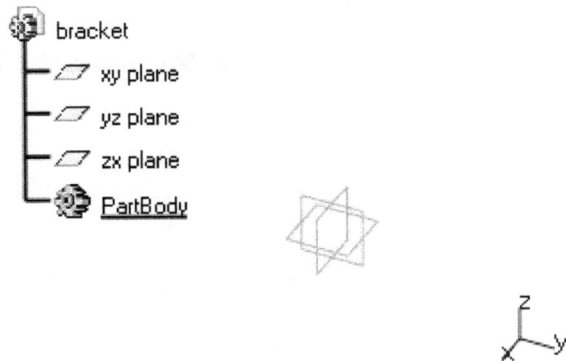

Figure 3–4

3.3 Sketching Planes

A new part always starts with three default reference planes. The model and specification tree display is shown in Figure 3–5. The planes are automatically named to match the directions of the coordinate system that they are parallel to, such as the XY plane.

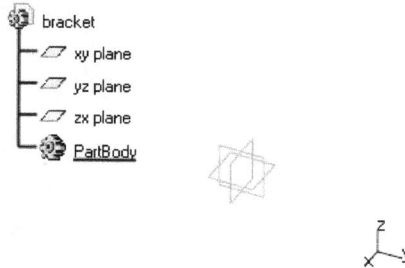

Figure 3–5

When you create a new part, the software uses the part name as the part number. To modify a part number, select the part name in the specification tree, right-click and select **Properties**. Enter the required part number in the *Part Number* field of the Properties dialog box, shown in Figure 3–6.

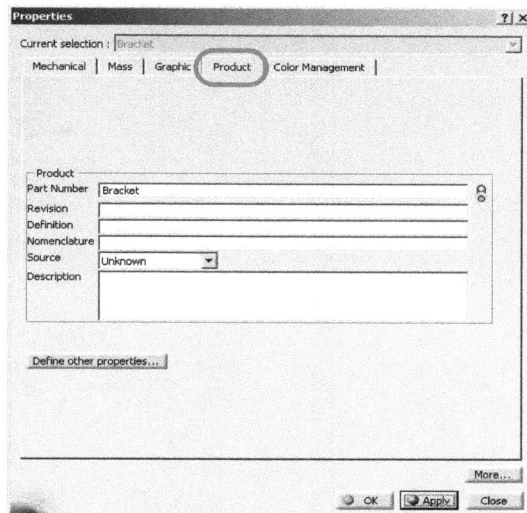

Figure 3–6

The part number is not the name of the CATPart file. When you first save the model, you are prompted for a filename and location. You can use different values for the part number and filename.

Reference Planes

All CATParts contain default reference planes as the first three features. The default reference planes remain the same size relative to screen, regardless of model size or zoom level, as shown in Figure 3–7.

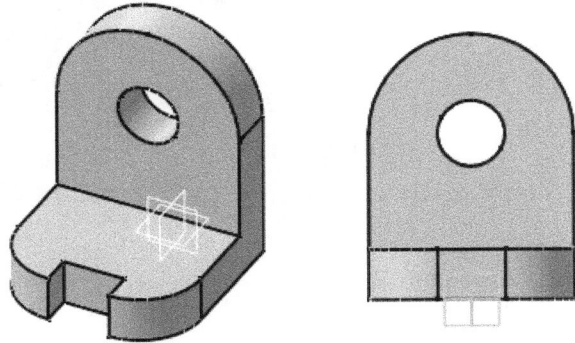

Figure 3–7

Planes cannot be displayed as shaded. This is for illustration only.

For better visualization, highlight each plane by placing the cursor over a reference plane in the specification tree or on the screen.

Default reference planes are useful for creating a new model because they provide a planar reference to place the first sketch. Figure 3–8 shows three shaded rectangular surfaces to help visualize the reference planes orientation.

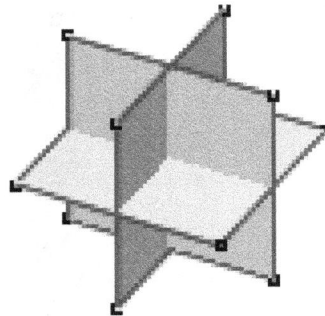

Figure 3–8

Selecting a Plane for Sketching

Selecting one plane over another impacts the Quick Views and the default orientation of the model. The YZ plane is considered the front of the part, as shown in Figure 3–9. However, this does not mean that you always sketch on the YZ plane.

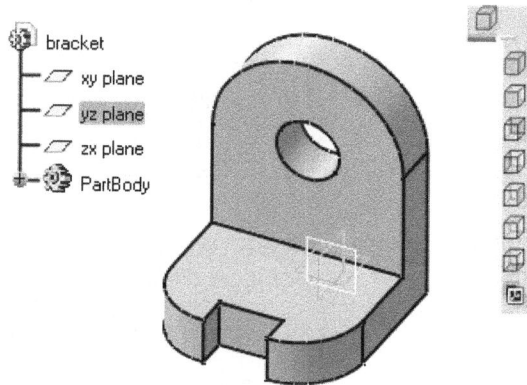

Figure 3–9

Sketch a front profile on the YZ plane, a side profile on the ZX plane, and a top profile on the XY plane.

The L-shape profile of a part is also a side profile. Therefore, the L-shape sketch of the bracket part is sketched on the ZX plane. The possible default orientations of a cylinder are shown in Figure 3–10 when a particular sketching plane is selected for sketching.

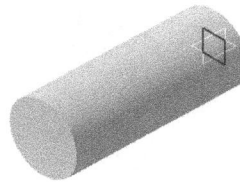

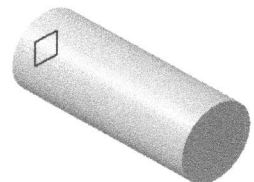

XY plane   *YZ plane*   *ZX plane*

Figure 3–10

3.4 Sketcher Workbench

How To: Create a Sketch

1. Select an appropriate sketching plane and click

   [✎] (Sketch).

2. Create your sketch.

3. Click [⬆] (Exit workbench) to complete the sketch.

Sketcher Grid

When you first enter the Sketcher workbench, the following objects display, as shown in Figure 3–11:

- Sketcher grid over your sketch plane

- Three default reference planes

- Horizontal and Vertical axes

- Compass

- Specification tree

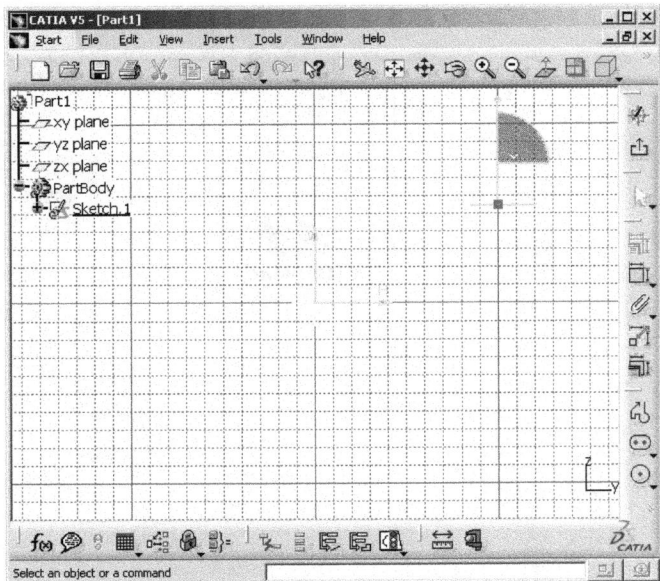

Figure 3–11

To modify the sketcher grid, select **Tools>Options**, and then select **Mechanical Design>Sketcher** in the Options dialog box that opens, as shown in Figure 3–12. You can define the following information on the sketcher display:

- Primary spacing

- Number of graduations

- Enable/disable the snap function

- Enable/disable the grid

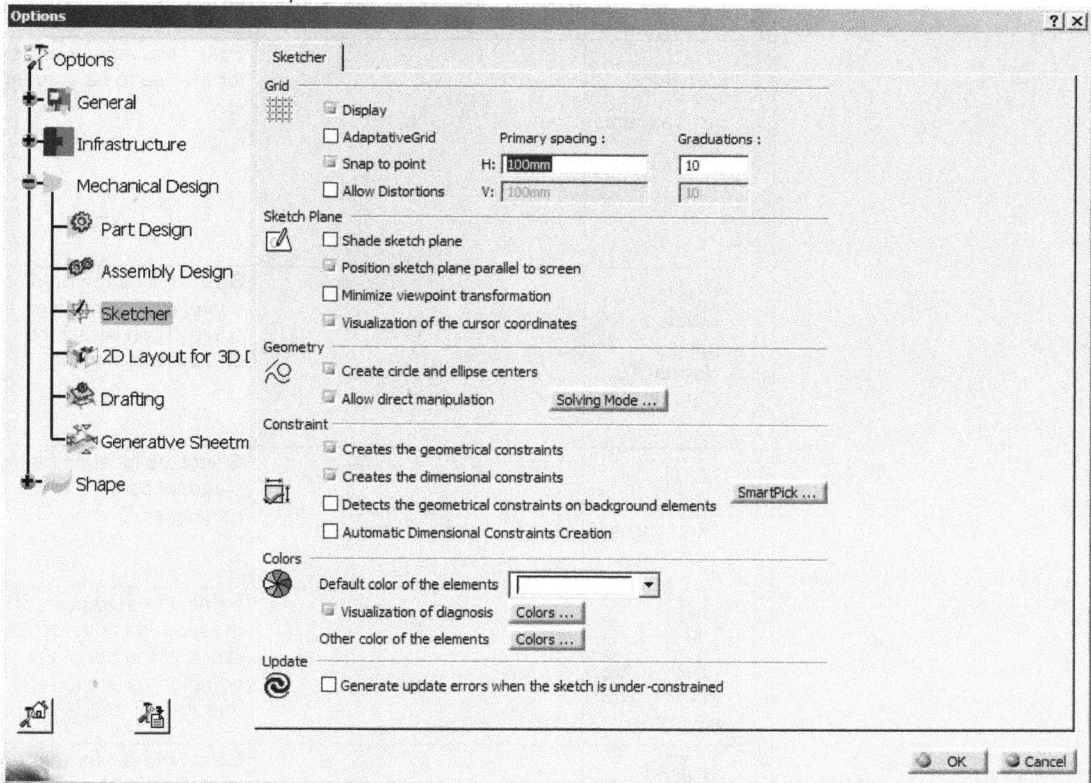

Figure 3–12

3.5 Basic Shapes

Other sketch tools are available. These are covered in a different chapter.

Once inside the Sketcher workbench, the feature's profile (or cross-section) must be sketched. The most commonly used tools for sketching are described as follows:

Icon	Sequence	Description
(Line)		Select the start and end points of the line.
(Bi-Tangent Line)		Select two arcs or circles for the line to be tangent to.
(Line Normal To Curve)		Select a location on a curve, or a point on a curve. Then select the end point of the line.
(Rectangle)		Select the location for two diagonal corners of the rectangle.
(3-Point Arc starting with limits)		Select the start point of the arc, end point of the arc, and then another point for the arc to pass through.
(Circle)		Select the center of the circle and a point on its perimeter to define the diameter.

 (Elongated Hole)		Select the center of each arc, and then select a location on the profile to define the diameter.
 (Corner)		Select the two lines the corner is tangent to, and then drag the corner out to the required size.
 (Chamfer)	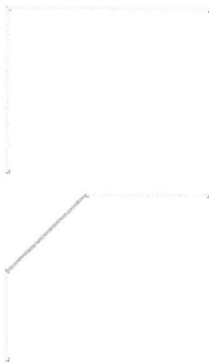	Select the two lines the chamfer contacts, and then drag the chamfer out to the required size.
 (Axis)		Select the start and end points of the axis.

Manual Definition

With many sketch tools, you can use another toolbar that contains additional functions for that specific type of geometry. Some of these options are described as follows:

Option	Description
Lines	Manually enter the coordinates of the start point, end point, line length, and angle into the Sketch Tools toolbar.

Start Point: H: 20mm	V: 20mm	L: 0mm	A: 0deg

Option	Description
Rectangle	Manually enter the coordinates of the first point, the coordinates of the second point, and the height and width of the rectangle.
Circle	Manually enter the coordinates for the circle's center and specify its radius.
Corner	Specify how to trim the existing lines when the corner is completed.

3.6 Profile Sketching

To create a connected series of lines and arcs, use

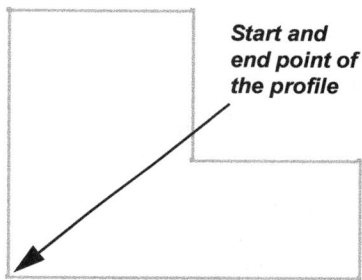 (Profile). Sketch a series of connected lines, then when you have formed a closed loop, the profile automatically terminates, as shown in Figure 3–13. You can also terminate the profile with an open loop by double-clicking the left mouse button at the end of the last line, as shown in Figure 3–14.

Start and end point of the profile

Double-click at the end to terminate

Figure 3–13   **Figure 3–14**

You can toggle from sketching a line to sketching a tangent arc (as shown in Figure 3–15) or three-point arc (as shown in Figure 3–16), by using the temporary icons in the Sketch tools toolbar. You return to sketching a line after you finish the arc.

Start (follow arrow) and end point of the profile

Tangent Arc

Select the Tangent Arc icon at this point

Select the Three Point Arc icon at this point

Three Point Arc

Start (follow arrow) and end point of the profile

Select the Tangent Arc icon at this point

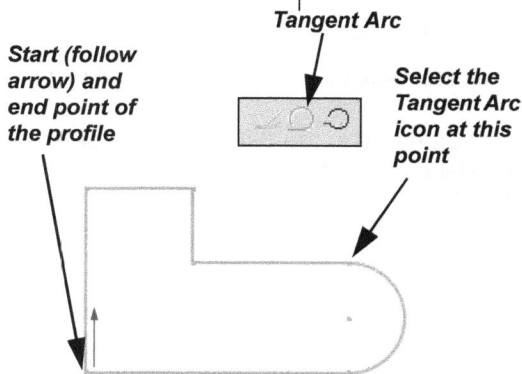

Figure 3–15

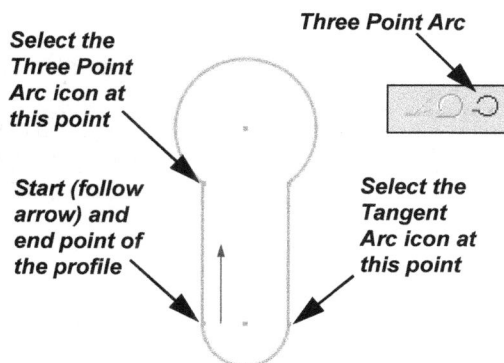

Figure 3–16

3.7 Sketcher Editing Operations

Trimming

 (Trim) extends or trims sketched entities to form a closed corner. Select each entity on the side of the intersection that you want to keep. Figure 3–17 shows three examples of trimming and extending line segments.

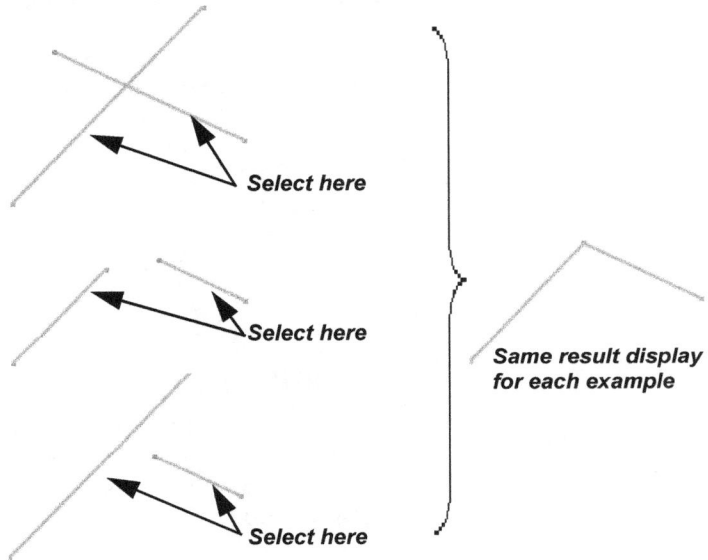

Figure 3–17

You can also choose to trim only the first selected entity by

clicking (Trim First Element) in the Sketch tools toolbar, and selecting the entity to which the first element should be trimmed, as shown in Figure 3–18.

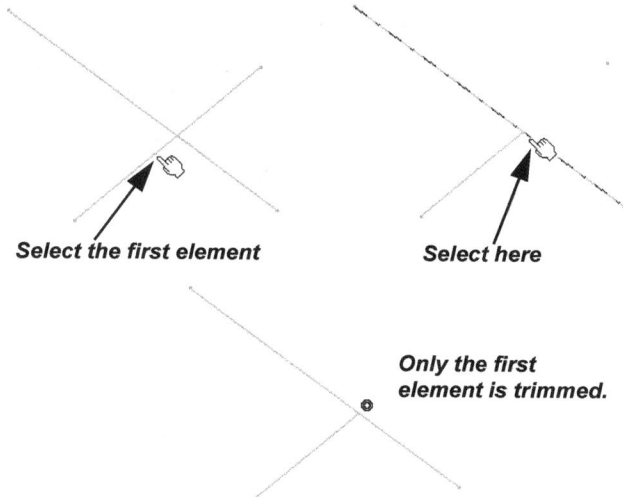

Select the first element   Select here

Only the first
element is trimmed.

Figure 3–18

Break   (Break) divides a sketched entity at its intersection with another sketched entity. To use the **Break** tool, select the feature you want to divide and select the intersecting feature. The intersection point is projected if the feature does not intersect the first entity.

- The **Break** tool is used to break circles into arcs using an intersecting line, as shown in Figure 3–19. Note that a closed entity, such as the circle, is also divided by an implicit 360° mark.

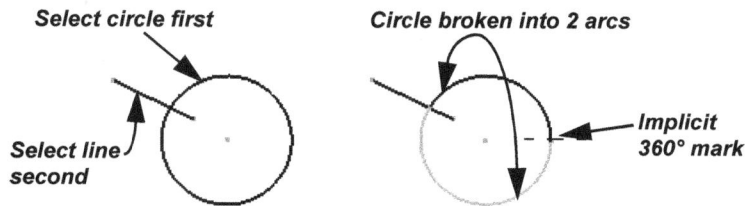

Select circle first   Circle broken into 2 arcs

Select line
second   Implicit
                360° mark

Figure 3–19

Quick Trim

(Quick Trim) deletes the selected portion of a feature. The software automatically breaks the element at its intersections with other sketched elements.

- The **Quick Trim** method is used to remove the arc segment between two vertical lines, as shown in Figure 3–20.

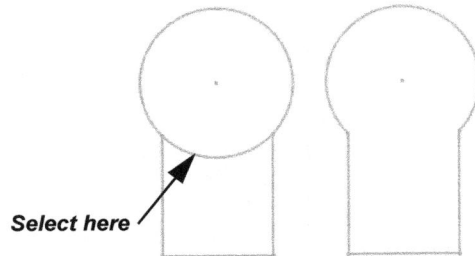

Select here

Figure 3–20

Delete and Undo

Pressing <Delete> enables you to remove portions (one or more lines) of a model or the entire sketch (rectangle).

- To completely eliminate a feature you just sketched, you can press <Ctrl>+<Z> or click (Undo). The keyboard shortcut executes the **Undo** command. CATIA records your previous actions, enabling you to undo multiple times.

3.8 Tips and Techniques

Repeating a Command

When you use any of the geometry creation icons, the command is automatically deactivated once you perform the action. However, by double-clicking on the icon, you can perform that command multiple times.

- Click ⬚ to deactivate it. This technique is more efficient than repeatedly selecting the same icon.

An active icon displays in an orange color.

Sketching in 3D

Sketching in a 3D orientation can be useful when solid geometry exists and you are sketching on the face of a previously defined feature.

- To return to the planar sketch view, click ⬚ (Normal View).

Construction Geometry

You can use construction geometry to help create lines, shapes, and points for your standard geometry. Construction geometry is useful when working with more complex sketches, as shown in Figure 3–21.

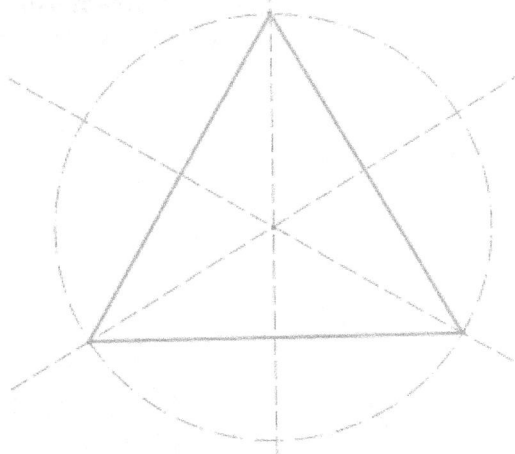

Figure 3–21

You can create construction geometry using one of the following methods:

Do not forget to return to Standard elements when you are done.

- Click ⌖ (Construction/Standard Element) in the Tools toolbar, as shown in Figure 3–22. Any geometry you sketch displays as construction geometry.

Construction/Standard Element

Figure 3–22

- Select the existing standard geometry and click

  ⌖ (Construction/Standard Element) to convert it to construction geometry.

Auto Search

Use the **Auto Search** tool to automatically select all entities that are connected to the selected entity.

- To use the **Auto Search** tool, select a sketched entity that belongs to the profile you want to select, then right-click and select *** object>Auto Search**, as shown in Figure 3–23. The continuous chain of entities is highlighted for the next operation.

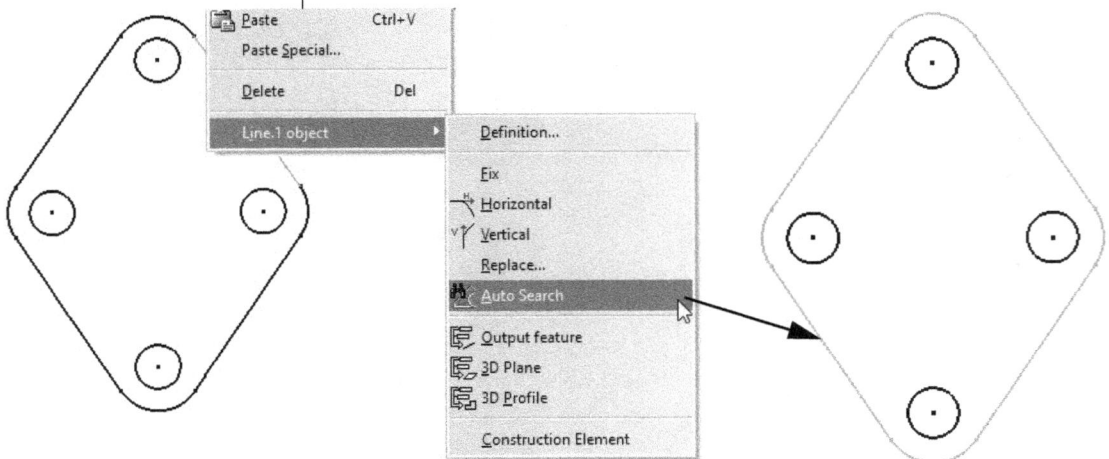

Figure 3–23

Sketching at Origin

If you select the origin of the sketch during the creation of a profile, CATIA automatically creates an implicit constraint between the vertex of the sketch and the origin. This constraint restricts the vertex of the profile from being moved at a later time, but can be broken by selecting the profile, selecting **Edit>Cut** and **Edit>Paste**. This pastes the profile on its original position without the constraint, so you can move it. This only works if the sketched entity has not been referenced by any other features. Any features that reference the entity being cut and pasted fail because the pasted item is considered a new sketched entity and does not maintain the references.

- This type of constraint can be used for a base feature since it is unlikely to move later. However, for other features that should be constrained to the origin, it is recommended to sketch offset from the origin and manually constrain the sketch to it. Figure 3–24 shows a circle that can be manually constrained to the origin using a **Coincident** constraint.

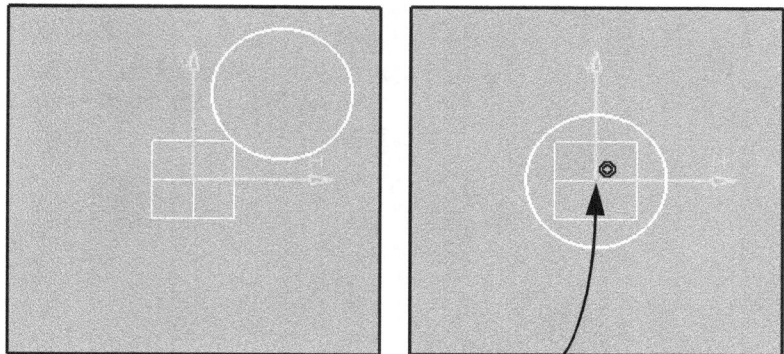

Coincident constraint

Figure 3–24

3.9 Specification Tree

The features you create are listed in the specification tree in the order in which you create them. Solid geometry features are listed under PartBody, as shown in Figure 3–25.

Sketches are automatically listed under the feature branch that uses them.

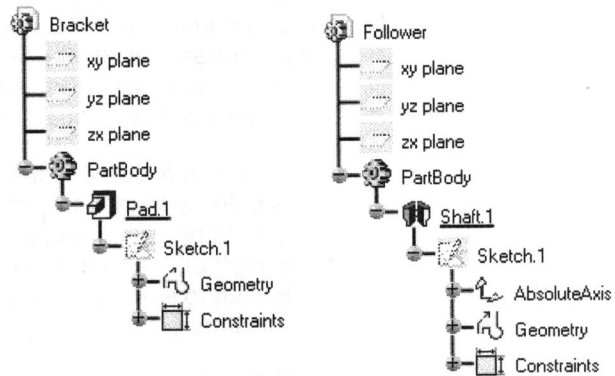

Figure 3–25

- A sketch is automatically hidden once referenced by a solid feature. Right-click on the sketch and select **Hide/Show** to toggle on its display.

Practice 3a

Sketching Basic Shapes

Practice Objectives

- Sketch a line, arc, rectangle, circle, and elongated hole.
- Trim overlapping shapes.

In this practice, you will create a sketch as shown in Figure 3–26. You will use various constraints to help constrain the sketch.

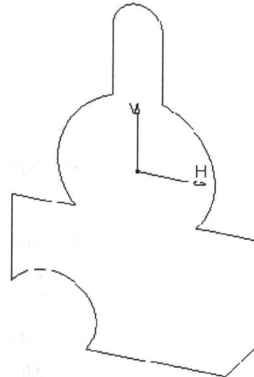

Figure 3–26

Task 1 - Create a new part and set the length units to millimeter.

1. Click [□] (New) to create a new part.

2. In the New dialog box, select the **Part** option and click **OK**, as shown in Figure 3–27.

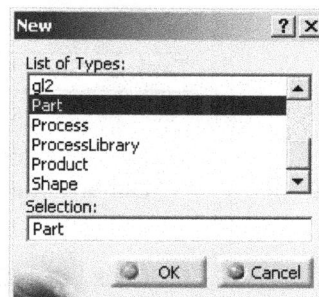

Figure 3–27

3. The New Part dialog box opens, as shown in Figure 3–28. Enter **Sketch_1** as the part name. If required, deactivate **Enable hybrid Design**.

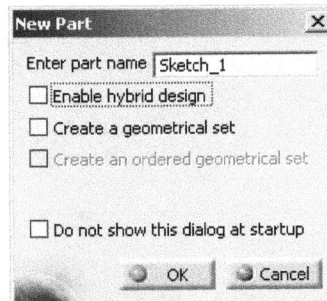

Figure 3–28

4. Click **OK** to create the new part model.

Task 2 - Select the sketching plane and enter the Sketcher workbench.

1. In the specification tree, select the YZ plane. Note which plane highlights on the screen.

2. Click (Sketch) to enter the Sketcher workbench. The selected reference plane displays parallel to the screen, as shown in Figure 3–29.

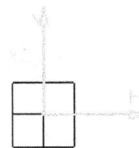

Figure 3–29

Task 3 - Sketch a circle.

Automatic Dimensional Constraints are discussed in more detail in a later chapter.

1. In the Sketch tools toolbar, ensure that (Automatic Dimensional Constraints) is toggled off.

2. Click (Circle) to sketch a circle.

3. Place the cursor over the intersection of the horizontal and vertical axes. Select the **0.0**, **0.0** location of the XY axis to define the circle's center point.

4. Drag the cursor and select a location to define the radius of the circle. The sketch displays as shown in Figure 3–30.

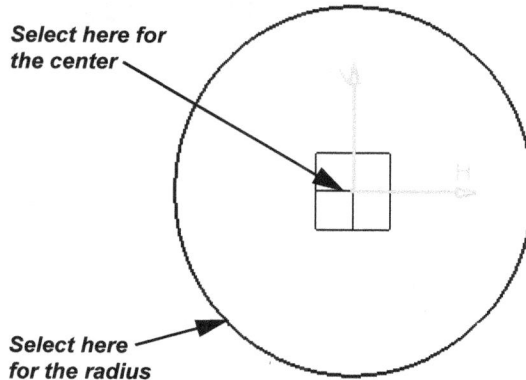

Select here for the center

Select here for the radius

Figure 3–30

Task 4 - Sketch a rectangle that overlaps the circle.

1. Click ▣ (Rectangle) to sketch a rectangle.

2. Select the first point of the rectangle and the second point of the rectangle, as shown in Figure 3–31.

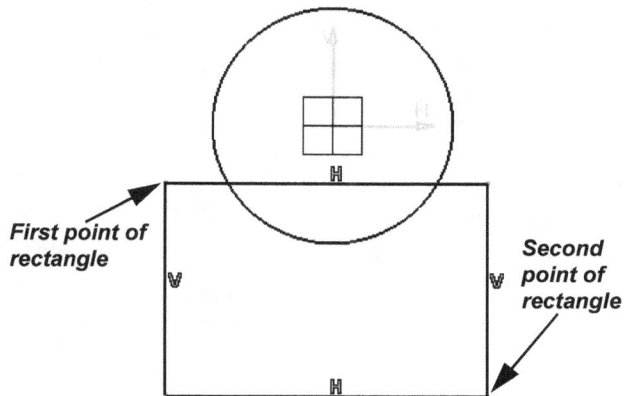

First point of rectangle

Second point of rectangle

Figure 3–31

Task 5 - Sketch a line.

1. Click [Line icon] (Line) to sketch a line.

2. Select the locations for the start and end points of the line, as shown in Figure 3–32.

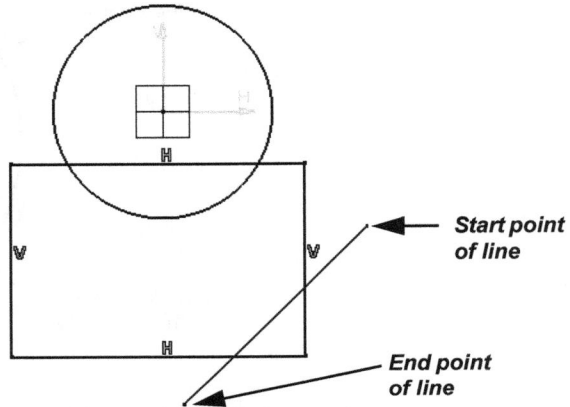

Figure 3–32

Task 6 - Sketch an arc.

1. Expand the [Circle icon] (Circle) flyout and click [Arc icon] (Three Point Arc) to sketch an arc.

Select the start point of the arc. Note that the lines of the rectangle highlight in orange when the cursor is over them. This color change indicates that the ends of the arc are aligned with that feature.

2. Select the second point that the arc passes through and select the end point of the arc, as shown in Figure 3–33.

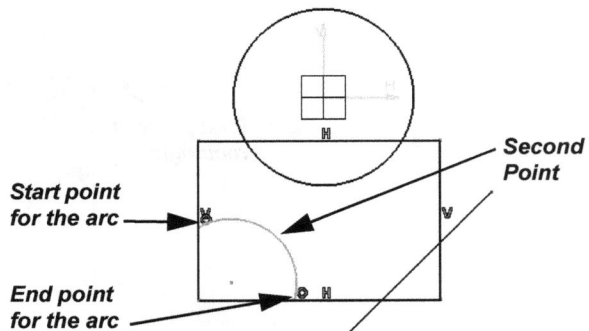

Figure 3–33

Task 7 - Sketch an elongated hole.

1. Expand the [⬜] (Rectangle) flyout and click [⊙] (Elongated Hole) to sketch an elongated hole.

2. Select the locations for the two arc centers, and a location to define the width of the elongated hole, as shown in Figure 3–34.

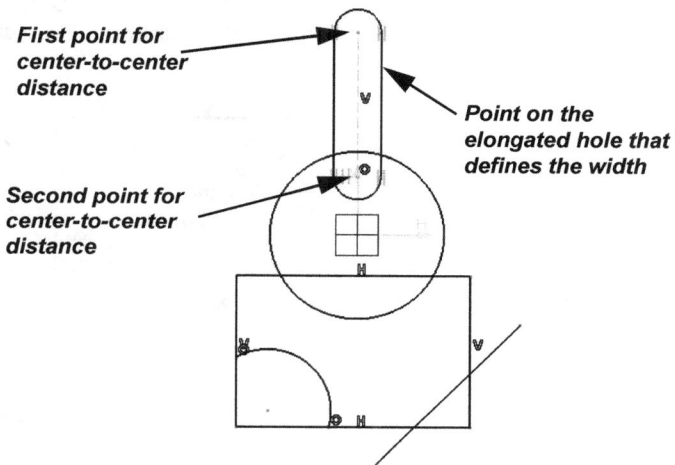

First point for center-to-center distance

Point on the elongated hole that defines the width

Second point for center-to-center distance

Figure 3–34

Task 8 - Trim the rectangle to the line and the circle.

Read Message area for your next selection.

1. Click [✂] (Trim) to trim the rectangle.

2. Select the line and the bottom of the rectangle, as shown in Figure 3–35.

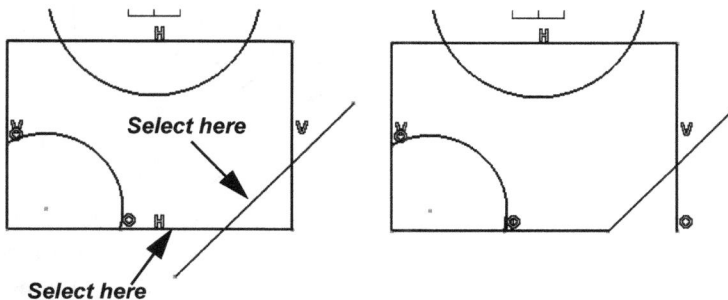

Select here

Select here

Figure 3–35

3. Note that ⊠ (Trim) is no longer highlighted. This means you have to click the icon again to perform another trim.

   Double-click on ⊠ (Trim) so you can trim multiple times.

4. Trim the other side of the rectangle and the line using the same technique. The elements to select are labeled **Trim #2** in Figure 3–36.

5. Trim two more times to trim the arc to the box. The elements to select are labeled **Trim #3** and **Trim #4** in Figure 3–36.

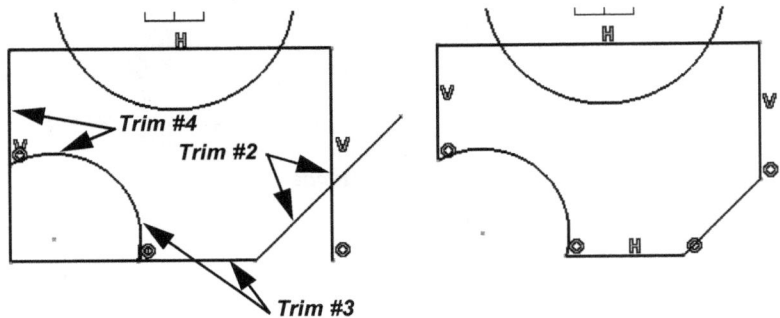

Figure 3–36

Task 9 - Trim the rectangle to the circle and the circle to the elongated hole using the Quick Trim method.

---

1. Expand the ⊠ (Trim) flyout menu and click ▱ (Quick Trim) to perform a **Quick Trim**.

2. Select the bottom of the circle to delete that segment, as shown in Figure 3–37.

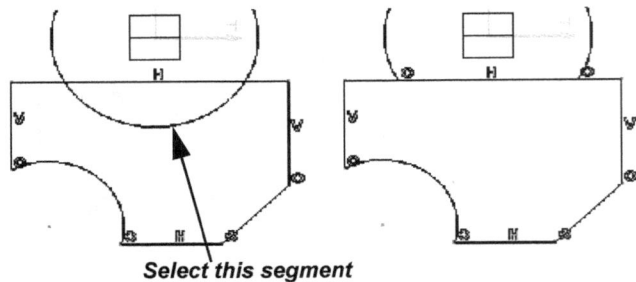

Select this segment

Figure 3–37

3. Double-click on ⬜ (Quick Trim) so you can trim multiple times.

4. Select the remaining intersecting segments to clean up the sketch, as shown in Figure 3–38.

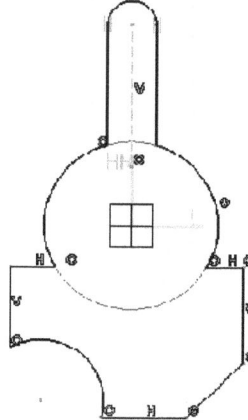

Figure 3–38

Task 10 - Save the part and exit the Sketcher workbench.

1. Click ⬆ (Exit workbench) to exit the Sketcher workbench. The sketch displays as shown in Figure 3–39.

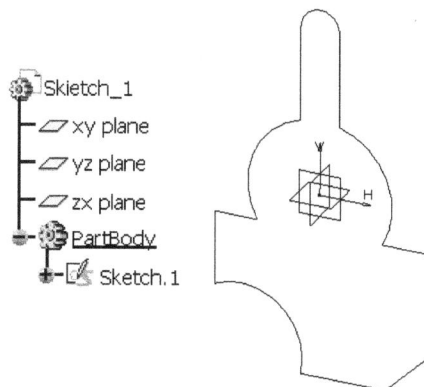

Figure 3–39

2. Click (Save) to save the part.

3. Accept the default part name of **Sketch_1.CATPart**.

4. Click **Save**.

5. Select **File>Close** to close the part window.

Practice 3b	# Profile Sketching

Practice Objective

- Use Profile Sketching to create lines and arcs.

In this practice, you will use the profile sketcher to create the sketch shown in Figure 3–40.

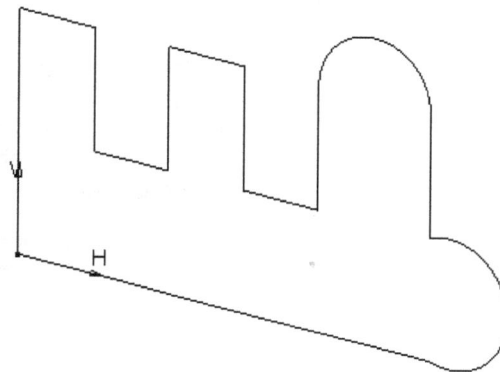

Figure 3–40

Task 1 - Create a new part and begin creating a sketch.

1. Click ☐ (New).

2. In the New dialog box, select **Part** and click **OK**.

3. Enter **Sketch_2** as the part name and click **OK**.

4. In the specification tree, select the YZ plane.

5. Click ◢ (Sketch).

Task 2 - Begin sketching a profile.

1. Ensure that the Sketch Tools toolbar displays and that

   ▦ (Automatic Dimensional Constraints) is toggled off.

2. Click ⏁ (Profile).

3. Place the cursor at the intersection of the horizontal and vertical axes, as shown in Figure 3–41. Press the left mouse button to begin sketching.

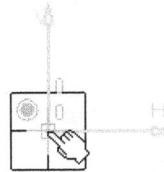

Figure 3–41

4. Sketch the series of connected vertical and horizontal lines, as shown in Figure 3–42. Note that the line turns blue when it is vertical or horizontal. Also note that the software displays a line to indicate when the cursor is coincident with other sketched elements.

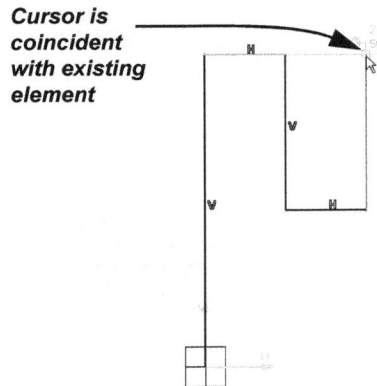

Figure 3–42

5. Continue sketching the profile until the section displays as shown in Figure 3–43. DO NOT end the profile yet.

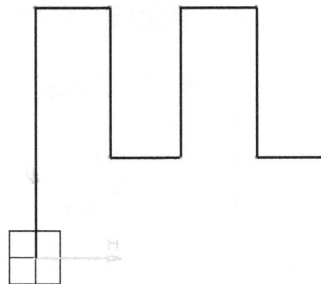

Figure 3–43

6. After selecting the end point of the last vertical line segment, click ⬭ (Tangent Arc) in the Sketch tools toolbar, as shown in Figure 3–44.

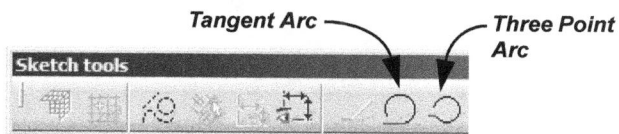

Figure 3–44

7. Drag the arc to **180°**, as shown in Figure 3–45. The arc highlights in blue once you reach 180°.

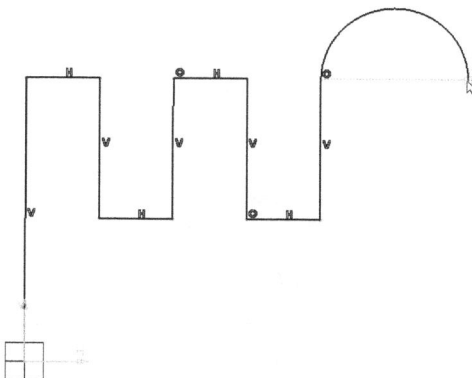

Figure 3–45

8. Draw a vertical line that is coincident with the intermediate horizontal lines, as shown in Figure 3–46.

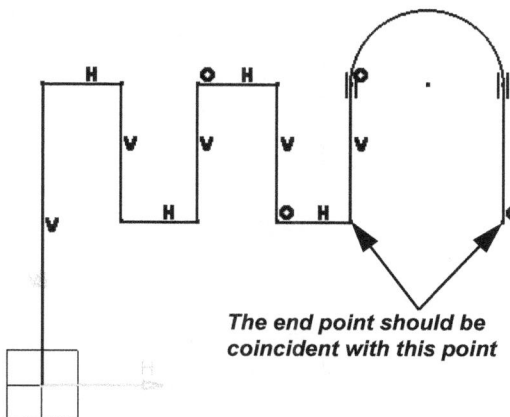

The end point should be coincident with this point

Figure 3–46

9. In the Tools toolbar, click ⬡ (Three Point Arc).

10. Sketch the three point arc shown in Figure 3–47. Try to make the end of the arc coincident with the horizontal axis and your last vertical line.

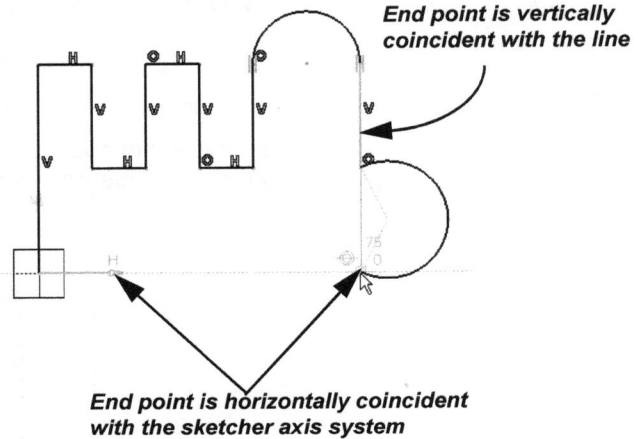

End point is vertically coincident with the line

End point is horizontally coincident with the sketcher axis system

Figure 3–47

11. Drag the last horizontal line and connect it to the start point to close the sketch as shown in Figure 3–48.

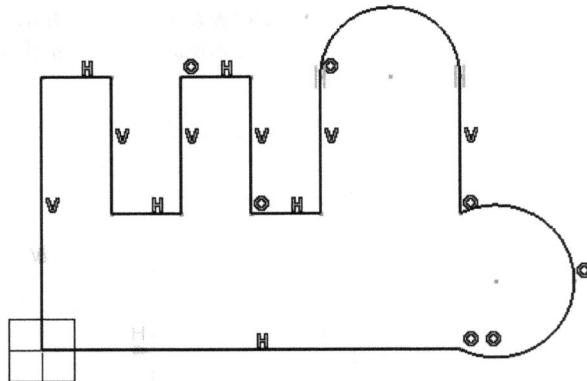

Figure 3–48

Task 3 - Select the profile.

In this task you will demonstrate the use of the **Auto Search** option by selecting the 13 entities of the sketch.

1. Select any entity in the sketch.

2. Right-click and select *** object>Auto Search**. The software highlights the entire profile.

3. Select anywhere on the background to clear the profile.

Task 4 - Exit the Sketcher workbench and save the part.

1. Click [⬆] (Exit workbench) to exit the Sketcher workbench.

2. Click [💾] (Save).

3. Accept the default name of **Sketch_2.CATPart**.

4. Click **Save**.

5. Select **File>Close** to close the part window.

Practice 3c

(Optional) Sketch Practice I

Practice Objective

- Create a sketch without instructions.

Create a new part called **SketchProfile** and sketch the profile shown in Figure 3–49. Use the YZ plane as the support for the sketch. Do not be concerned with the size of the profile; just ensure that the same shape is developed.

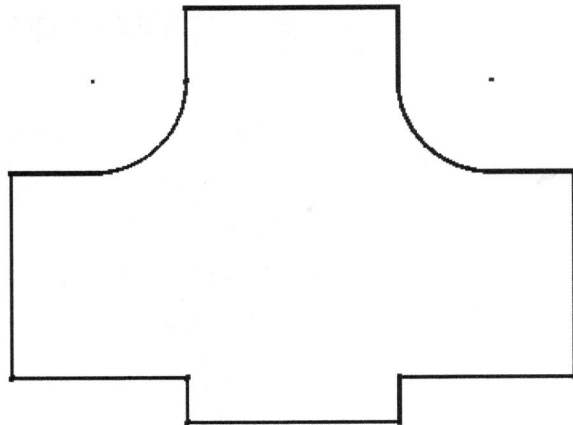

Figure 3–49

Practice 3d

(Optional) Sketch Practice II

Practice Objective

* Create a sketch without instructions.

Create a new part called **OutletProfile** and sketch the profile shown in Figure 3–50. Use the YZ plane as the support for the sketch. Do not be concerned with the size of the profile; just ensure that the same shape is developed.

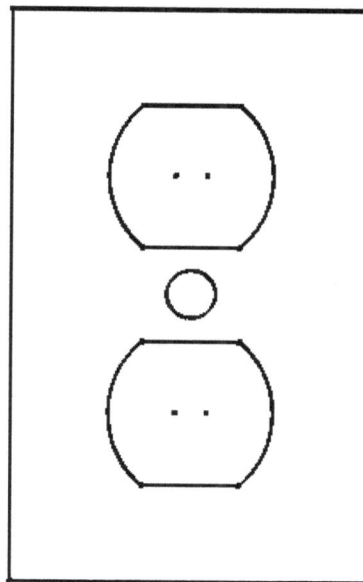

Figure 3–50

Chapter Review Questions

1. What is the process of accessing the Sketcher workbench?

   a. Select an appropriate sketch support and click .

   b. Click .

   c. When a CATIA part is created, the Sketcher workbench is immediately opened.

   d. Select an appropriate sketch support and click .

2. All new parts start with what features?

   a. Pads

   b. Pockets

   c. Surfaces

   d. Default Reference Planes and the Part Body.

3. Which default plane is considered the front of the part?

   a. XY plane

   b. ZX plane

   c. YZ plane

4. Which of the following statements best describes the default reference planes?

   a. They are the first solid feature.

   b. They have mass.

   c. They are the foundation of a part.

   d. They are not required and should be deleted.

5. If Figure 3–51 is shown in the Isometric view orientation, what is the sketching plane for the feature?

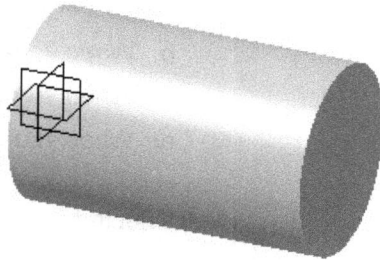

Figure 3–51

a. XY plane

b. ZX plane

c. YZ plane

6. Which of the following icons enables you to sketch construction geometry?

a.

b.

c.

d.

7. Sketches are automatically hidden once they are referenced by a solid feature.

a. True

b. False

8. Which tool is the most efficient method of creating a series of connected lines and arcs?

a.

b.

c.

d.

9. When is a profile terminated? (Select all that apply.)

   a. When you form a closed loop.

   b. When you click again.

   c. When you double-click.

   d. When you right-click and select **End Profile**.

10. Which of the following icons enables you to delete the selected portion of a feature?

   a.

   b.

   c.

   d.

Answers: 1.a, 2.d, 3.c, 4.c, 5.b, 6.c, 7.a, 8.b, 9.abc, 10.a

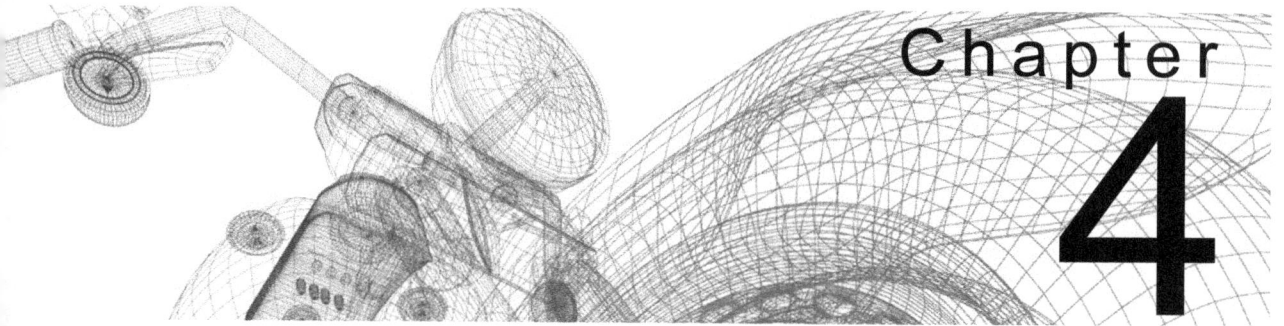

Chapter 4

Constraining Sketches

Constraints can be either geometric or dimensional. Geometric Constraints assess a relationship between geometric elements that forces a limitation, whereas dimensional constraints define the size and location of an element. In addition, the Auto Constraint feature creates the missing constraints to make the profile fully constrained.

Learning Objectives in this Chapter

- Understand the difference between Geometric, Dimensional, and Automatic Dimensional Constraints.
- Understand the advantages of using constraints to control sketches.
- Understand the various geometric constraints.
- Work with constraints and learn how to automatically constrain a sketch.
- Use the Edit Multi-Constraint dialog box to edit multiple dimensions before the section updates.
- Understand the system-defined constraint colors for the sketch status.
- Understand the Sketch Analysis dialog box and how to use its various tabs to analyze a sketch.

4.1 Constraints

Constraints define the size and location of a sketch. You can use two types of constraints, as shown in Figure 4–1.

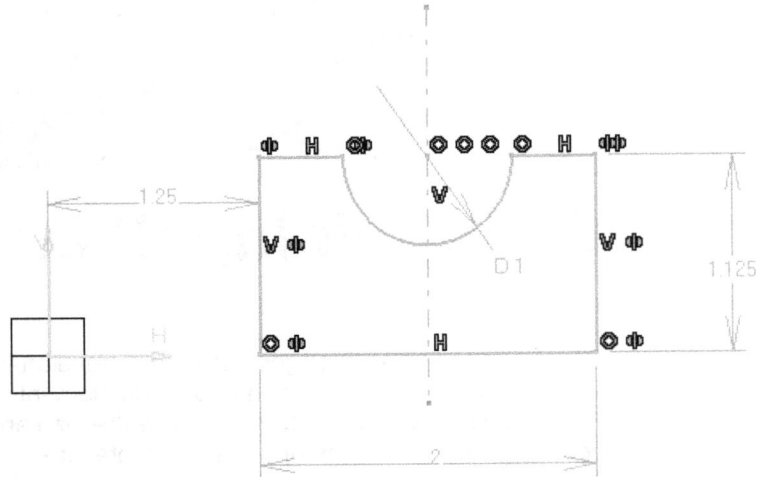

Figure 4–1

The constraints available, along with their icons in the Sketch Tools toolbar, are used to control their display. They are described as follows:

Icon	Constraint	Description
	Geometrical Constraints	Relationships between geometric elements that describe how they are oriented.
	Dimensional Constraints	Values used to define the size, distance, or angle of an element.
	Automatic Dimensional Constraints	Automatically apply the values used to define the size or angle of elements as you sketch.

You can develop sketches that are completely unconstrained or partially unconstrained. Thus, you do not need to place any unnecessary dimensions on a sketch. However, it is recommended that you fully constrain your sketches.

Figure 4–2 shows an example of a partially constrained sketch. Initially, the box is 50 wide. When this dimensional constraint is changed to 100, the software updates one side of the box and leaves the other side in its original state. If the design intent of this sketch is to create a rectangle, the current design of this part requires additional constraints to maintain the geometry over time.

Vertical

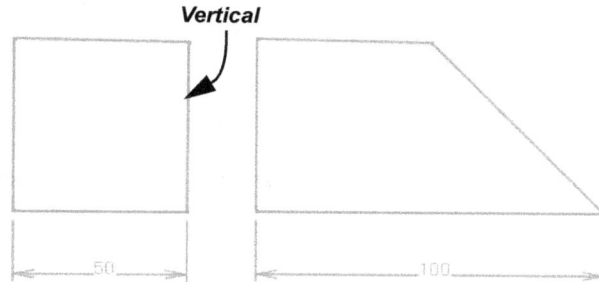

Figure 4–2

If you start constructing 3D solid models with features that are unconstrained, the models is more complex. Figure 4–3 shows an example of an unconstrained Pocket. If the block is made wider or taller, what happens to the Pocket? Should it remain centered on the block or should it remain the same distance from the right or left side? This unpredictable nature means that the designs must be thoroughly checked each time a change is made.

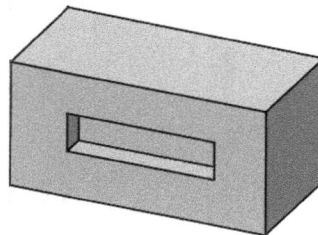

Figure 4–3

Advantages of Using Constraints

Using constraints has the following advantages:

- Dimensional constraints enable you to precisely define the size of your sketch and to quickly and accurately change its size.

- Geometric constraints enable you to incorporate design intent into your sketches, which automates the geometry update process.

4.2 Geometric Constraints

Geometric constraints are accessed using [icon] (Constraints Defined in Dialog Box). Geometric constraints consist of a relationship between geometric elements that forces a limitation of some type. For example, you can constrain a line in a sketch to be vertical. With the vertical constraint in place, the line is limited and cannot be at an angle.

The most commonly-used geometric constraints are described as follows:

Constraint	Example	Description
Horizontal		Use <Ctrl> to preselect the lines that are to be horizontal.
Vertical		Use <Ctrl> to preselect the lines that are to be vertical.

Parallelism	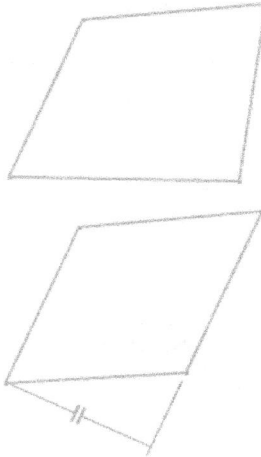	Select the first line to remain fixed, and select the second line to make parallel to the first.
Perpendicular	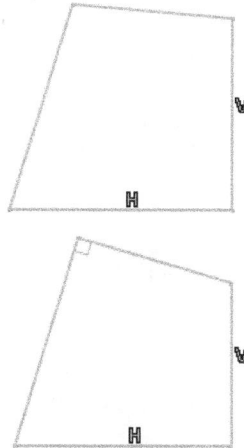	Use \<Ctrl\> to preselect lines to be perpendicular.
Concentricity	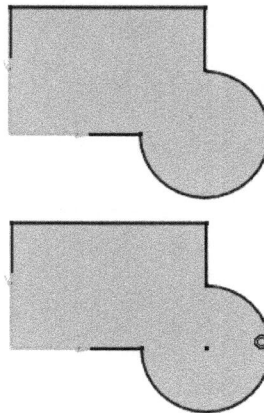	Select a curved edge of a Pad feature and the sketched circle. Concentricity only works with existing geometry.

Tangency	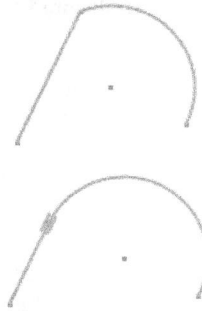	Use <Ctrl> to preselect the entities to be tangent.
Symmetry	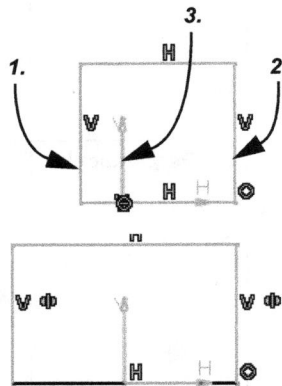	Press and hold <Ctrl> while selecting references in the following order: first symmetric element, second symmetric element, and symmetry reference.
Coincidence		Select end points of entities to be coincident with one another and/or to another point. For circles, you must select the circle centers.
	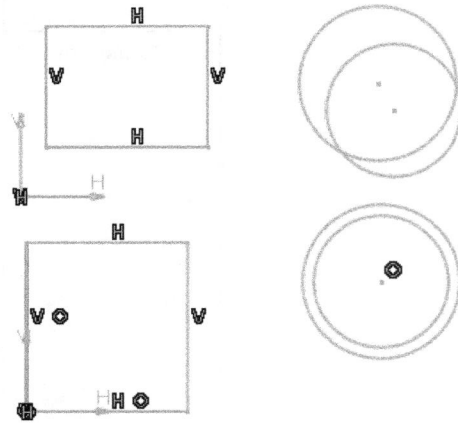	

How To: Apply a Constraint

1. Use <Ctrl> to preselect the elements in the correct sequence.

2. Click [⬚] (Constraints Defined in Dialog Box).

3. Select the required constraint in the Constraint Definition dialog box shown in Figure 4–4.

Only the constraints that are valid for the elements you selected are available.

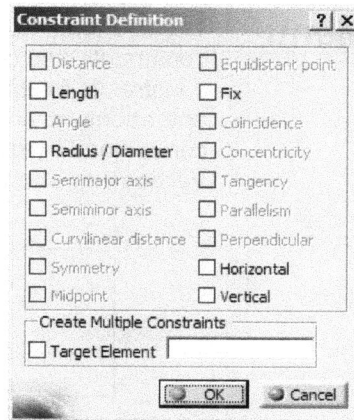

Figure 4–4

4. Click **OK**.

Note that you can apply constraints between entities using the **Create Multiple Constraints** option. In the Constraint Definition dialog box, enable **Target Element**, click in the *Target Element* field and select an element from the sketch. The selected element will drive the resulting constraints.

Three lines were selected in Figure 4–5, and the top line, **Line.3**, is used as the Target Element. When the **Distance** constraint is selected, the dimensions for the distance between the lines, are added, using **Line.3** as the baseline.

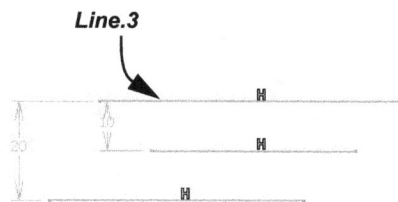

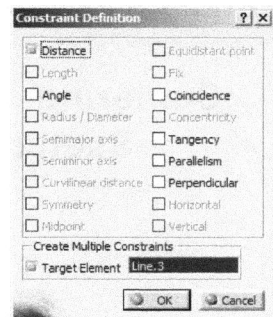

Figure 4–5

Deleting Constraints

Use one of the following methods to remove a constraint:

- Select the constraint symbol on the screen to highlight it, and press <Delete>.

- Select the constraint in the specification tree and press <Delete>.

Shortcut Menu

The shortcut menu provides access to frequently used geometric constraints and operations such as **Horizontal** or **Vertical** constraints for linear elements and **Close** or **Complement** operations for arcs. For example, a slanted line can be vertically constrained by right-clicking and selecting **Line.# object> Vertical**, as shown in Figure 4–6.

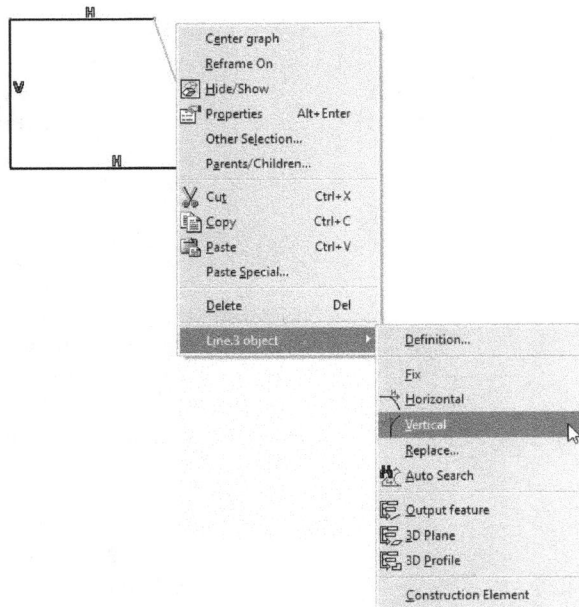

Figure 4–6

Centering a Sketch

To center a sketch on a part, sketch an axis and use the **Symmetry** constraint to constrain the axis to the middle of the part. Use <Ctrl> to multi-select the two edges of the part, and then the axis. Click (Constraints Defined in Dialog Box) and select **Symmetry**. When the **Symmetry** constraint is applied, the axis becomes centered, as shown in Figure 4–7.

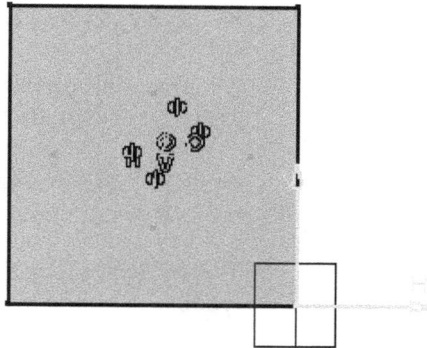

Figure 4–7

Fix Together Constraint

The **Fix Together** constraint constrains selected sketched elements together so that they can be moved as one entity.

How To: Fix Sketched Elements Together

1. Select the entities to add by drawing a selection box around them, or by multi-selecting with <Ctrl>.

2. Click 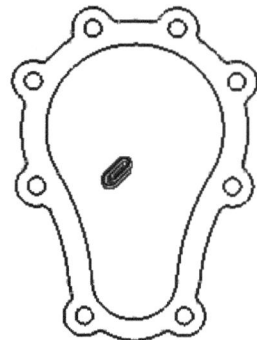 (Fix Together). The Fix Together Definition dialog box opens as shown in Figure 4–8.

3. Click **OK**. The sketch elements can be dynamically moved using the cursor, as shown in Figure 4–9.

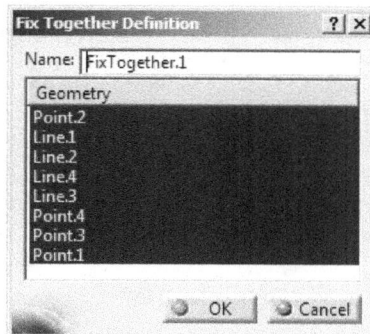

Figure 4–8

Figure 4–9

4.3 Dimensional Constraints

Dimensional constraints define an element's size and location. In most cases, you need to create several dimensions. Double-click on 🖼 (Constraint) to create as many dimensions as you require without having to click the icon every time.

The following topics describe how to create various dimension types.

Line Length Dimension

To dimension a line, select the line to be dimensioned and drag the dimension to the required location, as shown in Figure 4–10.

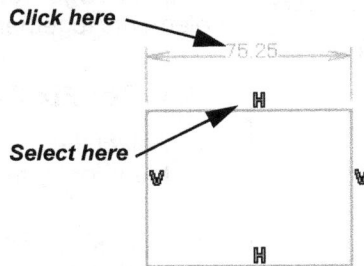

Figure 4–10

Distance between Parallel Lines

To dimension the distance between parallel lines, select the first line. A length dimension displays. Select the second line. The distance between the two lines displays. Click to place the dimension. An example is shown in Figure 4–11.

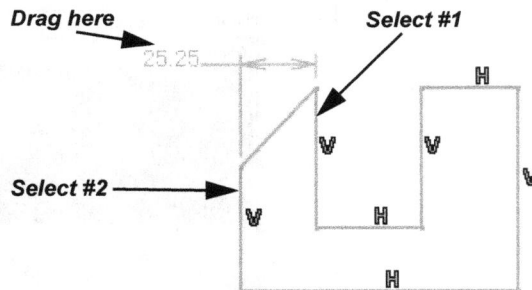

Figure 4–11

Arc Radius

To create an arc radius dimension, sketch a corner and the dimension is automatically created. To manually create an arc radius dimension, select the arc and click a location on the screen to place the dimension, as shown in Figure 4–12.

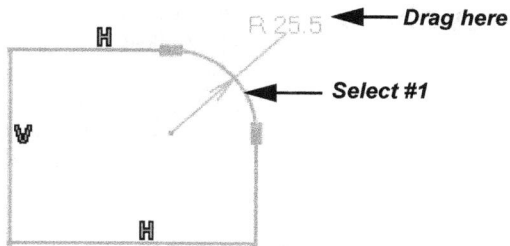

Figure 4–12

Arc Diameter

To dimension an arc as a diameter, you can use one of the following methods:

- A radius dimension displays by default when you select the arc. Before placing the dimension, right-click and select **Diameter**, as shown in Figure 4–13.

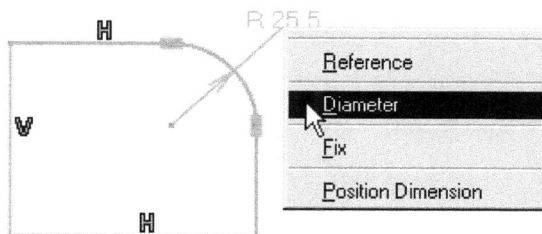

Figure 4–13

- Convert an existing arc radius dimension into a diameter dimension by double-clicking on the radius dimension. The Constraint Definition dialog box opens. Select **Diameter** in the drop-down list and click **OK** to complete the change, as shown in Figure 4–14.

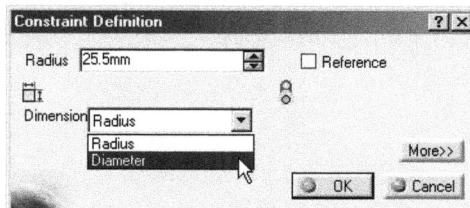

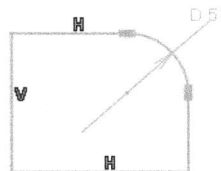

Figure 4–14

Revolved Diameter

When creating sketches for revolved features, only half of the profile is sketched. It is then revolved about the centerline. To create this dimension, select a line element and an axis. By default, a dimension representing the distance between the two parallel elements displays. Before placing the dimension, right-click and select **Diameter**, as shown in Figure 4–15.

The revolved diameter can only be created using an axis and not a construction line.

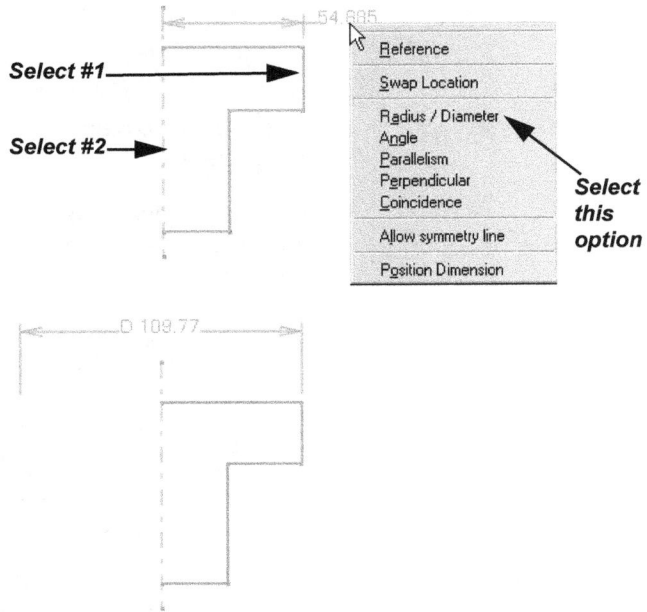

Figure 4–15

Angle Dimension

To create an angle dimension, select two non-parallel lines and an angle dimension displays. The dimension location determines how the angle dimension displays. The result of placing an angle dimension in four different locations is shown in Figure 4–16.

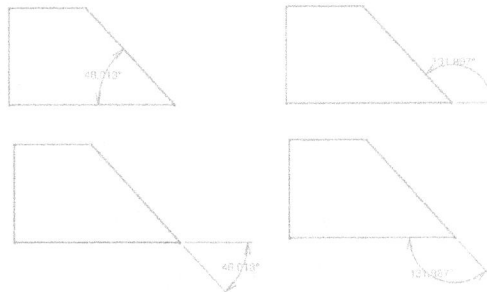

Figure 4–16

Point-to-Point Dimension

Point-to-point dimensions can be created between any two of the following elements:

- Center of an arc or circle

- End of a straight line

- Construction point

By default, the dimension displays as the absolute distance between the points. Before placing the dimension, use the shortcut menu to display the dimension as the horizontal or vertical distance between the points. These dimension options are shown in Figure 4–17.

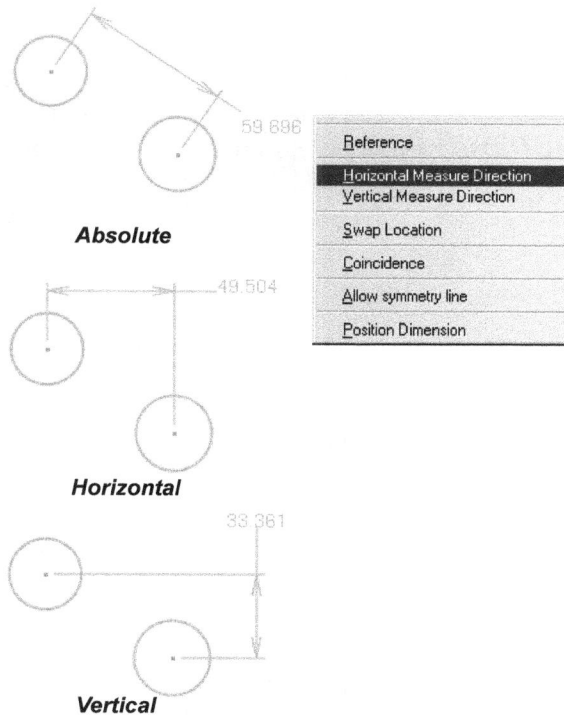

Absolute

Horizontal

Vertical

Figure 4–17

Line-to-Arc Tangent

You can also dimension to the arc center by selecting on the point.

To create a line-to-arc tangent dimension, select the line as the first element to dimension from. The line length dimension displays. Ignore this dimension and select the arc. The arc tangent dimension displays as shown in Figure 4–18.

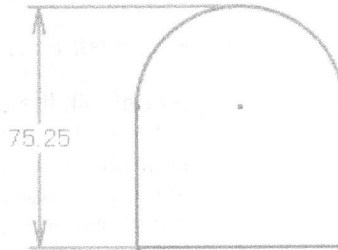

Figure 4–18

Arc Tangent-to-Arc Tangent

Select each of the arcs and drag the dimension to the required location. By default, the dimension displays as the absolute distance between the arc tangents, as shown in Figure 4–19.

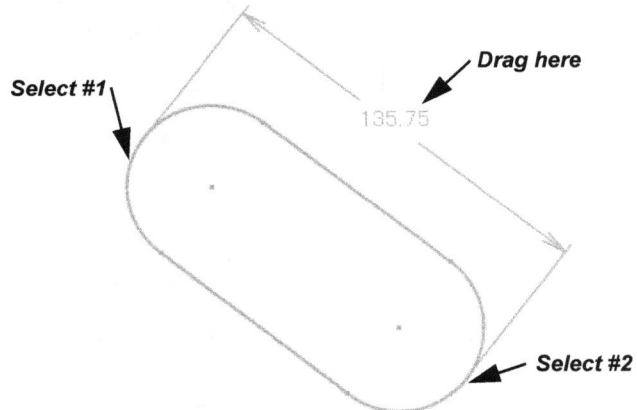

Figure 4–19

Before placing the dimension, you can use the shortcut menu to display the dimension as the horizontal or vertical distance between the arcs.

Shortcut Menu

Geometric Constraints can also be generated using

(Constraint) in conjunction with the shortcut menu. This enables you to double-click on the **Constraints** icon and create nearly all of the geometric and dimensional constraints for a profile with a single tool.

How To: Place Geometric Constraints Using the Shortcut Menu

1. Double-click on ⬚ (Constraint).
2. Select one or more geometric entities in your sketch.
3. Instead of clicking to place the dimension that displays, right-click to display the shortcut menu shown in Figure 4–20.

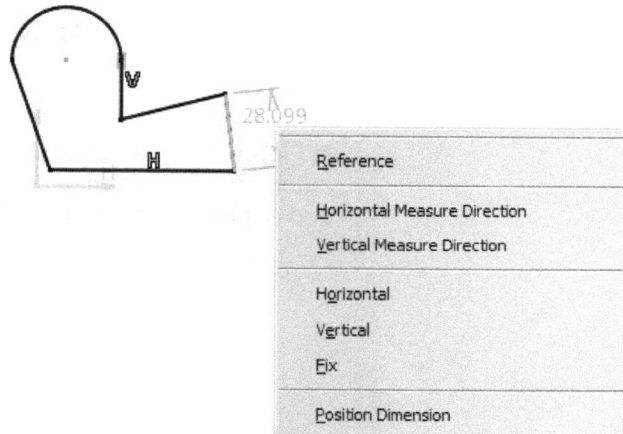

Reference

Horizontal Measure Direction
Vertical Measure Direction

Horizontal
Vertical
Fix

Position Dimension

Figure 4–20

4. Select the geometric constraint you want to apply to the selected geometry from the shortcut menu. The geometric constraint is now applied as shown in Figure 4–21.

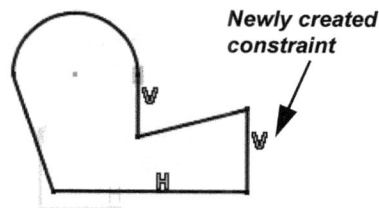

Newly created constraint

Figure 4–21

5. Repeat Steps 2 to 4 to place more geometric constraints.

6. Click ⬚ (Constraint) to deactivate the **Constraint** tool.

4.4 Automatic Dimensional Constraints

In the Sketch Tools toolbar, you can use [icon] (Automatic Dimensional Constraints), as shown in Figure 4–22, to automatically add dimensional constraints as you sketch geometry.

Figure 4–22

In Figure 4–23, as soon as the rectangle is sketched, the system automatically determined the required dimensions to constrain it and applied them accordingly.

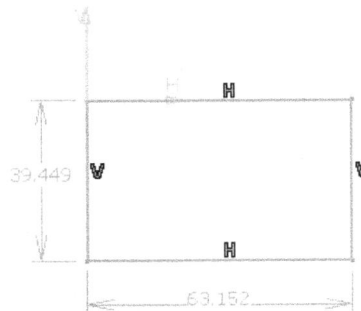

Figure 4–23

You can edit the dimensions to finalize them, as required. Automatic dimensional constraints are only applied to rectangles, circles, arcs and ellipses, and will only be added to define the size of an element, not its location relative to other elements.

4.5 Edit Multi-Constraint Dialog Box

The Edit Multi-Constraint dialog box enables you to modify the value of more than one dimension before updating the section. This is useful when modifying all dimensions of an oversized section. Typically, you would have to select the order of modification carefully to ensure that the modified dimension does not cause the section to fail. Using the **Edit Multi-Constraint** tool, you can modify all dimension values, and then preview and accept the changes.

The **Multi-Constraint** tool is found in the Constraint toolbar shown in Figure 4–24.

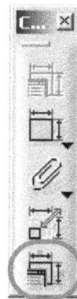

Figure 4–24

How To: Modify Dimensions Using the Edit Multi-Constraint tool

1. Click 🔲 (Edit Multi-Constraint) in the Constraint toolbar.
2. The Edit Multi-Constraint dialog box opens. The software displays the constraint name, initial value, current value, and the maximum and minimum tolerances for each dimension in the section as shown in Figure 4–25.

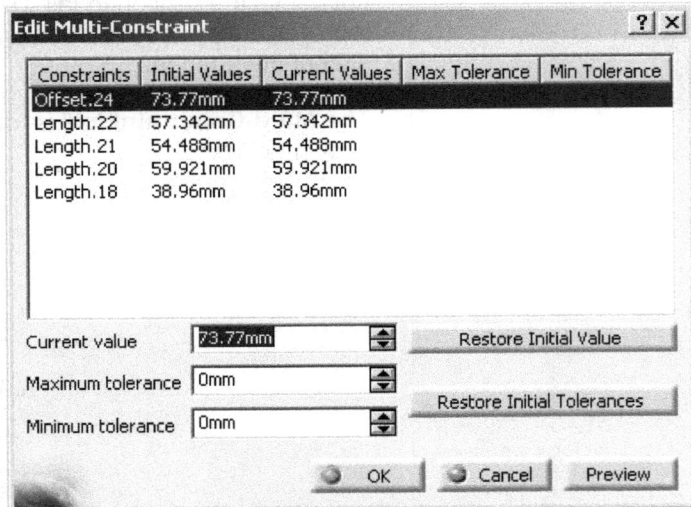

Figure 4–25

3. Select the dimension from the list or directly from the model. The corresponding dimension highlights in orange on the section.
4. In the *Current value* field, enter a new value. The dimension highlights in cyan to indicate that the initial value has been modified.
5. Once all dimensions have been modified, click **Preview** to preview the changes to the section.

6. Click **OK** to complete the changes. If an error occurs, click **Restore Initial Value** to undo the modification to the selected dimension.

Tips and techniques

- You can modify or restore multiple dimensions by using <Ctrl> to select them.

- Maximum and minimum tolerances can be added to any dimension by selecting it and entering the tolerance in the appropriate field.

- You can right-click in the *Current value* field in the Edit Multi-Constraint dialog box to access standard constraint editing options, as shown in Figure 4–26.

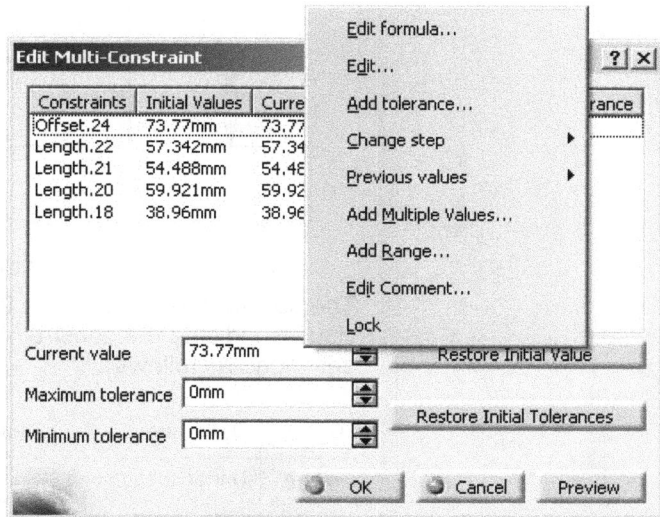

Figure 4–26

- For large, complex sections, click **Preview** frequently to update and test the section. If an error occurs, it is likely a dimension that was modified after the last preview.

- Selecting dimensions before clicking 🗒 (Edit Multi-Constraint) only adds those dimensions to the Edit Multi-Constraint dialog box.

4.6 Constraint Colors

To fully constrain your sketches, you must define the size and
location of the sketch. For the first sketch on a new part, you
must constrain the sketch to the horizontal and vertical axes, as
shown in Figure 4–27.

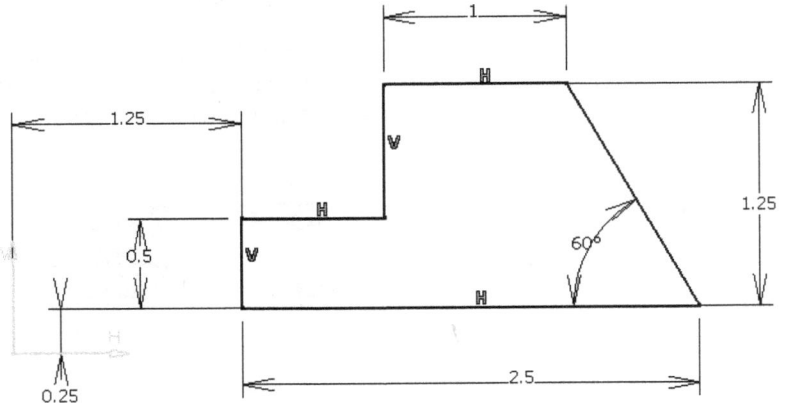

Figure 4–27

The software uses colors on the elements of your sketch to
visually indicate the constraint status. These colors are
described as follows:

Color	Definition	Description
White	Under constrained	Some degrees of freedom still remain for the element.
Green	Constrained	The geometry is completely fixed and cannot be moved without altering a dimensional value.
Purple	Over constrained	Too many dimensions or geometric constraints are on the element.
Red	Inconsistent	The sketch cannot be solved with the current combination of constraints and values.
Brown	Not changed	Geometry that is dependent on over-defined or inconsistent elements and is not up to date.

4.7 Sketch Analysis

Once the sketch is created and constrained, you can analyze the sketch by clicking (Sketch Analysis) or selecting **Tools> Sketch Analysis**. The Sketch Analysis dialog box opens as shown in Figure 4–28.

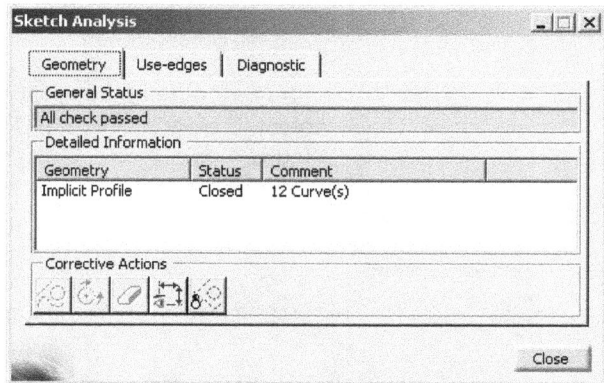

Figure 4–28

The following are examples of the types of analyses that can be performed:

- Ensure that the section meets the design intent.

- Ensure that the section is fully constrained.

- Check the status of projections and intersections.

- Perform corrective actions, as required.

Geometry Tab

The *Geometry* tab is used to analyze individual elements of the sketch. It displays the general status of the elements being analyzed. It is used to analyze the sketched elements and determine the status of each element in the model. The different values available in the *Status* column are described as follows:

Status	Description
Opened	A collection of sketched entities that form an open loop. Open loops can occur when the start and end points of a loop appear to be touching, but actually have a gap between them.

Closed	A collection of sketched entities that form a closed loop.
Isolated	A single sketched entity that is not touching or connected to any other geometry in the section. This could indicate a line which should be converted to a construction line, or a line which should belong to a loop of entities, but has gaps at either end.
Wrong Point	A sketched point is connected to existing geometry. This indicates that the point should be converted to a construction point to be a valid section to create 3D geometry.

The *Geometry* tab also displays detailed information about each selected element type and general comments, as shown in Figure 4–29.

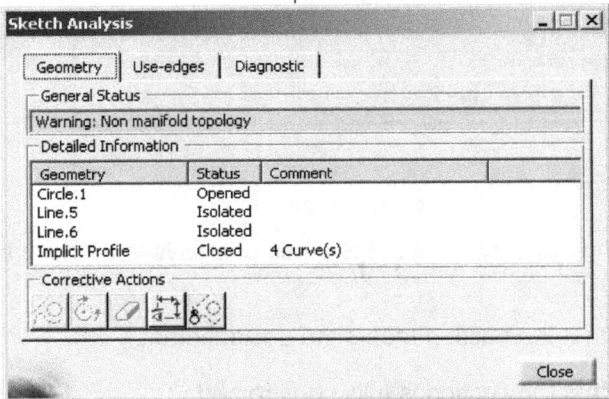

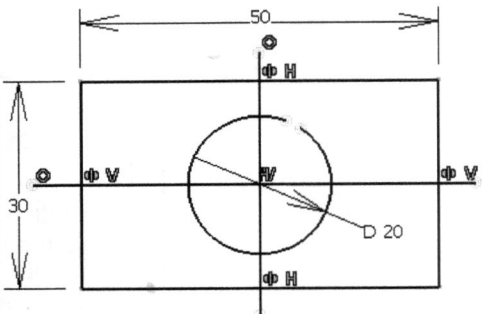

Figure 4–29

If you select an item in the Detailed Information area, the entity highlights on the screen, making it easier to find.

The sketch shown in Figure 4–29 has several problems. The detailed information displays that the circle is not closed (which is not the design intent) and that two line entities in the profile should be construction lines. The icons in the *Corrective Actions* area of the dialog box enable you to correct the problems in your sketch.

These icons are described as follows:

Icon	Description
	Changes the selected entity to a construction entity.
	Closes the open profile.
	Deletes the selected entity from the sketch.
	Toggles the display of constraints on and off in the sketch.
	Toggles the display of construction geometry on and off in the sketch.

The icons in the *Corrective Actions* area correct the problem, as shown in Figure 4–30. **Line.5** and **Line.6** were converted to construction entities using . **Circle.1** was closed using .

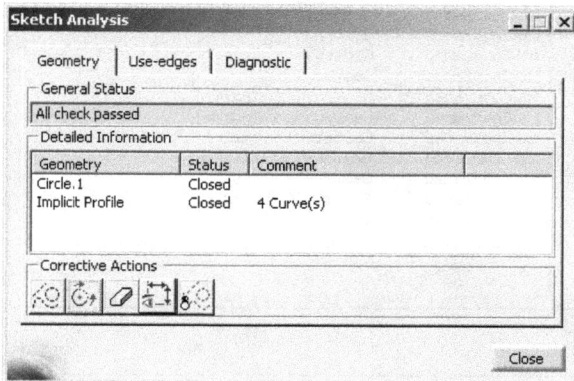

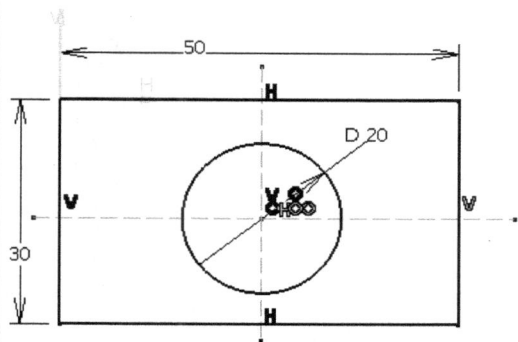

Figure 4–30

Use-edges

The *Use-edges* tab displays the status of all entities that are projected from existing geometry. The contents of this tab are discussed in detail once the concept of projecting 3D geometry has been introduced.

Diagnostic Tab

The *Diagnostic* tab provides a detailed summary of each sketched entity and the solving status of the sketch. A sketched entity can have one of the following three status values:

- **Under-Constrained:** Additional dimensions or constraints must be applied to the sketched entity.

- **Over-Constrained:** Too many dimensions or constraints have been applied to the element.

- **ISO-Constrained:** The entity is fully constrained.

The *Detailed Information* area lists all sketched entities, their current constraint status, and the type of entity (i.e., geometry, constraint, construction geometry, etc.), as shown in Figure 4–31.

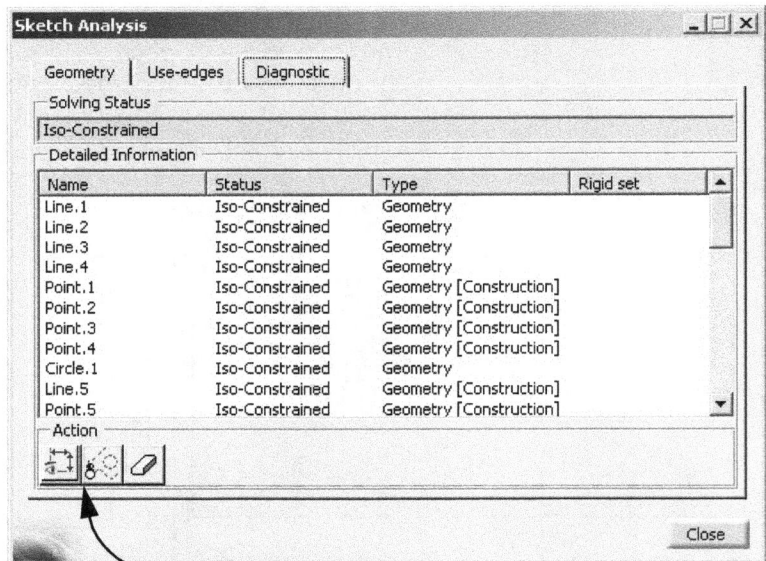

Hide/Show icons

Figure 4–31

The **Hide/Show** icons in the *Action* area can be used to simplify the screen. Select an entity in the *Detailed Information* area and select the appropriate icon to hide or show the entity.

You cannot edit the sketch while the tab is open. You must first exit the Sketch Analysis dialog box, solve any constraint issues, and re-open the dialog box to verify.

Sketch Solving Status

The Sketch Solving Status dialog box is used to determine the constraint status of the sketch. A sketch can either be under-constrained, over-constrained, or fully constrained (ISO-constrained). If the section is over-constrained or under-constrained, the software highlights the affected entities on the sketch.

Click (Sketch Solving Status) in the Tools toolbar to open the Sketch Solving Status dialog box, as shown in Figure 4–32.

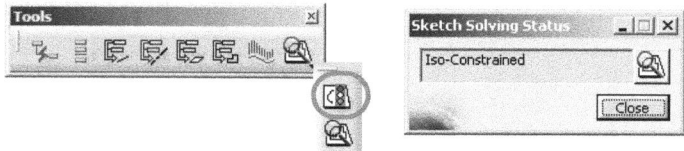

Figure 4–32

You can open the **Sketch Analysis** tool from this dialog box by clicking (Sketch Analysis).

4.8 Auto Constraint

If you are having trouble eliminating all degrees of freedom, you

can use (Auto Constraint) to fully constrain your sketch. The
Auto Constraint tool is found in the Constraint toolbar, as
shown in Figure 4–33.

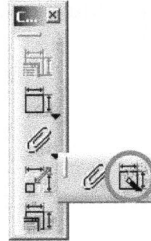

Figure 4–33

The Auto Constraint dialog box requires up to three sets of
information. These are described as follows:

Information	Description
Elements to be constrained	These elements of your sketch display in white. When in doubt, select your entire sketch.
Reference elements	These elements are what your sketch is located to. For new sketches, select the horizontal and vertical axes.
Symmetry lines	If you want your sketch to be symmetrical, select the horizontal axis, the vertical axis, or a sketched axis.

The Auto Constraint dialog box opens as shown in Figure 4–34.

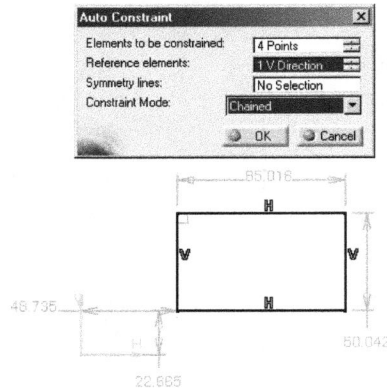

Figure 4–34

Practice 4a

Dimensions

Practice Objectives

- Create a sketched profile.
- Create the dimensions required to fully define a sketch,
- Recognize when a sketch is under-constrained or constrained.

In this practice, you will create the sketch shown in Figure 4–35. You will constrain the sketch using geometrical and dimensional constraints. You will also be able recognize whether a sketch is under-constrained or over-constrained.

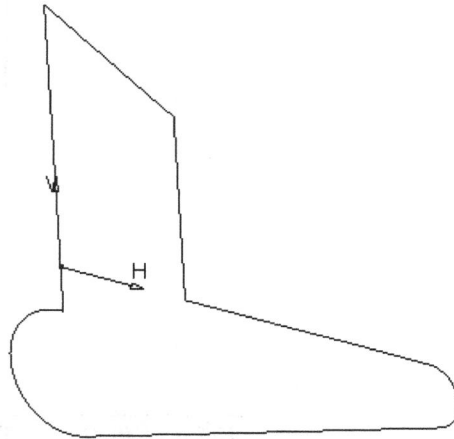

Figure 4–35

Task 1 - Create a new part and begin creating a sketch.

1. Click ☐ (New).

2. In the New dialog box, select **Part**, enter **Constraints_1** as the part name, and click **OK**.

3. In the specification tree, select the YZ plane.

4. Click ▨ (Sketch).

Task 2 - Begin sketching the profile.

1. Verify that the Sketch Tools toolbar is available.

The activated icon displays in orange.

2. Verify ⬛ (Geometrical Constraints) is selected to enable automatic geometric constraints.

3. Sketch the part profile shown in Figure 4–36 using

    ⬛ (Profile). Verify that the arcs are tangent in the locations shown.

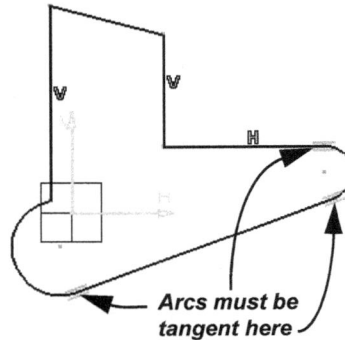

Arcs must be tangent here

Figure 4–36

Task 3 - Perform a sketch analysis.

1. In the Tools toolbar, click ⬛ (Sketch Solving Status). The Sketch Solving Status dialog box opens as shown in Figure 4–37.

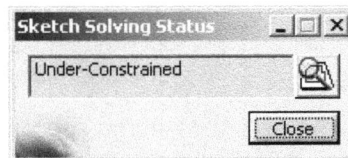

Figure 4–37

Design Considerations

The software reports that the section is under-constrained. Since no dimensions have been applied to the section, all entities are highlighted to indicate that they are under-constrained. You will apply dimensions to the section to constrain it in the part.

2. In the Sketch Solving Status dialog box, click ⬛ (Sketch Analysis). The Sketch Analysis dialog box opens as shown in Figure 4–38.

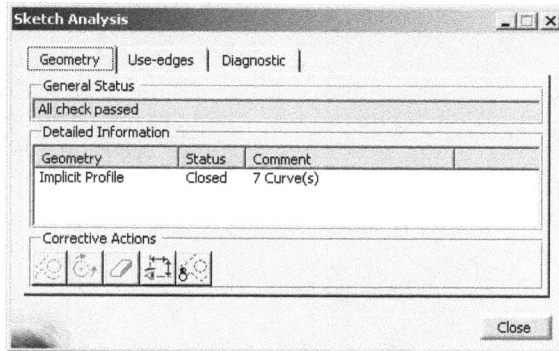

Figure 4–38

3. Verify that the software reports a closed status for the sketch and that only seven curves exist. If you receive a different result, verify that your section has been created correctly.

4. Close the Sketch Analysis dialog box.

Task 4 - Dimension the length of a straight line.

1. Click ⬛ (Constraint) to start constraining. The icon turns orange to indicate that it is active.

2. Select the vertical line shown in Figure 4–39. Click the dimension to the left side of the line. Do not modify the default values of your sketch. You will adjust them later.

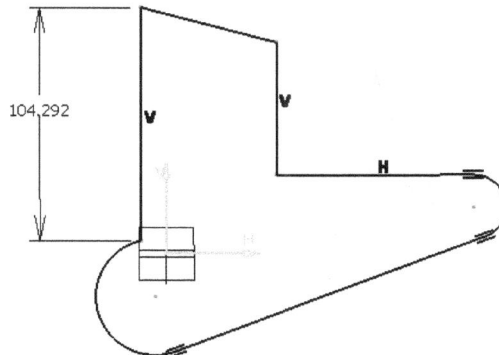

Figure 4–39

Task 5 - Dimension between parallel lines.

1. Note that [icon] (Constraint) is no longer active. Select it again to create another dimension.

2. Select the short vertical line, as shown in Figure 4–40. A length dimension displays. You do not want this dimension. Select the long vertical line, and a dimension displays for the distance between the two lines.

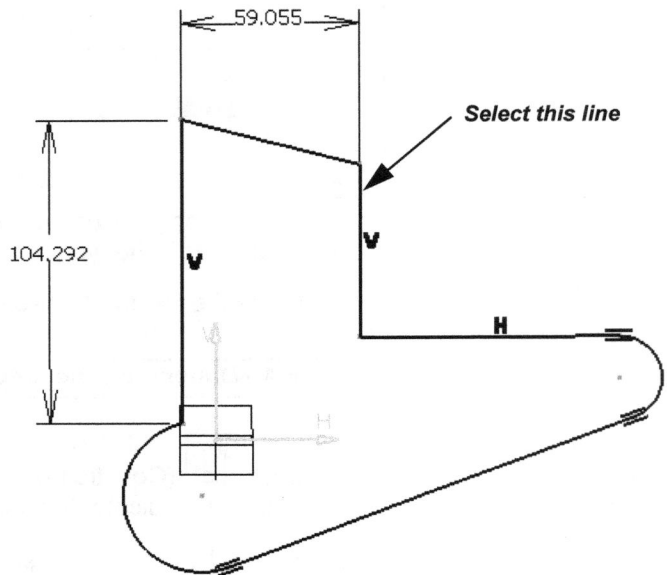

Figure 4–40

Task 6 - Enable continuous dimensioning and dimension the two arcs, one as a radius and one as a diameter.

1. Double-click on ⬚Ⅱ (Constraint) to enable continuous dimensioning. The icon remains orange until you select another action.

2. Select the arc on the left side and click the radius dimension outside the sketch, as shown in Figure 4–41.

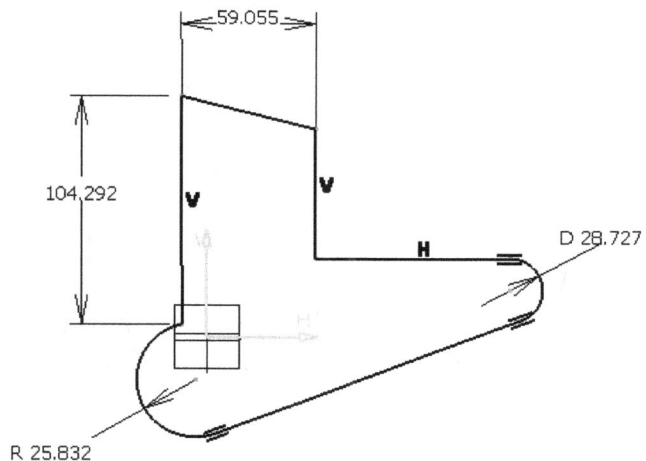

Figure 4–41

3. Select the arc on the right side, right-click and select **Diameter**.

Task 7 - Change the radius dimension to a diameter dimension.

1. Click 🔺 to terminate dimension creation.

2. Double-click on the radius dimension.

3. In the Constraint Definition dialog box, in the Dimension drop-down list, select **Diameter**.

4. Click **OK** to complete the change.

Task 8 - Create an angle dimension.

1. Double-click on ⬚ᵢ (Constraint).

2. Select the slanted line as the first element and the long vertical line as the second element, as shown in Figure 4–42. Before you place the dimension in its final location, move the cursor to other positions to preview the possible angle dimensions.

3. Place the angle dimension as shown in Figure 4–42.

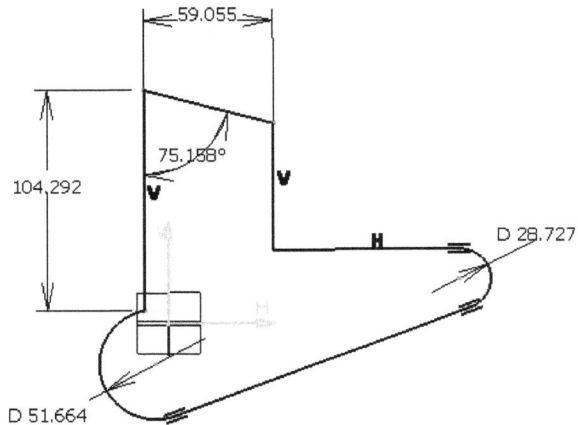

Figure 4–42

Task 9 - Create a horizontal dimension between the two arcs.

1. With ⬚ᵢ (Constraint) still be active, select each arc to initially create an absolute arc tangent dimension, but do not place the dimension.

2. Right-click and select **Horizontal Measure Direction**. The sketch displays as shown in Figure 4–43.

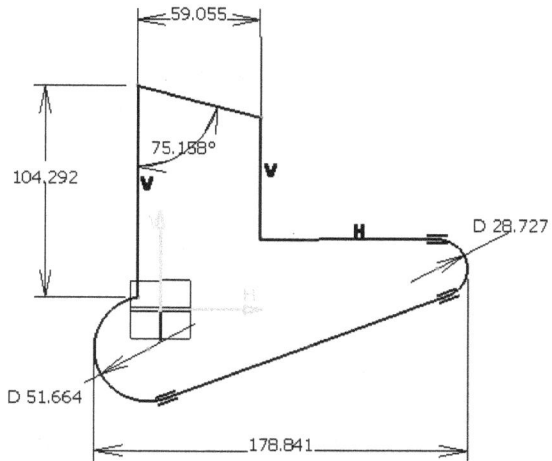

Figure 4–43

Task 10 - Create dimensions to fully constrain the sketch.

1. To finish constraining the shape of the sketch, create the two dimensions circled in Figure 4–44.

The 5.08 dimension is created by selecting the center point of the D51.664 arc and the 104.292 vertical line.

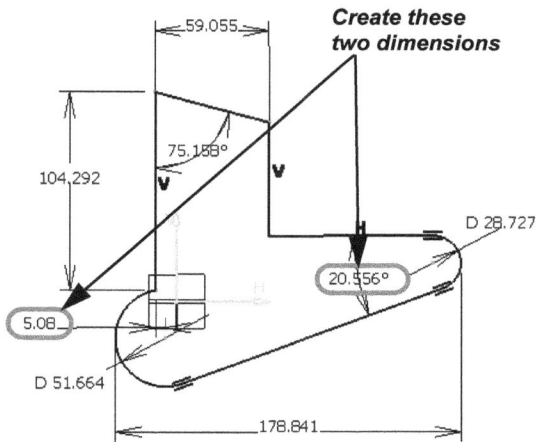

Figure 4–44

2. To constrain the location of the sketch relative to the datum planes, create the two dimensions circled in Figure 4–45. Create each dimension from the line to the horizontal or vertical axis.

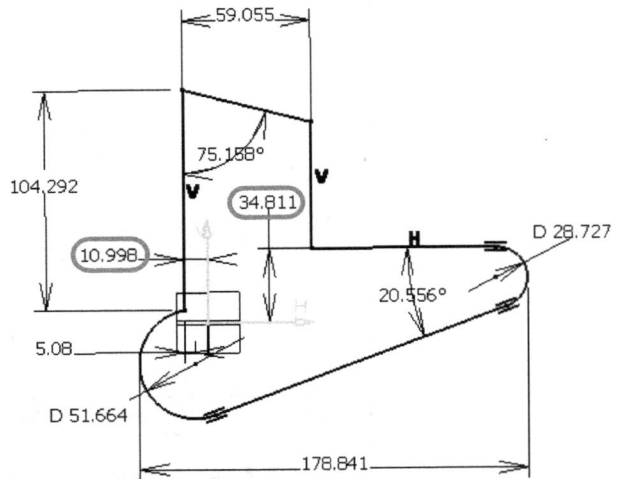

Figure 4–45

3. Click ▢ (Sketch Solving Status) to open the Sketch Solving Status dialog box, and verify that the software reports that the section is fully constrained, as shown in Figure 4–46.

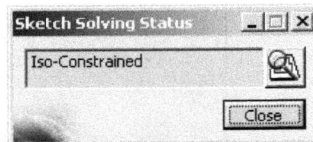

Figure 4–46

Task 11 - Over-constrain the sketch.

1. Create a dimension for the length of the angled line, as shown in Figure 4–47.

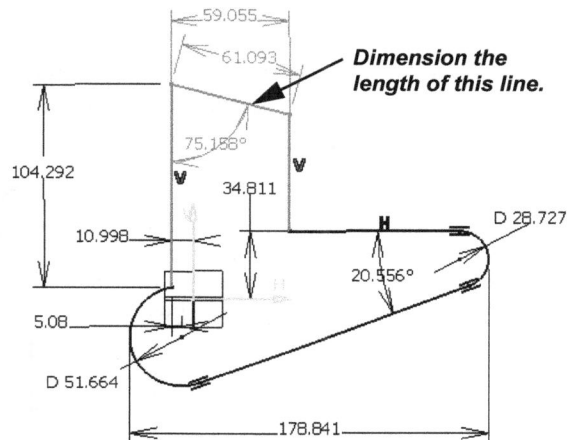

Dimension the length of this line.

Figure 4–47

The sketch is now over-constrained, as indicated by the purple color of the affected sketch entities.

2. Click ▣ (Sketch Solving Status). The software now reports that the sketch is over-constrained and highlights the three impacted sketch entities in orange.

3. Close the Sketch Solving Status dialog box.

Task 12 - Manipulate the dimensions.

1. Select the **59.055** dimension and press <Delete>. The sketch is once again correctly constrained.

2. Practice moving dimensions, as shown in Figure 4–48. Select the dimension number to move the dimension along the arrow. Select the arrow to move the dimension closer or farther from the sketch.

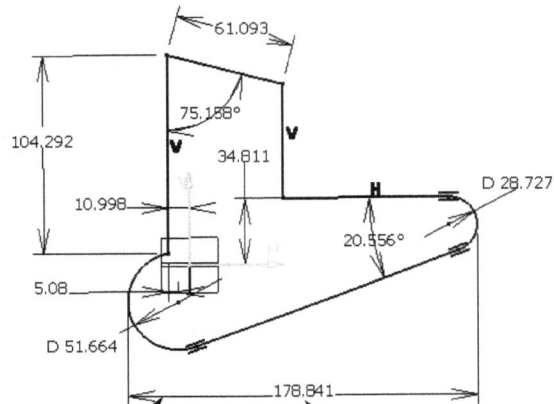

Click and drag here to move the dimension up and down.   **Click and drag here to move the dimension left and right.**

Figure 4–48

Task 13 - Modify the size of the dimensions.

1. Double-click on the **75.158** angle dimension.

2. In the *Value* field, enter **60.00** and click **OK**.

3. Click ⬛ (Edit Multi-Constraint). The Edit Multi-Constraint dialog box opens as shown in Figure 4–49. It contains all constraints in the sketch and their values.

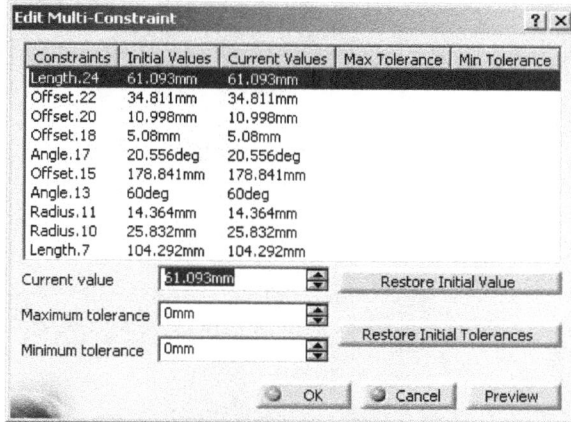

Figure 4–49

The constraint is highlighted in the sketch when you select it in the list.

Design Considerations

Be sure to enter half the diameter for the radius constraints, since both radius and diameter dimensions are represented using a radius.

4. In the Edit Multi-Constraint dialog box, select each dimension and modify its value in the field below the list to the value shown in Figure 4–50.

Note that all entities are green, indicating that the sketch is fully constrained.

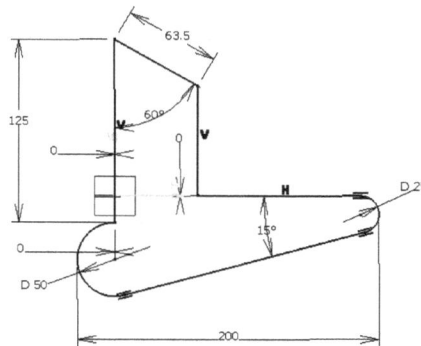

Figure 4–50

5. Click **Preview** to display the changes and then click **OK**.

Task 14 - Exit Sketcher and close the window.

1. Click ⬆️ (Exit workbench). The sketch displays as shown in Figure 4–51.

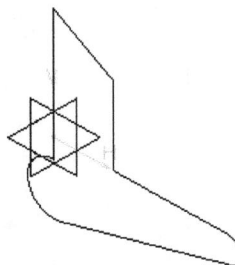

Figure 4–51

2. Click 💾 (Save) and save the part model.

3. Select **File>Close** to close the window.

<table>
<tr><td>

Practice 4b

</td><td>

Constraints

</td></tr>
</table>

Practice Objective

- Apply a variety of constraints to document the design intent of the sketch.

In this practice, you will create the sketch shown in Figure 4–52. You will gain an understanding of how geometrical constraints interact with one another. This practice will focus on driving the geometry through the use of constraints.

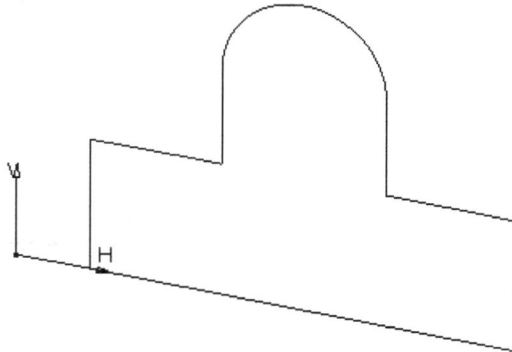

Figure 4–52

Task 1 - Create a new part and begin creating a sketch.

1. Click ☐ (New).

2. In the New dialog box, select **Part**, enter **Constraints_2** as the part name, and click **OK**.

3. In the specification tree, select the YZ plane.

4. Click ⬚ (Sketch).

Task 2 - Begin sketching the profile.

1. Ensure that the Sketch Tools toolbar is available.

2. Ensure that [ ] (Geometrical Constraints) is selected, to enable automatic geometric constraints.

3. Sketch the profile and the axis, as shown in Figure 4–53.

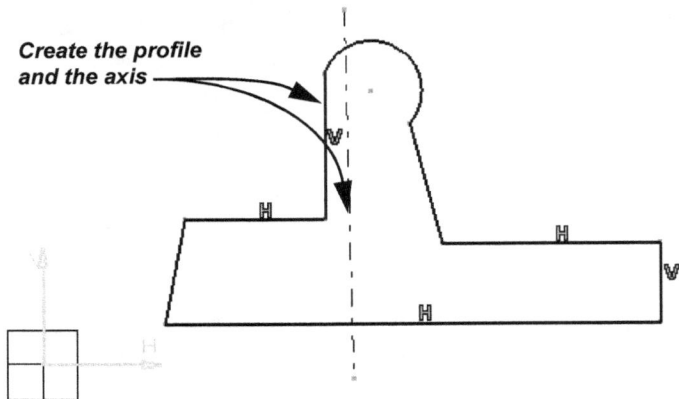

Create the profile and the axis

Figure 4–53

4. Use the Sketch Analysis to confirm that the section consists of one close profile that is constructed using 8 curves.

Task 3 - Make a slanted line vertical.

1. Select the slanted line shown in Figure 4–54.

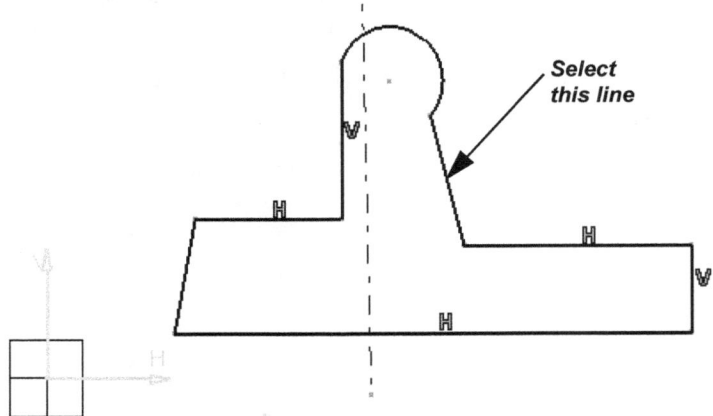

Select this line

Figure 4–54

2. Right-click and select **Line.# object>Vertical**, as shown in Figure 4–55.

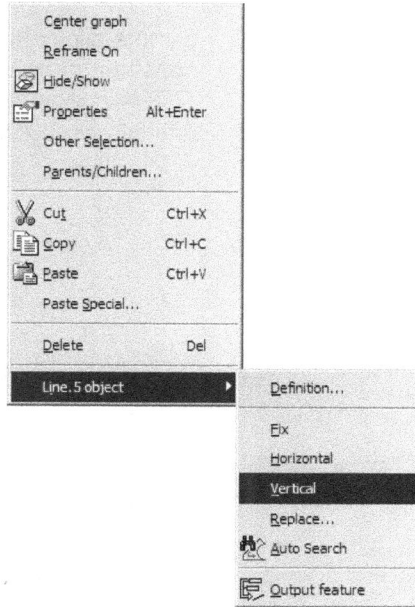

Figure 4–55

Design Considerations

This practice demonstrates the most efficient method of creating a geometric constraint in a sketch. Depending on the scenario, this might involve using a combination of icons and shortcut menu options. In each case, ⊞ (Constraints Definition) can be used instead. The corresponding option in the dialog box will be indicated in the margin. For example, the option for the **Horizontal** constraint displays as shown in Figure 4–56.

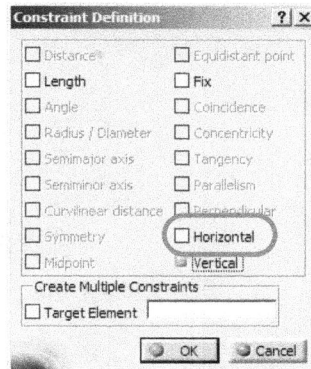

Figure 4–56

Task 4 - Make two lines coincident.

1. Double-click on ▢ (Constraint) to define a series of constraints. Select the horizontal lines shown in Figure 4–57. This will begin the creation of a dimension between the two entities. Do not place the dimension.

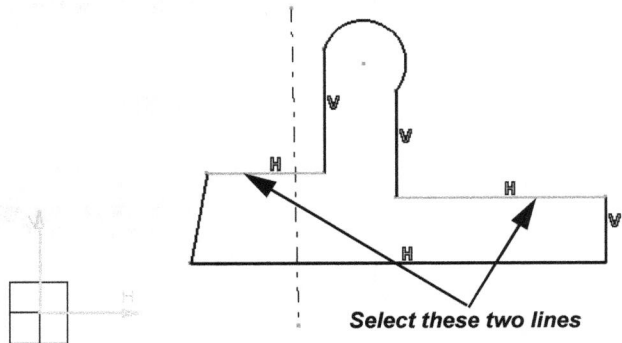

Select these two lines

Figure 4–57

2. Right-click and select **Coincidence**.

Task 5 - Make two lines parallel.

1. Select the vertical lines shown in Figure 4–58.

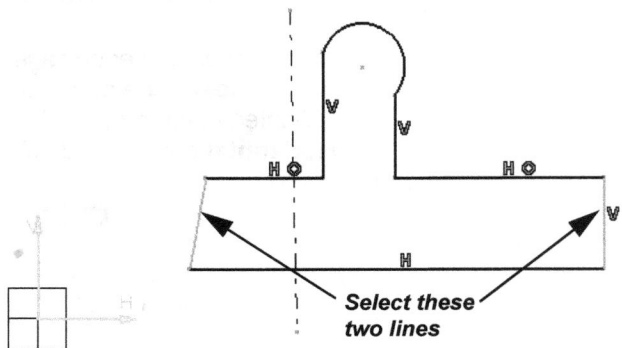

Select these two lines

Figure 4–58

2. Right-click and select **Parallelism**.

3. Place the parallel constraint using the left mouse button.

Task 6 - Make the arc tangent to the adjacent lines.

1. Select the arc and one of the adjacent straight lines as shown in Figure 4–59.

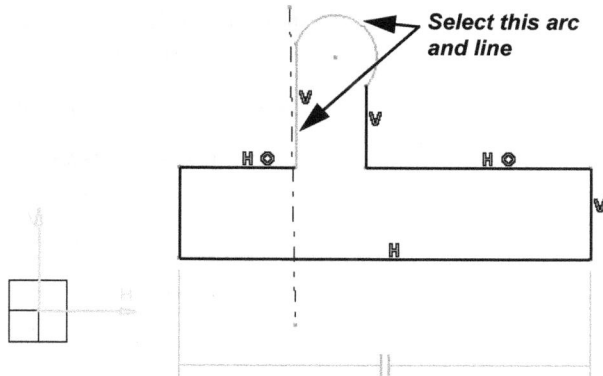

Figure 4–59

2. Right-click and select **Tangency**.

3. Repeat this task for the arc and for the line on the other side.

Task 7 - Make arc center coincident with a sketched axis.

1. Select the sketched axis and the center of the arc shown in Figure 4–60.

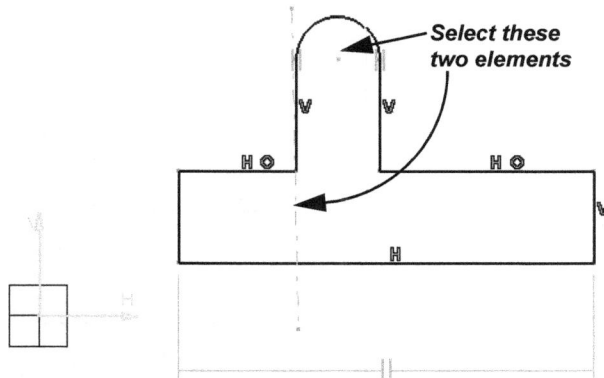

Figure 4–60

2. Right-click and select **Coincidence**.

Task 8 - Make the sketch symmetrical about the sketched axis.

To make two elements symmetrical about an axis, start by selecting the elements to be made symmetrical (in this case, two vertical lines). Once you have identified the symmetry constraint, select the symmetry element (in this case, the vertical axis).

1. Select the two vertical lines shown in Figure 4–61.

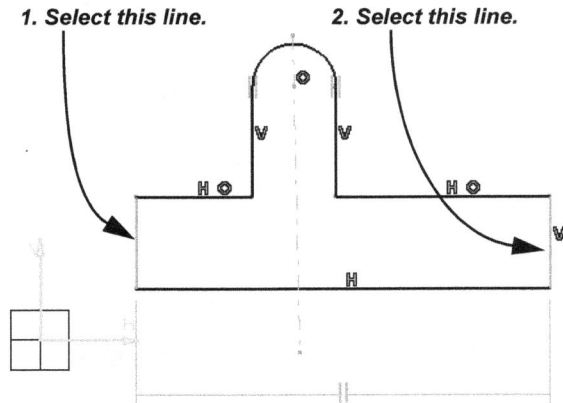

Figure 4–61

2. Right-click and select **Allow Symmetry Line**, as shown in Figure 4–62.

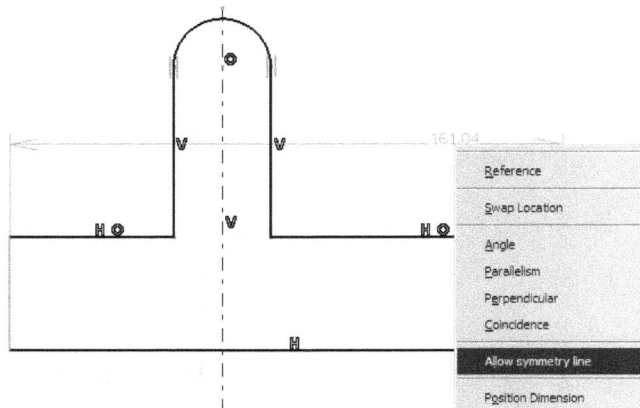

Figure 4–62

3. Select the axis shown in Figure 4–63 to complete the **Symmetry** constraint.

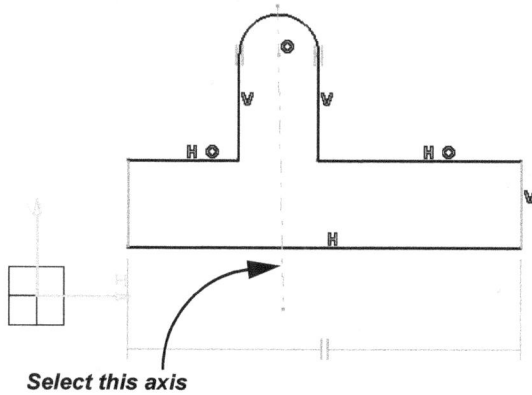

Select this axis

Figure 4–63

Task 9 - Constrain the sketch to the datum planes.

1. Create a **Coincidence** constraint between the bottom horizontal line and the horizontal axis, as shown in Figure 4–64.

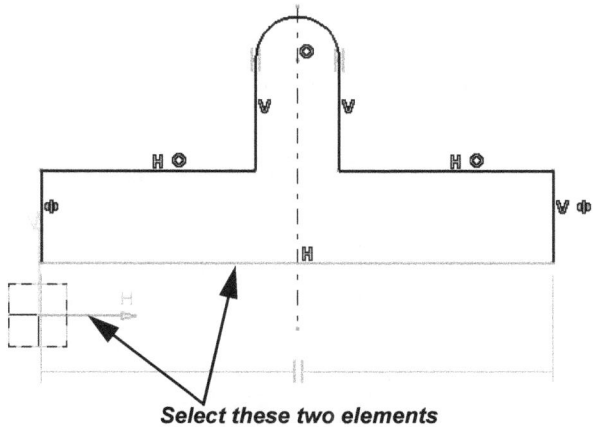

Select these two elements

Figure 4–64

2. Click to clear (Constraint) and to stop creating constraints.

Task 10 - Drag the sketch to test your constraints.

1. Select the vertical line on the far right side of the sketch and drag it left and right. The sketch updates to remain symmetrical.

2. Drag other elements to test your constraints, as shown in Figure 4–65.

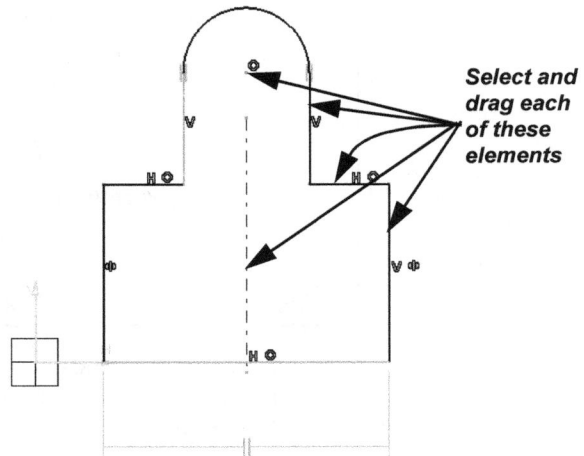

Figure 4–65

Task 11 - Dimension the section.

1. Add the dimensions and constraints shown in Figure 4–66. Adjust the dimension values accordingly.

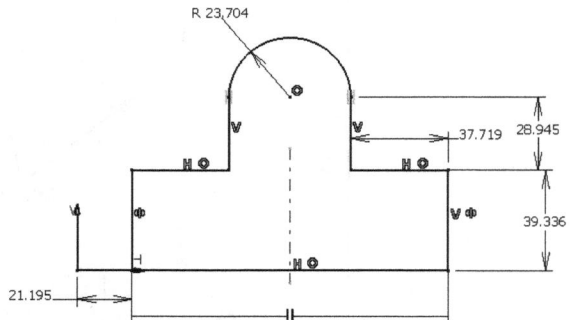

Figure 4–66

Task 12 - Exit the sketch and close the window.

2. Click (Exit workbench) to exit the sketch.

3. Click (Save) and save the part.

4. Select **File>Close** to close the window.

Chapter Review Questions

1. You can create an unconstrained sketch.

   a. True

   b. False

2. When a sketch is fully constrained, what color are the sketched entities?

   a. Red

   b. White

   c. Green

   d. Purple

3. What tool can you use to edit more than one constraint at one time?

   a. **Edit**

   b. **Edit Multi-Constraint**

   c. **Modify Constraints**

   d. None of the above.

4. Geometric constraints can be added using which tools? (Select all that apply.)

   a. (Constraint)

   b. (Edit Multi-Constraint)

   c. (Constraints Defined in Dialog Box)

   d. The shortcut menu.

5. What sketched entity must be present to create a revolved diameter dimension?

   a. An axis.

   b. A construction line.

   c. A line.

   d. The revolved diameter dimension can be created between any sketched entities.

6. Once created, how can you change a radius dimension to a diameter dimension?

   a. Right-click on the radius dimension and select **Diameter**.

   b. Double-click on the radius dimension and enter twice its value.

   c. Double-click on the radius dimension and select **Diameter** in the Dimension drop-down list.

   d. None of the above.

7. The **Sketch Analysis** tool can be used to perform corrective actions on sketches.

   a. True

   b. False

8. What displays in the Sketch Solving Status dialog box when a sketch is fully constrained?

   a. Fully Constrained

   b. Iso-Constrained

   c. Constrained

   d. None of the above.

9. How do you know whether a sketch is under-constrained?

   a. An under constrained sketch is, by default, white.

   b. When you use the **Sketch Solving Status** tool it reads Under-Constrained and highlights the affected entities on the sketch

   c. Use the **Sketch Analysis** tool. The *Diagnostic* tab indicates the status of each sketched entities.

   d. All of the above.

10. Select all of the following constraints that were used to sketch the geometry shown in Figure 4–67. (Select all that apply.)

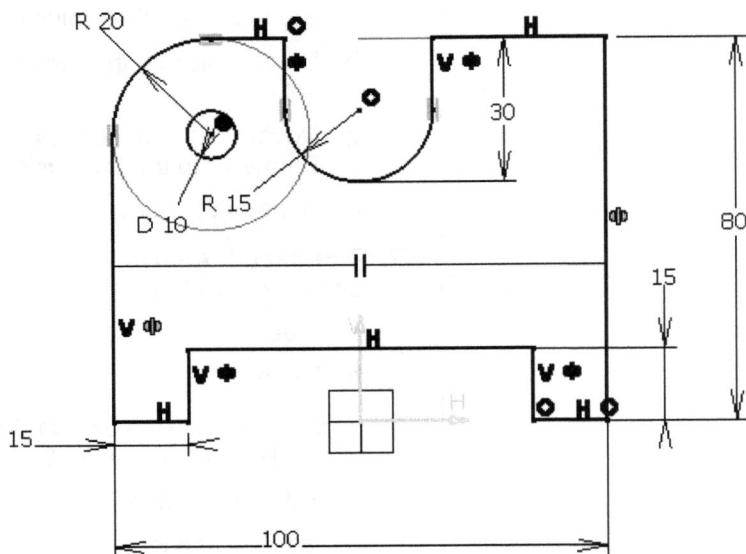

Figure 4–67

a. Tangent

b. Parallelism

c. Coincidence

d. Symmetry

e. Concentricity

f. Perpendicular

Answers: 1.a, 2.c, 3.b, 4.acd, 5.a, 6.c, 7.a, 8.b, 9.d, 10.abcde

Pad and Pocket Features

This chapter introduces the creation and modification of Pad and Pocket features, which serve as the foundation of your model. Understanding the various base features and the process of creating them will help you develop robust and flexible models. You will learn how to create pads to add material and pockets to remove material. When creating sketches for features, you can have sketches that form a closed loop, or sketches that are open, depending on the existing geometry. You will learn how to make changes to sketches.

Learning Objectives in this Chapter

- Use the various base features available.
- Use opened and closed sketches.
- Understand the basic process of creating a pad feature.
- Understand the restrictions on sketches used for pad features.
- Use the various options available for creating pad features.
- Understand the difference between a Pad and a Pocket.
- Understand the Limit options for the depth of Pad features.
- Learn how to use Open profiles.
- Learn about the types of changes that can be made to sketches, and the restrictions on those changes.

5.1 Base Features

When designing a new part, one of your first modeling decisions is to select which feature form to use as the Base feature. The Base feature is the first solid feature created in the model and it provides the foundation on which the entire model is constructed.

You can use one of the following features for your Base feature geometry:

- Pad
- Shaft
- Multi-sections Solid
- Rib

Figure 5–1 shows an example of a Pad feature.

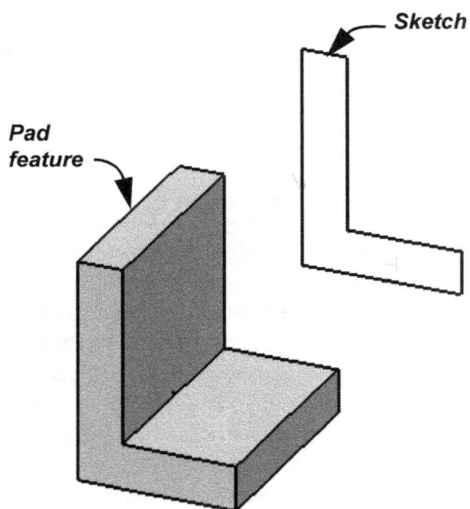

Sketch

Pad feature

Figure 5–1

5.2 Creating a Pad Feature

With a Pad feature, an existing sketch is extruded a specified distance to define the solid geometry.

How To: Create a Pad Feature

1. Select a profile or surface. The shape of a Pad is determined by the profile that is used to create the feature. Select the sketch. Selected items display in orange by default, as shown in Figure 5–2.

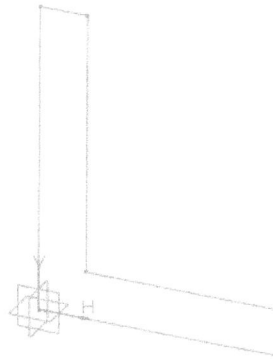

Figure 5–2

2. Click (Pad). The software initially constructs the Pad feature using the default values, as shown in Figure 5–3. The Pad Definition dialog box opens.

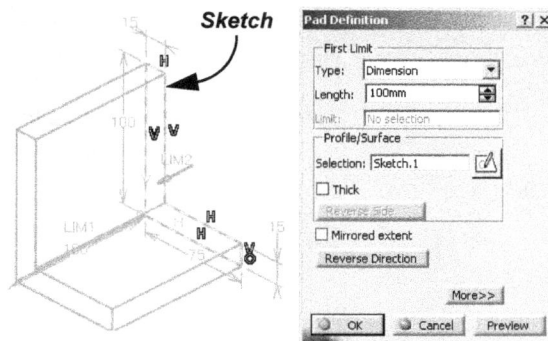

Figure 5–3

Additional limit types for Pad features are discussed later.

3. Specify Pad limit options.

   The distance that the sketch is extruded is known as the limit. The default limit type is dimension, which enables you to manually specify the extrusion distance. To specify the length of the feature, simply enter the distance in the *Length* field.

4. Click **Preview** to examine the geometry before completing the feature.
5. Click **OK** to complete the feature.

Mirrored Extent

The total depth of a Mirrored extent Pad feature is twice the length value entered in the Pad Definition dialog box.

You can select the **Mirrored extent** option in the Pad Definition dialog box to create geometry on both sides of the sketch, as shown in Figure 5–4.

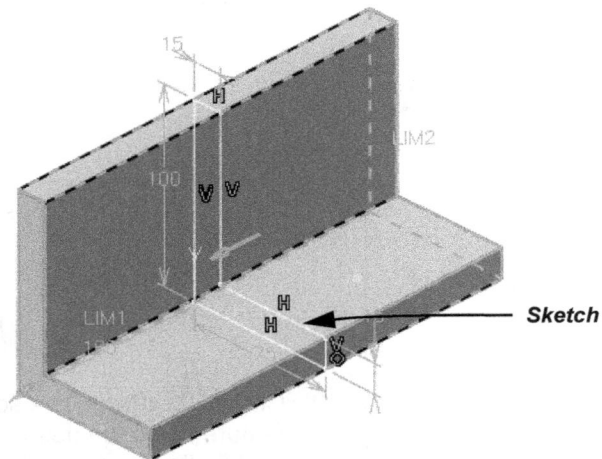

Figure 5–4

It is common practice to start a model with symmetrical geometry. This enables you to capture the design intent from the very beginning. Using this technique, additional features can be easily located relative to the center of the part and automatically remain centered, even when the size of the Base feature is changed.

Second Limit

Click **More** to fully expand the Pad Definition dialog box, as shown in Figure 5–5. By expanding the dialog box, you have access to a set of advanced feature options, such as the **Second Limit** distance. By changing the value from the default *zero* to a new value, you can create asymmetrical geometry about the sketch.

- You can enter a negative value for the First or Second Limit.

As a reference, the software displays an arrow to indicate the direction of the First Limit.

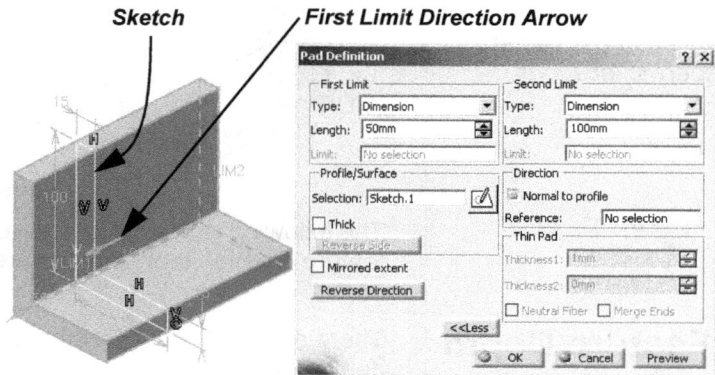

Figure 5–5

Sketch Restrictions for Pad Features

Not every sketch is valid for use with a Pad feature. Comparisons of valid and invalid sketches are described as follows:

Valid Sketch	Invalid Sketch	Description
		Multiple sections are acceptable, but they cannot intersect each other. You can use the trim function to eliminate the overlap condition.
		Open sections are not permitted for the first solid feature on the part unless the **Thick** option is used to create the Pad.

- If you try to create a Pad feature with an invalid section, an error message displays and you are not able to create the feature.

5.3 Pad Feature Options

As features are added to a model, planar surfaces of existing geometry can be selected as sketching planes, as shown in Figure 5–6.

To facilitate sketched feature creation, additional reference planes can be created at specific locations.

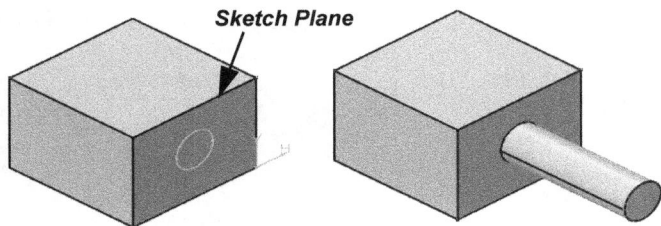

Sketch Plane

Figure 5–6

The following topics discuss several options available during Pad feature creation that help capture design intent.

Feature Depth Options

There are a number of methods that can be used to define the depth of a Pad feature. These options are shown in Figure 5–7.

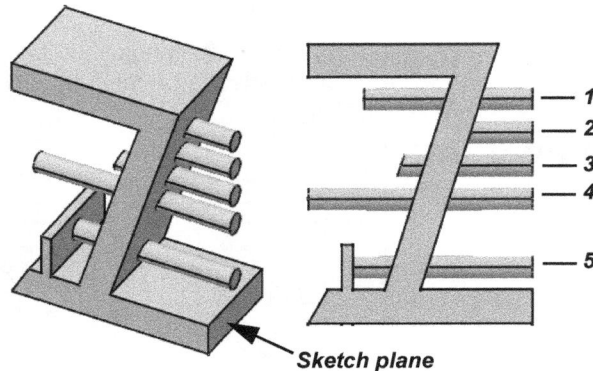

Sketch plane

Figure 5–7

The depth options, set in the *Type* drop-down list of the Pad Dialog box, are described as follows:

Example	Option	Description
1	**Dimension**	Manually enter length of feature.
2	**Up to next, with Offset**	Feature extruded to next solid surface that completely intersects sketch. Offset enables you to specify a positive or negative distance from that terminating plane.

3	Up to last, with Offset	Feature terminates at last solid surface that sketch completely intersects. Offset enables you to specify a positive or negative distance from that terminating plane.
4	Up to plane	Feature can be terminated at selected planar surface or reference plane.
5	Up to surface	Feature can be terminated at selected planar or non-planar surface that completely intersects sketch.

Second Limit Option

With Pad features, you can extrude the sketch on either side or both sides of the sketching plane. To access this functionality, click **More** in the Pad Definition dialog box.

For example, a circle is sketched on the planar surface of the Pad feature, as shown in Figure 5–8 and Figure 5–9.

- First limit type is **Dimension** with a length value of **20**.

- Second limit type is **Up to surface** and the cylindrical surface is selected.

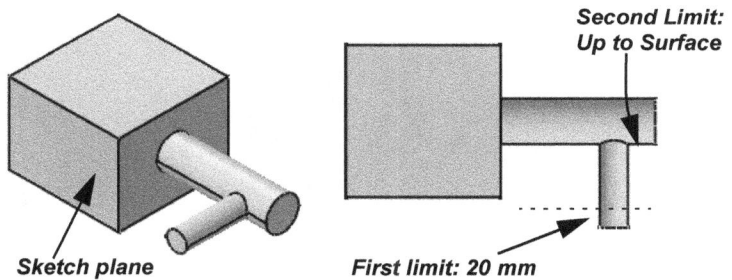

Sketch plane

Second Limit: Up to Surface

First limit: 20 mm

Figure 5–8

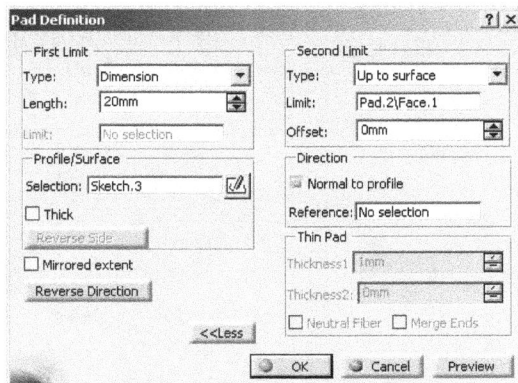

Figure 5–9

Non-Normal Direction

By default, Pads are extruded perpendicular (normal) to the sketch plane. You can disable this action by clearing the **Normal to Profile** option and selecting a straight line or edge to define the feature direction.

In the example shown in Figure 5–10, note that the sketch does not extend the entire length of the Pad feature. This sketch is used to define the direction only; the length of the line is not important.

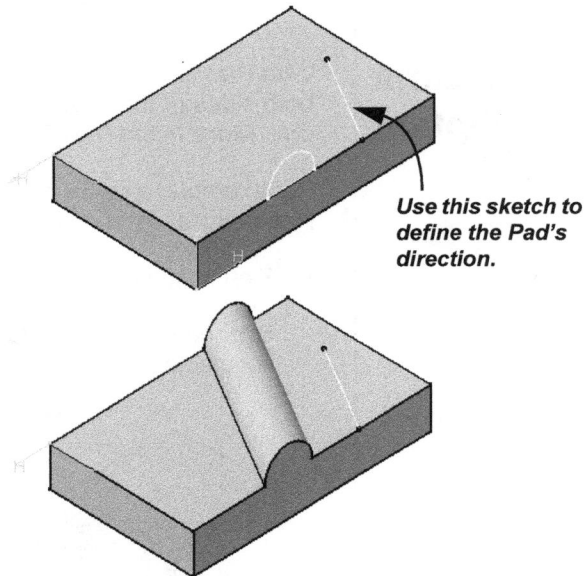

Use this sketch to define the Pad's direction.

Figure 5–10

Open and Closed Sketches

Your profile sketches do not have to form a closed loop. An open profile is acceptable under certain circumstances. However, the open end of the sketch must be bounded by existing geometry. This means the existing geometry must touch the open ends of the sketch at all times. If the Pad shown in Figure 5–11 is lengthened so that it extends off the part, the feature fails.

Using open profiles for feature creation increases update time and introduces instability into the model. A closed profile should be developed whenever possible.

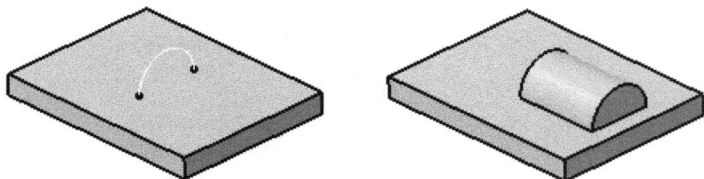

Figure 5–11

5.4 Pocket

A Pocket feature removes material by extruding a profile. It is similar to a Pad feature, except that a Pad adds material and a Pocket removes material, as shown in Figure 5–12.

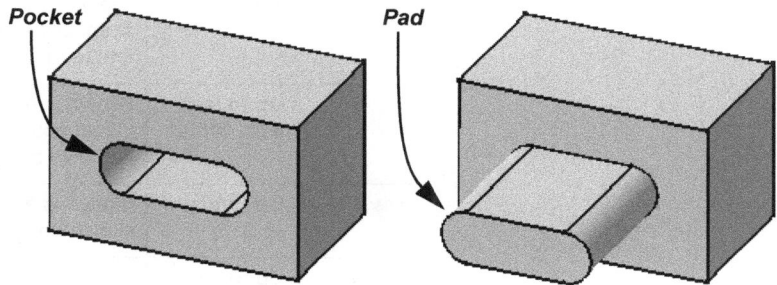

Figure 5–12

Limit Options

Several options are available to control the limits of a Pocket feature. These options are similar to those for the Pad feature, as shown in Figure 5–13.

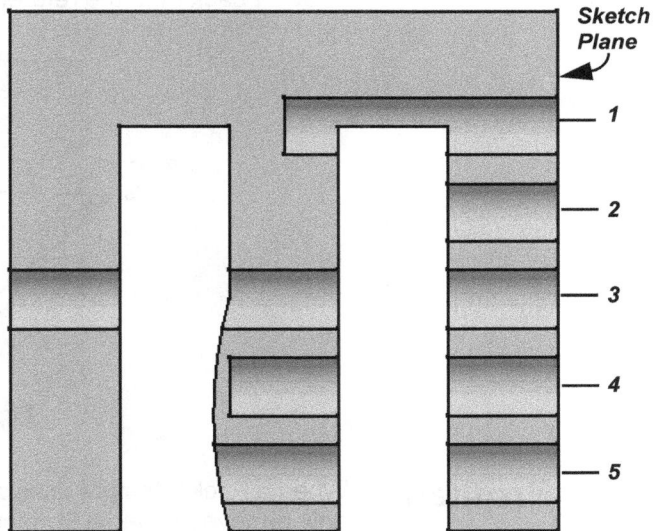

Figure 5–13

The limit options are described as follows:

Example	Option	Description
1	**Dimension**	Manually enter the depth of the Pocket.
2	**Up to next, with Offset**	Sketch is extruded to the next surface that intersects the entire sketch. Offset enables you to specify a positive or negative distance from that terminating plane.
3	**Up to last, with Offset**	Sketch is extruded through the entire model. Offset enables you to specify a positive or negative distance from that terminating plane.
4	**Up to plane**	Sketch is extruded to a specified plane. The sketch does not need to reside on the plane.
5	**Up to surface**	Sketch is extruded to a specified surface. The surface can be planar or non-planar. The surface must intersect the entire sketch.

All of the limit options, except for **Dimension**, have a default offset value of 0. You can change it to a positive value to extend the Pocket beyond the reference or change it to a negative value to pull it back from the reference, as shown in Figure 5–14.

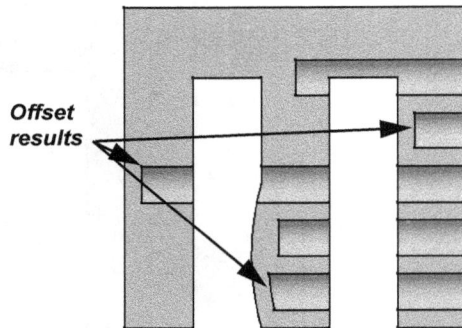

Offset results

Figure 5–14

Open Profiles

When a Pocket feature uses an open profile sketch, the software only removes material from one side of the sketch to the boundaries of the model. Clicking **Reverse Side** in the dialog box enables you to remove material on the other side, as shown in Figure 5–15.

If the open ends of the sketch are not coincident with the sides of the part, the software automatically extends them, as shown in Figure 5–16.

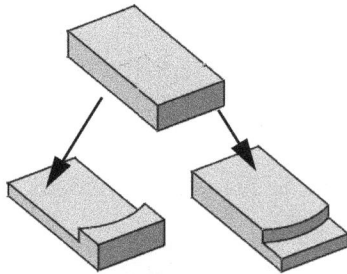

Figure 5–15

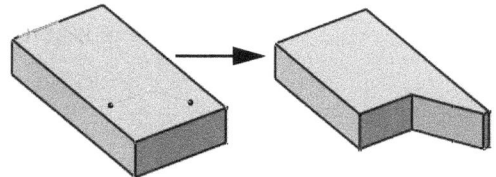

Figure 5–16

- Open profiles are subject to increased update time and introduce instability in the model. Avoid them whenever possible.

Other Feature Options

As is the case with Pads, Pocket features can have a unique second limit; they can be mirrored about the sketch and can be extruded in various ways, as shown in Figure 5–17.

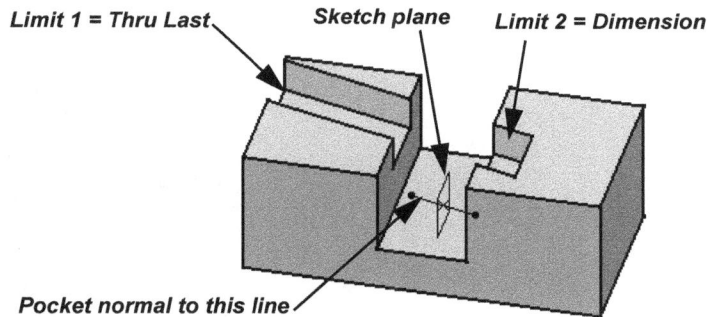

Limit 1 = Thru Last   *Sketch plane*   *Limit 2 = Dimension*

Pocket normal to this line

Figure 5–17

The Pocket Definition dialog box is shown in Figure 5–18.

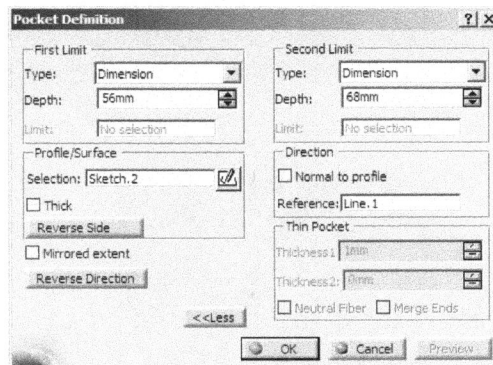

Figure 5–18

5.5 Making Changes to a Sketch

You can easily change the information of a feature, such as the length, sketch dimensions, shape of the sketch, and attributes of the feature (e.g., Mirrored extent).

The following topics discuss these changes in more detail.

**Dimensional
Changes**

How To: Change Dimensions

1. Double-click on a feature on the model to open its dialog box. The software also displays all dimensions of the feature, including the sketch dimensions.
2. Double-click on dimension to open the Constraint Definition dialog box.
3. Enter a new value and click **OK** to complete the change. The software automatically updates the geometry, as shown in Figure 5–19.

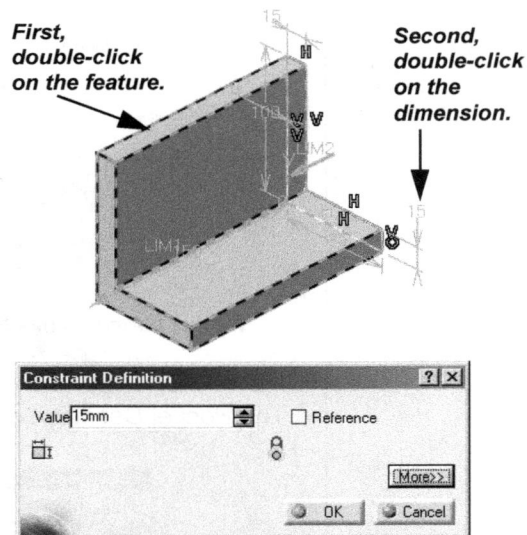

Figure 5–19

Changing the Sketch

The software automatically hides the sketch once you have used it for a Solid feature. To modify the sketch in the Sketcher workbench, you can use one of the following methods:

- Double-click on the sketch in the specification tree. Even if the sketch is hidden from the display, it displays in the Sketcher workbench.

- Click ☑ (Sketcher Workbench) in the dialog box for the feature, as shown in Figure 5–20. You enter the Sketcher workbench, where you can modify the sketch. When you exit Sketcher, you return to editing the feature in the Part Design workbench.

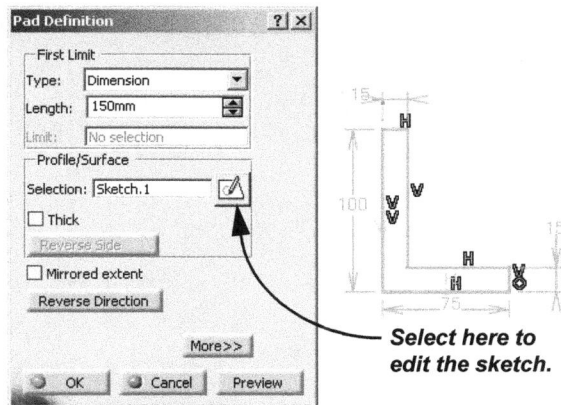

Figure 5–20

Deleting the Feature

Deleting a feature removes the geometry from the model. When a feature is deleted, the sketch remains. This enables you to use the sketch again, as required. Remember that you can use the **Undo** and **Redo** commands to restore features that are accidentally deleted or changed.

You can delete a Pad or a Pocket feature in one of the following ways:

- Select the feature in the specification tree and press <Delete>.

- Select the feature in the specification tree and select **Edit>Delete**.

- Select the feature in the specification tree, right-click and select **Delete**, as shown in Figure 5–21.

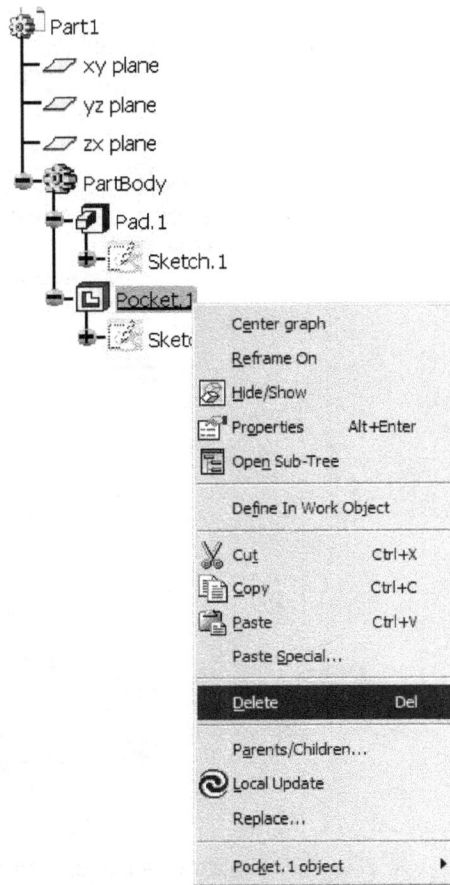

Figure 5–21

Change Restrictions

The only restriction to feature changes is on the feature form. You cannot change a Pad feature into a Pocket feature. You must delete the Pad feature, select the sketch, and then create a Pocket feature.

Practice 5a	# Creating and Modifying Pad Features

Practice Objectives

- Create a sketch to create a Pad feature.
- Modify a Pad feature.

In this practice, you will create Pad features and modify them using the Pad Definition dialog box. You will create the part shown in Figure 5–22.

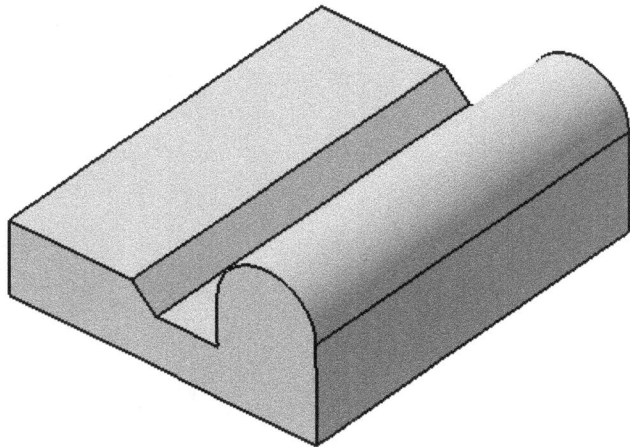

Figure 5–22

Task 1 - Create a new part.

1. Click [icon] (New).

2. In the New dialog box, select the **Part** option and click **OK**.

3. Enter **Pad_Sketch** as the part name, and click **OK**.

4. In the specification tree, select the YZ plane.

5. Click [icon] (Sketch).

Task 2 - Sketch the profile.

1. Sketch and constrain the part profile, as shown in Figure 5–23.

   - 50 (1.969 in)
   - 60 (2.362 in)
   - 25 (4.921 in)
   - 125 (4.921 in)
   - 20 (0.787 in)
   - 45 (1.772 in)

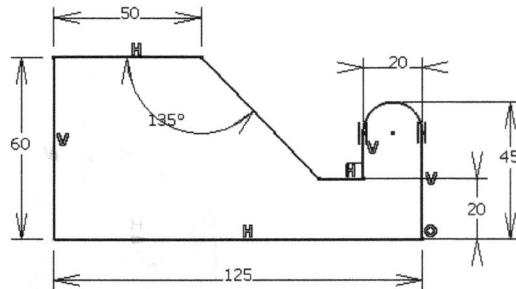

Figure 5–23

2. Click ⬆ (Exit workbench) to exit the Sketcher workbench.

Task 3 - Create a Pad feature from the sketch.

1. With the sketch highlighted, click 🔲 (Pad). The Pad Definition dialog box opens.

2. In the *Length* field, enter **75 (2.953 in)**. Click **OK** to complete the feature. The resulting geometry displays as shown in Figure 5–24.

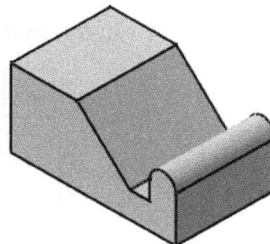

Figure 5–24

Task 4 - Make dimensional changes to the Pad feature.

1. Double-click on any face of the Pad feature. All of the dimensions of the feature display in green. The Pad Definition dialog box also opens.

2. Double-click on the *60* (2.362 in) dimension and change it to **30 (1.181 in)**, as shown in Figure 5–25.

*You can press <Enter> instead of clicking **OK**.*

3. In the Constraint Definition dialog box, click **OK**.

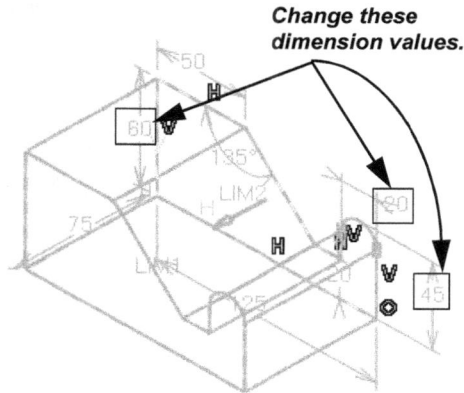

Figure 5–25

4. Repeat this process to change the *20* (0.787 in) dimension to **40 (1.575 in)** and the *45* (1.772 in) dimension to **60 (2.362 in)**.

5. Click **OK** in the Pad Definition dialog box to complete the dimensional changes and update the geometry. The resulting geometry displays as shown in Figure 5–26.

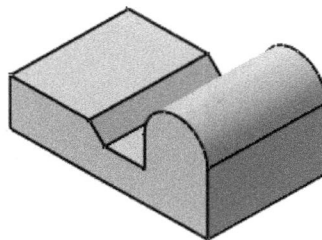

Figure 5–26

Task 5 - Change the attributes of the feature.

1. Double-click on the Pad feature again to open the Pad Definition dialog box.

2. Select the **Mirrored extent** option. The software previews the geometry in wireframe, as shown in Figure 5–27. The geometry is symmetrical about the sketch and has a total length of 150 (5.906 in).

Select this option

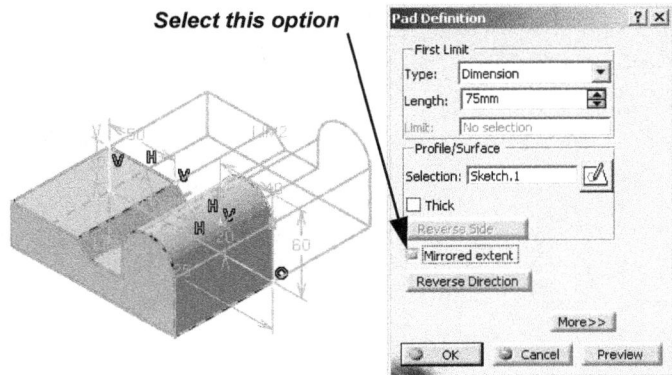

Figure 5–27

3. Clear the **Mirrored extent** option.

4. Click **More**. In the *First Limit* area, enter **50 (1.969 in)** for the length.

5. In the *Second Limit* area, enter **100 (3.937 in)** for the length. Click **Preview** and the resulting geometry displays as shown in Figure 5–28.

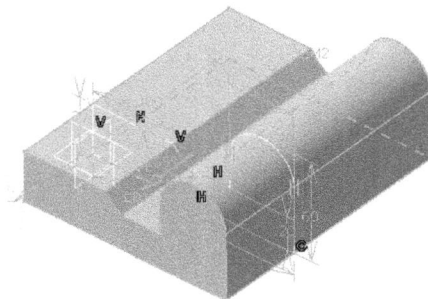

Figure 5–28

6. Click **OK** in the Pad Definition dialog box to complete the change and update the geometry.

Task 6 - Save the part and close the window.

1. Click ⬛ (Save) and save the part.

2. Select **File>Close** to close the window.

Practice 5b | Creating Pocket Features

Practice Objectives

- Create a sketch to create a Pocket feature.
- Modify a Pocket feature.

In this practice, you will create and modify three Pocket features. The first feature will represent a hole with a keyway Groove to accept a Shaft. The second feature will create a cylindrical elongated hole cutout on the flange of the part. The completed model displays as shown in Figure 5–29.

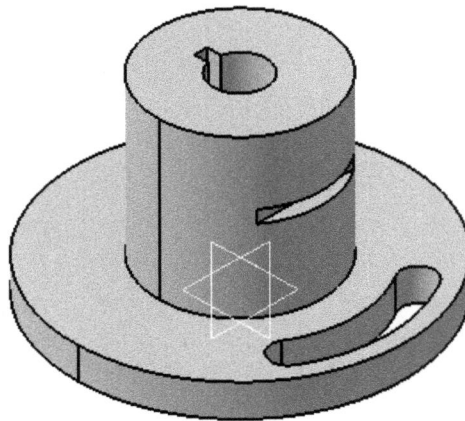

Figure 5–29

Task 1 - Open a model and create a profile on the top of it.

1. Click [] (Open).

2. Select **Pockets.CATPart** and click **Open**.

3. Select the top cylindrical face of the model and click [] (Sketch).

4. Sketch the profile as shown in Figure 5–30. Note that the arc is concentric with the cylindrical face and the keyway geometry is symmetrical about the vertical axis.

- 4 (0.157 in)
- 8 (0.315 in)
- 12 (0.472 in)

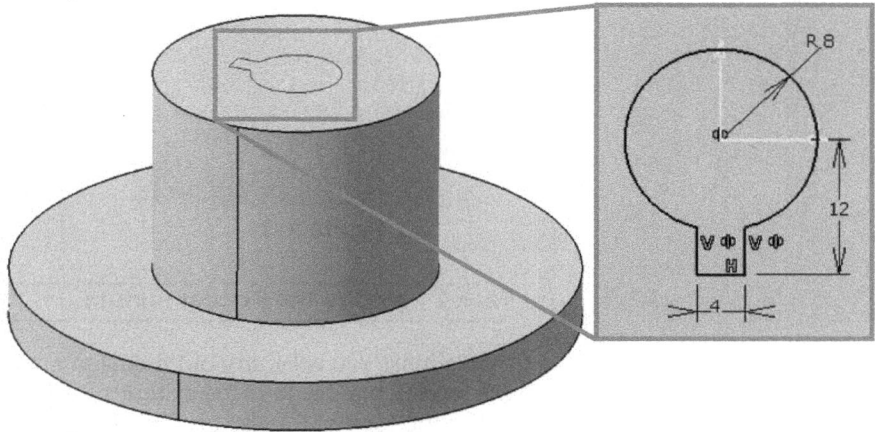

Figure 5–30

5. Exit the Sketcher workbench to complete the sketch.

6. With the sketch selected, click (Pocket). The Pocket Definition dialog box opens as shown in Figure 5–31, indicating a *Depth* of **33 (1.299 in)**.

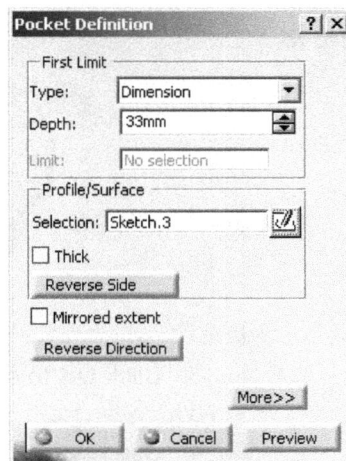

Figure 5–31

7. Verify that the arrow indicating direction points down into the part. Also confirm that the arrow indicating the material side, points toward the inside of the profile, as shown in Figure 5–32.

8. Enter a depth of **40 (1.575 in)** and click **OK**. The completed Pocket feature displays as shown in Figure 5–33.

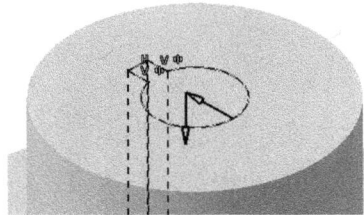

Figure 5–32

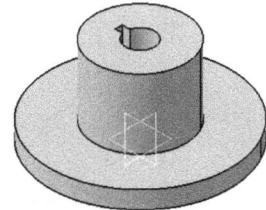

Figure 5–33

Task 2 - Modify the Pocket feature.

In this task, you will carry out a design change on the model. You will modify the depth of the cutout so that it will always extend up to the top face of the flange. This is done by modifying the depth options for the Pocket feature.

1. Locate the Pocket feature in the specification tree and double-click on it to open the Pocket Definition dialog box.

2. In the *First Limit* area, set *Type* to **Up to plane** and select the face as shown in Figure 5–34.

*Since the section does not entirely intersect the selected face, the **Up to surface** option cannot be used.*

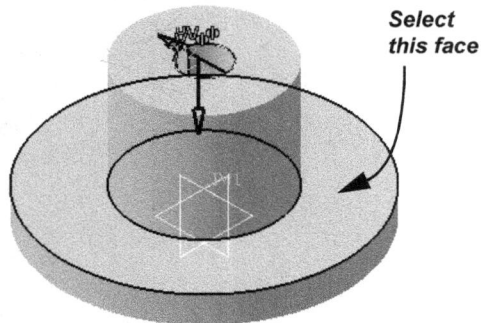

Figure 5–34

3. Click **OK** to complete the modification.

4. Use ▯ (Shading with Edges and Hidden Edges) View mode to review the depth of the feature.

5. Modify the depth of Pad.1 from *40* (1.575 in) to **50 (1.969 in)**. Review the model to verify that the Pocket feature is behaving correctly.

6. Once complete, return the model to the **Shading with Edges** display.

Task 3 - Create a second Pocket feature.

1. Select the face of the model as shown in Figure 5–35 and click [icon] (Sketch).

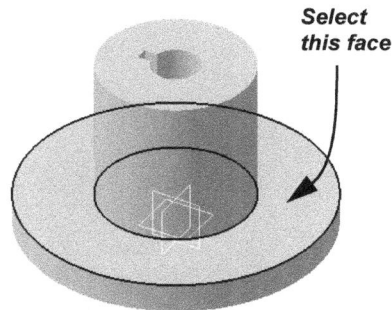

*Select
this face*

Figure 5–35

2. Sketch the profile as shown in Figure 5–36, using Cylindrical Elongated Hole. To create the angle dimension, create two construction lines that are symmetrical about the vertical axis and pass through the center of each arc.

- 5 (0.197 in)
- 40 (1.575 in)

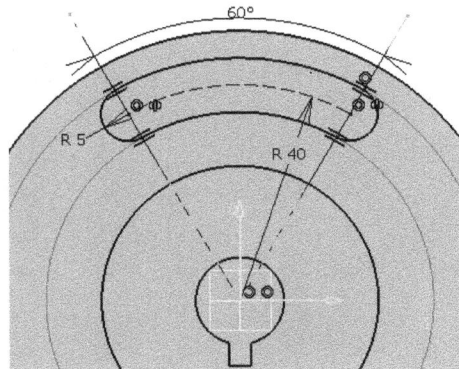

Figure 5–36

3. Exit the Sketcher workbench to complete the sketch.

4. Create a Pocket feature using the sketch just created. Define the depth using the **Up to last** option. The completed feature displays as shown in Figure 5–37.

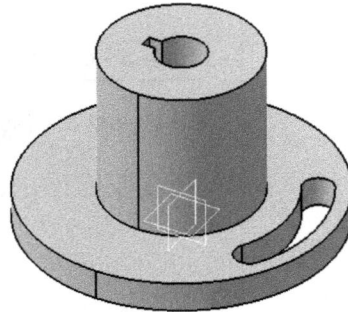

Figure 5–37

Task 4 - Create a Pocket using two limits.

In this task, you will sketch a profile for a Pocket feature on the YZ plane. Then you will create a Pocket feature that cuts material from both sides of the sketch plane.

1. Create a sketch on the YZ plane. Sketch the profile as shown in Figure 5–38.

   - 4 (0.157 in)
   - 10 (0.394 in)
   - 20 (0.787 in
   - 40 (1.575 in)

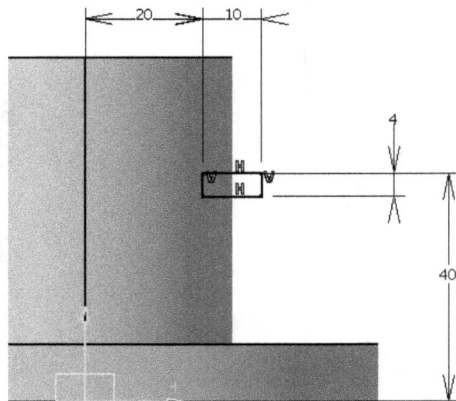

Figure 5–38

2. Exit the Sketcher workbench to complete the sketch.

3. Create a Pocket feature using the sketch just created.

4. Set the *First Limit* type as **Up to last**.

5. Click **More**. The Pocket Definition dialog box opens as shown in Figure 5–39.

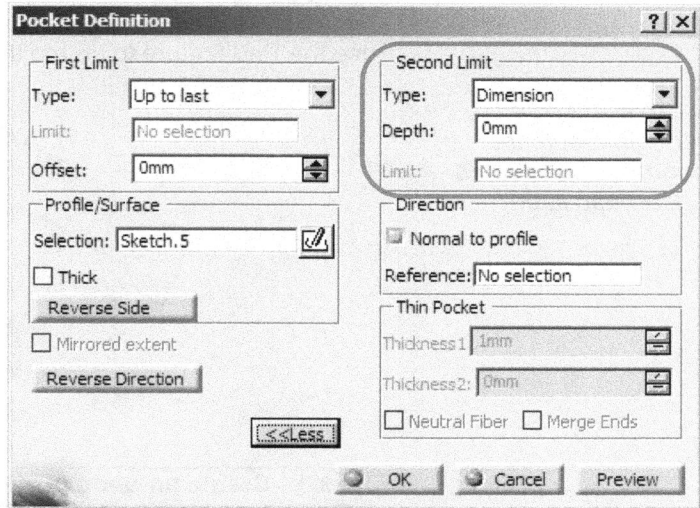

Figure 5–39

6. In the *Second Limit* area, set *Type* to **Up to last**.

7. Complete the feature. The model displays as shown in Figure 5–40.

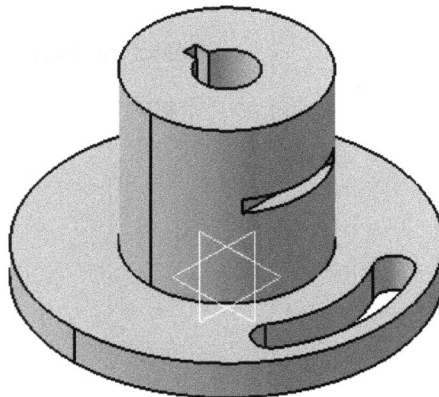

Figure 5–40

8. Save the model and close the window.

Practice 5c

Working With Open Sketches

Practice Objectives

- Correctly sketch and constrain an open profile.
- Use an open sketch to create a Pad feature.

In this practice you will add a Rib to a part, as shown in Figure 5–41. You will need to create an open profile sketch and use the Pad feature to create the Rib.

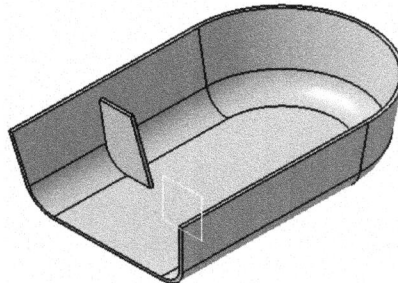

You can also use a stiffener to create the Rib geometry. Stiffeners are described later.

Figure 5–41

Task 1 - Create an open profile on the YZ plane.

1. Click (Open).

2. Select **Open_Sketch.CATPart** and click **Open**.

3. Set the model part length units to **millimeters** (mm).

4. Select the YZ plane and click (Sketch).

5. Sketch a horizontal and angled line as shown in Figure 5–42.

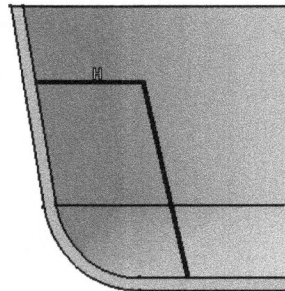

Figure 5–42

Design Considerations

To successfully use an open sketch as a Pad feature, the sketch must be fully constrained to other geometry. This way, CATIA knows how to extrude the open sections of the profile.

6. To constrain the open ends of the profile to existing geometry, click ⬚ (Constraints).

7. Select one of the open end points and the adjacent edge of the part, as shown in Figure 5–43.

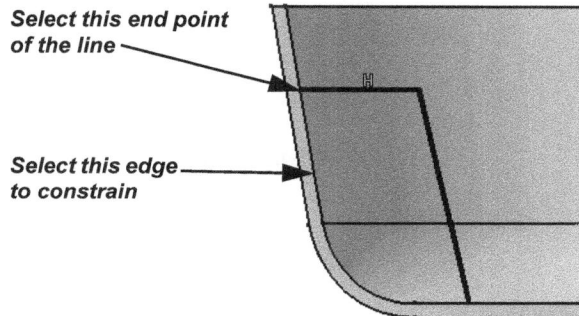

Select this end point of the line

Select this edge to constrain

Figure 5–43

8. Right-click and select **Coincidence**.

9. Repeat Steps 1 to 5 for the other open end.

10. Create the **12.5 (0.492 in)** and **32 (1.260 in)** dimensions as shown in Figure 5–44.

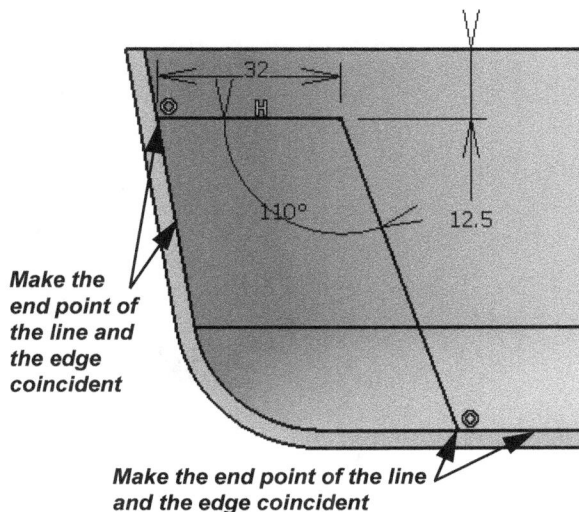

Make the end point of the line and the edge coincident

Make the end point of the line and the edge coincident

Figure 5–44

11. Exit the Sketcher workbench to complete the sketch. The part displays as shown in Figure 5–45.

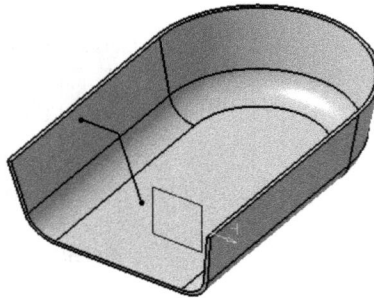

Figure 5–45

Task 2 - Create a Pad feature that represents the Rib's geometry.

1. Select the sketch and click (Pad).

2. Enter **1.60 (0.063 in)** for the length.

3. Select the **Mirrored extent** option to add material on both sides of the sketch plane.

4. Click **OK** to complete the feature. The part displays as shown in Figure 5–46.

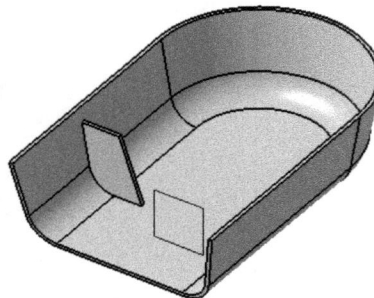

Figure 5–46

5. Click (Save).

6. Select **File>Close**.

Practice 5d | Pad and Pocket

Practice Objective

- Create a Pad feature and a Pocket feature.

In this practice, you will create the model shown in Figure 5–47 using Pad and Pocket features.

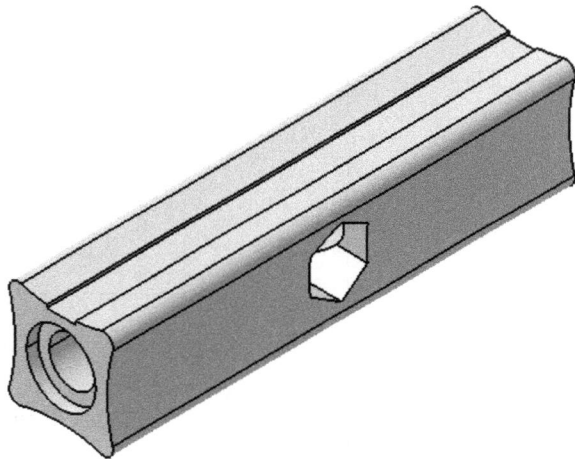

Figure 5–47

Task 1 - Create a Pad feature.

In this task, you will create a Pad feature to define the base feature for the model.

1. Create a new part called **Pad_Pocket.CATPart**.

2. Access the Sketcher workbench using the YZ plane as the sketch support.

3. To create the required profile, start by creating two centered rectangle construction squares, using dimensions of **80 (3.150 in)** and **100 (3.937 in)**, as shown in Figure 5–48.

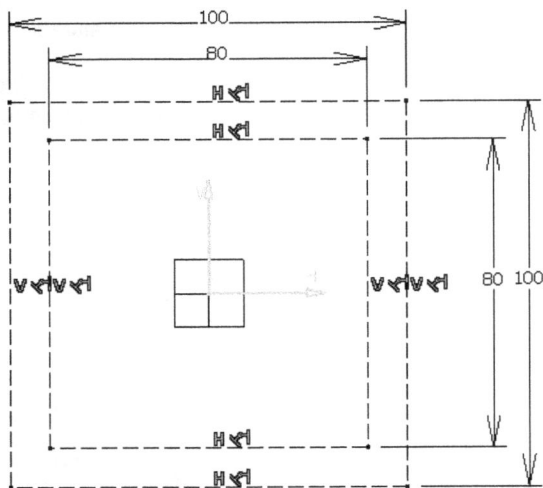

Figure 5–48

4. Click ⟳ (Three Point Arc).

5. Select the three points as shown in Figure 5–49 to create the arc.

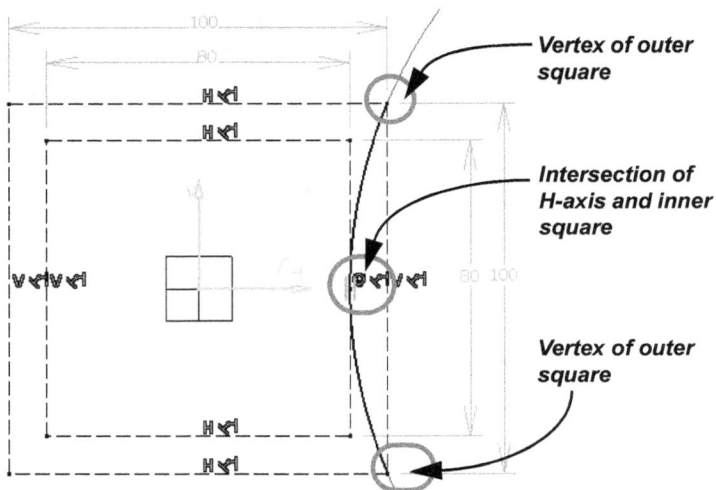

Vertex of outer square

Intersection of H-axis and inner square

Vertex of outer square

Figure 5–49

6. Create three more arcs using the method described in the previous step. The completed arcs display as shown in Figure 5–50.

7. Select one of the arcs. Right-click and select * **object>Auto Search**.

8. Click ⌐ (Corner).

9. Locate the Sketch Tools toolbar. With the **Corner** tool activated, the toolbar will update, enabling you to enter a radius. Enter **8 (0.315 in)**. The completed profile displays as shown in Figure 5–51.

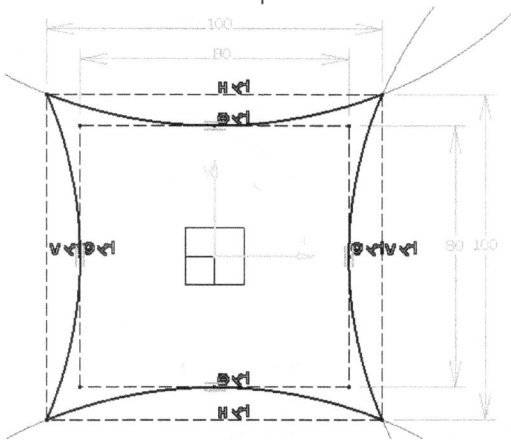

Figure 5–50

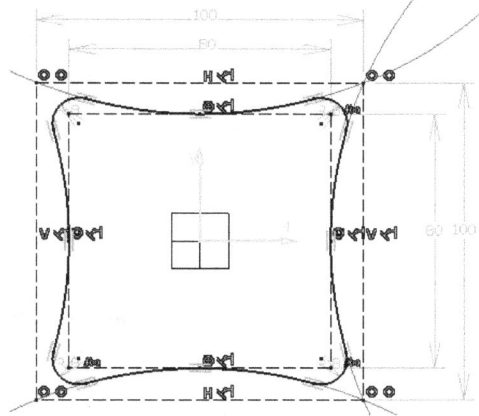

Figure 5–51

10. Exit the Sketcher workbench to complete the sketch.

Task 2 - Create a Pad feature.

1. Click 🗗 (Pad) and enter the following properties:

   • *Profile:* **Sketch.1**
   • *Length:* **400mm (15.748 in)**

2. Click **OK**.

Task 3 - Create a Pocket profile.

1. Create a sketch on the face as shown in Figure 5–52.

2. Sketch the **60 (2.362 in)** diameter circular profile as shown in Figure 5–53.

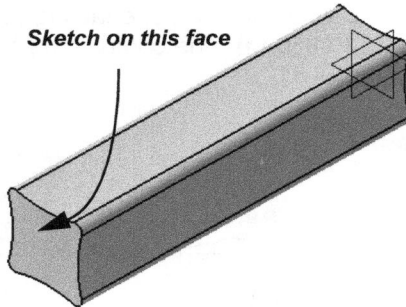

Figure 5–52

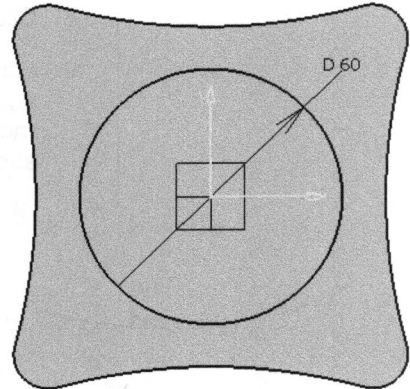

Figure 5–53

3. Exit Sketcher.

Task 4 - Create a Pocket.

1. Create a Pocket feature using the profile just created. Enter a depth of **10 (0.394 in)**. The completed feature displays as shown in Figure 5–54.

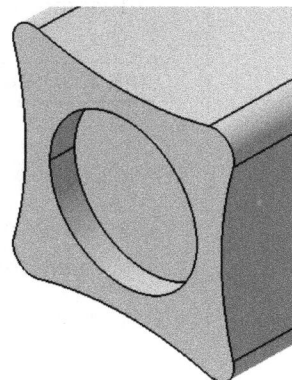

Figure 5–54

Task 5 - Create a through Pocket.

To create this Pocket, you will copy and paste a Sketch. This Sketch will act independently of the original profile.

1. In the specification tree, locate and select **Sketch.2**. This is the 60mm diameter profile used to create the previous Pocket feature.

2. Select **Edit>Copy**.

3. Select the face as shown in Figure 5–55.

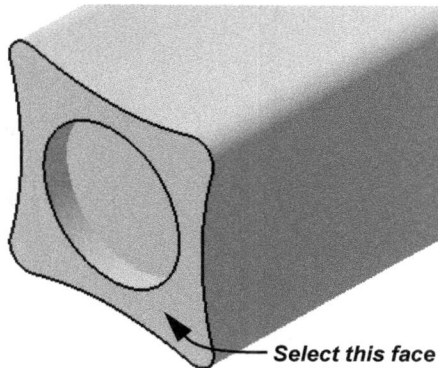

Select this face

Figure 5–55

4. Select **Edit>Paste**. The profile is pasted onto the part as **Sketch.3**, as shown in Figure 5–56.

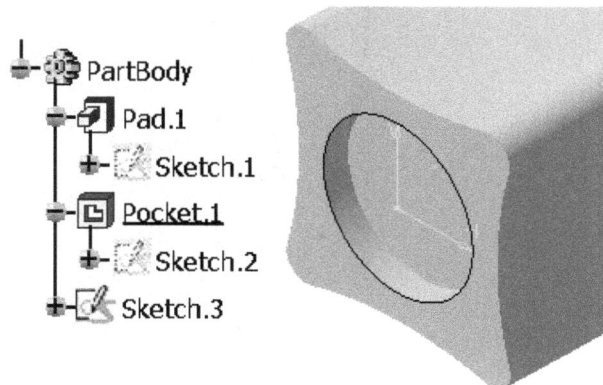

Figure 5–56

5. Edit **Sketch.3** and change the diameter from *60* (2.362 in) to **40 (1.575 in)**. Do not exit Sketcher.

6. Sketch and dimension a rectangular profile, as shown in Figure 5–57. Verify that the rectangle is symmetrical about the vertical axis.

- 10 (0.394 in)
- 20 (0.787 in)
- 38 (1.496 in)
- 40 (1.575 in)

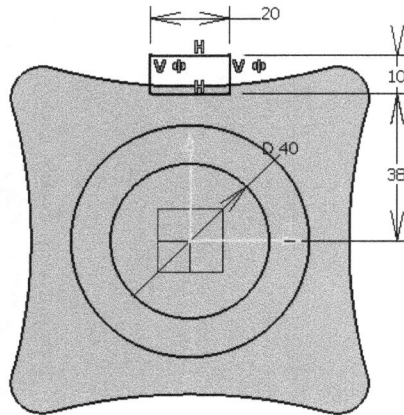

Figure 5–57

Design Considerations

Creating a profile that has more than one closed section has advantages and disadvantages. One advantage is that fewer sketched based features need to be created (in this case, one less sketch and Pocket will be created). However, the disadvantage is that the rectangular Pocket cannot be deactivated without deactivating the circular Pocket. Verify that you structure your model according to your design intent.

7. Create a Pocket feature using **Sketch.3**. Set the *First Limit Type* to **Up to last**. The model displays as shown in Figure 5–58.

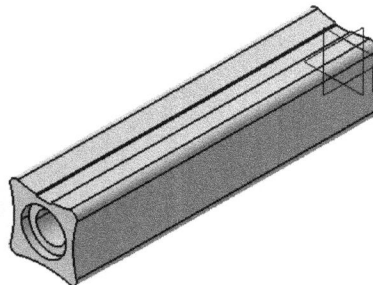

Figure 5–58

Task 6 - Create a Pocket.

1. Create a sketch on the ZX plane. Sketch the hexagonal profile using a dimension of **50 (1.969 in)**, as shown in Figure 5–59.

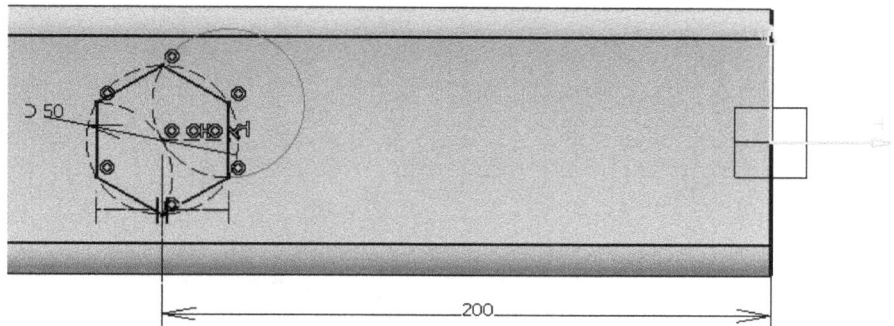

Figure 5–59

2. Create a Pocket feature that removes the hexagonal section from both sides of the sketch plane, using the **Up to last** option.

3. Hide the default reference planes. The completed model displays as shown in Figure 5–60.

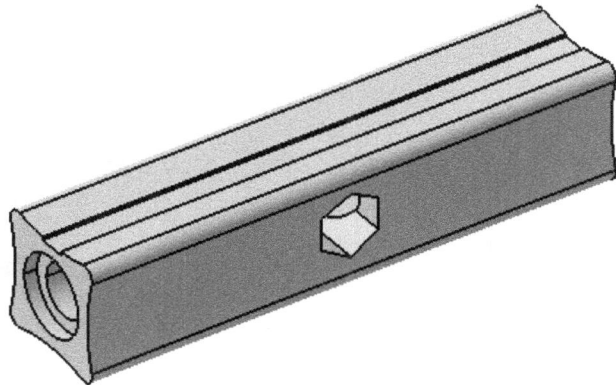

Figure 5–60

4. Save the model and close the window.

Practice 5e

(Optional) Additional Pockets

Practice Objective

- Create a Pocket feature.

In this practice, you will create the part shown in Figure 5–61. You will open an existing part and add two Pocket features.

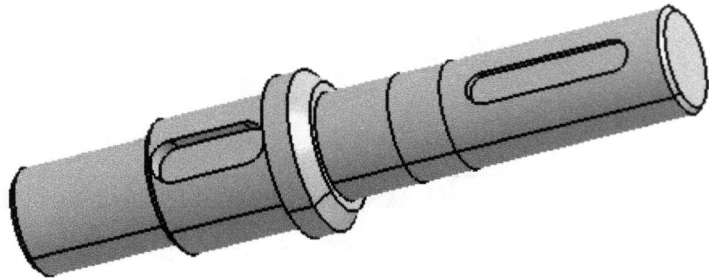

Figure 5–61

1. Open **Shaft.CATPart**.

2. Create the two Pocket features as shown in Figure 5–62. Place them in the approximate locations as shown with appropriate dimensioning schemes.

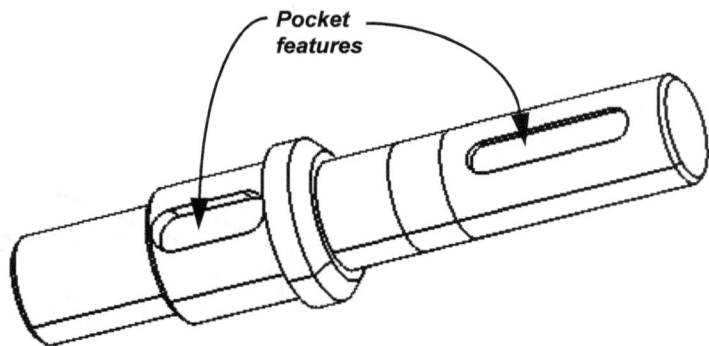

Pocket features

Figure 5–62

3. Click ⊟ (Save).

4. Select **File>Close**.

Practice 5f | (Optional) Crank

Practice Objective

- Create a part using pads without any instructions.

Create the **Crank.CATPart** shown in Figure 5–63.

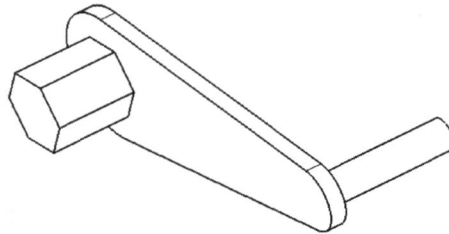

Isometric view
Scale: 1:1

Figure 5–63

Drawing views are shown in Figure 5–63 and Figure 5–64.

- 10 (0.394 in)
- 20 (0.787 in)
- 25 (0.984 in)
- 40 (1.575 in)

- 50 (1.969 in)
- 80 (3.150 in)
- 200 (7.874 in)

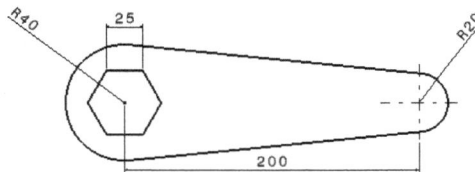

Front view
Scale: 1:1

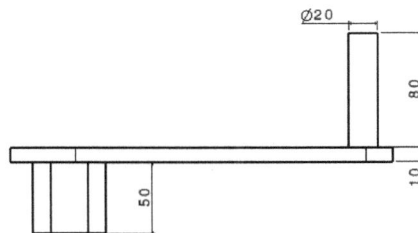

Top view
Scale: 1:1

Figure 5–64

Practice 5g

(Optional) Cylinder Block

Practice Objective

- Create a base feature and Pocket features without instruction

Create the **CylinderBlock.CATPart** model shown in Figure 5–65.

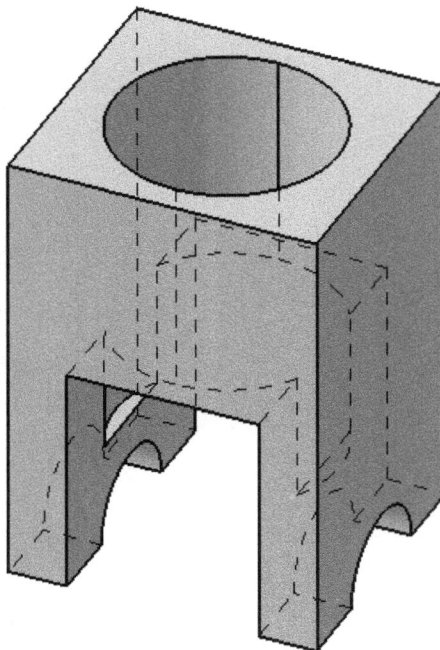

Figure 5–65

Drawing views are shown in Figure 5–66 and Figure 5–67.

- 31 (1.220 in)
- 35 (1.378 in)
- 103 (4.055 in)
- 120 (4.724 in)
- 130 (5.118 in)

- 150 (5.906 in)
- 165 (6.496 in)
- 192 (7.559 in)
- 250 (9.843 in)

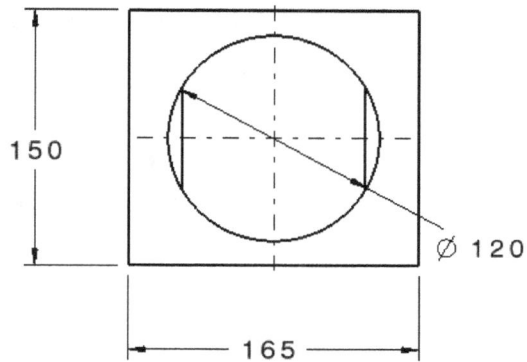

Figure 5–66

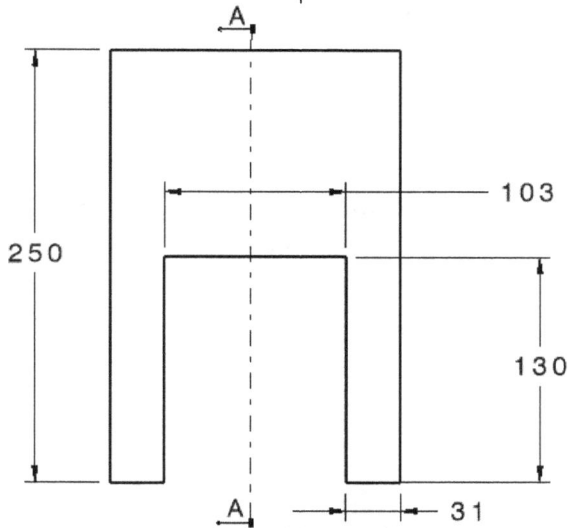

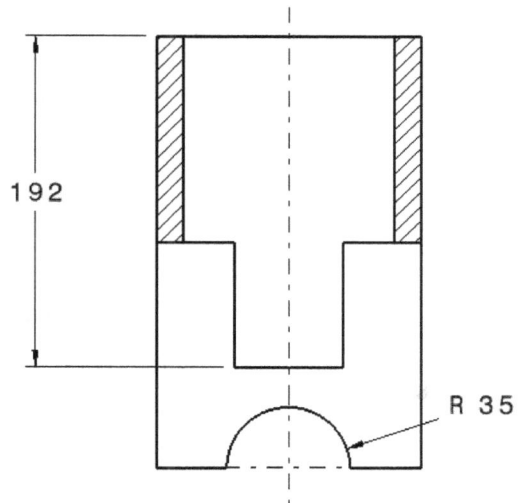

Figure 5–67

Chapter Review Questions

1. What is the general term for the first solid feature in a model?
   a. Foundation feature
   b. Base Feature
   c. Sketch
   d. Reference plane

2. Multiple profiles can be used as a profile for a Pad feature.
   a. True
   b. False

3. A Pad feature can be converted to a Pocket by changing its direction.
   a. True
   b. False

4. What option is used to create a Pad that is symmetrical to the sketch support?
   a. **Symmetric**
   b. **Mirror**
   c. **Mirrored Extent**
   d. None of the above.

5. To use the **Up to Surface** depth option, the terminating surface must completely intersect the sketch.
   a. True
   b. False

6. Which of the following are true, related to open sketches?
   a. An open profile can be used as the profile for a Pad when the open end of the sketch is bounded by existing geometry.
   b. Although you can use open profiles, it is good practice to create features using closed profiles wherever possible.
   c. Open profiles increase update time and introduce instability in the model.
   d. All of the above.

7. The sketch shown on the left side of Figure 5–68 is used to create a Pocket feature. What will the Pocket look like? Note the direction arrows in the image on the right side of Figure 5–68.

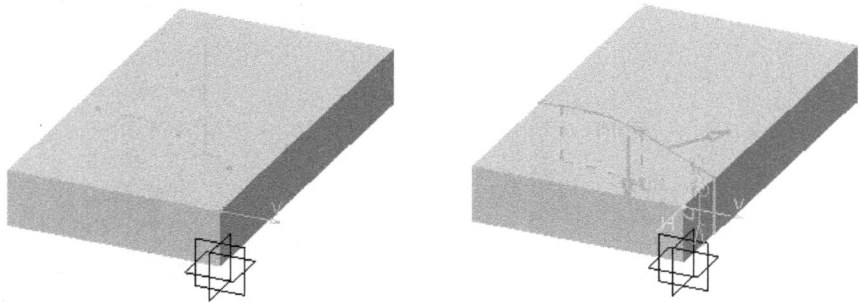

Figure 5–68

a. The Pocket feature would fail.

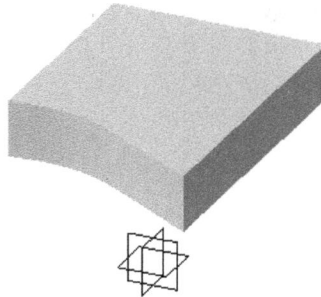

b.

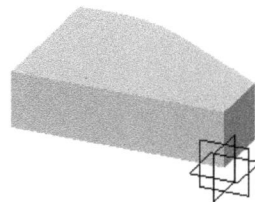

c.

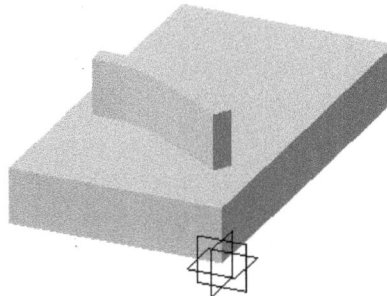

d.

8. In the specification tree shown in Figure 5–69, if you delete **Sketch.1**, **Pad.1** fails because **Sketch.1** is listed under the **Pad.1** branch of the feature tree, meaning **Pad.1** uses **Sketch.1** as its profile.

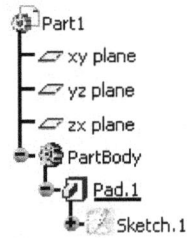

Figure 5–69

a. True

b. False

Answers: 1.b, 2.a, 3.b, 4.c, 5.a, 6.d, 7.c, 8.a

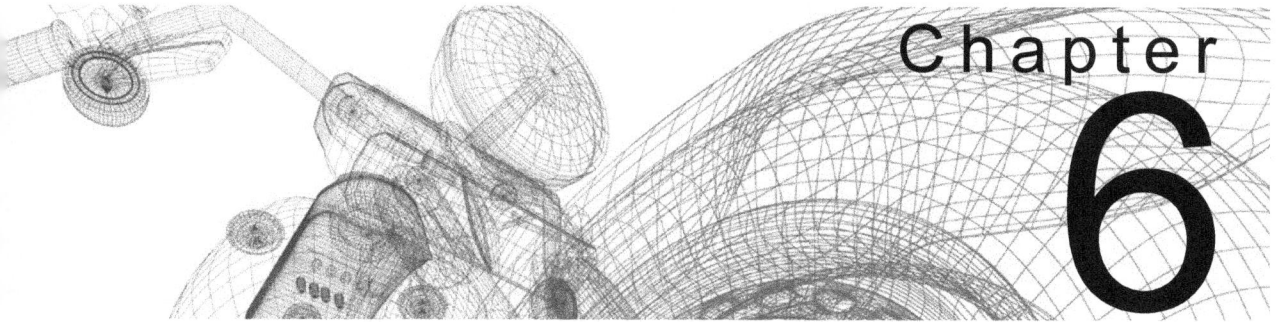

Chapter 6

Sketcher Tools and Techniques

It is important to understand all of the elements of the Sketcher workbench to work productively in CATIA. The Sketcher workbench has many useful tools that can help save time when designing and making changes.

Learning Objectives in this Chapter

- Understand the difference between a standard sketch and a positioned sketch.
- Use imported geometry.
- Understand the various methods of projecting entities from existing geometry into the sketch.
- Learn about the available tools for editing sketch entities.

6.1 Positioned Sketch

In CATIA, you can create a sketch in two different ways:

- Standard Sketch

- Positioned Sketch

Positioned Sketch

In a standard sketch, the sketch axis is free to move on the sketch support if the 3D geometry is modified. A positioned sketch enables you to select references to define the origin and orientation of the sketch support. This method enables the designer to incorporate the design intent of the model into the sketch. If you need to move the sketch relative to a geometric reference, you can define it during the creation of a positioned sketch. This provides more predictable results when modifying the geometry downstream.

How To: Create a Positioned Sketch

1. Click ▦ (Positioned Sketch). The Sketch Positioning dialog box opens, as shown in Figure 6–1.

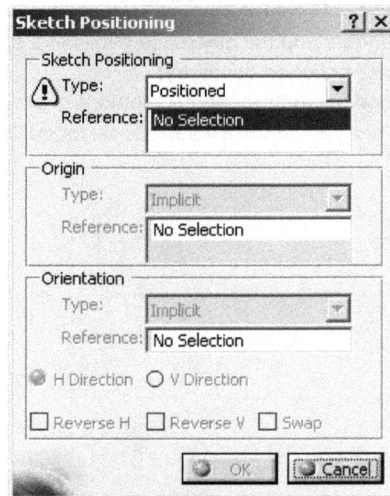

Figure 6–1

2. Verify that the **Positioned** option is selected in the Type drop-down list in the *Sketch Positioning* area.
3. Select a planar reference to define the sketch support. The sketch axis system displays on the part.

4. To define the location of the origin of the sketch axis system, in the *Origin* area, select an option in the Type drop-down list and select an appropriate reference, as shown in Figure 6–2.

Figure 6–2

Some of the more commonly used options are described as follows:

Option	Description
Projection point	The origin of the sketch is located at the projection of a selected point or vertex onto the sketch support.
Intersection 2 lines	The intersection of two lines creates a point. The origin of the sketch is located at the projection of this intersection point onto the sketch support.
Barycenter	The origin of the sketch is located at the projection of the center of the area of the selected entity.

5. To define the orientation of the sketch axis system, in the *Orientation* area, select an option in the Type drop-down list and select an appropriate reference as shown in Figure 6–3.

You can use the ***Reverse H***, ***Reverse V***, *and* ***Swap*** *options at the bottom of the dialog box to re-orient the sketch axis system.*

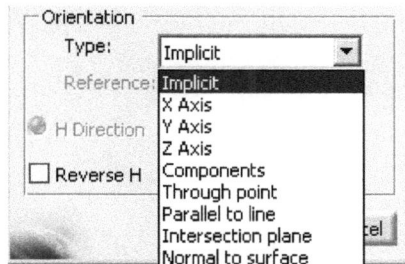

Figure 6–3

6.2 Copying and Importing Sketch Geometry

Copy and Paste

How To: Copy a Sketch from Another CATIA File into the Current File

1. Open the model that contains the sketch you want to copy.
2. Right-click sketch in the specification tree and select **Copy**, as shown in Figure 6–4.

Copying and pasting a sketch is a quick way of duplicating sketch geometry between part models or in the same part model.

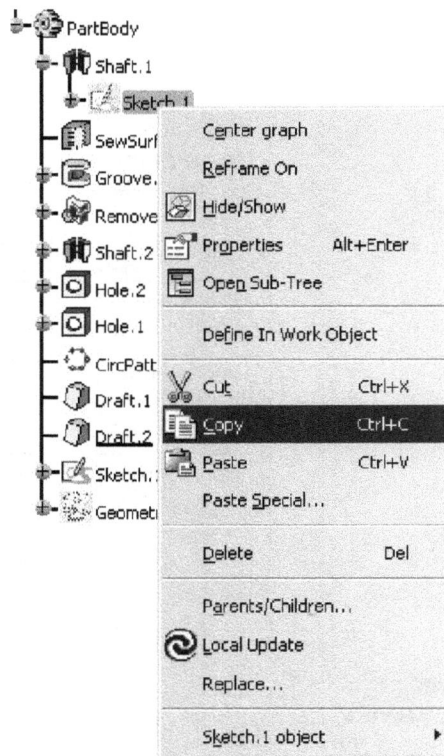

Figure 6–4

3. Activate the current file and select a plane or face as the support for the copied sketch. Right-click and select **Paste**, as shown in Figure 6–5. A copy of the sketch is created in the current model.

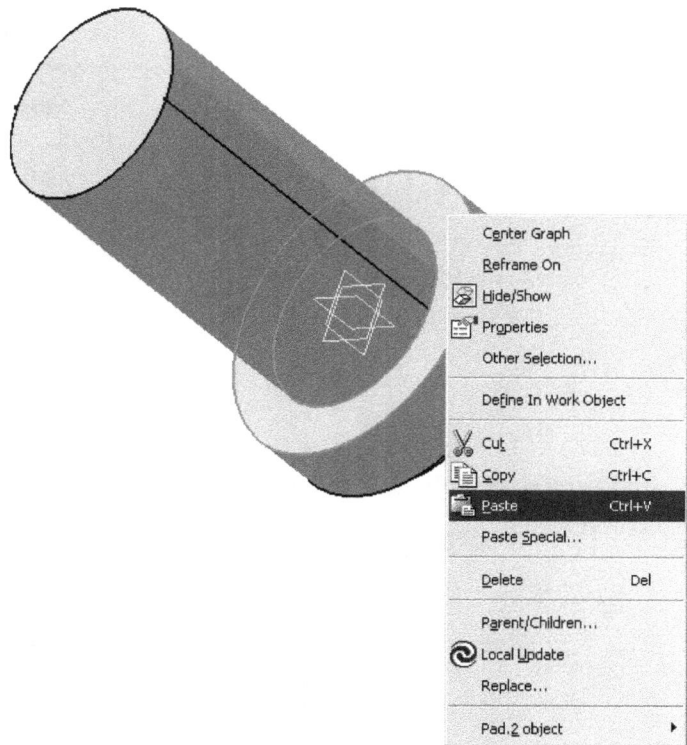

Figure 6–5

4. Verify that the sketch is correctly constrained by double-clicking on it in the specification tree to edit it and then using **Sketch Analysis** tool.

Imported Geometry

How To: Copy 2D Entities from an Imported File (DXF or IGES File)

1. Select **File>Open** and select the 2D file. The file opens in the Drafting workbench.
2. Select the required geometry in the sketch and select **Edit>Copy**.
3. Activate the current sketch and select **Edit>Paste** to paste the geometry into the sketch.

6.3 Projecting Geometry

The **3D Geometry** flyout options enable you to create sketches using existing 3D geometry. These options are shown in Figure 6–6.

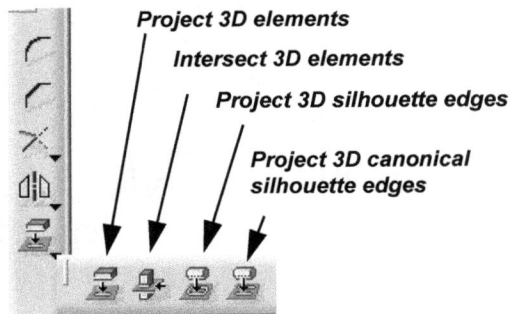

Project 3D elements

Intersect 3D elements

Project 3D silhouette edges

Project 3D canonical silhouette edges

Figure 6–6

Project 3D Elements

(Project 3D Elements) creates sketched geometry by projecting 3D entities such as edges and surfaces onto the 2D support. If the referenced geometry changes, the projected elements update accordingly. Projected entities display in yellow, indicating that they are locked in place. Locked entities cannot be translated, rotated, or scaled. However, they can be manipulated using the Relimitations toolbar options or by applying corners or chamfers.

If you select the curved surface of a cylindrical face, you can right-click and select **Select Boundary Edges** or **Select Axis** as shown in Figure 6–7.

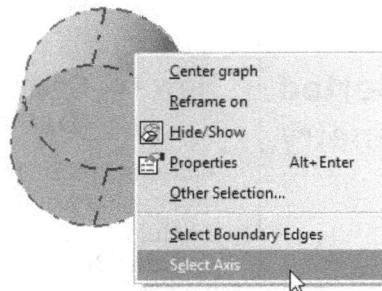

Figure 6–7

Intersecting 3D Elements

(Intersecting 3D Elements) creates a projected entity where the selected 3D entity intersects the support. Projected entities display in yellow, indicating that they are locked in place. As with projected 3D entities, you can still apply options from the Relimitation toolbar, corners, and chamfers to intersected 3D entities.

If you select the curved surface of a cylindrical face, you can right-click and select **Select Boundary Edges** or **Select Axis**.

Project 3D Silhouette Edges

(Project 3D Silhouette Edges) projects all of the silhouette edges of a feature onto the support. For example, the edge along the Spherical feature and adjacent planar surface (shown in Figure 6–8) are required references for the new geometry.

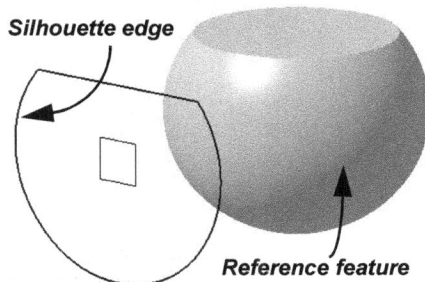

Figure 6–8

Project 3D Canonical Silhouette Edges

(Project 3D Canonical Silhouette Edges) only projects the silhouette edges of curved surfaces onto the support. In the example shown in Figure 6–9, the edge along the Spherical feature is a required reference for the new geometry.

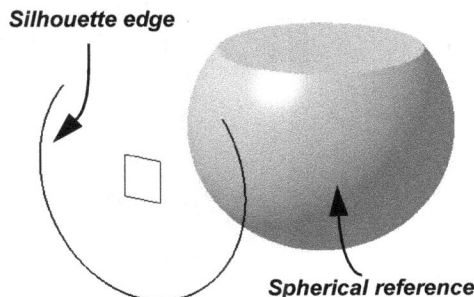

Figure 6–9

If the referenced geometry changes, the sketch also changes.

These four tools create a relationship between the sketched geometry and the referenced 3D geometry.

Sketch Analysis

To analyze and review the projections and intersections defined in a sketch, access the Sketch Analysis dialog box by clicking

. The dialog box is shown in Figure 6–10. Select the *Use-edges* tab, which displays the status of all entities that are projected from existing geometry. The cylindrical Pad in the center of the rectangle was referenced for a hole in the center of the new sketch.

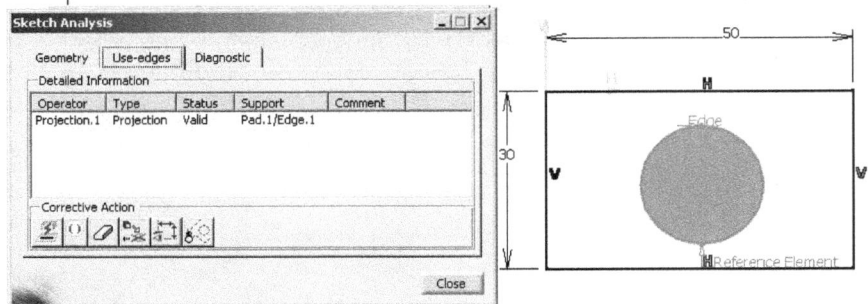

Figure 6–10

As with the *Geometry* tab, you can use the icons in the *Corrective Action* area of the dialog box to correct any problems with the referenced geometry. These icons are described as follows:

Icon	Description
	The entity is no longer linked to or referenced to 3D geometry.
( )	Toggles off/on the highlighted constraint in the detailed information area.
	Removes the highlighted geometry from the sketch.
	Replaces highlighted referenced geometry with selected geometry on the screen.
	Toggles the display of constraints.
	Toggles the display of construction geometry.

6.4 Editing Tools

To modify sketched geometry, use the Operations toolbar options. Figure 6–11 shows the Transformation toolbar options, which enable you to mirror, create symmetry, translate, rotate, scale, and offset 2D elements in your sketch.

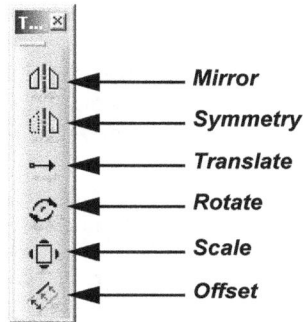

Figure 6–11

Mirror

Click 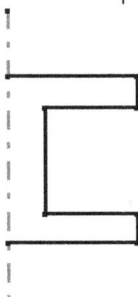 (Mirror) to symmetrically mirror sketched geometry about a line or axis, as shown in Figure 6–12.

Symmetry

Click (Symmetry) to symmetrically transform the selected geometry about a line or axis, as shown in Figure 6–13.

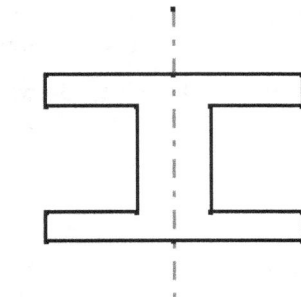

Figure 6–12

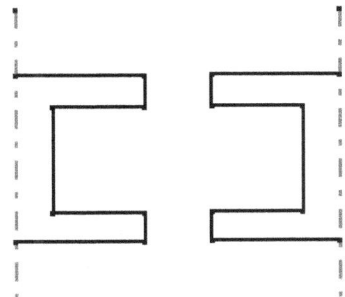

Figure 6–13

Translate

The **Translate** option moves sketched geometry you have selected along a translation vector.

How To: Create Translate Entities

1. Select the entities that you want to move, and click

   (Translate). The Translation Definition dialog box opens.

2. Select a location on the screen as the start point for the translation. The Translation Definition dialog box updates, as shown in Figure 6–14.

   Select Duplicate mode to create a copy of the selected entities in the new location. Clear it to move selected entities.

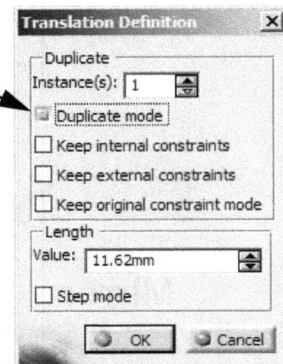

Figure 6–14

3. In the *Length* area, enter a specific value for the translation, or move the start point directly on the model to the required location.
   - If the **Step Mode** option is selected, the cursor snaps in increments of the value entered in the *Value* field.

4. Select the **Duplicate mode** option to keep the original sketch and create a copy of it in the new location.
5. Click **OK** to complete the definition.

Rotate

(Rotate) enables you to rotate sketched geometry using a method similar to that for translating.

How To: Create Rotate Entities

1. Select the entity or entities that you want to rotate, and click

   (Rotate) to open the Rotation Definition dialog box.

2. Select a location for the center of rotation and the dialog box updates as shown in Figure 6–16.

If the Step mode option is selected, each element is rotated from the previous element by the angle value. For example, if the value of angle is 10, the entities would rotate in 10 degree steps.

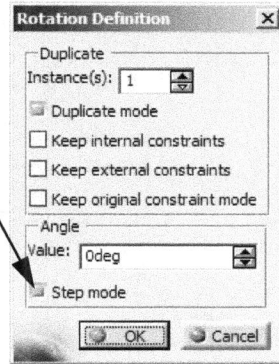

Rotation Definition

Duplicate
Instance(s): 1
Duplicate mode
☐ Keep internal constraints
☐ Keep external constraints
☐ Keep original constraint mode

Angle
Value: 0deg

Step mode

OK   Cancel

Figure 6–15

3. In the *Angle* area, enter a value for angle of rotation and click **OK**.
   - As with translation, selecting the **Duplicate mode** option keeps the original entities and rotates a copy of them to the new angle.

Scale

The **Scale** option resizes the selected sketched geometry using a scale factor.

How To: Create Scale Entities

1. Select the entities to edit and click ⟨Ị⟩ (Scale) to open the Scale Definition dialog box.
2. Select a location for the scaling centerpoint, and the Scale Definition dialog box updates, as shown in Figure 6–16.

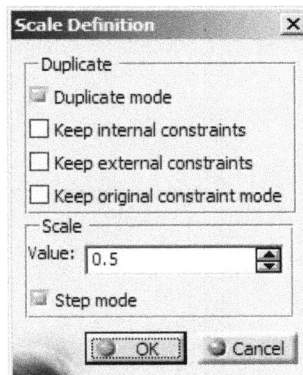

Scale Definition

Duplicate
Duplicate mode
☐ Keep internal constraints
☐ Keep external constraints
☐ Keep original constraint mode

Scale
Value: 0.5

Step mode

OK   Cancel

Figure 6–16

3. Enter the scale value and click **OK** to complete the definition.

For each of the Translate, Rotate, and Scale options, the following options apply:

Keep internal constraints	Preserves the internal constraints applied to the selected elements.
Keep external constraints	Preserves the external constraints applied to the selected elements.
Keep original constraints	Preserves the original constraints applied to the selected elements. The constraints defined in the original geometry are driving constraints.
Step mode	Enter a value, and dragged entities will move in increments matching the value. For example, if you enter a value of 10 for the Angle when rotating entities, the entities will rotate in increments of 10 degrees.

Offset

The **Offset** option enables you to create sketched entities by offsetting from existing sketched entities or from the edges of 3D geometry. Click (Offset) and select the entity that you want to offset. If offsetting from other sketched geometry, use the Sketch Tools toolbar options to define how to offset the entity. These options are described as follows:

Icon	Example	Description
(No Propagation)	Selected Edge	Offsets a single selected entity.

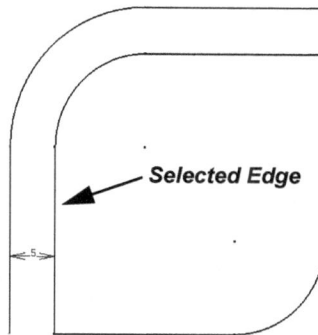

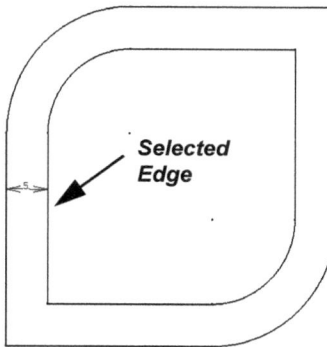

(Tangent Propagation)		Offsets the selected entity and any entities that form a tangent chain with it.
(Point Propagation)		Offsets the selected entity and any entities that form a chain with it.

Additionally, you can offset in both directions by clicking in the Sketch Tools toolbar. Offset in both directions can be applied to both sketched entities and edges of 3D geometry, as shown in Figure 6–17.

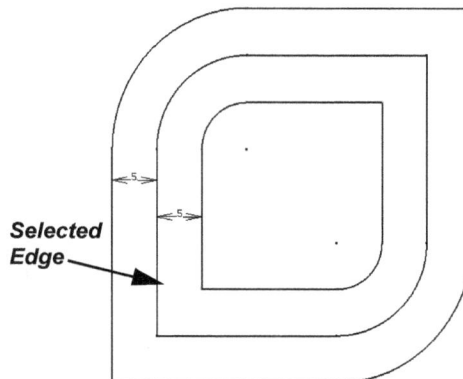

Figure 6–17

The offset can be repeated several times by entering the number of instances in the Sketch Tools toolbar. Each instance is offset from the previous one by the offset distance, as shown in Figure 6–18.

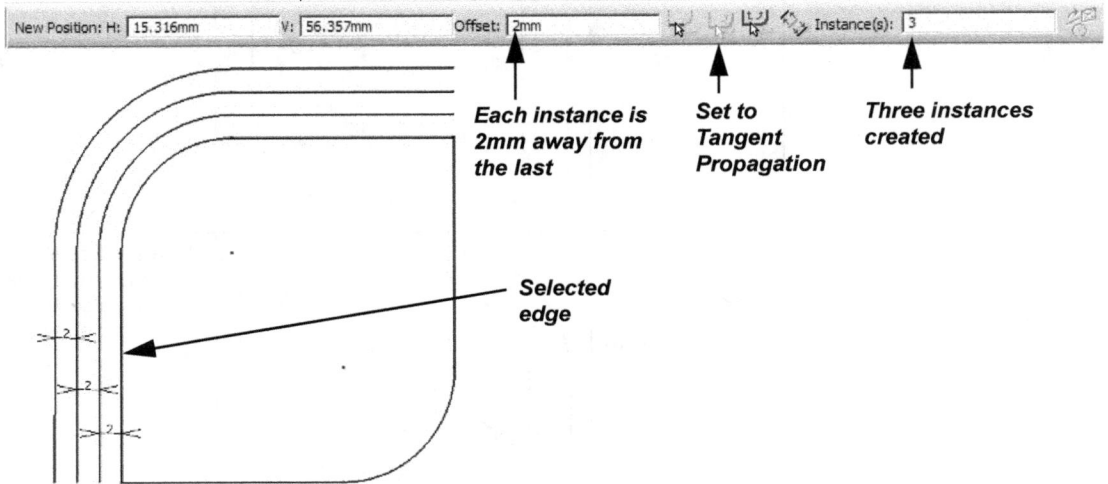

New Position: H: 15.316mm   V: 56.357mm   Offset: 2mm   Instance(s): 3

Each instance is 2mm away from the last

Set to Tangent Propagation

Three instances created

Selected edge

Figure 6–18

In addition to offsetting individual elements of a an existing 3D profile, you can offset an entire profile, provided it contains simple geometry such as lines, arcs and circles, and has no self-intersecting entities.

Practice 6a

Projecting 3D Geometry

Practice Objectives

- Project 3D geometry elements into a sketch.
- Offset sketched elements.

In this practice, you will practice using several projection tools in the Sketcher workbench. You will also offset some of these elements using a variety of methods. You are provided with existing solid and surface geometry and you will use these to create sketched elements. Upon completion, the model displays as shown in Figure 6–19.

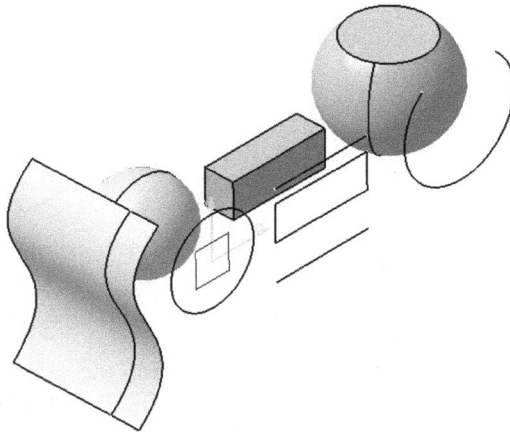

Figure 6–19

Task 1 - Open a part file and activate the Sketcher workbench.

1. Open the **SketchTools.CATPart** model.

2. Select the plane shown in Figure 6–20. Activate the Sketcher workbench.

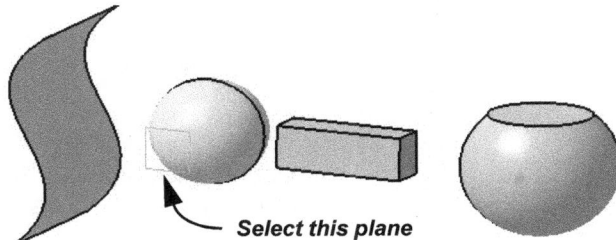

Select this plane

Figure 6–20

Task 2 - Project existing 3D geometry into the sketch.

In this task, you will project the edges of the rectangular Pad and the silhouette of the spherical surface onto the sketching plane. You will then create a sketcher entity at the intersection of the extruded surface and the sketch plane. The final geometry is shown in Figure 6–21.

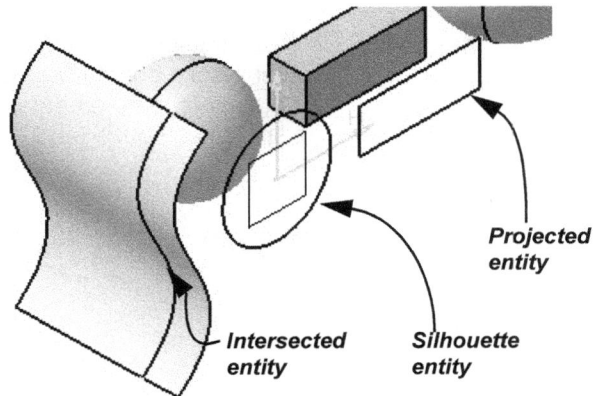

Projected entity

Intersected entity

Silhouette entity

Figure 6–21

1. Click (Project 3D Elements).

2. Select the top edge of the rectangular Pad, as shown in Figure 6–22. In the Projection dialog box, click **OK** and select a space on the background. A yellow line displays, which represents the edge projected into the sketch.

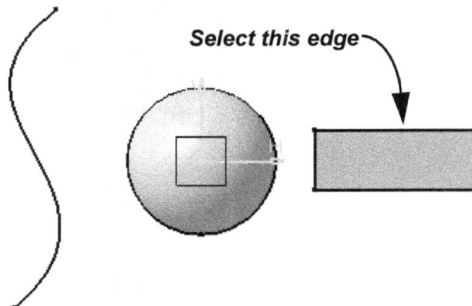

Select this edge

Figure 6–22

3. Double-click on (Project 3D Elements) and project the remaining three edges.

4. Click ⬜ (Isometric View). The view switches to Isometric, and the sketched elements display as shown in Figure 6–23.

5. Click ⬛ (Intersect 3D Elements).

6. Select the extruded surface and click **OK**. The element representing the intersection between the sketch plane and the Surface feature is created as shown in Figure 6–24.

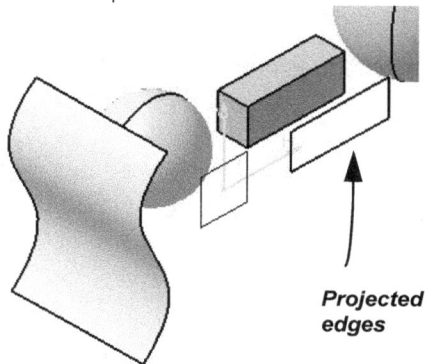

Projected edges

Figure 6–23

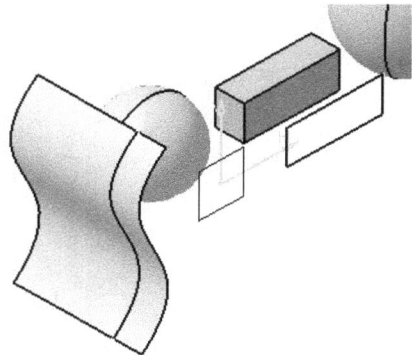

Figure 6–24

7. Select anywhere in the background to clear the selection of the intersection.

8. Click ⬛ (Project 3D Silhouette Edges).

9. Select the spherical surface. The silhouette edge of the surface is projected into the sketch plane as shown in Figure 6–25. Select in the background.

Select the spherical surface

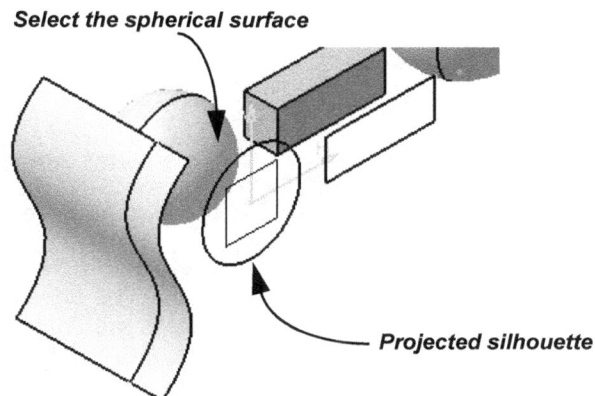

Projected silhouette

Figure 6–25

10. Click ![icon](Project 3D Silhouette Edges).

11. Select the spherical surface. The silhouette edges of the surface and adjacent edge are projected into the sketch plane as shown in Figure 6–26.

12. Select **Edit>Undo**.

13. Click ![icon](Project 3D Canonical Silhouette Edges).

14. Select the spherical surface. The silhouette edge of only the spherical surface is projected into the sketch plane as shown in Figure 6–27.

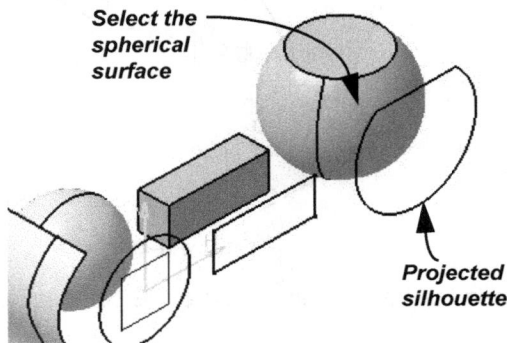

Figure 6–26

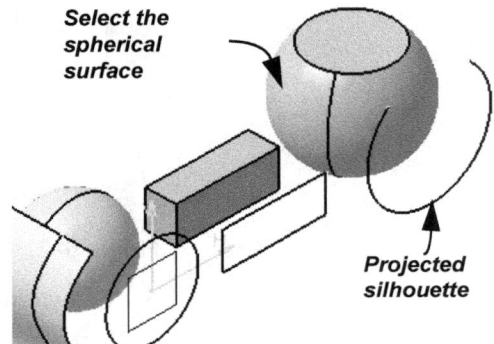

Figure 6–27

Task 3 - Create elements offset from the projected edges.

In this task, you will use the **Offset** option to make offset copies of the projected rectangle.

1. Click ![icon](Normal View) to orient the model to the sketch view.

2. In the Operations toolbar, click .

3. Select the top projected edge from the Pad.

4. Move the cursor up and click required .location to offset (**-10 (-0.394 in)**). The edge is offset to that location, and a parameter is automatically added by CATIA, as shown in Figure 6–28.

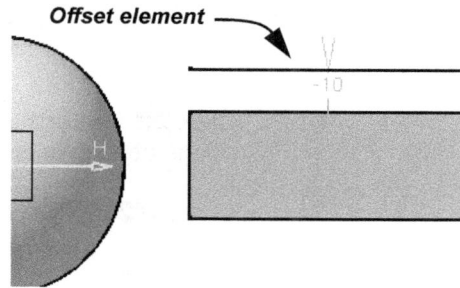

Figure 6–28

5. Click ![offset icon] (Offset) and select the bottom projected edge from the Pad.

6. In the Sketch Tools toolbar, in the *Offset* field enter **30 (1.181 in)**, as shown in Figure 6–29.

Enter either a positive or negative offset value to ensure that the element is positioned as shown in Figure 6–30.

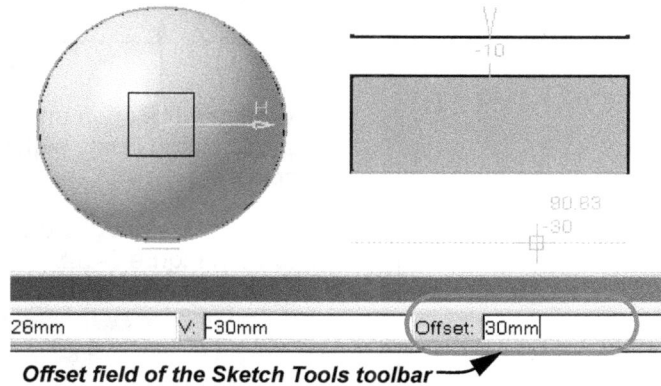

Figure 6–29

7. Press <Enter>. The sketch displays as shown in Figure 6–30.

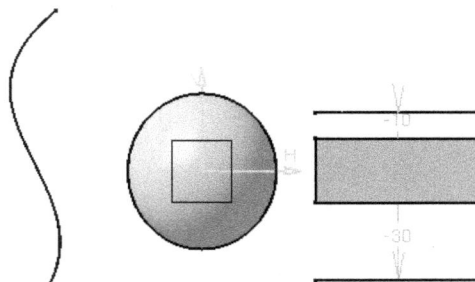

Figure 6–30

Task 4 - Analyze the sketch.

1. Click (Sketch Analysis). The Sketch Analysis dialog box opens as shown in Figure 6–31.

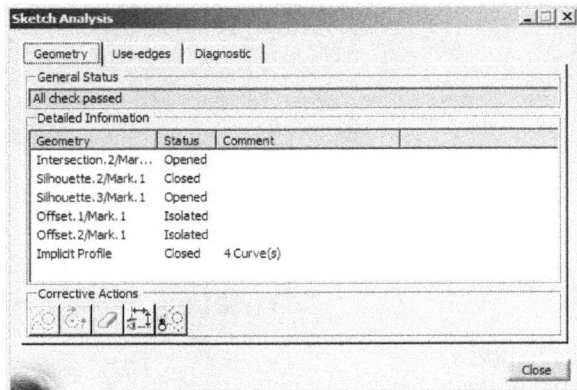

Figure 6–31

2. Investigate the open and closed sections listed under the *Status* column. They highlight as you select them in the display.

3. Select the *Use-edges* tab and note the projections listed as shown in Figure 6–32.

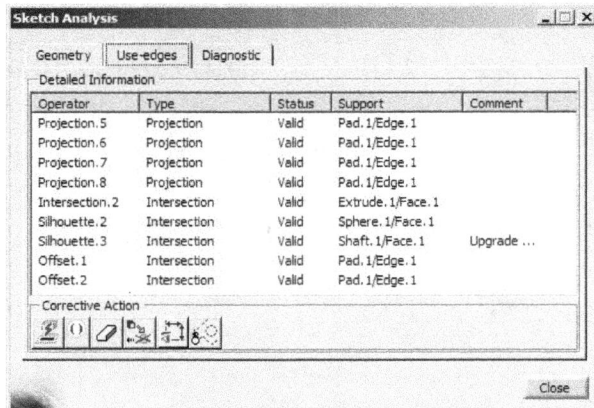

Figure 6–32

4. Click **Close**.

5. Exit the Sketcher workbench.

6. Save the model and close the file.

Practice 6b	# Sketcher Techniques

Practice Objectives

- Create and transform sketched elements.
- Create base solid geometry.
- Import a DXF file into Sketcher.

In this practice, you will create a part with a Pad as the base feature. You will then use the **Copy**, **Import**, and **Analysis** tools to create the feature shown in Figure 6–33.

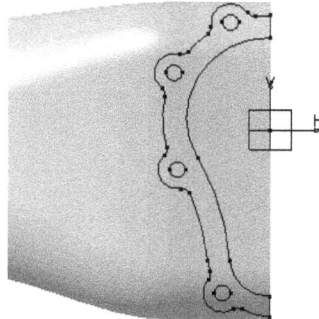

Figure 6–33

Task 1 - Import a DXF file.

1. Open **BlockLeft.CATPart**.

2. To switch the model orientation to the back view, click
   (Back View), as shown in Figure 6–34.

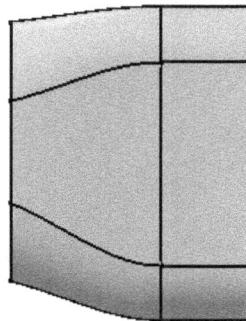

Figure 6–34

3. Select **File>Open**. In the Engine directory, select the **Interface.dxf** file. A new window opens with the DXF sketch.

4. In the specification tree, select **Main View**. Right-click and select **Copy**, as shown in Figure 6–35.

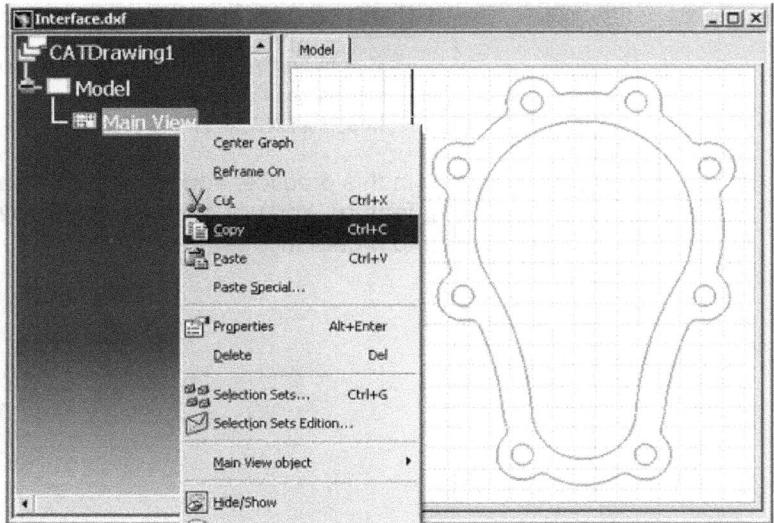

Figure 6–35

5. In the menu bar, select **Window>BlockLeft.CATPart** to switch back to the window containing the **BlockLeft.CATPart** 3D solid model.

6. Select the planar surface and paste the copied sketch geometry, as shown in Figure 6–36.

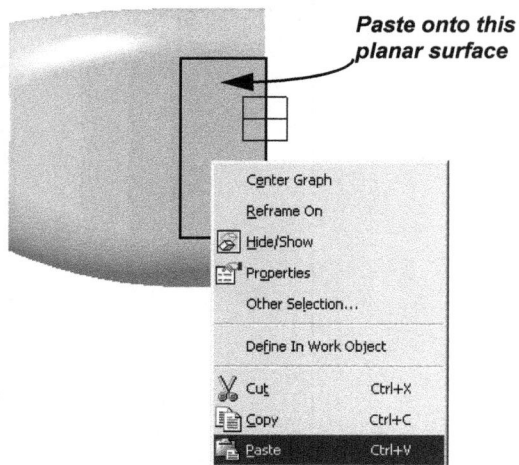

Figure 6–36

7. Click ⊹ (Fit All In). The imported sketch displays as shown in Figure 6–37.

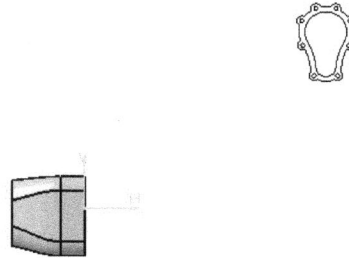

Figure 6–37

Task 2 - Modify the imported geometry.

1. Double-click on **Main View** sketch to activate the Sketcher workbench. Zoom in on the imported sketch.

Zoom in to ensure that the vertical line is coincident with the outer profile of the import geometry at the top and bottom. A geometric constraint can be applied as required.

2. Only half of the sketch is required. Sketch a line to separate the imported geometry into two symmetric sections, as shown in Figure 6–38.

3. Click ⬚ and select **location 1**, as shown in Figure 6–39. Hold the mouse button, drag the cursor to location 2, and release the mouse button. A selection trap is used to select all geometry in the rectangular trap.

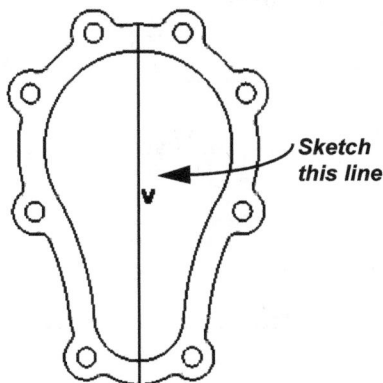

Sketch this line

Figure 6–38

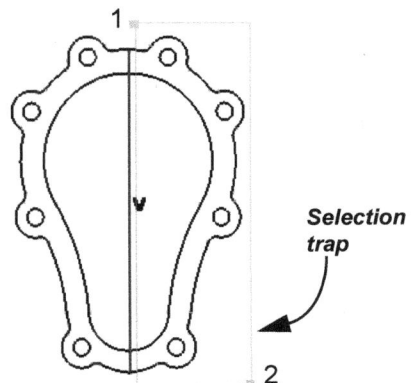

1

2

Selection trap

Figure 6–39

Only include geometry on the right side of the sketched vertical line in the selection trap.

4. Press <Delete>. The sketch updates as shown in Figure 6–40.

5. In the Relimitations toolbar, click 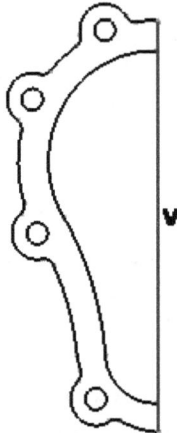 (Quick Trim) to activate the **Quick Trim** function.

6. Select the center of the sketched vertical line. The sketch updates as shown in Figure 6–41.

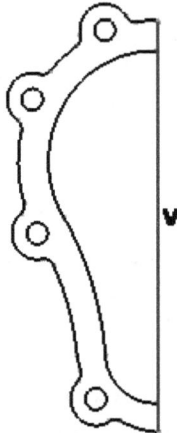
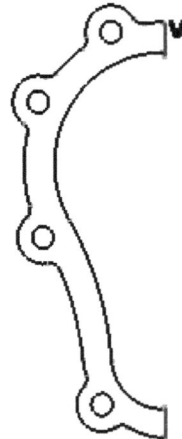

Figure 6–40   **Figure 6–41**

Task 3 - Analyze the sketch.

1. In the menu bar, select **Tools>Sketch Analysis**. The Sketch Analysis dialog box opens as shown in Figure 6–42.

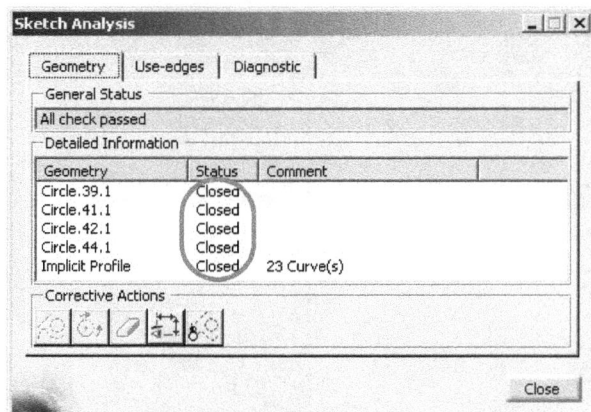

Figure 6–42

Ensure that the Status is set to **Closed** for all the geometry profiles that are listed in the dialog box. If it is not set to **Closed**, constrain the geometry to close all profiles.

2. Click **Close**.

Task 4 - Constrain the sketch.

1. Select the entire sketch using a selection trap.

2. Click [icon] (Fix Together) to constrain the relative positions of the imported entities. The Fix Together Definition dialog box opens as shown in Figure 6–43.

3. Click **OK** to complete the function. The sketch updates as shown in Figure 6–44.

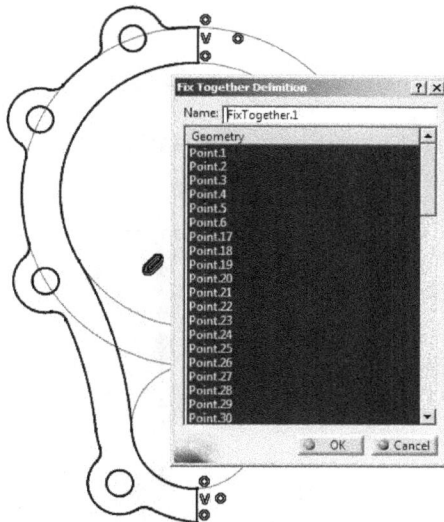

Figure 6–43

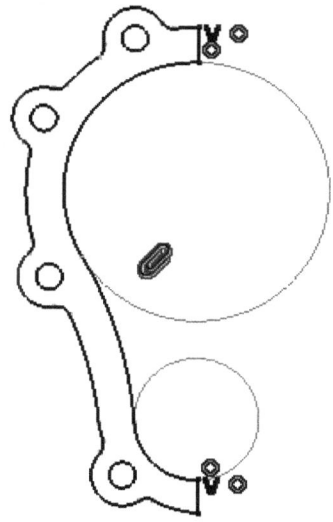

Figure 6–44

Task 5 - Position the imported sketch on the solid.

1. Drag the imported geometry closer to the solid by grabbing one of the elements in the sketch and holding the mouse button while you move the mouse.

2. Add a **Coincidence** constraint between the planar right face of the model and the lower vertical line of the imported geometry, as shown in Figure 6–45.

3. Add a dimension between the lower vertex of the imported geometry and the bottom vertex of the 3D model in the sketched view. The sketch updates as shown in Figure 6–46.

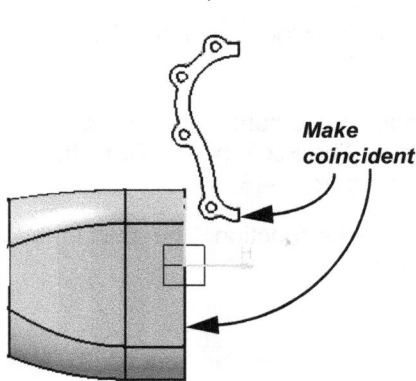

Make coincident

Figure 6–45

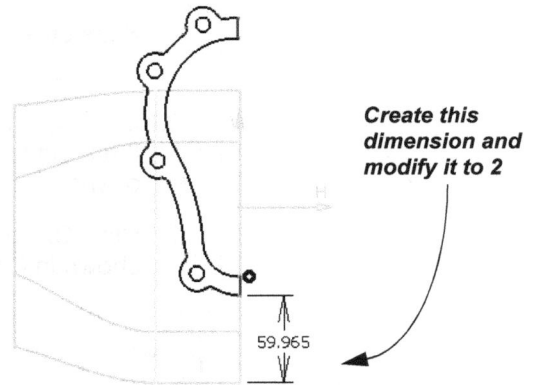

Create this dimension and modify it to 2

59.965

Figure 6–46

The model is shown without the auto-constraints for visual clarity.

4. Modify the value of the dimension to **2**. The model updates as shown in Figure 6–47.

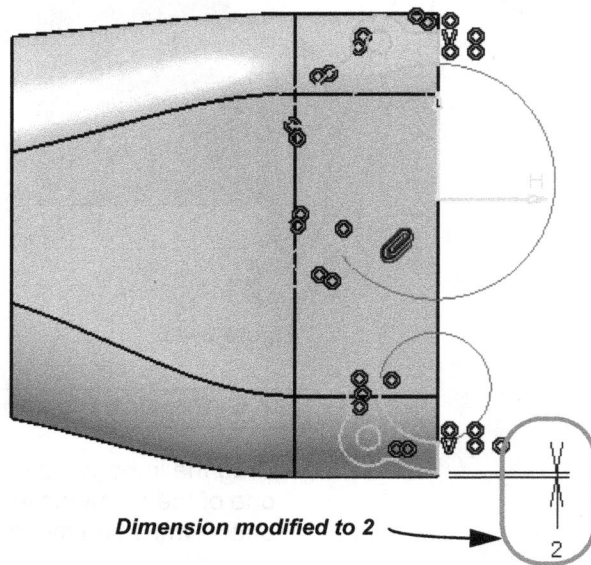

Dimension modified to 2

2

Figure 6–47

5. Click ▣ (Sketch Solving Status). Ensure that the message in the Sketch Solving Status dialog box indicates that the sketch is **Iso-Constrained**, as shown in Figure 6–48.

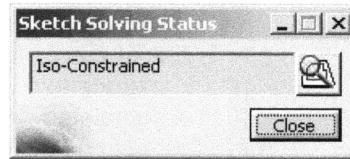

Figure 6–48

6. Click ▣ in the Sketch Solving Status dialog box.

7. Click ▣ to hide the constraints. The sketch displays as shown in Figure 6–49.

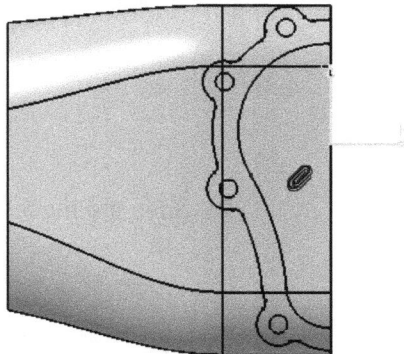

Figure 6–49

8. Click **Close**.

9. Exit the Sketcher workbench.

Task 6 - Develop the transmission interface.

In this task, you will use the imported sketch to create a Pad for the transmission interface of the engine block.

1. Create a Pad feature using the sketch you just created. The Pad should extend up to the solid in one direction and extrude to a depth of 10mm in the other direction. The completed part model displays as shown in Figure 6–50.

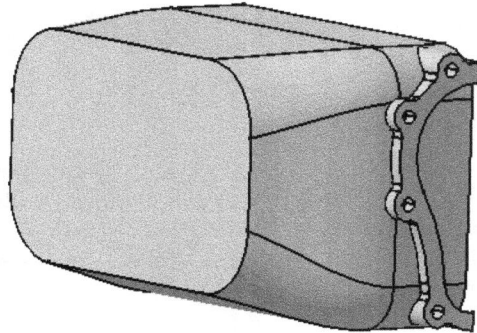

Figure 6–50

2. Save the model and close the window.

Chapter Review Questions

1. The two types of sketches in CATIA are Standard and Positioned.

   a. True

   b. False

2. A sketch cannot be copied between part models.

   a. True

   b. False

3. Which tools can be used to copy sketched entities? (Select all that apply.)

   a. <Ctrl>+<C>

   b. (Rotate)

   c. (Translate)

   d. (Scale)

4. Data imported into a sketch (i.e., from a DXF file) can be scaled, rotated, and translated.

   a. True

   b. False

5. Projected geometry can be scaled, rotated, and translated.

   a. True

   b. False

6. What does a sketched entity displayed in yellow indicate?

   a. The entity is over-constrained.

   b. The entity is under-constrained.

   c. The entity is locked.

   d. The entity has been imported from another file.

7. Which tool can be used to create the profile shown on the right side of Figure 6–51, from the entities shown on the left side of Figure 6–51?

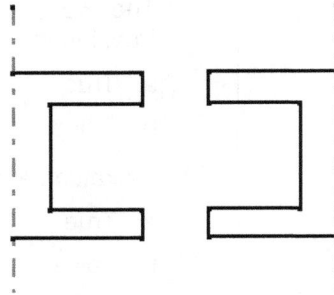

Figure 6–51

a. → (Translate)

b. (Mirror)

c. (Symmetry)

d. (Scale)

8. Multiple instances can be created with a single offset.

a. True

b. False

Answers: 1.a, 2.b, 3.abcd, 4.a, 5.b, 6.c, 7.c, 8.c

Sketcher Formulas

This chapter explores some advanced methods of dimension modification, such as Formulas and Equivalent Dimensions. Using formulas enables you to control the design intent in the sketch. You can also control the design intent by assigning equivalence between entities, so that changing one dimension will change multiple entities.

Learning Objectives in this Chapter

- Use formulas to control dimensional constraints in sketches, to ensure that your design intent is maintained.
- Use the Equivalent Dimension tool to establish a relationship between dimensions.
- Understand how the SmartPick tool can help in the creation of sketches.
- Use the Visualization to help clarify the display while sketching.

7.1 Formulas

To correctly convey the design intent, create a relationship between two or more dimensions in your sketch.

In the example shown in Figure 7–1, the design intent of the rectangular profile is that the height should always be half of the width. This can be achieved using the Formula Editor.

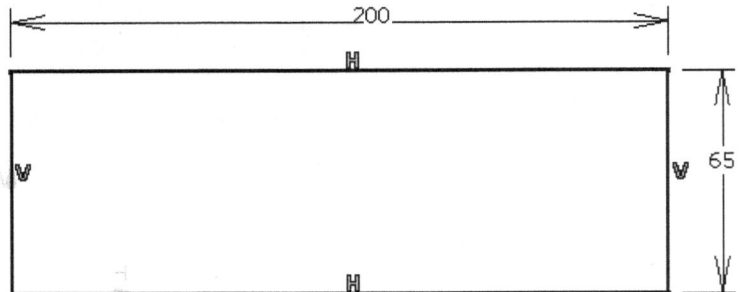

Figure 7–1

Before creating a formula, you must edit the dimension that you want to drive with the formula, called the base dimension. Drive the height of the rectangle by editing the 65mm dimension.

Right-click in the *Value* field and select **Edit formula**, as shown in Figure 7–2.

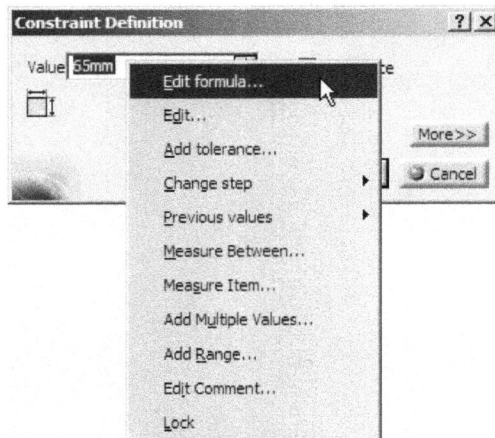

Figure 7–2

This technique does not work with diameter dimensions. To add a formula to a diameter dimension, right-click on the sketcher dimension and select **Radius.# object>Edit formula**.

The Formula Editor dialog box opens. It lists the driven parameter in the field at the top (in this case, **PartBody\ Sketch.1\Length.12\Length**) and enables you to enter the formula in the field shown in Figure 7–3.

Driven parameter   **Formula**

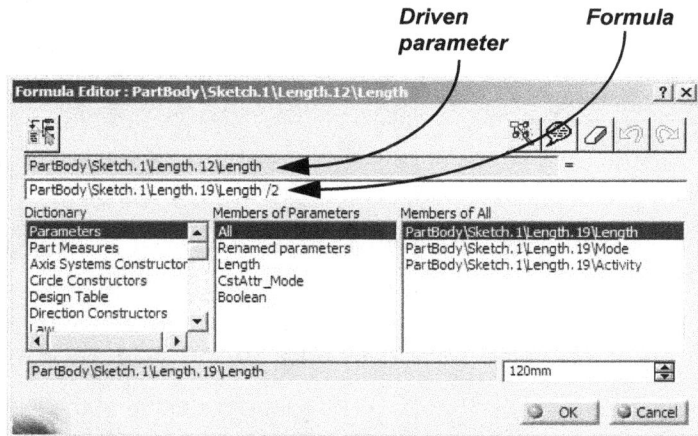

Figure 7–3

You can either type the formula directly into the dialog box or locate the driving dimension (**200mm**). By selecting the dimension, it is automatically added to the formula editor. This method ensures that no syntax errors are in the formula.

In this example, the **200mm** dimension is selected and added to the dialog box, as shown in Figure 7–4. The formula shown in the previous figure would make the two dimensions equal. In this case, the design intent is Height = Width/2, so a **/2** is added to the end of the formula, as shown in Figure 7–5.

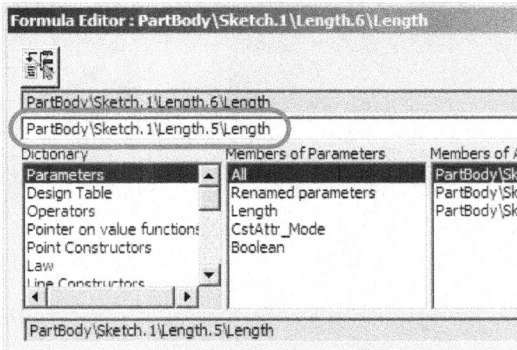

Figure 7–4

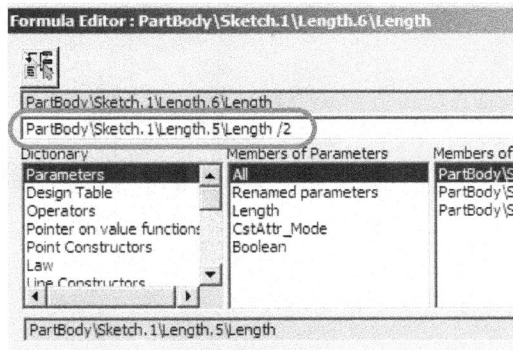

Figure 7–5

Once the formula has been entered, click **OK**. The *Value* field in the Constraint Definition dialog box is grayed out, as shown in Figure 7–6. The $f_{(x)}$ icon displays, which can be used to edit the formula.

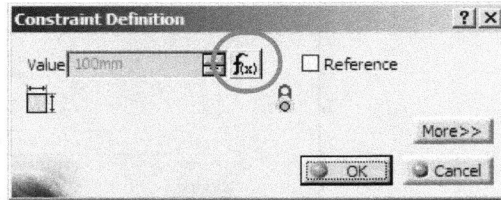

Figure 7–6

Since this dimension is driven by the relationship with the width dimension, a value cannot be entered. The only way to change the height of the rectangle is to:

- Change the value of the width dimension.

- Edit the formula using $f_{(x)}$.

- Delete the formula (right-click and select **Formula>Delete**).

The sketch updates automatically with the new height value of 100mm, and an icon displays next to the dimension to indicate that it is driven by a formula, as shown in Figure 7–7.

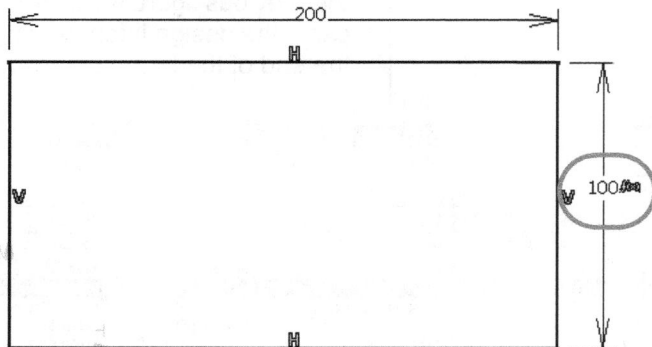

Figure 7–7

Displaying in the Specification Tree

To display formulas in the specification tree, select **Tools> Options>Infrastructure>Part Infrastructure>**Display tab. Select the options listed to toggle the display of features on or off in the specification tree. The *Display* tab is shown in Figure 7–8.

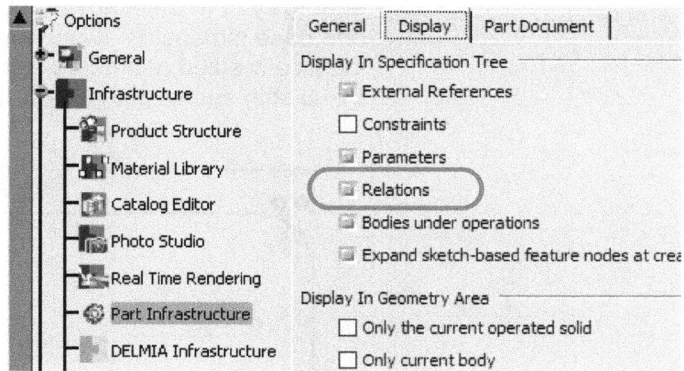

Figure 7–8

Figure 7–9 shows the specification tree with the **Relations** option enabled.

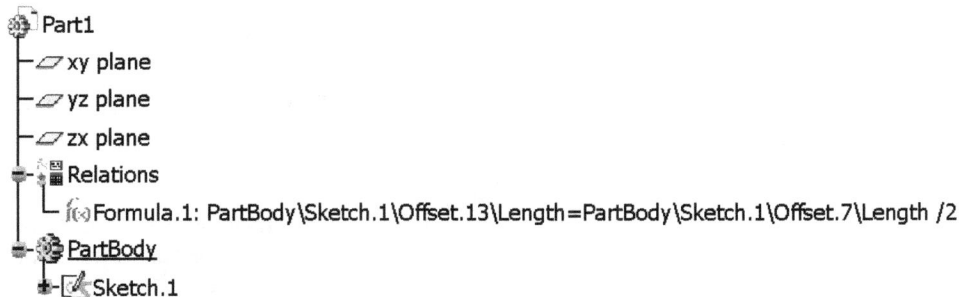

Part1
— xy plane
— yz plane
— zx plane
— Relations
  — Formula.1: PartBody\Sketch.1\Offset.13\Length=PartBody\Sketch.1\Offset.7\Length /2
— PartBody
  — Sketch.1

Figure 7–9

Select **Tools>Options>General>Display** to display the full text of a formula, and then select the *Tree Appearance* tab. The number of characters can be set to **Text-dependent** (shows all text) or to a maximum number of characters, as shown in Figure 7–10.

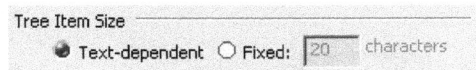

Tree Item Size
● Text-dependent ○ Fixed: [20] characters

Figure 7–10

7.2 Equivalent Dimensions

The **Equivalent Dimensions** tool is another method of creating a relationship between two or more dimensions. This tool enables you to drive any number of sketcher dimensions with one base dimension. It is useful for constraining a number of identically sized geometric elements, such as the four corners of the sketch shown in Figure 7–11.

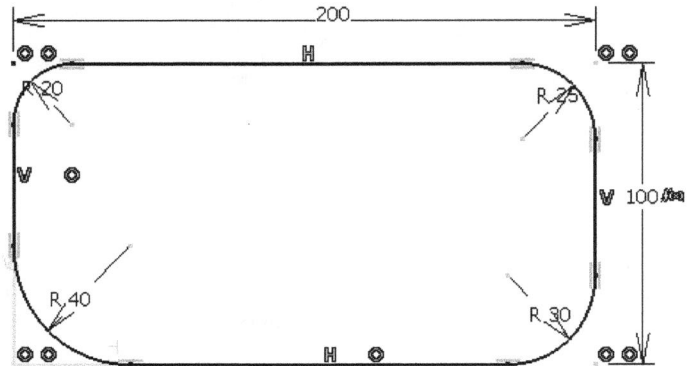

Figure 7–11

How To: Rotate Dimensions using the Equivalent Dimensions tool

1. Click 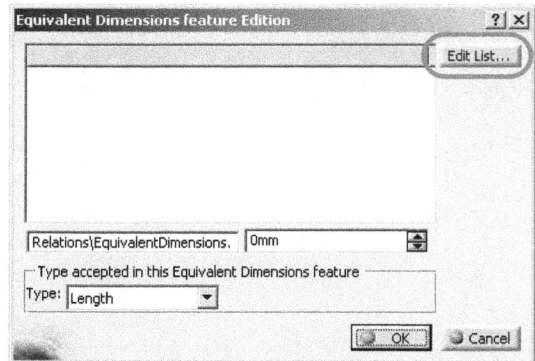 (Equivalent Dimensions) in the Knowledge toolbar, as shown in Figure 7–12. The Equivalent Dimensions dialog box opens, as shown in Figure 7–13.

Figure 7–12

Figure 7–13

2. Click **Edit List...** to add dimensions to the Equivalent Dimensions dialog box. A dialog box opens that lists all modifiable dimensions, as shown in Figure 7–14.

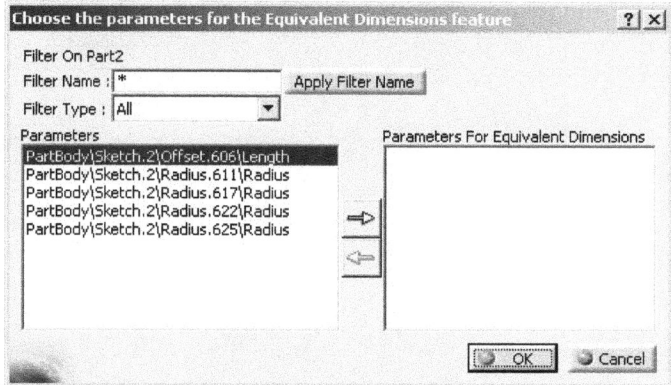

Figure 7–14

3. To add dimensions, highlight them (using <Ctrl> to multi-select) and then click ⇨ to move them to the *Parameters For Equivalent Dimensions* area. All radius dimensions are added, as shown in Figure 7–15.

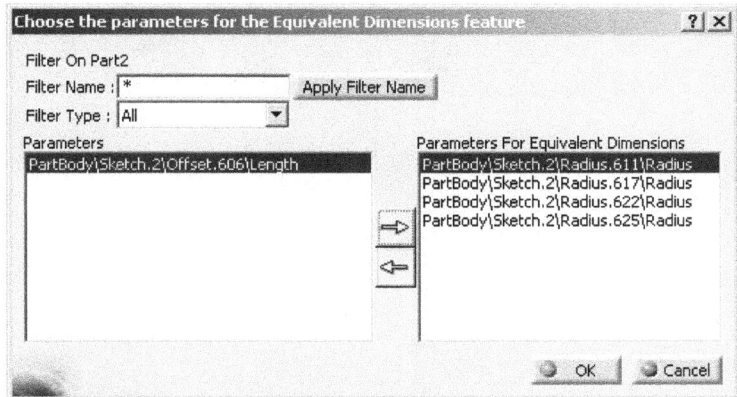

Figure 7–15

4. Click **OK** to return to the Equivalent Dimensions dialog box. Enter the equivalent dimension value in the field indicated in Figure 7–16. All dimensions are set to **10mm**.

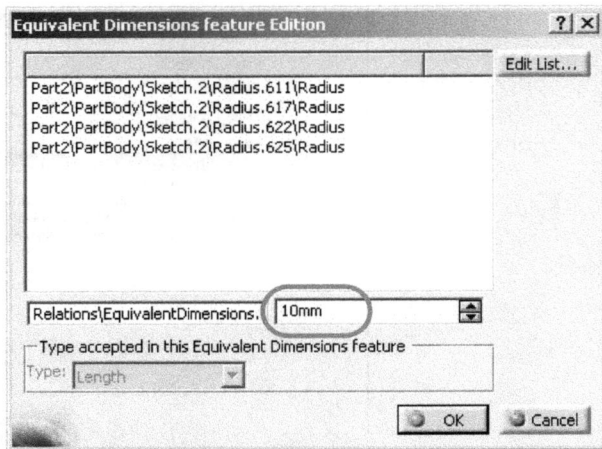

Figure 7–16

5. Once complete, click **OK** to return to Sketcher. The sketch updates with the equivalent dimensions, as shown in Figure 7–17. Note that a new branch has been added to the specification tree.

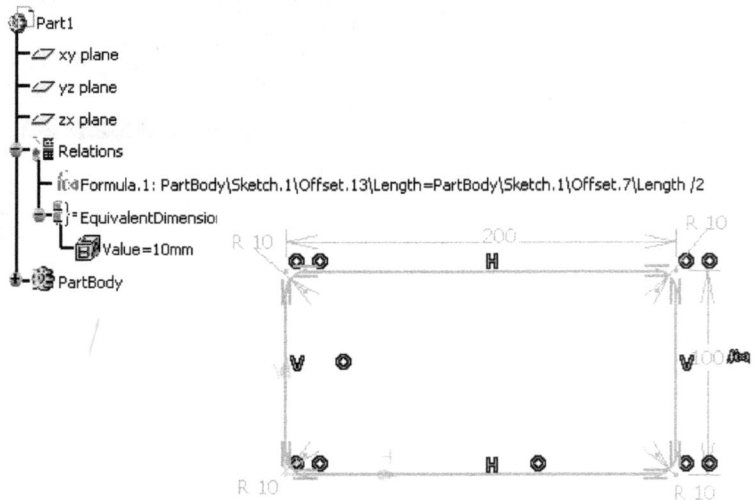

Figure 7–17

7.3 Sketch using SmartPick

SmartPick is an automatic tool used to ease the creation of a sketch. SmartPick is active anytime you create new geometry in Sketcher. As you sketch with SmartPick, it dynamically detects entities and adds positional and geometrical constraints to the geometry being created. The constraints being added display as symbols on the screen.

SmartPick detects the following entity positions and constraints:

• Support line and circles	• Tangency
• Alignment	• Concentricity
• Parallelism	• Horizontal and vertical
• Perpendicularity	• Midpoint

SmartPick only detects references and adds constraints to geometry in the active sketch. It does not snap to previously created features or sketches. If a reference to a previous feature is required, you must either project the 3D elements you want to reference into the current sketch, or sketch the geometry, unconstrained, and then add the required geometric constraints.

When SmartPick is active, the cursor changes to a crosshair symbol. The **H** and **V** coordinates for the cursor location display on the screen and in the Sketch Tools toolbar. All constraints detected by SmartPick display on the screen and are indicated by a change in color, as shown in Figure 7–18.

- Entities used to create the constraint display in orange and the constraint added displays in blue.

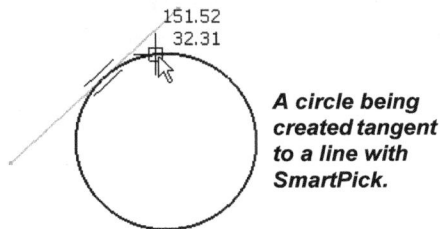

151.52
32.31

A circle being created tangent to a line with SmartPick.

Figure 7–18

Shortcut Menus

While sketching, the cursor becomes highlighted when moved over an existing sketched entity. Once highlighted, right-click on the entity to access its shortcut options.

For example, while creating a new line, the cursor is moved over an existing angled line. Right-click on the highlighted angled line to display the shortcut menu, as shown in Figure 7–19. The new line can be created so that it starts at the angled line's midpoint or its nearest end point.

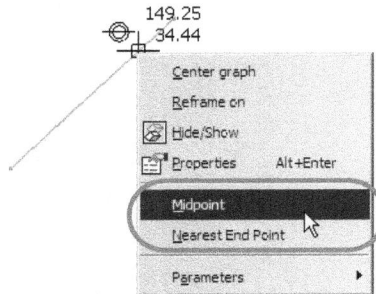

Figure 7–19

<Shift> and <Ctrl>

Use <Shift> and <Ctrl> to better control the creation of a constraint using SmartPick. If SmartPick detects a reference that is not required, you can temporarily deactivate the detection feature by pressing <Shift> as you sketch. You can also force the current constraint to snap using <Ctrl>. Once displayed, press <Ctrl> to keep the constraint snapped as you move the cursor.

SmartPick Options

You can control the type of constraints that SmartPick detects by changing the sketcher settings under **Tools>Option> Mechanical Design>Sketcher>SmartPick**. The available options are shown in Figure 7–20.

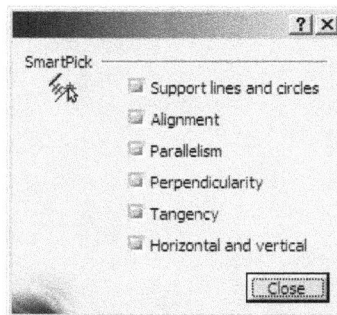

Figure 7–20

Constraint Tools

You can automatically generate geometric and dimensional constraints using the Sketch Tools toolbar in the Sketcher workbench shown in Figure 7–21.

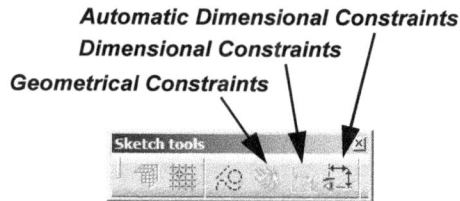

Automatic Dimensional Constraints
Dimensional Constraints
Geometrical Constraints

Figure 7–21

When you enable ⬚ (Geometrical Constraints), constraints detected are permanently added to the model.

• If the icon is toggled on (default setting), constraints are added to the sketch and updated when changes occur in the model.

• If the icon is toggled off, a permanent constraint is not added and does not update with changes to the model.

When you enable ⬚ (Dimensional Constraints), the software automatically creates dimensions for corner and chamfer elements. It also creates dimensions when you manually enter coordinates or manually specify feature size while you are sketching.

When you enable ⬚ (Automatic Dimensional Constraints), the software automatically creates dimensions as you sketch rectangles, circles, arcs, and ellipses.

7.4 Visualization Tools

Visualization tools display information about the internal geometry of a part or constraints of a sketch. They also simplify the display of a sketch by hiding information for complex sections. You can access these tools in the Visualization toolbar shown in Figure 7–22.

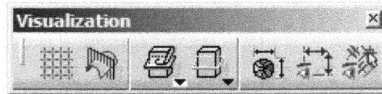

Figure 7–22

The icons are described as follows:

Option	Description
(Grid)	Toggle the sketch grid on and off.
(Cut Part by Sketch Plane)	Select to cut away the geometry in front of a sketch plane so that you can constrain the sketch to internal edges.
Visu3D flyout	This flyout contains three icons that control the display of existing model geometry in Sketcher. This functionality simplifies the view of a sketch by displaying 3D geometry in low light or by hiding it, thereby displaying only sketched geometry.
(Usual)	All modeling elements display in the sketch view.
(Low Light)	All solid and surface geometry displays in a low light gray color. All wireframe and sketch geometry displays normally. Elements cannot be selected from the model and must be selected from the specification tree.
(No 3D Background)	Only sketched elements created in the current section display. For example, the edges of an existing solid that have been projected onto the sketch display, but the geometry that was referenced is not. Elements can still be selected from the specification tree.

2D Visualization Mode flyout		This flyout contains six icons that control the display and selection of existing model geometry in Sketcher. This functionality simplifies the view of a sketch using the selected sketch plane.
	(Pickable visible background)	All geometry is visible and selectable.
	(No 3D Background)	No existing geometry displays.
	(Unpickable background)	All geometry is visible but cannot be selected.
	(Low intensity background)	Existing geometry is visible in a muted green color and can be selected.
	(Unpickable low intensity background)	Existing geometry is visible in a muted green color and cannot be selected.
	(Lock)	Model orientation is locked in the current sketch view.
(Diagnostics)		Select to enable/disable the display of constraint diagnostic colors for sketched entities.
(Dimensional Constraints)		Select to enable/disable the display of all dimensional constraints in the sketch.
(Geometrical Constraints)		Select to enable/disable the display of all geometrical constraints in the sketch.

Practice 7a

Sketcher Relations

Practice Objectives

- Create a relation in the sketcher using a formula.
- Create equivalent dimensions.

In this practice, you will create the sketch shown in Figure 7–23. The design requires the value of the dimension labeled A to be 1/2 of dimension B. It also requires that the three dimensions labeled X stay equal, and that the two radii labeled Y stay equal when changes occur. You will capture this design intent through the use of formulas and equivalent dimensions.

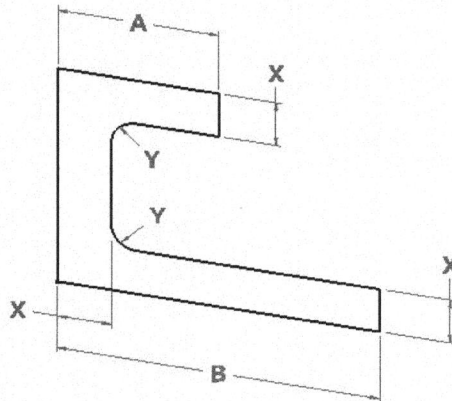

Figure 7–23

Task 1 - Create a new part model and rough sketch.

1. Create a new part named **ChannelSketch**.

2. Create a sketch on the YZ plane. Sketch the rough profile, as shown in Figure 7–24.

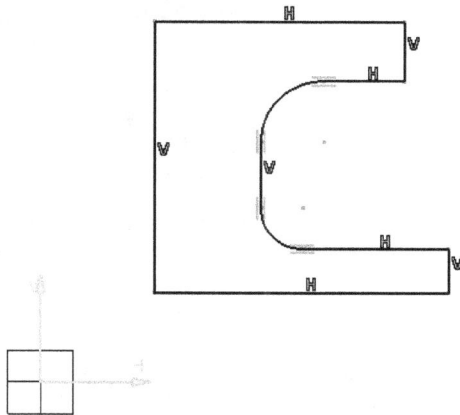

Figure 7–24

3. Constrain the lower left corner of the sketch to the sketch origin. Add dimensions and edit their values to those shown in Figure 7–25. Do not exit Sketcher.

- 10 (0.394 in)
- 15 (0.591 in)
- 20 (0.787 in)
- 25 (0.984 in)

- 80 (3.150 in)
- 100 (3.937 in)
- 120 (4.724 in)

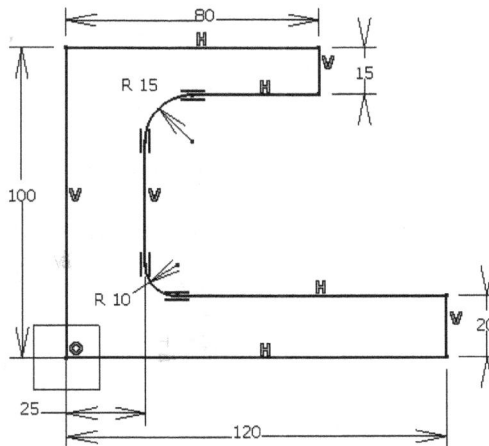

Figure 7–25

Task 2 - Add a formula to make the top length of the channel 1/2 of the bottom.

1. Click $f_{(x)}$ (Formula). The Formulas dialog box opens listing all of the system parameters.

2. Select the **80 (3.150 in)** length dimension from the sketch. The list jumps to that dimension, as shown in Figure 7–26.

Note that your parameter numbers will differ slightly from those shown in the images.

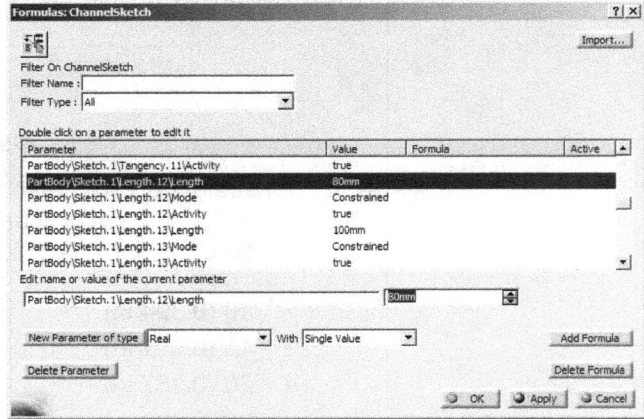

Figure 7–26

3. Click **Add Formula**. The Formula Editor dialog box opens, as shown in Figure 7–27.

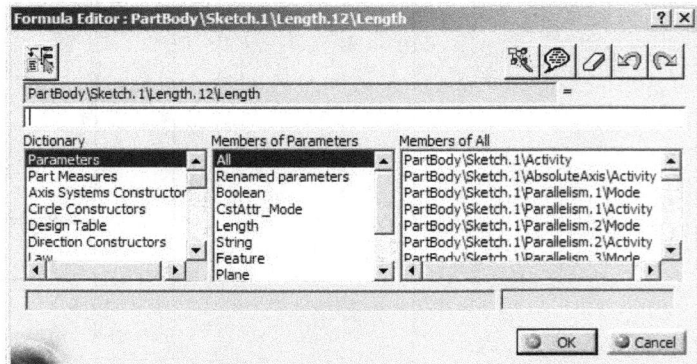

Figure 7–27

4. Select the **120 (4.724 in)** length dimension from the screen. In the Formula Editor dialog box, enter **/2** in the field, as shown in Figure 7–28. This sets the dimension of the top of the channel to be **1/2** of the bottom length of **120 (4.724 in)**.

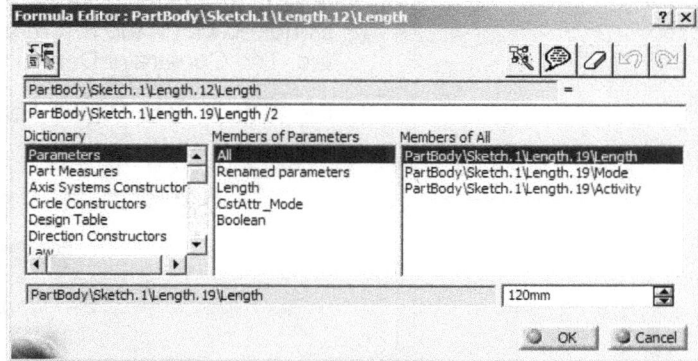

Figure 7–28

5. Click **OK** to exit the Formula Editor.

6. Click **OK** to exit the Formulas dialog box. The model will update to reflect the newly created formula.

Task 3 - Investigate the formula in the model.

---

1. Double-click on the **60 (2.362 in)** dimension to modify its value. This dimension is now driven by the formula and cannot be modified, as shown in Figure 7–29. Click **OK**.

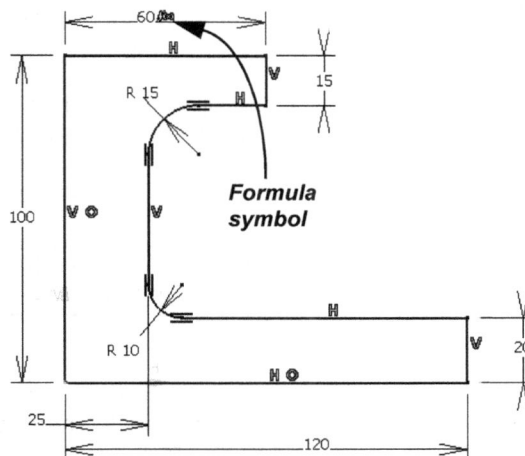

Figure 7–29

2. Double-click on the **120 (4.724 in)** dimension and enter **140 (5.512 in)** as the new value. Note the updated values.

Task 4 - Add a formula to make the fillet radii equal.

1. Double-click on the R15mm (0.591 in) dimension for the top arc. The Constraint Definition dialog box opens.

2. Right-click in the *Radius* field and select **Edit formula**, as shown in Figure 7–30.

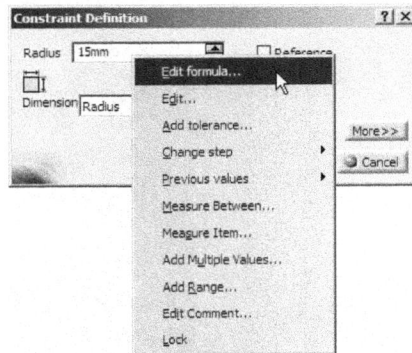

Figure 7–30

3. The Formula Editor dialog box opens. Select the **R10(0.394 in)** dimension.

4. Click **OK** to close the Formula Editor dialog box. Note the change in dimension values.

5. In the Constraint Definition dialog box, click **OK** to complete the relation.

6. Modify the parent radius dimension (on the bottom arc) to **5 (0.197 in)** and note the updated changes.

7. Modify the radius back to **10 (0.394 in)**.

Task 5 - Create an equivalent dimension for the thickness of the channel.

1. In the Knowledge toolbar, click (Equivalent Dimensions). The Equivalent Dimensions feature Edition dialog box opens, as shown in Figure 7–31. Note that *Type* is set to **Length**.

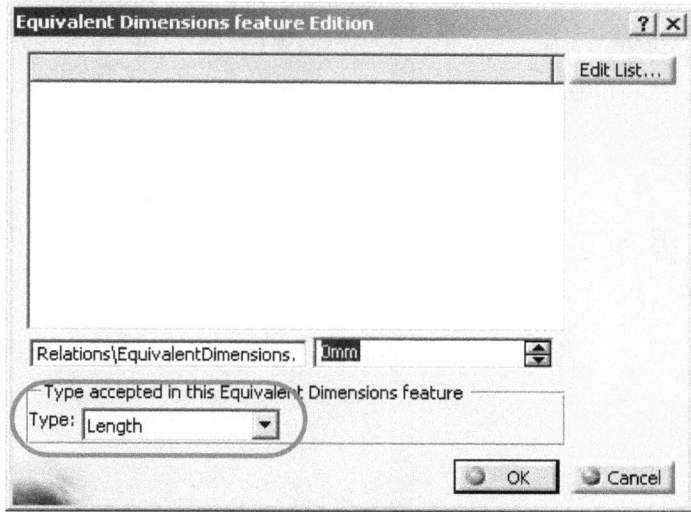

Figure 7–31

2. In the dialog box, click **Edit List**. A list of all sketch length dimensions display.

3. On the model, select the **20 (0.787 in)** dimension that represents the thickness of the lower flange. This dimension will be highlighted in the dialog box.

4. Click ⇨ to move the dimension to the right side of the dialog box.

5. Repeat Steps 3 and 4 for the two other flange thickness dimensions (**25 (0.984 in)** and **15 (0.591 in)**). The dialog box opens, as shown in Figure 7–32.

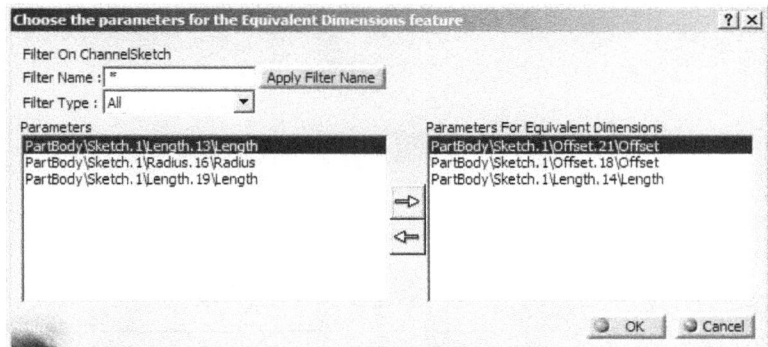

Figure 7–32

6. Click **OK**. The selected dimensions display as shown in Figure 7–33. The dimensions are driven by value at the bottom of the dialog box.

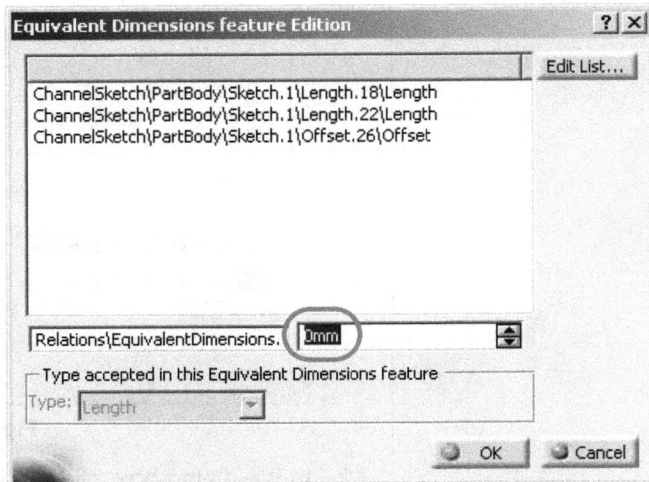

Figure 7–33

7. In the *Value* field, enter **10 (0.394 in)** and click **OK** to update all three dimensions. The profile displays as shown in Figure 7–34.

- 10 (0.394 in)
- 70 (2.756 in)
- 100 (3.937 in)
- 140 (5.512 in)

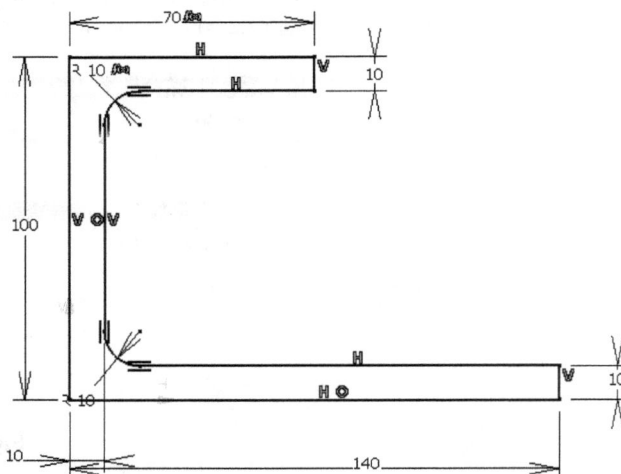

Figure 7–34

Task 6 - Edit an equivalent dimension.

1. Double-click on any of the three dimensions that drive the thickness of the channel. Note that ▣}= (Equivalent Dimensions) displays next to the *Value* field, as shown in Figure 7–35. This means that this dimension value is linked to other dimensions. If required, it can be used to change the definition of which dimensions are set as being equivalent.

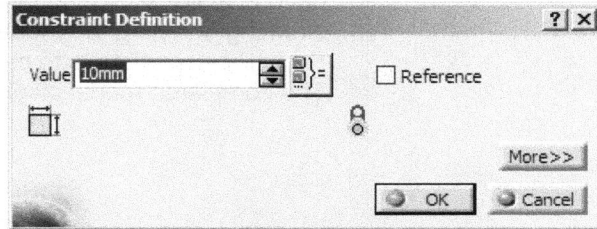

Figure 7–35

2. Enter **25 (0.984 in)** as the new value. All equivalent dimensions update, as shown in Figure 7–36.

   - 10 (0.394 in)
   - 25 (0.984 in)
   - 70 (2.756 in)
   - 100 (3.937 in)
   - 140 (5.512 in)

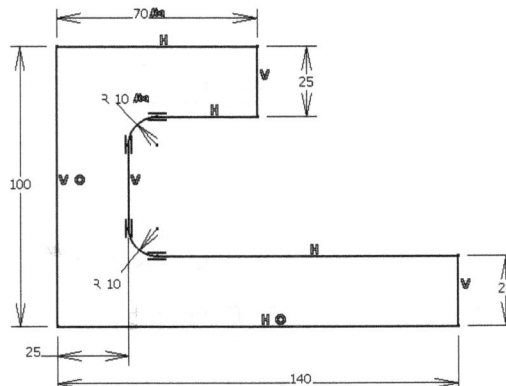

Figure 7–36

3. Click ⬆ (Exit workbench).

4. Save and close the model.

Practice 7b | # Set Visualization and SmartPick

Practice Objectives

- Create Equivalent Dimensions and a Formula.
- Manipulate SmartPick constraint creation.

In this practice, you will use the visualization options to control the display of existing solid geometry while in Sketcher. These options make sketching over existing geometry easier by dimming or hiding the model. You will also lock and disable SmartPick constraints to create the required sketched entities. The completed model displays as shown in Figure 7–37.

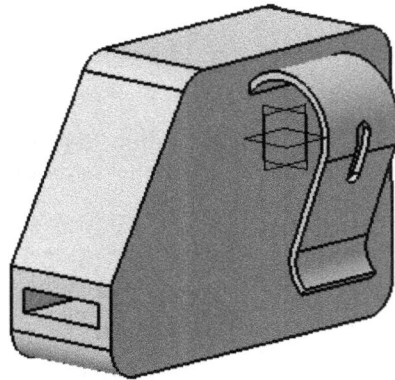

Figure 7–37

Task 1 - Create a new part and base feature.

1. Create a new part called **Clip.CATPart**.

2. Click ◫ (Positioned Sketch). Use the ZX Plane as the Sketch Reference.

3. Ensure that the orientation of the sketch is as shown in Figure 7–38.

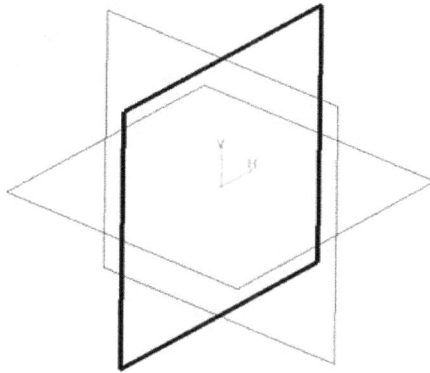

Figure 7–38

4. Click **OK** to enter the Sketcher workbench.

5. Create the sketch shown in Figure 7–39. Use the **Equivalent Dimension** tool to make all four radius dimensions equal.

- 20 (0.787 in)
- 55 (2.165 in)
- 60 (2.362 in)
- 150 (5.906 in)
- 180 (7.087 in)
- 240 (9.449 in)

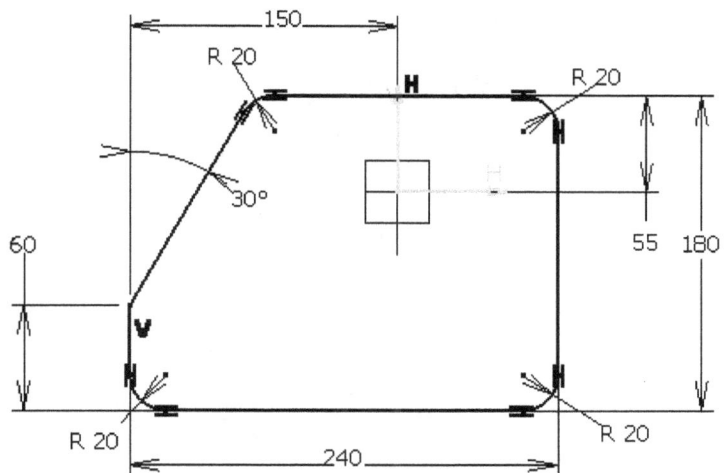

Figure 7–39

6. Exit the Sketcher workbench and use the sketch to create a Pad **80 (3.150 in)** in length, as shown in Figure 7–40. To obtain the correct direction of the Pad, in the Quick View toolbar, click ⬛ (Front View). The Absolute planes should be on the right side of the Pad.

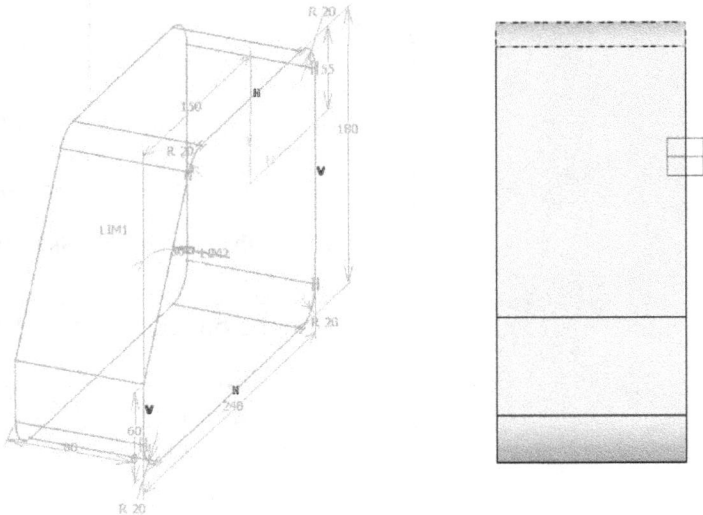

Figure 7–40

Task 2 - Modify the Visualization setting.

Design Consideration

In this task, you will create a sketch that will be used as the profile for the clip. This clip will be used in other models so it is important that unnecessary references are not used. In this situation, the design requirement is that the clip only references the three default reference planes. To accomplish this, you will use the **Visualization** tools, as shown in Figure 7–41.

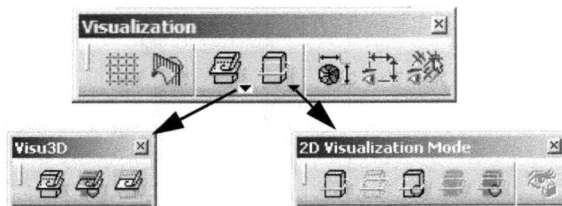

Figure 7–41

1. Access the Sketcher workbench using the YZ plane as the sketch support.

2. In the 2D Visualization Mode toolbar, click  (Unpickable low intensity background). The 3D geometry displays in a dark gray color, but you are not able to select it.

3. In the 2D Visualization Mode toolbar, click  (No 3D background). The solid geometry is removed from the display. This setting ensures that the base feature is not selected when dimensioning the sketch. It also helps with clarity when creating the geometry.

Task 3 - Create the sketched geometry.

1. Create the sketch shown in Figure 7–42.

- 5 (0.197 in)
- 20 (0.787 in)
- 37 (1.457 in)
- 40 (1.575 in)
- 64 (2.520 in)

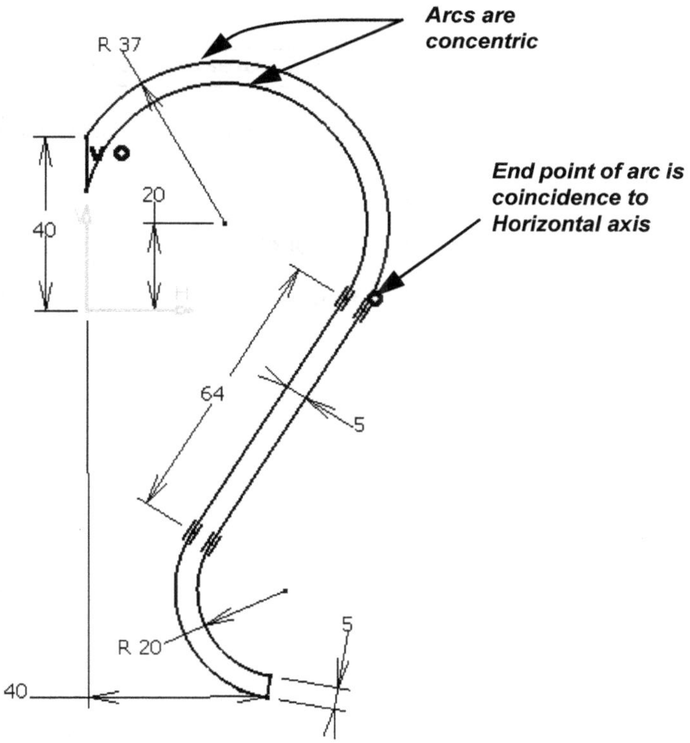

Arcs are concentric

End point of arc is coincidence to Horizontal axis

R 37
20
40
64
5
R 20
40
5

Figure 7–42

2. Exit the Sketcher workbench.

3. Deactivate ⬚ (No 3D Background) to display the 3D geometry.

4. Create a pad with a length of **30 (1.181 in)**. Select **Mirrored extent**. The model displays as shown in Figure 7–43.

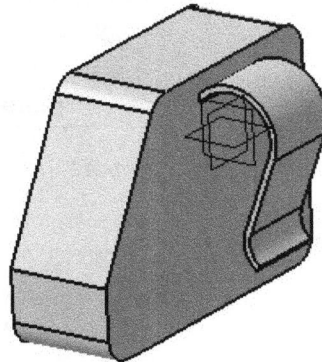

Figure 7–43

Task 4 - Create a pocket.

1. Access the Sketcher workbench using the ZX plane as the sketch support.

2. For clarity, in the Visu3D toolbar, click ⬚ (No Background).

3. Create the sketch using the dimensions **5 (0.197 in)** and **30 (1.181 in)**, as shown in Figure 7–44.

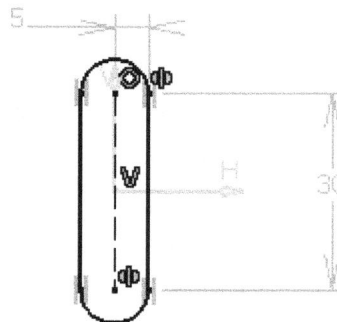

Figure 7–44

4. Exit the Sketcher workbench.

5. Create a Pocket feature to cut through the clip. Use the **Up to Last** depth option. The pocket direction might need to be reversed.

Task 5 - Create a pocket using formulas.

1. Click 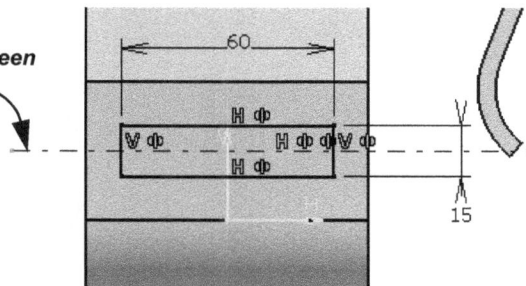 (Positional Sketch).

2. Select the surface of the part as the sketch support, as shown in Figure 7–45.

3. In the *Origin* area, select **Middle point**, as shown in Figure 7–46, and then select the edge shown in Figure 7–45.

Select this face as the sketch support

Select this edge to define the middle point reference

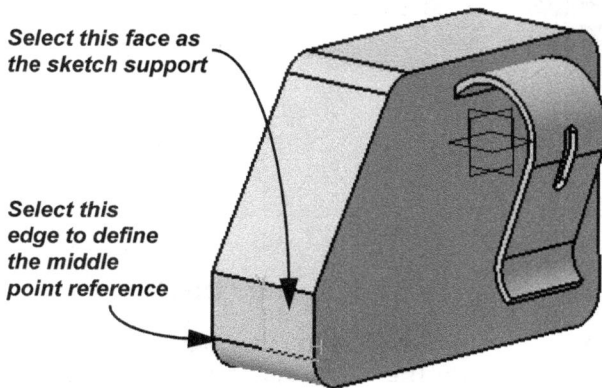

Figure 7–45

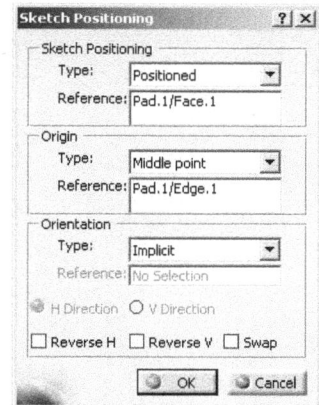

Figure 7–46

4. Click **OK** to access the Sketcher workbench.

5. Create the sketch using the dimensions **15 (0.591 in)** and **60 (2.362 in)**, as shown in Figure 7–47.

The axis is centered between the edges

Figure 7–47

6. To create a formula so that the **60 (2.362 in)** dimension is driven by the width of the Base feature, double-click on the **60 (2.362 in)** dimension.

7. Right-click in the *Value* field and select **Edit formula**.

8. In the specification tree, select **Pad.1**. In the Formula Editor dialog box, double-click on **PartBody\Pad.1\FirstLimit\ Length**.

9. Make this dimension equal to the length of the **Pad.1 - 20 (0.787 in)**, as shown in Figure 7–48.

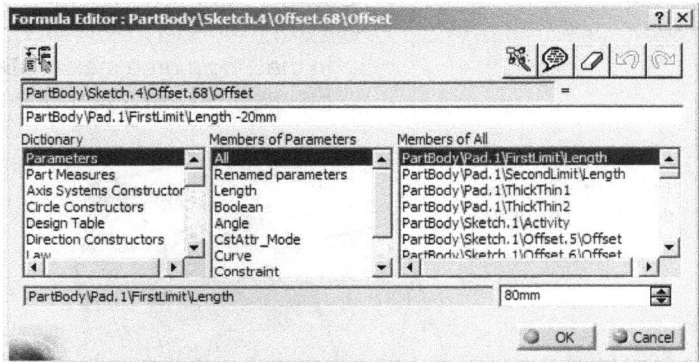

Figure 7–48

10. Click **OK** to close the Constraint Definition dialog box.

11. Exit the Sketcher workbench and create a Pocket feature **100 (3.937 in)** in length. The model displays as shown in Figure 7–49.

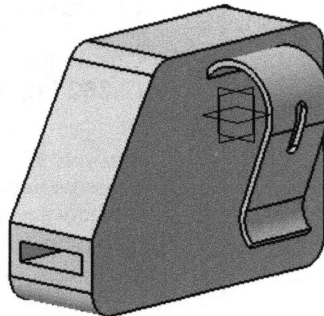

Figure 7–49

12. Save and close the file.

Chapter Review Questions

1. Review the profile shown in Figure 7–50. How many dimensions are driven by formulas?

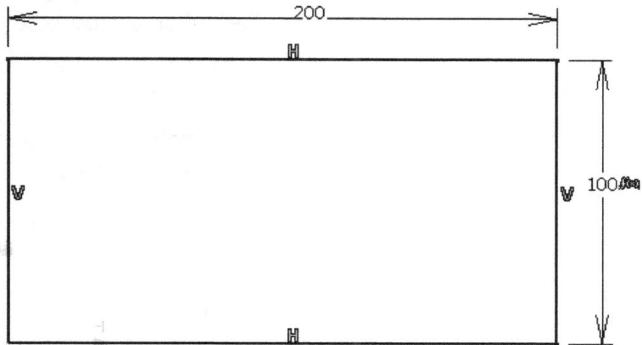

Figure 7–50

 a. 0

 b. 2

 c. 1

 d. It is impossible to tell.

2. The formulas: A = B, D = B/2, and C = A/2 can be created to center the hole and ensure that the length (dimension A) and width (dimension B) are equivalent as shown in Figure 7–51.

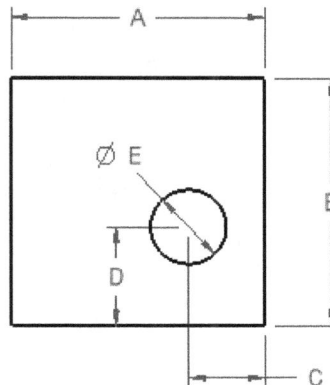

Figure 7–51

 a. True

 b. False

3. How can you tell that equivalent dimensions have been added to a model? (Select all that apply.)

   a. 🔧 displays next to dimensions that are equivalent.

   b. 📋 displays next to the *Value* field in the Constraint Definition dialog box.

   c. A branch is added under the **Relations** branch in the specification tree.

   d. A branch is added under the **Sketch** branch in the specification tree.

4. You can change the dimension value of a driven dimension.

   a. True

   b. False

5. Which key do you press to temporarily deactivate the SmartPick detection feature?

   a. <D>

   b. <Shift>

   c. <Alt>

   d. <Ctrl>

6. Which key do you press to force the current snapping of entities using SmartPick?

   a. <F>

   b. <Shift>

   c. <Alt>

   d. <Ctrl>

7. When 🖱 is highlighted, as shown in Figure 7–52, geometric constraints are automatically created.

Figure 7–52

   a. True

   b. False

8. Which tool can be used to cut a part by the sketching plane?

a.

b.

c.

Answers: 1.c, 2.a, 3.bc, 4.b, 5.b, 6.d, 7.a, 8.b

Reference Elements

There are several benefits to using reference elements when creating geometry. In the Part Design workbench, these elements consist of Point, Line, and Plane features.

Learning Objectives in this Chapter

- Understand how features display in the specification tree.
- Create necessary sketch planes when none are available.
- Create axis systems as reference frames for modeling.
- Understand the various methods of creating points, lines, and planes.
- Define reference elements.

8.1 Reference Elements

Reference elements are non-solid points, lines, and planes that aid in geometry creation. They do not have any volume, area, or mass properties, and they do not cause interference at the assembly level.

Feature Structure

All solid geometry is grouped under the PartBody branch in the specification tree.

- System-defined reference features, such as default reference planes, are always the first features of a model.

- User-defined reference features are automatically grouped in the Geometrical Set branch, which is automatically created by the software and lists all non-solid features, as shown in Figure 8–1.

This feature structure enables efficient navigation when selecting features in the specification tree.

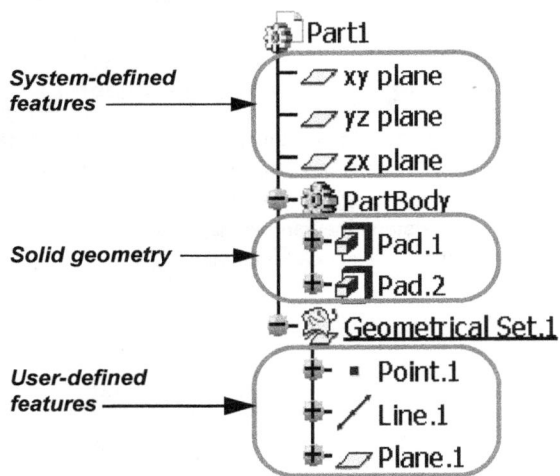

Figure 8–1

Sketch Plane Positioning

Figure 8–2 shows an example of a circular Pad Feature where the base feature geometry does not have a suitable planar face on which to sketch the circular profile. Additionally, the default reference planes are not in a suitable location. A reference plane can be created to provide the required sketching plane.

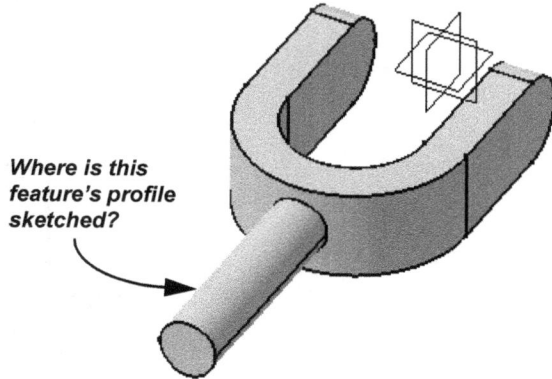

Where is this feature's profile sketched?

Figure 8–2

The creation of points and lines can also assist in the definition of a positioned sketch. The sketcher axis shown in Figure 8–3 was positioned using a point to locate the origin and a line to orient the vertical axis.

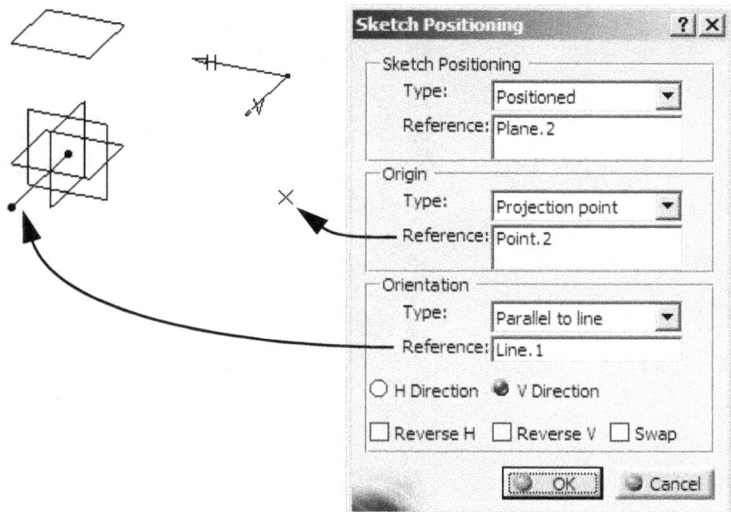

Figure 8–3

8.2 Axis Systems

An axis system is used to define a reference frame for a model, or portion of geometry in a part file. More than one axis system can be created for a model, as shown in Figure 8–4. The active axis system is shown with a solid line front and an orange color.

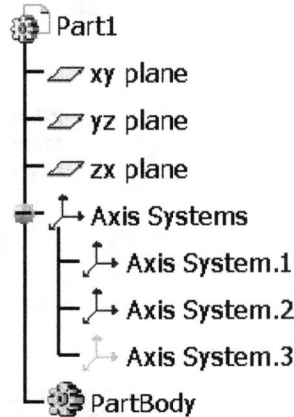

Figure 8–4

- To create an axis system, click 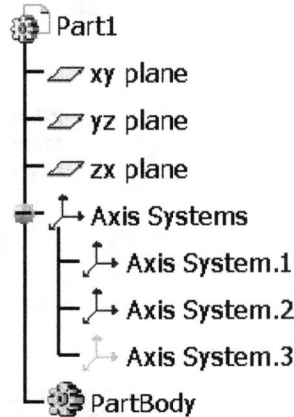 (Axis System) in the Tools toolbar. The Axis System Definition dialog box opens, as shown in Figure 8–5.

- The origin for each type of axis system is defined by selecting a point or vertex on the model. The origin can also be defined by right-clicking on the *Origin* field, as shown in Figure 8–6.

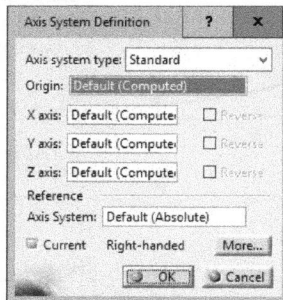

Figure 8–5

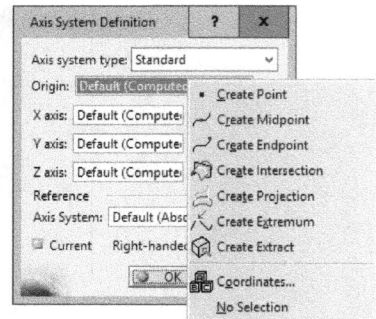

Figure 8–6

To introduce flexibility into the axis system, the origin is defined using the **Coordinates** option, which enables you to define the X-, Y-, and Z-coordinates relative to the part origin. The system can then be translated by modifying these coordinates.

All axis systems start in a default orientation about the origin and can be further defined by specifying the type and orientation references. These are described as follows:

Type	Orientation References
Standard	Select a reference to define the orientation of up to two axes (X, Y, Z). The orientation can be defined by selecting a point (the axis is oriented along a line between the point and the origin), a line, or a plane (defining a normal vector).
Axis rotation	Select a reference for the X-, Y-, or Z-axis. The axis system is then rotated about this axis by the specified angle measured from the specified reference.
Euler Angle	Define the origin, and enter an angle to define the orientation of the X-, Y-, and Z-axes.

8.3 Point Creation Methods

Points mark a location on a model and can be referenced by subsequent features. The methods used to create a point are described as follows:

Point Type		Description
Coordinates		Enter the X-, Y-, and Z-distances from an existing reference point or the origin of the part.
		Point at X=0, Y=0 and Z=0 · *Point at X=0, Y=2, Z=1*
		You can define the reference for the point using the following options:
	Point	The point's coordinates are measured from the selected point. By default, the coordinates are measured from the origin of the current local axis system.
	Axis System	The direction of the point's X-, Y-, and Z-coordinates are changed with respect to the selected axis system.
	Compass Location	If the compass is located on geometry, the X-, Y-, and Z-coordinates of the point can be set based on the compass location.
On Curve		Select an edge of a solid feature, a segment of a sketch, or a line for the point to be located on.
		Point at.50 (50%) ratio along arc
		You can define the location of the point along the edge using the following options:

	Ratio	Percentage along curve.
	Geodesic Distance	Distance measured along curve.
	Euclidean Distance	Absolute distance from a reference.
		The **Repeat object after OK** option enables you to specify additional points spaced at an incremental distance. There is also an option to create planes through points that are normal to the curve.
On Plane		Select the location for the point on a planar surface and specify the horizontal and vertical distances for the point. By default, the distances are relative to the origin of the part. Optionally, another reference point can be selected.

Origin

On Surface	Select the location for the point on a curved surface. By default, the point is created at the center of the surface. You can locate the point on the surface using one of the following:

- An edge.
- The surface normal of a plane.
- Points X, Y, and Z values using the shortcut menu. |

New point   **Center of surface**

Direction from center

Circle/Sphere/ Ellipse Center	Locate a point at the center of a circle, sphere, arc, or ellipse.
	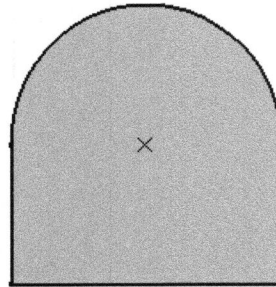
Tangent on Curve	Select a planar curve and a direction line. A point is placed at each tangent location relative to the direction line.
	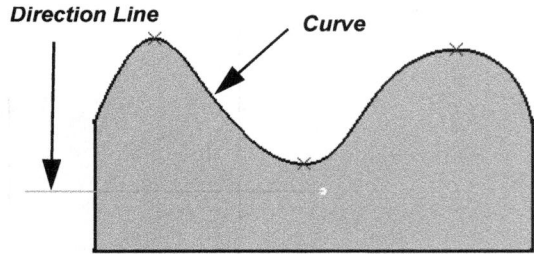
Between	Select two points and enter the ratio of the distance from the first point to the new point. You can use the **Reverse Direction** option to specify the distance from the second point to the new point. If the ratio is greater than one, the point is located on a virtual line extended beyond the two points.
	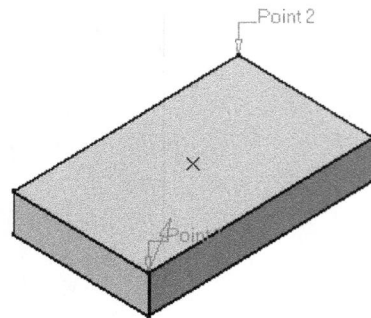

8.4 Line Creation Methods

Lines can define the axis of rotation for Shaft features, mark the center axis of cylindrical pads, and define the direction for non-normal pads. The methods you can use to create a line are described as follows:

Line Type	Description
Point-to-Point	Select two points or vertices for the line to connect. By default, a straight line between the two points or vertices is created. If required, you can select a support surface for the line to follow.
	Support surface for this line
	You can enter the distance for the start and end points of the line to extend beyond the two points.
Point-Direction	Select a starting point and an edge, line, or plane to define the line direction. Enter the length of the line.

Angle/ Normal to curve	Select the start point for the line and a line or edge to measure the angle relative to. Select a plane that has both the point and the line, and enter the angle.

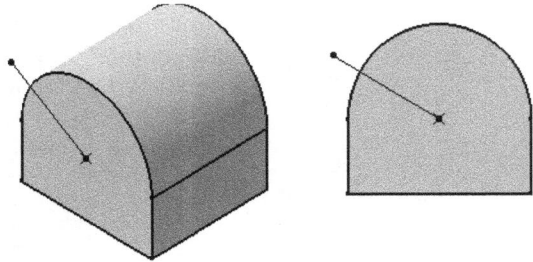

The **Repeat object after OK** option enables you to create a number of additional lines spaced at the same angle. These lines are not related to each other after they are created.

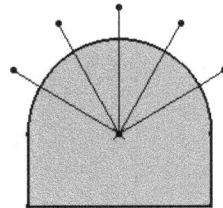

Tangent to curve	Select an edge for the line to be tangent to, and a point for the start of the line. Enter the line length.

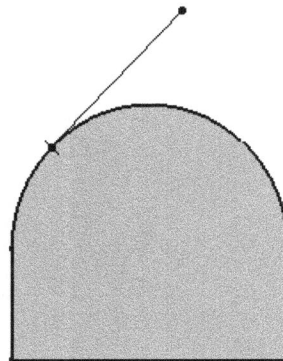

Normal to surface	Select a surface for the line to be perpendicular to, and a starting point. Enter the length of the line. 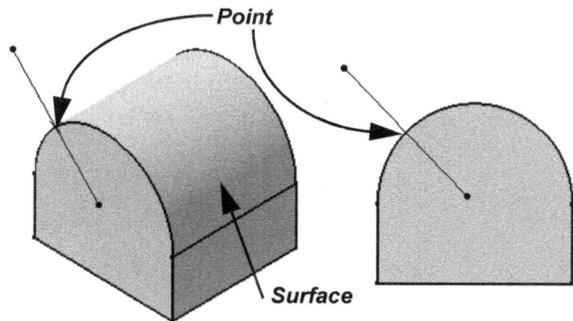 The **Mirror Extent** option constructs the line equally on each side of the point.
Bisecting	Select two lines or edges, and a new line is created that bisects them. If there is more than one solution, you can select the location for the bisecting line. 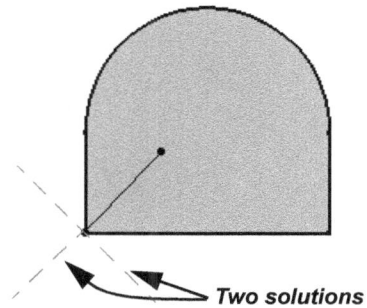

8.5 Plane Creation Methods

Planes can be used for sketch-based features, such as pads and shafts, and to provide a dimensional reference for other types of features. The methods you can use to create planes are described as follows:

Plane Type	Description
Offset from plane	Select a planar face on the model or a reference plane, and enter the offset distance.

Offset from this plane

Parallel through point	Select a planar face on the model or reference plane for the new plane to be parallel to, and select a point for the new plane to pass through.

Parallel to this face

Angle/Normal to plane	Select a line, edge, or axis for the plane to pass through, and a planar reference for the angle to be measured relative to.

Measure angle from here

Through three points	Select three points or vertices for the plane to pass through. 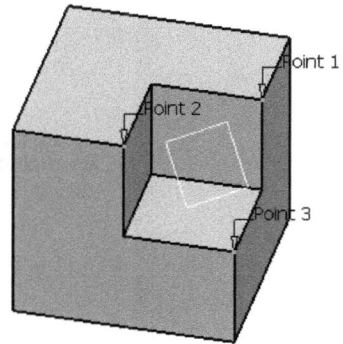
Through two lines	Select two lines, edges, or axes for the plane to pass through. 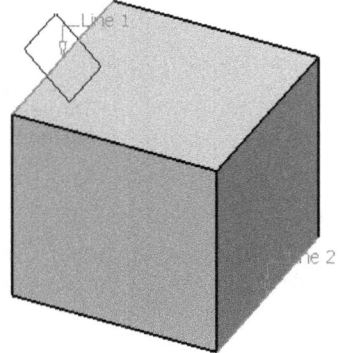
Through point and line	Select a point/vertex and a line/edge/axis for the plane to pass through. 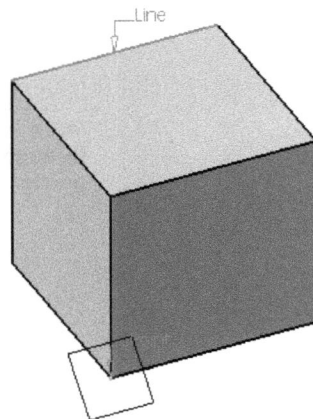

Through planar curve	Select a planar curve or sketched entity for the plane to pass through.	

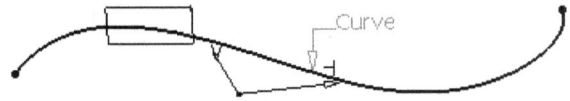

Normal to curve	Select a line, edge, or sketch segment for the new plane to be perpendicular to, and a point for the new plane to pass through.

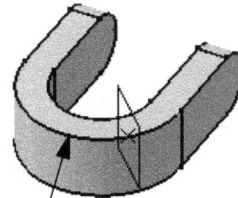

Plane is normal to this edge

Tangent to surface	Select a point that the new plane passes through, and a surface the new plane is tangent to.

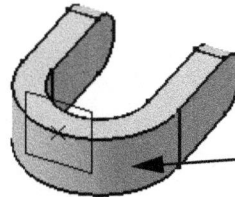

Tangent to this surface

Equation	Select a point and enter values for A, B, and C. The point defines the location of the plane while the A, B, and C values define vectors in the X-, Y-, and Z-directions. For example, A=1, B=0, C=0 creates a plane that is perpendicular to the X axis. Use **Normal to Compass** and **Parallel to Screen** to orient the plane as required.
Mean through points	Select three or more points to define the orientation of the plane. When more than three points are selected, the system uses the additional points to influence the orientation of the plane.

8.6 Reference Element Definition

The following topics are common to the creation of point, line, or plane reference elements:

- Implicit Axis Selection
- Lock Reference Element
- Shortcut Menus

Implicit Axis Selection

By default, cylindrical features do not display their axes. To reference the axis of a cylindrical feature, press <Shift> while holding the cursor over the feature. The axis shown in Figure 8–7 is useful for creating a plane that is at an angle to a planar reference and passes through the axis.

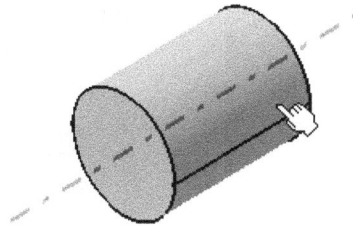

Figure 8–7

Lock Reference Element

If you need to create multiple instances of a type of reference element (e.g., point, line, or plane), you can lock the type of element you want to create.

- To efficiently create multiple offset reference planes, you can lock the **Offset from plane** Plane type, as shown in Figure 8–8.

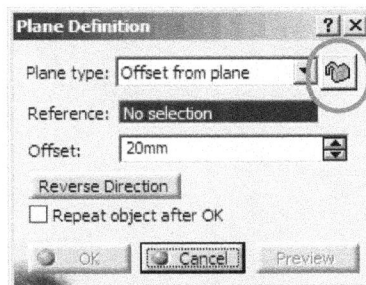

Figure 8–8

To lock the type, click . A locked type displays as , as shown in Figure 8–9.

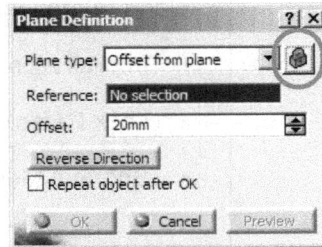

The lock stays active while CATIA is in session. If you exit the application and launch CATIA, the setting resets to default.

Figure 8–9

Shortcut Menus

The options available in the shortcut menu vary based on the type of input required.

You can access shortcut menu options when creating reference elements in the dialog boxes.

- To create a point on the fly while creating a **Parallel through point** reference plane on an edge, right-click in the *Point* field, as shown in Figure 8–10.

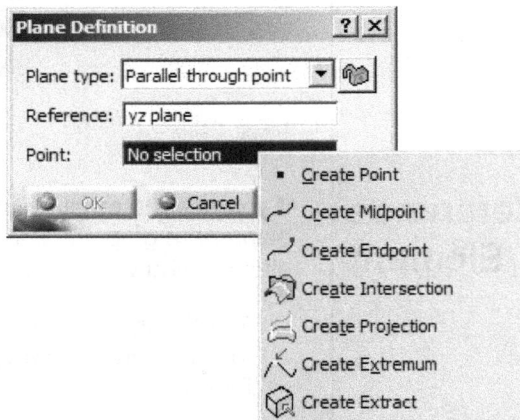

Figure 8–10

The creation of an element on the fly simplifies feature creation. It enables you to create required sub-elements without exiting the active feature.

- The element created on the fly is placed beneath the active feature in the specification tree. Figure 8–11 shows that the point created in the previous example is placed beneath the reference plane and hidden.

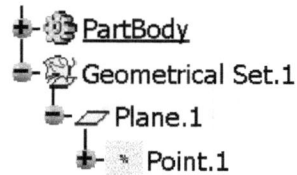

PartBody
Geometrical Set.1
Plane.1
Point.1

Figure 8–11

Practice 8a

Working with Feature Limits

Practice Objective

- Specify a different limit setting for each side of a mirrored extent Pad.

In this practice, you will create the part shown in Figure 8–12. You will create reference elements and use a different limit setting for the Pad feature.

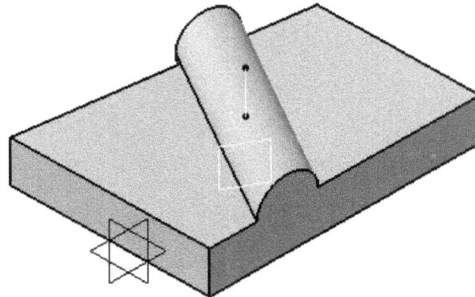

Figure 8–12

Task 1 - Open the part for use in this practice.

1. Click .

2. Select **Limit.CATPart** and click **Open**. Note that the right side of the part is perpendicular to adjacent surfaces, and the left side is angled.

Task 2 - Verify that the Reference Elements toolbar displays.

If you cannot see this toolbar, you might need to rearrange your toolbars by dragging them to new locations.

1. Select **View>Toolbars** and ensure that the **Reference Elements (Extended)** option is selected. This option adds icons for points, lines, and planes to your toolbar, as shown in Figure 8–13.

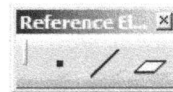

Figure 8–13

Task 3 - Create a point on the top face.

Design Considerations

This point will later be used as a reference point to constrain the profile sketch of a Pad feature. It will also be used as a starting point for a reference line.

1. Click ⬛ (Point).

2. In the Point type drop-down list, select **On surface**.

3. Select the top surface of the block.

4. Enter **0** for the *Distance*.

5. Click **OK** to complete the feature. A point is created on the center of the face, as shown in Figure 8–14.

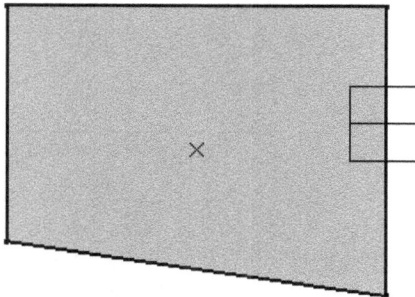

Figure 8–14

Task 4 - Create a line through the point and make it perpendicular to the top face of the part.

Design Considerations

This line will be perpendicular to the top face of the part and will pass through the point. It will be used as an axial reference for plane creation in later tasks.

1. Click ◢ (Line).

2. In the Line type drop-down list, select **Normal to surface**.

3. Select the top face as the surface that the line is perpendicular to, and select the point that the line will pass through, as shown in Figure 8–15.

4. Enter **20 (0.787 in)** for the *End* value. The length of the line is not important. It only needs to be long enough for you to see and easily select.

*Click **Reverse Direction** to orient the line in a direction that suits your preference. The direction or length of the line will not impact later features.*

5. Click **OK** to complete the feature. The part displays as shown in Figure 8–15.

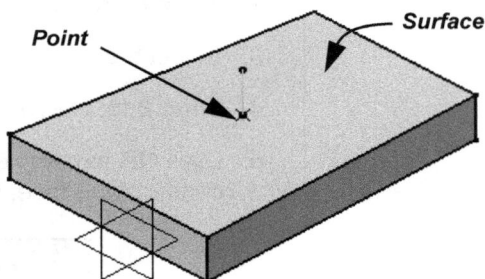

Point — Surface

Figure 8–15

Task 5 - Create a plane through the line at an angle to the YZ plane.

Design Considerations

This angled plane will use a default datum plane and the line as references. It will be used as a sketching plane for the profile of a Pad feature in the next task.

1. Click (Plane).

2. In the Plane type drop-down list, select **Angle/Normal to plane**.

3. Select the line as the rotation axis.

4. Select the YZ plane as the angular reference.

5. Enter **-60** for the angle.

6. Click **OK** to complete the feature. The part displays as shown in Figure 8–16.

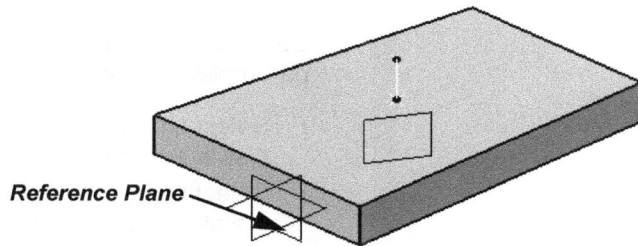

Reference Plane

Figure 8–16

Task 6 - Sketch a profile on the angled plane.

1. Select the angled plane and click [sketch icon] (Sketch).

2. Sketch a **25.0 (0.984 in)** diameter circle, as shown in Figure 8–17. Use the **Coincidence** constraint to constrain the center of the circle to the point.

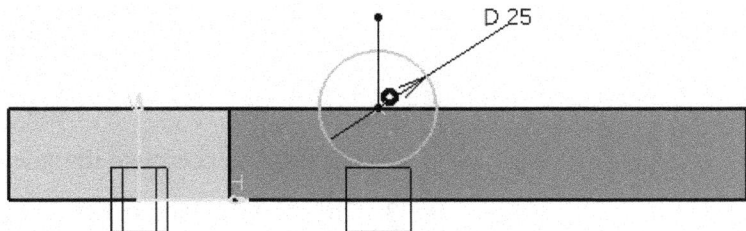

D 25

Figure 8–17

3. Click [exit icon] (Exit workbench) to complete the sketch.

Task 7 - Create a Pad feature using the circular sketch.

1. Select the sketch and click ▣ (Pad). Use the following parameters, as shown in Figure 8–18:

   • Select **Up to plane** for the First Limit Type and select the planar surface.
   • Select **Up to plane** for the Second Limit Type and select the planar surface.
   • Enter **6.00 (0.236 in)** offset for Limit 2.

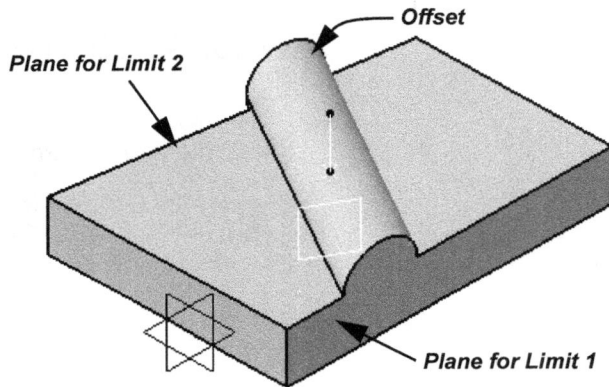

Figure 8–18

2. Click **OK** to complete the feature.

3. Save the part and close the file.

Practice 8b	# Reference Elements

Practice Objectives

- Create reference elements.
- Create solid features using reference elements.

In this practice, you will create the part shown in Figure 8–19. You will create reference elements to use as sketch planes. From these you will create the features.

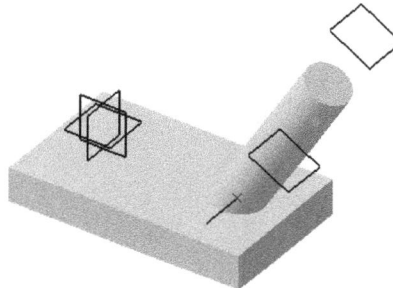

Figure 8–19

Task 1 - Open a model with an initial Pad feature.

1. Click [icon].

2. Select **Ref_Elements.CATPart** and click **Open**.

Task 2 - Create a point at the center of the part.

Design Considerations

The point you create here is used later to constrain the profile of a Pad feature. It is also used as a starting point for a line, which will serve as an axial reference for reference planes.

1. Select the top face of the part as shown in Figure 8–20.

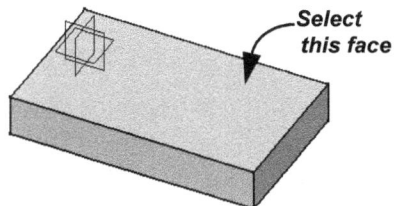

Select this face

Figure 8–20

2. Click ⬛ (Point) to create a point. The Point Definition dialog box opens.

3. The system has already selected **On Plane** in the *Point type*. Note the horizontal and vertical arrows on the model. They are located at the current origin of the model

4. Set the following, as shown in Figure 8–21:

   - *H* field: **38 (1.496 in)**
   - *V* field: **63.5 (2.500 in)**

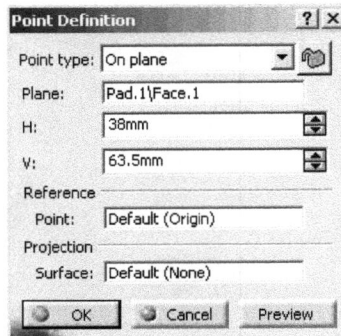

Figure 8–21

5. Click **OK**.

Task 3 - Create a line.

Design Considerations

This line will begin on the point you previously created. It is used as a pivot axis for several angled planes.

1. Click ╱ (Line) to create a line.

2. In the Line Definition dialog box, in the Line type drop-down list, select **Point-Direction.**

3. The **Point** option is now highlighted in the dialog box. Select the point you created in the previous task. The line begins at this point.

4. Ensure that the **Direction** option is now highlighted. In the specification tree or on the model, select the YZ plane. The line is perpendicular to this plane.

5. Ensure that the **Support** option is now highlighted. Select the top face of the part. The line resides on this plane.

6. Enter **25.00 (0.984 in)** in the End box. The length of the line is not important. It only needs to be long enough for you to see and easily select.

7. Click **OK** to complete the line. The resulting part displays as shown in Figure 8–22.

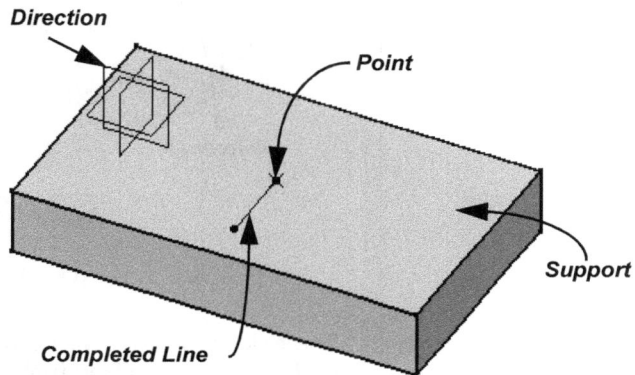

Figure 8–22

Task 4 - Create planes to locate a sketch.

Design Considerations

Using the previously created axis and one of the datum planes, you will create an angled plane. This plane will be used as a reference for the following plane that you will create.

1. Click (Plane) to create a plane.

2. In the Plane Definition dialog box, in the Plane type drop-down list, select **Angle/Normal to Plane.**

3. The **Rotation Axis** option is now highlighted. Select the line created in the previous task. The new plane passes through this axis.

4. The **Reference** option is now highlighted. Select the ZX plane as the plane to measure the angle from.

*You might need to enter **30** for the angle to obtain the result shown in Figure 8–23.*

5. Enter **-30** for the angle.

6. Click **OK** to complete the first plane. The resulting part displays as shown in Figure 8–23.

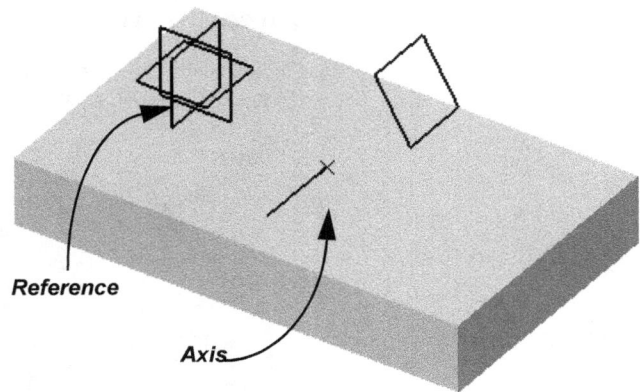

Figure 8–23

Design Considerations

The following plane will be used as a sketching plane for the profile sketch of a Pad feature. The plane will be offset from the angle plane.

7. Make the second plane offset from the first plane. You will use it as the sketching plane in the next task. Click

 (Plane) again.

8. Select **Offset from plane** in the Plane type drop-down list.

9. Select the first plane as the reference and enter **50.00 (1.969 in)** as the offset distance.

10. Click **OK** to complete the creation of this plane. The resulting part displays as shown in Figure 8–24.

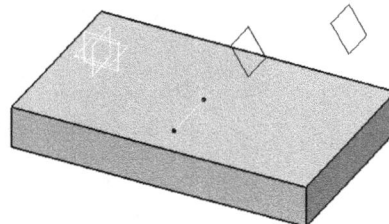

Figure 8–24

Task 5 - Create a sketch on the offset plane.

Design Considerations

This sketch will be used as a profile for a Pad feature. It is created on the offset plane and will be constrained to the point that you created earlier.

1. Select the offset plane and click ☐ (Positioned Sketch).

2. In the Origin Type drop-down list, select **Projection Point**.

3. Select **Point.1**. The Sketch Positioning dialog box opens as shown in Figure 8–25.

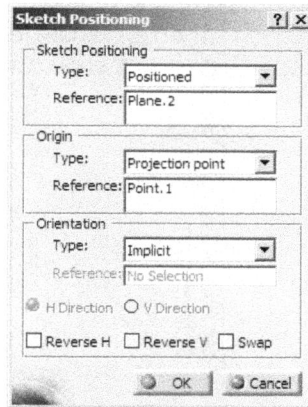

Figure 8–25

4. Click **OK** to enter the Sketcher workbench.

5. Sketch a **25 (0.984 in)** diameter circle centered on the origin as shown in Figure 8–26.

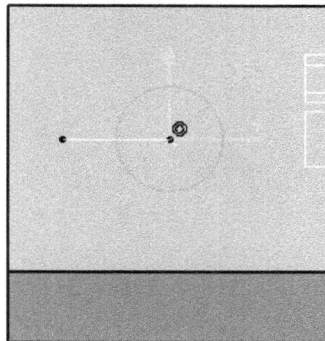

Figure 8–26

6. Click ⬆ (Exit workbench) to complete the sketch and exit the Sketcher workbench.

Task 6 - Create a Pad feature.

1. Select the sketch created in the last task and click 🔩 (Pad) to create a Pad feature.

2. If required, click **Reverse Direction** to extrude the profile toward the existing geometry.

3. In the Pad Definition dialog box, in the *First Limit* area, select **Up to next** in the Type drop-down list.

4. Click **OK** to complete this feature. The resulting part displays as shown in Figure 8–27.

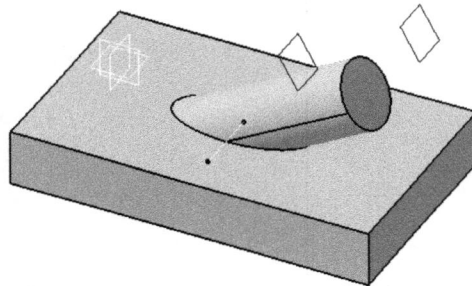

Figure 8–27

Task 7 - Modify the angle, offset distance, and location of the Pad feature.

1. Expand the specification tree to display the reference elements, as shown in Figure 8–28.

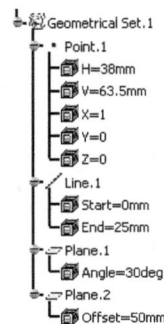

Figure 8–28

2. Double-click on **Offset=50mm (1.969 in)**, under the **Plane.2** branch. Set *Value* to **100.00 (3.937 in)** and click **OK**.

3. Double-click on **Angle=30deg**, under the **Plane.1** branch. Set *Value* to **60.00** and click **OK**.

4. Double-click on **V=63.5mm (2.500 in)**, under the **Point.1** branch. Set *Value* to **100.00 (3.937 in)** and click **OK**. The model displays as shown in Figure 8–29.

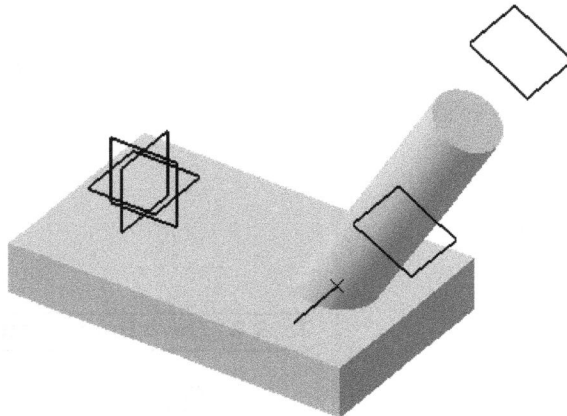

Figure 8–29

Task 8 - Rename the reference elements to more easily identify which features control the aspects of Pad.2.

1. In the specification tree, select **Point.1**, right-click, and select **Properties**.

2. In the *Feature Properties* tab, enter **Pad2: X&Y** as the *Feature Name*.

3. Repeat Step 2 and change the name of *Plane.1* to **Pad2: Angle**.

4. Repeat Step 3 and change the name of Plane.2 to **Pad2: Offset**. The specification tree displays as shown in Figure 8–30.

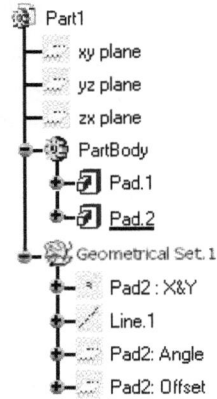

Specification tree icons with a gray background indicate that they are currently hidden from display.

Figure 8–30

Task 9 - Save the part and close the window.

1. Click (Save).

2. Select **File>Close**.

Practice 8c	# (Optional) Using Reference Elements

Practice Objectives

- Create reference elements.
- Create solid features using reference elements.

In this practice, you will complete the features of a coat stand by creating and using reference elements.

Task 1 - Create arms for the coat hanger.

1. Open **CoatStand.CATPart**. You must complete the model by adding arms to the main shaft.

2. Create an arm with the following, as shown in Figure 8–31 and Figure 8–32:

   - *length:* **300 (11.811 in)**
   - *radius:* **50 (1.969 in)**
   - *height:* **1500 (59.055 in)** (above the XY plane)
   - *angle:* **45** degrees (pointing upwards)
   - *rotation:* **45** degrees (from the YZ plane)

Figure 8–31	Figure 8–32

3. Then, create an arm with the following settings, as shown in Figure 8–33 and Figure 8–34:

- *length*: **600 (23.622 in)**
- *radius*: **50 (1.969 in)**
- *height*: **1200 (47.244 in)** (above the XY plane)
- *angle*: **45** degrees (pointing upwards)
- *rotation*: **45** degrees (from the YZ plane in the opposite direction as the other arm)

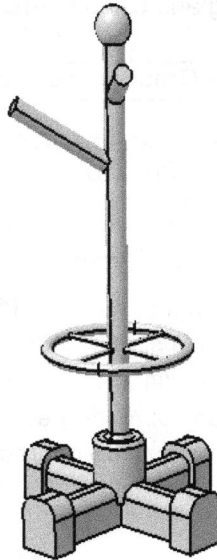 

Figure 8–33   **Figure 8–34**

Task 2 - Create pockets for the arms.

Create circular pockets with a *radius* of **30 (1.181 in)** halfway up each arm, as shown in Figure 8–35. Ensure that the pockets are perpendicular to the XY plane. The completed model displays as shown in Figure 8–36.

Figure 8–35

Figure 8–36

Chapter Review Questions

1. The default reference planes are the only reference planes that can exist in a model.

   a. True

   b. False

2. Which combination of constraints enables you to create the reference plane shown in Figure 8–37?

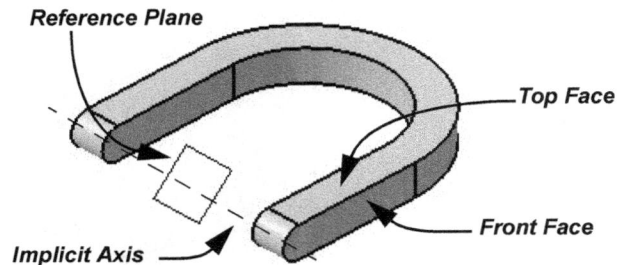

Figure 8–37

   a. Tangent to the Fillet and through the implicit axis of the Fillet.

   b. Through the implicit axis of the Fillet at an angle to the front face.

   c. Through the implicit axis of the Fillet at an angle to the top face.

   d. Through the top face at an angle to the front face.

3. Which of the following are valid constraint combinations to create a reference plane? (Select all that apply.)

   a. Through two edges.

   b. Offset from a surface.

   c. Parallel to a plane and through a point.

   d. Tangent to a surface and through a point.

4. Which of the following are valid constraint combinations to create a reference line? (Select all that apply.)

   a. At the intersection of two planes.

   b. Through the center of a circle.

   c. Through two points.

   d. Parallel to a line.

5. Which of the following statements is true regarding the specification tree shown in Figure 8–38?

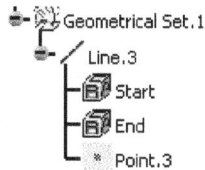

Figure 8–38

a. A point was created first and then used to create the line.

b. The point was created on the fly while creating the line.

c. The point was automatically created by CATIA when the vertex of existing geometry is used as the point reference.

d. A line was created and then a point.

6. Points, lines, and planes affect the mass properties of a model.

a. True

b. False

7. Where are user-defined reference features placed in the specification tree? (Assume that the **Hybrid** design option is not active).

a. In the Geometrical Set branch.

b. In the Annotations branch.

c. In the Features branch.

d. None of the above.

8. A Point-Point line type that lies on a support surface is always a straight line.

a. True

b. False

Answers: 1.b, 2.c, 3.abcd, 4.cd, 5.b, 6.b, 7.a, 8.b

Shaft and Groove Features

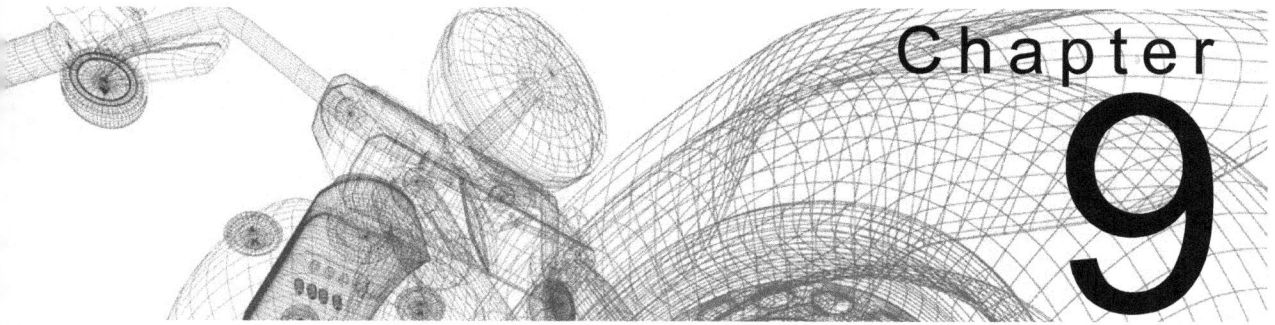

The Shaft and Groove features are used in a similar way to the Pad and Pocket features, except that their sketches rotate about an axis. This chapter covers the requirements for sketches used in Shaft features. Additionally, you will learn how to create grooves to remove material from the model and how you can create grooves on both planar and cylindrical surfaces.

Learning Objectives in this Chapter

- Learn the steps required to create a shaft feature.
- Understand the restrictions on sketches used for shaft features.
- Learn the steps required to create a groove feature.
- Create grooves on cylinders.

9.1 Shaft Feature

A Shaft feature consists of an existing sketch rotated about an axis. Figure 9–1 shows an example of a section rotated 360° about a sketched axis.

You can also use the vertical axis of the sketch.

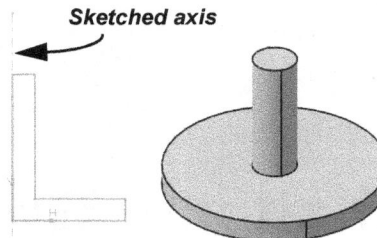

Sketched axis

Figure 9–1

General Steps

Use the following general steps to create a Shaft feature:

1. Select a profile.
2. Initiate the creation of a Shaft.
3. Select a rotational axis.
4. Specify **Shaft limit** options.
5. Complete the Shaft feature.

Step 1 - Select a profile.

The shape of a Shaft is determined by the profile that is used to create the feature.

• By default, selected items display in orange, as shown in Figure 9–2.

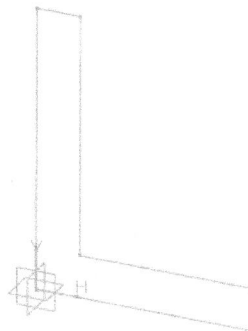

Figure 9–2

Sketch Restrictions

The sketch you select for a Shaft feature requires valid sketch geometry and an axis. The valid and invalid combinations of geometry and axis are described as follows.:

Sketch	Shaft Geometry	Description
		This is a closed sketch with the axis on the edge of the profile.
		This is a closed sketch with the axis offset from the profile. The result is a hole in the Shaft.
	Invalid	This is a closed sketch with the axis inside the profile. A Shaft feature cannot sketch geometry on both sides of the axis of rotation, since the geometry would overlap.
		This is an open sketch with the axis coincident with the open ends of the profile. This sketch is valid, because the axis closes the sketch.
	Invalid	This is an open sketch with the axis offset from the profile. This sketch is invalid, because no sketched geometry exists that generates a surface on the inside of the hole in the Shaft.

Step 2 - Initiate the creation of a Shaft.

To create a shaft, click [Shaft] (Shaft). The software initially creates the feature using the default values shown in the Shaft Definition dialog box in Figure 9–3

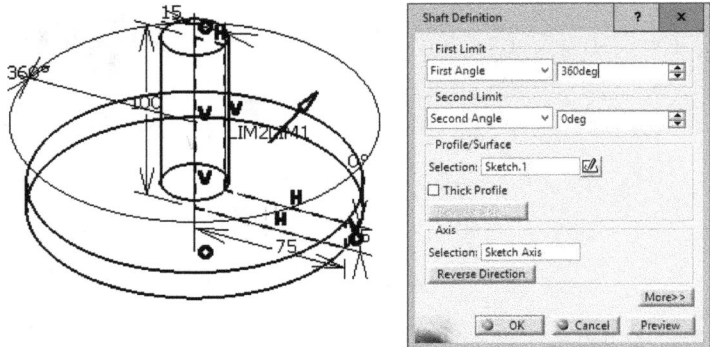

Figure 9–3

Step 3 - Select a rotational axis.

To create the Shaft feature, the rotational axis about which the profile is going to be revolved is required. By default, the software uses the first sketched axis created in the profile. If the sketch does not contain an axis, click [icon] in the Shaft Definition dialog box to alter the sketch without leaving the definition of this feature.

- While in the Sketcher workbench, click [Axis] (Axis) to sketch an axis, as shown in Figure 9–4.

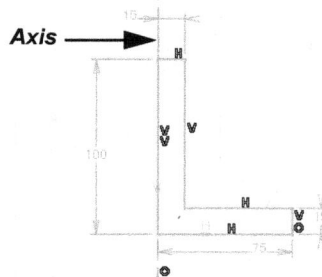

Figure 9–4

- Alternatively, you can select an existing edge, line, or axis. Figure 9–5 shows the selected vertical absolute axis of the sketch.

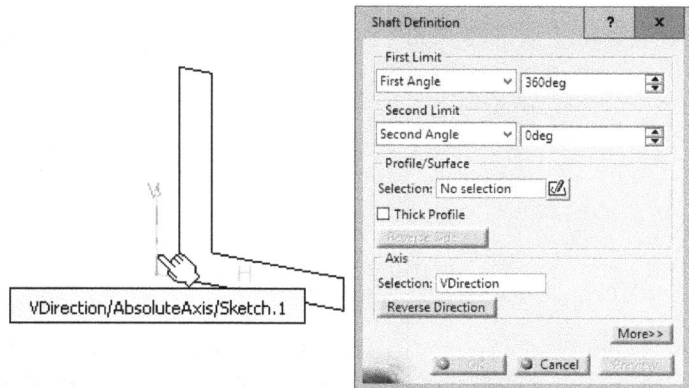

VDirection/AbsoluteAxis/Sketch.1

Figure 9–5

Step 4 - Specify Shaft limit options.

The angle that the sketch is rotated through is known as the limit. By default, the sketch is rotated 360° about the axis. This value can be changed, as required.

Rotation Angle

The default rotation angle is 360°. If you enter a smaller angle, the sketch is rotated in the direction indicated by the first angle direction arrow, as shown in Figure 9–6.

First angle direction arrow

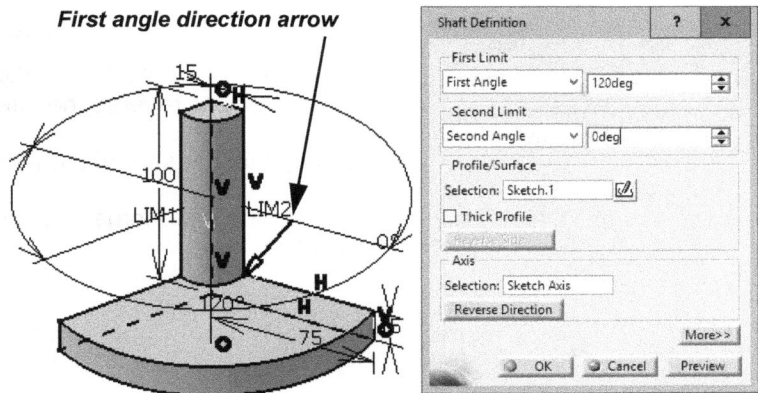

Figure 9–6

Entering a negative first angle value enables you to specify the angle of material to be removed from a 360° Shaft, as shown in Figure 9–7.

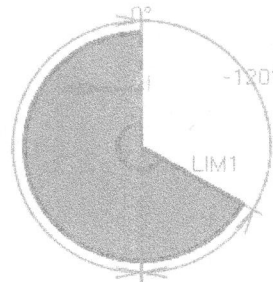

Figure 9–7

You can also change the default zero value of the second angle to rotate the sketch to the opposite side, as shown in Figure 9–8.

The sum of the first and second angles must be greater than zero and no more than 360°.

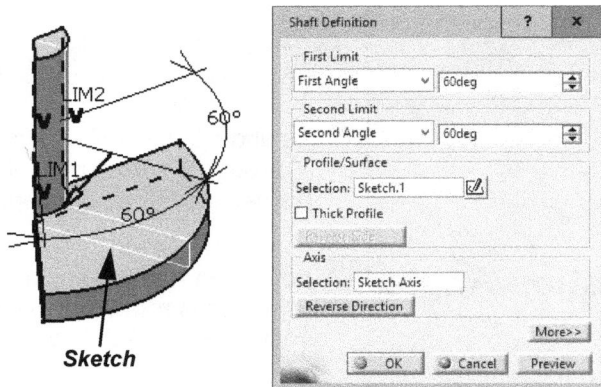

Figure 9–8

- Entering **0** for *First angle* and a value for the *Second angle* enables you to reverse the direction of the Shaft feature.

- Ensure that the sum of the two angles is 360 degrees or less.

- To examine the geometry before you complete the feature, click **Preview**.

In addition to entering the *First Angle* and *Second Angle* limits, you can apply any of the following limiting types, which are similar to those used for Pad and Pocket features:

- **First Angle or Second Angle**: Creates a feature up to the defined angle value.

- **Up to next**: Creates a feature up to the next intersecting feature.

- **Up to last**: Creates a feature up to the last intersecting feature.

- **Up to plane**: Creates a feature up to the defined plane.

- **Up to surface**: Creates a feature up to the defined surface.

Step 5 - Complete the Shaft feature.

Click **OK** to complete the feature.

9.2 Groove Feature

A Groove feature removes material by rotating a sketch about an axis, as shown in Figure 9–9. It is similar to the Shaft feature, except that material is removed, instead of being added.

- As with the Shaft feature, you can accept the default value of 360° for the first limit and 0 for the second limit value. Figure 9–10 shows a model where the first limit value is changed to 90° and the second limit value is changed to 45°.

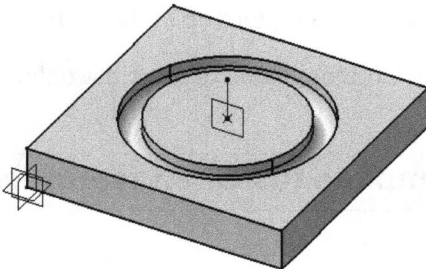

Figure 9–9

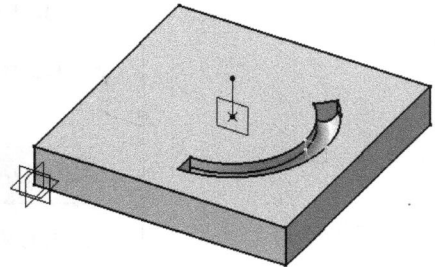

Figure 9–10

In addition to entering the *First Angle* and *Second Angle* limits, you can apply any of the following limiting types:

- **First Angle or Second Angle**: Creates a feature up to the defined angle value.

- **Up to next**: Creates a feature up to the next intersecting feature.

- **Up to last**: Creates a feature up to the last intersecting feature.

- **Up to plane**: Creates a feature up to the defined plane.

- **Up to surface**: Creates a feature up to the defined surface.

Requirements

To create a Groove feature, you must meet the following requirements:

- You must provide a rotation axis for the sketch. It can be a line, a sketched axis in the profile, or the implicit axis.

- Your profile must only be on one side of the axis.

- The section must be closed.

Grooves on Cylinders

To create a Groove feature on a cylindrical feature, a sketch plane must pass through the center of the cylindrical feature. If a suitable plane does not exist, you can use the **Angle/Normal to Plane** option when creating the reference plane. An axis must be selected as a placement reference.

- To select an implicit axis, hold <Shift> and place the cursor over the cylinder to highlight it, as shown in Figure 9–11. You can then select this axis as the rotation axis for the new plane.

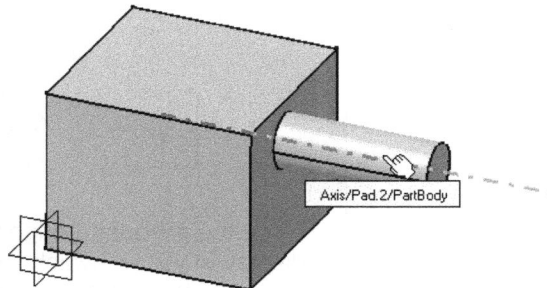

Axis/Pad.2/PartBody

Figure 9–11

Rotation Axis

The implicit axis can be used to define the rotation axis for the Groove feature. This reduces the need to create additional line or sketched axis features.

Silhouette Edges

In some cases, you might need to constrain the sketch so that one or more sketched entities are coincident with the silhouette edge of the cylinder, as shown in Figure 9–12.

This horizontal line of the sketch must be coincident with the silhouette edge of the cylinder.

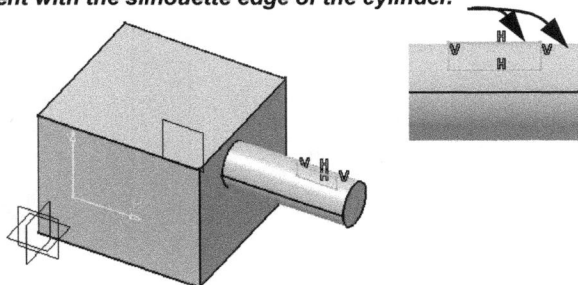

Figure 9–12

You cannot apply a coincidence constraint between the line and the silhouette edge. Therefore, click (Project 3D Canonical Silhouette Edge) and select the cylinder. This copies the top and bottom edges into the sketch, as shown in Figure 9–13.

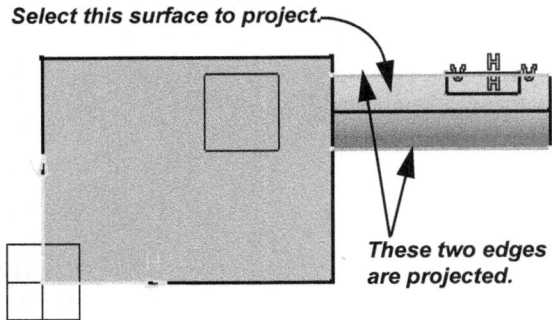

Select this surface to project.

These two edges are projected.

Figure 9–13

Once the silhouette edges are copied into your sketch, they display in yellow, which indicates projected geometry. To complete your sketch, use one or a combination of the following methods:

- Delete the top or bottom silhouette edge that is not required.

- Convert the silhouette edge to construction geometry, and constrain your sketch to it.

- Leave the silhouette edge as a geometry element.

Dimension the Remaining Material Diameter

If the design intent is to control the diameter of a Groove feature, create a diameter dimension between the bottom of the sketch and the sketched axis, as shown in Figure 9–14.

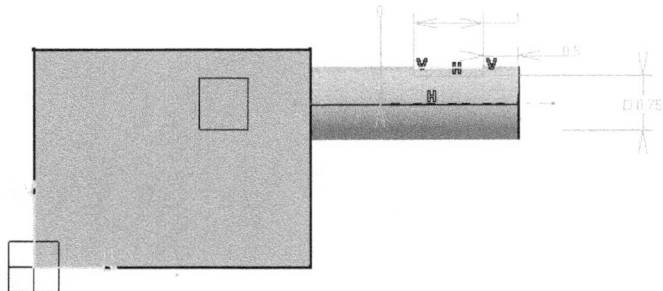

Figure 9–14

Practice 9a	# Shaft & Groove Features

Practice Objective

- Create a Shaft feature and a Groove feature.

In this practice, you will create the part shown in Figure 9–15. The base feature for the model is created using a Shaft feature by revolving a profile about the Y-axis. A Groove feature is then used to develop the lubrication grooves.

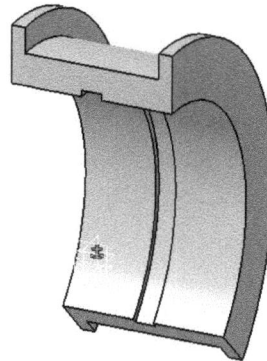

Figure 9–15

Task 1 - Create a new part.

1. Click ⬜ (New).

2. In the New dialog box, select the **Part** option and click **OK**.

3. Name the part **Bearing** and click **OK**.

Task 2 - Create a sketch.

1. Create a sketch on the YZ plane.

2. Sketch the horizontal axis, as shown in Figure 9–16. This will define the rotational axis of the Shaft feature.

Figure 9–16

3. Sketch the profile as shown in Figure 9–17. Verify that the vertical elements are symmetrical about the vertical axis, and that the top horizontal elements are coincident.

- 2 (0.079 in)
- 5 (0.197 in)
- 9 (0.354 in)
- 24 (0.945 in)
- 60 (2.362 in)

*To create the diameter dimension, right-click and select **Radius/ Diameter**.*

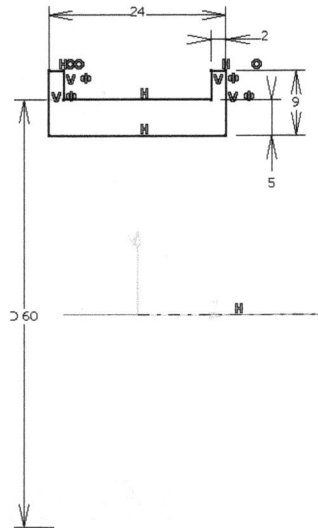

Figure 9–17

4. Click ⬆️ (Exit workbench) to exit the Sketcher workbench.

Task 3 - Create a datum plane for use later in this practice.

1. In the Reference Elements toolbar, click ▱ (Plane).

2. In the Plane Definition dialog box, in the Plane type drop-down list, select **Angle/Normal to plane**.

3. Right-click in the *Rotation axis* field and select **Y Axis**, as shown in Figure 9–18.

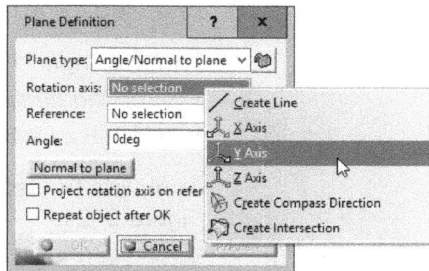

Figure 9–18

4. For the *Reference*, select **yz plane** in the Specification Tree.

5. Edit the angle to **100**, as shown in Figure 9–19.

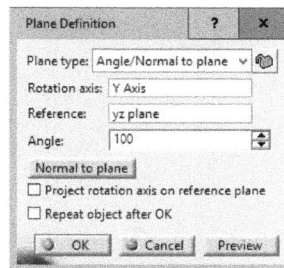

Figure 9–19

6. Click **OK** in the Plane Definition dialog box.

Task 4 - Create a Shaft feature.

---

1. Select **Sketch.1**.

2. Click [icon] (Shaft). The Shaft Definition dialog box opens as shown in Figure 9–20.

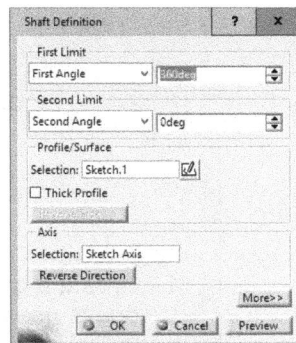

Figure 9–20

3. Enter the following parameters to define the Shaft feature:

- *First angle:* **180deg**
- *Second angle:* **0deg**
- Click **Reverse Direction**.

4. Complete the feature. The model displays as shown in Figure 9–21.

Figure 9–21

Task 5 - Create a Groove feature.

In this task, you will create a feature to represent the lubrication Groove on the inside diameter of the bearing. The completed feature displays as shown in Figure 9–22.

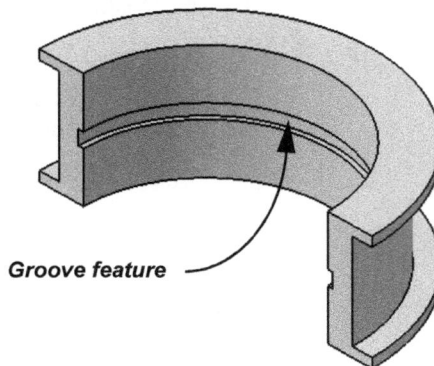

Groove feature

Figure 9–22

1. Create a positioned sketch on the YZ plane. To define the origin, use the **Middle Point** type and select the edge shown in Figure 9–23.

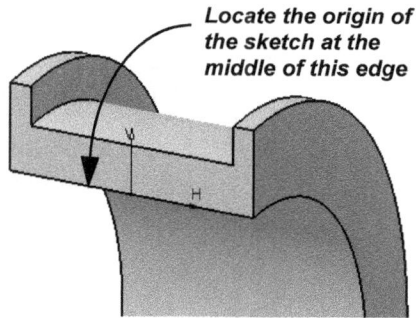

Locate the origin of the sketch at the middle of this edge

Figure 9–23

2. Sketch the profile shown in Figure 9–24, using the dimensions of **1 (0.039 in)** and **3 (0.118 in)**. Verify that the profile is symmetrical about the vertical sketch axis.

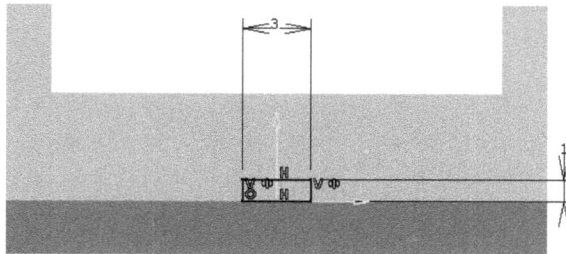

Figure 9–24

3. Exit Sketcher.

4. With the sketch preselected, click (Groove). The Groove Definition dialog box opens as shown in Figure 9–25.

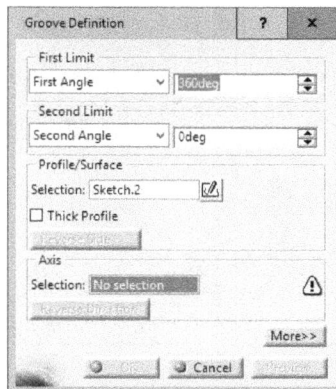

Figure 9–25

Design Considerations

Note ⚠ next to the *Selection* field in the *Axis* area. An axis was not sketched into the profile used for the Groove, so a rotation axis for the feature is not automatically defined.

5. Select the **Shaft.1** feature to select its axis. The Groove Definition dialog box updates as shown in Figure 9–26.

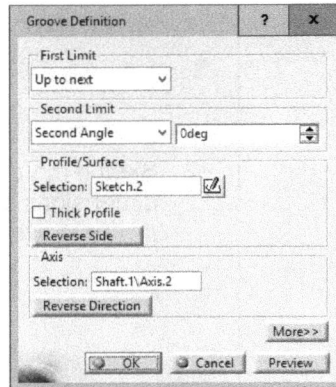

Figure 9–26

You might need to click **Reverse Direction** *to get the required result.*

6. Modify the options in the Groove Definition dialog box so that the resulting feature displays as shown in Figure 9–27.

Figure 9–27

Task 6 - Change the shaft to reference the datum plane.

1. In the Specification Tree, double-click on **Shaft.1**.

2. In the Shaft Definition dialog box, select **Up to plane** from the First Limit drop-down list.

3. Select **Plane.1** in the Specification Tree.

4. Click **OK**.

5. In the Update Diagnosis Shaft.1 dialog box, click **Sub Elements**.

6. In the Sub Elements in Error dialog box, click **OK**. The model updates as shown in Figure 9–28.

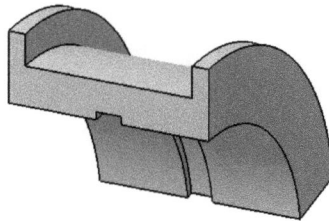

Figure 9–28

Task 7 - Edit the angle of the plane.

1. In the Specification Tree, right-click on **Plane.1** and select **Plane.1 object>Edit Parameters**.

2. Edit the *100* angle dimension to **45** and click **OK**.

3. In the Tools toolbar, click (Update All). The model updates as shown in Figure 9–29.

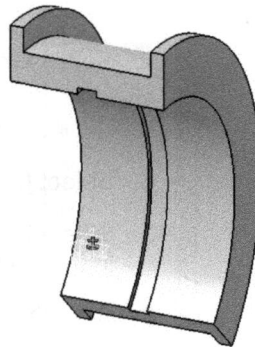

Figure 9–29

4. Save the model and close the window.

Practice 9b

Groove Features

Practice Objectives

- Create a Groove feature.
- Locate revolved sketches to cylindrical geometry.

In this practice, you will create the part shown in Figure 9–30. The part will consist of two Groove features. You will also use silhouette projections to locate a sketch onto cylindrical geometry.

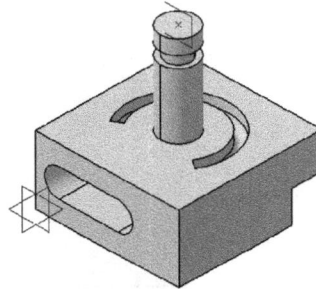

Figure 9–30

Task 1 - Create a point.

Design Considerations

This point will mark the center of the cylinder. It will be used as a reference for a plane, which will be used to create the two profiles in this task.

1. Click (Open).

2. Select **Groove.CATPart** and click **Open**.

3. Click (Point) in the Reference Elements toolbar.

4. Select **Circle/Sphere/Ellipse center** as the point type.

5. Select the circular edge on the top of the cylinder, as shown in Figure 9–31.

6. Click **OK** to complete the feature.

7. Click (Plane) and select **Parallel through point** as the plane type.

8. Select the YZ plane as the parallel reference for the new plane, and select the point to locate the plane.

9. Click **OK** to complete the feature. The new point and plane display as shown in Figure 9–31.

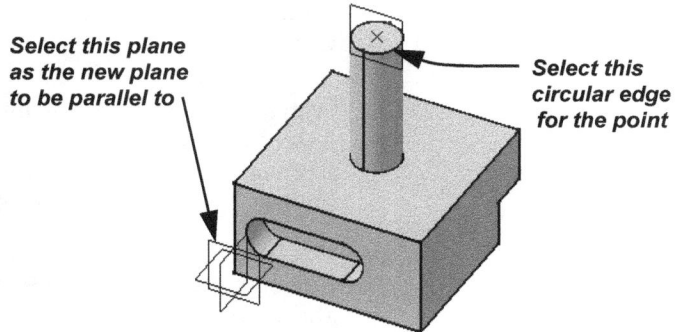

Select this plane as the new plane to be parallel to

Select this circular edge for the point

Figure 9–31

Task 2 - Create a sketch to be used for a Groove feature.

1. Create a positioned sketch on the newly created reference plane, using **Point.1** as the origin.

2. Click (Profile) to sketch the shape. Dimension the width and height of the shape, as shown in Figure 9–32.

   • 22.5 (0.886 in)
   • 32 (1.260 in)
   • 95 (3.740 in)

This sketched profile should be closed to avoid feature failure.

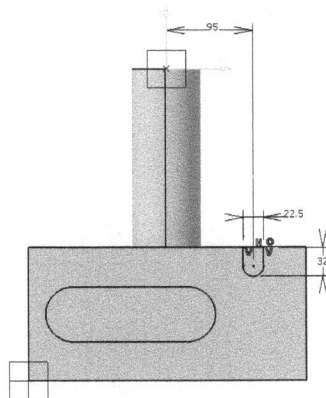

Figure 9–32

3. Constrain the horizontal line of the sketch with the horizontal edge of the part.

4. Dimension the center of the arc to the vertical sketcher axis.

5. When the sketch is fully constrained, click [icon] (Exit workbench).

6. With the sketch still highlighted, click [icon] (Groove) to create a Groove feature. The software does not automatically build a preview of the Groove because the sketch does not have an axis. Note that the axis selection box is active.

7. Place the cursor over the cylinder. The implicit axis displays. Select this axis and click **Preview**. The feature displays as shown in Figure 9–33.

8. Set the *First Angle* as **90** and click **Preview**. Set the *Second Angle* as **150** and click **Preview**. The part displays as shown in Figure 9–33.

9. Select and drag the **LIM1** and **LIM2** tags of the Groove to dynamically modify the rotation angles.

10. When you have set the limits to an angle similar to that shown in Figure 9–33. Click **OK**.

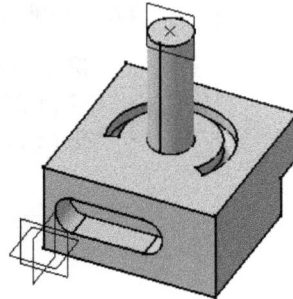

Figure 9–33

Task 3 - Create a sketch for a Groove feature on the cylinder.

1. Create a positioned sketch on the newly created reference plane using **Point.1** as the origin.

2. Select **View>Zoom Area** and zoom into the top of the cylinder by dragging a box around it.

3. Click (Project 3D Elements) and select the cylinder then click **OK**. This creates an axis that is automatically constrained to the center of the cylinder, as shown in Figure 9–34.

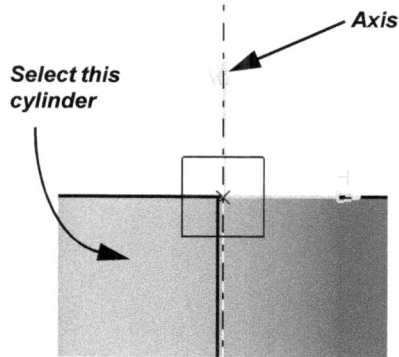

Select this cylinder

Axis

Figure 9–34

4. Click (Project 3D Canonical Silhouette Edges).

5. Select the cylinder. Two vertical lines display. The warning message box opens, as shown in Figure 9–35.

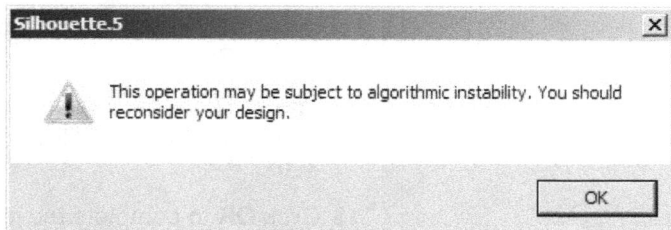

Silhouette.5

This operation may be subject to algorithmic instability. You should reconsider your design.

OK

Figure 9–35

Design Considerations

The warning message displays to make you aware that features using silhouette edge projections in a sketch might become unstable. CATIA occasionally loses references to silhouetted edges. Use caution when using this type of projection in your models.

6. Click **OK**.

7. With the two silhouette projections selected, click

 (Construction/Standard Element). The silhouette edges are now changed to construction lines.

8. Select the background area of the display to clear the geometry and click [icon] (Construction/Standard Element) to return to Standard Element creation.

9. Sketch and dimension the rectangle as shown in Figure 9–36. Verify that the right vertical edge of the rectangle is coincident with the construction line.

- 25 (0.984 in)
- 27 (1.063 in)
- 32 (1.260 in)

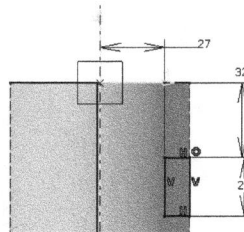

Figure 9–36

10. Exit the Sketcher workbench.

11. With the sketch highlighted, click [icon] (Groove). Note that the sketch axis is automatically selected as the rotational axis for the Groove feature.

12. The software has maintained your previous values for the first and second angles. Reset these values to rotate the sketch 360°.

13. Click **OK** to complete the feature. The part displays as shown in Figure 9–37.

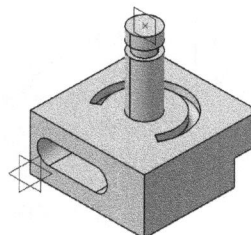

Figure 9–37

14. Click [icon] (Save).

15. Select **File>Close**.

Practice 9c

(Optional) King Chess Piece

Practice Objective

- Create Pad and Shaft features without instructions.

Create a new part called **King_Piece** with a part number of **03051976**, as shown in Figure 9–38. Exact dimensions are not required.

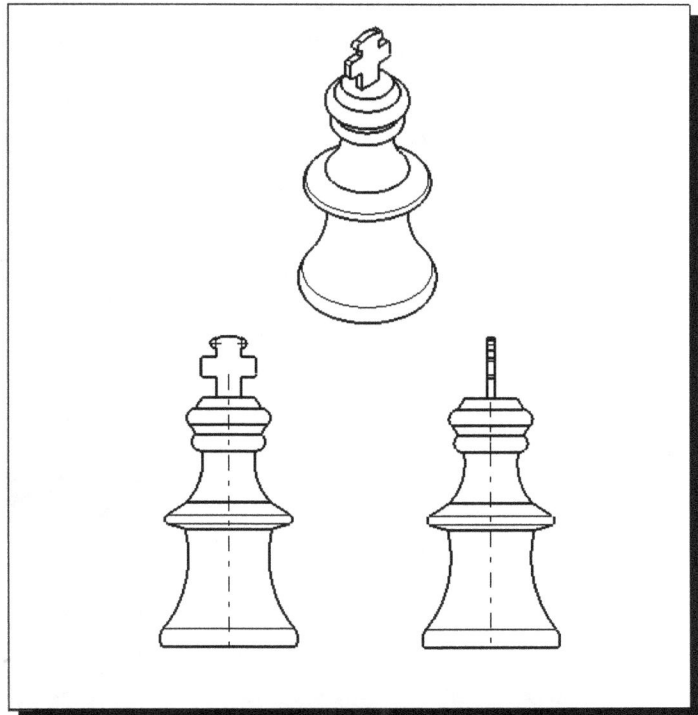

Figure 9–38

Practice 9d

(Optional) Creating Shafts and Grooves

Practice Objective

- Create Shaft and Groove features with minimal instruction.

In this practice, you will create a model of a spinning top using Shaft and Groove features. The completed model is shown in Figure 9–39. As a good practice, create an axis system in the drawing as a foundation for building features.

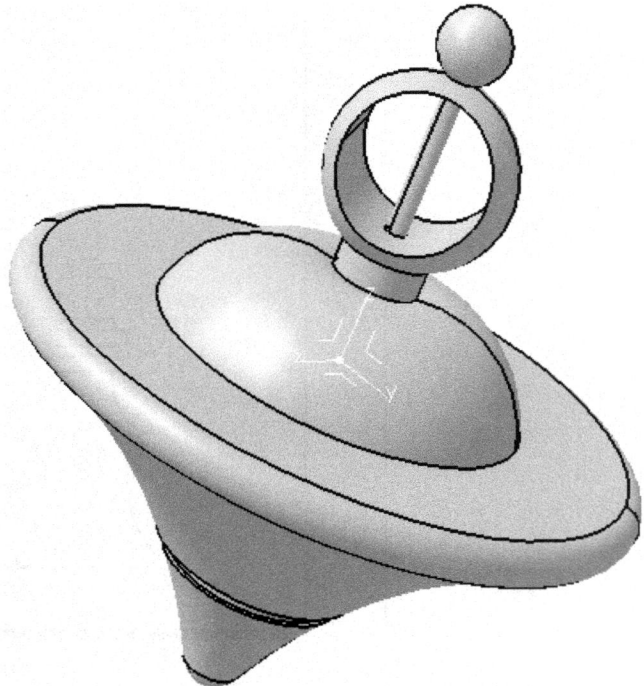

Figure 9–39

Task 1 - Create a new model.

1. Create a new part called **SpinningTop.CATPart**.

2. Use the dimensioned drawings in Figure 9–40, Figure 9–41, Figure 9–42, Figure 9–43, and Figure 9–44 to create the required geometry.

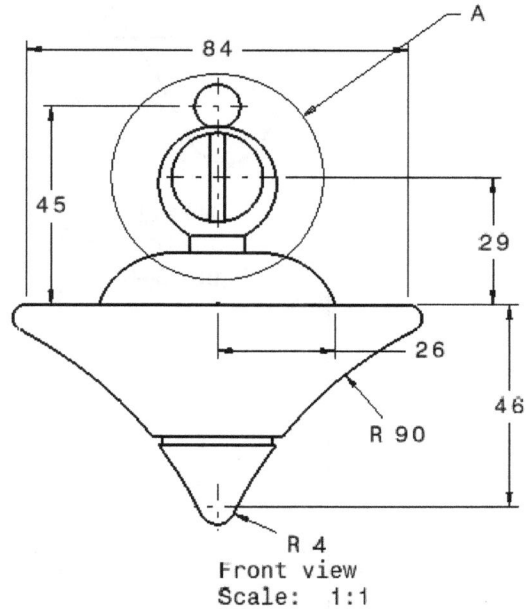

Front view
Scale: 1:1

Figure 9–40

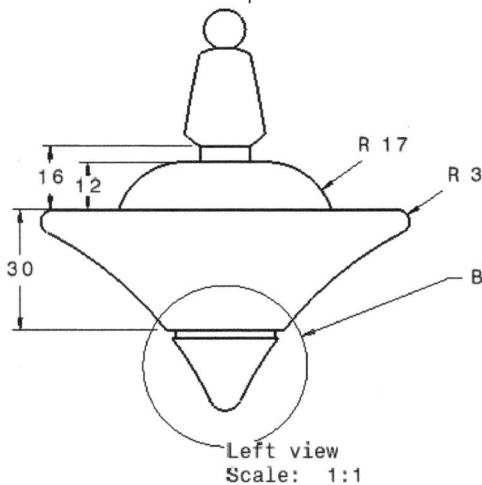

Left view
Scale: 1:1

Figure 9–41

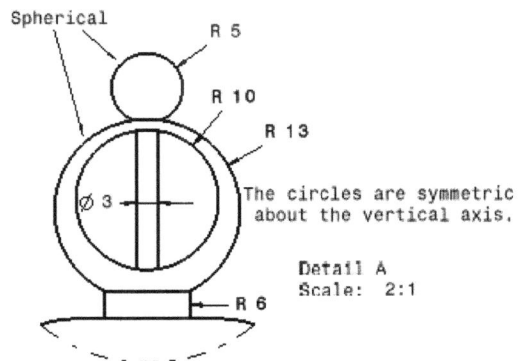

The circles are symmetric about the vertical axis.

Detail A
Scale: 2:1

Figure 9–42

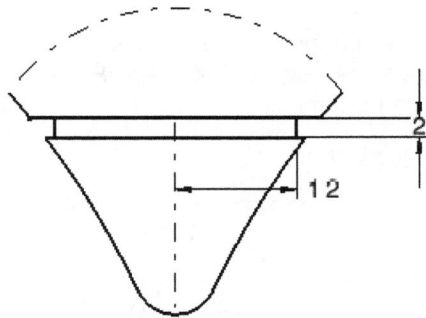

Detail B
Scale: 2:1
Figure 9–43

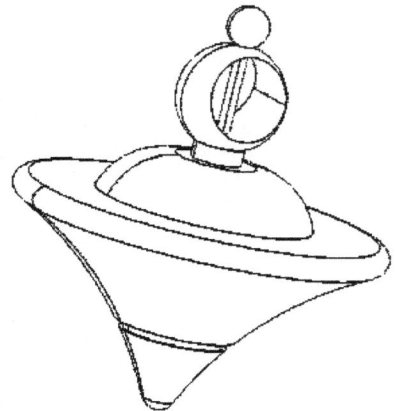

Isometric view
Scale: 1:1
Figure 9–44

Chapter Review Questions

1. You mistakenly use a sketch to create a Pad feature, when you really intended to create a Shaft. What do you need to do to fix this?

   a. Right-click the pad and select **Convert to Shaft**.

   b. Right-click the Pad and select **Pad.object>Definition**. In the Pad Definition dialog box, select **Shaft**.

   c. Delete the Pad and use the sketch to create a Shaft feature.

   d. None of the above.

2. Which of the following profiles is not valid for use in creating a Shaft feature?

   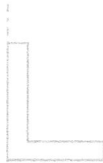

   a.

   b.

   c.

   d.

3. Which of the following are valid selections as an axis for a Shaft or Groove feature? (Select all that apply.)

   a. An axis created inside the sketch.

   b. An existing edge.

   c. The vertical absolute axis of a sketch.

   d. The implicit axis of an existing feature.

4. The profile for a Groove feature must lie completely to one side of the axis of revolution.

   a. True

   b. False

5. A Groove is required on the side of the cylindrical feature shown in Figure 9–45. What feature is required to aid in the creation of the Groove feature?

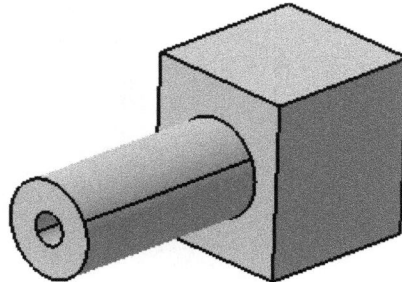

Figure 9–45

   a. A construction line.

   b. A sketch support.

   c. A point.

   d. None of the above.

6. What will be projected onto the sketch if the Cylindrical feature, shown in Figure 9–46 is projected using the **Project 3D Elements**?

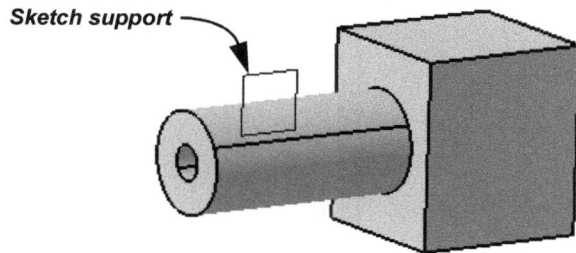

Sketch support

Figure 9–46

a. The side edges of the cylinder

b. The implicit axis of the cylinder.

c. The edges of the hole in the cylinder.

d. None of the above.

7. What is going to be projected onto the sketch if the Cylindrical feature, shown in Figure 9–46, is projected using the **Project 3D Canonical Silhouette Edges** icon?

a. The side edges of the cylinder

b. The implicit axis of the cylinder.

c. The edges of the hole in the cylinder.

d. None of the above.

Answers: 1.c, 2.c, 3.abcd, 4.a, 5.b, 6.b, 7.a

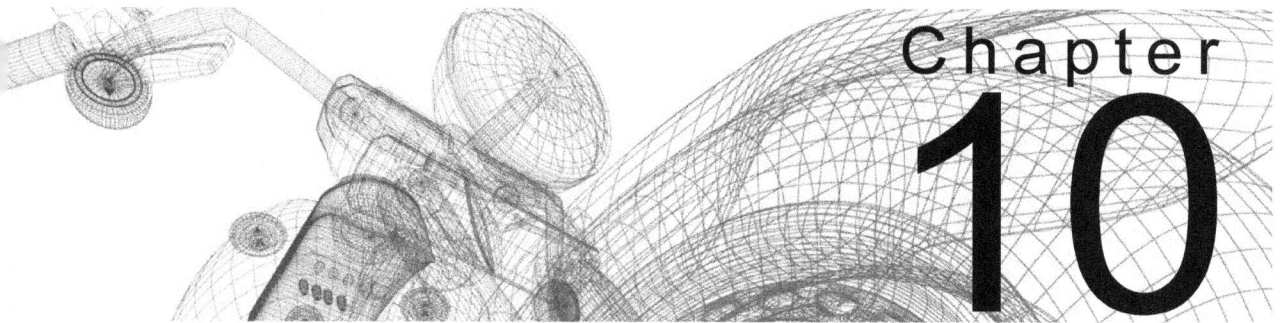

Feature Management

CATIA provides several tools to simplify the display of your model. Three of these tools are Search, Hide/Show, and Activate/Deactivate. Using these tools will increase your overall efficiency. You can also use Selection Sets to quickly select groups of features at the same time.

Learning Objectives in this Chapter

- Use Search in complex models to find specific objects.
- Show and hide features to simplify the display and make working with complex models more efficient.
- Understand how hidden features display in the specification tree.
- Learn how to Activate and Deactivate objects.
- Learn how to group features using selection sets.

10.1 Search for Features

In complex models with a large number of features, locating specific features in the model might become difficult. The **Search** tool enables you to locate and select the feature in the specification tree using a variety of search parameters.

- Select **Edit>Search** to perform a search. The Search dialog box opens and it displays the results of a sample search for a feature with a name containing the string **Rib,** as shown in Figure 10–1.

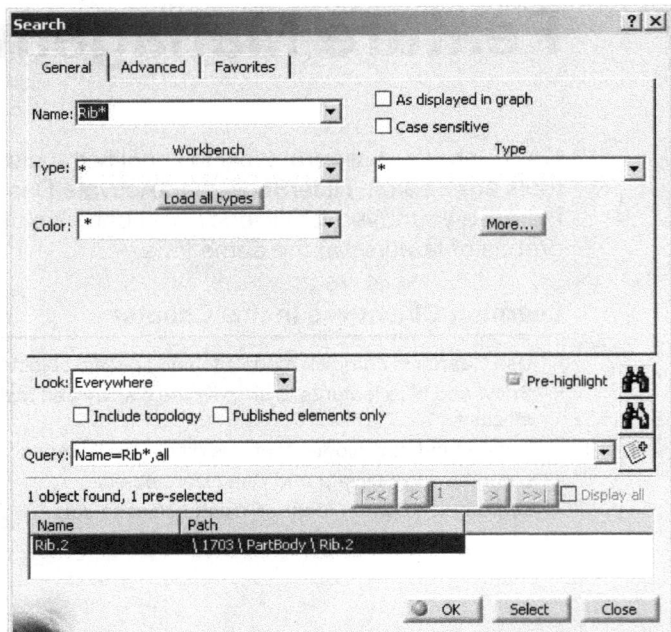

Figure 10–1

When you select the found objects, the features are highlighted in the main window and specification tree. The feature can be selected for use in the current operation by clicking **Select**.

- The *Advanced* tab provides options to define more search parameters.

- The *Favorites* tab provides access to search results that have been stored using (Add to favorites).

10.2 Hide and Show

CATIA contains two default display spaces - invisible and visible. You have been working in visible space. As you create additional features and your models become more complex, the display area of the screen becomes cluttered. To simplify the display, the **Hide** and **Show** commands can be used to move features between the two spaces.

A model with all elements visible is shown in Figure 10–2.

Sketches are normally hidden after they are referenced by a feature. They are shown here for illustration purposes.

The display shows many elements that no longer need to be shown.

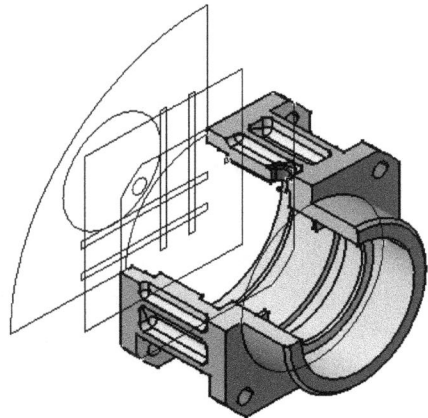

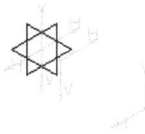

Figure 10–2

The model shown includes all of the sketches, lines, and reference planes. Individual features can be moved from the visible space to the invisible space by using one of the following methods:

- Click ⬚ (Hide/Show) in the View toolbar and select the feature(s) to hide/show. You can also use this method in reverse.

- Select the feature in the display area or in the specification tree, right-click, and select **Hide/Show**. When a feature is switched to the invisible space, it no longer displays. However, the features still exist.

To select all features of a particular type, use the **Hide** or **Show** commands in the **Tools** menu, as shown in Figure 10–3.

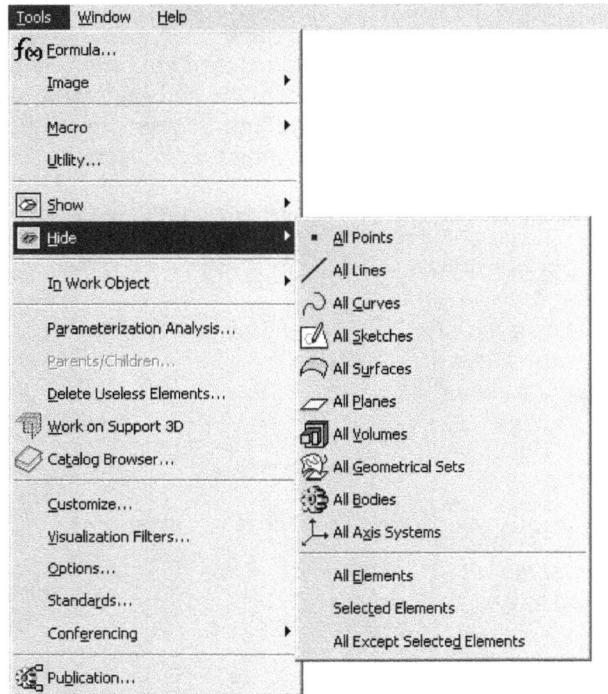

Figure 10–3

As a result, the display area is much less cluttered. Figure 10–4 shows the same model as the one shown in Figure 10–2, except that all sketches, planes, points, and axis systems are hidden from visible space.

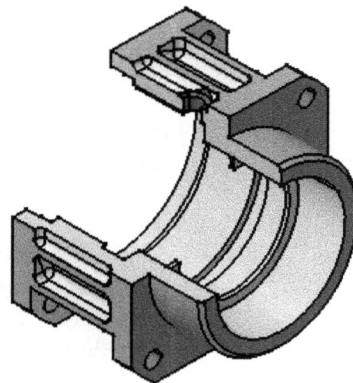

Figure 10–4

Indication of Hidden Features

The specification tree displays hidden features as faded or grayed icons, as shown in Figure 10–5.

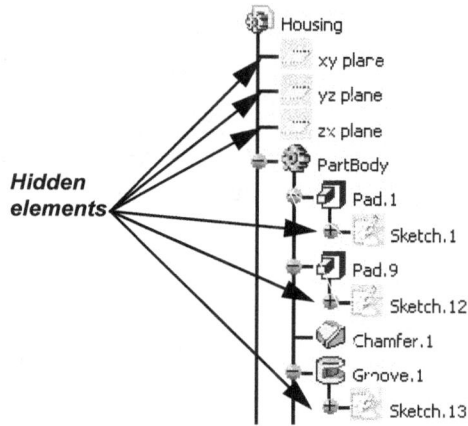

Figure 10–5

- To swap between the visible working space and invisible working space, click ✎ (Swap visible space) in the View toolbar. Hidden features are shown in a separate working space (i.e., invisible). Click the icon again to return to the visible working space.

- To make individual features visible after they have been hidden, select them in the specification tree, right-click and select **Hide/Show**.

Tips and Techniques

Use the **Hide** and **Show** commands carefully. Although no real harm can be done to your model, the **Hide** and **Show** commands can produce unexpected results if you select inactive features, or select the wrong types of features.

- A feature in the specification tree that affects the mass properties of the model cannot be hidden without hiding all solid features. To control the display of solid features independently, the feature must be deactivated.

10.3 Activate and Deactivate

If features are deactivated, the update sequence time decreases.

When features are added to the model, the software updates them with any changes made. When a change occurs that forces subsequent features to change drastically, the update can fail. To deactivate a feature and help solve an update failure, select the feature, right-click and select the feature object name (e.g., **Hole.1 object**), and then select **Deactivate**, as shown in Figure 10–6.

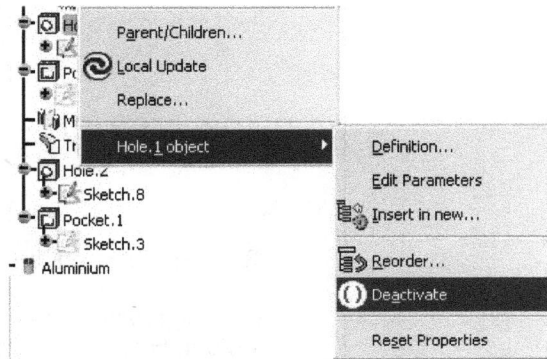

Figure 10–6

The **Deactivate** option temporarily removes the feature from the update sequence. This enables you to keep the feature as currently defined, without deleting it. The feature icon displays with a deactivation symbol in the specification tree, as shown for the **Hole.1** object in Figure 10–7.

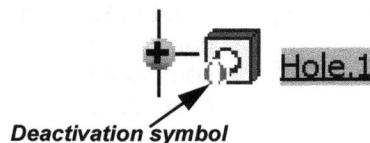

Deactivation symbol

Figure 10–7

You can modify any previous features to help solve an update failure. Once solved, the feature can be returned to the update sequence by selecting it in the specification tree, right-clicking on the feature object name, and selecting **Activate**.

Features should only be deactivated temporarily. If they are not required, they should be deleted from the model.

You can use the **Deactivate** option to:

- Reduce the chance of unwanted parent/child relationships.

- Make models run faster.

- De-feature the model for Finite Element Analysis purposes.

- Try alternative designs for a feature.

To avoid accidentally referencing a Fillet feature when creating additional features, deactivate the Fillet feature on your model, as shown in Figure 10–8. Deactivating fillets is one way to help CATIA run faster for modeling design and Finite Element Analysis.

- You can also deactivate specific features and create alternative types. This option enables you to keep fillets for use at a later time without having to recreate them.

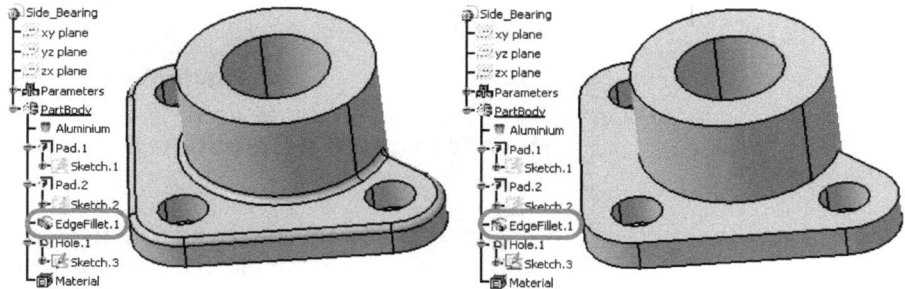

Figure 10–8

Once the design is finalized, it is recommended that you delete all unused features, rather than keep them deactivated in the model. If not deleted, these features can unnecessarily increase file size and cause confusion to someone else using this file at a later time.

Parent/Child Considerations

If a parent feature is selected for deactivation, its children must also be deactivated. Children features that are impacted by deactivating the parent are highlighted in the specification tree and the model. Figure 10–9 shows the **Hole.1** feature selected for deactivation and the Deactivate dialog box. The Draft feature is the child feature and is consequently deactivated.

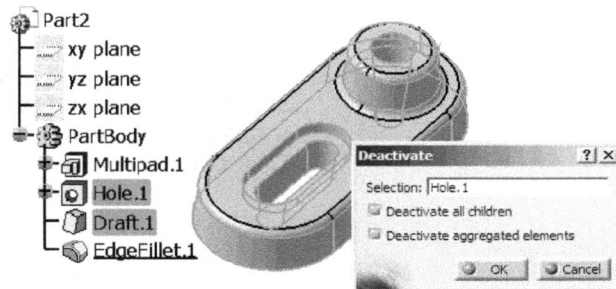

Figure 10–9

10.4 Creating Selection Sets

Selection sets enable you to define groups of features that can be quickly selected at the same time. This function is ideal for groups of features that are selected often. For example, you can quickly deactivate and activate fillet, chamfer, and other dress-up features by adding them to a selection set.

- The Selection Sets toolbar is shown in Figure 10–10.

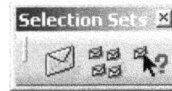

Figure 10–10

How To: Create a Selection Set

1. Click (Selection sets edition) to create a selection box. The Selection Sets Edition dialog box opens, as shown in Figure 10–11.

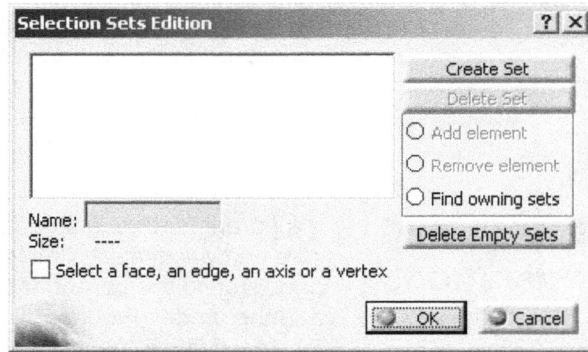

Figure 10–11

2. Click **Create Set** and enter a name for the set in the *Name* field.
3. With the new set highlighted, select the **Add element** option. Select features in the specification tree to add to the set. The **Select a face, an edge, an axis or a vertex** option, enables you to select geometry from the model.
4. Click **OK** to complete the creation of the set.

5. Click (Selection sets) to select a feature. The Selection Sets Selection dialog box opens, as shown in Figure 10–12.

Figure 10–12

6. Select the set from the list and click **Select**. Close the dialog box to complete the selection.

Practice 10a | # Feature Management

Practice Objectives

- Simplify the model display using the Hide/Show commands.
- Activate and deactivate features.
- Create and use selection sets.

In this practice, you will use feature management techniques to modify a part. You will use the **Hide/Show**, **Activate/Deactivate** and **Selection Set** commands. In addition, you will learn the properties of these commands and how they affect the model display.

Features are selected for visual clarity.

Task 1 - Hide reference geometry and sketch features.

1. Click [ ] (Open). Select **BlockMgt.CATPart** and click **Open**. Note that the reference elements and feature sketches are also displayed.

2. View the invisible space by clicking [ ] (Swap visible space). The background changes to the invisible space color. Some measurements are hidden in the model. Therefore, they display in the invisible space.

3. Return to the visible space by clicking [ ] (Swap visible space).

4. Using <Ctrl>, select the three default reference plane features.

5. Right-click over any of the selected features in the display area and select **Hide/Show**.

6. The planes are removed from visible space and added to invisible space. Click [ ] (Swap visible space) to switch to invisible space. The three planes display as shown in Figure 10–13.

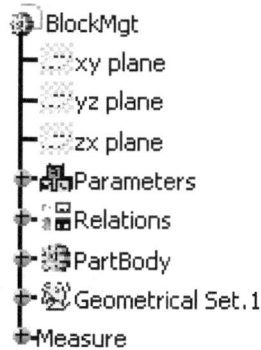

Figure 10–13

7. Click (Swap visible space) to switch back to visible space.

8. By default, sketches that are used to create other features, such as pads, grooves, pockets, etc., are automatically hidden from display. Currently, they are all set to display. Select **Tools>Hide>All Sketches** to remove all sketches from visible space. The model updates, as shown in Figure 10–14.

Note that all hidden feature icons are grayed in the specification tree.

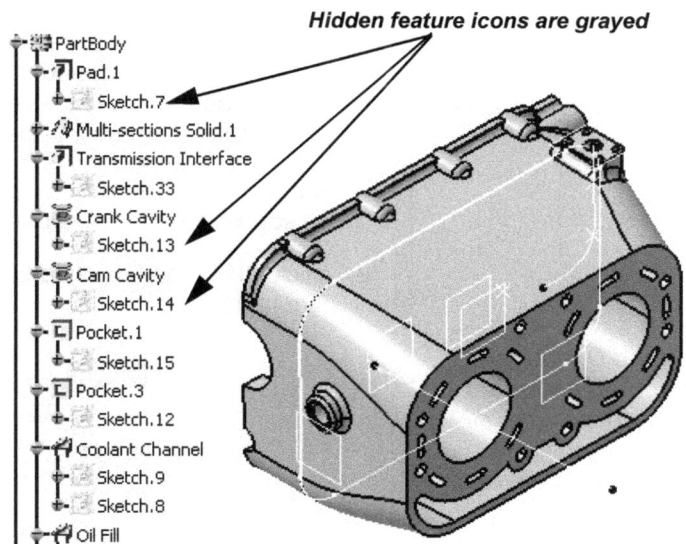

Hidden feature icons are grayed

Figure 10–14

9. Reference geometry features are still set to display in visible space. Right-click on **Geometrical Set.1** and select **Geometrical Set.1 object>Hide Components**.

10. Click ⌖ (Swap visible space) to switch to invisible space.

11. Switch back to visible space.

Task 2 - Attempt to hide a Hole feature.

1. Select the **Hole.5** feature in the specification tree, right-click and select **Hide/Show**. If you are unable to locate the feature in the specification tree, you can select any other solid feature to hide.

   Note that the contents of the PartBody switch to invisible space. Solid features cannot be hidden or shown independently from the rest of the PartBody solid features.

2. Select the **Hole.5** feature in the specification tree again, right-click and select **Hide/Show** to return PartBody to visible space.

Task 3 - Deactivate the Hole feature.

Design Considerations

As shown in Task 2, individual solid geometry features cannot be hidden independently. However, you can deactivate the individual solid features independently.

1. Right-click on the **Hole.5** feature in the specification tree and select **Hole.5 object>Deactivate**.

2. Click **OK** in the Deactivate dialog box, as shown in Figure 10–15.

*Select the **Deactivate aggregated elements** option to deactivate all geometry grouped below the main element node being deactivated.*

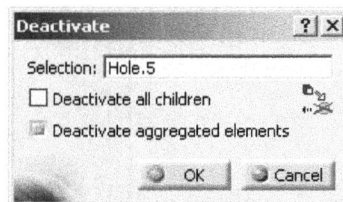

Figure 10–15

The Hole feature is deactivated and removed from visible space, as shown in Figure 10–16.

Deactivation symbol displays on feature icon

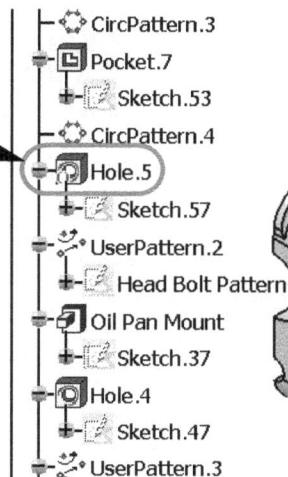

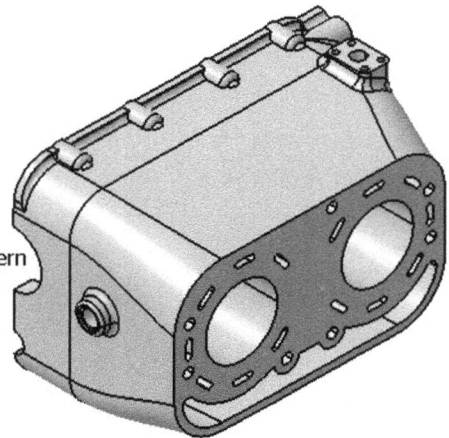

- CircPattern.3
- Pocket.7
  - Sketch.53
- CircPattern.4
- Hole.5
  - Sketch.57
- UserPattern.2
  - Head Bolt Pattern
- Oil Pan Mount
  - Sketch.37
- Hole.4
  - Sketch.47
- UserPattern.3

Figure 10–16

Design Considerations

The feature is not switched to invisible space because it is deactivated and therefore no longer updates with the rest of the model. In this case, deactivation is useful in illustrating the manufacturing process of the model for a marketing presentation. The last step is to drill the hole in the part. To obtain a graphic of the model without the hole, it is recommended to deactivate the feature, generate the graphic, and then re-activate the feature, rather than deleting the feature.

3. In the specification tree, select the deactivated **Hole.5** feature. Right-click, and select **Hole.5 object>Activate**.

4. Click **OK** then click in the background to clear the selection. The model returns to the active state.

Task 4 - Deactivate the Fillet features.

---

1. Click [icon] (Selection sets edition). You might need to display the Selection Sets toolbar to access the icon (check the top toolbar). The Selection Sets Edition dialog box opens.

2. Click **Create Set**.

3. Enter **FilletSet** in the *Name* field. Select the **Add element** option as shown in Figure 10–17.

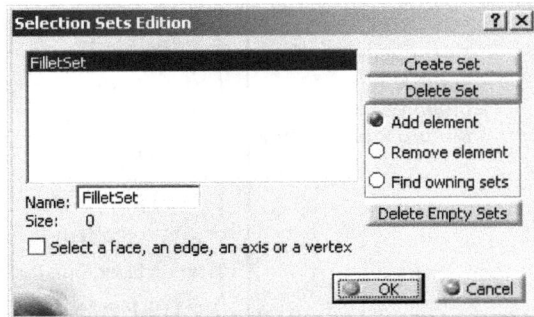

Figure 10–17

Design Considerations

*The Windows shortcut keys for **Find** (<Ctrl>+ <F>) also opens the Search dialog box.*

You must perform a search operation to locate the Fillet features to add to the selection set. Searching is the most efficient way to locate and select all of the Fillet features in the model.

4. Select **Edit>Search**. The Search dialog box opens.

5. In the workbench **Type** menu, select **Part Design** and select **Type>Fillet**. The Search dialog box opens as shown in Figure 10–18.

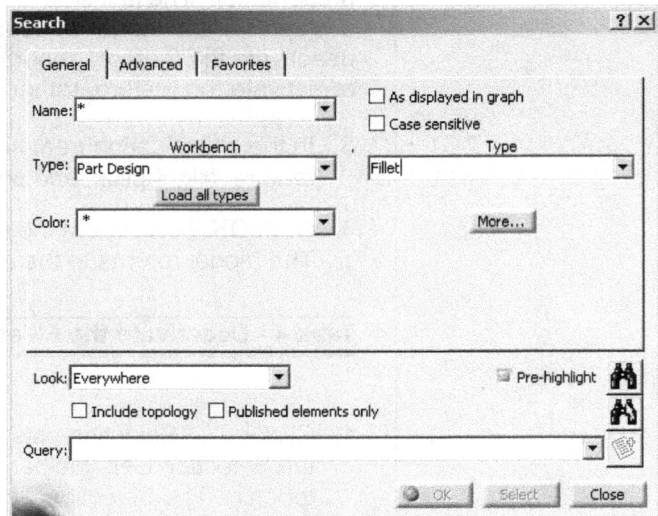

Figure 10–18

6. Click (Search) to start the search. The results of the search is shown in Figure 10–19.

7. In the Search dialog box, click **OK** to add the Fillet features to the selection set. The Fillet feature is highlighted in the model and the specification tree. In the Selection Sets Edition dialog box, *Size* updates to **10**, as shown in Figure 10–20.

10 objects found, 10 pre-selected	
Name	Path
EdgeFillet.1	\ BlockMgt \ PartBody \ EdgeFillet.1
EdgeFillet.2	\ BlockMgt \ PartBody \ EdgeFillet.2
EdgeFillet.3	\ BlockMgt \ PartBody \ EdgeFillet.3
EdgeFillet.4	\ BlockMgt \ PartBody \ EdgeFillet.4
EdgeFillet	\ BlockMgt \ PartBody \ EdgeFillet
EdgeFillet.6	\ BlockMgt \ PartBody \ EdgeFillet.6
EdgeFillet.7	\ BlockMgt \ PartBody \ EdgeFillet.7
EdgeFillet.8	\ BlockMgt \ PartBody \ EdgeFillet.8
EdgeFillet.9	\ BlockMgt \ PartBody \ EdgeFillet.9
EdgeFillet.10	\ BlockMgt \ PartBody \ EdgeFillet.10

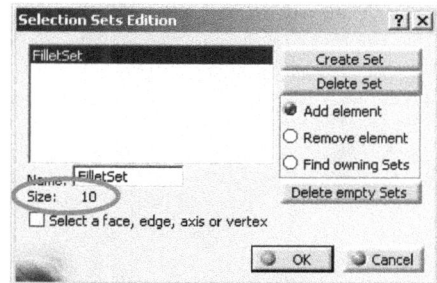

Figure 10–19

Figure 10–20

8. Click **OK** to close the Selection Sets Edition dialog box. The Fillet features should still be selected.

9. In the menu bar, select **Edit>Selected objects>Deactivate**. The Fillet features are deactivated from the model, as shown in Figure 10–21.

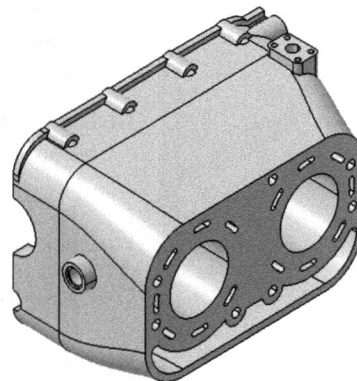

Figure 10–21

10. Clear the Fillet features by clicking in the background.

You can also click

 (Selection sets) to open the Selection Sets Selection dialog box.

11. Click (Find Owning Selection Sets). The Selection Sets Edition dialog box opens as shown in Figure 10–22.

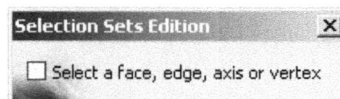

Figure 10–22

12. In the specification tree, select any of the Fillet features. The Selection Sets Selection dialog box opens as shown in Figure 10–23.

Figure 10–23

Design Considerations

When many unnamed or ambiguous selection sets (e.g., groups of fillets) exist and are difficult to distinguish, use **Find Owning Selection Sets** to locate the required set. Selection sets are accessed through the **Selection Sets** icon. Therefore, remember to name your selection sets meaningfully.

13. In the list, select **FilletSet** and click **Select**. Close the Selection Sets Selection dialog box to complete the selection. The Fillet features are highlighted in the specification tree.

14. Right-click on a Fillet feature in the specification tree and select **Selected objects>Activate**.

15. Click ⊞ (Save).

16. Close the file.

Task 5 - Clean up the display of other models.

1. Open three models worked on previously.

2. Practice modifying the display of the models by hiding/showing features. Use the different methods described here.

3. Save the parts and close the windows.

Chapter Review Questions

1. Which of the following feature types can be hidden using the **Hide/Show** command? (Select all that apply.)

   a. Points

   b. Planes

   c. Sketches

   d. Pads

2. Deactivating a feature does not modify children of that feature.

   a. True

   b. False

3. When you deactivate a feature, it continues to be part of the update sequence.

   a. True

   b. False

4. Visible space contains any features that are shown. Invisible space shows features that have been hidden.

   a. True

   b. False

5. A selection set can be used to select individual edges.

   a. True

   b. False

6. By default, sketches that are used to create other features, such as Pads, are automatically hidden from display.

   a. True

   b. False

Answers: 1.abc, 2.b, 3.b, 4.a, 5.a, 6.a

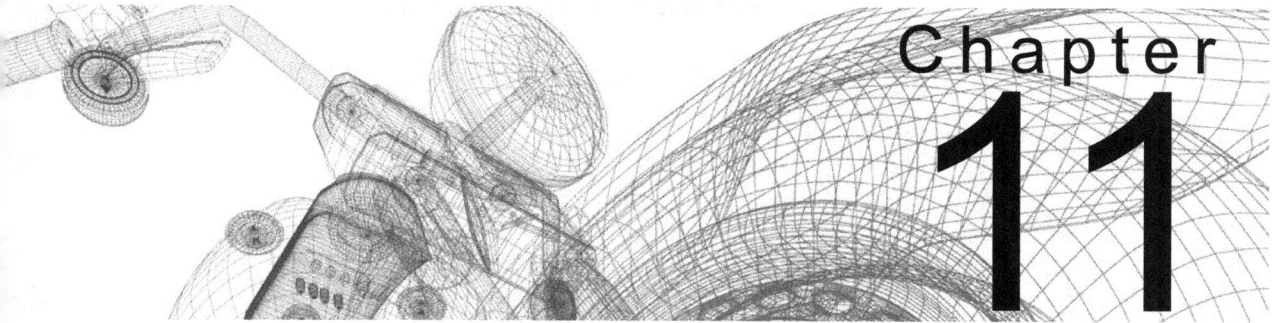

Introduction to Dress-Up Features

In this chapter, you are introduced to three basic types of dress-up features. You learn how to create these features and how to select appropriate references for them. Dress up features enable you to create some of the finishing geometry on your models, such as fillets, chamfers, and holes.

Learning Objectives in this Chapter

- Review the three types of dress-up features.
- Create edge fillets and holes.
- Understand the various selection techniques for edge fillets.
- Understand the five types of holes.
- Learn about chamfer features.
- Understand the Reverse, Symmetric extents, and Corner Cap options.
- Review some best practices for working with dress-up features.

11.1 Dress-Up Features

Figure 11–1 shows the three types of dress-up features available:

- Edge fillet

- Chamfer

- Hole

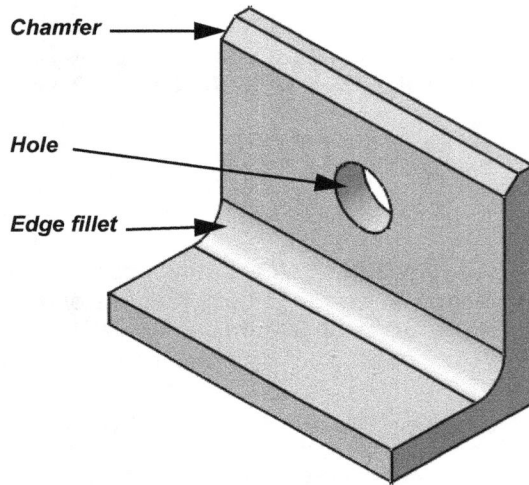

Figure 11–1

A dress-up feature does not require sketching. When you select a dress-up feature for creation, the software implies its shape and you select references, which locate the feature relative to existing geometry.

11.2 Creating Edge Fillets

An **Edge Fillet** is used to round a sharp edge. The software builds circular shaped geometry that is tangent to the two adjacent surfaces of the selected edge, as shown in Figure 11–2.

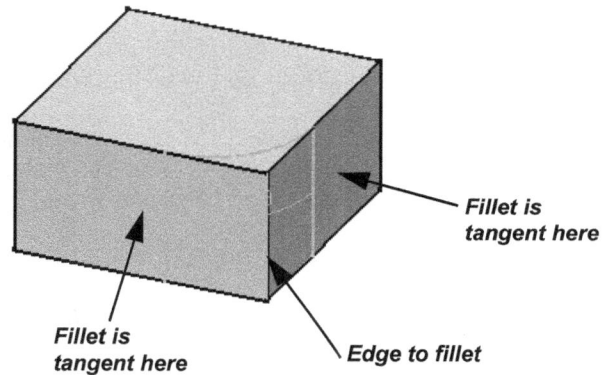

Fillet is tangent here

Fillet is tangent here

Edge to fillet

Figure 11–2

- A fillet can add or remove material in the model, as shown in Figure 11–3.

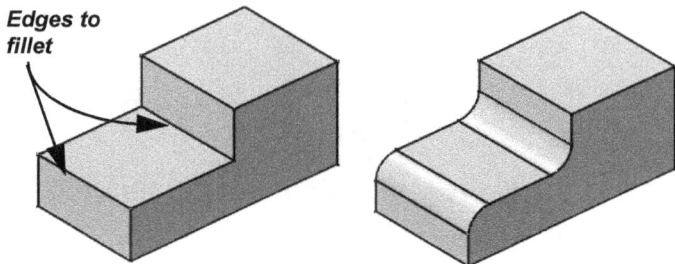

Edges to fillet

Figure 11–3

General Steps

Use the following general steps to create an edge fillet:

1. Identify the edges to be filleted.
2. Select a selection mode.
3. Specify the fillet radius.
4. Complete the feature.

Step 1 - Identify the edges to be filleted.

Click 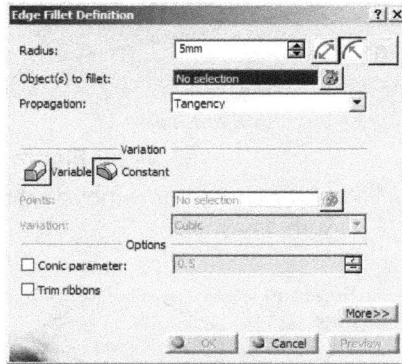 (Edge Fillet) to create a Fillet feature. The Edge Fillet Definition dialog box opens and the *Object(s) to fillet* field is activated. Select the edges and/or faces to fillet. The software adds the selected references to the dialog box, as shown in Figure 11–4.

The references that have been selected can be reviewed by clicking  to open the Fillet objects dialog box, as shown in Figure 11–5. Use this dialog box to review, replace, and remove selected fillet references.

Figure 11–4

Figure 11–5

Edge Identification Methods

Individually Selecting Edges

You can select as many edges as required for one Fillet feature, as shown in Figure 11–6. When preselecting the edges, hold <Ctrl>. Each edge is highlighted in red as you select it. For hidden edges, you can spin the model to select them or set the display to show them.

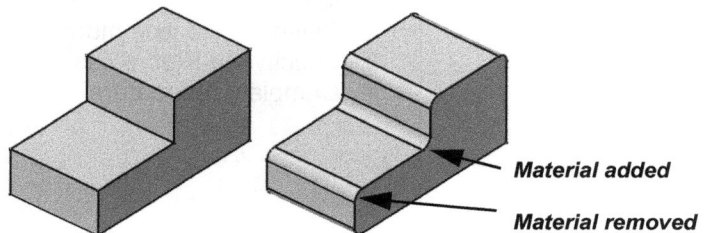

Material added

Material removed

Figure 11–6

Selecting a Surface

When you select an entire surface for filleting, the software automatically highlights all of the edges on the surface's boundary in orange and applies a fillet to each edge, as shown in Figure 11–7. If the surface contains inner edges, those are filleted as well, as shown in Figure 11–8.

Selected surface

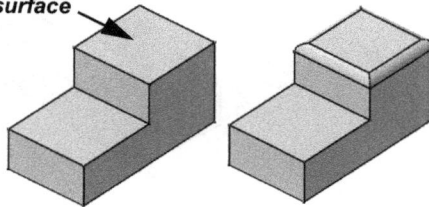 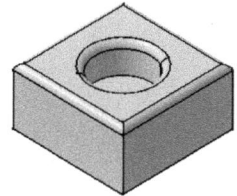

Figure 11–7   **Figure 11–8**

When you select a cylindrical surface for filleting, the software creates fillets on the edges at the top and bottom of the surface, as shown in Figure 11–9.

Select this cylindrical surface

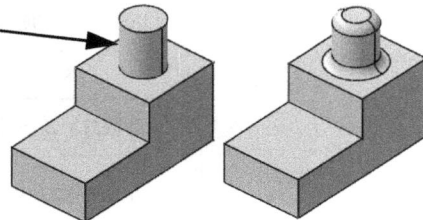

Figure 11–9

Selecting a Vertex.

You can create a fillet on three adjacent edges by selecting a vertex. The software places a fillet on the three intersecting edges, as shown in Figure 11–10.

Select this vertex   Three edges are filleted

Figure 11–10

Combinations

Experiment with different combinations of edge identification methods until you can efficiently select the edges for filleting, as shown in Figure 11–11.

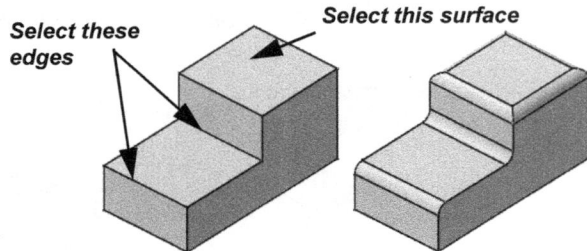

Select these edges

Select this surface

Figure 11–11

Clearing an Edge

To remove an edge or face from the feature at a later time, double-click on the Fillet feature and select the edge you want to remove. The first time you select an edge, it is included in the fillet. The second time you select it, it is removed from the fillet.

Step 2 - Select a selection mode.

When you select an edge to be filleted, the software automatically continues to fillet the adjacent edges that are tangent to your selected edge. This process, known as selection mode, enables you to create fillets more efficiently, without manually select each edge along a continuous chain.

The Edge Fillet Definition dialog box provides options for controlling the selection mode. They are described as follows:

Setting	Description
Tangency	Fillet continues along adjacent edges of selected edge until non-tangency condition is encountered (default value).
Minimal	Disables propagation and only selected edge is filleted.
Intersection	Intersection edges of selected features with the current solid are filleted. In this selection mode, parts features are used instead of part edges.

Intersection with selected features	Intersection edges of selected features are filleted. Part features are used instead of part edges.

- Examples for Tangency and Minimal selection modes are shown in Figure 11–12.

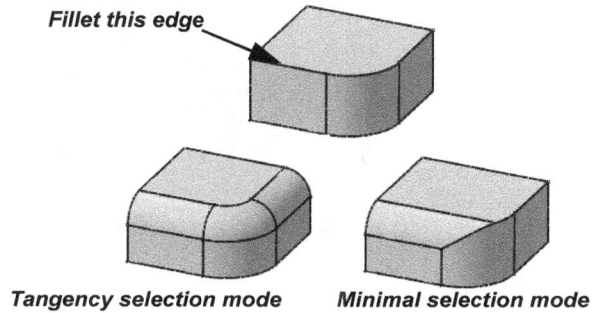

Fillet this edge

Tangency selection mode   **Minimal selection mode**

Figure 11–12

This option is only available when an edge has been selected.

Changing the option for selection mode (for Minimal and Tangency) only works for straight edges. When a curved edge is selected as the reference for a fillet, the software always continues the fillet to adjacent tangent edges.

- An example for Intersection selection mode is shown in Figure 11–13.

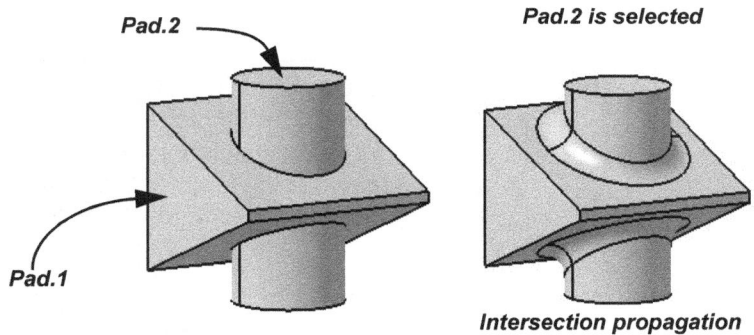

Pad.2

Pad.2 is selected

Pad.1

Intersection propagation

Figure 11–13

- An example for Intersection with selected features is shown in Figure 11–14.

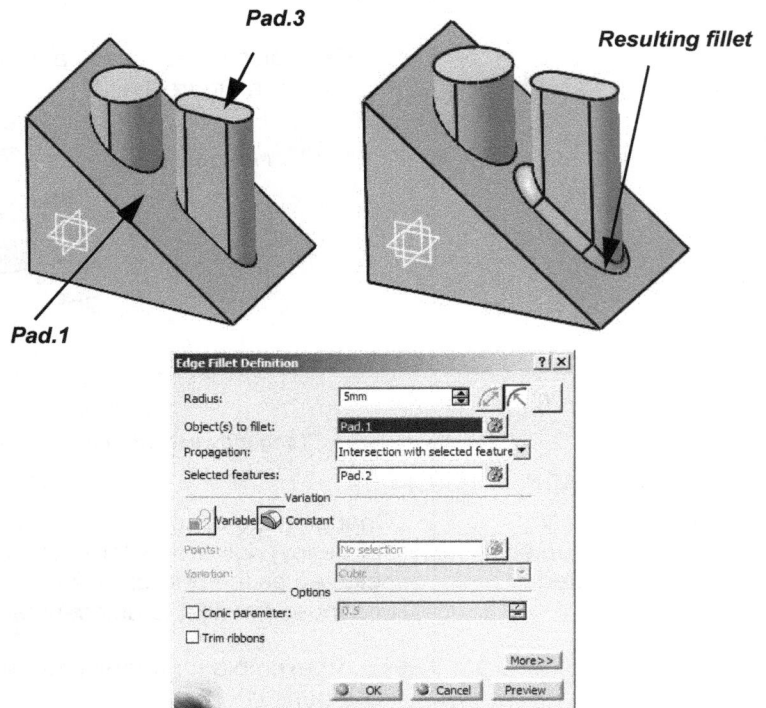

Pad.3

Resulting fillet

Pad.1

Figure 11–14

Step 3 - Specify the fillet radius.

The radius value entered is applied to all of the edge fillets created in the feature. If you want to have separate radius values for the edges, you must create them as separate fillet features.

Step 4 - Complete the feature.

Click **OK** to complete the Edge Fillet feature.

11.3 Creating Chamfers

A Chamfer feature creates a flat, beveled surface between two faces that are adjacent to an edge. Similar to Fillet features, chamfers behave in the following ways:

- They can add or remove material from the model, as shown in Figure 11–15.

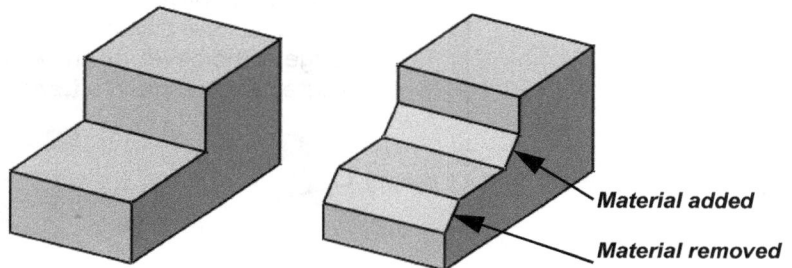

Material added

Material removed

Figure 11–15

- You can select edges or surfaces to be chamfered. When you select a surface, all of the edges on the surface's boundary are chamfered.

- Chamfer features follow the same selection rules as Fillet features, as shown in Figure 11–16.

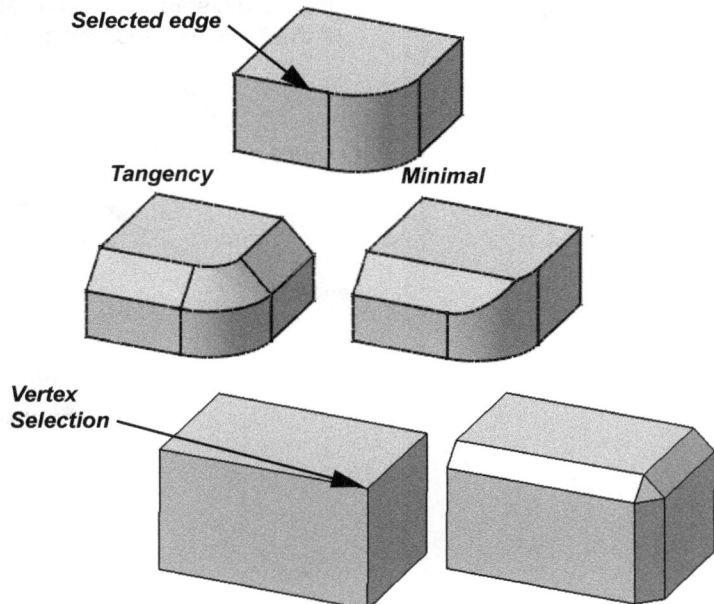

Selected edge

Tangency   *Minimal*

Vertex Selection

Figure 11–16

How To: Create a Chamfer Feature

1. Select the edges to chamfer. Similar to Fillets, chamfer edges can be selected individually, or propagated by using propagation methods.

2. The Dimension mode for a chamfer can be defined in the Mode drop-down list in the Chamfer Definition dialog box. It dictates how the chamfer is dimensioned.

   The **Length1/Angle** option creates a chamfer where the length equals the distance from the edge to be chamfered to the edge of the bevel, as shown in Figure 11–17. The angle is measured with respect to **Length1**).

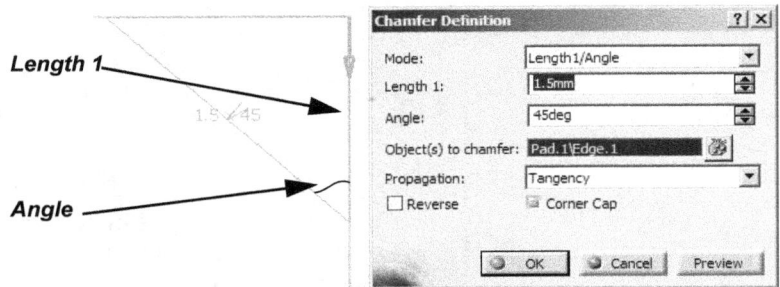

Figure 11–17

Another method of defining the size of the chamfer is to select **Length1/Length2** in the Mode drop-down list. You enter the distance from the edge to be chamfered to the edge of the bevel on each side, as shown in Figure 11–18.

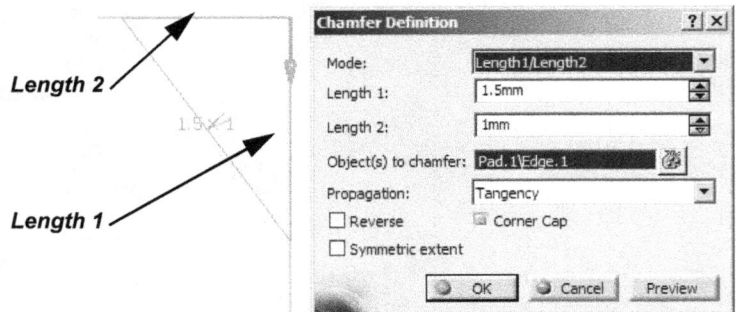

Figure 11–18

3. Select the **Reverse** option in the Chamfer Definition dialog box to flip the direction of the chamfer dimensions. The **Corner Cap** option creates a clean corner when more than two edges converge, as shown in Figure 11–19.

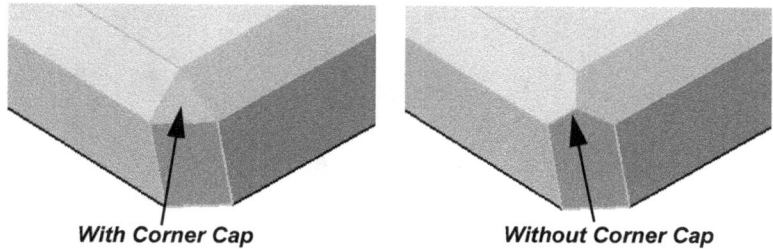

With Corner Cap   **Without Corner Cap**

Figure 11–19

4. Click **OK** to complete the feature.

11.4 Creating Holes

You can create five types of holes, as shown in Figure 11–20.

Simple   *Tapered*   *Counterbored*   *Countersunk*   *Counterdrilled*

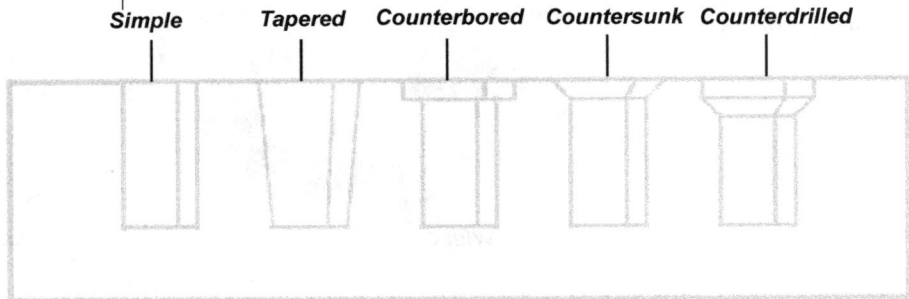

Figure 11–20

The parameters used to define the size of the holes change with each type. The parameter values are set in the Hole Definition dialog box as shown in Figure 11–21.

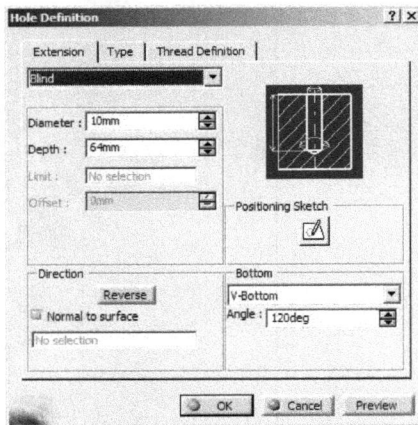

Figure 11–21

- With a simple hole, you must specify the hole diameter and the depth of the hole.

- With a countersunk hole, you must provide the diameter and depth of the hole, and the depth and angle of the countersink.

General Steps

Use the following general steps to create a Hole feature:

1. Select references for the hole.
2. Position the hole.
3. Specify **Hole** options.
4. Complete the feature.

Step 1 - Select references for the hole.

The dimension scheme is initially determined by the references you select. For example, if you select a face on which to locate the hole, and two edges as references the hole has a linear dimensioning scheme, as shown in Figure 11–22.

When selecting references, you must select an edge for locating the hole, not a surface or plane.

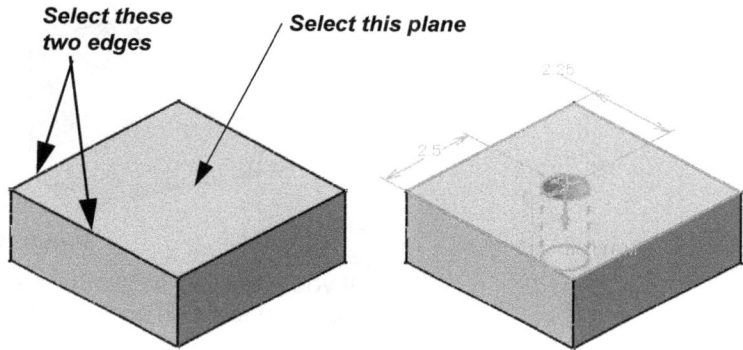

Select these two edges

Select this plane

Figure 11–22

Selecting references to define the location of the hole is optional. You can select the placement plane for the hole and have the software locate the hole at the exact location you selected on the face.

- If you select a surface and a circular edge, the software locates the hole on the plane and coaxial to the center of the circular arc, as shown in Figure 11–23.

You can also select the cylindrical surface as the reference for the coaxial hole.

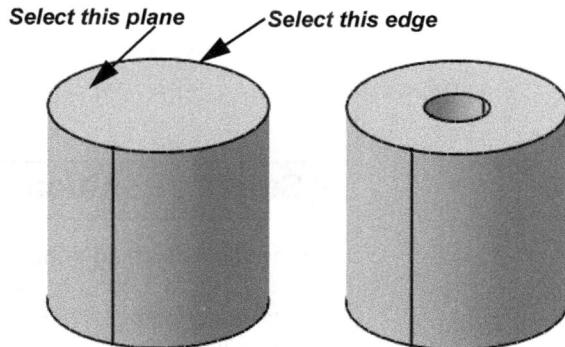

Select this plane

Select this edge

Figure 11–23

- If you preselect a face and a point, the software locates the hole on the plane and it is automatically constrained to the point, as shown in Figure 11–24.

Select this point   *Select this face*

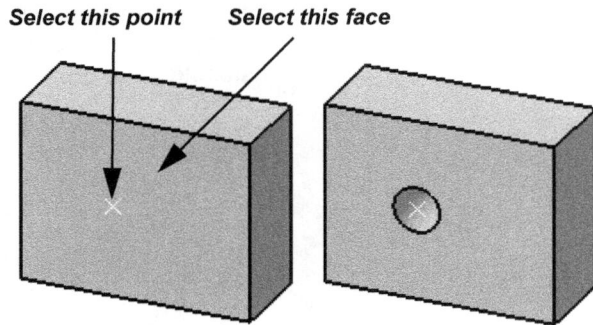

Figure 11–24

- If you preselect a cylindrical surface, the hole is placed at the selected location and normal to the cylindrical surface, as shown in Figure 11–25.

The location of the hole in the cylinder and the distance from the end of the cylinder are undefined.

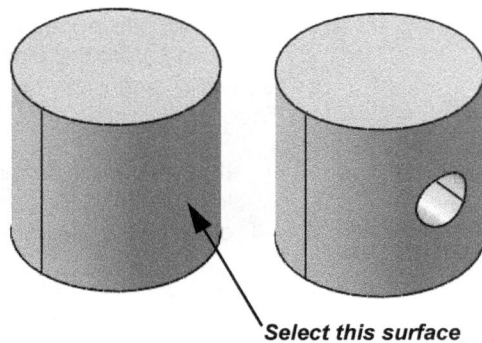

Select this surface

Figure 11–25

Step 2 - Position the hole.

If the dimensioning schemes described above do not capture your design intent, click ⬛ in the Hole Definition dialog box to manually create dimensions that locate the feature. When you enter the Sketcher workbench, the center of the hole is marked with an asterisk (*). You can drag the asterisk to a new location and create dimensions to the asterisk from edges, surfaces, or planes.

A positioning sketch is used to locate a hole in a circle with an angle dimension, as shown in Figure 11–26. A construction circle is used to define the diameter of the bolt circle, and an axis is used to locate the asterisk around the circle.

An asterisk marks the
hole center.

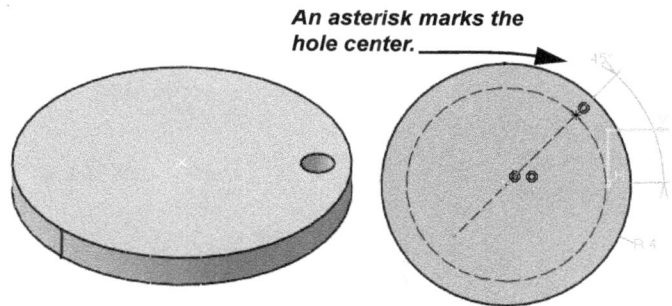

Figure 11–26

Figure 11–27 shows an example of a hole on a cylindrical face. If you want to precisely locate the hole, you can use the positioning sketch to dimension the asterisk vertically on the cylinder. You can also apply a coincidence constraint between the asterisk and a plane that passes through the center of the cylinder.

An asterisk is
coincident with the
angled plane.

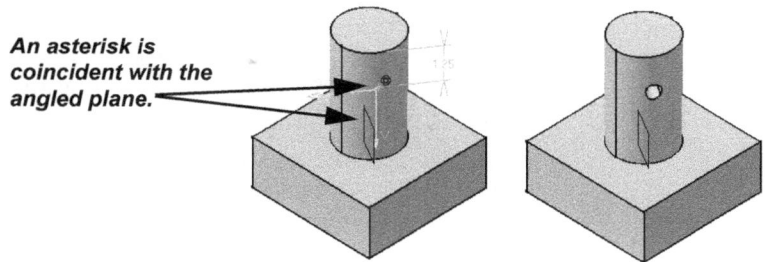

Figure 11–27

Positioning sketches can also be used to constrain holes that are initially created as unconstrained.

Step 3 - Specify Hole options.

Depth Options

The **Blind** hole depth option is identical to the **Dimension** depth option for pads and pockets.

Similar to previously discussed features, there are many options available for you to capture your design intent of the hole, as shown in Figure 11–28.

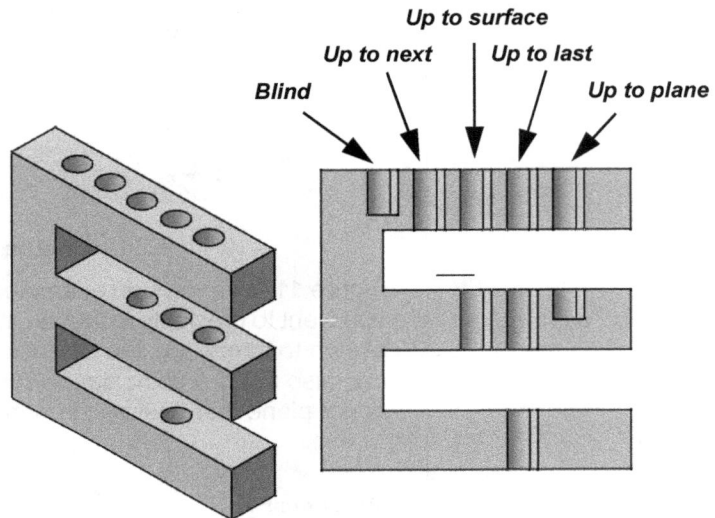

Figure 11–28

Hole features that have a depth option other than **Blind** can take advantage of the offset parameter, as shown in Figure 11–29. The default offset value of **0** can be changed to a positive value to extend the hole deeper or to a negative value to make the hole shallower.

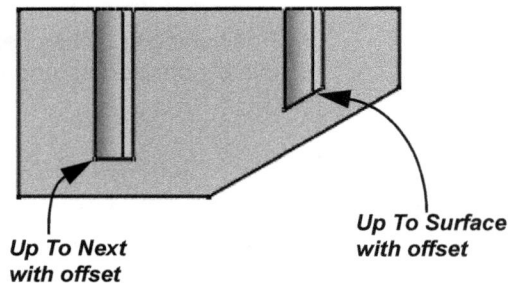

Figure 11–29

If you do not know the exact depth of a **Blind** hole, you can select the BOTTOM tag on the screen and dynamically drag the hole to a depth that suits your preferences.

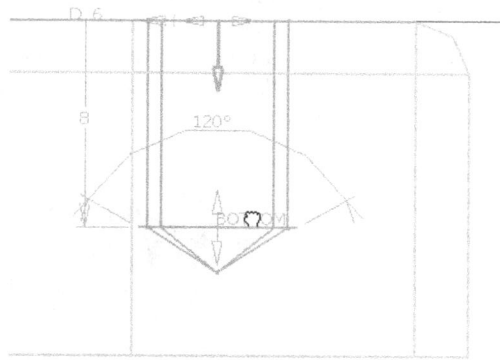

Figure 11–30

By default, the first **Blind** depth hole created will default to
V-Bottom. You can specify an angle of the sharp point, as
shown in Figure 11–31.

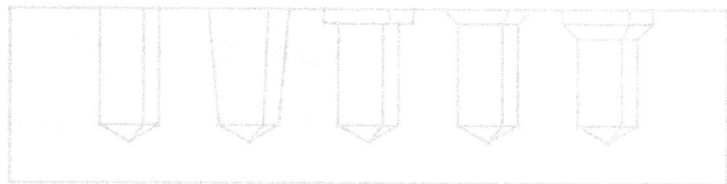

Figure 11–31

You can change the bottom option to **Flat**, resulting in a hole
similar to that shown in Figure 11–32.

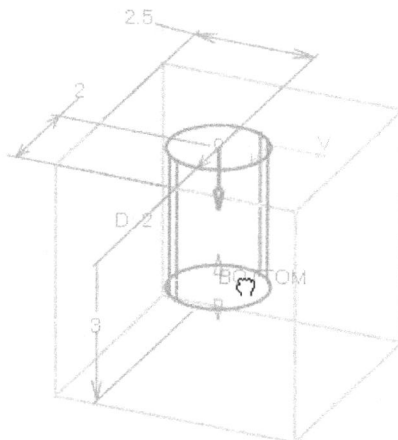

Figure 11–32

Any subsequent holes will default to the setting of the previously
created hole.

Hole Direction

You can zoom in and drag the hole-to-edge dimensions outside the geometry for easier access.

When you select the planar face of an existing feature to create a hole, it removes material on one side of that plane only, as shown in Figure 11–33. Click **Reverse** in the Hole Definition dialog box to drill the hole in the opposite direction.

Hole placement plane

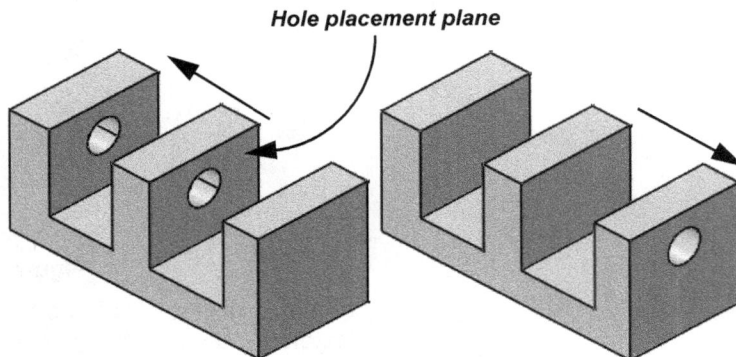

Figure 11–33

Step 4 - Complete the feature.

Click **OK** to complete the Hole feature.

11.5 Modeling Considerations

Use the following guidelines when working with dress-up features:

- Do not locate features on the tangent edges of fillets or the beveled edges of chamfers, as shown in Figure 11–34. This establishes a parent/child relationship between these features. If the parent feature (fillet or chamfer) is deleted from the model, the child feature fails and requires additional work to maintain the geometry over time.

Do not locate dimensions to tangent edges of fillets

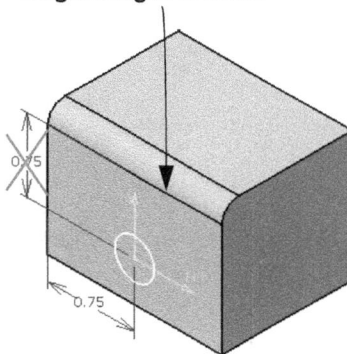

Locate dimensions to a planar surface

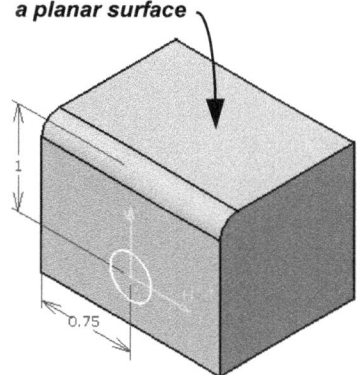

Figure 11–34

- When creating a dimension in the Normal view, the software creates a dimension to the first edge. Figure 11–34 shows the vertical dimension that was created to the tangent edge of the Fillet. It is recommended to orient the model in a 3D view and dimension from the circle's center to a planar surface.

- To prevent the above scenario, put fillets and chamfers into the model as late as possible in the design.

- Create holes, fillets, and chamfers as separate features instead of including them in one sketch for a Pad feature, as shown in Figure 11–35. This makes it easier for you to make changes to the model at a later time and enables you to create your sketches more quickly.

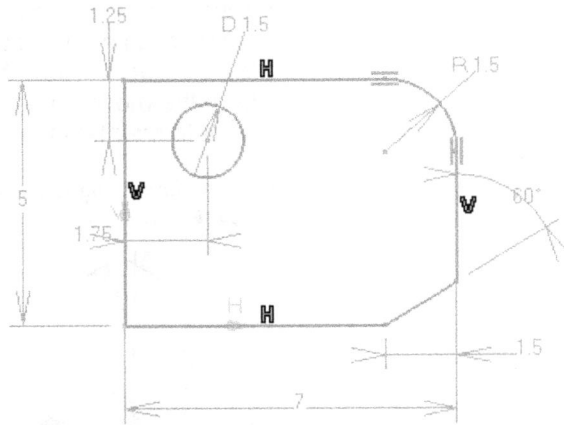

Figure 11–35

Practice 11a	# Creating Holes, Fillets, and Chamfers

Practice Objectives

- Create a Fillet feature using several edge selection methods.
- Create and change Chamfer features.
- Create Hole features.

In this practice, you will add various dress-up features such as holes, fillets, and chamfers to a part, as shown in Figure 11–36. You will learn how different hole placement methods are affected as a model is modified, how different edge selection techniques can be used to create a Fillet feature, and how to create a Chamfer feature.

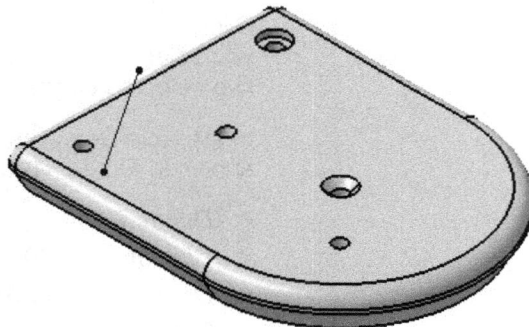

Figure 11–36

Task 1 - Create a hole that is located to two sides of the part.

1. Click [Open icon] (Open).

2. Select **Dressup_Features.CATPart** and click **Open**.

Design Considerations

This hole will reference two edges of the part. By preselecting the face and two edges, the hole is automatically created on the face and references the two selected edges. This method enables the Hole feature to update with the edges if the part is modified. The hole will always remain a set distance from the edges.

3. Select the top face of the part, as shown in Figure 11–37. The face's edge highlights in orange.

4. Hold <Ctrl> and select the two edges, as shown in Figure 11–37. The selected edges highlight in red.

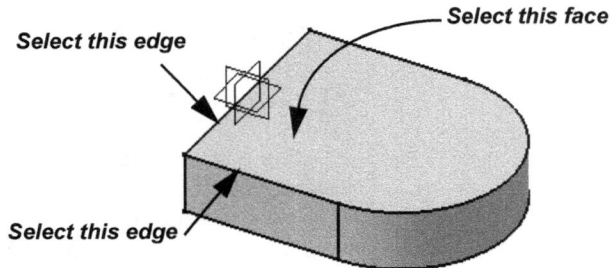

Figure 11–37

5. Click (Hole). A hole is placed in the exact location where you selected the face. The hole is also dimensioned to the two selected edges.

6. In the Hole Definition dialog box, set the following options, as shown in Figure 11–38.

- *Depth*: **Blind**
- *Diameter*: **25.00 (0.984 in)**
- *Depth*: **63.50 (2.500 in)**
- Bottom drop-down list: **V-Bottom**
- *Angle*: **135**

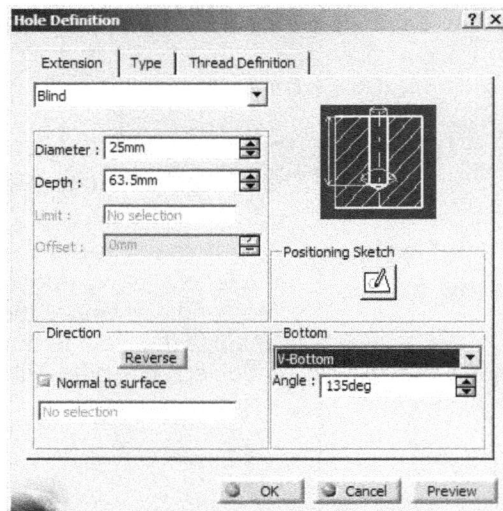

Figure 11–38

7. Double-click on the edge-to-hole dimensions in the model and set each value to **75.00 (2.953 in)**, as shown in Figure 11–39.

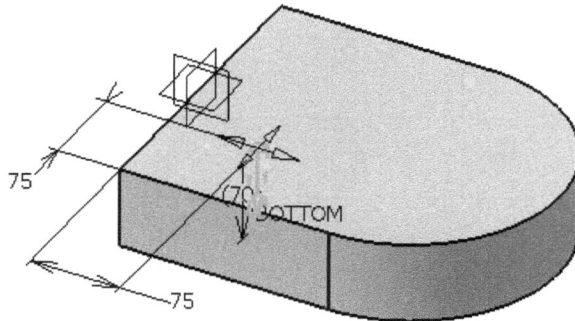

Figure 11–39

8. Click **OK** to complete the feature.

Task 2 - Create a hole at the center of an arc.

Design Considerations

By preselecting the face and arc, the hole is automatically created at the center of the arc. Using this method enables the Hole feature to remain centered on the part. If the arc radius is increased or decreased, the hole always remains at the center regardless of how far apart the edges move.

1. Select the top face of the part again, hold <Ctrl> and select the curved edge of the arc, as shown in Figure 11–40.

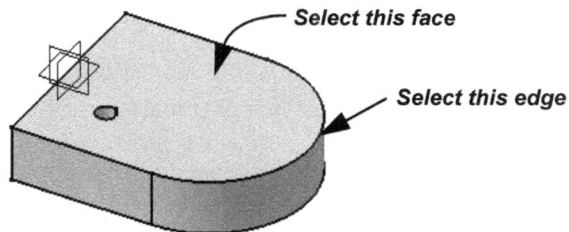

Figure 11–40

2. Click [icon] (Hole). A new hole is placed at the center of the arc. Note that the hole has the same characteristics as the previous hole, such as *Diameter*, *Depth*, and *Bottom* settings.

3. Select **Up to Last** for the depth.

4. In the dialog box, select the *Type* tab and select **Countersunk** for the hole.

5. Enter **12.50** (0.492 in) as *Depth* of the countersink, as shown in Figure 11–41.

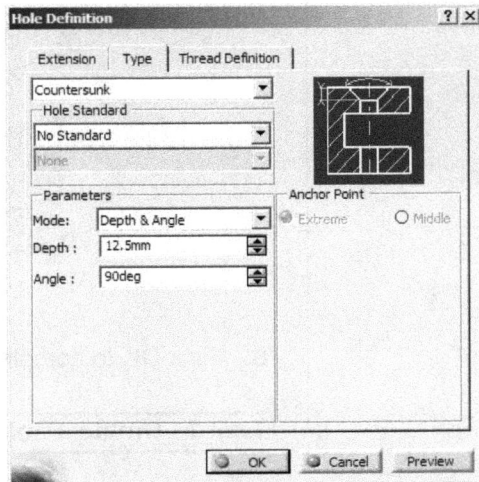

Figure 11–41

6. Click **OK** to complete the feature.

Task 3 - Create an under constrained hole.

Design Considerations

This hole will be placed on the surface of the part. It will not be constrained to any edges. If the part is modified, the hole's position will remain unaffected due to the lack of constraints.

1. Select the top face of the part and click (Hole). A Hole feature is placed at the exact location that you selected on the top face, as shown in Figure 11–42. Since you did not select any edges or surfaces to which the hole is located, its position is unconstrained.

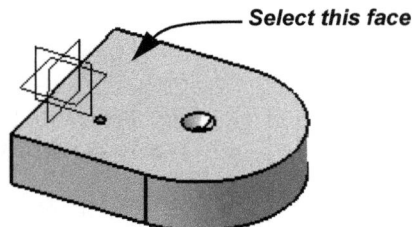

— *Select this face*

Figure 11–42

2. In the dialog box, select the *Type* tab and select **Counterbored** for the hole.

3. Set the following:

   - *Diameter:* **50.00 (1.969 in)**
   - *Depth*: **12.50 (0.492 in)** (default value)

4. Click **OK** to complete the feature.

Task 4 - Make the part wider to see the impact of constrained and under-constrained features.

---

1. On the model or in the specification tree, double-click on the Pad feature to display the dimensional constraints.

2. Change the 250 (9.843 in) dimension as **380 (14.961 in)** and the 300 (11.811 in) dimension as **625 (24.606 in)**, as shown in Figure 11–43.

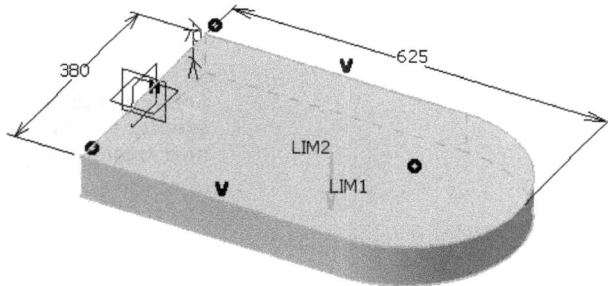

Figure 11–43

3. Click **OK** to complete the change. The first hole remains **75.00** (2.953 in) from each edge, as shown in Figure 11–44. The countersunk hole remains coaxial with the center of the arc. The counterbored hole remains in the same location at which it was originally placed.

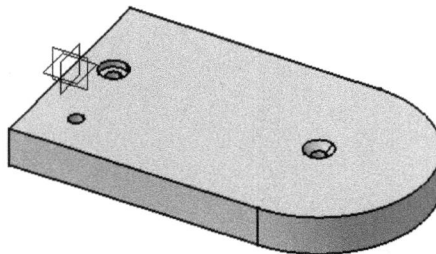

Figure 11–44

Task 5 - Change the counterbore hole to have dimensional constraints.

1. Double-click on the counterbored hole to begin the process of editing the feature.

2. In the Hole Definition dialog box, click ⬛ to enter the Sketcher workbench to dimension the location of the hole.

3. The asterisk (*) indicates the current location of the hole center. Select and drag the asterisk closer to the left side of the part as shown in Figure 11–45.

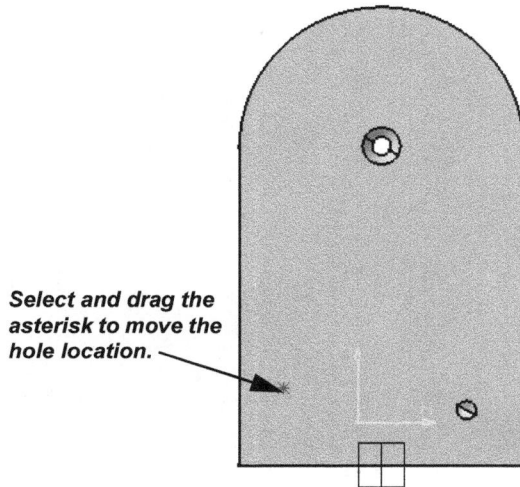

Select and drag the asterisk to move the hole location.

Figure 11–45

4. Double-click on ⬛ (Constraint) and create dimensional constraints from the asterisk to the two edges of the model, as shown in Figure 11–46.

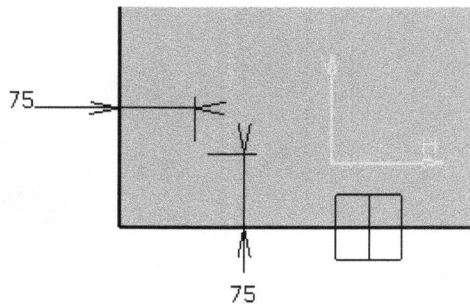

Figure 11–46

5. Set the values to **75.00 (2.953 in)** for each dimension.

6. Click ⬆ (Exit workbench) to exit the sketching environment.

7. Click **OK** to complete the feature.

8. Change the width of the Pad feature from 380 (14.961 in) to **500 (19.685 in)** to verify that the counterbored hole works with the design intent. The part displays as shown in Figure 11–47.

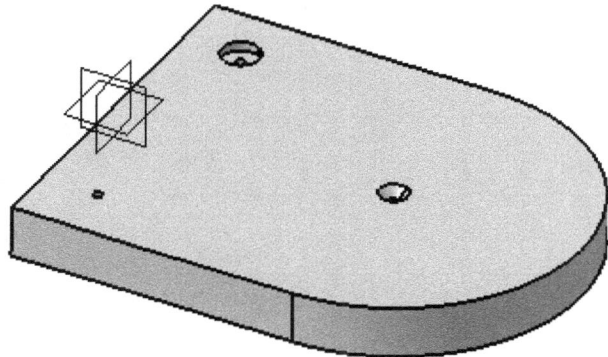

Figure 11–47

Task 6 - Create another simple hole.

Design Considerations

You will create this hole similar to the counterbored hole you previously created. However, you will use the positioning sketch function to develop a radial dimensioning scheme for the hole.

1. Select the top face of the part and click ▣ (Hole). Set the following:

   • *Depth type*: **Blind**
   • *Depth value*: **25.0 (0.984 in)**
   • *Bottom*: **Flat**

2. Select the *Type* tab and select **Simple** for the *hole type*.

3. Return to the *Extension* tab and click ✎.

4. Ensure that ⊙ (Construction/Standard Element) is highlighted, and click ⊙ (Circle). Sketch a construction circle that is approximately centered on the countersunk hole, as shown in Figure 11–48.

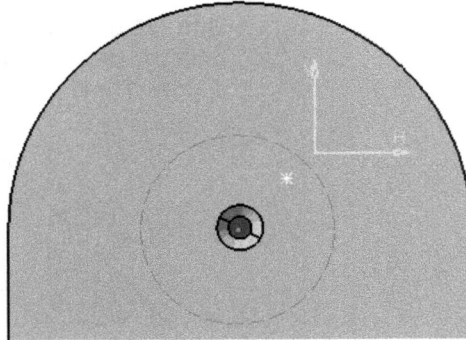

Figure 11–48

5. Select the construction circle, hold <Ctrl> and select the large arc of the Pad feature. Click 🗔 (Constraints Defined in Dialog Box).

6. Select the **Concentricity** constraint and click **OK**.

7. Select the construction circle, hold <Ctrl> and select the asterisk. Click 🗔 (Constraints Defined in Dialog Box).

8. Select the **Coincidence** constraint and click **OK**.

9. Create the diameter dimension for the construction circle.

10. Change the *circle diameter* to **265 (10.433 in)**, as shown in Figure 11–49.

11. The final item required in the positioning sketch is an angle dimension for the location of the hole around the circle. Click ⎢ (Axis) to create an axis.

12. Sketch the line passing through the center of the construction circle and the asterisk, as shown in Figure 11–49.

13. Create the angle dimension between the axis and the vertical plane.

14. Change the *Angle value* to **45**, as shown in Figure 11–49.

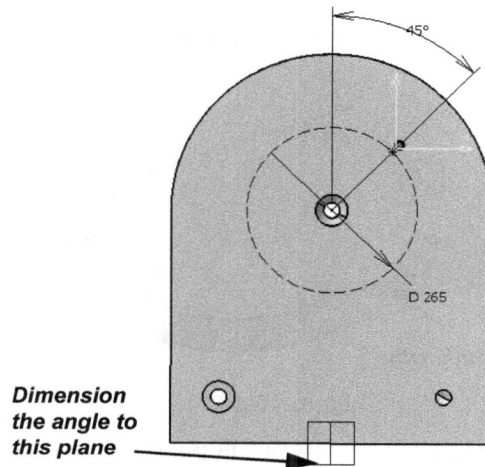

Figure 11–49

15. Click ⬆ (Exit workbench) to exit the sketching environment.

16. Click **OK** to complete the feature.

___

Task 7 - Create a Fillet feature on the top edge of the Pad.

___

1. Click 🖻 (Edge Fillet) to create a Fillet feature.

2. Select the straight edge of the Pad feature, as shown in Figure 11–50.

3. Enter **25.00 (0.984 in)** for *Radius* and click **Preview**. The fillet continues beyond the selected edge and stops when it reaches a sharp corner, as shown in Figure 11–51. This is a result of the default **Tangency** selection mode.

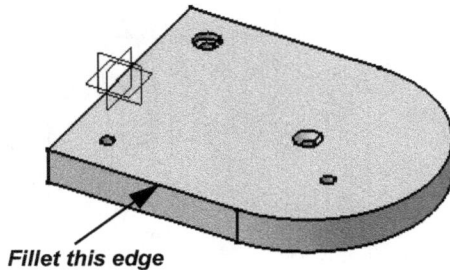

Fillet this edge

Figure 11–50

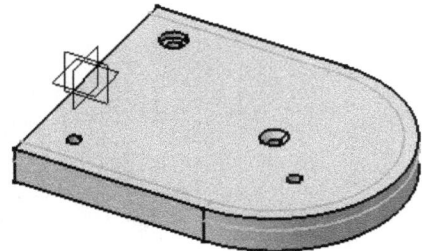

Figure 11–51

*When prompted with a warning that the edges will be replaced by normal edges, click **OK**.*

4. In the Selection mode drop-down list, select **Minimal.** Click **Preview** again. Only the selected edge is filleted.

5. Return the selection mode to **Tangency**.

6. The Objects to fillet lists one edge. Select the three edges to be filleted, as shown in Figure 11–52. You can rotate the model or switch to hidden line display to select the hidden edge.

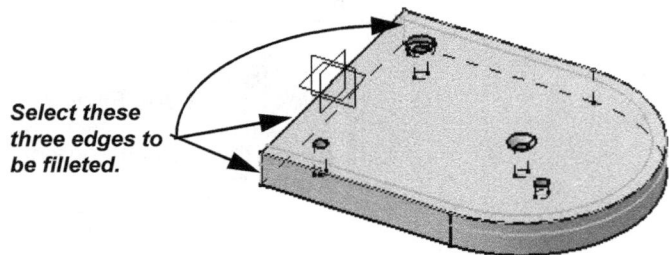

Select these three edges to be filleted.

Figure 11–52

7. Click **OK** to complete the feature.

Task 8 - Create a Chamfer feature on the bottom edge.

1. Click ▱ (Chamfer) to create a Chamfer feature and select the bottom edge of the part, as shown in Figure 11–53.

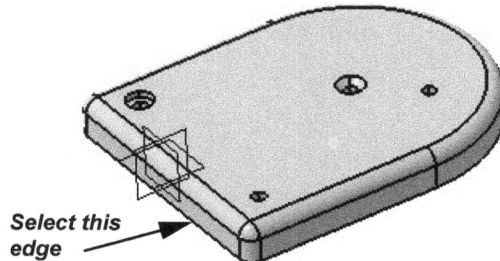

Select this edge

Figure 11–53

2. Set the following:

   - *Length 1*: **38.00 (1.496 in)**
   - *Angle*: **30**

3. Go to the **Front** quick view and zoom in on the chamfered edge.

4. Set the *Display* to **Wireframe (NHR)**.

5. Click the **Reverse** option a few times and note that it enables you to flip the direction of the chamfer, as shown in Figure 11–54.

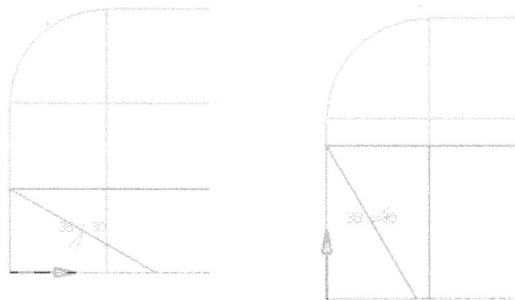

Figure 11–54

6. Keep the **Reverse** option selected, click **OK** to complete the feature, and then return the view mode to

 (Shading With Edges) and click (Isometric View). The model displays as shown in Figure 11–55.

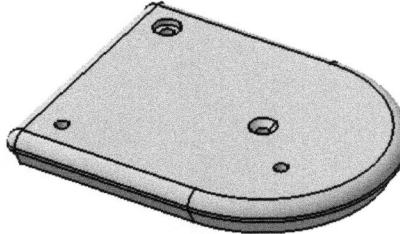

Figure 11–55

Task 9 - Create an angled hole.

In this task, you will create an angled hole. The angle of the hole will be controlled by a line you will create.

1. Click (Line).

2. In the Line type drop-down list, select **Angle/Normal to curve**. Right-click in each of the following fields and set the following options:

   • *Curve*: **Z Axis**
   • *Support*: **ZX plane**
   • *Point*: **Create Point**

3. Using the **Coordinates** point type, create the point. Locate the point at **0, 0, 0**, as shown in Figure 11–56.

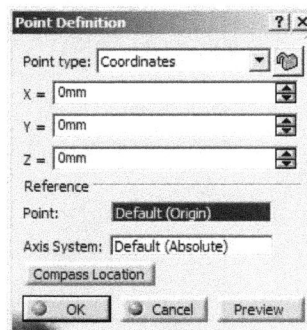

Figure 11–56

4. Click **OK** to create the point and return to the Line Definition dialog box. Set the following:

   - *Angle:* **135**
   - *End:* **150 (5.906 in)**

5. Click **OK** to complete the line. The line displays as shown in Figure 11–57.

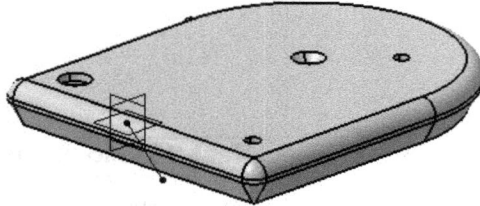

Figure 11–57

6. Create a new Hole feature anywhere on the top surface of the model. Set the following:

   - *Type* tab:
     - *Change Counterbored to* **Simple**
   - *Extension* tab:
     - *Diameter:* **25mm (0.984 in)**
     - *Depth*: **50mm (1.969 in)**

7. Clear the **Normal to surface** option located at the bottom left corner of the Hole Definition dialog box and set *Bottom* to **Flat**. Select the line you just created, as shown in Figure 11–58.

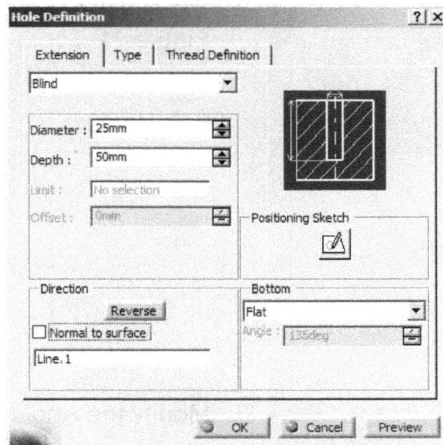

Figure 11–58

8. Complete the feature. The model displays as shown in Figure 11–59.

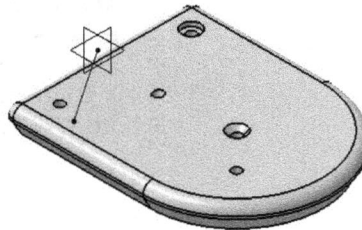

Figure 11–59

Task 10 - Modify the line angle.

Design Considerations

The angle of this Hole feature can now be controlled by modifying the Line feature used to define the direction.

1. Select the *Left* quick view and change the *Display* to **Wireframe (NHR)**. The angled hole displays as shown in Figure 11–60.

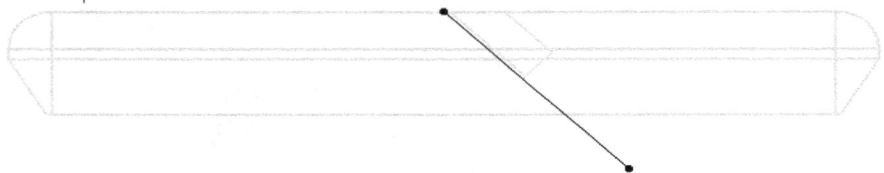

For clarity, the other hole features have been deactivated

Figure 11–60

2. Expand the Line feature in the specification tree, as shown in Figure 11–61.

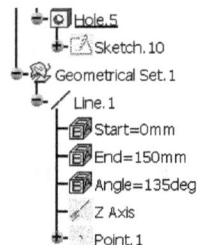

Figure 11–61

3. Modify the Angle parameter. Change the *Angle* to **155**.

4. The angle of the hole updates.

5. Save and close the file.

Practice 11b | (Optional) Link

Practice Objective

- Create a part without instructional steps.

Create the **Link.CATPart** shown in Figure 11–62.

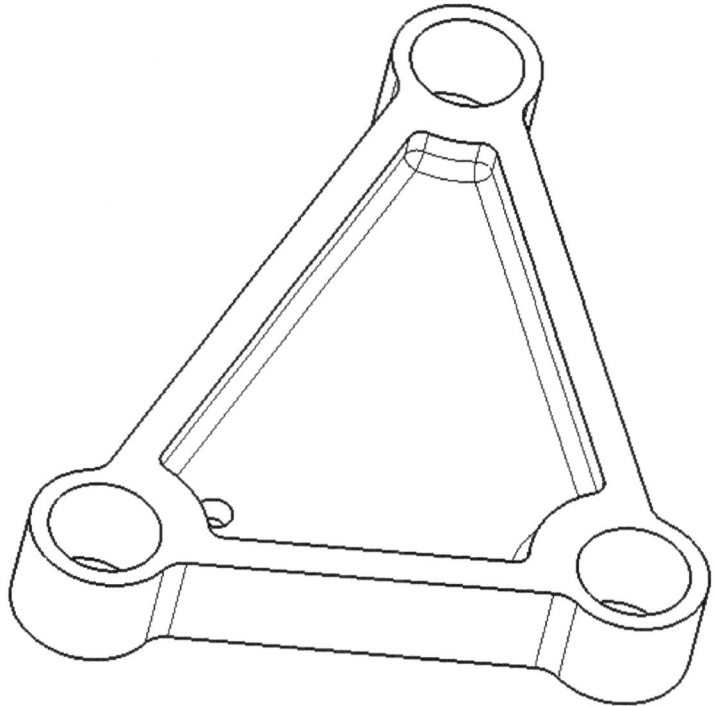

Figure 11–62

Drawing views are shown in Figure 11–63.

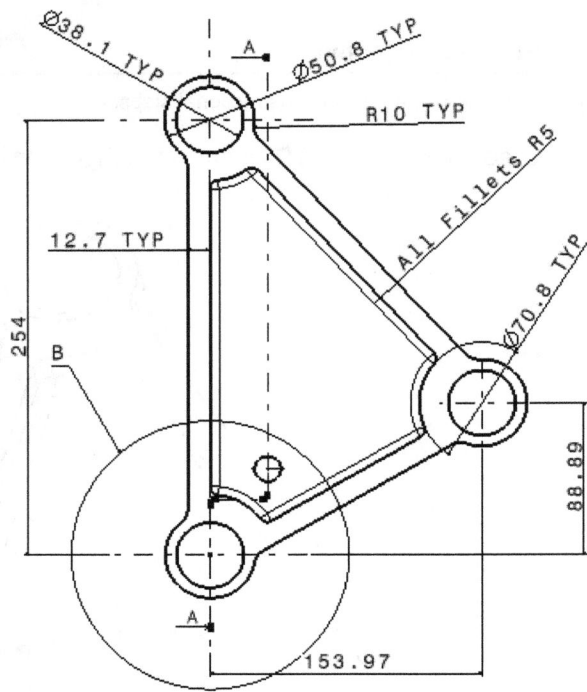

Front view
Scale: 1:1

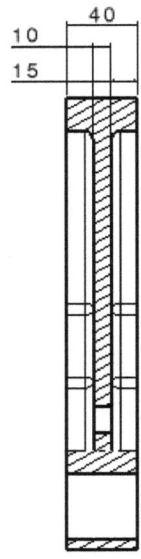

Section view A-A
Scale: 1:1

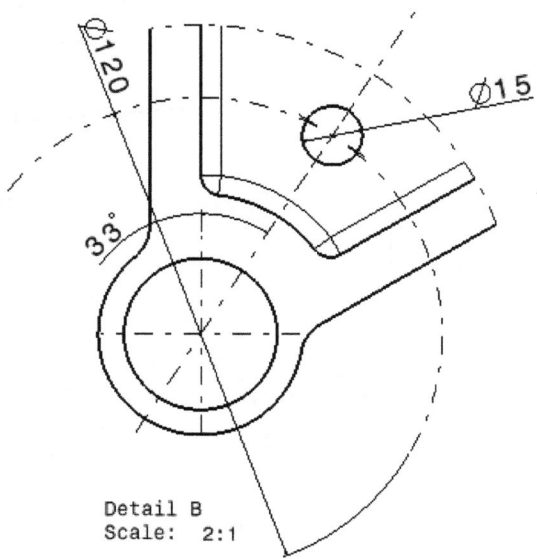

Detail B
Scale: 2:1

Figure 11–63

Practice 11c | (Optional) Crankshaft

Practice Objective

- Create a part without instructional steps.

Create the **Crankshaft.CATPart** shown in Figure 11–64.

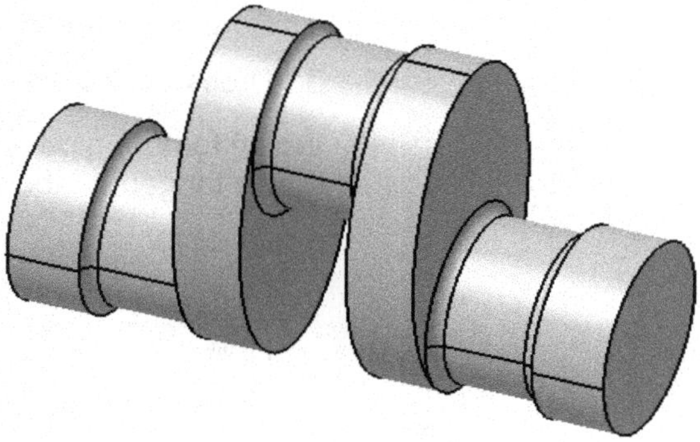

Figure 11–64

Drawing views are shown in Figure 11–65.

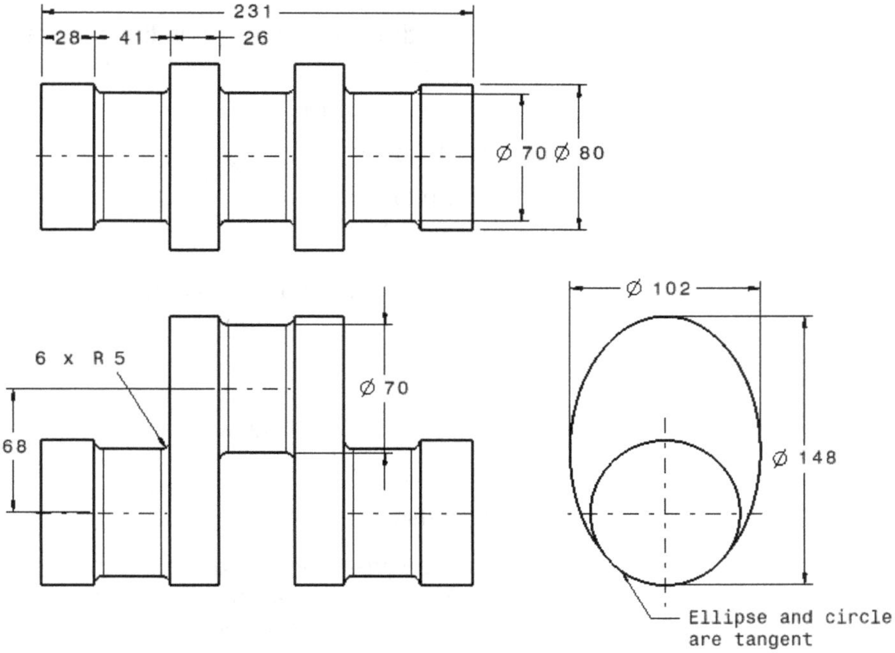

Figure 11–65

Chapter Review Questions

1. _____ features represent features for which a shape is predefined.

   a. Sketched Features

   b. Solid Features

   c. Surface Features

   d. Dress-up features

2. Which feature type taught in this chapter creates a feature that is tangent to the adjacent faces of the resultant feature?

   a. Chamfer

   b. Fillet

   c. Hole

   d. None of the above.

3. Fillets on multiple edges can be controlled by one dimension.

   a. True

   b. False

4. Select the hole depth option that requires you to specify a dimension.

   a. Up to Surface

   b. Up to Next

   c. Up to Last

   d. Blind

5. Fillets can add or remove material.

   a. True

   b. False

6. Chamfer features always remove material.

   a. True

   b. False

7. You can create a coaxial Hole without entering the sketcher workbench by preselecting the planar surface and circular edge of the cylindrical feature.

   a. True

   b. False

8. Why is it considered bad practice to dimension to filleted or chamfered edges?

   a. Dimensioning to filleted or chamfered edges creates a parent/child relationship.

   b. If the fillet/chamfer is deleted, the child features are also deleted.

   c. It is better to dimension to stable features that are not likely to be removed or dramatically changed.

   d. All of the above.

Answers: 1.d, 2.b, 3.a, 4.d, 5.a, 6.b, 7.a, 8.d

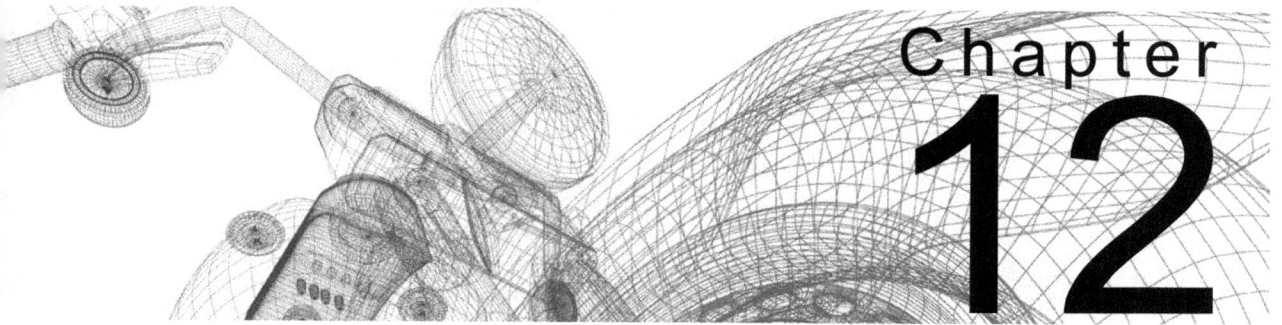

Advanced Dress-Up Features

In this chapter you learn how to work with various types of fillets to further refine your designs. Additionally, you learn how to effectively use dress-up features such as the Shell, Draft and Pocket features to modify and manipulate the geometry model to better fulfill the desired design intent.

Learning Objectives in this Chapter

- Use the various fillet types, such as Variable Radius, Tritangent, Face-face, and Chordal.
- Use a uniform wall thickness by creating a Shell feature.
- Select individual surfaces to shell with unique thicknesses.
- Create pad and pocket features that automatically contain draft and filleted edges.
- Learn how the order in which features are created affects the resulting geometry.
- Learn how to reorder features.

12.1 Additional Fillet Features

The Edge Fillet feature is the most basic of the fillet features. The four additional Fillet features are:

* Variable Radius

* Tritangent

* Face-face

* Chordal

Variable Radius Fillet

When using a **Variable Radius Fillet**, a different radius value can be entered at locations along the edge. To create a variable radius fillet, click ⬚ (Edge Fillet) to open the Edge Fillet Definition dialog box, then click ⬚ (Variable), as shown in Figure 12–1.

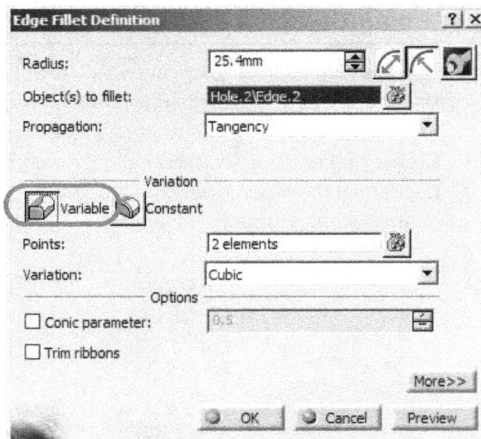

Figure 12–1

A Variable Radius fillet allows for varying radius values at the vertices and points along the selected edge, as shown in Figure 12–2.

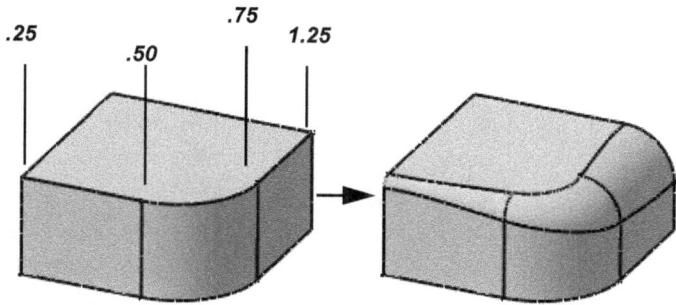

Figure 12–2

When you begin the creation of a variable radius fillet, the software assigns the entered *Radius* value to each end of the selected chain of edges, as shown in Figure 12–3.

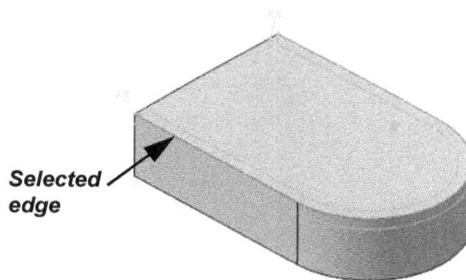

Selected
edge

Figure 12–3

You can add or remove vertices or points along the edge in the *Points* field in the Variable Radius Fillet Definition dialog box, as shown in Figure 12–4. The software adds a radius value at that location. To change a radius value, double-click on it and enter a new value.

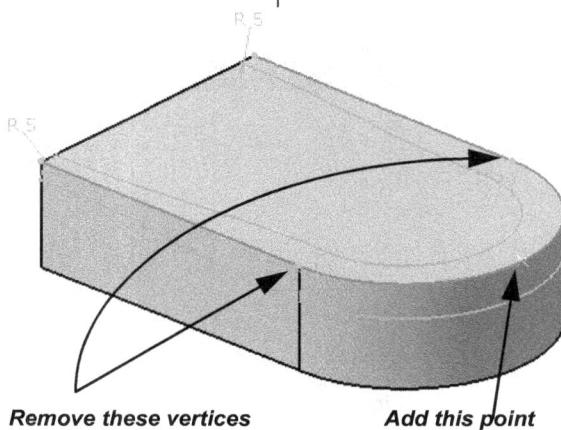

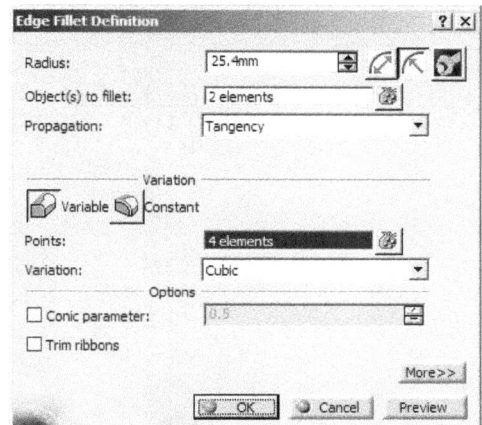

Remove these vertices   *Add this point*

Figure 12–4

To remove a point or vertex, select the point near the dimension on the model. In addition, [icon] can be clicked in the Variable Radius Fillet Definition dialog box to display a list of points, as shown in Figure 12–5. To remove a point from the Point Elements dialog box, select the point and click **Preview**.

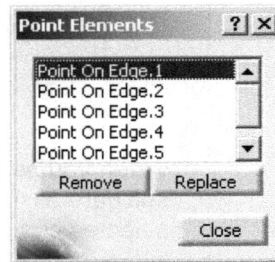

Figure 12–5

You can also use reference planes to identify where you want to control a variable radius fillet. The software intersects the plane with an edge and places a radius dimension at that location.

- To quickly edit all of the variable radius values, click

  [icon] (Edit Fillet Values) to open the Fillet Values dialog box as shown in Figure 12–6.

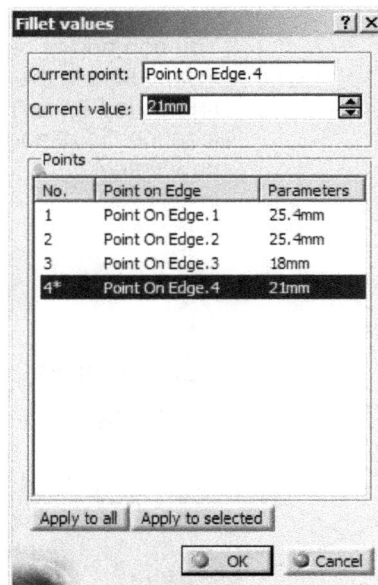

Figure 12–6

- **Apply to all** enables you to edit individual radius values and set all of the values to be the same.

- **Apply to selected** enables you to select several values and set them to be the same.

Note that you can change back to a constant radius fillet by clicking ![icon] (Constant) in the Edge Fillet Definition dialog box. If you added any additional radius points for a variable radius round however, they will be lost.

Tritangent Fillet

A **Tritangent Fillet** creates a fillet that is tangent to three surfaces, as shown in Figure 12–7.

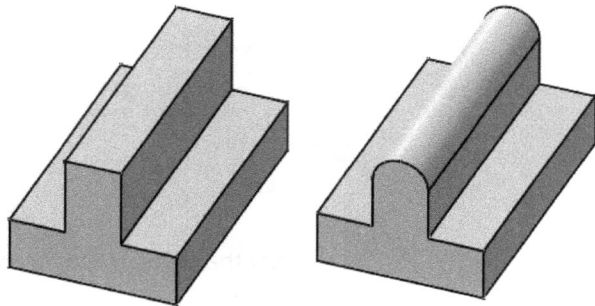

Figure 12–7

To create a tritangent fillet, click ![icon] (Tritangent Fillet) and specify two faces to fillet and a face to be removed, as shown in Figure 12–8. Faces can also be preselected; however, you must select the two parallel faces to be filleted first and then select the face to be removed.

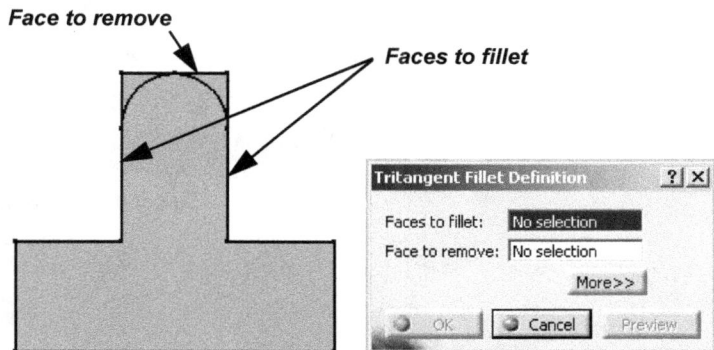

Figure 12–8

The three faces you specify for the tritangent fillet do not need to be planar or parallel, as shown in Figure 12–9.

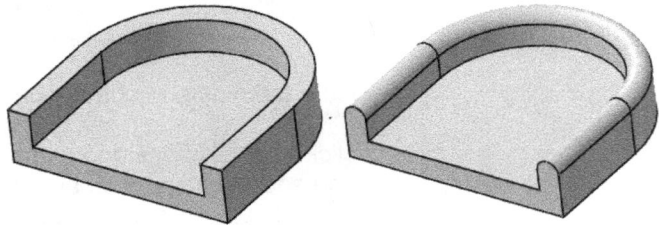

Figure 12–9

You can trim tritangent fillets to a plane, face, or surface by clicking **More** in the Tritangent Fillet Definition dialog box and clicking the *Limiting element(s)* field, as shown in Figure 12–10.

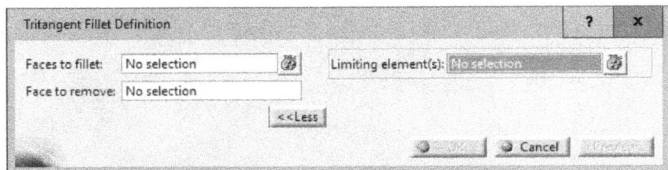

Figure 12–10

Select the plane, face, or surface to to limit the extend of the fillet.

Face-Face Fillet

A **Face-Face Fillet** is used when no intersection occurs between the surfaces that the fillet is tangent to, as shown in Figure 12–11.

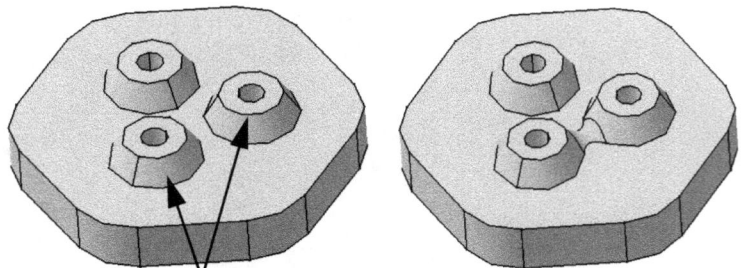

Select these two faces
Figure 12–11

To create a face-face fillet, click 🦋 (Face-Face Fillet). A face-face fillet can also be used to fillet between the two surfaces shown in Figure 12–12.

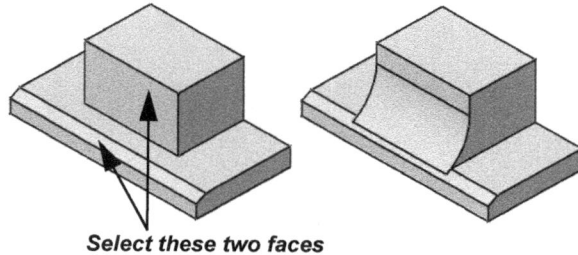

Select these two faces

Figure 12–12

Face-face fillets fail to update if the radius value is not large enough to span between the surfaces, or if the radius is so large that it extends beyond the two faces.

Depending on the geometry, there can be circumstances in which the selection of two surfaces could result in more than one possible fillet. For example, the selection of the rounded surface and the base surface shown in Figure 12–13 could result in a fillet to one side or the other of the upper pad feature.

You can use the **Near Point** option in the Face-Face Fillet Definition dialog box to select the nearest point to the side on which you want the round to be created, as shown in Figure 12–14.

Fillet could be created on either side

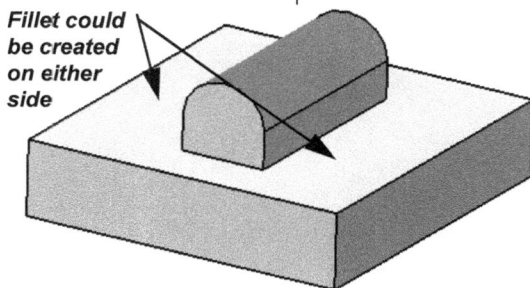

Figure 12–13

Selected point

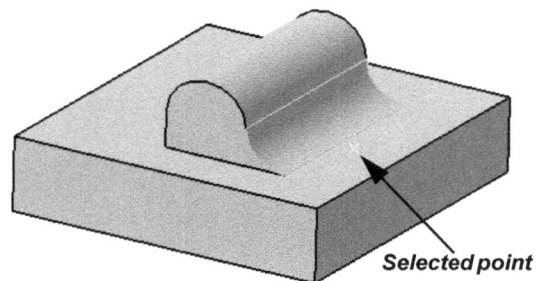

Figure 12–14

Chordal Fillet

A **Chordal Fillet** creates a fillet that is measured by a chord length, rather than radius value. Figure 12–15 shows an example of a cross-section of a chordal fillet. The measurements show what a chord looks like in comparison to a radius measurement.

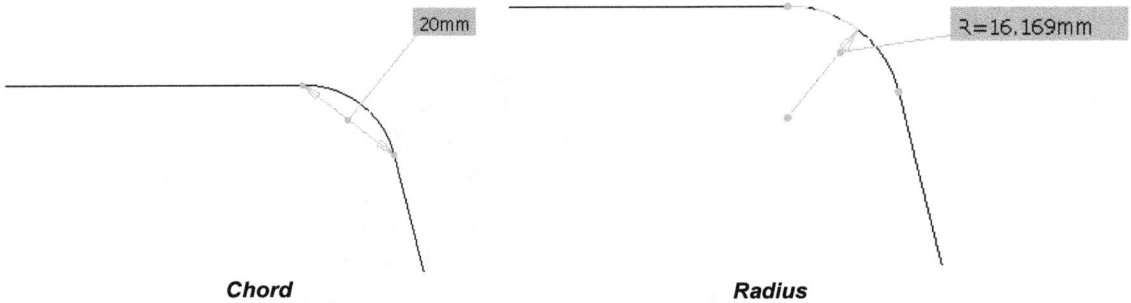

20mm

R=16.169mm

Chord

Radius

Figure 12–15

To create a chordal fillet, click [icon] (Edge Fillet) to open the

Edge Fillet Definition dialog box, then click [icon] (Chordal) and specify the edges to fillet. Complete the fillet by entering a *Chordal length* value, as shown in Figure 12–16.

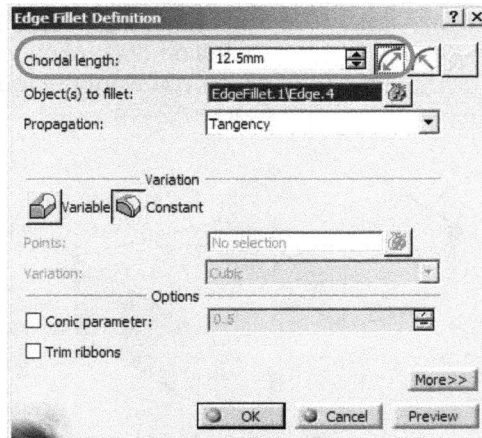

Figure 12–16

Variable Chordal Fillet

By default, chordal fillets use a constant chordal length. However, different chordal lengths can be defined at selected points by clicking (Variable). You can add or remove vertices or points along the selected edge in the *Points* field in the Edge Fillet Definition dialog box. The software adds a chordal length value at each location. To change the value, double-click on it and enter a new value.

To remove a point or vertex, select the point near the dimension on the model, or click , select the point in the Point Elements dialog box, and click **Remove**.

12.2 Draft Feature

The Draft feature adjusts the surface of existing geometry. Draft is typically required for injection molded parts and castings to enable the part to be released from the mold. It should not be used to make angled cuts on features unless the intent is to mold the part. Figure 12–17 shows an example of a Draft feature.

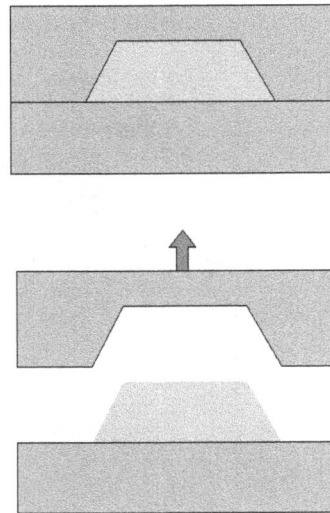

Figure 12–17

When you create a Draft feature, you are required to specify the following information:

- Neutral element

- Pull direction

General Steps

Use the following general steps to create a Draft feature:

1. Start the creation of the Draft feature.
2. Select the faces to draft.
3. Select a neutral element.
4. Specify a pull direction.
5. Complete the feature.

Step 1 - Start the creation of the Draft feature.

Click [ ] (Draft Angle) to create a Draft feature. The Draft Definition dialog box opens as shown in Figure 12–18.

Figure 12–18

Note that two types of drafts can be defined in this dialog box.

- [ ] (Constant) defines a constant draft feature.

- [ ] (Variable) defines a variable draft feature. A variable draft feature enables you to define multiple draft angles for a single draft surface, as shown in Figure 12–19. The angles are defined at points or vertices on the model.

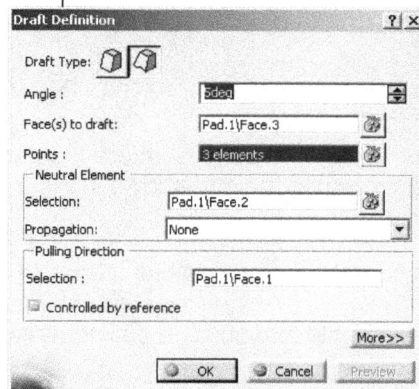

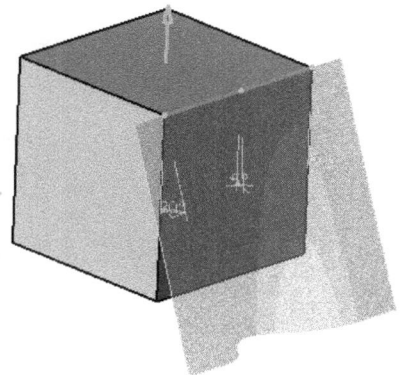

Figure 12–19

Step 2 - Select the faces to draft.

Specify the faces to draft by selecting them on the model.

Selection By Neutral Face

The **Selection by neutral face** option enables you to automatically select the faces to draft, based on the selected neutral element. Any face that is bounded by the neutral element is drafted, as shown in Figure 12–20.

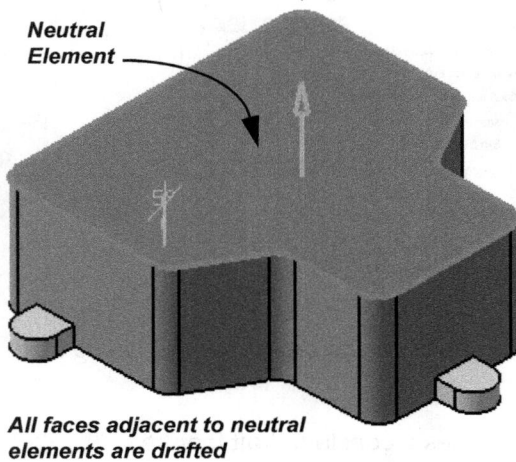

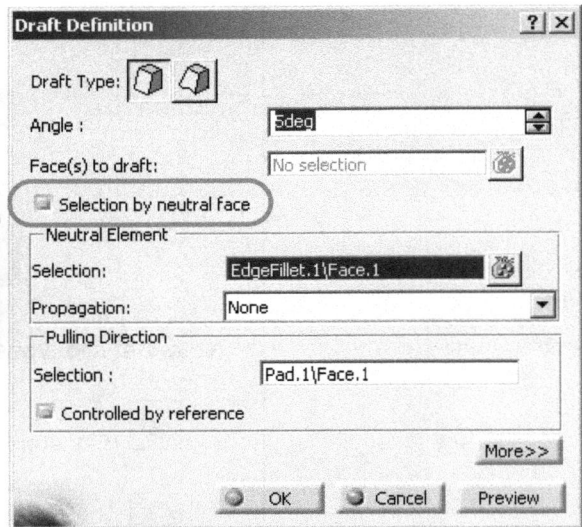

Neutral Element

All faces adjacent to neutral elements are drafted

Figure 12–20

If this option is selected, the *Face(s) to draft* field is grayed out and the faces are determined by the selection of the neutral element.

Step 3 - Select a neutral element.

The neutral element defines where the part maintains its original size. For example, the part shown in Figure 12–21 is initially **5.50** units wide.

Three different neutral element scenarios are shown in Figure 12–21, where the model maintains the **5.50** value at the neutral element location. The pulling direction for each instance is upward.

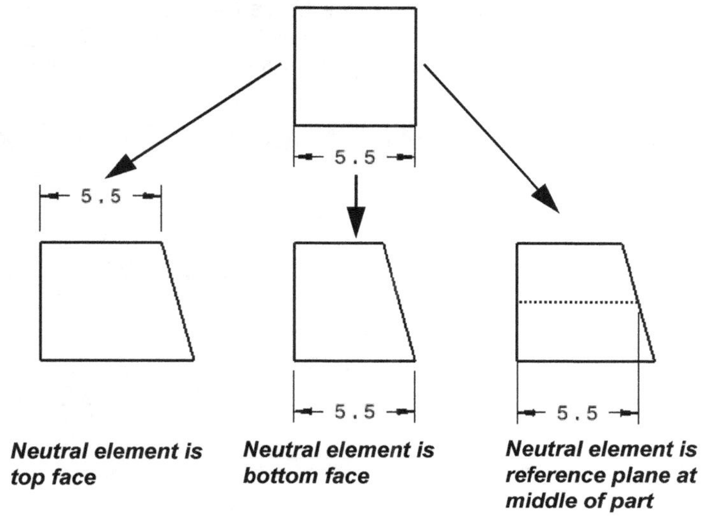

Neutral element is top face — **Neutral element is bottom face** — **Neutral element is reference plane at middle of part**

Figure 12–21

The implicit edge between the neutral element and the faces being drafted defines the start point of the draft. This edge can be developed from a planar or non-planar neutral element.

Consider the drain cap model shown in Figure 12–22. The curved end surface of the model is used as the neutral element because it provides the required start point for the draft angle.

Due to the shape of the neutral element face, the pulling direction cannot be determined automatically and must be manually defined by selecting a planar or linear reference. In this example, the YZ plane is selected.

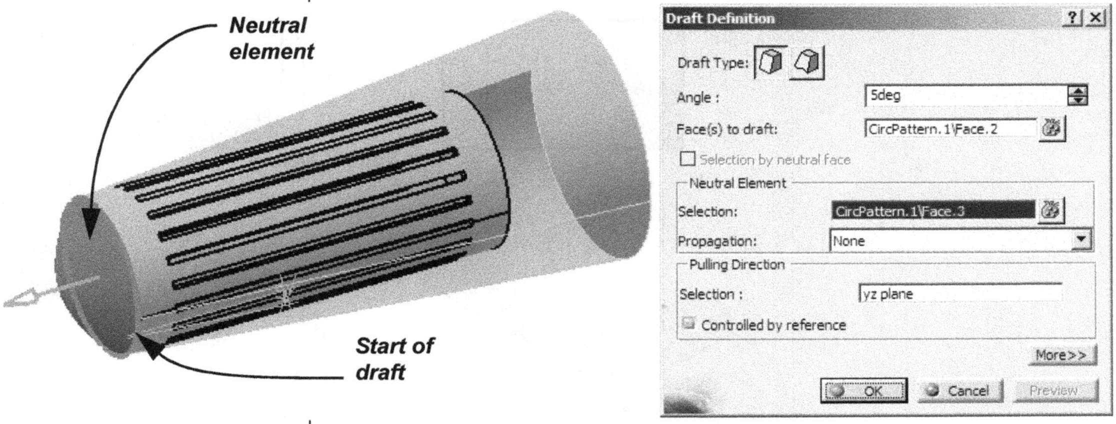

Figure 12–22

Draft Form

Click **More** for additional options to control the Draft feature, as shown in Figure 12–24. The Draft Form drop-down list enables you to refine the details of the draft.

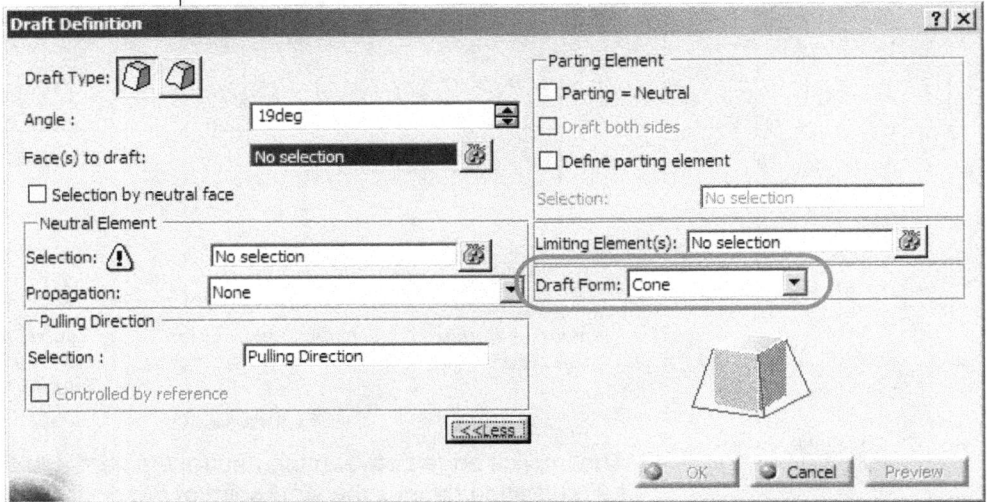

Figure 12–23

Figure 12–24

- **Cone** is the default value in the Draft Form drop-down list. With this option selected, a standard or non-radial Draft is created.

- With the **Square** option, a radial Draft is created that adds curvature to the resulting face, as shown on the right side of Figure 12–25.

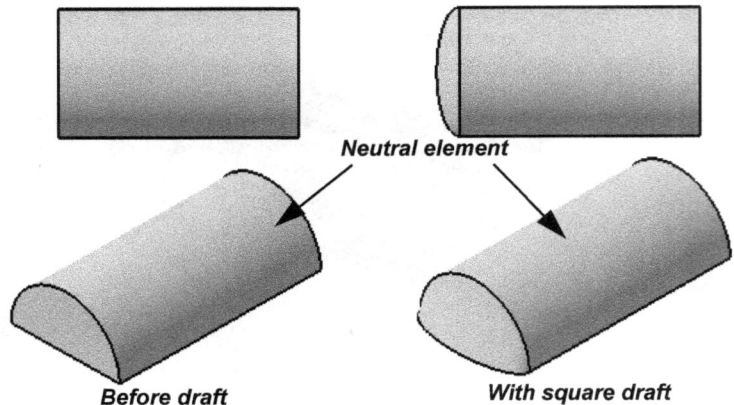

Neutral element

Before draft

With square draft

Figure 12–25

Step 4 - Specify a pull direction.

The pull direction defines the positive Draft direction. Select a planar surface as the reference for the pull direction. The normal vector of the surface reference defines the direction the mold is pulled apart. Clicking on the pull direction arrow to change its direction. The results of selecting different surfaces for the pull direction are shown in Figure 12–26.

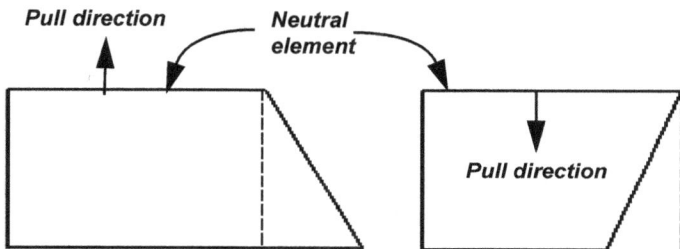

Figure 12–26

Step 5 - Complete the feature.

Click **OK** to complete the feature.

12.3 Creating Shell Features

The Shell feature removes selected surfaces from the model. It leaves a hollowed out solid of a specified wall thickness, as shown in Figure 12–27.

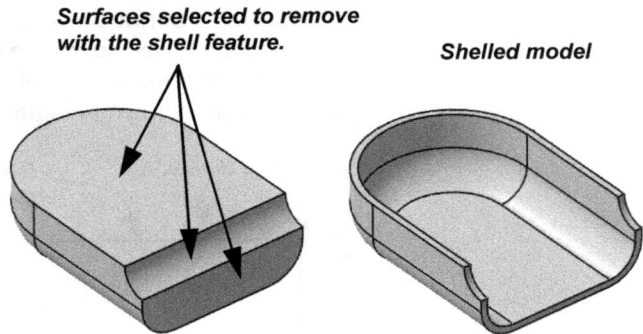

Surfaces selected to remove with the shell feature.

Shelled model

Figure 12–27

How To: Create a Shell Feature

1. Click ⬦ (Shell) to create a Shell feature. The Shell Definition dialog box opens as shown in Figure 12–28.

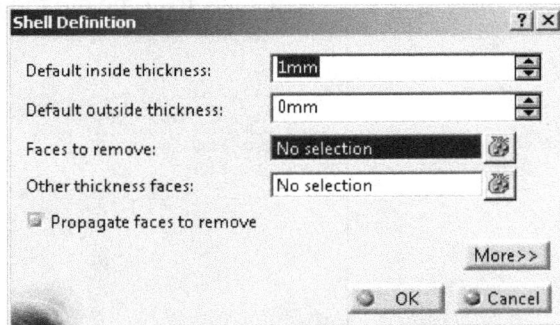

Figure 12–28

2. Select the surfaces to remove. Surfaces to be removed can be selected before or after clicking the **Shell** icon. Selected faces are shown in Figure 12–29. In CATIA, selected surfaces display in magenta.

Surfaces to remove

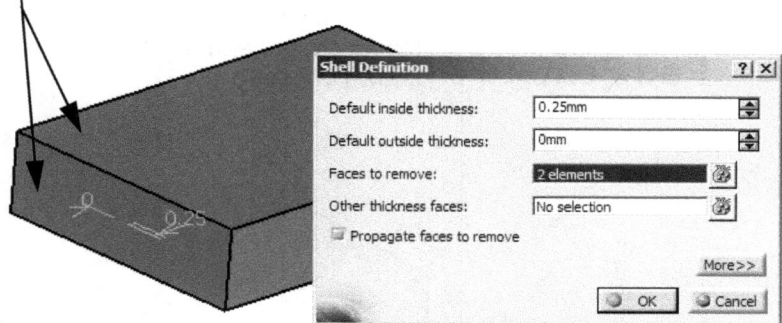

Figure 12–29

3. Use the Shell Definition dialog box to define the wall thickness. The wall thickness value can be offset from the inside and/or outside of the model. Different combinations of inside and outside thickness are shown in Figure 12–30.

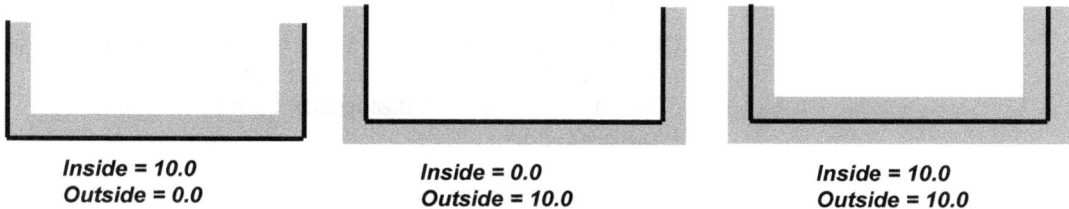

Inside = 10.0   *Inside = 0.0*   *Inside = 10.0*
Outside = 0.0   *Outside = 10.0*   *Outside = 10.0*

Figure 12–30

You can select additional surfaces to specify a different wall thickness, as shown in Figure 12–31.

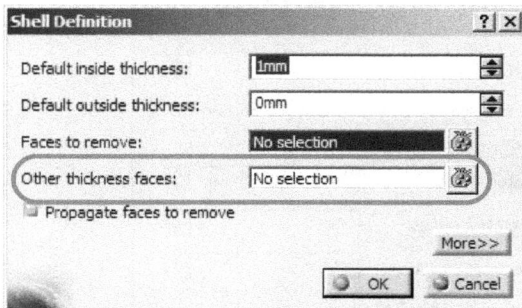

Select the back face as the surface to have a different thickness.

Figure 12–31

4. Click **OK** to complete the Shell feature.

12.4 Drafted Filleted Pad and Pocket Features

Drafted Filleted Pad Feature

A drafted filleted Pad enables you to quickly create a Pad feature that is drafted and has three different sized edge Fillets, as shown in Figure 12–32.

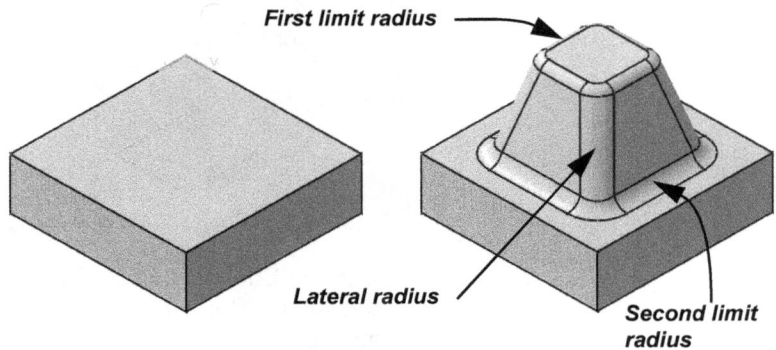

Figure 12–32

- Click (Drafted Filleted Pad) from the toolbar and select the sketch to be used for the Pad feature. The Drafted Filleted Pad Definition dialog box opens, as shown in Figure 12–33.

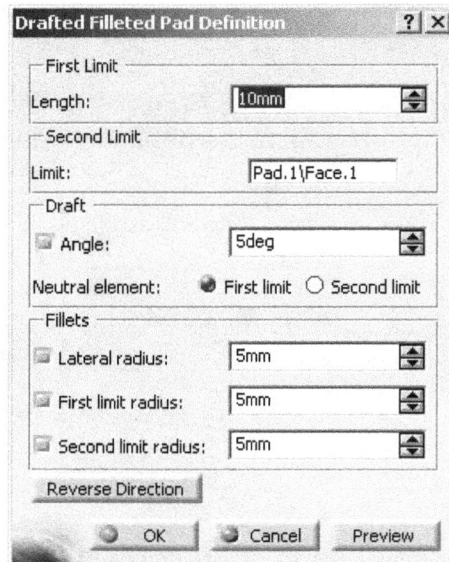

Figure 12–33

Note the options for the Draft and the three Radius features. Clearing these options eliminates them from the feature. You can create a drafted filleted Pad feature without a second limit radius.

Once the drafted filleted Pad feature is created, all five features are listed separately in the specification tree, as shown in Figure 12–34. From this point, any changes to the features must be performed on the individual features.

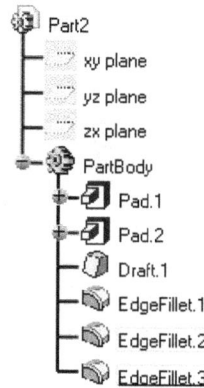

Creating a drafted filleted Pad feature is a quick way to initially create the five features.

Figure 12–34

Drafted Filleted Pocket Feature

A drafted filleted Pocket is similar to the drafted filleted Pad, except that material is removed instead of being added, as shown in Figure 12–35.

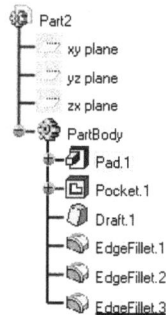

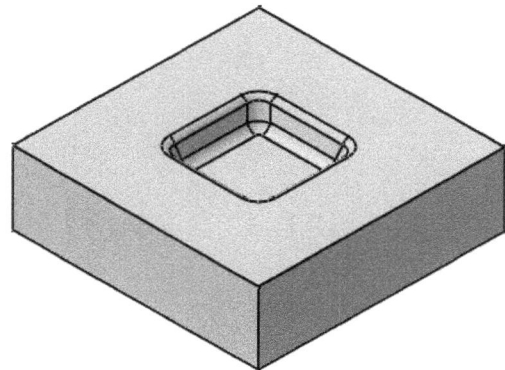

Figure 12–35

12.5 Impact of Feature Order on Geometry

CATIA is a feature-based solid modeler. The order in which the features are created is important and can have a dramatic impact on the resulting geometry. Figure 12–36 shows an example of a model that consists of two Pad features and a Shell feature. Note the order of feature creation in the specification tree. Figure 12–37 shows the same three features in a different order, as shown in the specification tree.

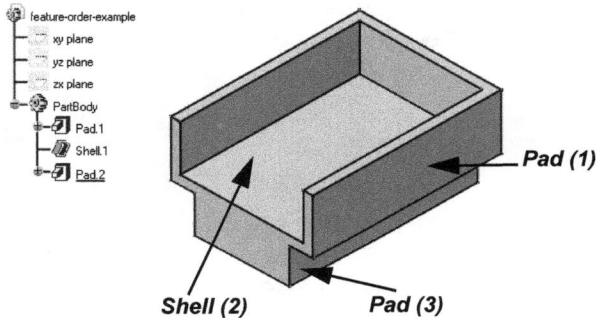

Pad (1)

Shell (2)   Pad (3)

Figure 12–36

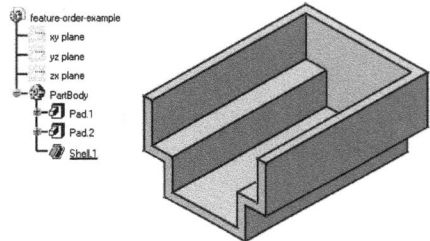

Figure 12–37

Feature Reorder

An advantage of feature-based solid modeling is that features can be easily reordered to change their sequence in the model. This saves time since you do not have to delete several features and recreate them in a new sequence.

How To: Reorder a Feature

1. Select the feature to be reordered in the specification tree. Right-click and select **Shell.# object>Reorder**, as shown in Figure 12–38.

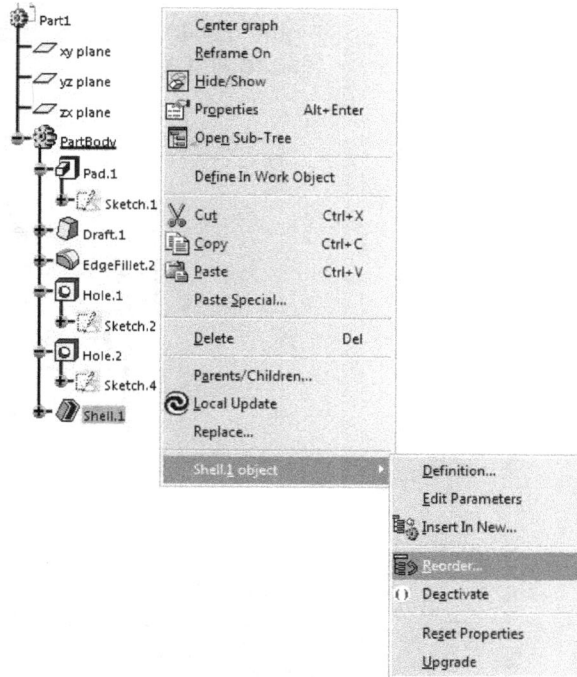

Figure 12–38

When Inside is selected, the feature is positioned at the bottom of the selected body or geometrical set.

2. Specify the new location of the feature. You can reorder a feature **Before** the selected feature, **After** the selected feature, or **Inside** a body or geometrical set, by selecting the appropriate option in the Reorder drop-down list, as shown in Figure 12–39.

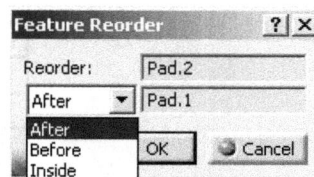

Figure 12–39

3. Click **OK** to complete feature reorder.

Define in Work Object

By default, when features are added to a model, they are added at the end of the feature list. The **Define in Work Object** option is used to insert new features between existing features. To access this option, select the feature in the specification tree, right-click and select **Define In Work Object**.

Figure 12–40 shows an example model that consists of a Pad feature and a Hole feature.

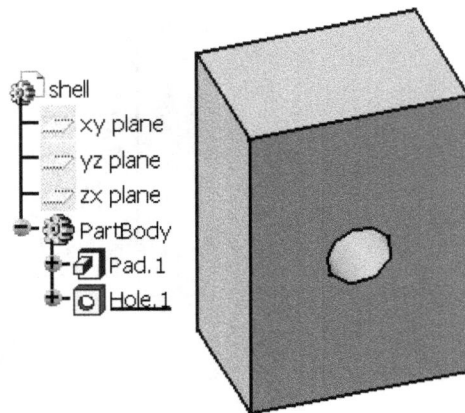

Figure 12–40

A Shell feature added to the model would be placed as the last feature in the specification tree and it would include the surface of the Hole. To insert the Shell before the Hole (or after the Pad), select **Pad.1**, right-click and select **Define In Work Object**. The **Hole.1** feature is removed from display, as shown in Figure 12–41. **Pad.1** is underlined, indicating that it is the work object.

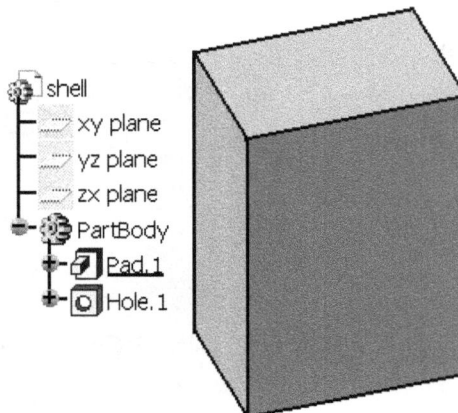

Figure 12–41

New features are added between the Pad and Hole features, as shown in Figure 12–42. To restore all features, select **PartBody**, right-click and select **Define In Work Object**, as shown in Figure 12–43.

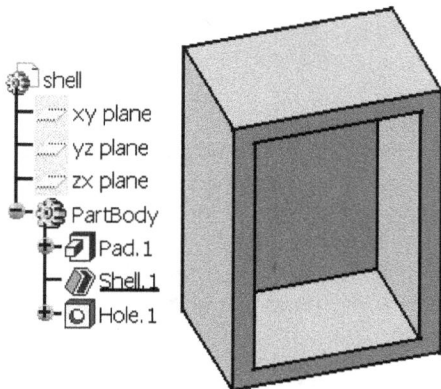

Figure 12–42

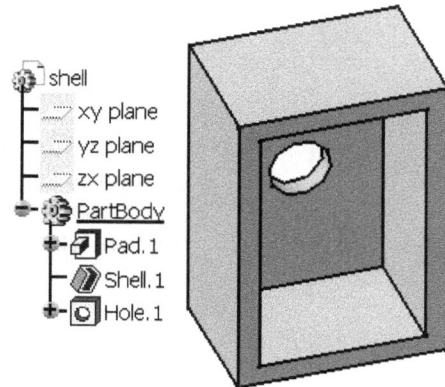

Figure 12–43

Restrictions

If one feature references another, a parent/child relationship is established between the two features. This means one feature is dependent on the other for an aspect of its definition and the software does not enable you to reorder the child feature before the parent feature. Figure 12–44 shows an example where the elongated Hole feature is dimensioned to the circular Hole feature.

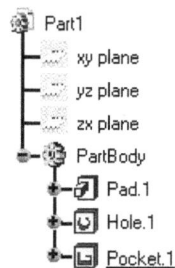

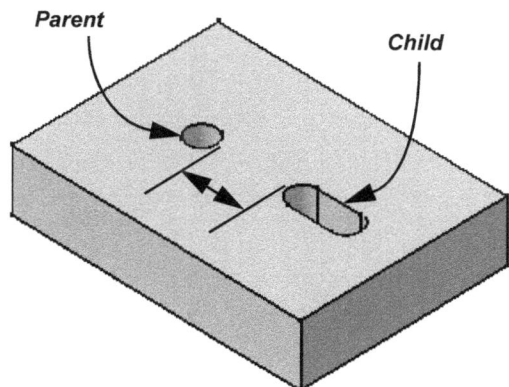

Figure 12–44

Practice 12a

Creating Additional Dress Up Features

Practice Objectives

- Create a Tritangent and Variable Fillet.
- Create a Draft and a Drafted Filleted Pad.
- Create a Shell.

In this practice, you will create the part shown in . Since many features are used to create the part, you will use the **Reorder** function to rearrange the features to achieve the final design. When using the Shell feature, the creation order of features is important. Remember that incorrect ordering of features that are to be shelled can cause the creation of undesirable geometry.

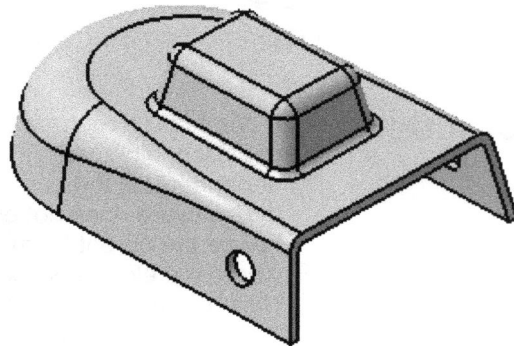

Figure 12–45

Task 1 - Create the base feature.

1. Create a new part called **Cover**.

2. Create a sketch on the XY plane with the dimensions **75 (2.953 in)** and **120 (4.724 in)**, and constraints shown in Figure 12–46. Note the symmetry constraint.

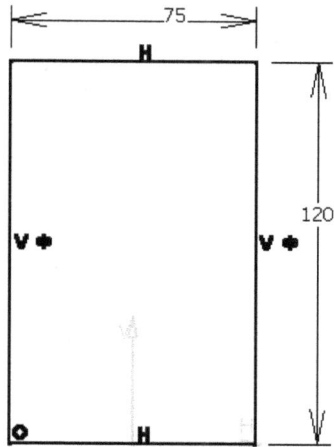

Figure 12–46

3. Create a Pad feature with a *length* of **30.0 (1.181 in)**, as shown in Figure 12–47.

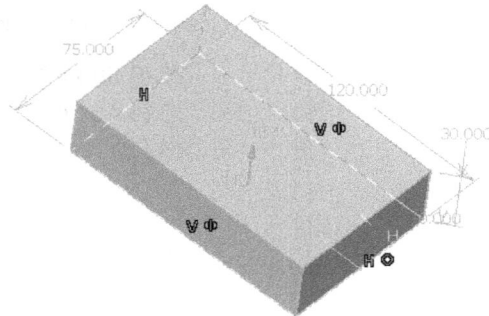

Figure 12–47

Task 2 - Create a sketch for use with a drafted filleted Pad feature.

---

1. In the specification tree, select the three default reference planes, right-click and select **Hide/Show**.

2. Create a positioned sketch using the following parameters:

   • *Sketch Positioning Reference:* Top face of the part
   • *Origin Type:* **Middle point**
   • *Origin Reference:* Top, right edge of the part

The model displays as shown in Figure 12–48.

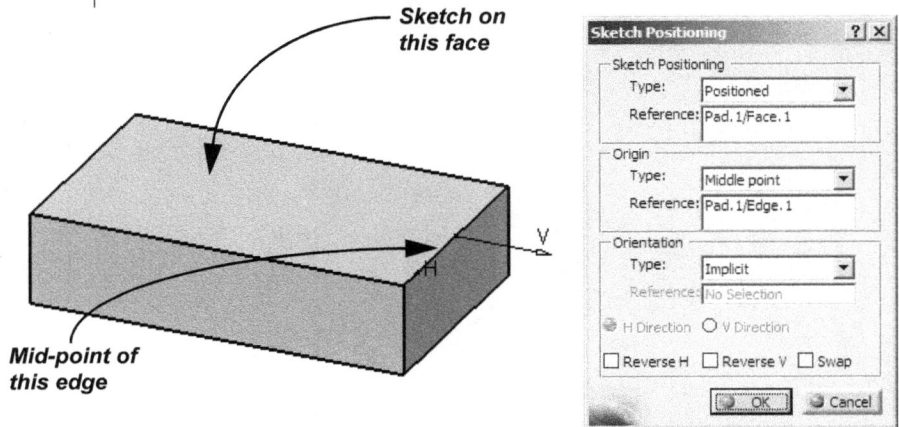

Figure 12–48

3. Sketch a rectangle approximately in the center of the top face.

4. Add a symmetry constraint to center the rectangle about the YZ plane.

Since the YZ plane is hidden, select it in the specification tree.

5. Create the dimensions shown in Figure 12–49.

- 25 (0.984 in)
- 30 (1.181 in)
- 45 (1.772 in)

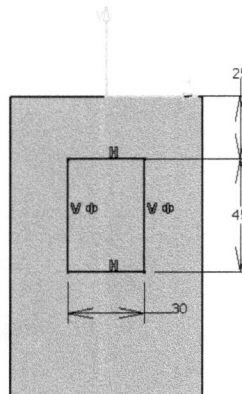

Figure 12–49

6. Exit the Sketcher workbench.

7. With the sketch still highlighted, click ![Drafted Filleted Pad icon] (Drafted Filleted Pad) to create a Drafted Filleted Pad. The Drafted Filleted Pad Definition dialog box opens.

8. Enter **20.0 (0.787 in)** for the *length*.

9. Select the *top face* of the part as the second limit.

10. Enter the values shown in Figure 12–50.

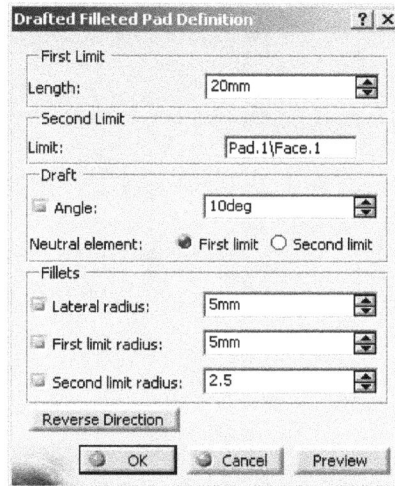

Drafted Filleted Pad Definition

First Limit
Length: 20mm

Second Limit
Limit: Pad.1\Face.1

Draft
☐ Angle: 10deg
Neutral element: ⦿ First limit ○ Second limit

Fillets
☐ Lateral radius: 5mm
☐ First limit radius: 5mm
☐ Second limit radius: 2.5

Reverse Direction

OK   Cancel   Preview

Figure 12–50

11. Click **OK** to complete the feature. The model displays as shown in Figure 12–51.

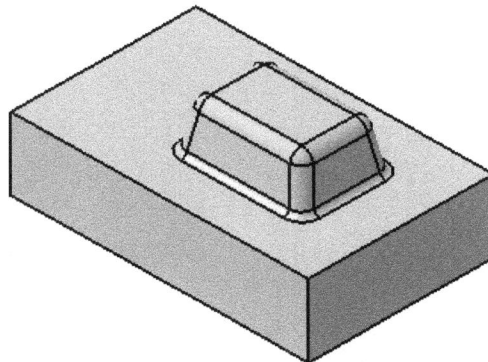

Figure 12–51

Task 3 - Create a Tritangent Fillet feature.

1. Click ⬚ (Tritangent Fillet) to create a Tritangent Fillet. The Tritangent Fillet Definition dialog box opens as shown in Figure 12–52.

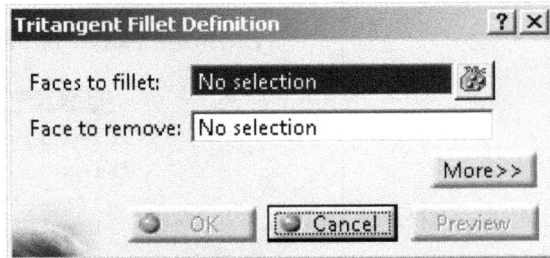

Figure 12–52

2. Make the following selections:

   - *Faces to fillet:* Select the two long faces of the Pad
   - *Face to remove:* Select the hidden back face of the Pad

   The faces are shown in Figure 12–53.

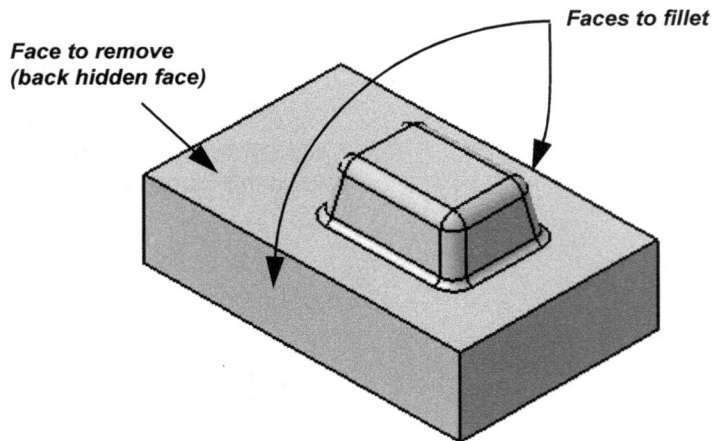

Faces to fillet

Face to remove (back hidden face)

Figure 12–53

3. Click **OK** to complete the feature.

Task 4 - Create a Hole feature.

**Design
Considerations**

The following Hole feature demonstrates the importance of feature order. You will draft the vertical faces of the part. If the Hole is created after the Draft feature, the Hole will be perpendicular to the drafted surface. To maintain the design intent of the part, you create the Hole before the Draft so that it is extruded perpendicular to the vertical face.

1. Create a Hole feature in the location shown in Figure 12–54 by preselecting the appropriate face and edges.

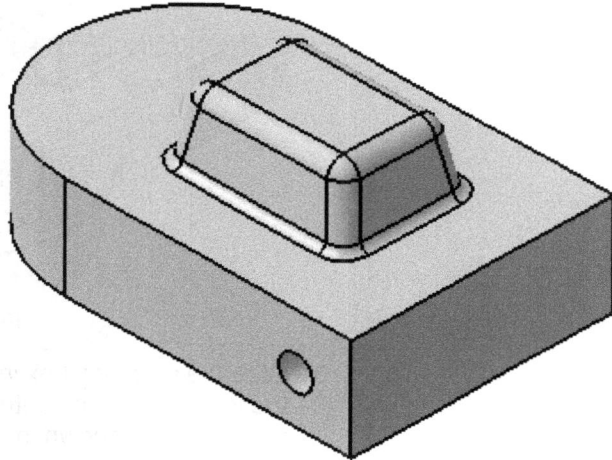

Figure 12–54

2. Modify the hole dimensions to **12 (0.472 in)** and **16 (0.630 in)**, as shown in Figure 12–55.

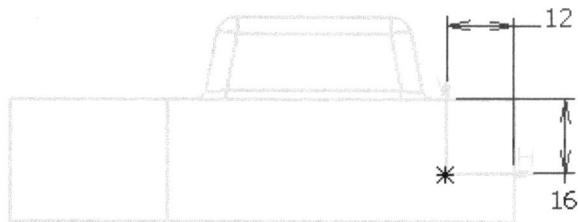

Figure 12–55

3. Set the following:

- *Depth option:* **Up To Last**
- *Diameter value*: **10.00 (0.394 in)**
- *Bottom type:* **Flat**

Task 5 - Create a Draft feature.

1. In the toolbar, click ⬚ (Draft Angle). The Draft Definition dialog box opens.

2. Select the two surfaces shown in Figure 12–56. The draft surfaces turn maroon as a visual indicator.

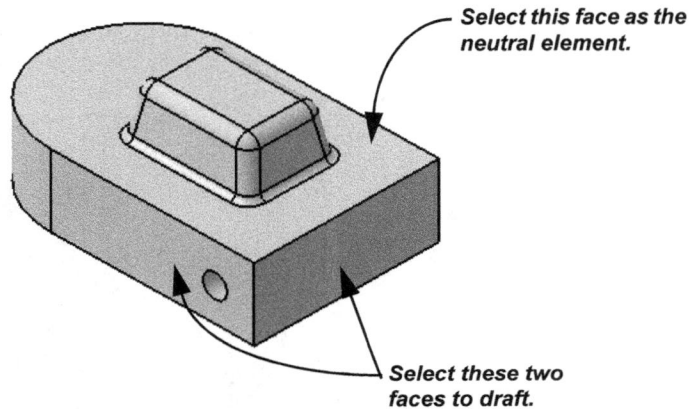

Select this face as the neutral element.

Select these two faces to draft.

Figure 12–56

3. Click the selection box in the *Neutral Element* area and select the top face as the neutral element. The Draft Definition dialog box opens as shown in Figure 12–57.

Figure 12–57

4. Adjust the pulling direction arrow to face up, as shown in Figure 12–58.

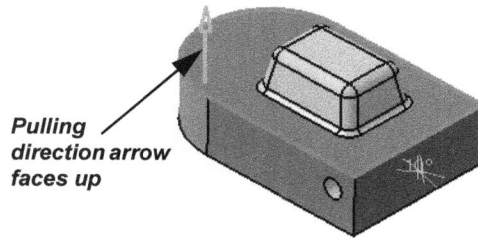

Pulling
direction arrow
faces up

Figure 12–58

5. Enter **10** in the *Angle* field.

6. Click **OK** to complete the feature.

7. Use different quick views to view the result.

Task 6 - Create a point to mark the middle of the arc at the top of the part.

Design Considerations

This point will be positioned at the center of the arc on the part. It will be used to define a radius in a Variable Radius Fillet feature that you create in this task.

1. Click [ ] (Point) and select **On Curve** as the *point type*.

2. Select the arc edge as the curve reference and click **Middle point** to locate the point at the midpoint of the arc, as shown in Figure 12–59.

3. Click **OK** to complete the feature.

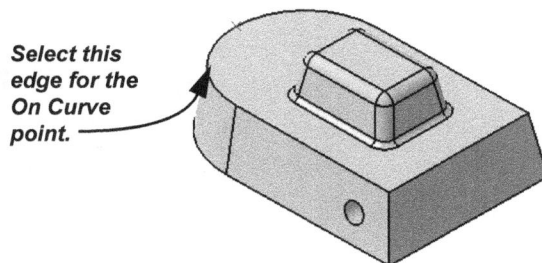

Select this
edge for the
On Curve
point.

Figure 12–59

Task 7 - Create the variable Radius Fillet feature.

1. Click 🔲 (Edge Fillet) to open the Edge Fillet Definition dialog box, then click 🔲 (Variable) to create a variable radius fillet.

2. Select one of the edges, which automatically selects all three edges, as shown in Figure 12–60.

Select one of these three edges

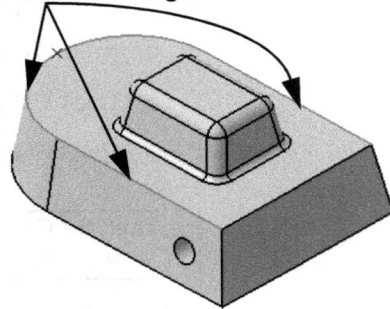

Figure 12–60

3. Enter **5.0 (0.197 in)** for the *radius*.

4. Select the *Points* field to activate it and select the point you previously created, to add it to the location in which you are specifying a radius value.

5. Enter **15.0 (0.591 in)** for the *radius* (double-click on the 5.0 (0.197 in) value at the point). The Parameter Definition dialog box opens for you to enter a new value, as shown in Figure 12–61.

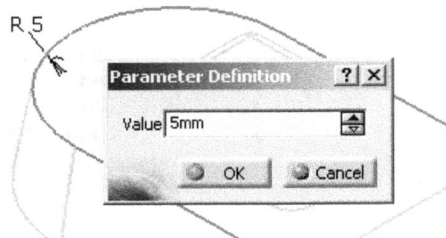

Figure 12–61

6. Click **Preview** to verify that the geometry is created in the required manner.

7. Click **OK** to complete the feature.

Small points display at each vertex along the chain of edges. Note the number of vertices listed in the Points field in the Variable Edge Fillet Definition dialog box.

8. Hide the Point feature from display. The part displays as shown in Figure 12–62.

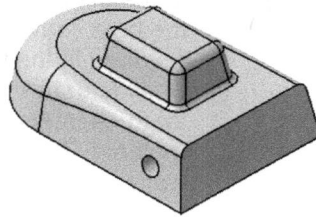

Figure 12–62

Task 8 - Create a Shell feature to hollow out the model.

1. Click 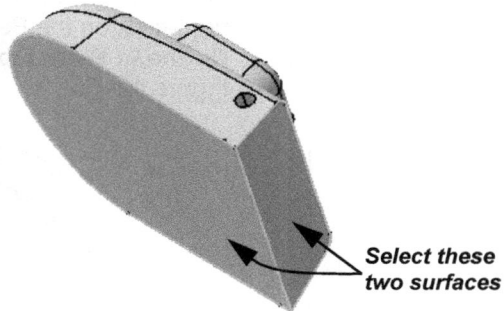 (Shell) to add a Shell feature.

2. Select the two surfaces shown in Figure 12–63.

Select these two surfaces

Figure 12–63

3. Enter **3.0 (0.118 in)** for the *inside thickness*.

4. Click **OK** to complete the feature. The feature hollows out around the hole, as shown in Figure 12–64.

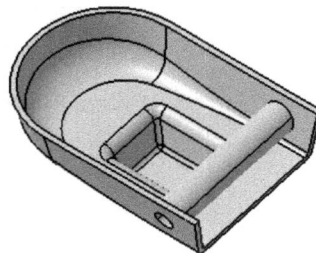

Figure 12–64

Design Considerations

Task 9 - Reorder the Hole feature after the Shell feature.

In the previous task, the Shell feature removed material around the hole, leaving a column of material. This geometry is not required in the final part. Reordering the Hole feature after the Shell feature eliminates this problem. Now that there are no features intersecting the part, the shell removes all the inside material. The hole then removes material from only the two side walls.

1. Right-click on the Hole feature in the specification tree and select **Hole.1 object>Reorder**.

2. By default, the Hole feature will be located **After** the selected feature. Leave this as the default option.

3. In the specification tree, select **Shell.1** and click **OK** in the Feature Reorder dialog box.

4. The Hole feature might not currently be the active object (indicated by an underline in the specification tree). If it is not, right-click on the PartBody in the specification tree and select **Define In Work Object**. The model displays as shown in Figure 12–65.

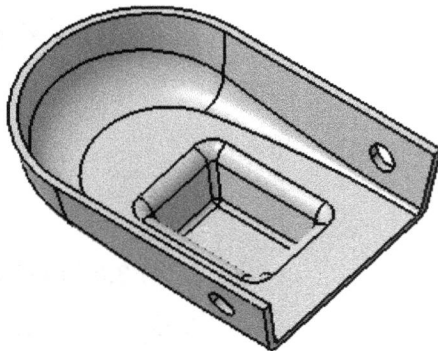

Figure 12–65

5. Click ![save icon] (Save).

6. Select **File>Close**.

Practice 12b	# Phone Cover

Practice Objectives

- Create a Draft with a non-planar neutral element.
- Create a Fillet.

In this practice, you will create Draft features in a mold-injected telephone cover so that it can be easily removed from its manufacturing die, as shown in Figure 12–66. To preserve the required profile for the top of the phone cover, a non-planar neutral element must be used for one of the Draft features. When a non-planar neutral element is used, a pulling direction should be specified, as the default might no longer fulfill your design intent. Remember that the direction of pull is perpendicular to the pulling direction plane.

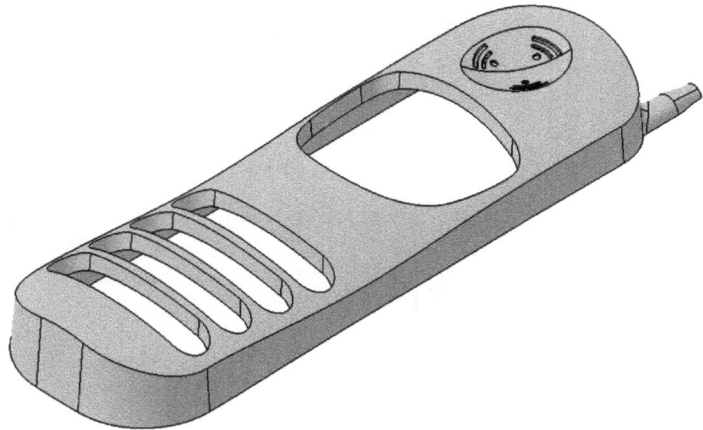

Figure 12–66

Design Considerations

This plastic part will be manufactured using injection molding. For the part to be easily separated from the manufacturing die, some of its faces must be drafted. Consider which faces should be drafted to optimize the manufacturing time of the part.

Task 1 - Create a draft on the exterior surfaces.

1. Select **File>Open** and select **PhoneCover.CATPart**.

2. Click ⬡ (Draft Angle).

3. Enter **8deg** for the *draft angle*.

4. Select the face shown in Figure 12–67 as the face to draft.

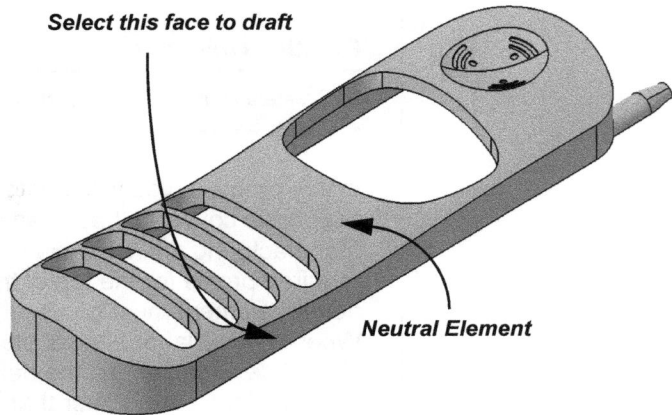

Select this face to draft

Neutral Element

Figure 12–67

Design Considerations

The Draft Angle feature uses tangency propagation to automatically select tangent faces and reduce the amount of time consumed by selecting individual faces to draft.

5. Select the top face of the phone cover as the Neutral Element.

6. Select the XY plane as the pulling direction.

7. Verify that the direction of the arrow defining the pulling direction will enable the part to be removed from the die.

The Draft Definition dialog box opens as shown in Figure 12–68.

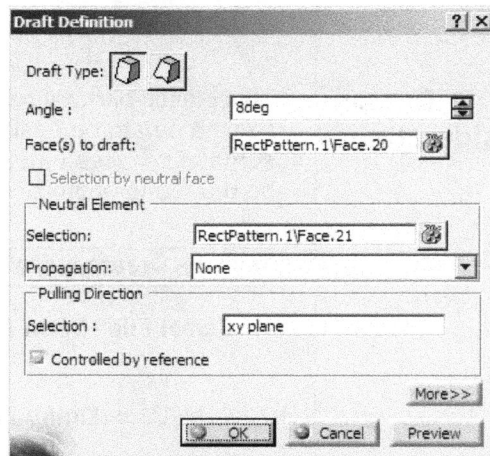

Draft Definition

Draft Type:

Angle : 8deg

Face(s) to draft: RectPattern.1\Face.20

☐ Selection by neutral face

Neutral Element

Selection: RectPattern.1\Face.21

Propagation: None

Pulling Direction

Selection : xy plane

☐ Controlled by reference

More>>

OK   Cancel   Preview

Figure 12–68

8. Click **OK** to complete the feature.

9. Rename the newly created draft feature as **Exterior**.

Task 2 - Create a draft on the interior surface.

Design Considerations

To maintain uniform thickness of the phone cover wall, the interior body surface must be drafted at the same angle as the exterior body surface.

1. Rotate the part to reveal the interior body surface, as shown in Figure 12–69.

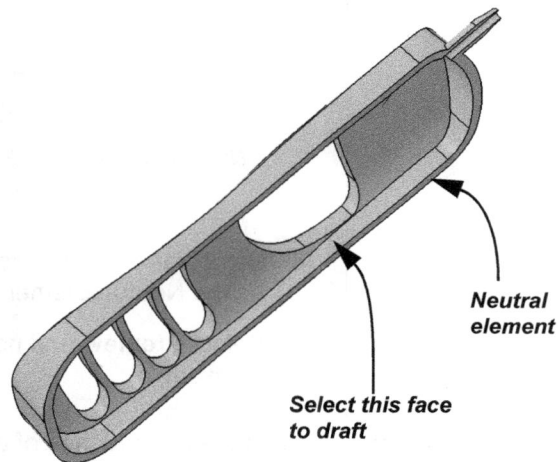

Neutral element

Select this face to draft

Figure 12–69

2. Click (Draft Angle).

3. Enter **8deg** as the *draft angle*.

4. Select the interior edge surface as the face to draft, as shown in Figure 12–69.

5. Select the bottom face of the phone cover as the Neutral Element.

6. Select the XY plane as the pulling direction, and click the orange arrow to change the direction so that it points toward the bottom of the phone.

7. Click **OK** to complete the feature.

8. Rename the newly created Draft feature as **Interior**.

Task 3 - Create a draft on the end of the antenna silo.

1. Click ⬛ (Draft Angle).

2. Enter **8deg** as the *draft angle*.

3. Select the end surface of the antenna silo as the face to draft, as shown in Figure 12–70.

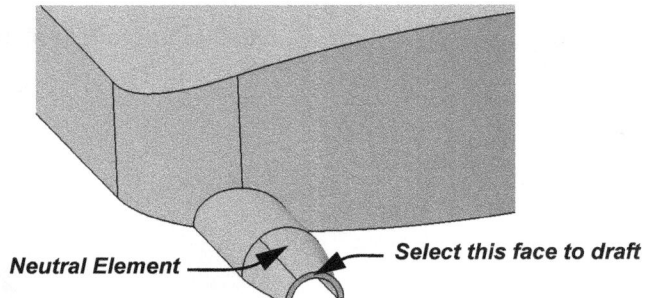

Neutral Element —————→   ←————— *Select this face to draft*

Figure 12–70

4. Select the curved surface of the **multi-sections solid** feature as the Neutral Element.

5. Select **Preview** and note the Feature Definition Error message.

Design Considerations

Because the end face of the antenna silo is radial, the default conic draft form cannot be used because parts of the face will be parallel (tangent) to the pulling direction. The square draft form type must be used to create a draft on a radial surface.

6. Click **More**. In the Draft Form drop-down list, select **Square.**

7. Click **OK** to complete the feature.

8. Rename the newly created draft feature as **Antenna**.

Task 4 - Create a draft on the keypad and LCD display cutouts.

1. Click ⬛ (Isometric view).

2. Click ⬛ (Draft Angle).

3. Enter **4deg** as the *draft angle*.

4. Select the faces shown in Figure 12–71 as the faces to draft.

Select these faces to draft

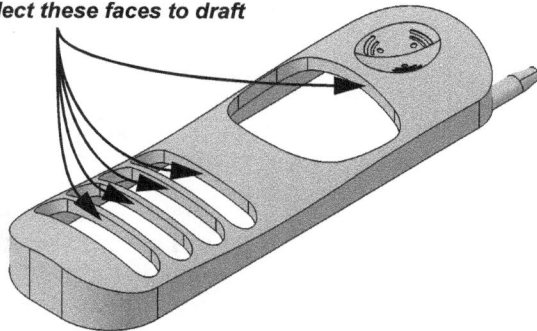

Figure 12–71

5. Select the XY plane as the pulling direction.

6. Select the top face of the phone cover as the Neutral Element.

7. Click **OK** to complete the feature.

8. Rename the newly created Draft feature as **Keypad&LCD**.

Task 5 - Create a draft on the speaker holes.

1. Click [icon] (Draft Angle).

2. Enter **10deg** as the *draft angle*.

3. Zoom in on and select the faces shown in Figure 12–72 as the faces to draft for all three instances of the speaker holes pattern.

Select these faces to draft

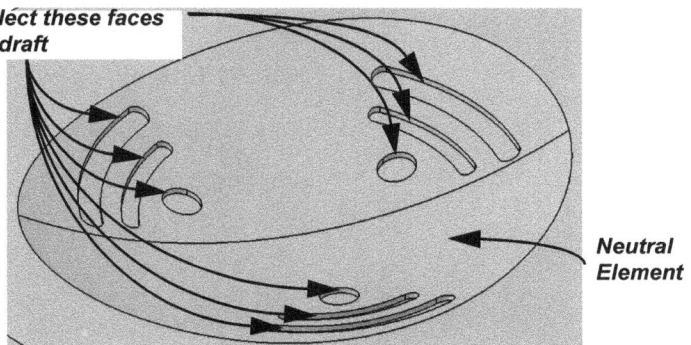

Neutral Element

Figure 12–72

4. Select the indented speaker surface as the Neutral Element.

5. Select the XY plane as the pulling direction.

6. Click **OK** to complete the feature.

7. Rename the newly created Draft feature as **SpeakerHoles**.

Task 6 - Fillet the antenna to the exterior body surface.

Design Considerations

The Fillet feature is used to remove sharp edges and corners. With this injection-molded plastic part, leaving the corner between the antenna and cover body sharp creates a stress riser. Adding a fillet acts as a stiffener and aids in fulfillment of the design intent (in the case of a telephone, this might be the user requirement of durability).

1. Click ⬚ (Edge Fillet).

2. Select one of the two parts of the edge joining the antenna to the exterior body surface as the objects to fillet, as shown in Figure 12–73.

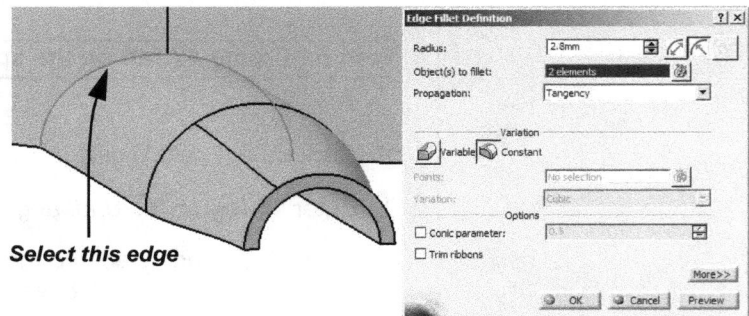

Figure 12–73

3. Enter **2.8 (0.110 in)** as the *Radius*.

4. Click **OK** to complete the feature.

5. Rename the feature as **Fillet-2.8mm**.

6. Save and close the file.

Design Considerations

Make a habit of creating Edge Fillets as your final design features. Edge Fillets interfere with the implementation of other dress-up features, such as Chamfer and Draft Angle. Although advanced features, such as a Reflect Line Draft enables you to draft filleted geometry, they should only be used as a last resort. The increased complexity of advanced features unnecessarily increases model size and system resource consumption.

Practice 12c | (Optional) Tank

Practice Objective

- Create a part without instructional steps.

Create the **Tank.CATPart** as shown in Figure 12–74.

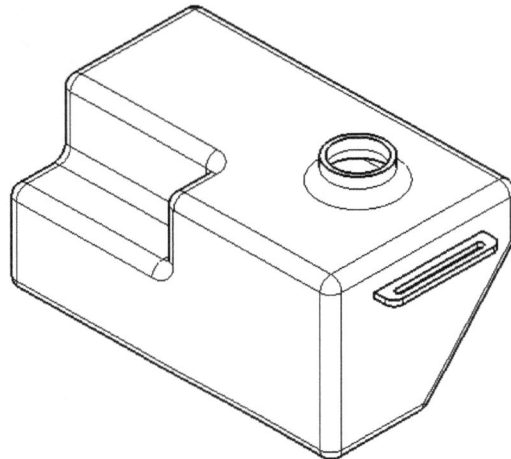

Figure 12–74

Drawing views are shown in Figure 12–75.

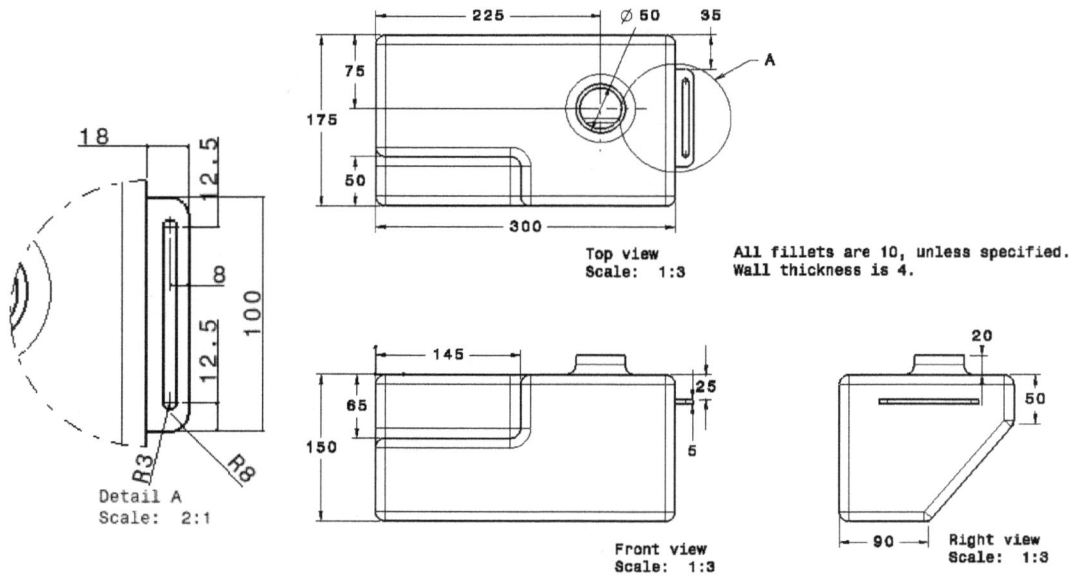

All fillets are 10, unless specified.
Wall thickness is 4.

Top view
Scale: 1:3

Detail A
Scale: 2:1

Front view
Scale: 1:3

Right view
Scale: 1:3

Figure 12–75

Practice 12d | (Optional) Connecting Rod

Practice Objective

- Create a part without instructional steps.

Create the **ConnectingRod.CATPart** shown in Figure 12–76.

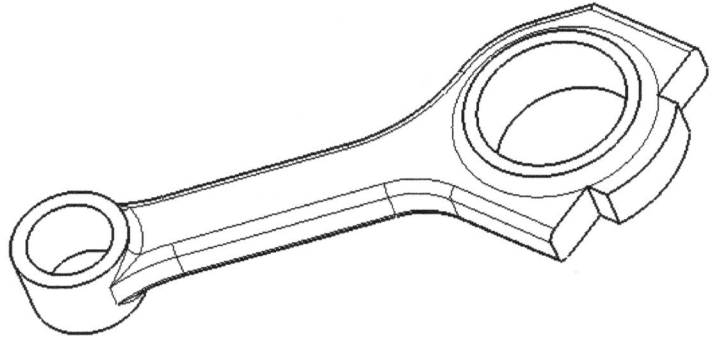

Figure 12–76

Drawing views are shown in Figure 12–77 and Figure 12–78.

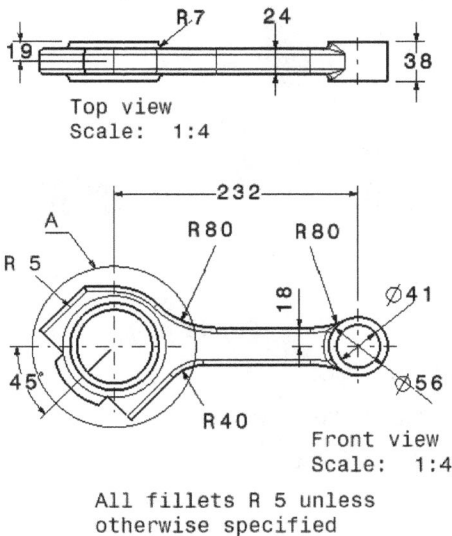

Top view
Scale: 1:4

Front view
Scale: 1:4

All fillets R 5 unless
otherwise specified

Figure 12–77

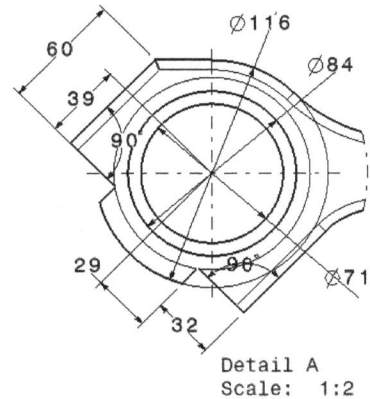

Detail A
Scale: 1:2

Figure 12–78

Chapter Review Questions

1. The wall thickness of a Shell is always a constant thickness.
   a. True
   b. False

2. A child feature can be reordered above its parent in the specification tree.
   a. True
   b. False

3. A radius value of **0** is acceptable when creating a variable radius Fillet.
   a. True
   b. False

4. Which tool is used to create the model shown on the right side of Figure 12–79?

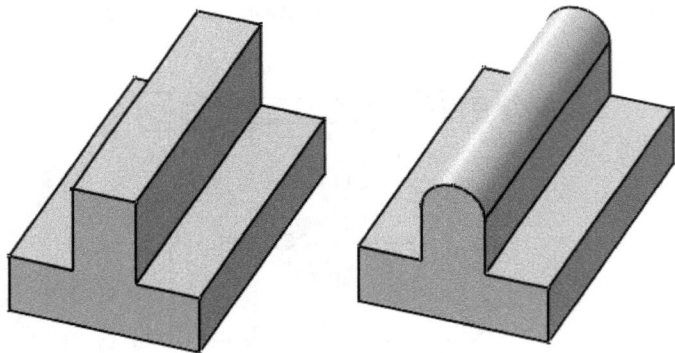

Figure 12–79

   a. Tritangent fillet
   b. Variable Radius fillet
   c. Face-Face Fillet
   d. Edge Fillet

5. Which tool is used to create a Fillet where no intersection between the surfaces to be filleted exists?

   a. Tritangent fillet

   b. Variable Radius fillet

   c. Face-Face Fillet

   d. Edge Fillet

6. Which of the following statements is true regarding create a draft? (Select all that apply.)

   a. Multiple surfaces can be selected for drafting.

   b. Multiple faces can be selected when defining the pull direction.

   c. A planar surface is required as the reference for the pull direction.

7. The pull direction used to create the Draft shown in pull direction to produce the Draft shown in Figure 12–80 is

   _____.

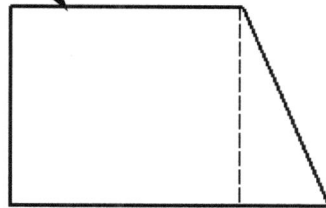

Figure 12–80

   a. Leftward

   b. Rightward

   c. Upward

   d. Downward

8. A Drafted Filleted Pad feature creates a single feature in the specification tree.

   a. True

   b. False

Answers: 1.b, 2.b, 3.a, 4.a, 5.c, 6.ac, 7.c, 8.b

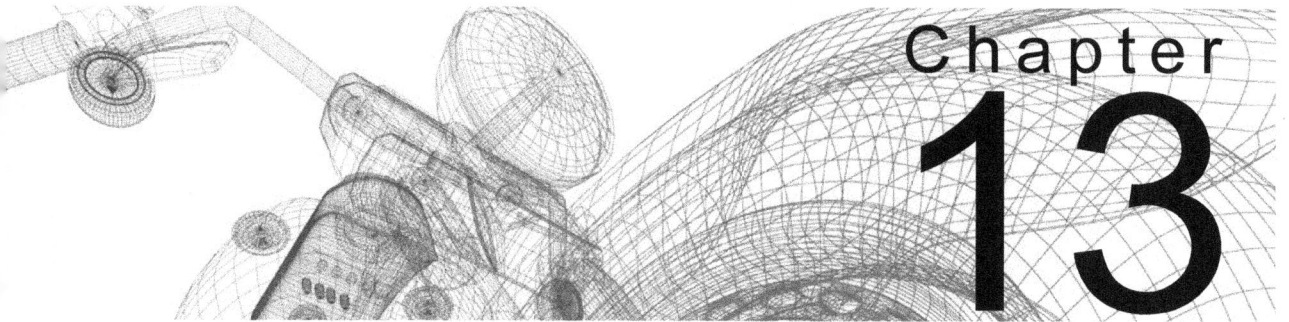

Feature Duplication

In this chapter, you learn how to duplicate features using patterns or the Copy/Paste command. You also learn how to use the Mirror command to mirror selected parts of an assembly. Using these tools will increase your modeling efficiency and help you build robust models.

Learning Objectives in this Chapter

- Create rectangular and circular patterns.
- Copy, paste, and mirror features.
- Understand user patterns for creating non-uniform patterns.
- Create formulas to control design intent.
- Understand system parameter names and how to use them to create formulas.
- Learn to display formulas and parameters in the specification tree.
- Edit and delete formulas and user-defined parameters.
- Use and create various types of parameters, including user-defined parameters.

13.1 Pattern Features

Patterns are used to quickly duplicate geometry. Once the initial feature(s) is created, several instances of the same geometry can be patterned by a specified dimensional increment. The pattern can be created as a rectangular or circular pattern. If any dimension changes in the original feature, the instances update to the new dimensions.

Step 1 - Specify the reference direction.

Rectangular Pattern

When creating a rectangular pattern, features can be patterned along an edge in one or two directions. The initial Hole feature shown in Figure 13–1 is duplicated using a rectangular pattern in the first direction only. The direction of the pattern is defined by the part edge. This edge is selected as the reference element in the Pattern Definition dialog box.

Using the *Second Direction* tab in the dialog box, the hole can be patterned in a second direction, as shown in Figure 13–2.

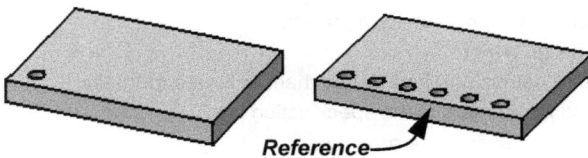

Reference—

Figure 13–1

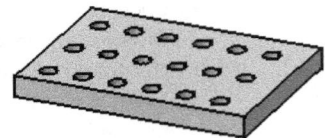

Figure 13–2

After defining the second direction, the **Identical instances in both directions** option is made available. If selected, the pattern is created with the number of instances provided in the **Instance(s)** box in the First Direction tab, The number of instances in the second direction is set to match that of the first direction. If you change the number of instances in the first direction, the instances in the second direction automatically update.

Circular Pattern

When creating a circular pattern, features can be patterned by a set angle. Select a feature or a line to serve as an axial reference for the circular pattern. The Hole feature shown in Figure 13–3 is patterned about an axial reference defined by the center Pad.

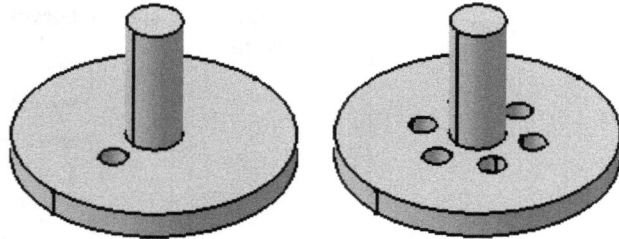

Figure 13–3

Step 2 - Specify the reference parameters.

Rectangular Pattern

Rectangular patterns can be defined by selecting one of the following combinations:

- Instance(s) & Spacing

- Instance(s) & Length

- Spacing & Length

- Instance(s) & Unequal Spacing

Circular Pattern

The dialog box updates according to the selected parameter type. Selecting the appropriate parameter scheme establishes the appropriate driving dimensions.

Circular patterns can be defined by selecting one of the following parameter options:

Option	Description
Instance(s) & Angular Spacing	Define the pattern by the number of instances and the spacing between the instances. Parameters: Instance(s) & angular spacing Instance(s): 3 Angular spacing: 90deg Total angle: 180deg
Instance(s) & Total Angle	The spacing between the instances is calculated by dividing the total angle by the number of instances. Parameters: Instance(s) & total angle Instance(s): 4 Angular spacing: 39.333deg Total angle: 118deg

Angular Spacing & Total Angle	The number of instances is calculated by dividing the total angle by the angular spacing between the instances. The calculated value for the number of instances is always rounded up. 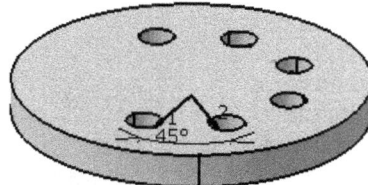
Complete Crown	The angular spacing between instances is calculated by dividing the complete crown (i.e., 360 deg) by the number of instances. 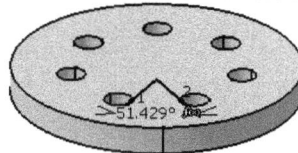
Instance(s) & Unequal Angular Spacing	You can specify different angular values between different instances. 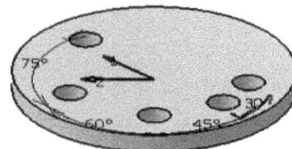

The pattern can also be defined by defining parameters in the *Crown Definition* tab in the Circular Pattern Definition dialog box. A crown definition creates an additional circle pattern, as shown in Figure 13–4.

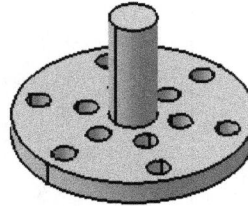

Figure 13–4

The dialog box updates according to the selected parameter type. Selecting the appropriate parameter scheme establishes the appropriate driving dimensions.

Crown definition patterns can be defined by selecting one of the following parameter options:

Option	Description
Circle(s) & Circle Spacing	The additional pattern rows are defined by entering the number of circles (including the original) and the spacing between rows.
Circle(s) & Crown Thickness	The additional pattern rows are defined by entering the number of circles (including the original) and the distance to the last row.

Circle Spacing & Crown Thickness	The number of additional pattern rows is calculated by dividing the distance to the last row by the spacing between the rows. The calculated value is always rounded up.

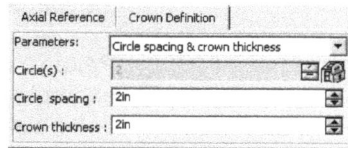

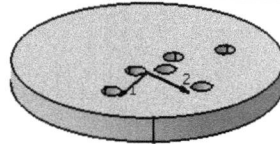

Step 3 - Remove instances, if required.

While creating the pattern, you can easily remove an instance by selecting it while the Pattern Definition dialog box is active. The wireframe outline of the instance to be deleted is removed. All other instances remain in their offset position. The rectangular pattern shown in Figure 13–5 has the interior instances removed.

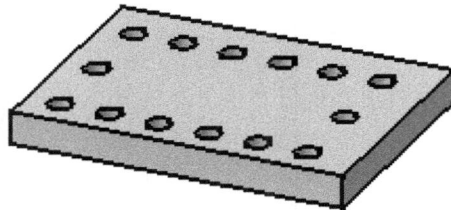

Figure 13–5

Pattern Multiple Features

In previous examples, only one feature is selected for duplication. You can also create a pattern using multiple features. To pattern multiple features, preselect the features at the same time using <Ctrl>, then click ⠿ (Rectangular Pattern) or ◇ (Circular Pattern). Figure 13–6 shows an example of patterning multiple features. The circular pad, draft, and hole are all patterned in one operation.

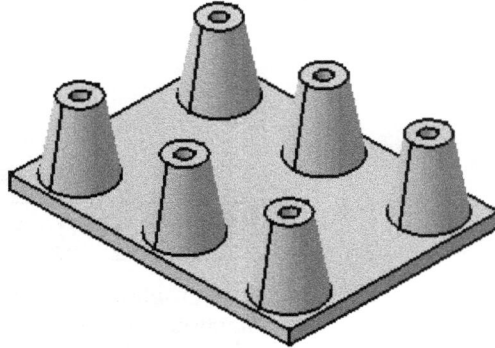

Figure 13–6

13.2 Creating User Patterns

User patterns are used when the pattern is not uniform and when you only need particular instances of a circular or rectangle pattern.

How To: Create a User Pattern

1. Select features for a user pattern as you would for the other types of patterns. Click (User Pattern) to open the User Pattern Definition dialog box, as shown in Figure 13–7.

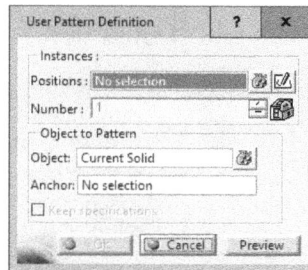

Figure 13–7

Specify positions to place the instances. These positions are marked by points that must be in the same body as the feature you are patterning. Since you cannot pattern features outside of the current body, you must create points in the Sketcher workbench, and then use the points as the positions. Select the *Positions* field in the User Pattern Definition dialog box, and select a point or a sketch from the specification tree.

Alternatively, click (Sketch) next to the *Positions* field and sketch a set of points.

2. Change the position of the anchor, if required.

The anchor is the point on each instance where the position marker is located. By default, CATIA uses the center of gravity (center of the feature) of each instance. If this position is not correct, you can change it by changing the anchor location. To change the anchor location, select the *Anchor* field and then select a point on each instance to act as the new anchor.

- The anchor shown in Figure 13–8 is left as the center of gravity.
- The anchor shown in Figure 13–9 is set to the top of the feature.

Location of position marker

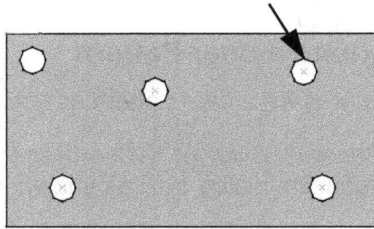

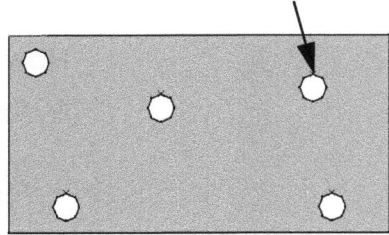

Location of position marker

Figure 13–8

Figure 13–9

3. Remove instances and validate the pattern. You can remove instances from the pattern by selecting the position marker (anchor) of the instance while in the User Pattern Definition dialog box. The instance is removed from the display. Select the position marker again to return the instance to the display.
4. Click **OK** once you complete the pattern.

Patterns on the Fly

If you are creating a feature that you know will be patterned, you can create it on the fly in the Pattern dialog box. Click

(Rectangular Pattern), (Circular Pattern) or (User Pattern), then, in the Pattern Definition dialog box, right-click on the *Object* field and select the feature that you want to create, as shown in Figure 13–10.

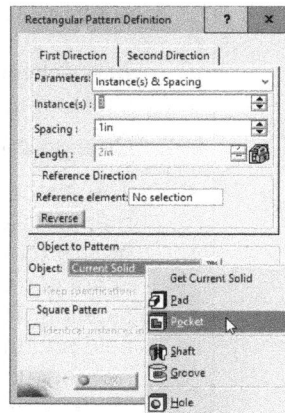

Figure 13–10

Once the feature is created, continue the pattern definition using the techniques previously described.

13.3 Copy Features

The **Copy/Paste** command is another way to duplicate features. The original circular pad is copied to new positions, as shown in Figure 13–11.

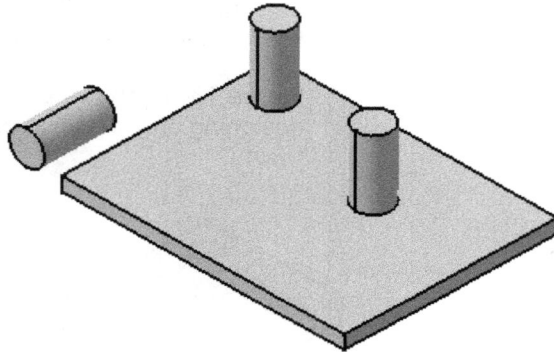

Figure 13–11

The pasted feature is placed directly on top of the original feature if the same placement plane is used. To change the position of the copied feature, the sketch must be redefined. The copied feature remains independent of the original feature.

You can also use <Ctrl>+<C> to copy and <Ctrl>+<V> to paste.

• To copy a feature, select the feature(s), right-click and select **Copy**. Select the new reference pad, right-click and select **Paste**.

13.4 Mirror Features

The **Mirror** command enables you to mirror selected features about a specified surface or reference plane. To use the **Mirror** command, select the features to be mirrored and click

(Mirror) in the Transformation Features toolbar. Complete the feature by selecting the mirroring plane or surface.

Figure 13–12 shows a symmetrical part that can be created by designing only a portion of it. In this example, the part is mirrored twice.

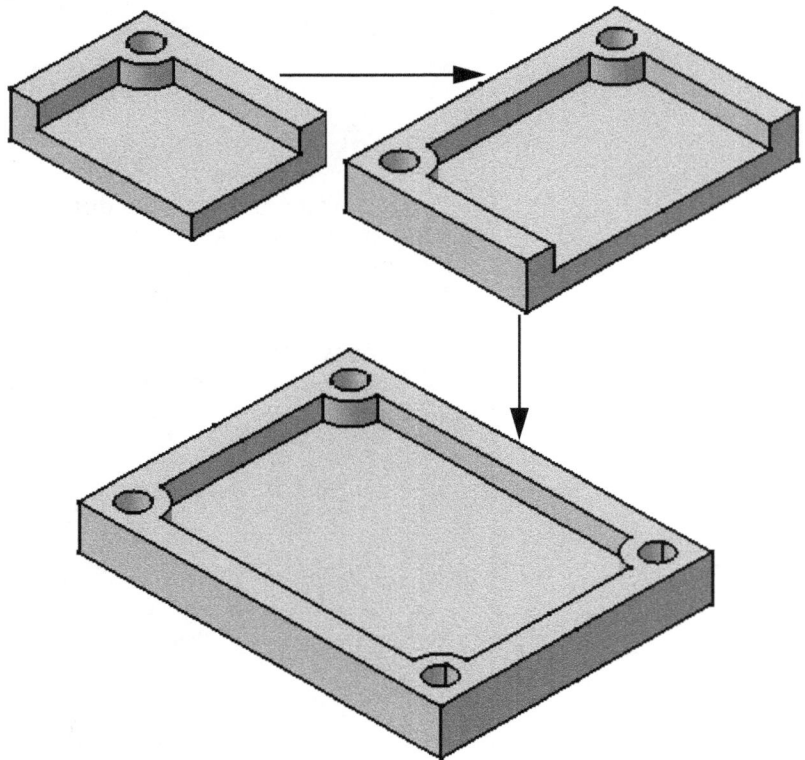

Figure 13–12

13.5 Formulas

A CATIA model can consist of one or many features, known as the intrinsic properties of the model. The software creates a system-defined parameter for every intrinsic property of a model. System- and user-defined parameters can be used in a formula.

Formulas are features that define or constrain a parameter. Using formulas enables you to fully capture the design intent of the model.

Figure 13–13 shows an example of a model whose design intent is model is to ensure that the hole feature is centered on the block even if the size the block changes in the future. A formula can be defined to capture this intent.

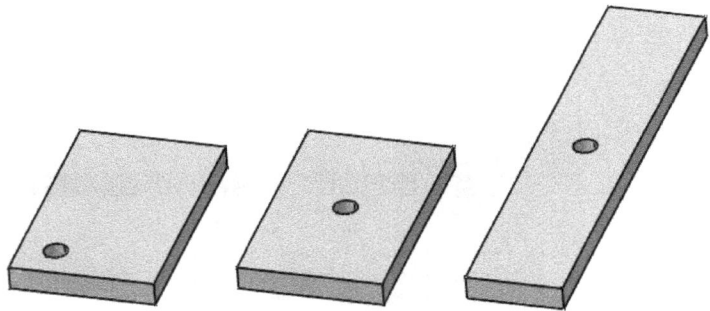

Figure 13–13

A formula is a relation that uses operators and functions to perform operations on parameters. An example of a formula is shown in Figure 13–14.

f(x) Formula.1: PartBody\Sketch.1\Length.5\Length=PartBody\Sketch.1\Length.6\Length *2

Figure 13–14

The left side of a relation is the parameter to be constrained and the right side is the statement used to control the feature.

13.6 Formulas Dialog Box

To create a formula (or function), click $f_{(x)}$ (Formula) in the toolbar. The Formulas dialog box opens as shown in Figure 13–15. The Formulas dialog box enables you to perform the following actions:

- Display the list of parameters.

- Create parameters and formulas.

- Import external files.

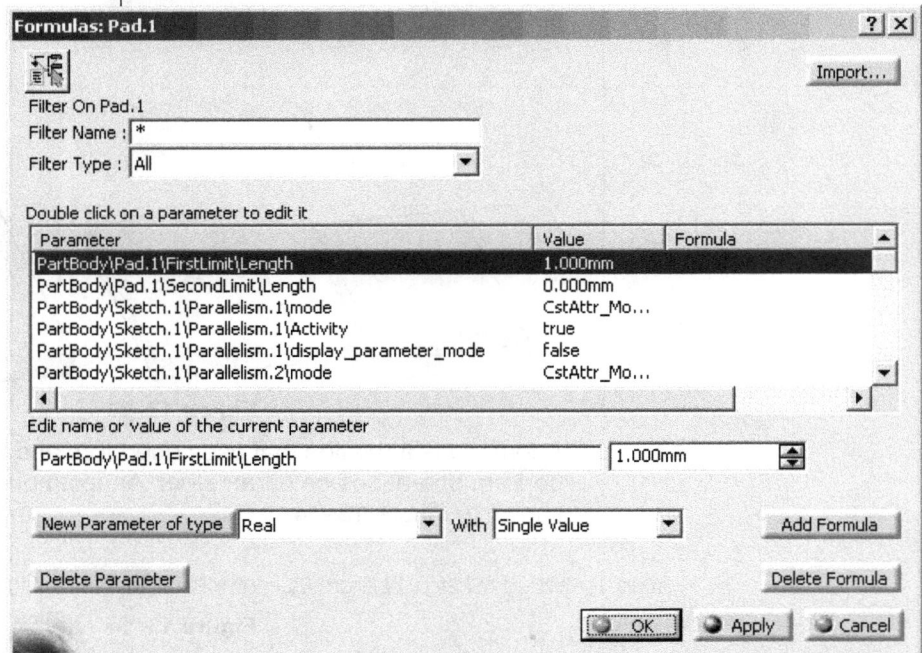

Figure 13–15

To access system or user-defined parameters, select a feature in the specification tree or from the model display and click

$f_{(x)}$ (Formula). By default, all the parameters associated with that feature display in the *Parameter* area.

Parameter Area

The *Parameter* area lists all of the parameters associated with the selected feature, as shown in Figure 13–16. If a feature is not selected before opening the Formulas dialog box, all model parameters display by default.

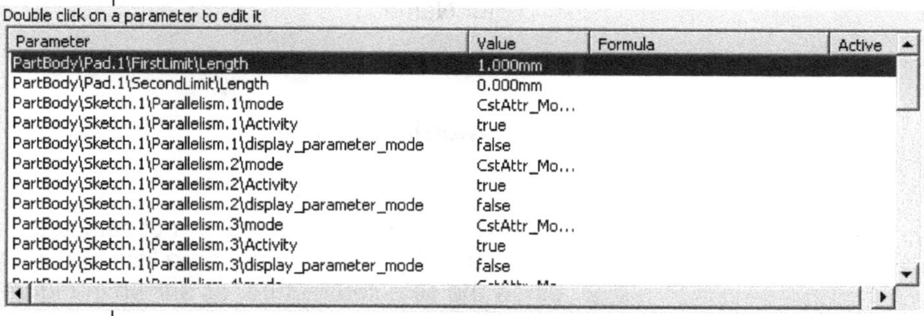

Double click on a parameter to edit it

Parameter	Value	Formula	Active ▲
PartBody\Pad.1\FirstLimit\Length	1.000mm		
PartBody\Pad.1\SecondLimit\Length	0.000mm		
PartBody\Sketch.1\Parallelism.1\mode	CstAttr_Mo...		
PartBody\Sketch.1\Parallelism.1\Activity	true		
PartBody\Sketch.1\Parallelism.1\display_parameter_mode	false		
PartBody\Sketch.1\Parallelism.2\mode	CstAttr_Mo...		
PartBody\Sketch.1\Parallelism.2\Activity	true		
PartBody\Sketch.1\Parallelism.2\display_parameter_mode	false		
PartBody\Sketch.1\Parallelism.3\mode	CstAttr_Mo...		
PartBody\Sketch.1\Parallelism.3\Activity	true		
PartBody\Sketch.1\Parallelism.3\display_parameter_mode	false		
PartBody\Sketch.1\Parallelism.4\mode	CstAttr_Mo...		

Figure 13–16

Edit Name or Value of Current Parameter

The *Edit name or value of the current parameter* box displays the selected parameter, as shown in Figure 13–17. The value box on the right side is not available if this parameter is already constrained by a formula.

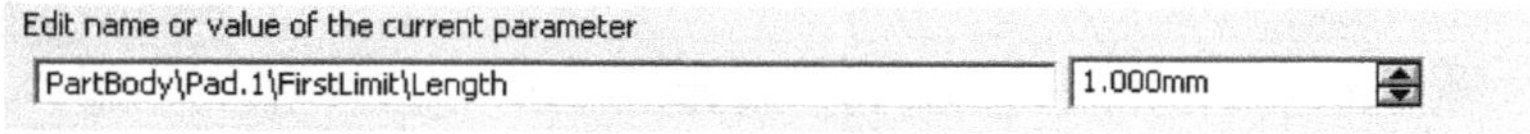

Edit name or value of the current parameter

| PartBody\Pad.1\FirstLimit\Length | 1.000mm |

Figure 13–17

Right-clicking on the value box opens a shortcut menu that enables you to redefine the parameter, as shown in Figure 13–18.

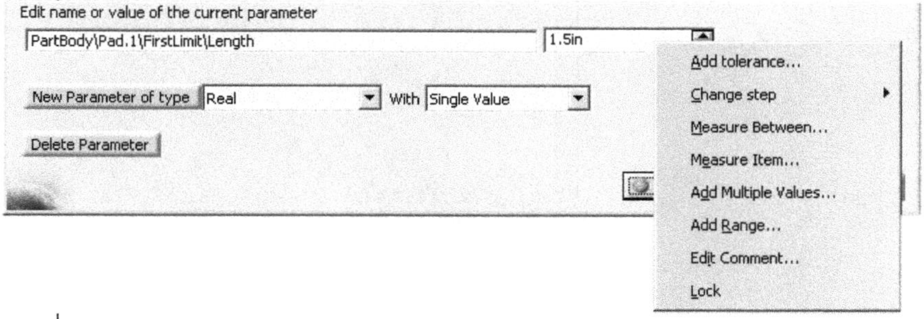

Edit name or value of the current parameter

| PartBody\Pad.1\FirstLimit\Length | 1.5in |

New Parameter of type | Real ▼ | With | Single Value ▼

Delete Parameter

Add tolerance...
Change step ▶
Measure Between...
Measure Item...
Add Multiple Values...
Add Range...
Edit Comment...
Lock

Figure 13–18

Filter Area

The *Filter* area in the Formulas dialog box enables you to narrow the parameter list using the following types of filters:

- Incremental option

- Filter Name

- Filter Type

Incremental Option

By default, 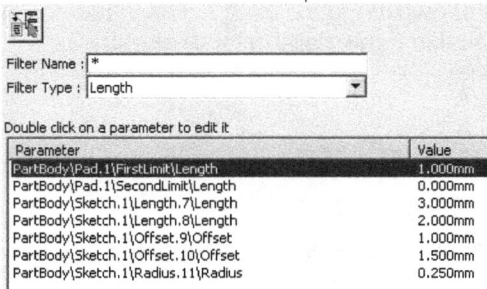 (Incremental) is not selected. When this option is not selected, the *Parameter* area lists the first level of features below the selected feature, as shown in Figure 13–19. If you click 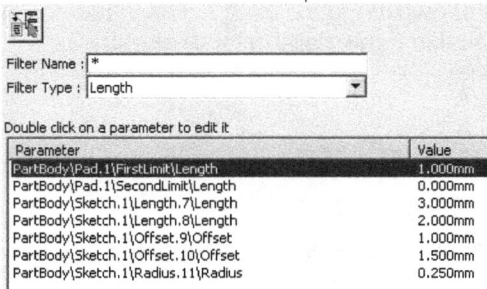 (Incremental), the *Parameter* area only lists one feature below the selected feature, as shown in Figure 13–20.

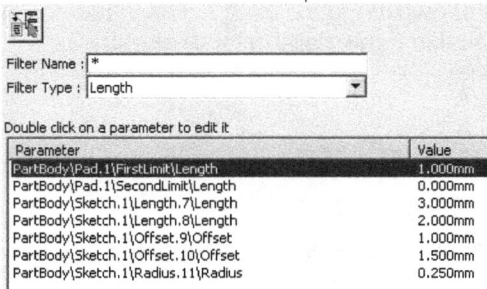

Figure 13–19

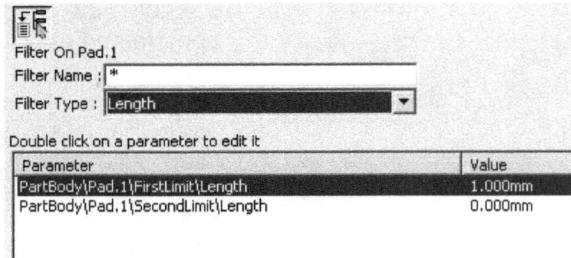

Figure 13–20

Filter Name

The *Filter Name* field enables you to specify a feature name to narrow the list of parameters displayed. Figure 13–21 shows the parameter list before entering a filter name value. Figure 13–22 shows the parameter list after **pad** has been entered in the *Filter Name* field. The software displays only the parameters containing the word "pad".

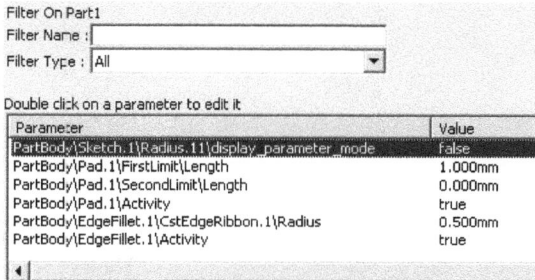

Figure 13–21

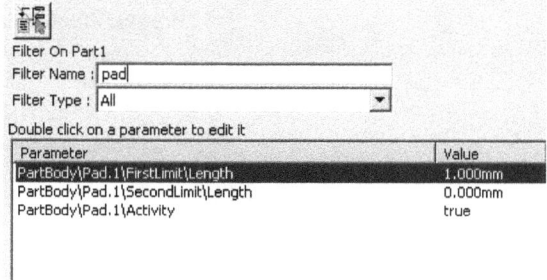

Figure 13–22

Filter Type

The value entered for filter name is not case-sensitive.

The *Filter Type* field enables you to specify the parameters to be displayed based on the type of parameter selected, as shown in Figure 13–23. Figure 13–24 shows the parameter list after *Filter Type* has been set to **Length**.

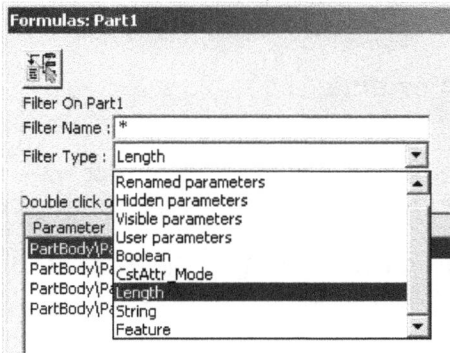

Figure 13–23

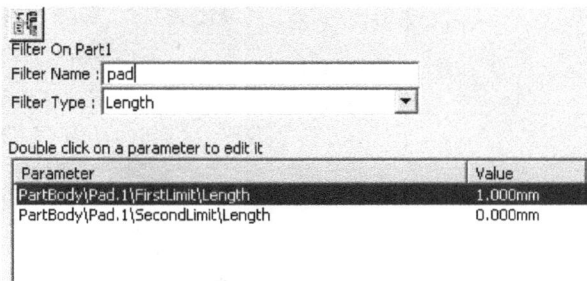

Figure 13–24

13.7 Create a Formula

Determining System Parameter Names

Place the cursor over a dimension in the Sketcher workbench to display a note with the name of the system-defined parameter. The dimension types and their corresponding parameter names are described as follows:

Dimension Type	Intrinsic Parameter Name
Radius Dimension	R. 1.2508 Radius.5
Line Length	1.7921 Length.8
Distance Between Two Parallel Lines	6.0989 Offset.7
Angle Between Two Lines	31.938° Angle.10

Creating a Formula

How To: Create a Formula

1. Click $f_{(x)}$ (Formula). The Formulas dialog box opens.
2. Select one or more feature(s) on the model to display their dimensions.
3. Select an intrinsic parameter name from the parameter list or select a dimension on the display. The formula drives this dimension.
4. Click **Add Formula**. The Formula Editor dialog box opens. Enter a formula and/or select another dimension to relate.
5. Click **OK** in the Formula Editor dialog box.
6. Click **OK** in the Formulas dialog box. The function symbol

   R. 2.5000 displays next to driven dimension.

13.8 View and Edit Formulas

Displaying in the Specification Tree

To display formulas and parameters in the specification tree, select **Tools>Options>Infrastructure>Part Infrastructure** and select the *Display* tab. Select the options to toggle the display of features on or off in the specification tree, as shown in Figure 13–25.

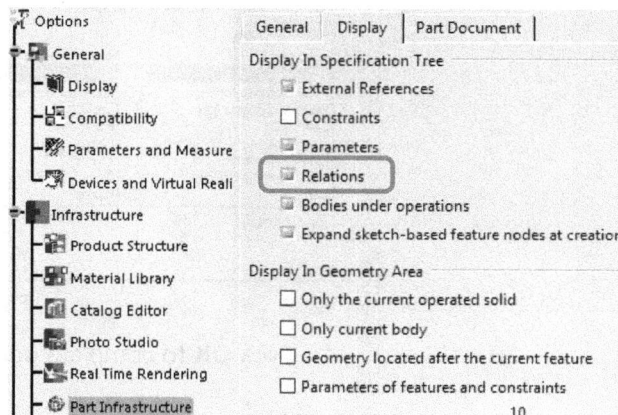

Figure 13–25

Figure 13–26 shows the specification tree with the relations display option enabled.

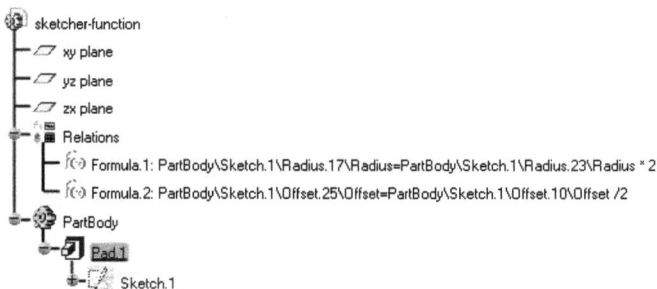

Figure 13–26

Select **Tools>Options>General>Display** to display the full text of a formula, then select the *Tree appearance* tab. The number of characters can be set to text-dependent (shows all text) or to a maximum number of characters, as shown in Figure 13–27.

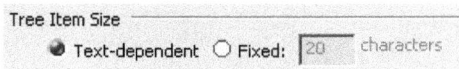

Figure 13–27

Edit and Delete a Formula

How To: Edit a Formula

1. Expand the relations branch in the specification tree.
2. Double-click on the relation to be edited.
3. Make changes using the Formula Editor dialog box, as shown in Figure 13–28.

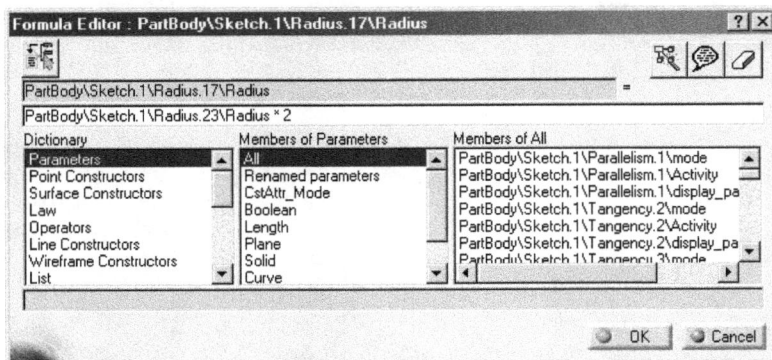

Figure 13–28

4. Click **OK** to complete editing the formula.

How To: Delete a Formula

1. Select the formula in the specification tree.
2. Press <Delete> or right-click and select **Delete**.

13.9 Create User-Defined Parameters

A user-defined parameter created in CATIA consists of a parameter name and a parameter value, which enable you to incorporate additional information into the model. Like system-defined parameters, they can be constrained by relations and used as an argument in a relation.

Types of Parameters

A few common parameter types include the following:

- Real Number

- Integer

- String

How To: Create a User-Defined Parameter

1. Click 𝑓(𝑥) (Formula). The Formulas dialog box opens, as shown in Figure 13–29.

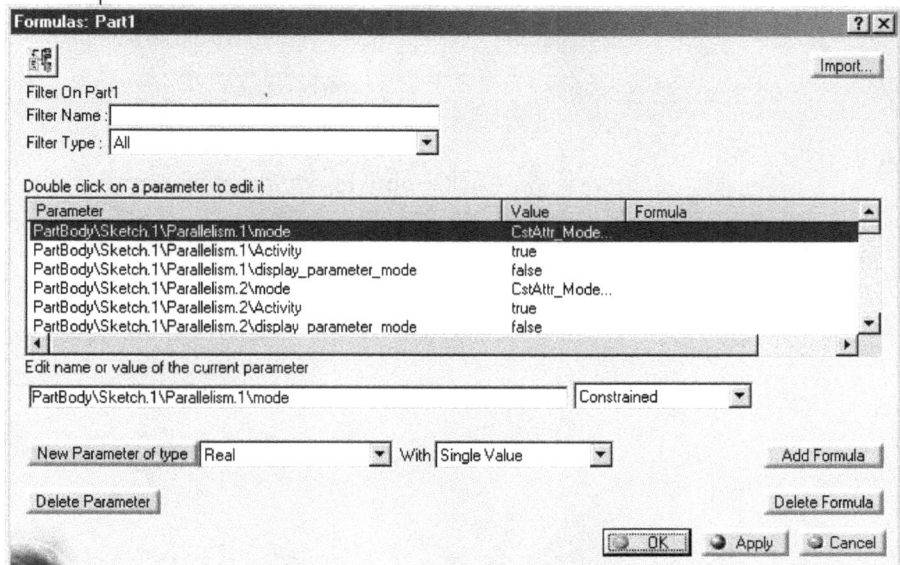

Figure 13–29

2. In the New Parameter of type drop-down list, select the type of parameter as shown in Figure 13–30.

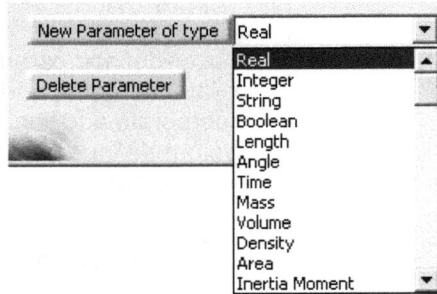

Figure 13–30

3. Click **New Parameter of type**. The dialog box updates with the additional input fields.
4. Enter a name and a value for the parameter, as shown in Figure 13–31.

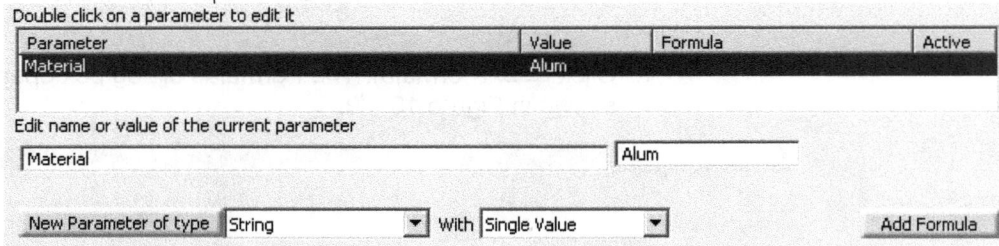

Figure 13–31

5. Click **Apply** to add the new parameter to the parameter list.
6. Click **OK**.

13.10 View and Edit User-defined Parameters

Displaying Parameters

To display the user-defined parameters in the specification tree, select **Tools>Options>Infrastructure>Part Infrastructure**. Select the *Display* tab and select the **Parameters** option, as shown in Figure 13–32.

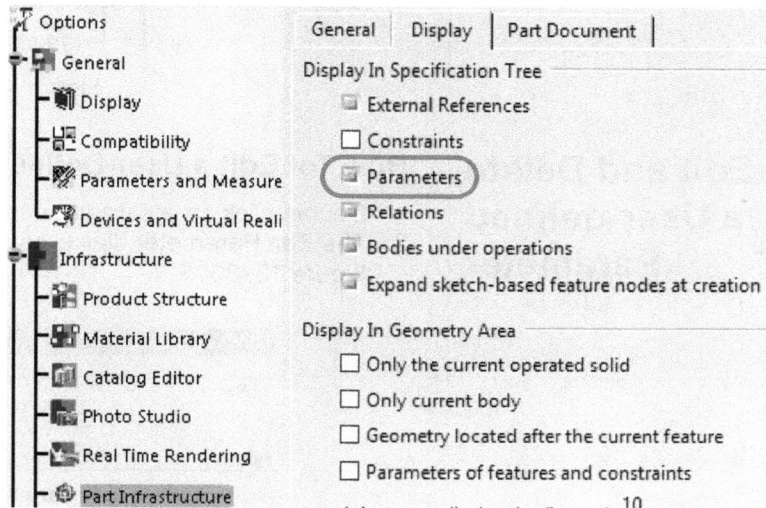

Figure 13–32

To display the user-defined parameter value in the specification tree, select **Tools>Options>General>Parameters and Measures** and select the *Knowledge* tab. Select the **With value** option, as shown in Figure 13–33.

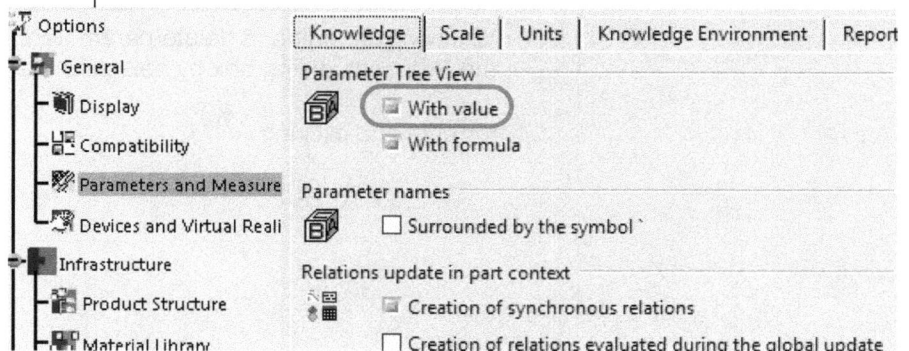

Figure 13–33

The specification tree is shown in Figure 13–34 listing a user-defined parameter of type string named material, which has a value of **Alum**.

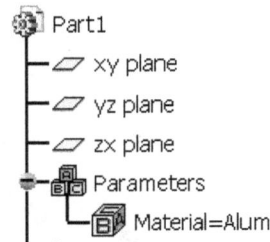

Figure 13–34

Edit and Delete a User-defined Parameter

How To: Edit a User-Defined Parameter

1. Double-click on a parameter in the specification tree.
2. The Edit Parameter dialog box opens as shown in Figure 13–35.

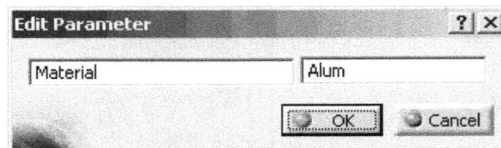

Figure 13–35

3. Make the changes as required.

How To: Delete a User-Defined Parameter

1. Select the parameter in the specification tree.
2. Press <Delete> or right-click and select **Delete**.

• You can also edit and delete parameters and formulas using the Formulas dialog box by selecting the parameter or formula and clicking $f_{(x)}$.

Practice 13a | Patterning

Practice Objectives

- Duplicate a feature using a rectangular and circular pattern.
- Modify circular and rectangular patterns.

In this practice, you will create the two parts shown in Figure 13–36. Each of these parts will consist of a patterned feature. The patterns are later modified, and some patterned instances are removed from the patterns manually.

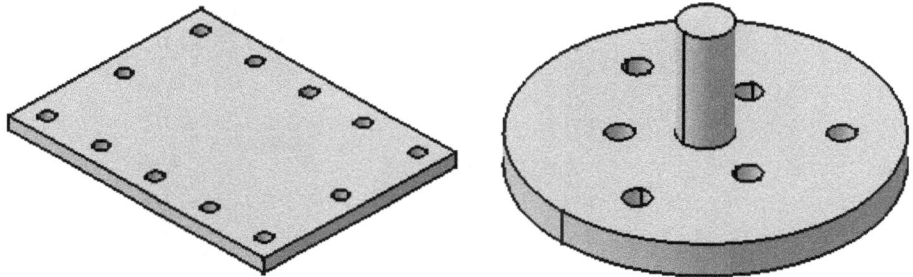

Figure 13–36

Task 1 - Open the part pattern1.

1. Select **File>Open** and select **Pattern_Rect.CATPart**.

2. In the specification tree, select **Hole.1** and click

   ▦ (Rectangular Pattern). The Rectangular Pattern Definition dialog box opens.

3. Set the following, as shown in Figure 13–37:

- *Parameters:* **Instance(s) & Spacing**
- *Instance(s):* **5**
- *Spacing:* **25 (0.984 in)**

Figure 13–37

4. Select the *Reference element* field, and select the front edge as the reference direction, as shown in Figure 13–38.

5. Click **Reverse**, if required, to position the holes on the plate.

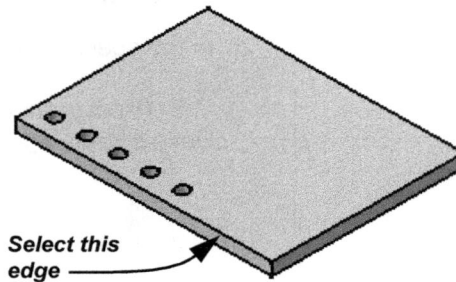

Select this edge

Figure 13–38

6. Click **OK** to finish the pattern definition. The pattern is not evenly spaced about the plate.

Task 2 - Modify the pattern for equal spacing.

1. In the specification tree, double-click on the **RectPattern.1** feature. The Rectangular Pattern Definition dialog box opens.

2. Select **Instance(s) & Length** in the Parameters drop-down list.

3. The original hole is located 15mm (0.591 in) from the part edges and the part is 200mm (7.874 in) long in this direction. Change the length to **170 (6.693 in)**.

4. Click **OK** to display the new pattern, as shown in Figure 13–39.

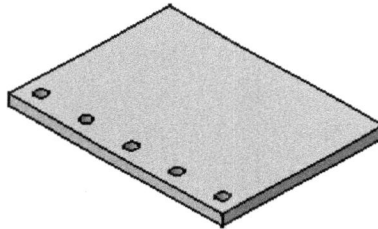

Figure 13–39

Task 3 - Modify the pattern for two directions.

1. In the specification tree, double-click on **RectPattern.1**.

2. Select the *Second Direction* tab.

3. Position three instances of the holes centered on the Pad, as shown in Figure 13–40. The holes are 15mm (0.591 in) from the Pad edge and the part is 150mm (5.906 in) long in this direction.

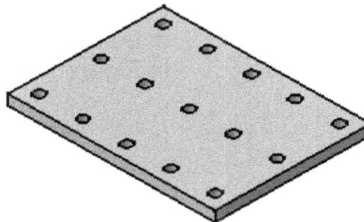

Figure 13–40

Task 4 - Remove the three holes in the center.

1. In the specification tree, double-click on **RectPattern.1**.

2. Select the dots at the center of the three holes that are in the center of the Pad.

3. Click **OK**. The model displays as shown in Figure 13–41.

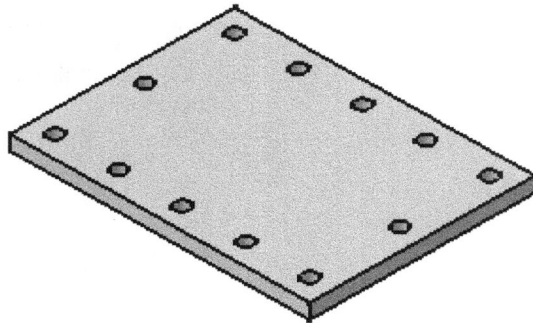

Figure 13–41

4. Save the model and close the window.

Task 5 - Open the part Pattern_Circ.

1. Select **File>Open** and select **Pattern_Circ.CATPart**.

2. In the specification tree, select **Hole.1**. Click ⬥ (Circular Pattern). The Circular Pattern Definition dialog box opens.

3. In the Parameters drop-down list, select **Complete crown** and enter **6** in *Instance(s)*.

4. Select the cylindrical surface as the reference element. The **Pattern** tool will use the implicit axis as the reference direction. The Circular Pattern Dialog box displays as shown in Figure 13–42.

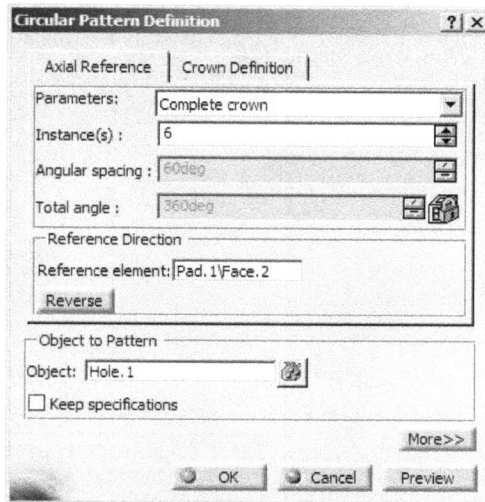

Figure 13–42

5. Click **OK** to finish the pattern creation. The part displays as shown in Figure 13–43.

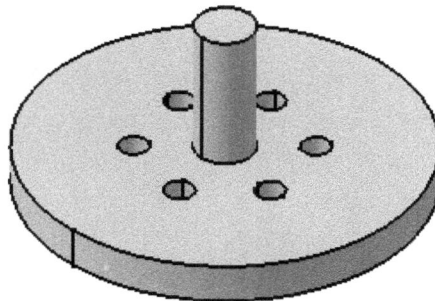

Figure 13–43

Task 6 - Add a second direction for the circular pattern.

1. In the specification tree, double-click on **CircPattern.1**.

2. Select the *Crown Definition* tab and set the following:

    - *Circle(s)*: **2**
    - *Circle Spacing*: **25 (0.984 in)**

3. Click **OK** to finish the pattern creation. The model displays as shown in Figure 13–44.

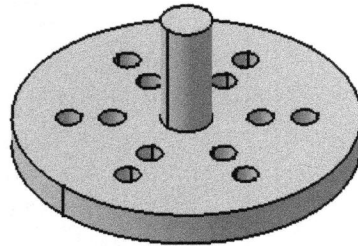

Figure 13–44

Task 7 - Remove instances from the pattern.

1. Redefine the pattern and remove instances so that the model displays as shown in Figure 13–45.

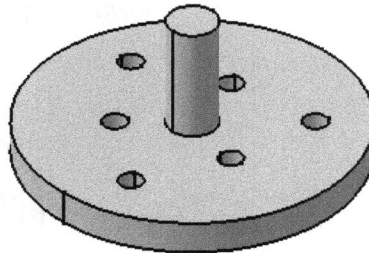

Figure 13–45

2. Save the model and close the window.

Practice 13b | User Patterns

Practice Objective

- Create a user pattern.

In this practice, you will create a user pattern of multiple features to create the boss for the screws and to hold the two halves of the tape measure together. The completed model with a user pattern of three screw boss instances is shown in Figure 13–46.

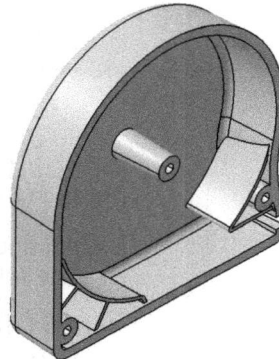

Figure 13–46

Task 1 - Create a user pattern.

1. Open **TapeMeasureBack.CATPart**.

2. Preselect the following three features, as shown in Figure 13–47:

   - **Pad.2**
   - **Hole.1**
   - **Draft.3**

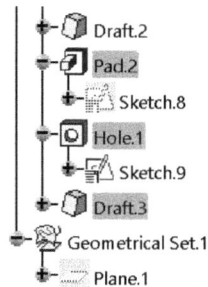

Figure 13–47

3. Click 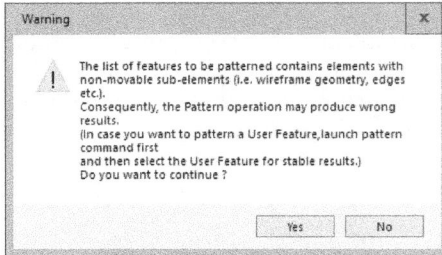 (User Pattern). A warning message opens as shown in Figure 13–48. Click **Yes** to open the User Pattern Definition dialog box shown in Figure 13–49.

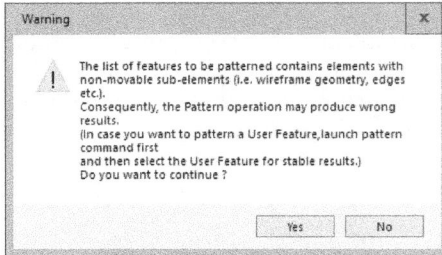

Figure 13–48

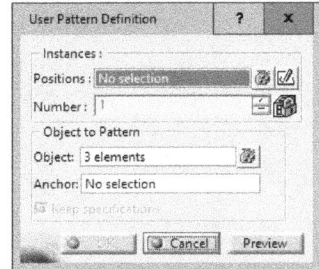

Figure 13–49

4. Click 🖉 (Sketch) next to the *Positions* field and select the **zx plane** in the specification tree.

5. Sketch and dimension the 3 points shown in Figure 13–51. Use the following dimensions:

- 28 (1.102 in)
- 36 (1.417 in)
- 38 (1.496 in)

Image shown in Wireframe for clarity.

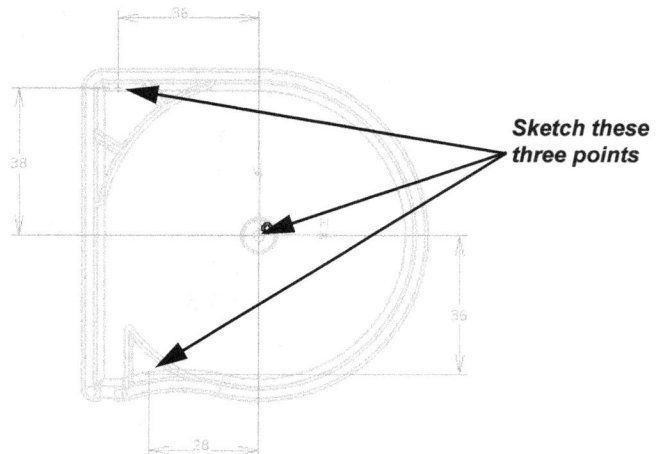

Sketch these three points

Figure 13–50

6. Exit the Sketcher workbench.

7. Click **OK** in the User Pattern Definition dialog box. The model updates as shown in Figure 13–51.

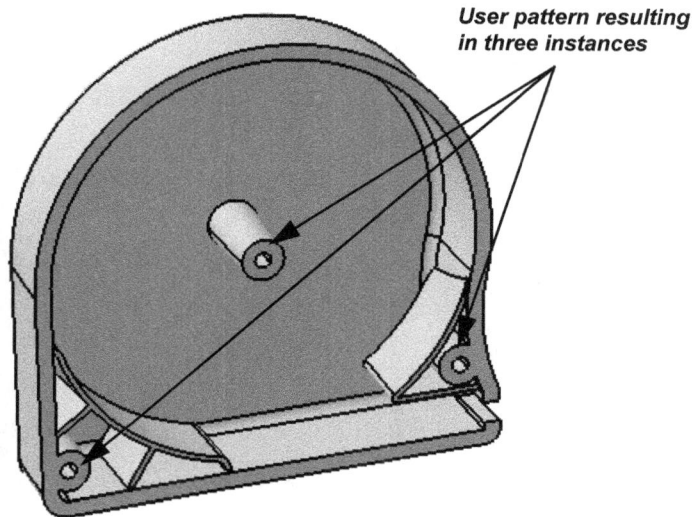

User pattern resulting in three instances

Figure 13–51

Task 2 - Create a Pocket feature.

1. Create a positioned sketch on the planar surface as shown in Figure 13–52.

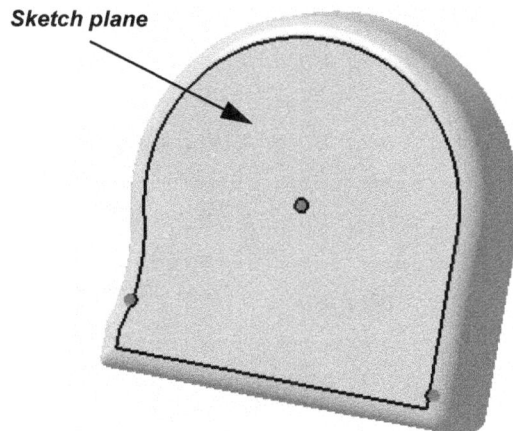

Sketch plane

Figure 13–52

2. Create a sketch by offsetting the circular edge of the existing hole by **1.5 (0.059 in)**, as shown in Figure 13–53.

3. Exit the Sketcher workbench.

4. Click 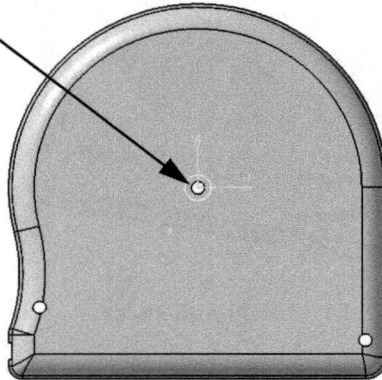 and define the Pocket by setting the *depth* to **1.5 (0.059 in)**.

The completed Pocket is shown in Figure 13–54.

Offset the edge by 1.5

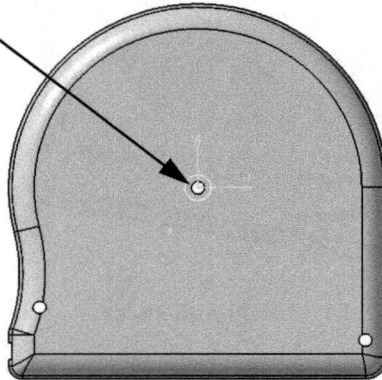

Figure 13–53

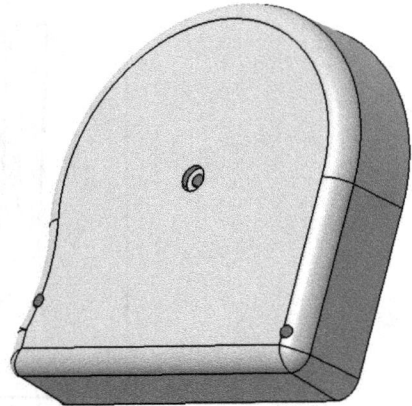

Figure 13–54

Task 3 - Create a user pattern.

1. Select the Pocket you just created and click (User Pattern).

2. In the specification tree, select **Sketch.13**, which was established when creating the pattern for the Pad, Hole, and Draft.

3. Click **OK** and the completed Pocket user pattern displays as shown in Figure 13–56.

4. Click 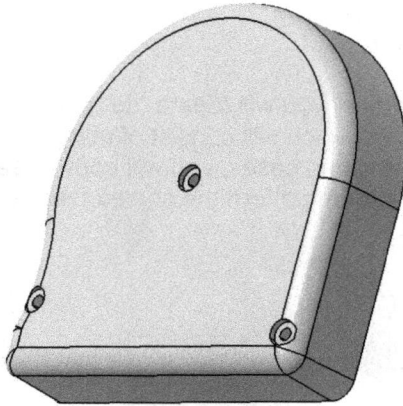 (Isometric View) and save the model. The model displays as shown in Figure 13–56.

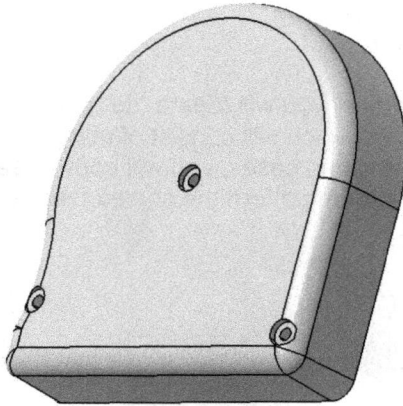

Figure 13–55

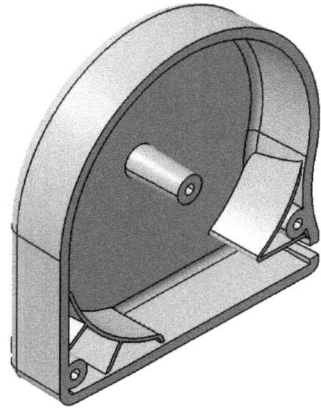

Figure 13–56

Design Considerations

A user pattern enables you to pattern multiple features and use the same positioning sketch multiple times as shown in Figure 13–57.

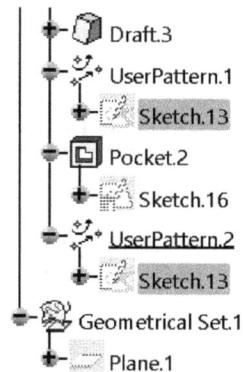

Figure 13–57

5. Save the model and close the window.

Practice 13c | Mirror

Practice Objectives

- Mirror features.
- Create patterns.

In this practice, you will create the part shown in Figure 13–58which will consist of mirrored and patterned features. In some cases, you will copy a feature into a mirrored feature and then pattern the copied feature.

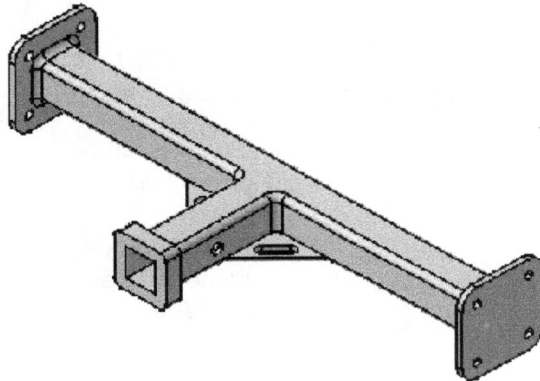

Figure 13–58

Task 1 - Open T_Support.

1. Select **File>Open** and select **T_Support.CATPart**.

2. Create the rectangular pattern of **Hole.2**, as shown in Figure 13–59. Enter **89.2 (3.512 in)** for the *spacing*.

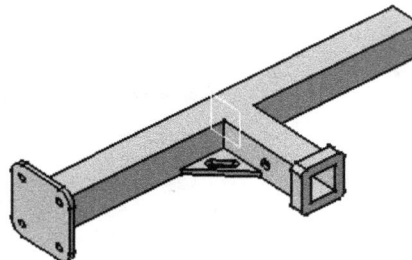

Figure 13–59

Task 2 - Mirror the mounting area to the other side.

1. Using <Ctrl>, select **Pad.4** and **EdgeFillet.3**.

2. Click [icon] (Mirror). You are prompted for the mirroring element.

3. In the specification tree, select plane ZX and click **OK**. The model displays as shown in Figure 13–60.

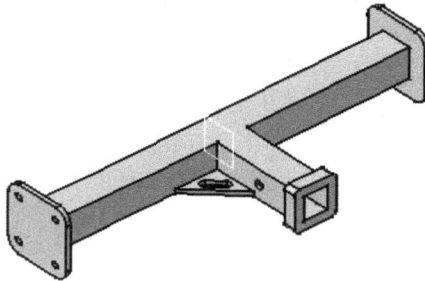

Figure 13–60

Task 3 - Copy a Hole feature.

1. Select **Hole.2** in the specification tree.

2. Select **Edit>Copy**.

3. Select the mirrored Pad surface, as shown in Figure 13–61. Select **Edit>Paste**.

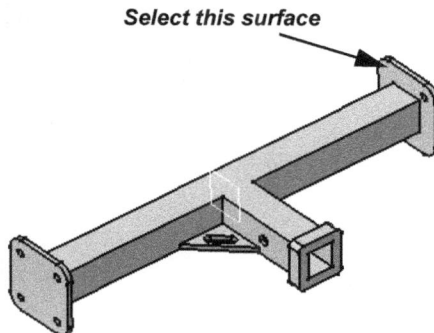

Select this surface

Figure 13–61

4. Create the rectangular pattern for **Hole.3**, as shown in Figure 13–62.

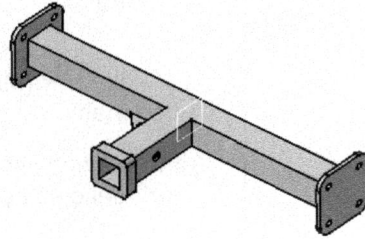

Figure 13–62

Task 4 - Mirror the stiffener and Pocket features.

1. In the specification tree using <Ctrl>, select **Stiffener.1** and **Pocket.1**.

2. Mirror the features about plane ZX, as shown in Figure 13–63.

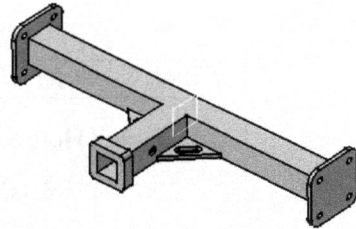

Figure 13–63

Task 5 - Finish the model.

1. Finish the model by adding **9.525 (0.375 in)** edge fillets where required. Use Figure 13–64 as a reference.

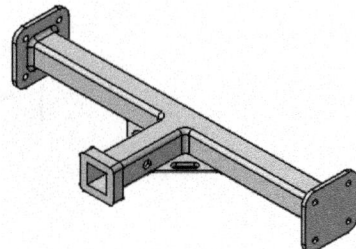

Figure 13–64

2. Save the model and close the window.

Practice 13d | (Optional) Piston

Practice Objective

- Create more complex geometry without instructions

Create a new part called **Piston** with a part number of **02051875**. Refer to the drawing shown in Figure 13–65 for dimension values.

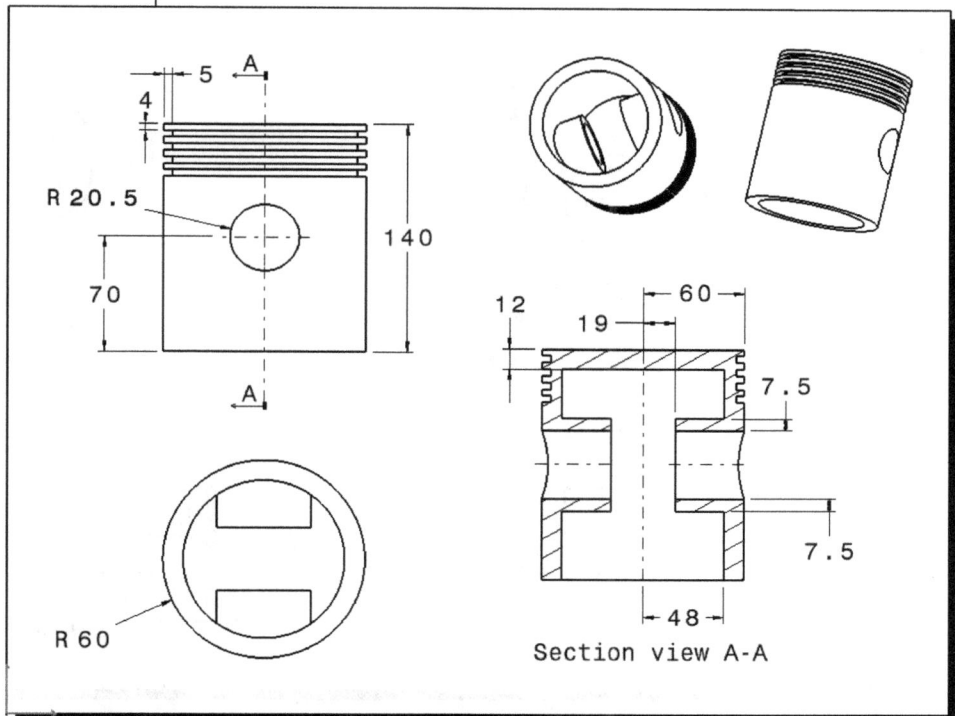

Figure 13–65

Practice 13e | (Optional) Flange

Practice Objective

- Duplicate features without instructions

Create a new part called **Flange** with a part number of **0311892**. Refer to the drawing shown in Figure 13–66 for dimension values.

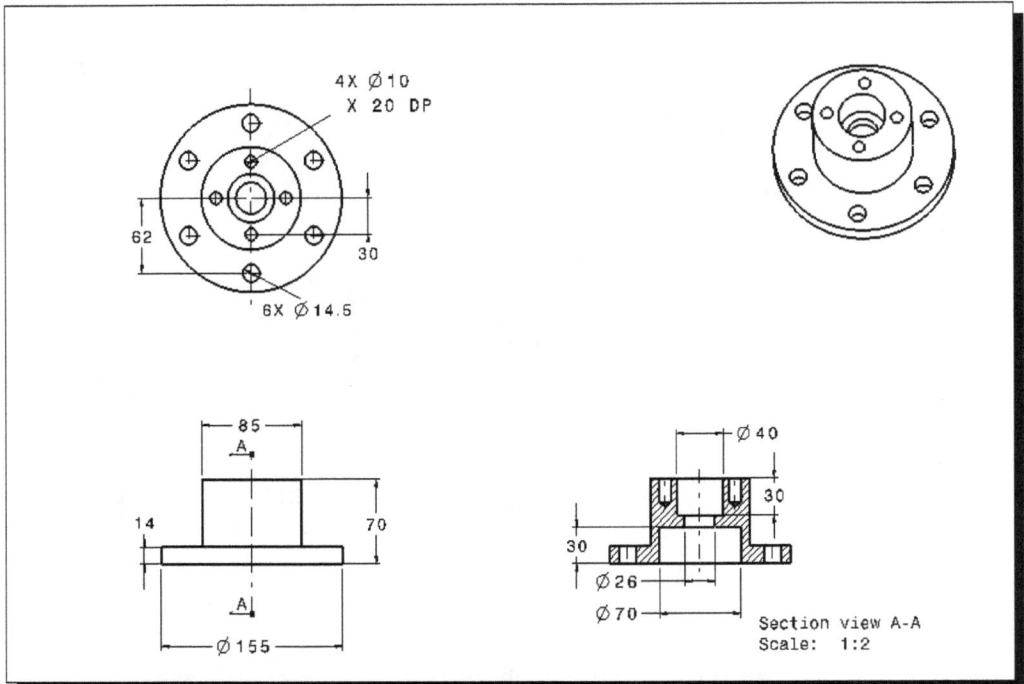

Figure 13–66

Practice 13f | Relations

Practice Objective

- Create a relation using formulas.

In this practice, you will create the part shown in Figure 13–67. The design requires the hole feature to remain located at the center of the part, regardless of changes to the main part. You will use formulas to create a relation to constrain the hole feature to the center of the part.

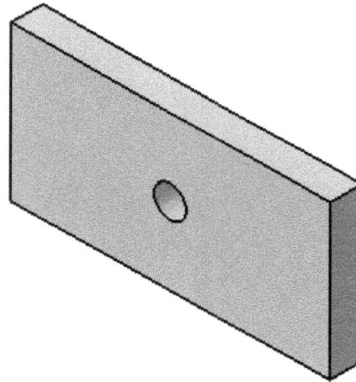

Figure 13–67

Task 1 - Create a new part model.

1. Create a new part file.

2. Create a sketch with the dimensions and constraints, as shown in Figure 13–68. Select the YZ plane as the sketching plane.

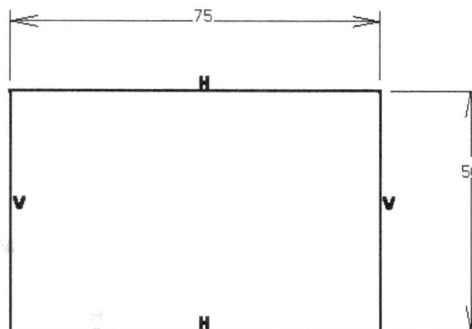

Figure 13–68

3. Create a pad feature that is 12.5 in height. Click
   ▢ (Isometric view) so that the model displays as shown in
   Figure 13–69.

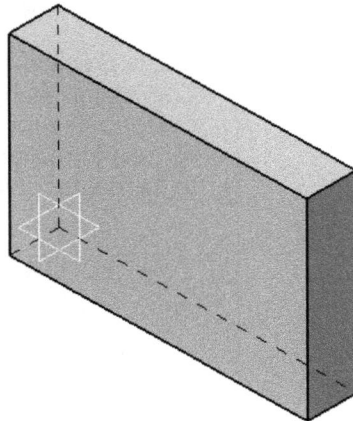

Figure 13–69

4. Save the part and enter **Relations** as the name.

Task 2 - Create a relation using a formula.

1. Click $f_{(x)}$ (Formula). The Formulas dialog box opens, listing
   all of the system parameters.

2. In the specification tree, select **Sketch.1**. The dimensions
   used to constrain the sketch display.

3. In the Formulas dialog box, in the Filter Type drop-down list,
   select **Length** as shown in Figure 13–70.

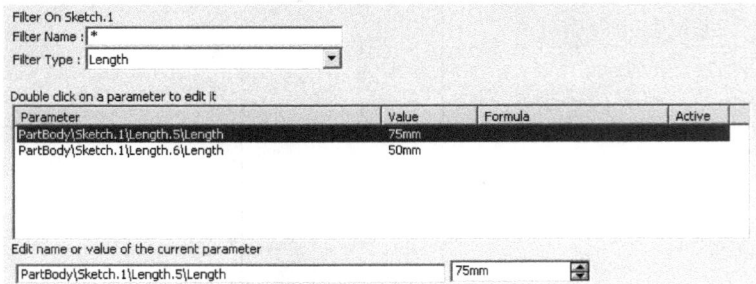

Filter On Sketch.1
Filter Name : *
Filter Type : Length

Double click on a parameter to edit it

Parameter	Value	Formula	Active
PartBody\Sketch.1\Length.5\Length	75mm		
PartBody\Sketch.1\Length.6\Length	50mm		

Edit name or value of the current parameter

PartBody\Sketch.1\Length.5\Length   75mm

Figure 13–70

4. Select the **75 (2.953 in)** parameter.

5. Click **Add Formula**.

6. The Formula Editor dialog box opens, as shown Figure 13–71. Select the **50 (1.969)** dimension from the model display.

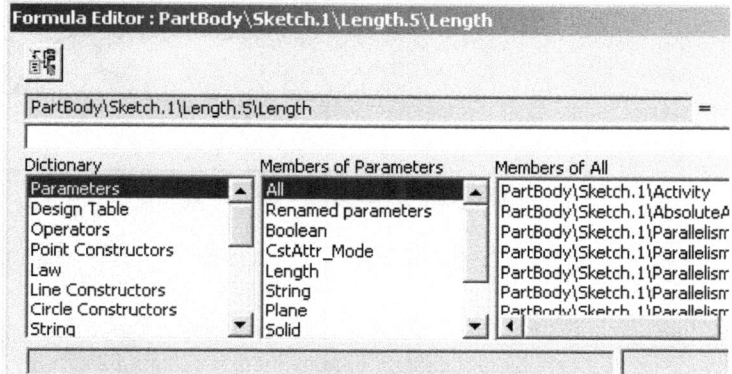

Formula Editor : PartBody\Sketch.1\Length.5\Length

PartBody\Sketch.1\Length.5\Length   =

Dictionary	Members of Parameters	Members of All
Parameters	All	PartBody\Sketch.1\Activity
Design Table	Renamed parameters	PartBody\Sketch.1\AbsoluteA
Operators	Boolean	PartBody\Sketch.1\Parallelism
Point Constructors	CstAttr_Mode	PartBody\Sketch.1\Parallelism
Law	Length	PartBody\Sketch.1\Parallelism
Line Constructors	String	PartBody\Sketch.1\Parallelism
Circle Constructors	Plane	PartBody\Sketch.1\Parallelism
String	Solid	◄

Figure 13–71

7. Enter ***2** in the field, as shown in Figure 13–72.

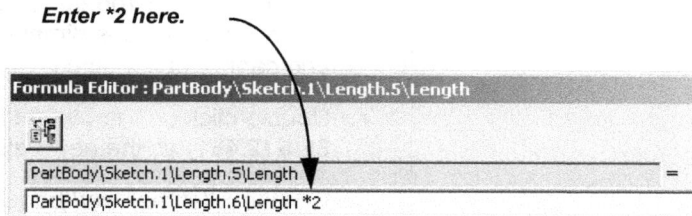

Enter *2 here.

Formula Editor : PartBody\Sketch.1\Length.5\Length

PartBody\Sketch.1\Length.5\Length   =
PartBody\Sketch.1\Length.6\Length *2

Figure 13–72

This sets the **75 (2.953 in)** parameter to be two times the **50 (1.969)** parameter.

8. Click **OK**.

9. Click **Apply** and **OK**.

10. The model updates to reflect the newly created formula.

Task 3 - Investigate the formula in the model.

1. In the specification tree, double-click on **Sketch.1**.

2. The sketch opens as shown in Figure 13–73. Note the updated value (**100.00 (3.937in)**) and the appearance of the function symbol.

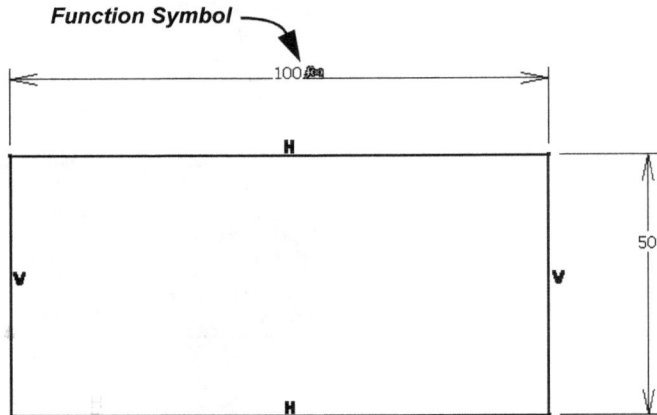

Figure 13–73

3. Double-click on **100.00 (3.937in)** dimension to modify its value. Note that this dimension is now driven by the formula and cannot be modified. Click **OK**.

4. Double-click on the **50.00 (1.969 in)** dimension and enter **62.5 (2.461)** as the new value. Note the updated values.

5. Exit the Sketcher workbench and save the model.

Task 4 - Create a hole feature.

1. Create a Hole feature with a **12.5 (0.492 in)** diameter, using the **Up To Next** depth option.

2. Dimension the hole as shown in Figure 13–74.

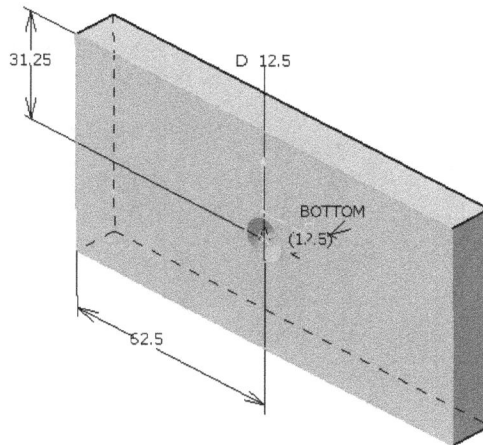

Figure 13–74

The design intent of this part is to keep the Hole feature centered on the part. Using the above dimensions, the hole is centered.

3. Modify the 62.5 (2.461 in) dimension of **Pad.1** to **75.00 (3.937in)**. Did the hole feature remain in the center of the

   part? Click (Undo) to undo the modification.

Task 5 - Create a relation to center the hole feature.

Design Considerations

Create a relation to ensure that the hole always remains in the center of the part regardless of the part dimensions. Without a relation, the hole will not remain in the center if the part is modified. If we add a relation where the hole remains at the midpoint of the length and the midpoint of the width of the part, the hole will remain centered as the part is updated.

1. Click (Formula). The Formulas dialog box opens.

2. Select the Hole feature. The dimensions for the Hole feature display.

3. Select the **62.50 (2.461 in)** dimension of the Hole feature.

4. Click **Add Formula**. The Formula Editor dialog box opens.

5. In the specification tree, select **Pad.1**. The sketch dimensions of **Pad.1** display.

6. Select the **125.00 (4.921)** dimension.

7. Add **/2** to the pad sketch length parameter, as shown in Figure 13–75.

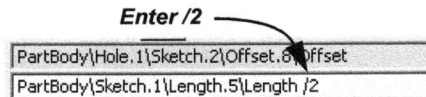

Enter /2 —————

```
PartBody\Hole.1\Sketch.2\Offset.8\Offset
PartBody\Sketch.1\Length.5\Length /2
```

Figure 13–75

8. Click **OK**.

9. Repeat Steps 2 to 8 for the **31.25 (1.230 in)** dimension of the hole and the **62.5 (2.461 in)** dimension of **Pad.1**.

10. Click **OK** and **Apply** to complete the definition of the formula.

11. Modify the 62.5 dimension of **Pad.1** as **75.0 (3.937in)**.

12. Has the design intent of this part been captured? Which dimensions can be directly modified? Which dimensions cannot be directly modified?

Task 6 - Display the relation features in the specification tree.

---

1. Select **Tools>Options>Infrastructure>Part Infrastructure**.

2. Select the *Display* tab and select **Relations**. Click **OK**. The specification tree updates to display the relation features you have created.

3. Change the text displayed for the relation features by selecting **Tools>Options>General>Display**. Select the *Tree appearance* tab.

4. Select the **Text-dependent** option and click **OK**. Note the changes in the specification tree.

5. Click [save icon]. Select **File>Close**.

Practice 13g | Relations II

Practice Objectives

- Create formulas to define a relation.
- Create user-defined parameters.

In this practice, you will modify an existing part by creating formulas and relations. The design require the wall thickness remain at one-eighth of the height, regardless of changes to the height. You will create a relation between the wall thickness and the height of the part to achieve the design intent.

Task 1 - Open an existing model.

1. Open the **Shell_Relation.CATPart** part file.

2. Investigate the features in the specification tree that make up this part.

Task 2 - Create a relation to capture the design intent.

A structural analysis of this part indicates that a relationship between the height of the part and the wall thickness must exist. To maintain the structural integrity of the part, the wall thickness must be a function of the height by a factor of 0.125.

1. Click $f_{(x)}$ (Formula). In the specification tree, select the **Shell.1** feature. Select the shell thickness dimension **1.60 (0.063 in)** as the dimension to be driven.

2. Click **Add Formula**.

3. Select the **9.5** (0.374 in) length (height) dimension on **Pad.1** and multiply the parameter by **0.125**. Apply the formula to complete the formula definition.

4. Flex the model by modifying the height value from 9.5 (0.374 in) to **12.50 (0.492 in)**.

5. Modify the height value again to **25.0 (0.984 in)**. Note the wall thickness of the shell updates.

Task 3 - Add a relation using the Constraint Definition dialog box.

1. In the specification tree, double-click on **Pad.1**. The dimensions for **Pad.1** display.

2. Double-click on the **38 (1.496 in)** dimension. The Constraint Definition Dialog box opens.

3. Right-click on the value field and select **Edit Formula...** as shown in Figure 13–76.

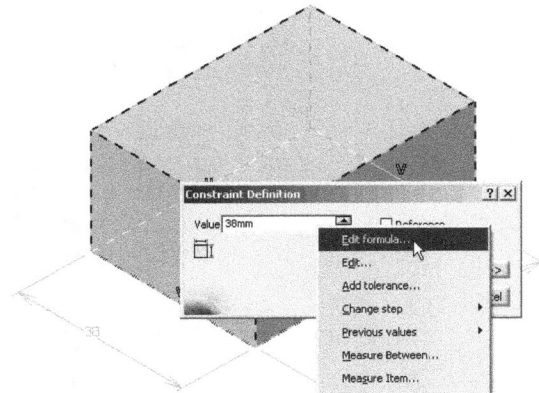

Figure 13–76

4. The Formula Editor dialog box opens. Select the **50 (1.969 in)** dimension.

5. Add **/2** to the parameter.

6. Click **OK** in the Formula Editor dialog box.

7. Click **OK** in the Pad Definition dialog box. The model updates and displays as shown in Figure 13–77.

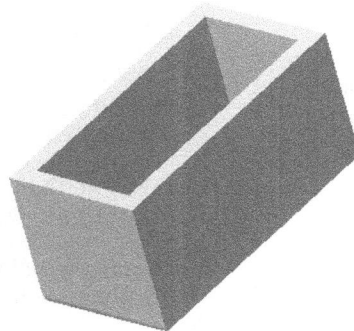

Figure 13–77

8. Save the model.

Task 4 - Create a user-defined parameter.

1. Click $f_{(x)}$ (Formula).

2. In the New parameter of type drop-down list, select **String** as shown in Figure 13–78.

Figure 13–78

3. Click **New Parameter of type**.

4. Enter **Material** as the name and **6061 Alum** as the value as shown in Figure 13–79.

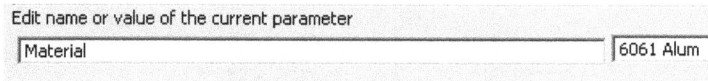

Figure 13–79

5. Click **OK**.

Task 5 - Display the parameter and its value in the specification tree.

---

1. Select **Tools>Options>Infrastructure>Part Infrastructure**. Select the *Display* tab and select **Parameters**.

2. Click **OK**. The specification tree updates to display the user-defined parameter feature you have created.

3. Display the parameter value in the specification tree by selecting **Tools>Options>General>Parameters and Measures**.

4. Select the *Knowledge* tab and select **With Value**. Click **OK**.

If the parameter is not displayed in the specification tree, select Tools>Options> Infrastructure>Part Infrastructure. Select the Display tab and select the Parameters option.

5. The specification tree updates to display this information, as shown in Figure 13–80.

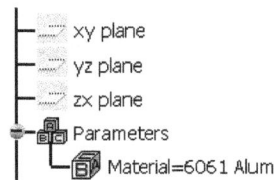

Figure 13–80

6. Click .

7. Select **File>Close**.

Chapter Review Questions

1. The model shown in Figure 13–81 has a rectangular pattern of holes created in one direction. What was the number of pattern instances defined in the dialog box?

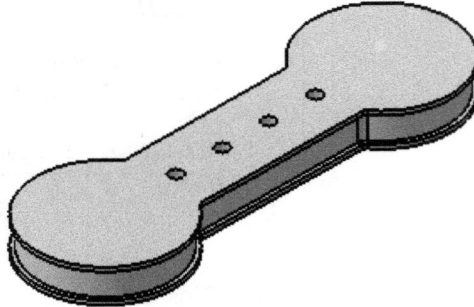

Figure 13–81

   a. 1

   b. 3

   c. 2

   d. 4

2. Which reference element(s) can be used as a reference for mirroring features?

   a. Plane

   b. Point

   c. Axis

3. You can mirror individual features or the entire part body.

   a. True

   b. False

4. When you delete a pattern, all occurrences of the Pattern feature are deleted including the original feature?

   a. True

   b. False

5. Multiple features can be Patterns at the same time.

   a. True

   b. False

6. To create the pattern shown in Figure 13–82, you could create a rectangular pattern in two directions and toggle off the instances that are not required.

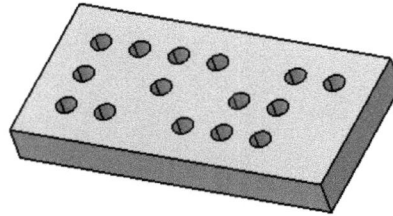

Figure 13–82

   a. True

   b. False

7. Copied features remain dependent on the source feature.

   a. True

   b. False

8. A PartBody contains five features. If the entire current solid is mirrored, how many features are listed in the specification tree?

   a. 5

   b. 10

   c. 6

   d. 11

9. A mirrored feature is dependent on the source geometry.

   a. True

   b. False

Answers: 1.d, 2.a, 3.a, 4.b, 5.a, 6.a, 7.b, 8.c, 9.a

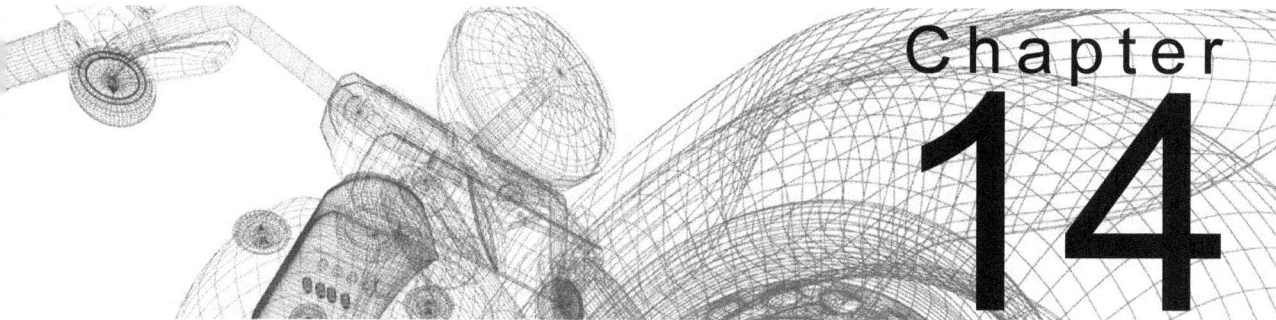

Thin Features

This chapter introduces solid features that enable the use of thin cross-sections by prompting you to input a thickness value.

Learning Objectives in this Chapter

- Create pads and pockets from open or closed sections using the Thick option.
- Learn how to quickly add stiffeners to a model.

14.1 Thin Pads and Pockets

Pad and Pocket features are created from sketches whose entities are closed, or otherwise closed by existing geometry. Solid material is either added to or subtracted from the enclosed area of the sketch.

Using the **Thick** option, you can apply solid material to one or both sides of an open sketch. Solid material can also be applied to the inside or outside area of a closed sketch. The **Thick** option offsets a section and adds or removes material between the original sketch and the offset section.

Thin Pads

To create a thin Pad, select **Thick** in the Pad Definition dialog box, as shown in Figure 14–1.

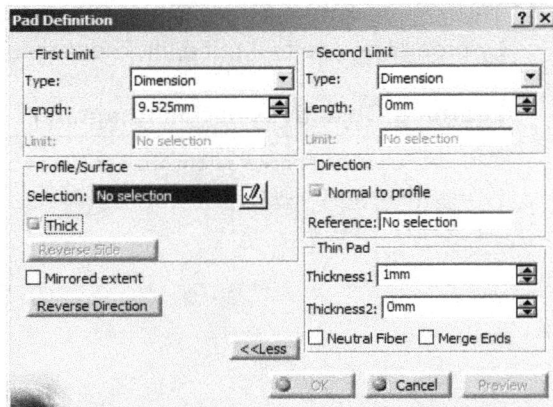

Figure 14–1

The base feature shown in Figure 14–2 has a constant thickness applied to one side of the open section sketch.

A thickness can be applied to both sides of the sketch.

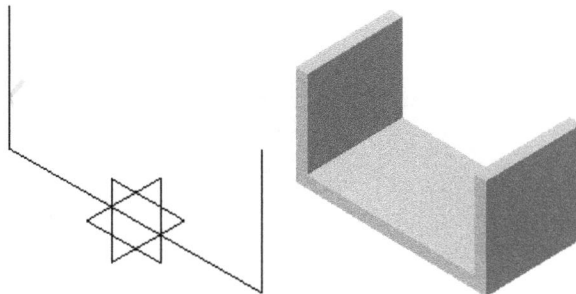

Figure 14–2

Thin Pockets

The **Thick** option can also be applied to a Pocket feature. Figure 14–3 shows a sketch that can be used to create a thin Pocket. The result of the offset displays with and without the **Merge Ends** option selected.

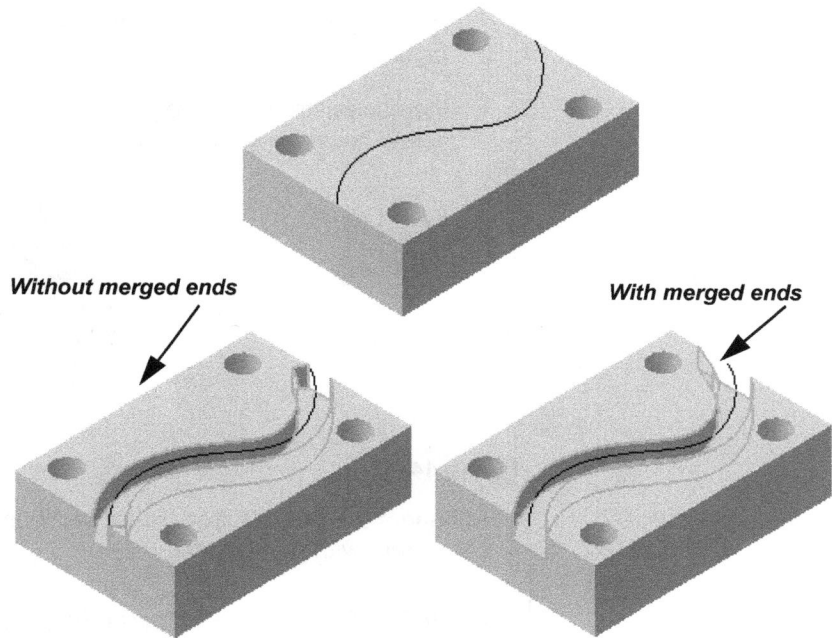

Without merged ends

With merged ends

Figure 14–3

14.2 Stiffeners

A Stiffener feature adds material to your model. The Stiffener is used for two main reasons:

- Provides extra rigidity on a thin wall, as shown in Figure 14–4.

- Increases structural integrity, as shown in the example of the screw boss in Figure 14–5.

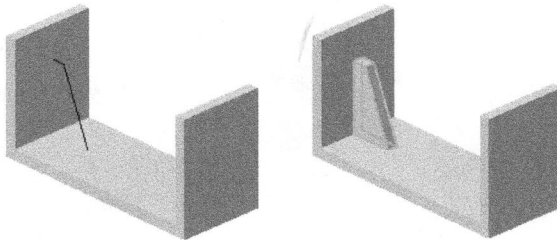

Figure 14–4

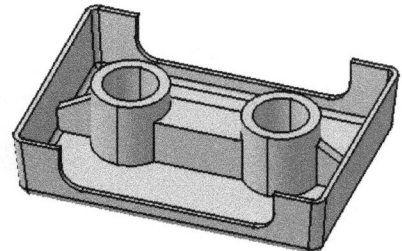

Figure 14–5

Stiffeners are created from open sections, whose end points are coincident with part edges.

How To: Create a Stiffener Feature

1. Click ![icon] (Stiffener). The Stiffener Definition dialog box opens as shown in Figure 14–6.

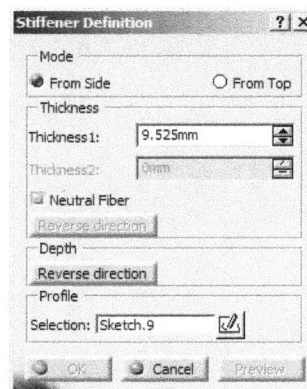

Figure 14–6

Applying thickness in both directions is limited, depending on the geometry present.

2. Select the sketch and apply the thickness in one or both directions using the fields in the dialog box.
3. Specify the mode. The **From Side** option creates the Stiffener parallel to the sketch plane, as shown in Figure 14–7. The **From Top** option creates the Stiffener perpendicular to the sketch plane, as shown in Figure 14–8.

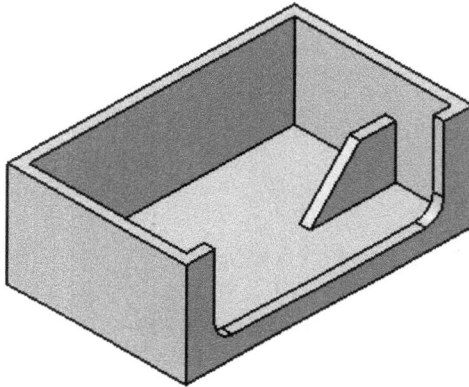

Figure 14–7

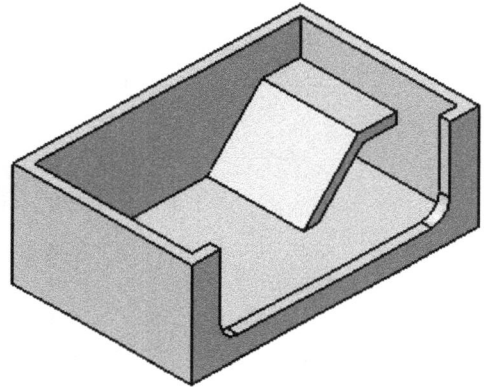

Figure 14–8

Practice 14a | Creating Additional Features I

Practice Objective

- Create a thin Pad and a thin Pocket.

In this practice, you will add features to an electrical plug for a computer monitor.

Task 1 - Create a sketch for a thin Pad.

1. Click [image: Open icon] (Open).

2. Select **Plug.CATPart** and click **Open**.

Design Considerations

The top face of the model requires a raised surface. Create two rectangular Pads for this purpose. The sketch profile will be used to create a thin Pad, which will then be patterned to create the second Pad.

3. Select the top face of the part and click [image: Sketch icon] (Sketch) to enter the Sketcher workbench.

4. Sketch a rectangle as shown in Figure 14–9.

5. Add a symmetry constraint to center the rectangle on the horizontal axis.

6. Dimension the section, as shown in Figure 14–10.

- 3.125 (0.123 in)
- 6.25 (0.246 in)
- 25 (0.984 in)

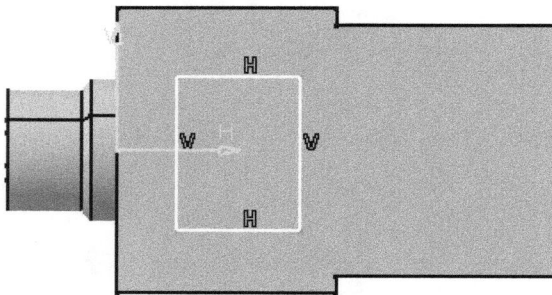

Figure 14–9

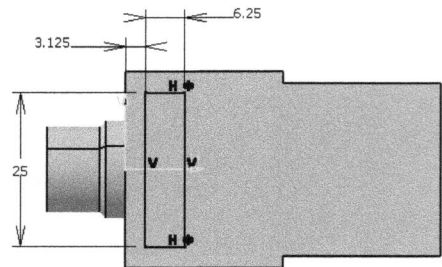

Figure 14–10

7. Click ⬆ (Exit workbench) when the sketch is completed.

Task 2 - Create a thin Pad.

1. With the sketch still highlighted, click ▣ (Pad) to create a Pad. The Pad Definition dialog box opens.

2. Set the *Length* to **1.600 (0.063 in)**.

Thin Pads can add material to either side of the cross-section.
Thickness1 *indicates the thickness of material added to the inside of the section, while*
Thickness2 *determines the thickness of the material added to the outside.*

3. In the *Profile/Surface* area, select **Thick**. The Pad Definition dialog box expands and the Thin Pad section opens.

4. To add material to the inside of the section, set the following:

   • *Thickness1*: **1.600 (0.063 in)**
   • *Thickness2*: **0**

   The Pad Definition dialog box is shown in Figure 14–11.

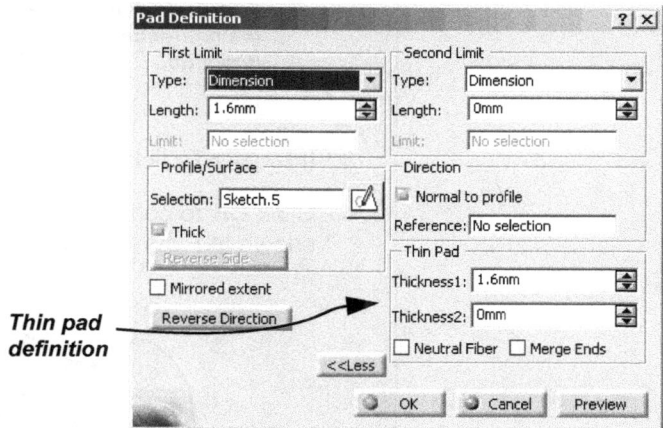

Thin pad definition

Figure 14–11

5. Click **OK** to complete the feature. The model displays as shown in Figure 14–12.

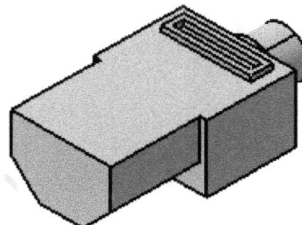

Figure 14–12

Task 3 - Pattern the thin Pad.

1. With the thin Pad highlighted, click ⊞ (Rectangular Pattern) to pattern the feature. Set the following:

   - *Number of instances*: **2**
   - *Spacing*: **12.5 (0.492 in)**

2. Select the *Reference element* box and select the side of the thin Pad, as shown in Figure 14–13.

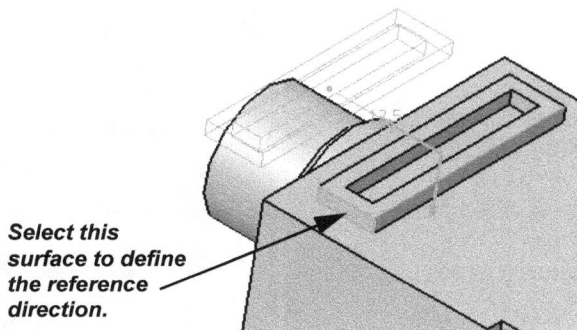

Select this surface to define the reference direction.

Figure 14–13

3. If required, click **Reverse** so that the pattern lies on the part.

4. Click **OK** to complete the pattern. The model displays as shown in Figure 14–14.

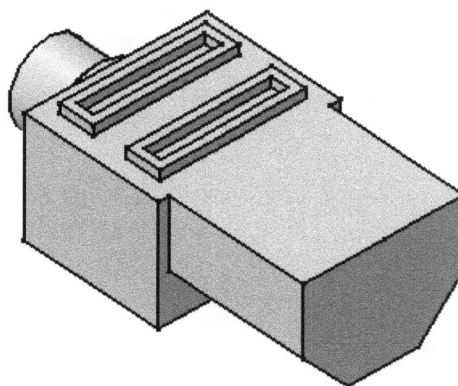

Figure 14–14

Task 4 - Create a sketch for a thin Pocket.

Design Considerations

Create the three thin Pockets for the plug sockets. The individual lines will be used as profiles for thin Pocket features.

1. Select the face shown in Figure 14–15 and click 🖊️ (Sketch).

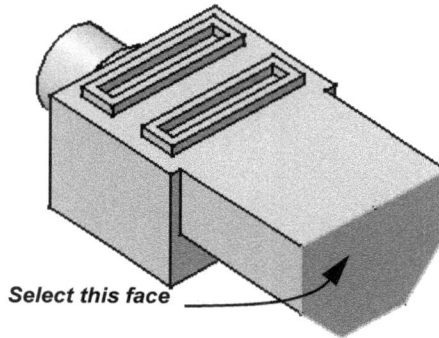

Select this face

Figure 14–15

2. Sketch the section shown in Figure 14–16. The section consists of three vertical lines.

3. Make the upper two lines symmetrical about the vertical axis.

4. Dimension the section as shown in Figure 14–17 using the dimensions of **6.25 (0.246 in)**, **3.8 (0.150 in)** and **19 (0.748 in)**.

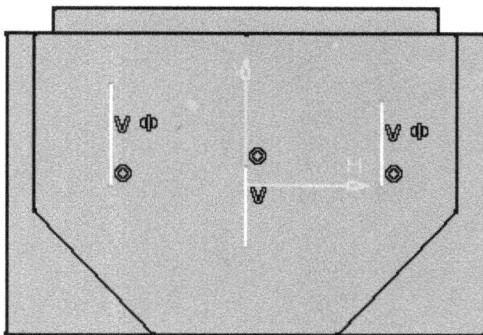

Figure 14–16

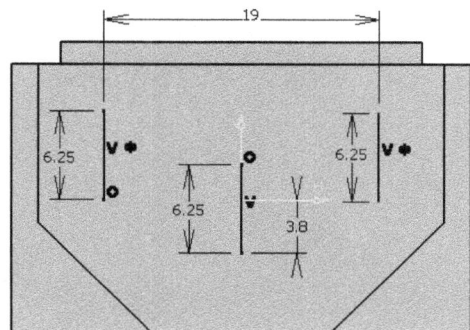

Figure 14–17

5. Click 📤 (Exit workbench) when the sketch is completed.

Task 5 - Create the thin pocket.

1. With the sketch highlighted, click [icon] (Pocket) to create a Pocket.

2. The Feature Definition Error dialog box opens as shown in Figure 14–18. Click **Yes** to continue to the Pocket Definition dialog box.

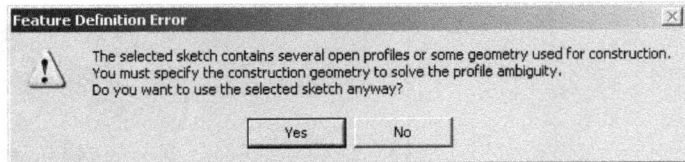

Feature Definition Error

⚠ The selected sketch contains several open profiles or some geometry used for construction. You must specify the construction geometry to solve the profile ambiguity. Do you want to use the selected sketch anyway?

Yes   No

Figure 14–18

3. Set the *Depth* to **19.00 (0.748 in)**.

4. In the *Profile/Surface* area, select the **Thick** option. The dialog box expands and the *Thin Pocket* area displays.

5. Select the **Neutral Fiber** option and enter **3.2 (0.126 in)** in the *Thickness1* field. The total thickness of the thin pocket is set to 3.2mm (0.126 in).

6. Click **OK** to create the thin Pocket. The model displays as shown in Figure 14–19.

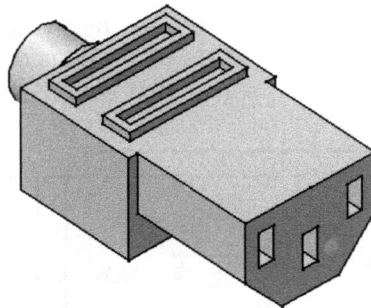

Figure 14–19

7. Click [icon] (Save).

8. Select **File>Close**.

Practice 14b | Creating Additional Features II

Practice Objectives

- Create a thin Pad.
- Create a Tap, a Thread, and a Stiffener.

In this practice, you will add two tapped bosses to a part using thin Pad and Thread features. These bosses will require support, so you will also create Stiffener features, as shown in Figure 14–20. Since the Stiffeners are created from open profiles, you will use the **Project 3D Silhouette Edges** tool to project the edges of the thin Pad features.

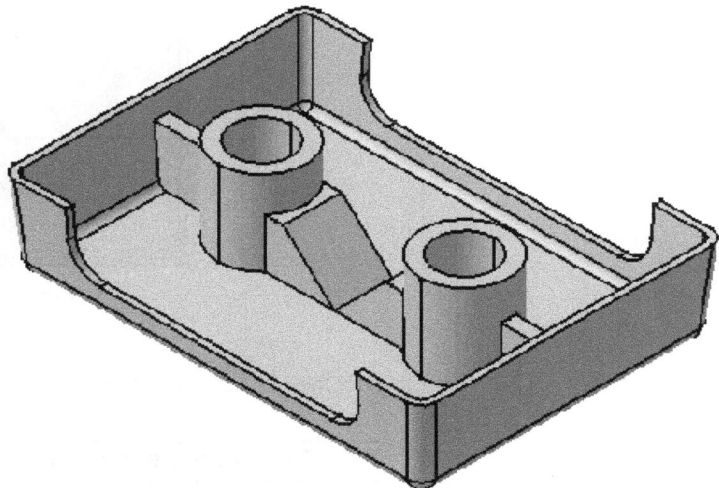

Figure 14–20

Task 6 - Create a sketch for a thin Pad.

1. Click (Open).

2. Select **Lid.CATPart** and click **Open**.

Design Considerations

The following profiles will be constrained to the datum axis. They will be used to create thin Pads, which will later be threaded.

3. Select the surface shown in Figure 14–21 and enter the Sketcher workbench.

4. Sketch the section shown in Figure 14–21 using the dimensions of **38 (1.496 in)** and **90 (3.543 in)**. Make the two entities symmetrical about the horizontal axis.

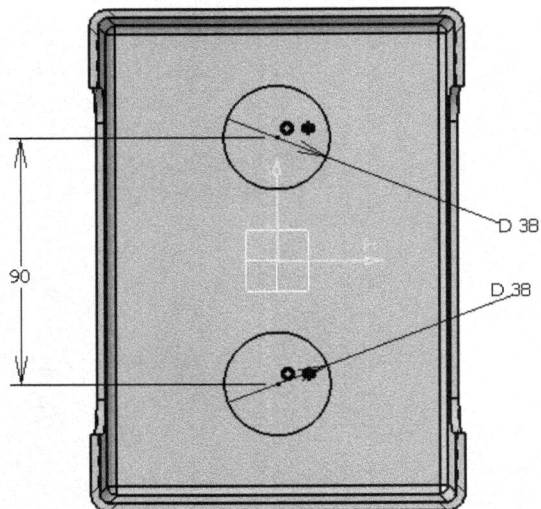

Figure 14–21

5. Click ⬆ (Exit workbench) when the sketch is completed.

Task 7 - Create the thin Pad.

---

1. With the section highlighted, click 🗗 (Pad).

2. Enter a *length* of **38.00 (1.496 in)**.

3. Select the **Thick** option.

4. Select the **Neutral Fiber** option and enter **6.4 (0.252 in)** in the *Thickness1* field. The total thickness is now 6.4mm (0.252 in).

5. Click **OK** to complete the feature. The model is shown in Figure 14–22.

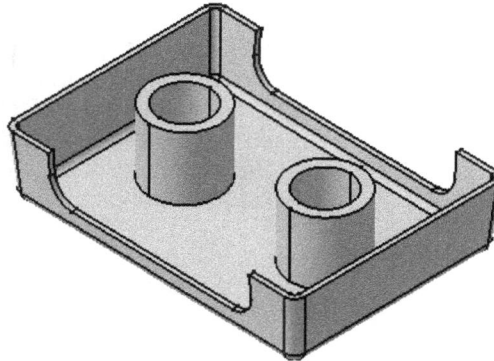

Figure 14–22

Task 8 - Create a sketch for the stiffener.

In this task, you will define the profile of a Stiffener feature using a positioned sketch. The origin of this sketch will be located on the inside face of the lid so that the stiffener profile can snap to this surface. You will start creating a point that defines the origin.

1. Select **Tools>Show>All Planes**.

2. Create a reference point using the **On plane** option. Select the inside face of the lid and enter an *H* and *V offset* of **0mm**, as shown in Figure 14–23.

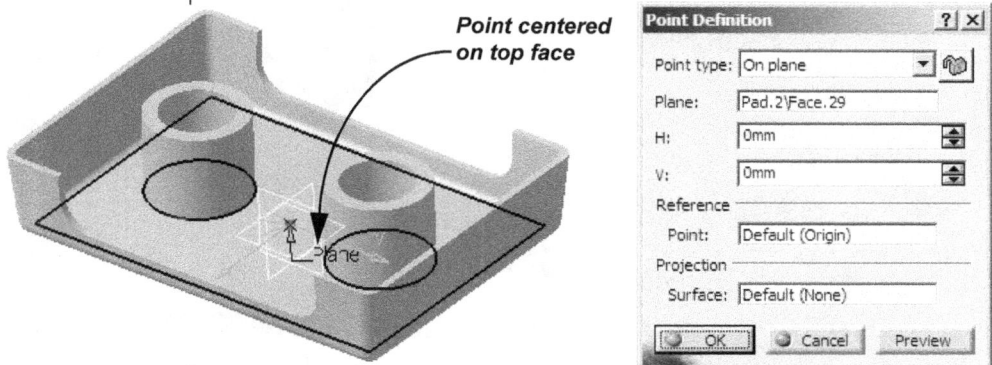

Figure 14–23

3. Create a positioned sketch on the YZ plane. Locate the origin using the **Projection point** option and select the point just created.

Design Considerations

A Stiffener is created from an open section, whose end points are coincident with two surfaces on the part. To constrain the section, the use projections and cutting the part by the sketch plane to make the existing 3D geometry available in the sketch. Projections should be converted to construction elements so that they are not used in the profile of the Stiffener.

- In the sketch you are about to create, you will need to project the edges of the cylinder and the lid onto the sketch plane.

  This is done by clicking ![icon] (Project 3D Canonical Silhouette Edges) and selecting the cylinder.

- Additionally, you can select edges from the sketch plane of

  the part by clicking ![icon] (Cut Part by Sketch Plane). Note that edges selected using the **Cut Part by Sketch Plane** tool are not projected onto the sketch. However, constraints made to the edges are constrained in the sketch plane.

Figure 14–24 shows the resulting silhouette projection and cut part when the edge of the sketch plane is selected.

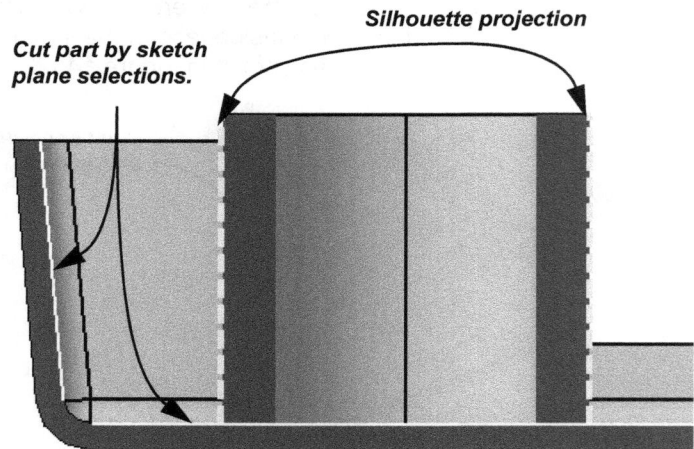

Cut part by sketch plane selections.

Silhouette projection

Figure 14–24

4. Sketch the two open sections shown in Figure 14–25, using the dimensions **3.2 (0.126 in)** and **19 (0.748 in)**. Use the projection methods discussed in the Design Considerations to correctly constrain the section.

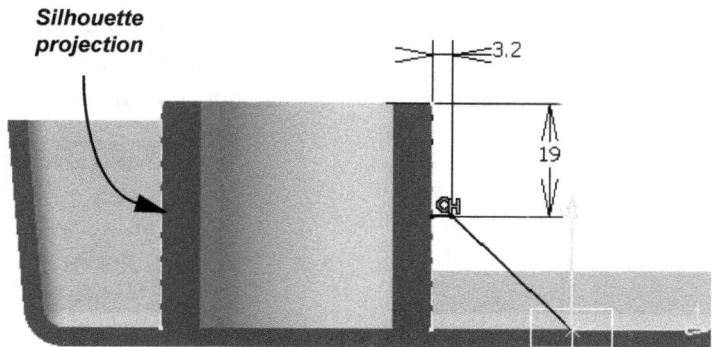

Silhouette projection

Figure 14–25

5. When the sketch is completed, click ⬆ (Exit workbench).

Task 9 - Create a stiffener.

Design Considerations

Unlike a Pad feature, when the Stiffener is created, it does not extrude the open profile in two directions. The Stiffener feature will follow the curvature of the cylindrical part which it supports. The Stiffener tool is found in the Sketch-Based Features toolbar, as shown in Figure 14–26.

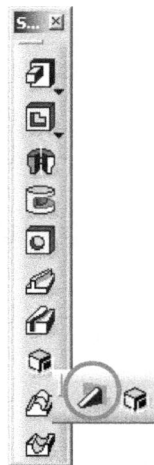

Figure 14–26

1. With the sketch preselected, click (Stiffener). The Stiffener Definition dialog box opens as shown in Figure 14–27. Make the following selections:

   - *Mode:* **From Side**
   - *Thickness1:* **3.2mm (0.126 in)**
   - Select **Neutral Fiber**.

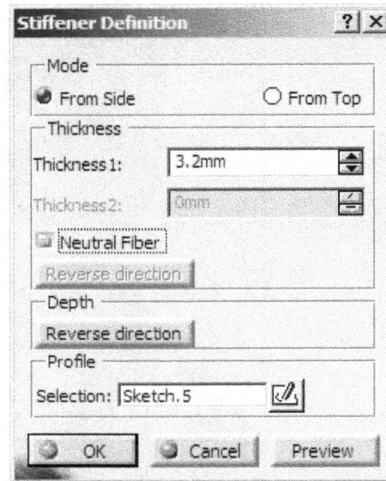

Figure 14–27

2. Click **OK** twice to complete the feature. The model displays as shown in Figure 14–28.

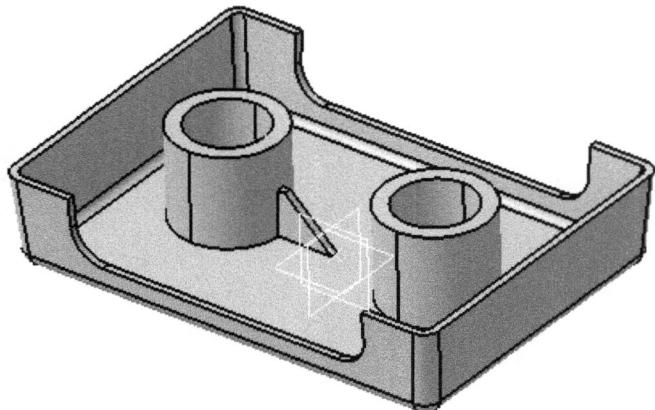

Figure 14–28

Task 10 - Modify the depth of the stiffener.

1. In the specification tree, double-click on the Stiffener feature.

2. Modify *Thickness1* to **25.00 (0.984 in)**.

3. Click **OK** to update the feature. The model displays as shown in Figure 14–29. Note that the Stiffener adapts to follow the cylindrical face that its section is aligned.

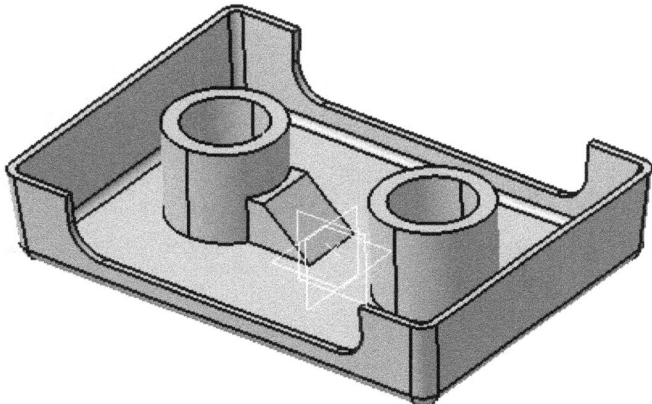

Figure 14–29

Task 11 - Create additional stiffeners (optional).

1. Create a sketch on the YZ plane. Sketch the profile shown in Figure 14–30, using a dimension of **12.5 (0.492 in)**. Remember to use 3D projections to correctly constrain the profile.

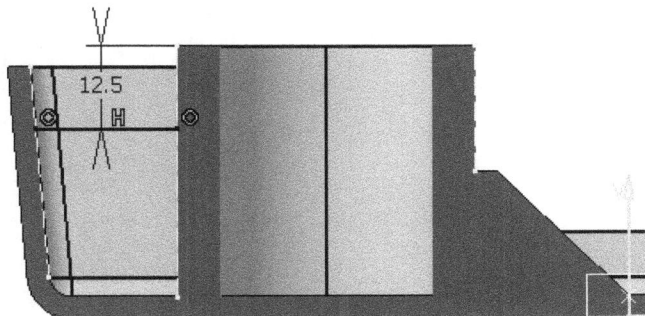

Figure 14–30

2. Create a second Stiffener feature with a *Width* of **6.25 (0.246 in)**.

3. Select **PartBody** in the specification tree and select **Tools> Hide>All Except Selected Elements**. The model displays as shown in Figure 14–31.

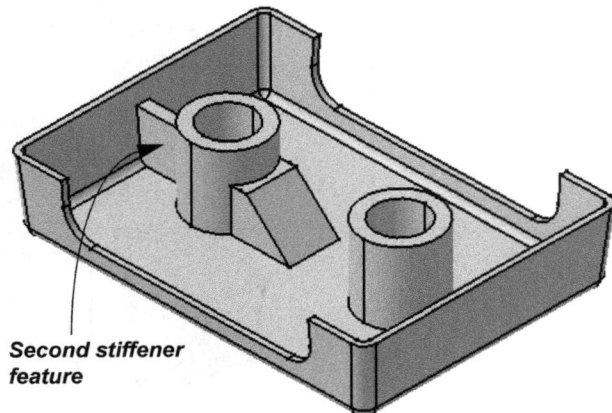

Second stiffener feature

Figure 14–31

4. Create two additional Stiffener features on the YZ plane to support the right cylindrical boss. Use the dimension scheme and values used to create the stiffeners supporting the left cylindrical box. The finished model displays as shown in Figure 14–32.

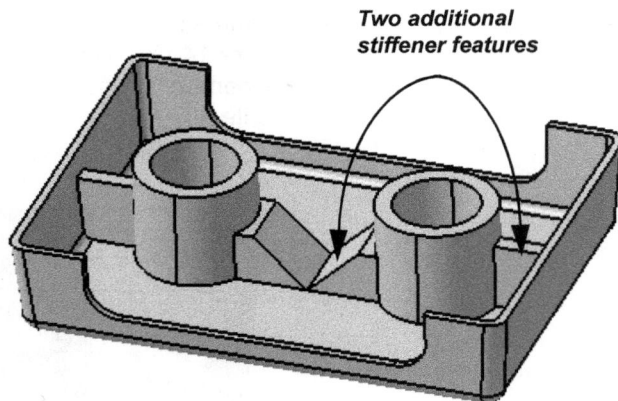

Two additional stiffener features

Figure 14–32

5. Click 🖫 (Save).

6. Select **File>Close**.

Practice 14c | (Optional) Axle Bracket

Practice Objective

- Create a part without any instructions.

Create the **AxleBracket.CATPart** shown in Figure 14–33.

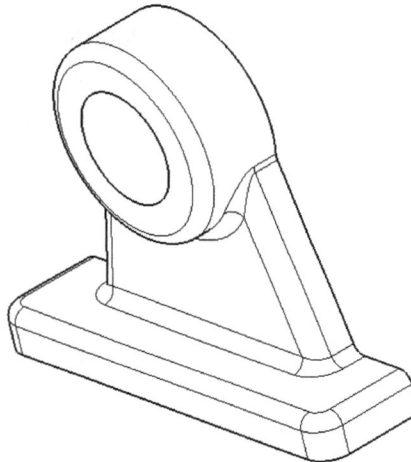

Figure 14–33

Drawing views are shown in Figure 14–34 and Figure 14–35.

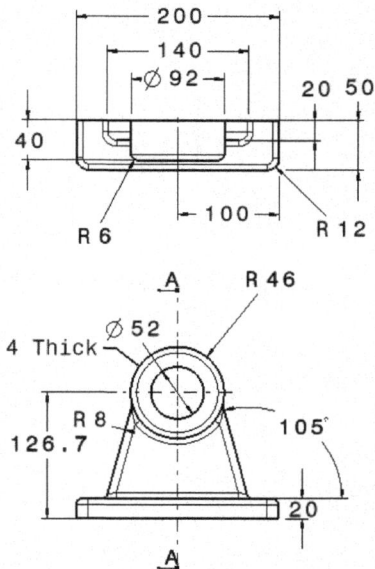

Figure 14–34

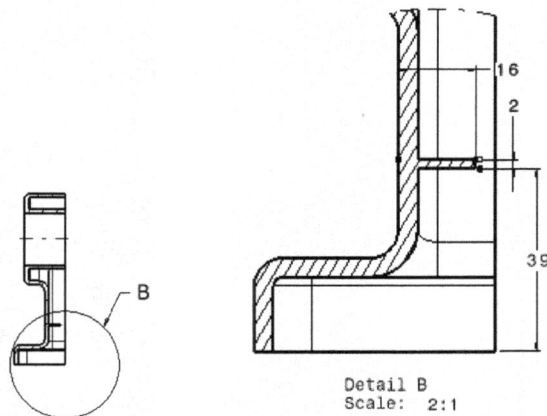

Figure 14–35

Chapter Review Questions

1. A closed profile cannot be used to create a thin Pad.
   a. True
   b. False

2. Using the **Thick** option, where can material be added?
   a. One side of the profile only.
   b. One or both sides of the profile.
   c. Both sides of the profile only.
   d. None of these.

3. A Stiffener can be an open or closed profile.
   a. True
   b. False

4. The end points of a Stiffener profile must be coincident with an existing part edge.
   a. True
   b. False

5. The thickness of a Stiffener is always applied symmetrically about both sides of the profile.
   a. True
   b. False

6. Which Stiffener mode creates a Stiffener that is parallel to the sketch plane?
   a. From Side
   b. From Top

7. Which option is used to apply solid material equally to both sides of an open sketch?
   a. Neutral Plane
   b. Neutral Fiber
   c. Symmetric
   d. None of the above.

Answers: 1.a, 2.b, 3.b, 4.b, 5.b, 6.a, 7.b

Parent/Child Relationships

Parent/Child relationships are an important aspect of CATIA, as they control how features interact with one another. In this chapter you learn how to create and modify parent/child relationships and how to use them to your advantage.

Learning Objectives in this Chapter

- Understand the impact of Parent/Child relationships.
- Understand the various ways in which Parent/Child relationships can be created.
- Investigate Parent/Child relationships.
- Learn how to change existing Parent/Child relationships.
- Use the Replace command to replace features with Parent/Child relationships.
- Investigate feature failures.

15.1 Establishing Parent/Child Relationships

A parent/child relationship is the dependency of one feature on another. The independent feature is referred to as the parent and the dependent feature is referred to as the child.

- Modifying a parent feature can also affect the children of that feature. For example, if a child feature is dimensioned to an edge of a parent feature and modifying the parent moves this edge, the child feature moves accordingly. If the parent feature is deleted, the system no longer contains enough information to update the child feature's location. In this case, the child feature must be edited.

There are a several ways of establishing parent/child relationships that can help you capture design intent.

Sketching Plane

Default reference planes are automatically created by the software and are used as a sketching plane for the base feature, as shown in Figure 15–1. Additionally, default reference planes cannot be deleted or modified, so they make stable parent references.

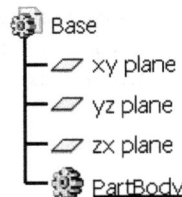

Figure 15–1

The references used to constrain additional reference features, such as reference points, lines, and planes become parents to these features, as shown in Figure 15–2.

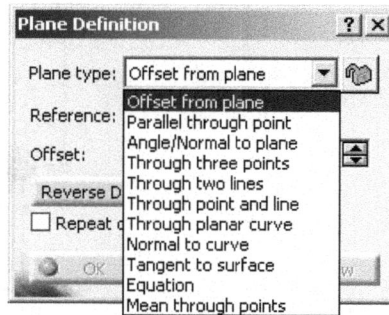

Figure 15–2

If a user-defined reference plane is used as a sketching plane, these references become parents to the sketch and the resulting geometry.

Planar surfaces of existing geometry can be selected as a sketch plane, as shown in Figure 15–3. This surface becomes a parent to the new sketch and subsequent geometry.

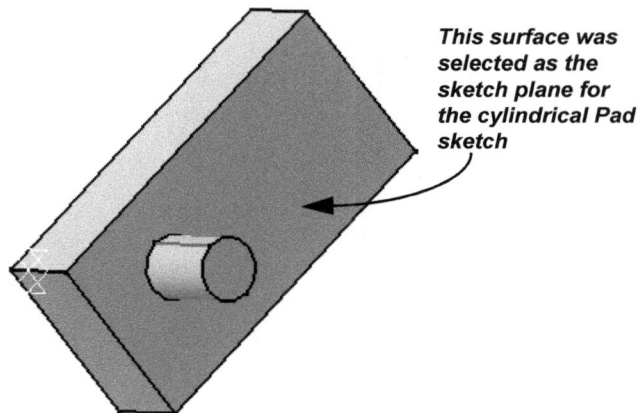

This surface was selected as the sketch plane for the cylindrical Pad sketch

Figure 15–3

Sketch

The sketch from which sketched features derive their geometry are parents to the solid geometry, as shown in Figure 15–4.

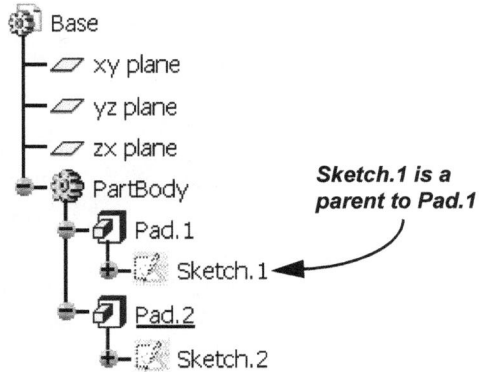

Sketch.1 is a parent to Pad.1

Figure 15–4

Sketch Constraints

Constraints meant for the creation of sketch geometry can create a dependency between features, as shown in Figure 15–5.

The sketched line was made coincident with the surface of the Pocket.

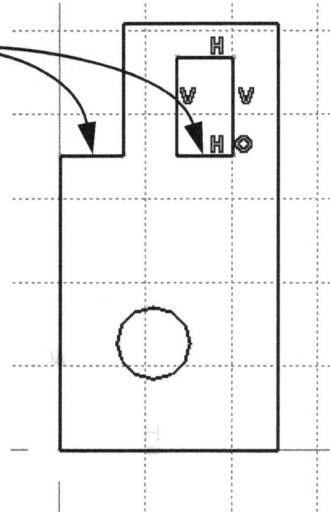

Figure 15–5

The resulting geometry is shown in Figure 15–6.

If modifications are made to the referenced Pocket feature, the coincident constraint maintains the design intent, as shown in Figure 15–7.

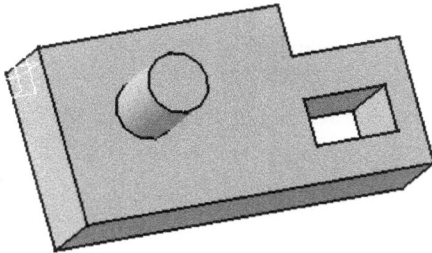

Figure 15–6

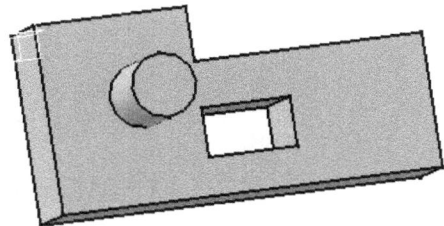

Figure 15–7

Dimensioning References

When dimensioning sketches to existing geometry, a parent/child relationship is established between the sketch and the geometry it is dimensioned to. If dimensions have not been specified to locate the sketch, the software automatically positions the sketch relative to the system-defined AbsoluteAxis, as shown in Figure 15–8.

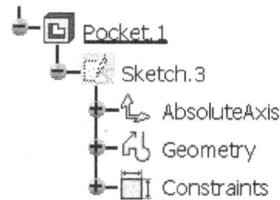

Figure 15–8

Note the relative coordinate values of initial sketch geometry, as shown in Figure 15–9.

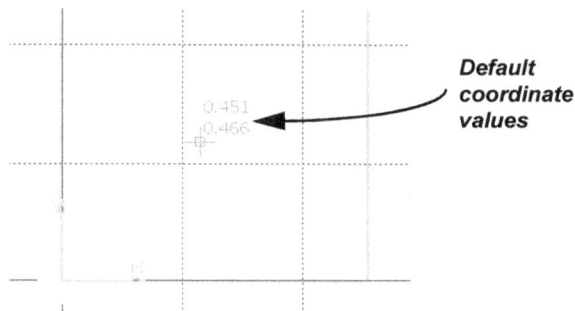

Default coordinate values

Figure 15–9

Projection of 3D Geometry

If the projected 3D geometry tools are used to create sketch geometry, a parent/child relationship is established between the sketch and the existing geometry being projected, as shown in Figure 15–10.

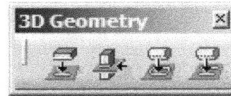

Figure 15–10

In Figure 15–11, the Rib feature is dependent on the cylindrical Pad features.

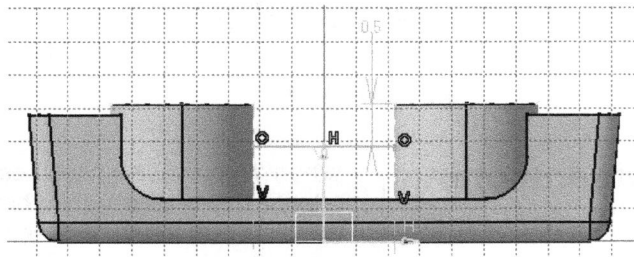

Figure 15–11

Depth Options

Consider the **Up to plane** option used in the example, as shown in Figure 15–12. Note the effect of modification to the parent feature, as shown in Figure 15–13.

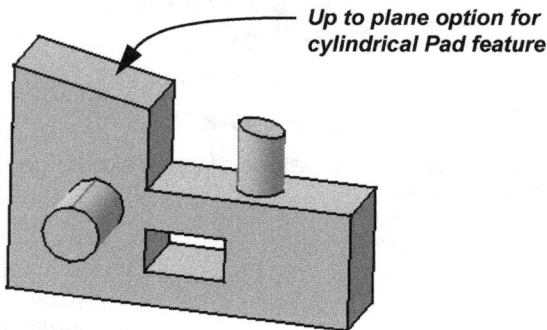

Up to plane option for cylindrical Pad feature

Figure 15–12

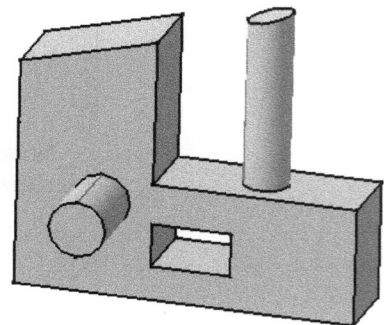

Figure 15–13

Alternatively, you can
select **Tools>
Parent/Children** after
selecting the feature.

15.2 Investigating Parent/Child Relationships

The **Parent/Children** tool displays information about the parents and children of a selected feature. To activate the **Parent/Children** tool, select a feature in the specification tree or on the screen, right-click and select **Parents/Children**, as shown in Figure 15–14.

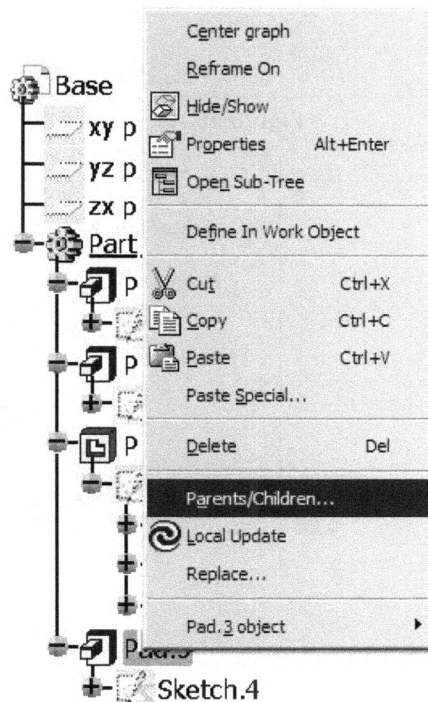

Figure 15–14

The Parents and Children dialog box opens as shown in Figure 15–15. Double-clicking on the sketch item lists the parents and children of that item, as shown in Figure 15–16 for the model in Figure 15–17.

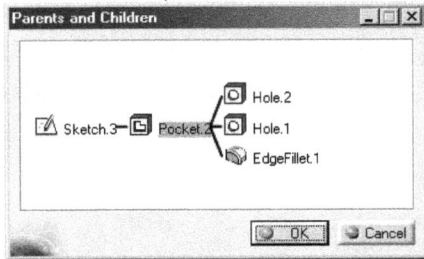

Figure 15–15

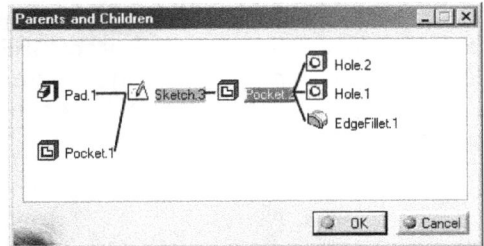

Figure 15–16

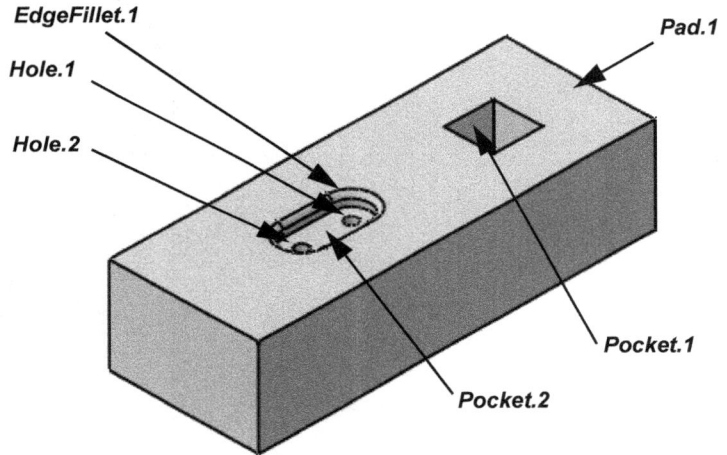

Figure 15–17

15.3 Changing Parent/Child Relationships

Changing the Sketch Plane

If the sketch plane of a sketched feature is changed, the solid geometry derived from that sketch follows the location of the sketch. To change the sketch plane reference of a sketch, select it from the specification tree, right-click and select **Sketch.# object>Change Sketch Support**, as shown in Figure 15–18.

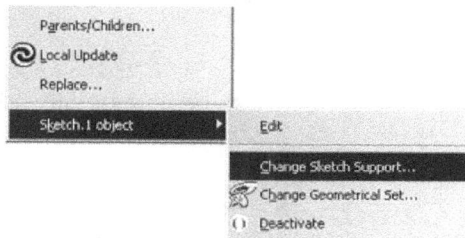

Figure 15–18

The Sketch Positioning dialog box opens as shown in Figure 15–19. The AbsoluteAxis for the sketch displays.

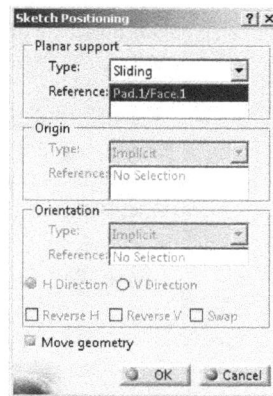

Figure 15–19

The sketch support type can be defined as either **Sliding**, **Positioning**, or **Isolated**, as shown in Figure 15–20.

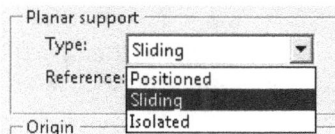

Figure 15–20

Sliding	Maintains the original orientation of the AbsoluteAxis sketch.
Positioning	Enables you to change the origin and direction of the H and/or V direction of the AbsoluteAxis.
Isolated	Breaks all absolute axis links with the AbsoluteAxis.

Sketch Dimensions

The parent/child relationships created by a dimensioning scheme can be changed by editing the sketched feature and deleting dimensions while in the Sketcher workbench.

Sketcher Constraints

A parent/child relationship created through the use of constraints can be changed by editing the sketched feature and deleting the constraints while in the Sketcher workbench.

Depth Option

The Depth option of a solid geometry feature can be changed by editing the Pad or Pocket and selecting a different depth option reference or a different depth option.

Replace

The **Replace** command enables you to replace a feature that has parent/child relationships. This option is not available for solid elements, but can be accessed in sketches and wireframe and surface designs.

For example, consider a Pocket with a fillet child. If you need to change the section of the Pocket, modifying the sketch using **Cut** and **Paste** causes the fillet to fail. Instead, create a new section and replace the section.

How To: Replace the Parent/Child Relationships of a Sketched Entity

1. Create the replacing entity.
   - In this example, the hexagonal section of the Pocket is replaced with a rectangular section. An edge fillet references the Pocket feature and fails if the geometry of the section is deleted and re-created. Therefore, the rectangular section is created in a new sketch and used to replace the hexagonal sketch.
2. In the specification tree, select the hexagonal sketch feature, right-click and select **Replace**.

3. In the specification tree, select the rectangular sketch to replace the hexagonal sketch. The Replace dialog box opens as shown in Figure 15–21. Depending on the references selected for the feature being replaced, you might have to go through each edge in the list and manually specify from the sketch which edge to replace it with.

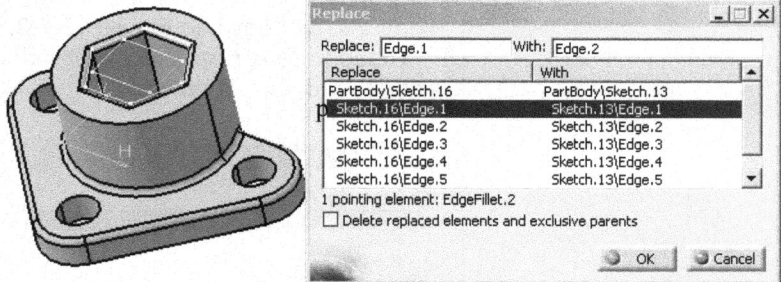

Figure 15–21

4. Click **OK** to replace the section. The feature updates to reflect the change. The replacement is shown in Figure 15–22.

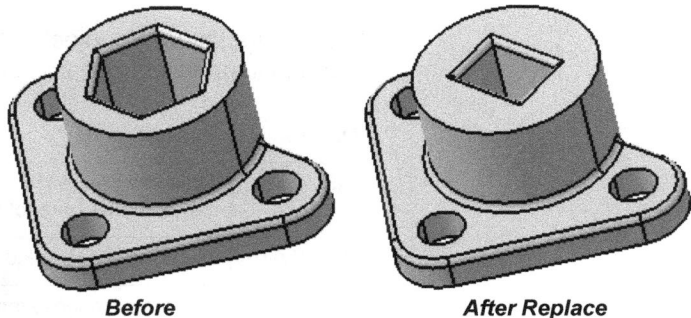

Before   *After Replace*

Figure 15–22

You can also use the **Replace** command if you need to replace a section (with a parent/child relationship) that was automatically constrained to the origin. In this case, copying and pasting the sketch causes the children features to fail. However, you can maintain parent/child relationships by replacing the section with a duplicate sketch.

15.4 Feature Failure

Modifications to the part model are common during the course of product design. Depending on the magnitude of the changes, subsequent features might fail as a result of parent/child relationship disruption. When a feature fails, the Update Diagnosis dialog box opens and provides troubleshooting options, as shown in Figure 15–23. The **Update Diagnosis** tool is used to repair parent/child relationships when the **Replace** command cannot be used.

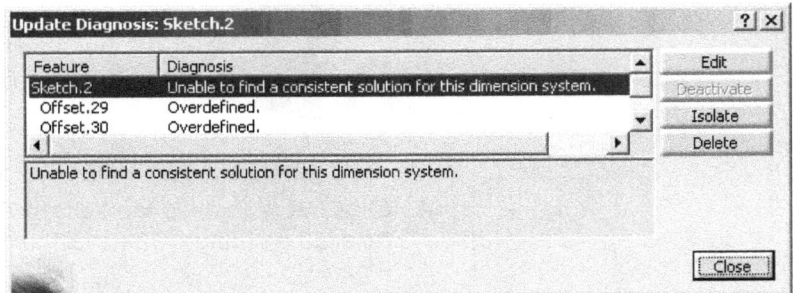

Figure 15–23

The feature failure troubleshooting options available in the Update Diagnosis dialog box are described as follows:

Option	Description
Edit	Activates the Failed Feature dialog box so that modifications can be made to resolve the failure.
Deactivate	Deactivates the failed feature.
Isolate	Deletes all inconsistent parent/child relationships.
Delete	Deletes the selected failed feature.

The type of feature that has failed determines the options available in the Update Diagnosis window. For example, a failed dress-up feature (fillet, draft, or shell) cannot be isolated because dress-up features are dependent on solid body parent elements.

Two common feature failure types and solutions are available:

• Draft Angle Failure

• Fillet Failure

Draft Angle Failure

Figure 15–24 shows an example of a drafted Pad. The rectangular profile sketch is changed to a semi-circle so that three drafted faces are removed.

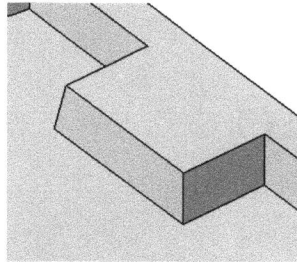

Figure 15–24

The Update Diagnosis dialog box opens as shown in Figure 15–25.

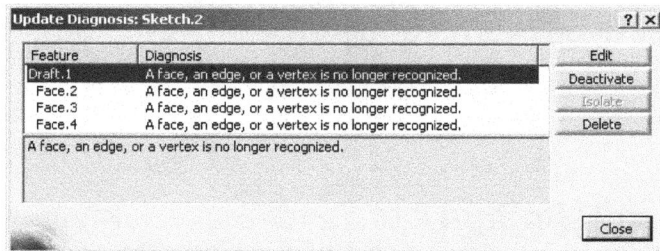

Figure 15–25

Since the Draft.1 feature is a child of the Pad feature, the three faces that were removed with the original Pad are no longer recognized and prevent the model from updating. The Draft feature cannot be isolated because it is driven by existing geometry. Deactivating the Draft feature toggles it off temporarily, but does not resolve the issue. **Delete** removes the feature from the model.

When selecting **Edit**, the Feature Definition Error opens, as shown in Figure 15–26. The three faces specified in the Update Diagnosis dialog box cannot be used because they no longer exist.

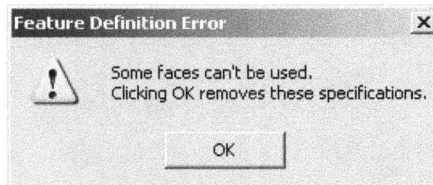

Figure 15–26

After closing the Feature Definition Error dialog box, the Draft Definition dialog box opens, as shown in Figure 15–27. The three faces removed during the creation of the semi-circular Pad are highlighted in the model display. The new semi-circular Pad face can be added as a face to draft. The model updates when the Draft Definition dialog box is closed.

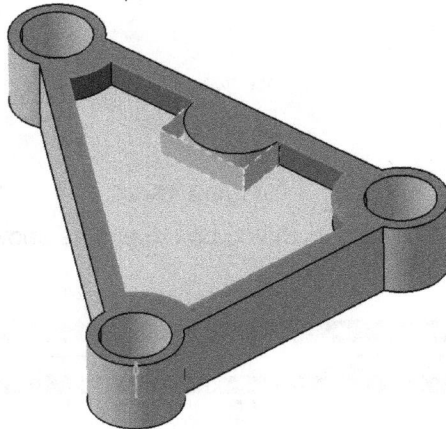

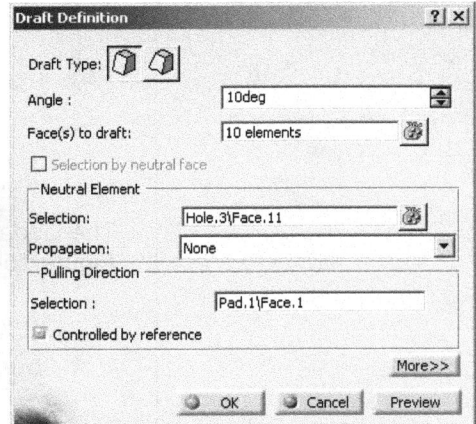

Figure 15–27

Fillet Failure

It is not recommended to create constraints using the edges of a fillet. If improper fillets result from poor design technique or designer oversight, they can be repaired. Figure 15–28 shows an example of a wedge Pad.

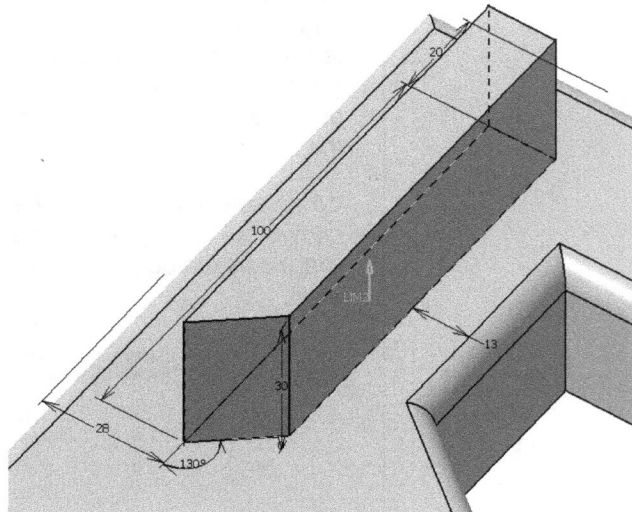

Figure 15–28

The wedge is constrained to the edge of a fillet by the 13mm dimension. When the Fillet feature is removed from this edge, the Update Diagnosis dialog box opens as shown in Figure 15–29. This indicates that a parent/child relationship has failed and that the constraint is no longer recognized.

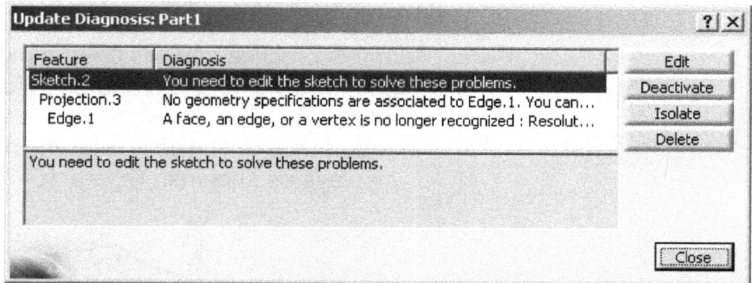

Figure 15–29

By isolating the sketch feature, the failed constraint is removed and **Sketch.2** becomes under-constrained. The former constraint edge is saved as an external reference (construction) line in the sketch.

- Select the **Edit** option to repair the parent/child relationship issue. The part automatically enters the Sketcher workbench and the damaged constraint can be reconnected to the non-filleted edge by selecting **Reconnect**, as shown in Figure 15–30.

- The parent/child relationship has been reconciled, and the part updates when you exit the Sketcher workbench.

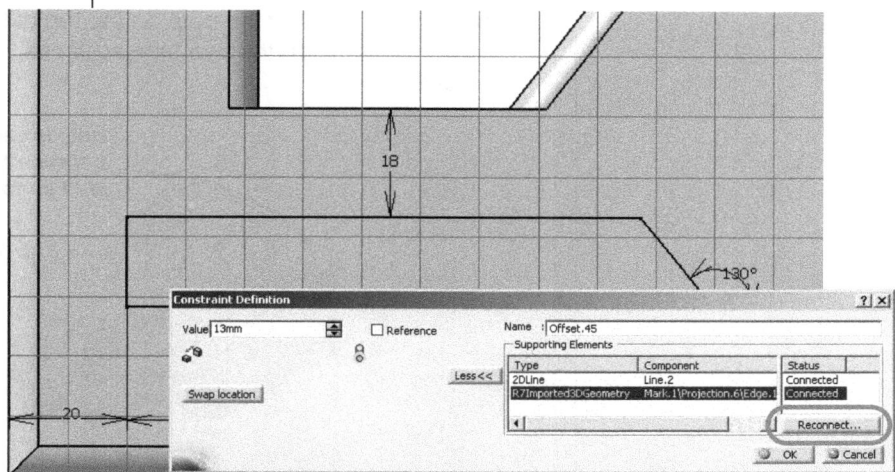

Figure 15–30

Practice 15a | Parent/Child Relationships

Practice Objectives

- Edit parent/child relationships.
- Resolve feature failure.

In this practice you will open a model and modify it to create the part. You will analyze and edit parent/child relationships and resolve feature failure. In addition, you will observe the importance of correctly referencing features. The final part model displays as shown in Figure 15–31.

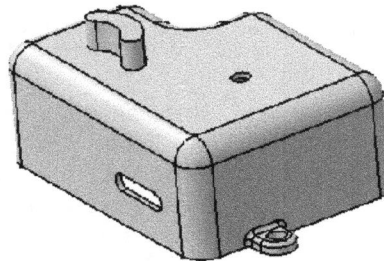

Figure 15–31

Task 1 - Investigate the part.

1. Open **Enclosure.CATPart**.

2. Verify that the model units are set to millimeters (mm).

3. Note the location of the hole on the top of the part. The hole is centered between the two side surfaces, as shown in Figure 15–32.

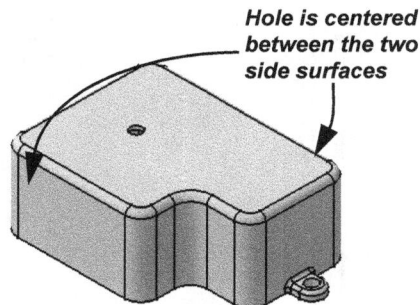

Hole is centered between the two side surfaces

Figure 15–32

4. Change the *radius* of the top Fillet feature to **15mm (0.591 in)**. The model displays as shown in Figure 15–33. The hole is no longer positioned in the middle of the part.

Vent hole is no longer in the middle of the part.

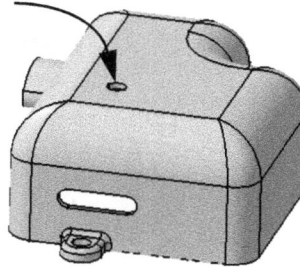

Figure 15–33

Task 2 - Investigate the Vent Hole feature.

1. In the specification tree, right-click on the Sketch Vent feature and select **Parents/Children**. The Parents and Children dialog box opens as shown in Figure 15–34.

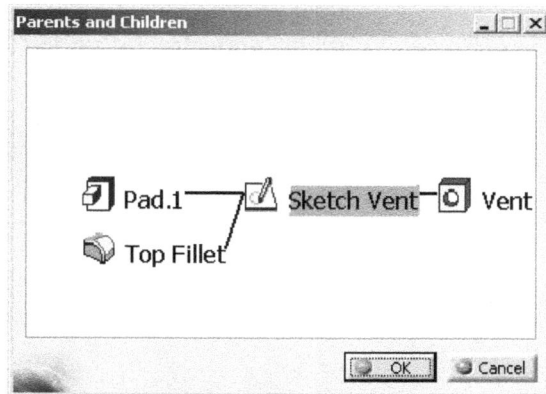

Figure 15–34

- Pad.1 and Top fillet are parents to the Vent hole. When the fillet radius changed, the hole moved because of this relationship.

2. Close the Parents and Children dialog box.

Task 3 - Change the parent/child relationship of the Vent hole.

1. Double-click on the Sketch Vent sketch feature in the specification tree to modify it. Note the 34.5 (1.358 in) dimension to the edge of the top Fillet feature, as shown in Figure 15–35.

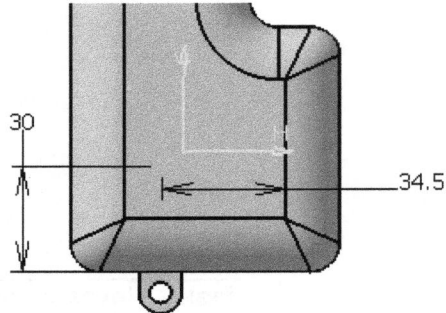

Figure 15–35

2. Delete the 34.5 (1.358 in) dimension.

3. Create a new dimension from the hole center to the right side surface of the part. Modify the *value* to **34.5 (1.358 in)**, as shown in Figure 15–36.

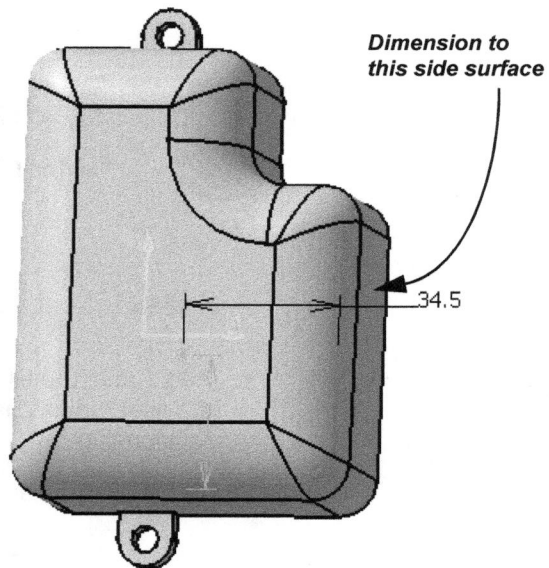

Figure 15–36

4. Exit the Sketcher workbench.

5. Modify the *Top fillet* to **7.5 (0.295 in)**. The model displays as shown in Figure 15–37. Note that the position of the Vent hole remained in its intended position.

Figure 15–37

6. Investigate the parent/child information of the Sketch Vent feature again. Note that the top **Fillet** feature is no longer a parent of the Vent Hole feature, as can be seen in Figure 15–38.

Figure 15–38

Task 4 - Change the sketch plane reference of a feature.

In this task, you will incorporate the design change shown in Figure 15–39.

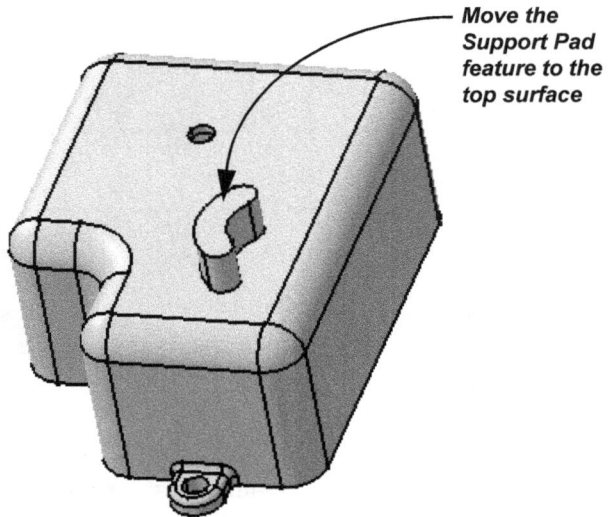

Move the Support Pad feature to the top surface

Figure 15–39

1. In the specification tree, select the Sketch Support sketch feature. Right-click and select **Sketch Support object> Change Sketch Support**. The Sketch Positioning dialog box opens, as shown in Figure 15–40.

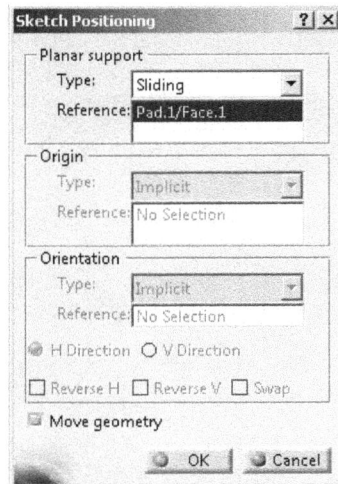

Figure 15–40

2. To change the sketching plane, select the top surface shown in Figure 15–41. The model turns red.

Select the top surface

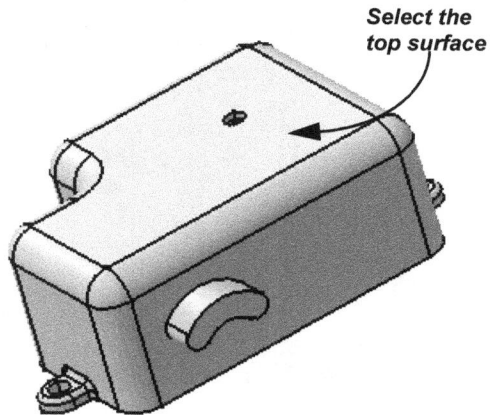

Figure 15–41

3. Click **OK** to accept the modification. The model displays as shown in Figure 15–42.

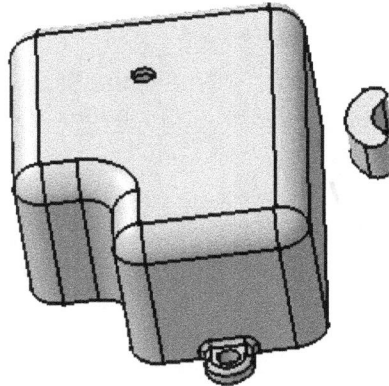

Figure 15–42

4. In the specification tree, double-click on Sketch Support to activate the Sketcher workbench.

5. Click and drag a box around the sketch to select the entire sketch, as shown in Figure 15–43.

6. Drag the sketch to a location similar to the one shown in Figure 15–44.

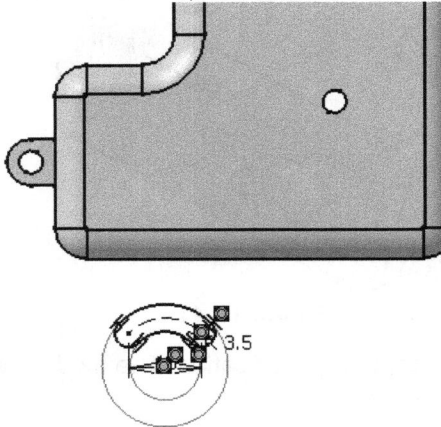

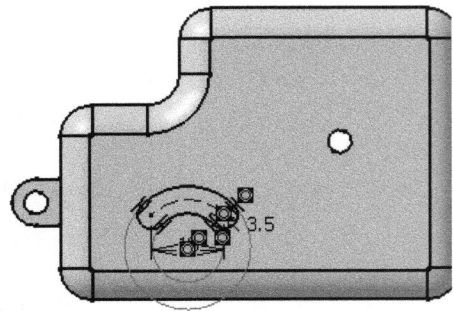

Figure 15–43   **Figure 15–44**

7. Exit the Sketcher workbench. The model displays as shown in Figure 15–45.

Figure 15–45

Task 5 - Resolve a feature failure.

Design Considerations

In this task, you will cause a feature failure by changing the sketch support of the Pocket feature, as shown in Figure 15–46. Then you will resolve this feature failure.

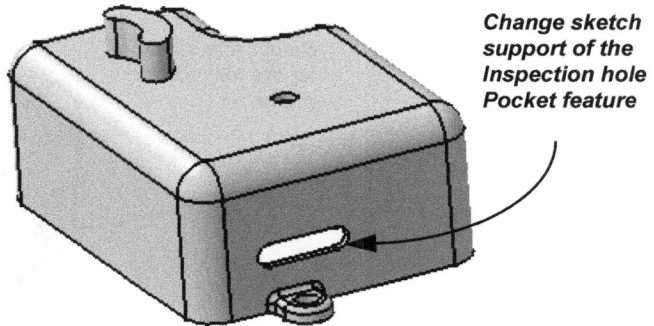

Change sketch support of the Inspection hole Pocket feature

Figure 15–46

1. Investigate the sketch before it is moved by double-clicking on the Sketch Inspection sketch feature in the specification tree. The sketch is now activated in the Sketcher workbench.

2. Note the dimensions (3 (0.118 in), 15 (0.591 in), and 18 (0.709 in)) and constraints that were used to place the sketch in Figure 15–47. Which dimensions and/or constraints locate the sketch vertically? Horizontally?

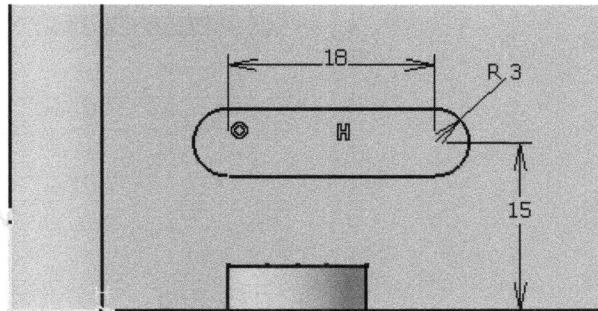

Figure 15–47

3. Exit the Sketcher workbench without making any changes.

4. Select the Sketch Inspection sketch feature in the specification tree. Right-click and select **Sketch Inspection object>Change Sketch Support**.

5. Click **OK** to accept the warning.

6. Select the surface shown in Figure 15–48.

Select this surface as the new sketch plane

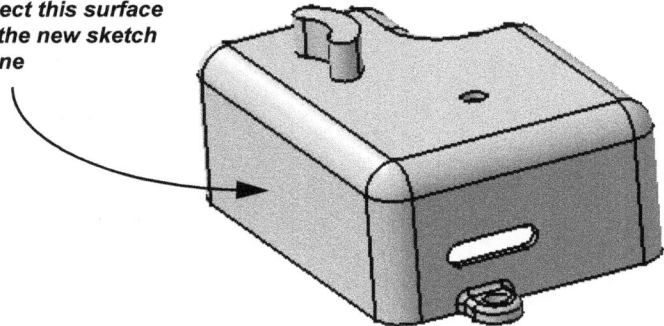

Figure 15–48

7. Click **OK** in the Sketch Positioning dialog box.

8. The Update Diagnosis dialog box opens as shown in Figure 15–49. It indicates that a feature failure has occurred.

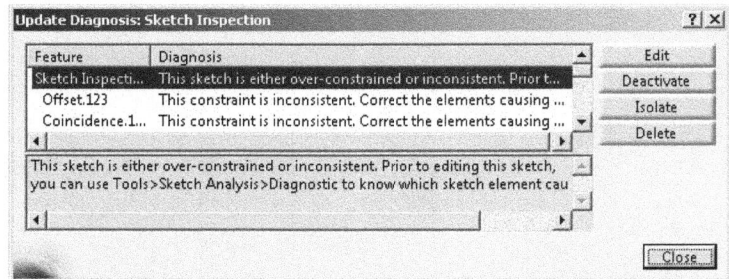

Figure 15–49

9. Click **Edit**.

10. The software activates the failed sketch feature in the Sketcher workbench, as shown in Figure 15–50. Note the resulting 15 (0.591 in) dimension. Drag the cursor over the dimensions if they are too dark to see on the screen.

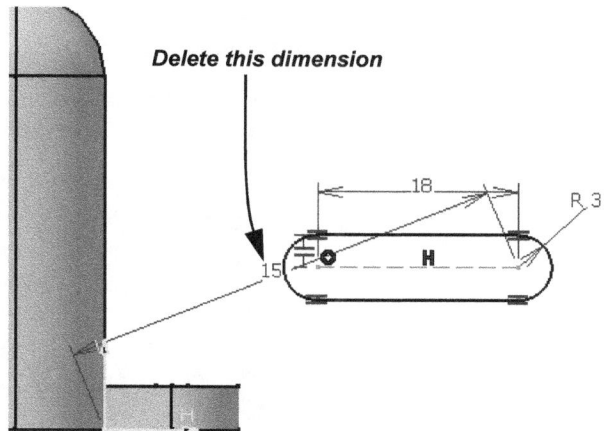

Delete this dimension

Figure 15–50

11. Delete the 15 (0.591 in) dimension.

12. Select the entire sketch and attempt to move it to the left onto the model. Note that it moves up and down but not left or right.

13. Delete the **Coincident** constraint between the sketch and the geometry below the sketch, as shown in Figure 15–51.

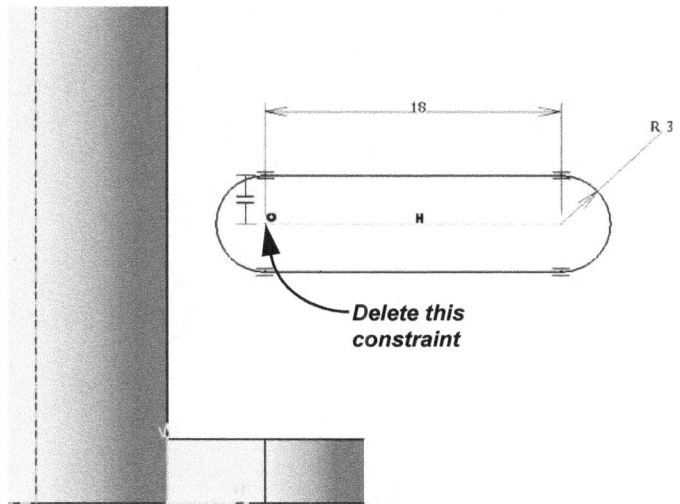

Delete this constraint

Figure 15–51

14. Select the entire sketch again and move it onto the model, as shown in Figure 15–52.

15. Using the correct values, add the dimensions (**15 (0.591 in) 20 (0.787 in)**) shown in Figure 15–52.

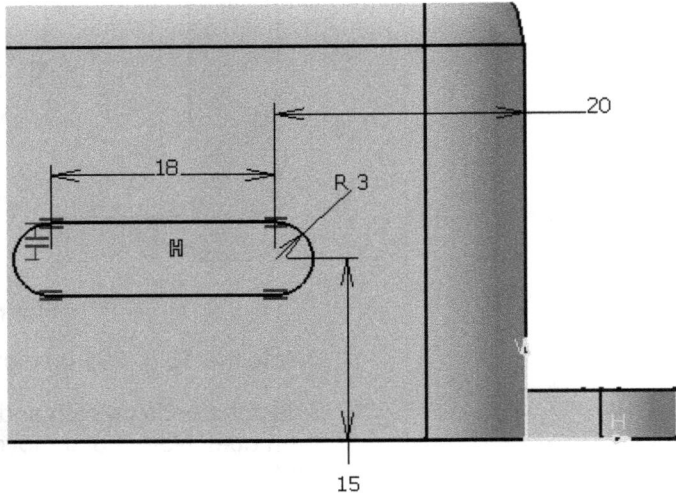

You can also use the **Translate** *operation in Sketcher to move the sketched entities.*

Figure 15–52

16. Exit the Sketcher workbench. The model displays as shown in Figure 15–53.

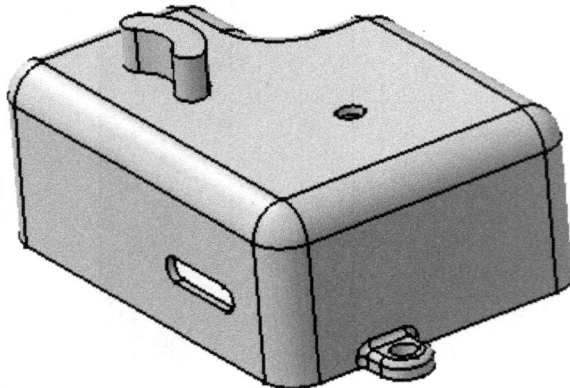

Figure 15–53

17. Click (Save).

18. Select **File>Close**.

Practice 15b | Resolving Failed Features

Practice Objectives

- Edit a sketch profile.
- Resolve Draft and Fillet feature failure.

In this practice you will modify the profile of a sketch that controls Pocket, Draft, and Fillet features as shown in Figure 15–54. After the profile has been modified, you will resolve feature update failures resulting from the modification of the sketch, which is a parent feature.

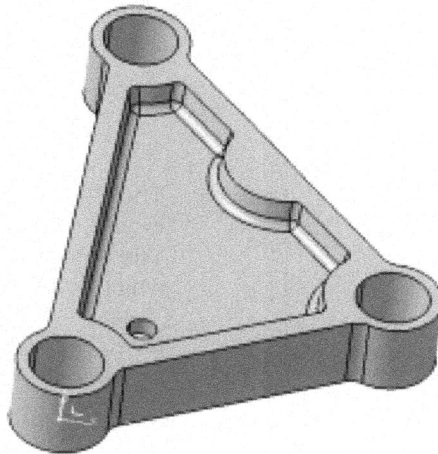

Figure 15–54

Task 1 - Investigate the part.

In this task, you will use the **Parents/Children** tool to locate and edit the sketch that drives the main Pocket feature.

1. Open **FeatureResolve.CATPart**.

2. Verify that the model units are set to millimeters (mm).

3. Right-click on the face shown in Figure 15–55. Select **Parents/Children**.

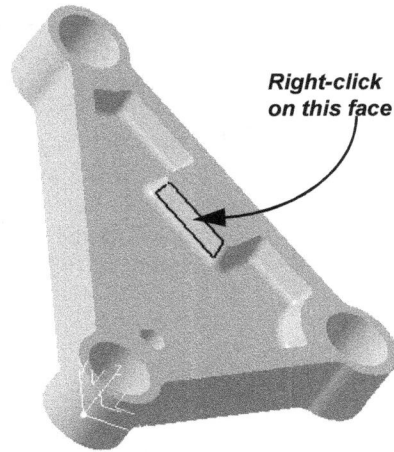

Right-click on this face

Figure 15–55

- The Parents and Children dialog box opens as shown in Figure 15–56. Note that the feature selected was **Draft.1**. The software shows the parents of the Draft feature, which are **Pocket.1** and **Pad.1**.

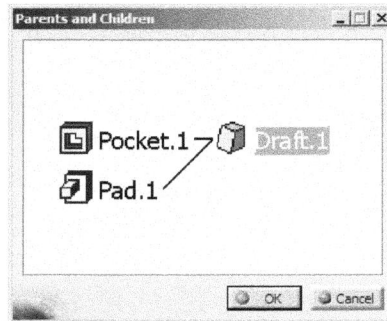

Figure 15–56

4. Locate the sketch that is parent to the **Pocket.1** feature in the Parents and Children dialog box. To do this, double-click on **Pocket.1**.

5. Right-click on the **Sketch.2** feature and select **Edit**, as shown in Figure 15–57. The Sketcher workbench is activated.

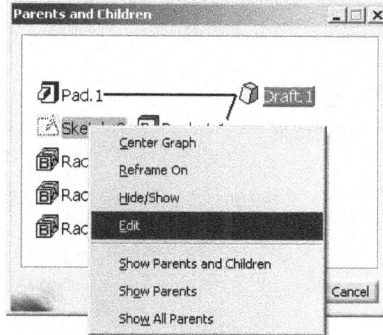

Figure 15–57

Task 2 - Modify the sketch.

1. In the sketch profile, delete the three lines shown in Figure 15–58.

2. Add an arc of radius **30.0mm (1.181 in)** in place of the three deleted lines, as shown in Figure 15–59. Trim as required.

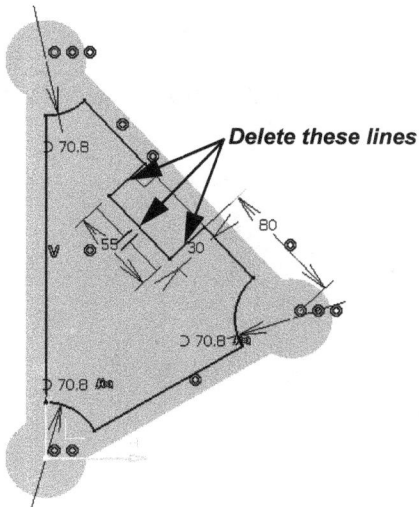

Figure 15–58

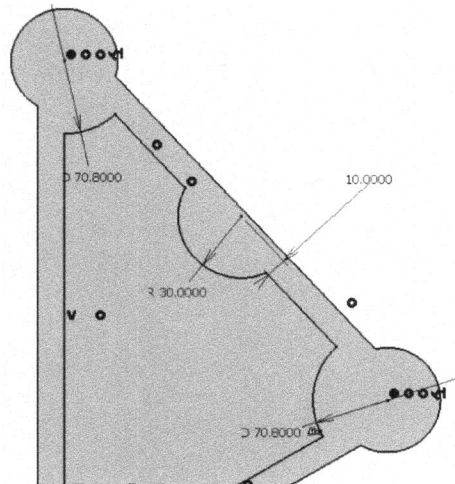

Figure 15–59

3. Exit the Sketcher workbench.

Task 3 - Resolve the update error of the Draft.1 feature.

The Update Diagnosis dialog box opens, as shown in Figure 15–60.

Design Considerations

During the modification of the Sketch.2 profile, the three faces driving the **Draft.1** feature were removed, along with the three sketched lines. When working with complex parts, check the parent/child relationships of a sketch feature before modifying its profile. Analyze whether it is more efficient to repair resultant failures or to create a new sketch and subsequent dress-up features.

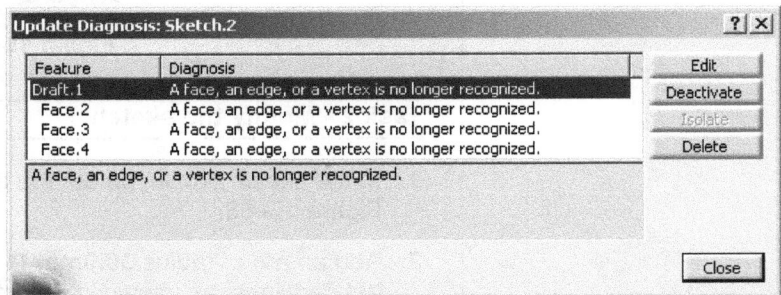

Figure 15–60

1. In the Update Diagnosis dialog box, select **Draft.1.** Click **Edit**. The Feature Definition Error dialog box opens, along with a graphical representation of the unrecognized faces, as shown in Figure 15–61.

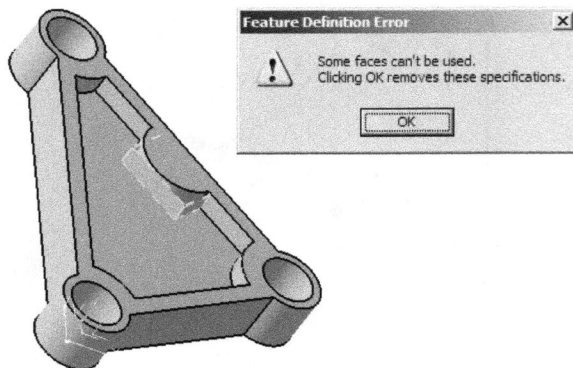

Figure 15–61

2. In the Feature Definition Error dialog box, click **OK** to remove the three faces from the draft definition. The Draft Definition dialog box opens, as shown in Figure 15–62.

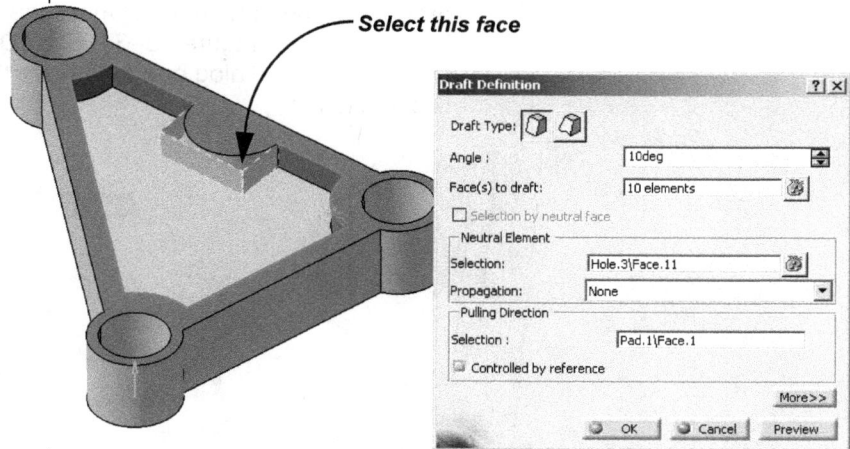

Select this face

Figure 15–62

3. Select the *Face(s) to draft* field and then select the newly created cylindrical face, as shown in Figure 15–62.

4. Click **OK** to finish resolving the **Draft.1** feature failure.

Task 4 - Resolve the update error of the EdgeFillet.1 feature.

The modification of **Sketch.2** has also affected the EdgeFillet.1 feature. The Update Diagnosis dialog box reports that four edges are no longer recognized, as shown in Figure 15–63.

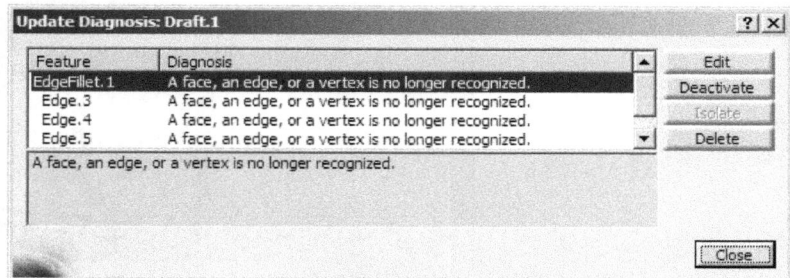

Figure 15–63

1. Select the **EdgeFillet.1** feature in the Update Diagnosis dialog box. Click **Edit** to begin resolving the feature failure.

2. The Feature Definition Error dialog box opens, along with a graphical representation of where the filleted edges used to be, as shown in Figure 15–64. Click **OK** in the Feature Definition Error dialog box to remove the four edges from the fillet definition.

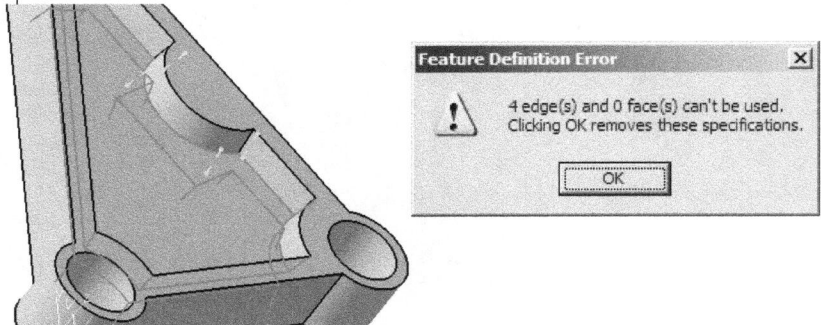

Feature Definition Error ✕

⚠ 4 edge(s) and 0 face(s) can't be used. Clicking OK removes these specifications.

OK

Figure 15–64

3. The Edge Fillet Definition dialog box opens. Select the *Object(s) to fillet* field and select the three edges shown in Figure 15–65.

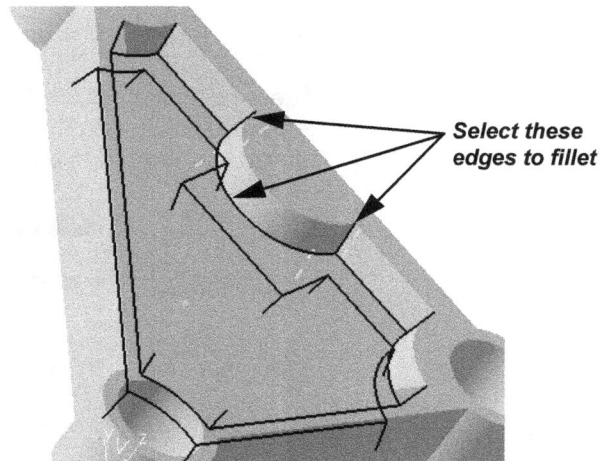

Select these edges to fillet

Figure 15–65

4. Click **OK** to finish resolving the **EdgeFillet.1** definition. The updated part displays as shown in Figure 15–66.

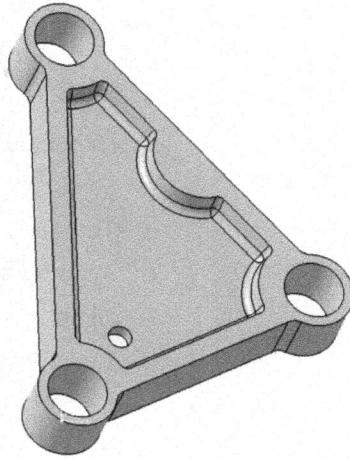

Figure 15–66

5. Save and close the file.

Chapter Review Questions

1. Which of the following actions create feature relationship when sketching a feature? (Select all that apply.)
   a. Selecting the Sketch support.
   b. Dimensioning the length of a line.
   c. Projecting an existing edge to create a new entity.
   d. Trimming two entities in the new sketch.
   e. Aligning a new entity with an existing entity.
   f. Dimensioning new entities to existing geometry.
   g. Selecting the **Blind depth** option.
   h. Selecting the **Up to Surface depth** option.

2. A plane can be a parent of another plane.
   a. True
   b. False

3. Default reference planes cannot be deleted or modified.
   a. True
   b. False

4. In Figure 15–67, **Pad.1** and **Pocket.1** are parents of **Sketch.3,** and **Sketch.3** is a parent of **Pocket.2**. **Hole.2, Hole.1, EdgeFillet.1** are in turn, children of **Pocket.2**.

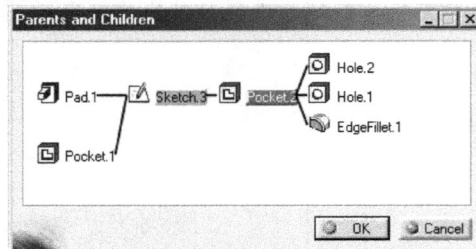

Figure 15–67

   a. True
   b. False

5. In Figure 15–67, deleting **Pocket.1** will not affect **Pocket.2**.
   a. True
   b. False

6. Which of the following depth options will not create a parent/child relationship? (Select all that apply).

   a. Up to Surface

   b. Up to Last

   c. Up to Plane

   d. Blind

7. You can isolate a Fillet.

   a. True

   b. False

8. A feature is deleted from a model. The Update Diagnosis dialog box opens and indicates that a Fillet and a Pocket feature have both failed. You deactivate both features, which means you have resolved the failure.

   a. True

   b. False

Answers: 1.acefh, 2.a, 3.a, 4.a, 5.b, 6.bd, 7.b, 8.b

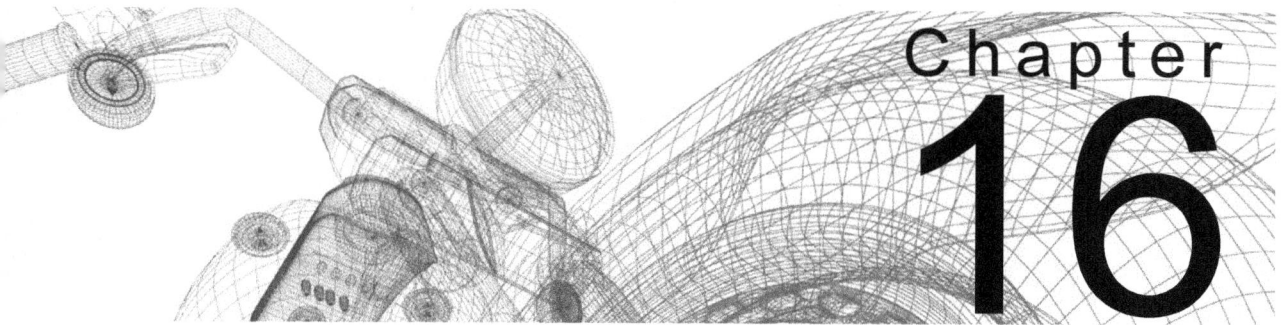

Part Information

CATIA provides you with several tools that can be used to obtain information about a part's measurements and inertia. You can also use the feature investigation tools to determine how the model was constructed.

Learning Objectives in this Chapter

- Use measure entities.
- Update measurements that result from a model modification.
- Learn how to measure between items.
- Understand Standard, Chain, and Fan modes.
- Apply material to a model.
- Measure 2D and 3D inertia.
- Position a section plane to visualize a 3D section of the model.

16.1 Measuring Items

The **Measure Item** tool is a one-click measurement tool that enables you to select one of the following items in the specification tree or on screen to measure:

- Point

- Edge (straight or curved)

- Surface (flat or curved)

- PartBody

Click 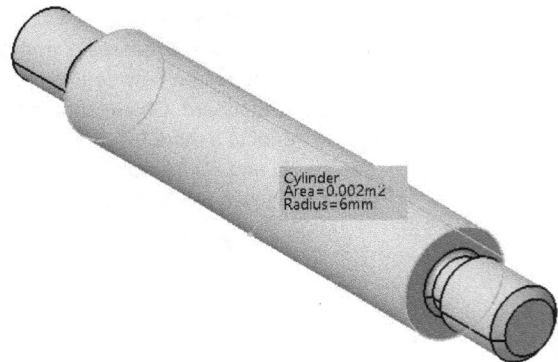 (Measure Item) in the Measure toolbar to open the Measure Item dialog box, as shown in Figure 16–1. The measurements results depend on what you select and what result settings are in place. The results for a curved surface are shown in Figure 16–2.

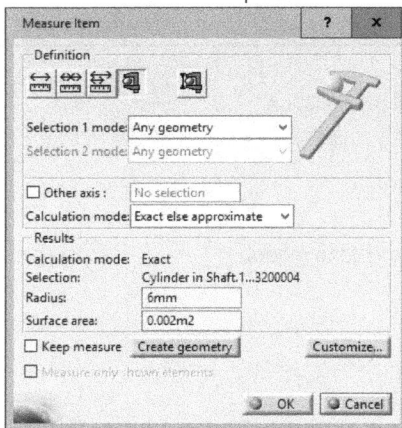

Figure 16–1

Figure 16–2

You can use the *Selection 1 mode* and *Selection 2 mode* drop-down lists to set the entities to measure.

Note that to measure the thickness, you can either select **Thickness** from the selection mode drop-down list or click

(Measures the Thickness).

The measure item results can be customized for the selected item by clicking **Customize**. The Measure Item Customization dialog box opens as shown in Figure 16–3.

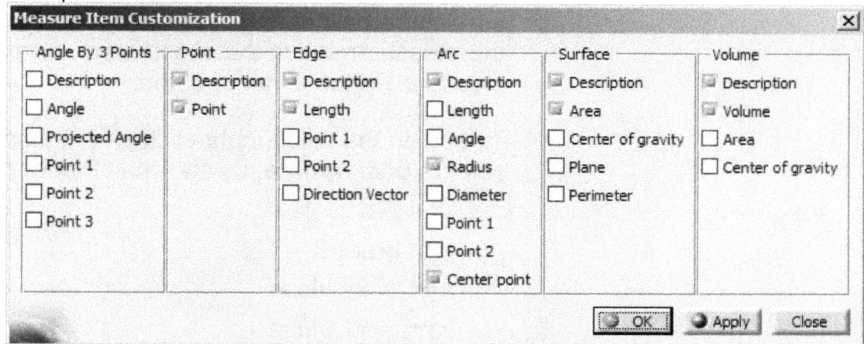

Figure 16–3

Once an item is measured, you can save the measurement with the model data by selecting the **Keep Measure** option in the Measure Item dialog box, as shown in Figure 16–4.

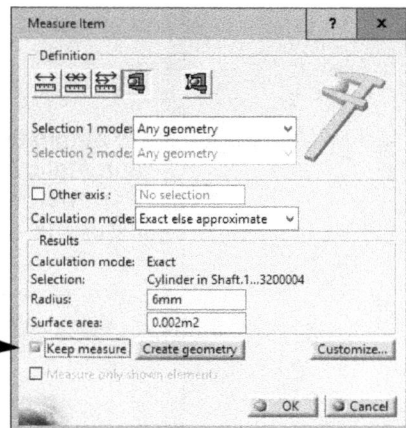

Select to save measurement with model data.

Figure 16–4

The measurement is then added to the specification tree, as shown in Figure 16–5.

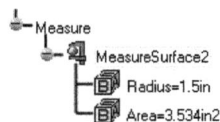

Figure 16–5

16.2 Updating Measurements

If modifications are made in the model that result in a change to a measured value (e.g., geometry change), ⌖ displays next to the measurement in the specification tree, indicating that the measured value is not updated.

To update the value, right-click on the measurement name and select **Local update**, as shown in Figure 16–6.

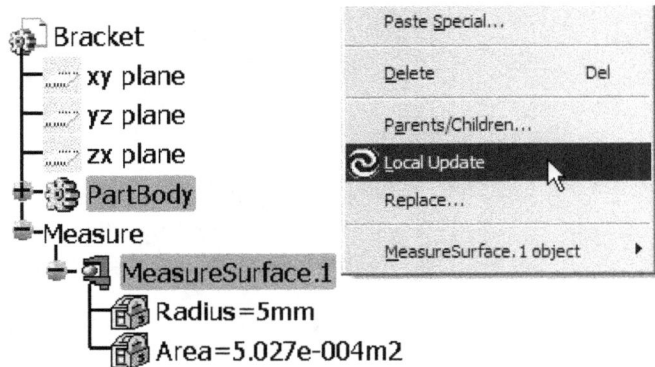

Figure 16–6

To automate the update of these measurements, enable the automatic update options under **Tools>Options>General> Parameters and Measure>***Measure Tools* tab, as shown in Figure 16–7.

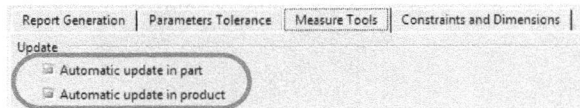

Figure 16–7

16.3 Measuring Between Items

Click ⟷ (Standard) in the Measure toolbar to open the Measure Between dialog box, as shown in Figure 16–8.

Measure Between Modes

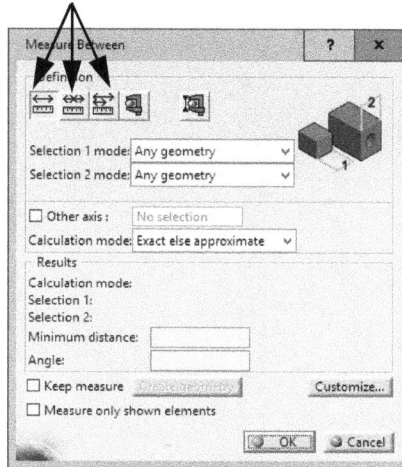

Figure 16–8

The three modes of Measure Between tools available are described as follows:

- Standard

- Chain

- Fan

Standard Mode Measure Between

The **Standard Mode Measure Between** tool is the default Measure Between mode. It is a two-click measurement tool that enables you to measure between two selected items of the same or mixed types. You can select from the specification tree or on the screen. The different selectable item types for the **Measure Between** tool are shown in Figure 16–9.

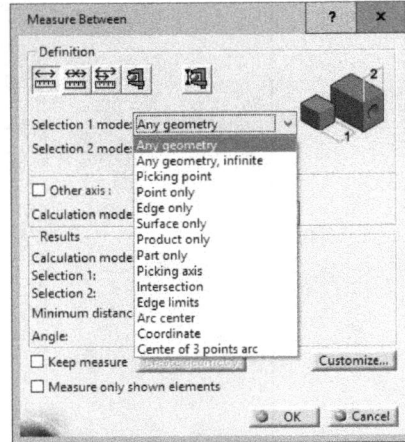

Figure 16–9

- Using **Any geometry**, the software enables you to measure between geometry of any type. If this causes difficulty in selecting a specific type of element, select a more applicable element in the menu.

- **Any geometry, infinite** extends the selected plane, curve, or line infinitely to obtain an accurate minimum distance.

- **Standard Mode Measure Between** is a two-click tool that can be used to take measurements, such as the distance between items or angle between items.

An example of a measurement between two selected surfaces is shown in Figure 16–10. The results can be saved and customized using the same method as the **Measure Item** tool.

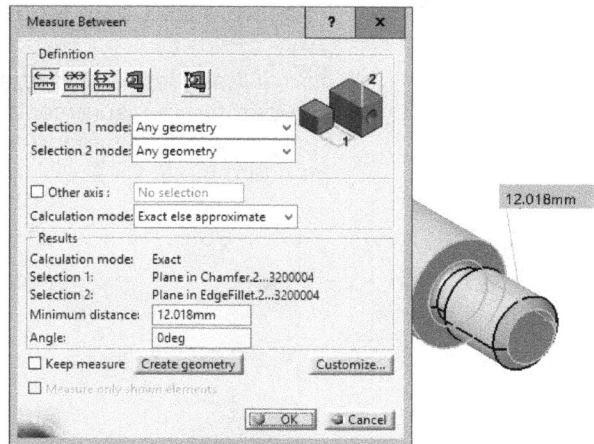

Figure 16–10

When selecting hole and arc centers, you can display an axis by moving the cursor over the approximate center of the hole and arc, as shown in Figure 16–11.

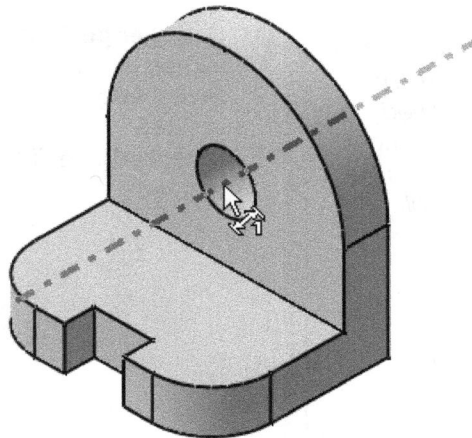

Figure 16–11

Chain Mode Measure Between

The **Chain Mode Measure Between** tool enables you to quickly gather multiple measurements between pairs of selected items in a chain.

To activate the **Chain Mode Measure Between** tool, click

(Chain) in the Measure Between dialog box. Figure 16–12 shows three measurements that can be created using four item selections in Chain mode rather than six item selections in Standard mode.

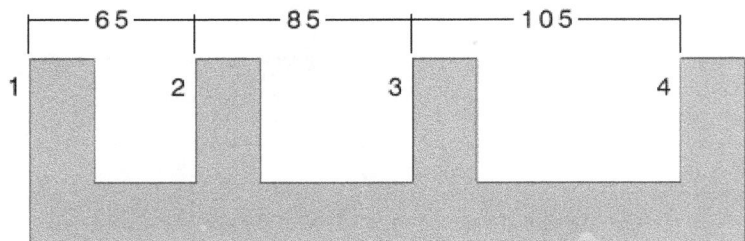

Figure 16–12

How To: Create Measurements using Chain mode

Figure 16–12 shows an example of measurements using chain mode:

1. Select **edge 1** and **edge 2**. The measurement distance of 65 inches is created.
2. Select **edge 3**. The measurement distance of 85 inches is created.
3. Select **edge 4**. The measurement distance of 105 inches is created.

*After the first measurement is created, the software creates measurements between any newly selected items and the last selected item. The results can be saved and customized using the same method as the **Measure Item** tool.*

Fan Mode Measure Between

The **Fan Mode Measure Between** tool enables you to quickly gather multiple measurements between one base item and any number of other items. To activate the **Fan Mode Measure Between** tool, click ⬚ (Fan) in the Measure Between dialog box.

The three measurements shown in Figure 16–13 can be created using four item selections in Fan mode rather than six item selections in Standard mode.

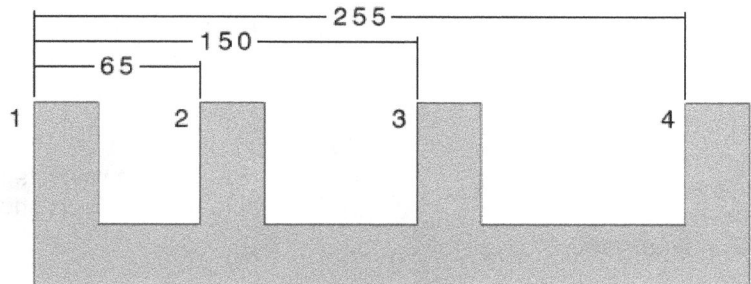

Figure 16–13

*After the first measurement is created, the software creates measurements between any newly selected items and the first selected item (base item). The results can be saved and customized using the same method as the **Measure Item** tool.*

How To: Create Measurements using Fan mode

Figure 16–13 shows an example of measurements using Fan mode:

1. Select **edge 1** and **edge 2**. The measurement distance of 65 inches is created.
2. Select **edge 3**. The measurement distance of 150 inches is created.
3. Select **edge 4**. The measurement distance of 255 inches is created.

Measuring with Reference Elements

In situations where the part geometry is complex, such as models created using surfacing techniques, it is difficult to find planar references to measure between. In this case, reference elements can be constructed to generate an exact measurement reference.

- Consider the simplified example shown in Figure 16–14. In this case, a measure between operation referencing the top and bottom faces can report the minimum and maximum distances. The software is free to select the location on the curved surface from which the measurement is made.

Another option is to use **Customize> Components**. *This reports the X, Y, and Z components of a measurement, enabling you to extract the required direction.*

- To measure the distance between an exact location on the top surface, a reference point can be created to define the location, as shown in Figure 16–15.

- To further define the type of measurement, a reference plane can be created. This restricts the measurement direction to be normal to the plane, as shown in Figure 16–16.

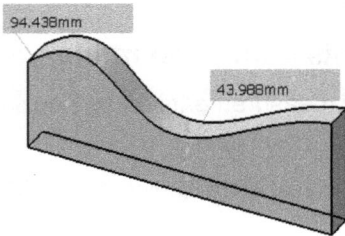

Figure 16–14

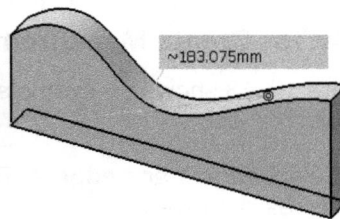

Figure 16–15

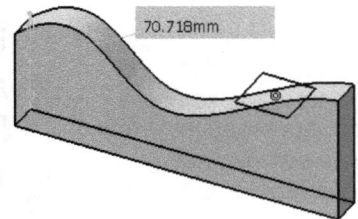

Figure 16–16

16.4 Measuring Inertia

Before measuring the inertia of the model, it is recommended that you first define the model's material properties.

Apply a Material

When you apply a material to a model, the properties of the model (such as density and Young's modulus) are defined. This ensures that accurate inertia values are computed for the model.

How To: Apply a Material

1. Click ![icon] (Apply Material) to define the material for the model. The Library dialog box opens as shown in Figure 16–17.

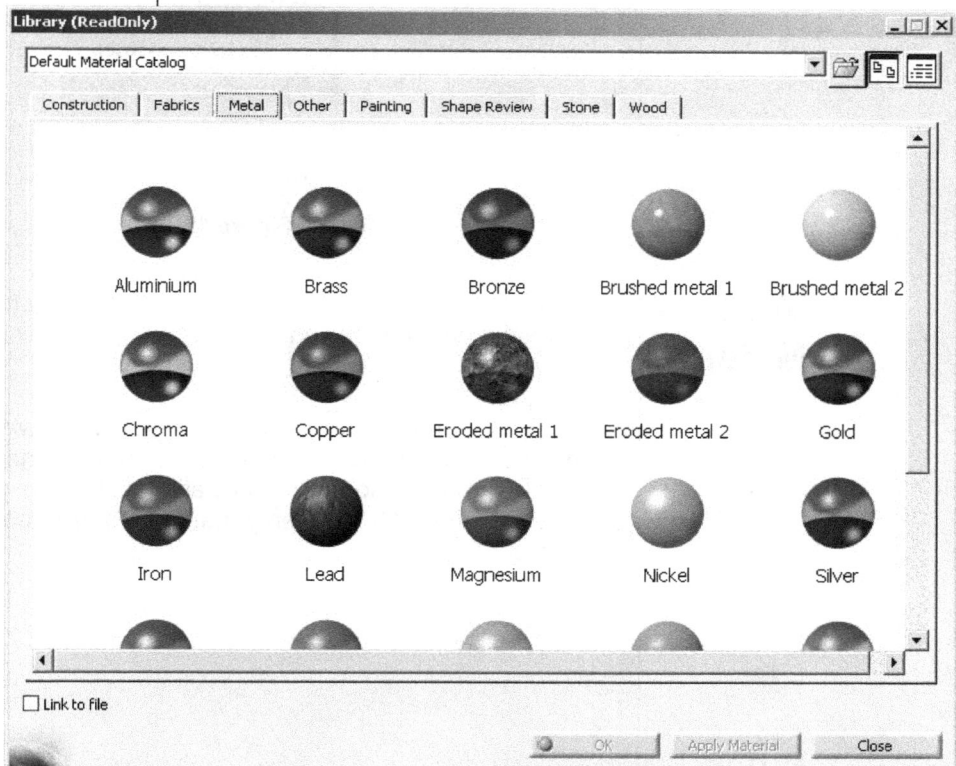

Figure 16–17

By placing the material into a part body, you can measure the inertia of each body. By placing the material into the part number, you apply one material to the entire part. To measure its inertia, you must select the part number in the specification tree.

2. Double-click on a graphic representing the required material in the dialog box to view the material properties.
3. Select a material from the dialog box and drag it onto the part body or part number. The material is listed in the specification tree, as shown in Figure 16–18. All properties for the selected material are defined for the model to which the material is applied. The properties are also used in the inertia calculations.

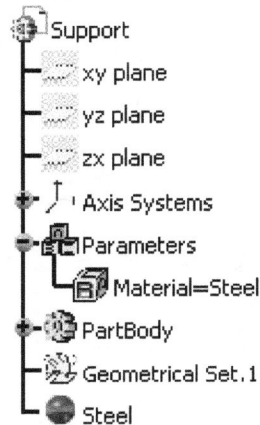

Support
— xy plane
— yz plane
— zx plane
Axis Systems
Parameters
Material=Steel
PartBody
Geometrical Set.1
Steel

Figure 16–18

Viewing the Material

The model can also be viewed in a custom View mode with the material rendering applied.

Click ▨ (Shading with Material) or select **View>Render Style>Customize View** to apply the material rendering to a model. The View Mode Customization dialog box opens as shown in Figure 16–19. Verify that the **Material** option is selected.

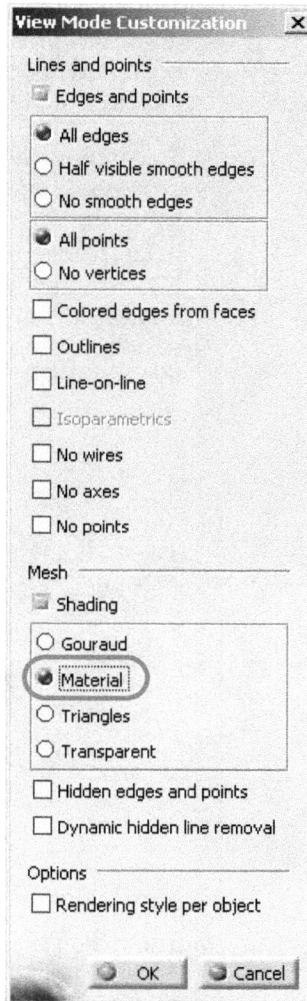

Figure 16–19

Measure Inertia 3D

The inertia of an object is defined as the property by which it retains its present velocity (speed and direction) so long as it is not acted upon by an external force. An equivalent definition of inertia is the resistance of an object to a change in its motion.

To compute the model inertia using the model's current material properties, select a model to create measurements for and click

![inertia icon] (Measure Inertia) in the toolbar. With ![icon] (Measure Inertia 3D) selected, you can select 3D entities (such as features or bodies) in the specification tree and measure their inertia. The results display in the Measure Inertia dialog box, as shown in Figure 16–20.

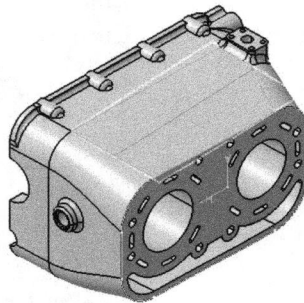

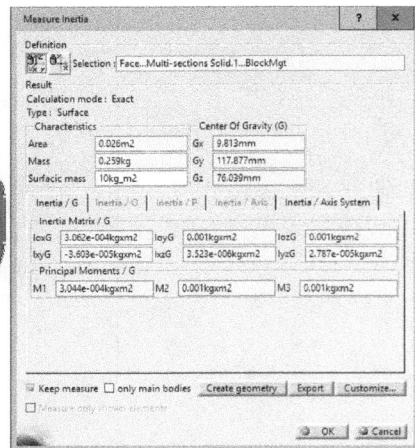

Figure 16–20

The dialog box reports the following information:

- Characteristics, such as volume, area, mass, and density.

- The center of gravity relative to the origin of the part.

- Inertia data of the part.

The inertia data of the part can be measured with respect to a variety of elements by selecting one of the following tabs.

Tab	Meaning
Inertia / G	Measure inertia with respect to the center of gravity of the model.
Inertia / O	Measure inertia with respect to the origin of the model.
Inertia / P	Measure inertia with respect to a selected point.
Inertia / Axis	Measure inertia with respect to a selected axis.
Inertia / Axis System	Measure inertia with respect to a selected axis system.

The *Inertia / G* tab is activated by default. To activate the other four tabs, click **Customize** to open the Measure Inertia Customization dialog box shown in Figure 16–21.

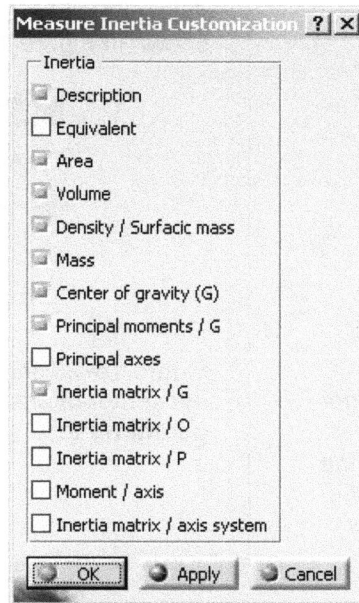

Figure 16–21

Each tab displays a variety of inertia data that is relevant to the measurement reference. For example, the following parameters are reported for an Inertia / G calculation.

Parameter	Meaning
Iox	Area moment of inertia about the X-axis.
Ioy	Area moment of inertia about the Y-axis.
Ioz	Area moment of inertia about the Z-axis.
Ixy	Mass moment of inertia on the XY plane.
Ixz	Mass moment of inertia on the XZ plane.
Iyz	Mass moment of inertia on the YZ plane.

The **Measure Inertia** tool also enables you to create a point and/or an axis system at the center of gravity in the part. To create geometry, click **Create geometry** in the Measure Inertia dialog box. The Creation of Geometry dialog box opens as shown in Figure 16–22.

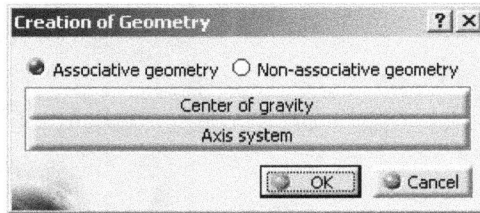

Figure 16–22

The results of the Measure Inertia tool can be saved and customized using the same method as the Measure Item tool.

Figure 16–23 shows an example of an axis system and a point at the center of gravity that has been created using the **Create geometry** tool.

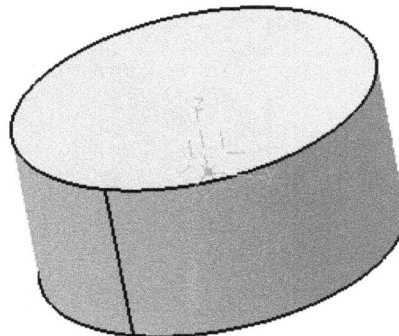

Figure 16–23

Measure Inertia 2D

Measuring the inertia of a section or surface is useful for rapidly determining the structural properties of complex shapes. With

![icon] (Measure Inertia 2D) selected, you can select solid faces from the model and measure their two-dimensional inertia properties. This tool is identical to its 3D counterpart, except that certain calculations that do not apply to two-dimensional surfaces (mass, density, volume, etc.) are not present, as shown in Figure 16–24.

Only the Inertia / G tab is available when measuring in 2D.

*Note that **Create geometry** is not available when measuring inertia in 2D.*

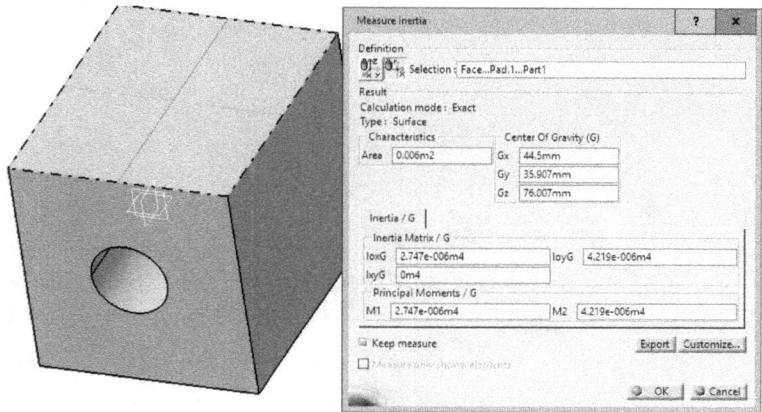

Figure 16–24

16.5 Dynamic Sectioning

The Dynamic Sectioning enables you to position a section plane to visualize a 3D section view of a part, as shown in Figure 16–25. The section plan can be dynamically adjusted.

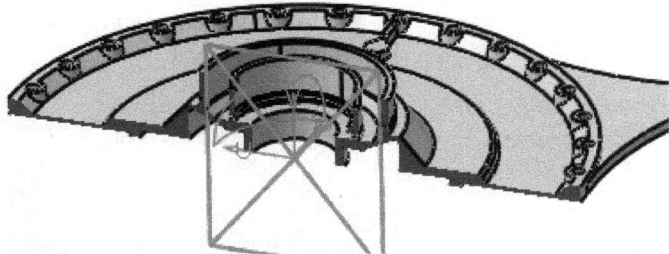

Figure 16–25

To use the Dynamic Sectioning tool, click [icon] (Dynamic Sectioning) from the Dynamic Sectioning toolbar. A red section plane is automatically displayed on the model.

The location of the section plane can dynamically be modified. To adjust the position, select an edge, surface, plane, or curve in the model. If you are selecting a reference in the model, a purple section plane locater icon displays, as shown in Figure 16–26.

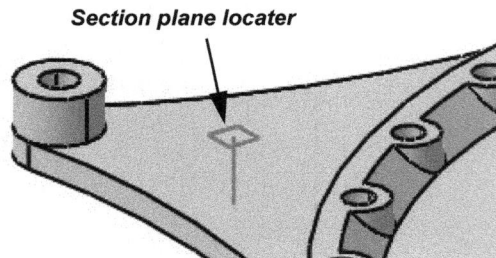

Section plane locater

Figure 16–26

To translate the section plane along about the selected reference, hover the cursor over the red section plane, as shown in Figure 16–27. When the green arrow displays, click and drag the plane to the required location. The model is dynamically cut about the section plane as you click and drag.

To rotate the section plane, hover the cursor over one of the red arcs on the section plane compass. Click the arc, and drag the section plane to the required location, as shown in Figure 16–28.

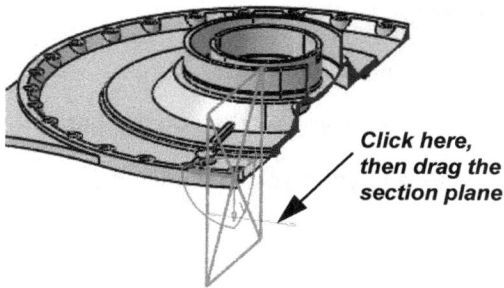

Click here, then drag the section plane

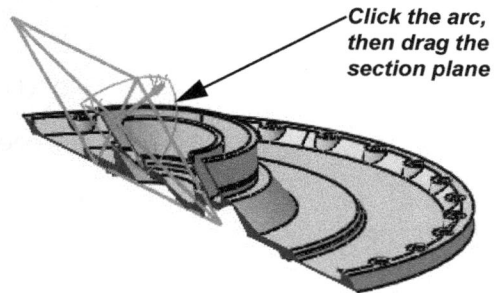

Click the arc, then drag the section plane

Figure 16–27   **Figure 16–28**

The section plane can be adjusted repeatedly. When done using the Dynamic Sectioning tool, deactivate by clicking the **Dynamic Sectioning** icon.

16.6 Feature Investigation

CATIA provides several tools to investigate a model. The investigation tools can be used to determine how a model is constructed. These tools are useful if:

- A model is created by someone else.

- It has been a long time since you worked on the part.

- The model is complex and you need to modify the feature structure.

Scanning the Model

Scanning the model enables you to review the construction history of a model, one feature at a time. This is helpful when working with models that are created by other users. The **Scan** tool enables you to review and replay the design, giving you an idea of the model creator's design intent and modeling techniques.

To use the **Scan** tool, select **Edit>Scan or Define In Work Object**. The Scan dialog box opens, as shown in Figure 16–29. Use the control icons to play, step forward, rewind, or stop the model at the current feature creation location.

Figure 16–29

By default, the **Structure** option is selected in the Scan dialog box. With this setting, the software replays the features of the active body based on the feature order displayed in the specification tree. Features in other bodies or geometrical sets are not replayed.

If the **Update** option is selected, the software replays the features in the model in the order in which they are updated, as shown in Figure 16–30.

Figure 16–30

Figure 16–31 shows an example of a part that was created by first adding a reference plane that was used as a support for **Sketch.1**. The scan order, based on the **Structure** or **Update** option, is shown in Figure 16–31.

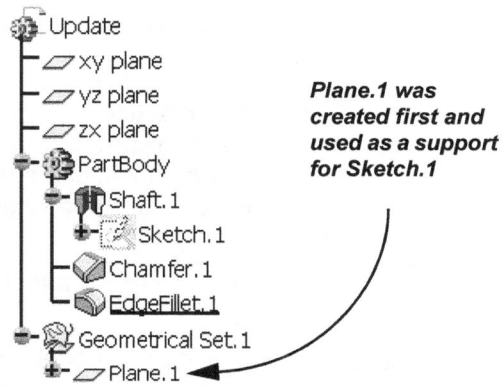

Figure 16–31

	Structure	Update
1	Shaft	Plane.1
2	Chamfer	Sketch.1
3	EdgeFillet.1	Shaft.1
4	**End**	Chamfer.1
5		EdgeFillet.1
6		**End**

Practice 16a | Take Measurements

Practice Objectives

- Review the feature creation history.
- Assign a material to the part.
- Determine the mass, volume, and surface area of the part.

In this practice, you will use the **Scan** tool to view the model's creation history. You will also assign a material to the part, take measurements of the part, and analyze some of its properties, such as mass and volume.

Task 1 - Open a part and scan the model.

Design Considerations

Scanning the model is another way of reviewing its creation history. This is often a helpful tool if you did not create the model, but need to update it. The **Scan** tool enables you to review the creation process and grasp the original designer's design intent.

1. Open **Support_Info.CATPart**. Note the feature order in the specification tree to review how the model is created.

2. Select **Edit>Scan or Define In Work Object** to activate the **Scan** tool.

3. Click |◄◄| to reset the model to the first feature created. The model displays as shown in Figure 16–32. A Pad is the first feature created for the model.

4. Click |►| and note the addition of a second Pad feature.

5. Click |►| to automatically play the addition of the remaining features, as shown in Figure 16–33.

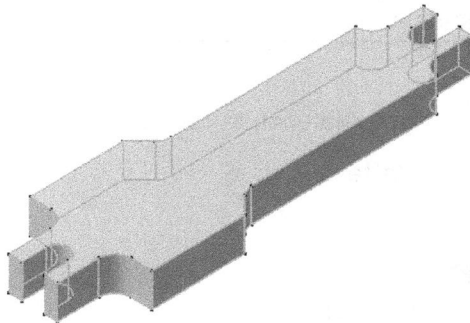

Figure 16–32

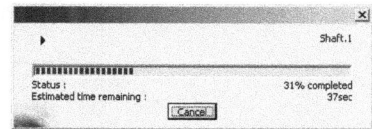

Figure 16–33

6. Close the **Scan** tool.

Task 2 - Review some of the parent/child relations in the model.

---

1. Expand PartBody in the specification tree to display the features under **PartBody**.

2. A design change requires that the Shaft support of **Pad.6** be modified. Before making modifications, it is recommended to review which child features rely on **Pad.6** as a parent. Select the **Pad.6** feature in the specification tree, right-click and select **Parents/Children**. The Parents and Children dialog box opens, as shown in Figure 16–34.

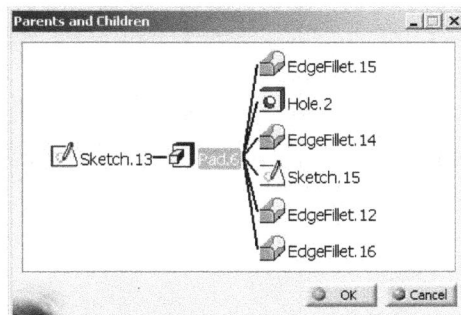

Figure 16–34

All items listed on the right side of **Pad.6** are child features that reference **Pad.6**. Modifications to **Pad.6** might result in modifications or failures with the child features. The parent feature (**Sketch.13**) is listed on the left side of **Pad.6**.

3. Double-click on various items in the dialog box to see further levels of the parent/child relations.

Task 3 - Assign iron as the model material before you calculate inertia.

1. Click (Apply Material) to open the material library.

2. Select the *Metal* tab.

3. Drag Iron (Iron) onto the model and click **OK** in the Library dialog box.

4. Double-click on the Iron feature listed in the specification tree, as shown in Figure 16–35.

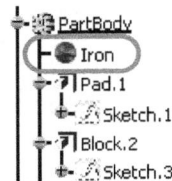

Figure 16–35

5. The Iron Properties dialog box populates with the feature properties. Review the properties and note the density value. Close the dialog box.

Task 4 - Display the model with iron material.

1. Click (Shading with Material). The model is rendered with the material applied to it, as shown in Figure 16–36.

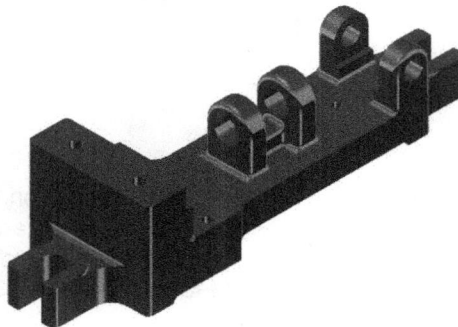

Figure 16–36

Task 5 - View inertia results using the iron material properties.

1. Select the part body in the specification tree and click

    (Measure Inertia) to measure the model inertia. The resulting data displays in the Measure Inertia dialog box, as shown in Figure 16–37.

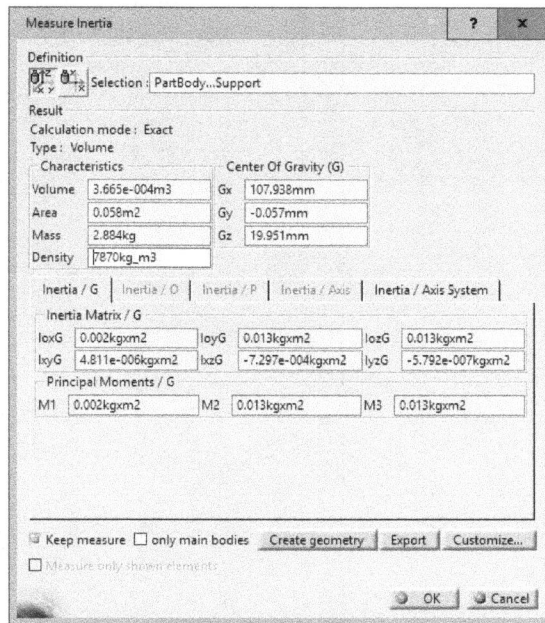

Figure 16–37

Note that the density value displayed is that of iron, shown in the Properties dialog box from Task 4. Note the surface area value. This might be important if the part is powder-coated or plated. Also note the volume value. This might be important in calculating the material cost of molded or cast parts.

2. Review the other measurements that are calculated. Close the dialog box.

3. Change the View mode back to (Shading with Edges), as required.

Task 6 - Measure inertia with respect to an axis system.

1. Expand the specification tree right-click on **Axis System.1** and select **Hide/Show**.

2. Select the PartBody in the specification tree and click

   (Measure Inertia) to measure the model inertia.

3. Click **Customize** and select the **Inertia matrix / axis system** option, as shown in Figure 16–38.

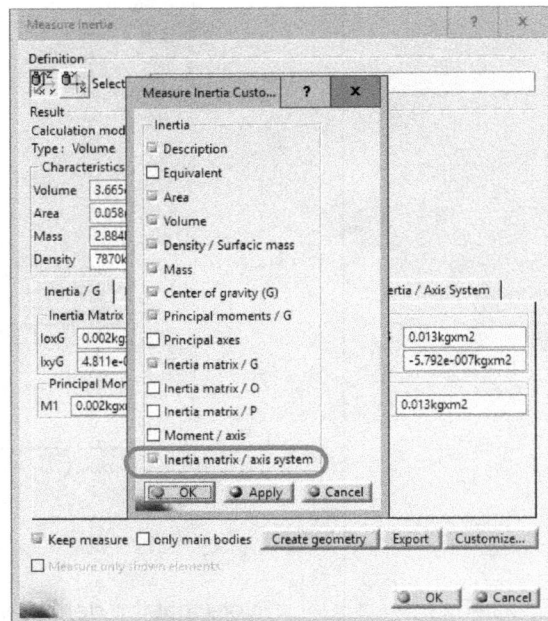

Figure 16–38

4. Click **OK** and select the *Inertia / Axis System* tab.

5. Select the **Select Axis System** option and select **Axis System.1** as the axis system, as shown in Figure 16–39.

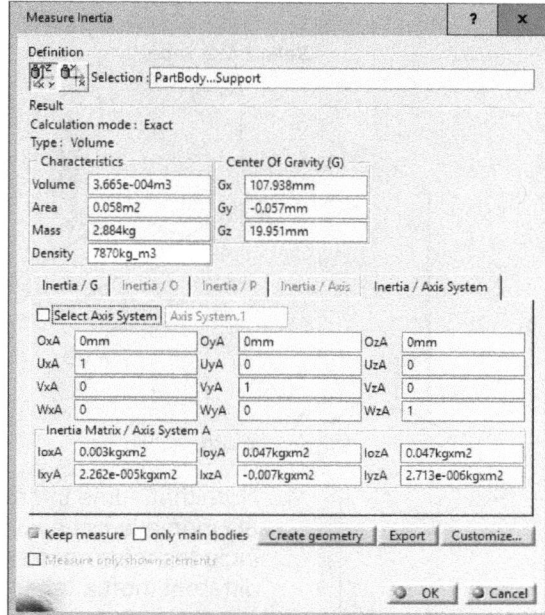

Figure 16–39

6. Note how the values of the Inertia Matrix are different than the values measured in the *Inertia / G* tab

7. Close the dialog box.

Task 7 - Measure inertia in 2D.

1. Click (Measure Inertia) to measure the model inertia.

2. Click (Measure Inertia 2D).

3. Select the surface shown in Figure 16–40. The Measure Inertia dialog box opens as shown in Figure 16–41.

Select this face

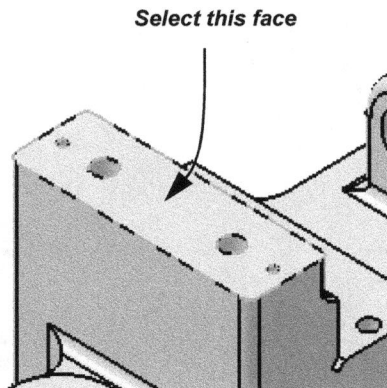

Figure 16–40

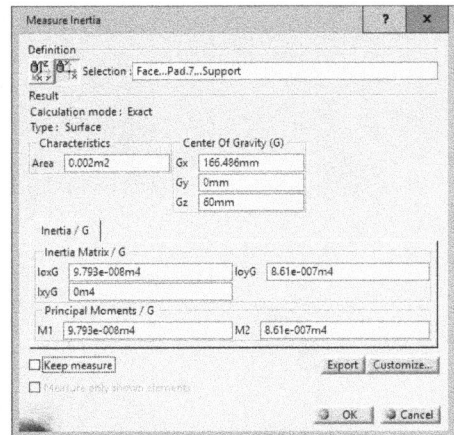

Figure 16–41

4. Note that some information that is present when measuring 3D inertia is not available when measuring 2D inertia. This includes information such as the volume, density, and the different inertia tabs (*Inertia / O, Inertia / P,* etc.).

5. Close the dialog box.

Task 8 - Take a series of one-click measurements.

1. Click ▧ (Measure Item) to make some one-click measurements.

*If the units for the area calculation are incorrect, select **Tools>Options> Parameters and Measure**, select the Units tab and set the Area units to square meter.*

2. Select the cylindrical surface shown in Figure 16–42. Note that both the area and radius display.

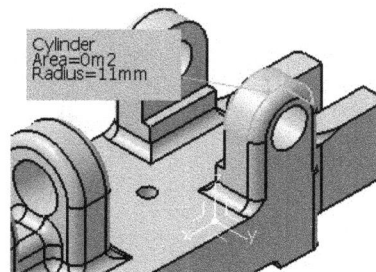

Figure 16–42

Note that you obtain an area of 0m^2. This is because the area of the cylindrical surface is relatively small. You can determine the correct area by changing the number of decimal places displayed for measurement.

3. Select **Tools>Options>Parameters and Measure>***Units* tab.

4. Select **Area** in the *Units* field.

5. Change the value in the *Decimal places for read/write numbers* field to **7**, as shown in Figure 16–43.

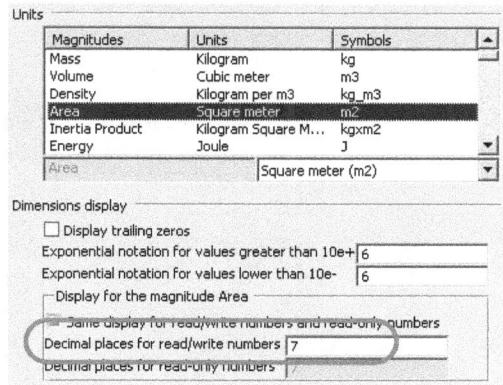

Decimal places cannot be set globally. You must set the number of decimal places for each type of unit individually.

Magnitudes	Units	Symbols	
Mass	Kilogram	kg	
Volume	Cubic meter	m3	
Density	Kilogram per m3	kg_m3	
Area	Square meter	m2	
Inertia Product	Kilogram Square M...	kgxm2	
Energy	Joule	J	
Area		Square meter (m2)	

Dimensions display
☐ Display trailing zeros
Exponential notation for values greater than 10e+ [6]
Exponential notation for values lower than 10e- [6]
Display for the magnitude Area
Same display for read/write numbers and read-only numbers
Decimal places for read/write numbers [7]
Decimal places for read-only numbers [7]

Figure 16–43

6. Click **OK** to close the Options dialog box.

7. Repeat the measurement of the cylindrical surface. The results display as shown in Figure 16–44.

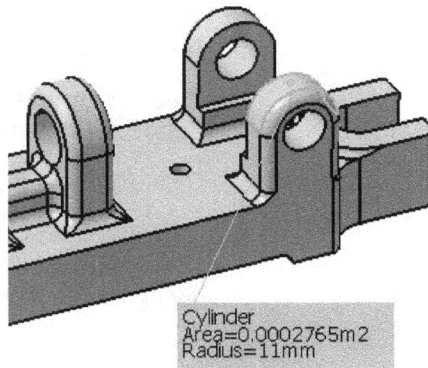

Cylinder
Area=0.0002765m2
Radius=11mm

Figure 16–44

8. Take additional one-click measure item measurements for different items in the model, including flat surfaces, the part body, and a vertex.

9. Close the Measure Item dialog box.

Task 9 - Take a series of measure between measurements.

1. Click ⟷ (Measure Between) to take some measure between measurements.

2. Activate the Standard Measure Between mode by clicking ⟷ (Standard) in the Measure Between dialog box.

3. Select the flat face and hole axis to measure between, as shown in Figure 16–45.

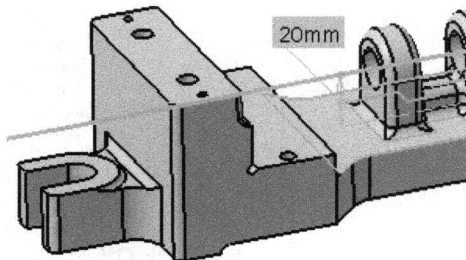

Figure 16–45

4. Note that the Angle dimension is calculated in the dialog box but not on the model. This dimension is not required.

5. Click **Customize** to customize the results.

6. Clear the **Angle** option in the *Panel* column in the Measure Between Customization dialog box.

7. Click **Apply** and **OK**.

8. Repeat Step 3 for a different flat face and hole axis. Note that only the distance is measured and displayed in both the dialog box and on the model.

9. Practice making additional measurements using Standard mode.

10. Set the named view to top by clicking ⬛ (Top).

11. Activate the **Chain Mode Measure Between** tool by clicking

    ⬛ (Chain) in the Measure Between dialog box.

12. Select **Edge 1** and **Hole 1**, as shown in Figure 16–46.

13. Once the measurement displays, continue to select **Hole 2**, followed by **Hole 3**, **Hole 4**, and finally **Edge 2**. The measurements display in order, as shown in Figure 16–47.

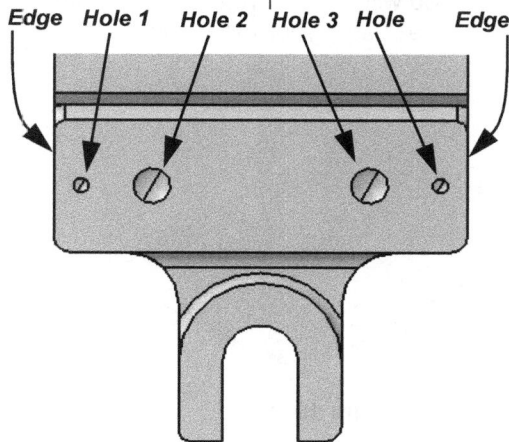

Edge Hole 1 Hole 2 Hole 3 Hole Edge

Figure 16–46

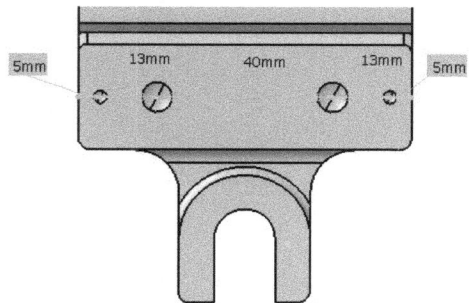

Figure 16–47

*To show all measurements at once, select the **Keep Measure** option in the Measure Between dialog box to save measurements with model data.*

14. Hide the parameters you have just created.

15. Activate the Fan Mode Measure Between tool by clicking

    ⬛ (Fan) in the Measure Between dialog box.

16. Repeat steps 12 to 13 and compare the results with the results in Figure 16–47.

17. Hide the parameters you have just created.

18. Click ⬛ (Save).

19. Select **File>Close**.

Practice 16b | Measuring with Reference Geometry

Practice Objective

- Create reference geometry to perform measure operations.

In this practice, you will develop packaging for the game controller as shown in Figure 16–48. To create a box for the part, you will first determine the maximum width, height, and length of the model. To do this, you will develop reference geometry, such as points and planes, to assist in your measurements.

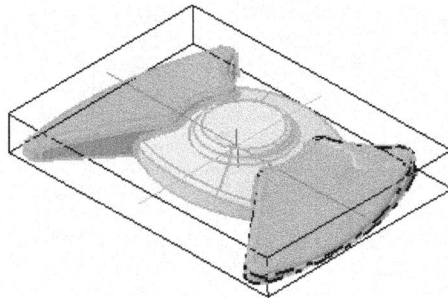

Figure 16–48

Task 1 - Open GameController.CATPart and take a measurement.

1. Open **GameController.CATPart**.

1. Click ⟷ (Standard) and measure between the two arc edges on the bottom of the model, to obtain the overall height of the model, as shown in Figure 16–49.

   The software reports the distance between the centers of the two arcs, as shown in Figure 16–50. To obtain the overall height of the part, 153.355 mm (6.038 in), additional reference geometry must be developed.

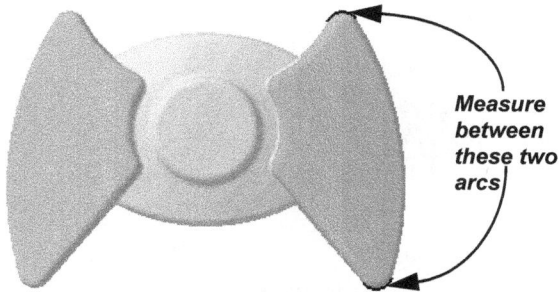

Figure 16–49

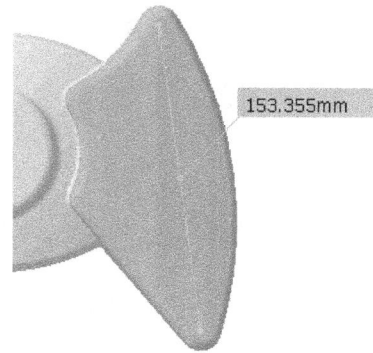

153.355mm

Figure 16–50

2. Cancel the measurement.

Task 2 - Create reference geometry.

In this task, you will build reference points that mark the extremities of the two arc edges previously measured. The **Tangent on curve** option is used in this case, as it forces the software to locate the outermost point of the selected curve when viewed from the selected plane.

1. Create a reference point using the following parameters:

   - *Point Type:* Tangent on curve
   - *Curve:* Select the arc edge shown in Figure 16–51.
   - *Direction:* ZX plane

   The resulting point displays as shown in Figure 16–52.

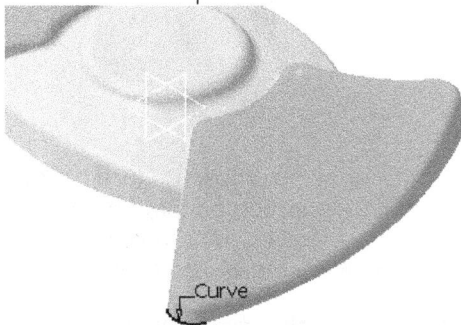

Curve

Figure 16–51

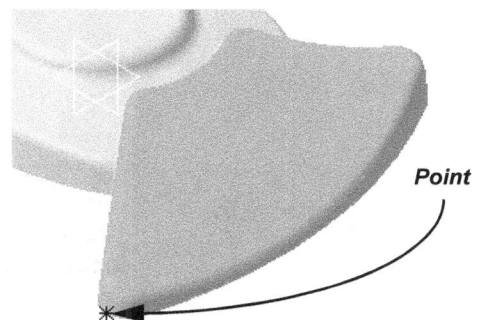

Point

Figure 16–52

2. Repeat this process to create a point on the top arc edge. The point displays as shown in Figure 16–53.

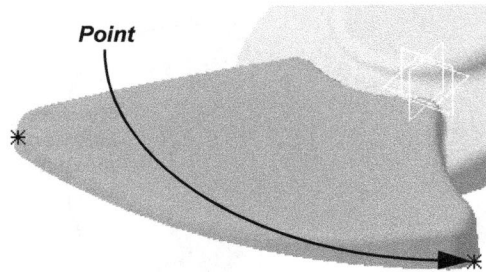

Figure 16–53

Task 3 - Take a measurement between points.

1. Repeat the Measure Between operation, selecting the two points created. The resulting measurement, 173.194 mm (6.819 in), displays as shown in Figure 16–54.

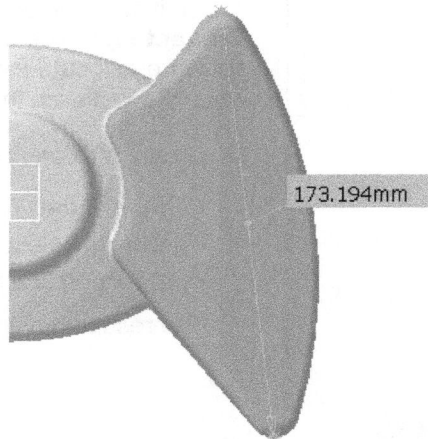

Figure 16–54

Design Considerations

The measurement still does not show the true height of the model. Since it cannot be guaranteed that the two points are vertically aligned, you can use the **Measure Between** tool to obtain the components of the measured distance.

2. Click **Customize** and enable the **Components** option in both the *3D* and the *Panel* columns. The dialog box updates to display the X, Y, and Z components of the measurement. The true height of the model is approximately 171.96mm (6.770 in).

Task 4 - Use reference planes to display distance in one direction.

In this task, you will build reference planes through the point elements. Measuring between two reference planes ensures that the measured distance is in the exact required direction. This also enables you to keep only the required component(s) of a measurement and display it on the model.

1. Create a reference plane using the following options:

   - *Plane type:* **Parallel through point**
   - *Reference:* **YZ plane**
   - *Point:* **Point.1**

   The completed reference plane displays as shown in Figure 16–55.

2. Create a second reference plane that is parallel to the YZ plane and through Point.2. The model displays as shown in Figure 16–56.

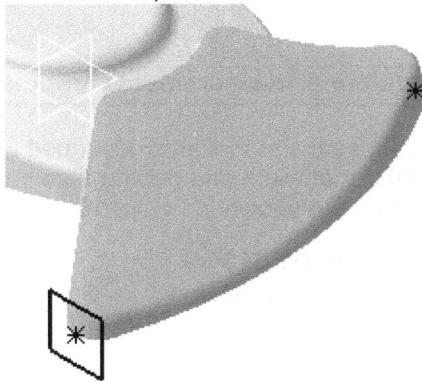

Figure 16–55

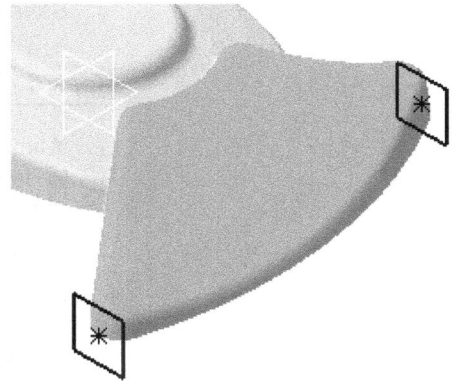

Figure 16–56

3. Measure between the two reference planes just created. Ensure that the **Keep Measure** option is enabled. The model displays the dimension 171.961 mm (6.770 in), as shown in Figure 16–57.

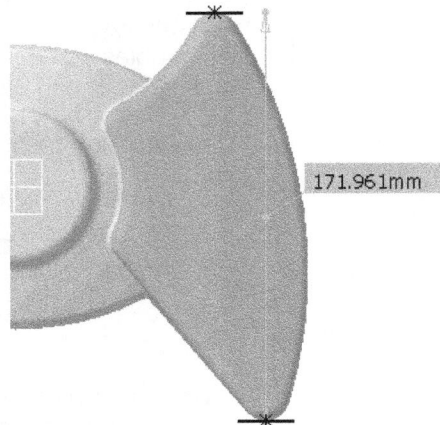

171.961mm

Figure 16–57

4. Save the model and close the file.

Task 5 - Take additional measurements (optional).

---

1. If time permits, use the techniques described in this practice to determine the true width and depth of the model. The measured values are shown in Figure 16–58.

- *Width:* **241.62mm (9.513 in)**
- *Depth:* **30.28mm (1.192 in)**

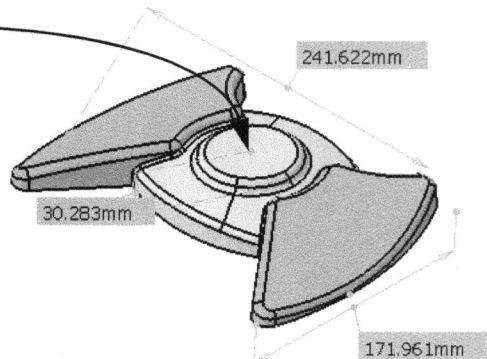

Assume that the highest point on the model is at the center.

241.622mm

30.283mm

171.961mm

Figure 16–58

2. Save the model and close the file.

Chapter Review Questions

1. Which of the following items can be measured using the **Measure Item** tool? (Select all that apply).

   a. Point

   b. Edge

   c. Two planes

   d. Flat Surface

2. You can switch between **Measure Item** and **Measure Between** without closing the dialog box.

   a. True

   b. False

3. Measurements are always stored with the model data.

   a. True

   b. False

4. Measurement data is stored in the Results branch of the specification tree.

   a. True

   b. False

5. In Figure 16–59, the icon indicates that the measurement has not been updated.

   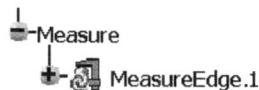

   Figure 16–59

   a. True

   b. False

6. When material is applied to a model, the properties (density, etc.) are defined which permits accurate inertial values.

   a. True

   b. False

7. The **Create Geometry** tool enables you to create an axis system and a point at the center of gravity.

   a. True

   b. False

Answers: 1.abd, 2.a, 3.b, 4.b, 5.a, 6.a, 7.a

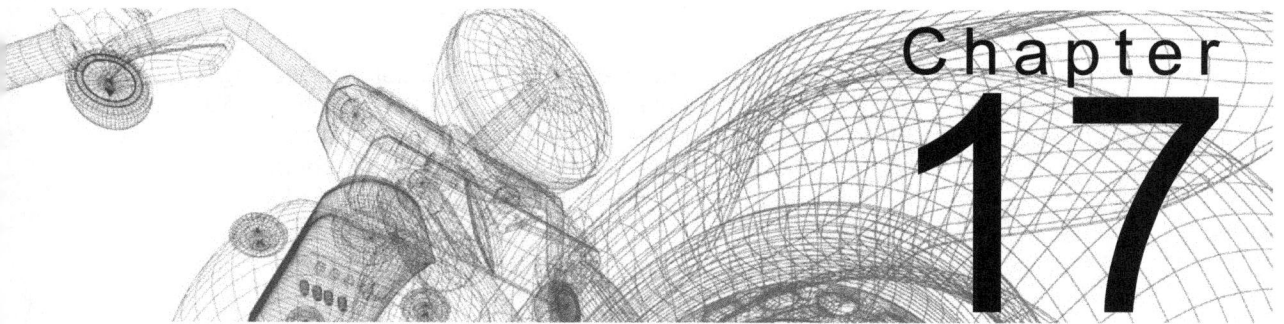

Rib and Slot Features

Sketched features previously covered include the Pad, Shaft, Pocket, and Groove. Rib and Slot features differ slightly in that they require two sketches, a profile, and a center curve.

Learning Objectives in this Chapter

- Learn about Rib and Slot features.
- Understand the various options available for Rib and Slot features.

17.1 Ribs and Slots

The sketch plane of the profile must intersect the center curve.

A Rib feature adds material to your model by sweeping a sketched profile along a center curve, keeping the profile normal to the center curve at all points. Figure 17–1 shows an example of a Rib. A slot is similar to a Rib feature, except that it removes material from your model by sweeping a profile along a center curve.

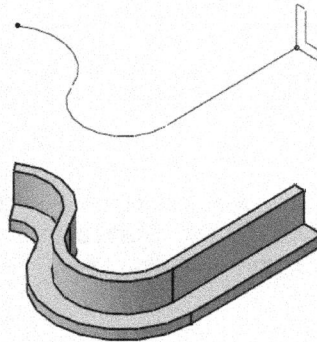

Figure 17–1

How To: Create a Rib Feature

1. Click (Rib) to open the Rib Definition dialog box, which prompt for profile selection and a center curve sketch, as shown in Figure 17–2.

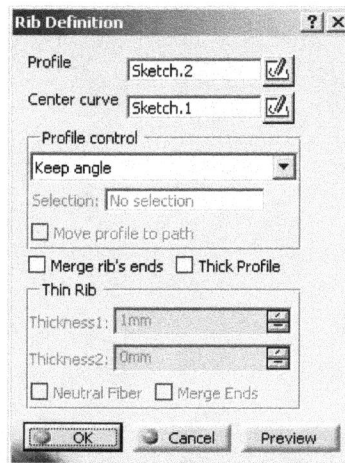

Figure 17–2

2. Specify the center curve. The center curve defines the path that the profile sketch follows. It must intersect the sketch plane of the profile.

3. Select a profile sketch to follow the center curve. As the profile follows the center curve, it can be controlled using the Profile control options. Three options are available from the drop-down list in the *Profile control* area.

The Profile control options are described as follows:

Profile Control Option	Description
Keep angle	Maintains the existing angle between the profile sketch plane and center curve.
Pulling direction	Sweeps profile relative to a specified direction. A plane or edge can be selected.
Reference surface	Maintains angle value relative to the axis of the profile and a selected surface.

4. Click **OK** to complete the feature.

Slots

Slot features remove material from your model by sweeping a profile along a center curve. Slot features are created using a similar method to ribs. To create a slot, click (Slot). Figure 17–3 shows an example of a slot.

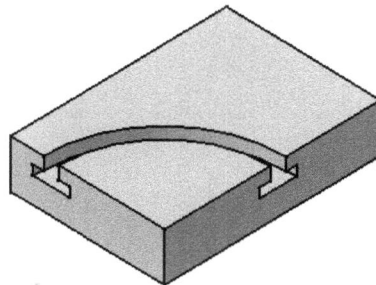

Figure 17–3

17.2 Rib and Slot Options

Merge Ends

The **Merge ends** option enables the profile to continue its trajectory and merge with a surface. Since the center curve is defined on the cup's surface, the profile does not extend into the cup body. However, if the **Merge ends** option is selected, the geometry merges with the cup body, as shown in Figure 17–4.

Figure 17–4

Center Curve

When specifying the center curve, an existing sketch can be used. If an existing sketch is not available, you can click

 (Sketch) and create a new sketch on the selected plane. The center curve can also be specified by selecting an existing edge on a part surface, as shown in Figure 17–5.

Only one edge can be selected for the center curve.

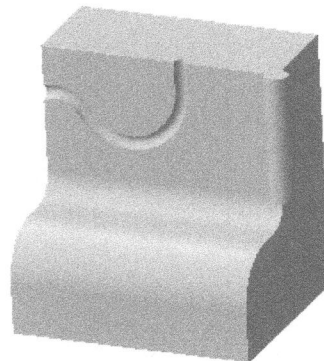

Figure 17–5

If entities in your center curve are non-tangent, sharp corners are produced. Note the difference in geometry from tangent entities compared to non-tangent entities, as shown in Figure 17–6.

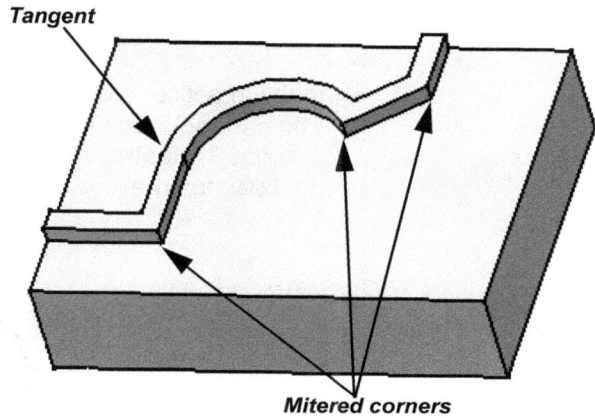

Figure 17–6

Overlapping Geometry

If the cross-section overlaps itself as it travels along the center curve, the feature aborts, as shown in Figure 17–7. If this occurs, modify the profile or the center curve.

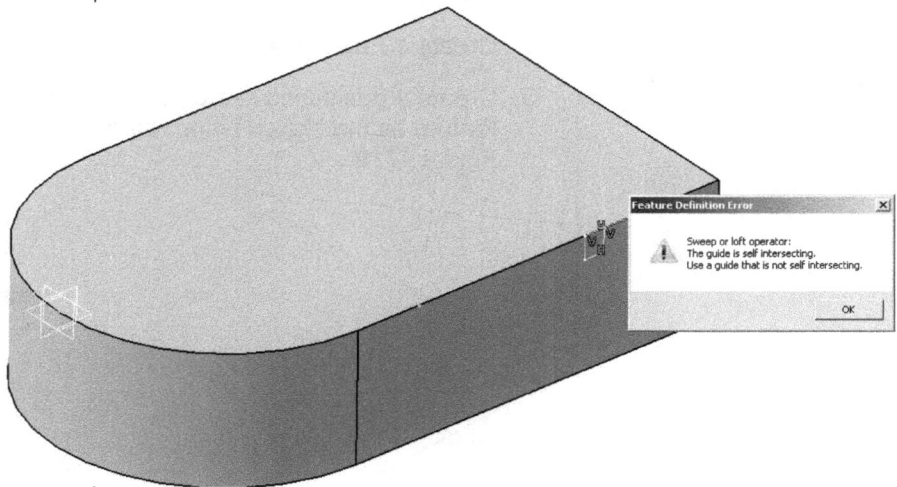

Figure 17–7

Practice 17a | Slots and Ribs

Practice Objective

- Create and modify a Slot and a Rib

In this practice, you will create the part shown in Figure 17–8. The part requires Slot and Rib features. You will also modify the slot and Rib features to merge their ends flush with the surface of the base feature.

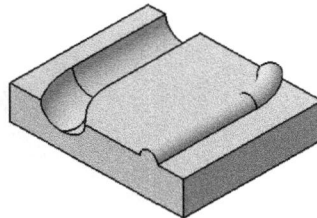

Figure 17–8

Task 1 - Create a Slot feature.

1. Create a new part named **Rib_Slot.CATPart**.

2. Create a Pad 200 x 250 x 50 thick.

Verify that the model units are set to millimeters.

3. Create a positioned sketch using the top surface of the Pad feature as the sketch plane reference as shown in Figure 17–9.

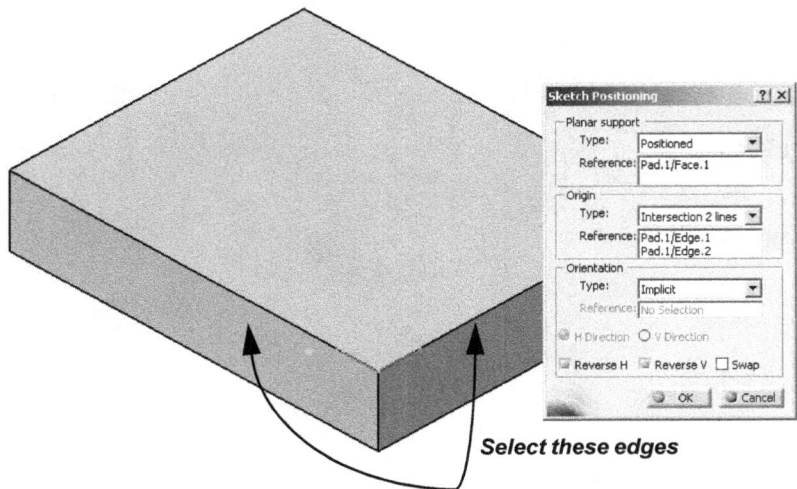

Select these edges

Figure 17–9

4. Dimension and constrain the sketch, as shown in Figure 17–10. It is used later for the center curve of a Slot feature.

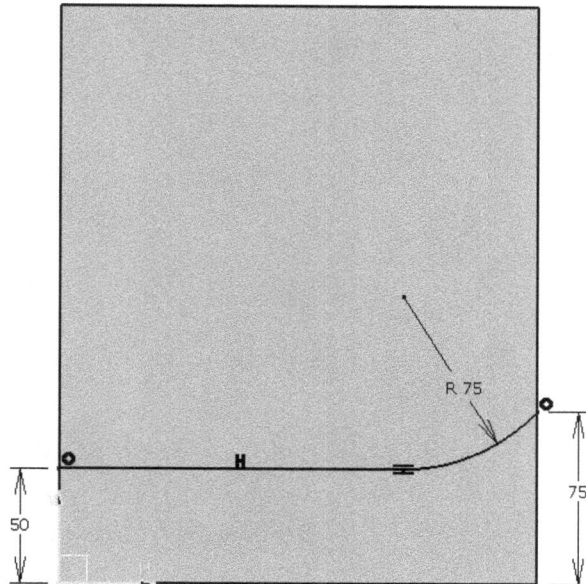

Figure 17–10

5. Create a positioned sketch with the sketch plane and origin defined, as shown in Figure 17–11.

6. Sketch a circle with a *radius* of **25** and constrain it to the origin, as shown in Figure 17–12.

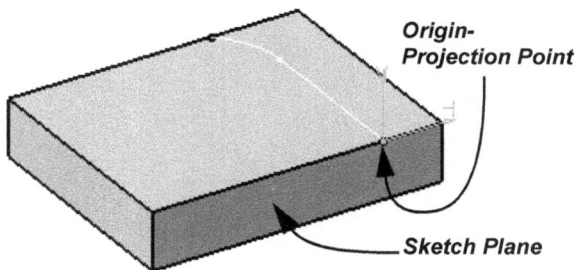

Figure 17–11

Figure 17–12

7. Create a Slot feature by clicking 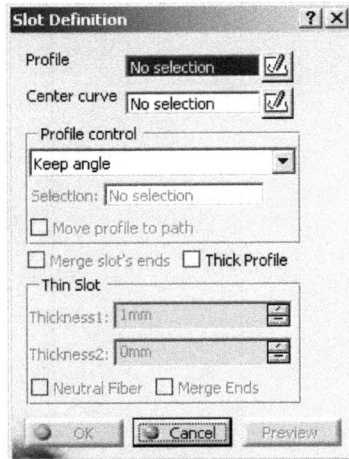 (Slot). The Slot Definition dialog box opens, as shown in Figure 17–13.

Figure 17–13

8. Select the following:

   • *Profile:* **Sketch.3** (if not already selected)
   • *Center curve:* **Sketch.2**

9. Click **OK**. The Slot feature displays as shown in Figure 17–14.

10. Double-click on the Slot feature to modify it.

11. Select the **Merge slot's ends** option and click **OK** in the Slot Definition dialog box. The slot displays as shown in Figure 17–15.

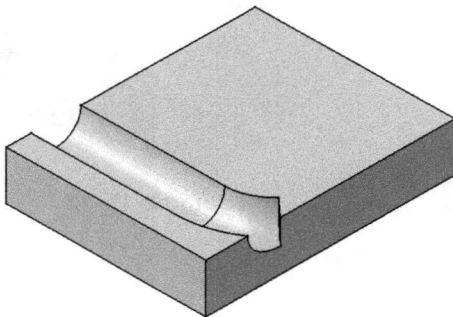

Figure 17–14

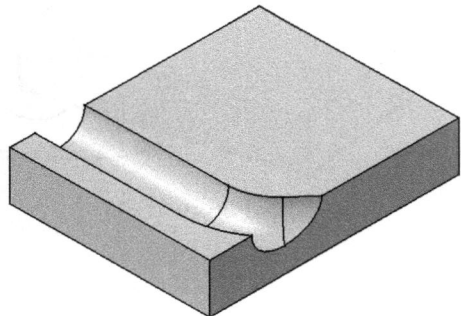

Figure 17–15

12. Double-click on the sketch of the slot center curve and modify the *arc radius* to **100.0**.

13. Exit the sketch and view the change in geometry.

Task 2 - Create a Rib feature.

1. Create a sketch, as shown in Figure 17–16.

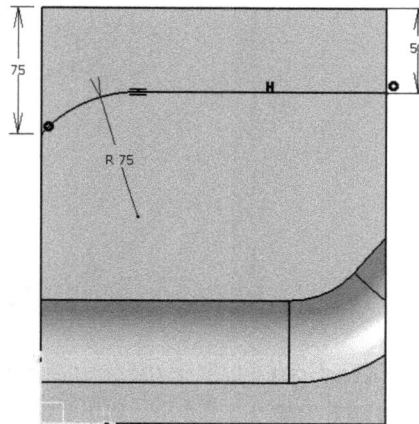

Figure 17–16

2. Create a Positioned Sketch on the back face as the planar support and select the end point of the previous sketch as the Origin, as shown in Figure 17–17.

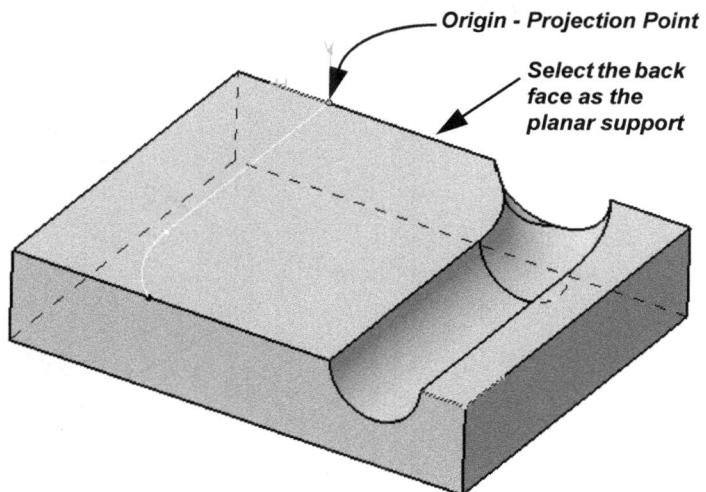

Figure 17–17

3. Click ⬜ (No 3D Background) in the 2D Visualization Mode toolbar.

4. Create an arc profile as shown in Figure 17–18. Click ⬜ (No 3D Background) in the 2D Visualization Mode toolbar to toggle it off.

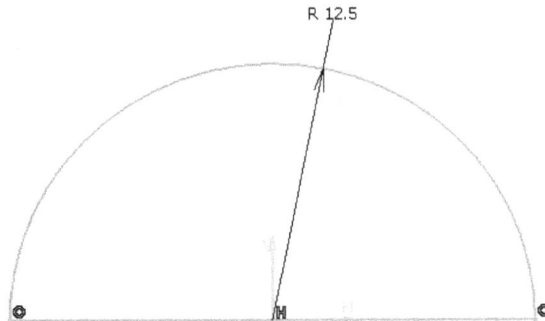

R 12.5

Figure 17–18

Design Considerations

It is recommended to close the profile section (recommended) for Rib and Slot features. The software uses the top face of the part to close the section since the arc is coincident. An open section can often cause unstable results during feature creation and downstream modifications. A closed profile provides a more robust model.

*Ensure that the **Merge ends** option is cleared.*

5. Click ⬜ (Rib) to create a Rib and select the appropriate profile and center curve sketches. The Rib feature displays as shown in Figure 17–19.

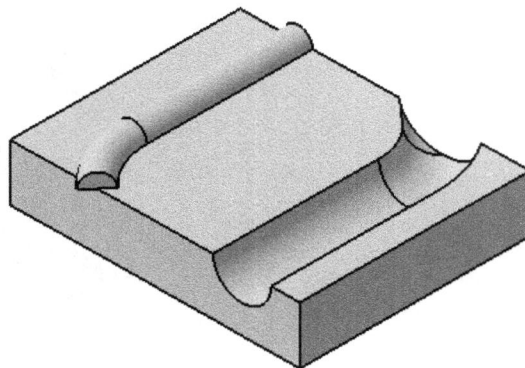

Figure 17–19

Design Considerations	You cannot merge ends with a surface that does not intersect the cross-section. Since the center curve does not cause the Rib to fully intersect the face, the **Merge Ends** option must be cleared.

Task 3 - Modify the profile control of the Rib feature.

1. Double-click on **Rib.1** in the specification tree. The Rib Definition dialog box opens.

2. Select **Pulling direction** in the Profile Control drop-down list, as shown in Figure 17–20.

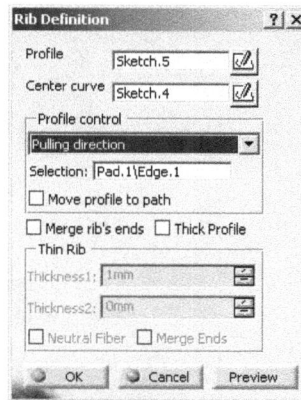

Figure 17–20

3. Select the edge shown in Figure 17–21 to define the pulling direction.

4. Click **OK** to complete the change. The part displays with the edge of the Rib feature now flush with the face of the part, as shown in Figure 17–22.

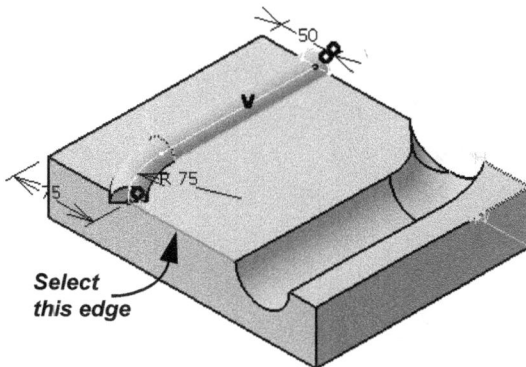

Select this edge

Figure 17–21

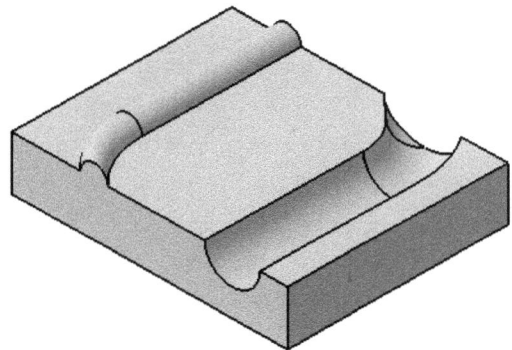

Figure 17–22

Task 4 - Save the part and close the window.

1. Click (Save).

2. If time permits, create the slot shown in Figure 17–23.

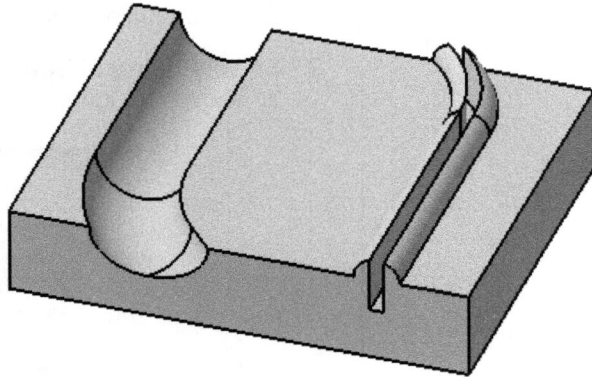

Figure 17–23

3. Select **File>Close**.

Practice 17b | Car Exhaust

Practice Objective

- Create a thick Rib feature.

In this practice, you will create two thick Rib features to define the geometry for the pipe and the tip of a car exhaust system. The completed model displays as shown in Figure 17–24.

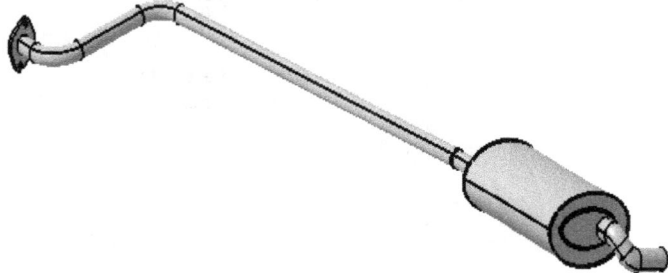

Figure 17–24

Task 1 - Open a part model.

1. Open **CarExhaust.CATPart**. The model consists of two separate geometry items: the exhaust flange and the silencer. Each piece of geometry has been created in a separate body, which displays in the specification tree. In addition, two curves have been created that are used later as the center curves for the two Rib features.

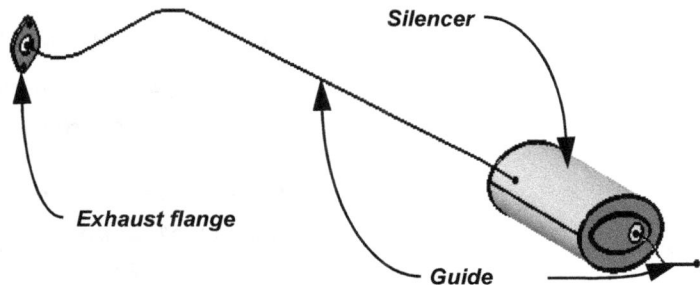

Figure 17–25

2. Verify that the PartBody is the active object.

Task 2 - Create the profile for the first Rib.

1. Create a sketch on the planar surface of the exhaust flange, as shown in Figure 17–26.

2. Prepare the sketch to insert the pipe into the hole of the flange. To create a parametric relationship between the pipe and the flange, use the edge of the flange geometry. Click

    (Project 3D Elements) and select the circular edge of the flange, as shown in Figure 17–27.

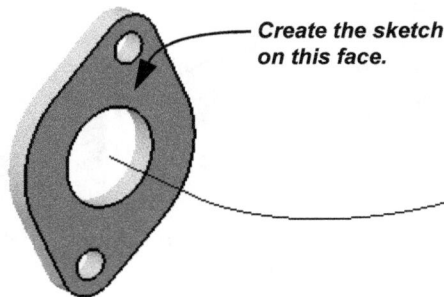

Create the sketch on this face.

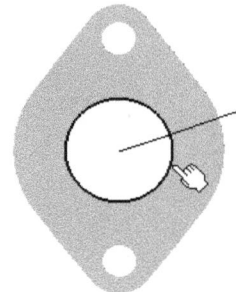

Figure 17–26   **Figure 17–27**

3. Exit the sketch.

Task 3 - Create the exhaust pipe.

In this task, you will use a Rib feature to define the shape of the exhaust pipe. The Rib will use the circular section for its profile and the polyline curve for the guide curve.

1. Create a Rib feature. Make the following selections:

    -   *Profile:* Select the circular sketch just created
    -   *Center curve:* **GuideCurve.1** from the PolylinePoints body
    -   *Thick Profile:* Select this option
    -   *Thickness1:* **0mm**
    -   *Thickness2:* **2mm (0.079 in)**

    The completed Rib is shown in Figure 17–28.

Figure 17–28

Task 4 - Create the exhaust tip.

In this task, you will create the exhaust tip geometry using a Rib feature. You will be given a minimum amount of instruction to complete this task. The completed Rib is shown in Figure 17–29.

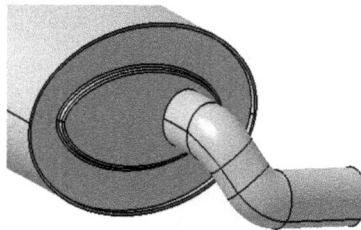

Figure 17–29

1. Create a sketch that has the circular section shown in Figure 17–30 projected onto the sketch plane.

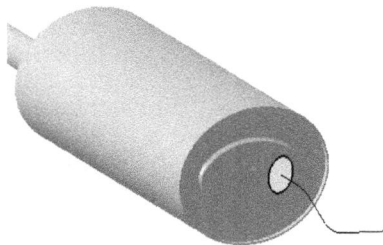

Figure 17–30

2. Create a Rib feature using this sketch and **GuideCurve.2**. Select the **Thick Profile** option and add a *thickness* of **2mm** to the outside of the circular profile.

Task 5 - Save the part and close the window.

1. Click (Save).

2. Select **File>Close**.

Practice 17c | (Optional) Dipstick

Practice Objective

- Create a model with limited instructions.

In this practice, you will create two Rib features for a dipstick. One Rib feature will define the handle and the second will define the stick. The guide curves for each Rib have been created for you. The completed model is shown in Figure 17–31.

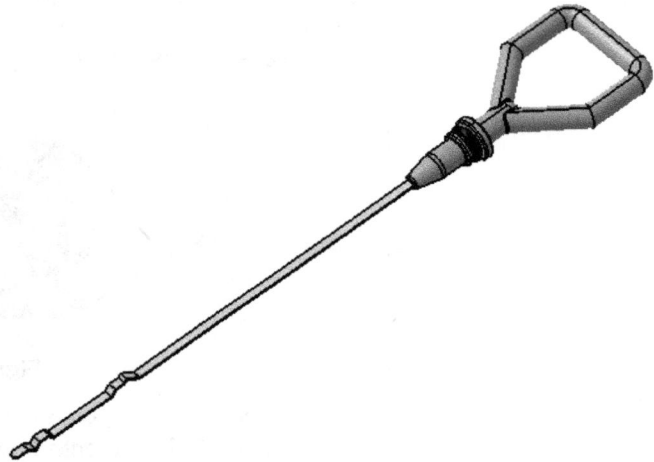

Figure 17–31

1. Open **Dipstick.CATPart**.

2. Show the two reference planes from **Geometrical Set.2.**

3. To build the two Rib features, use positioned sketches to build the profiles for the ribs, and rename the features.

The drawing shown in Figure 17–32 is provided for dimensional information.

- 1 (0.039 in)
- 5 (0.197 in)
- 11.8 (0.465 in)
- 14 (0.551 in)

- 72 (2.835 in)
- 315 (12.402 in)
- 416 (16.378 in)

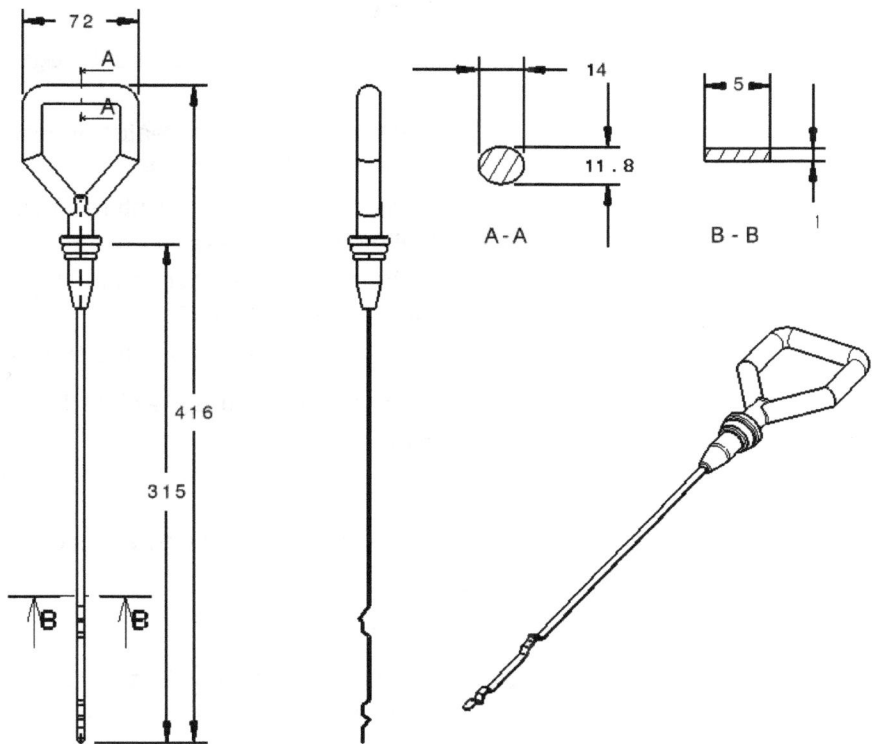

Note: The Rib feature should be used to create the handle and stick. Additional details can be added, such as Edge Fillets, if time permits.

Figure 17–32

Chapter Review Questions

1. Which two elements must be defined to create a Rib feature?

    a. Profile

    b. Datum Plane

    c. Axis

    d. Center Curve

2. Which of the following statements regarding Rib features is true?

    a. A Rib creates a single feature whose geometry is blended between multiple profiles.

    b. A Rib creates a single feature whose geometry is swept along a defined path.

    c. A Rib can only be added to the model after the base feature has been created.

    d. A Rib path must intersect the sketch support of the profile.

3. The profile of a Rib must be closed.

    a. True

    b. False

4. Multiple edges can be selected as the center curve.

    a. True

    b. False

5. Non-tangent entities in the center curve of a Rib or Slot produce sharp corners while tangent entities produce smooth corners.

    a. True

    b. False

6. The Slot feature profile and center curve shown in Figure 17–32 fails because _____.

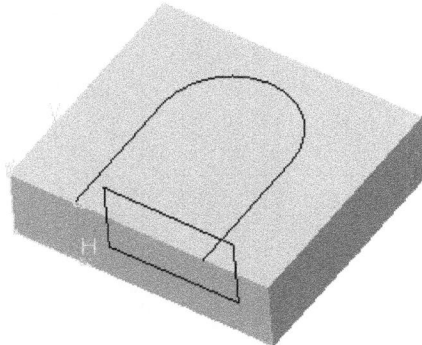

Figure 17–33

   a. The rectangular section is not fully in the solid.

   b. A rectangular shape cannot be used to follow a tangent curve.

   c. The resulting geometry overlaps itself.

   d. None of the above.

7. The _____ option can be used to blend the ends of a rib into existing geometry.

   a. Merge Ends

   b. Smooth Ends

   c. Blend Ends

   d. None of the above.

8. When creating a Rib or Slot, use the _____ option to maintain the angle value relative to the axis of the profile and the selected surface.

   a. Keep Angle

   b. Reference Surface

   c. Pulling Direction.

   d. None of the above.

Answers: 1.d, 2.b, 3.b, 4.b, 5.a, 6.c, 7.a, 8.b

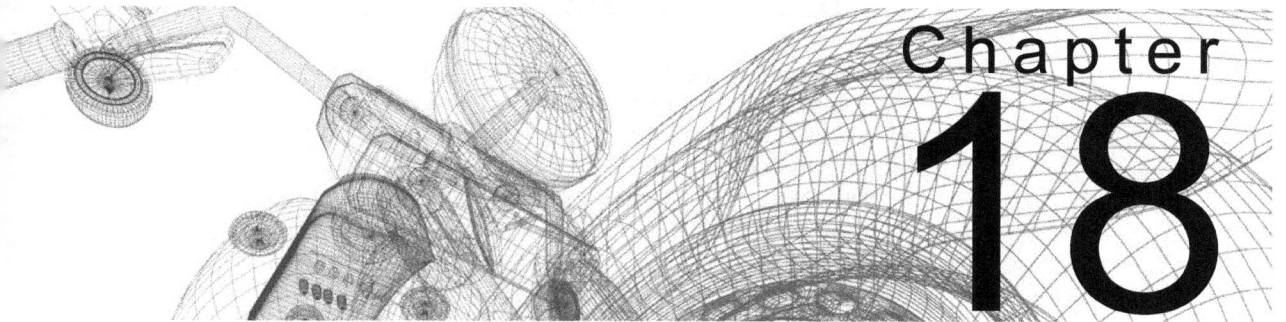

Multi-sections Solid Features

A Multi-sections Solid feature is an additional feature that can add or remove material from your model. Multiple offset sketches are selected and the software creates the transitional surfaces between the selected sketches to create the feature.

Learning Objectives in this Chapter

- Create multi-section solids to create complex geometry.
- Create multi-section solids to create transitions between existing geometry.

18.1 Multi-sections Solids

Multi-sections solids are used to create complex geometry or transitional surfaces between existing geometry. Multi-sections solids add material to your model. An example of this feature is shown in Figure 18–1. Removed multi-sections solids behave similar to multi-sections solids, except that they remove material from your model.

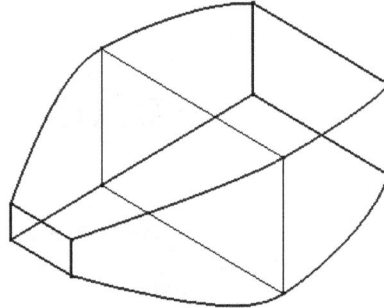

Figure 18–1

How To: Create a Multi-sections Solid

The order of section/sketch selection is important because the transitional surfaces are created in order between the sections.

1. Create all sketches that are required for the feature.

2. Click ![icon] (Multi-sections Solid) to open the Multi-sections Solid Definition dialog box, as shown in Figure 18–2.

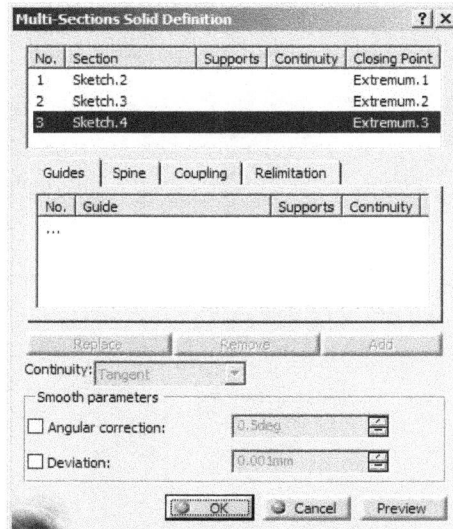

Figure 18–2

Closing Point

3. Select the sketches in the order of creation and click **OK** to complete the feature.

When the sketched sections are selected, the software selects a default closing point at one of the vertices in the sketch. The position of the closing point is used to calculate how the software connects the vertices. Figure 18–3 shows the closing points for the three sections.

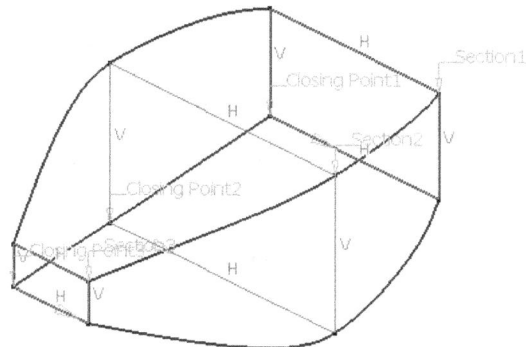

Figure 18–3

If the closing points are not aligned and are pointing in the same direction, the transitional surfaces appear to twist as the software connects the vertices. The closing point of the last section is moved, as shown in Figure 18–4.

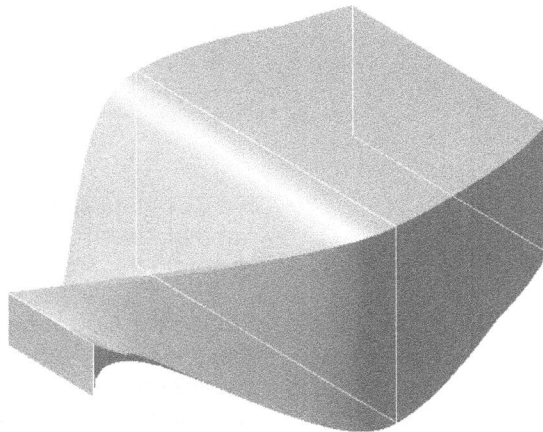

Figure 18–4

Editing Closing Points

*If a closing point is removed, it can be created again by right-clicking and selecting **Create Closing Point**.*

There are several ways to modify a closing point. One is to change a closing point location by right-clicking on the Closing Point# tag on the screen and selecting **Edit Closing Point** or **Remove**. A new location in the sketch can now be selected. Another method is to right-click on the Closing Point# tag on the screen and select **Replace**. Select another point to become the new closing point.

- If a closing point is pointing in the wrong direction, zoom in on the arrow and select it to toggle the arrow direction.

Coupling

The **Coupling** option is used to define the transitions between the sections. These options are described as follows:

Coupling Option	Description
Ratio	If the sections are connected at positions, the ratio is computed by the percentage of the section profile. This option is recommended when non-equal numbers of vertices are present in the sketch sections.
Tangency	If the sections have the same number of tangency discontinuity points, the points are coupled together between sections.
Tangency then curvature	If the sections have the same number of tangency and curvature discontinuity points, tangency discontinuity points are coupled together between sections, and then curvature discontinuity points are coupled together between sections.
Vertices	If the sections have the same number of vertices, these points are coupled together between sections.

- If a **Coupling** option is used and the criteria described are not met, an error message displays when attempting to generate the Multi-sections Solid feature.

- Setting the **Coupling** option to **Vertices** results in an error message when attempting to create transitions between a square and a circular section. This error occurs because the circular section does not have any vertices to couple with the square section.

Removed Multi-sections Solids

Removed Multi-sections Solids features behave similar to multi-sections solids, except that they remove material from your model. The software joins multiple sections by connecting vertices. Click (Removed Multi-sections Solid) to create a removed multi-sections solid. Proceed using the same steps as the multi-sections solids.

Practice 18a

Basic Multi-sections Solid Features

Practice Objectives

- Create a Multi-sections Solid feature.
- Create a Removed Multi-sections Solid feature.

In this practice, you will create a model using a Multi-sections Solid and Removed Multi-sections Solid features. During the creation of Multi-sections features, pay careful attention to closing points of the sections. If they are not correctly placed, the Multi-sections feature will contort. The final model should display as shown in Figure 18–5

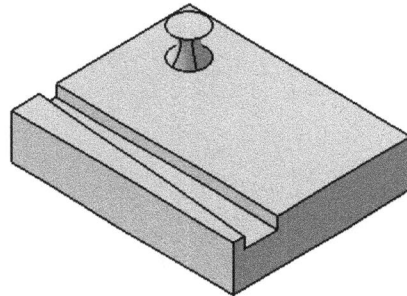

Figure 18–5

Task 1 - Create the base feature geometry.

1. Create a new part called **Basic_Multi-sections Solid.CATPart**

2. Use the XY plane for the sketching plane and create a **Pad** feature, **200 x 250 x 50**, as shown in Figure 18–6.

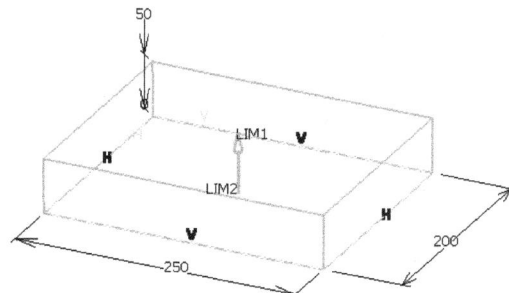

Figure 18–6

Task 2 - Create a Multi-sections Solid feature.

1. In the Reference Elements toolbar, click ▱ (Plane) to create a reference plane.

2. Create a plane *offset* **25** from the top surface of the Pad. Select the **Repeat object after OK** option to create multiple copies.

3. Click **OK**. The Object Repetition dialog box opens. Do the following:

   - *Instance(s)* field: **1**
   - *Mode for Repetition:* leave **Absolute**
   - Clear the **Create in a new body** option.

4. Click **OK**. The updated model displays as shown in Figure 18–7.

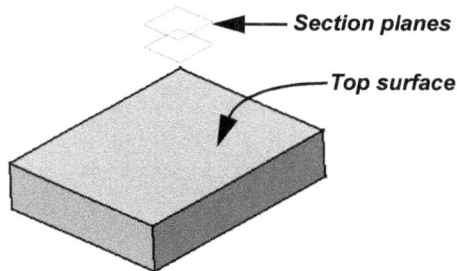

Figure 18–7

Design Considerations

The reference planes that you have just created will be used as sketching planes to create sections for the multi-sections solid.

5. Ensure that the PartBody is active. To set the active body, right-click on PartBody in the specification tree and select **Define In Work Object**, as shown in Figure 18–8.

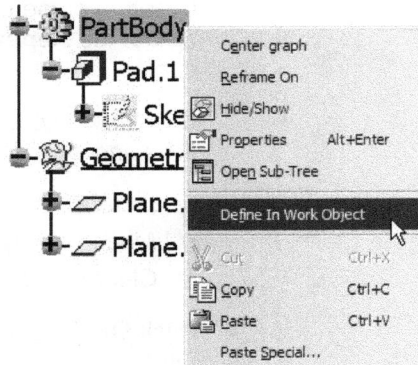

Figure 18–8

6. Select the top surface of the Pad and click (Sketch) to enter the Sketcher workbench.

7. Sketch a **37.5** diameter circle with constraints, as shown in Figure 18–9.

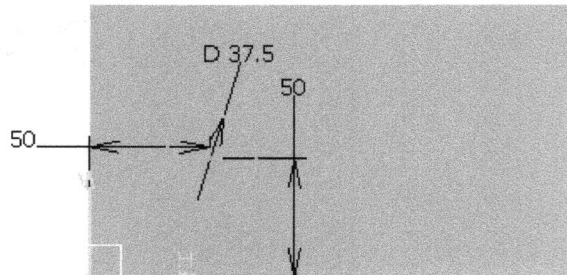

Figure 18–9

8. Click (Exit workbench) when the sketch profile is complete.

Task 3 - Create a sketch to be used for the Multi-sections Solid feature.

1. Select the plane shown in Figure 18–10. Click

    (Positioned Sketch).

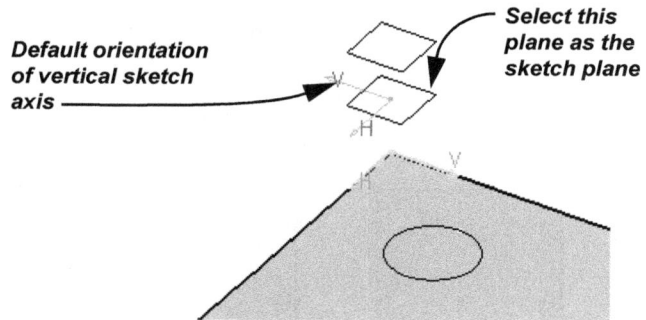

Default orientation of vertical sketch axis

Select this plane as the sketch plane

Figure 18–10

2. Leave the *Origin Type* as **Implicit.**

3. By default, the orientation (Horizontal and Vertical sketch axes) displays as shown in Figure 18–10. The Vertical sketch axis is flipped in the opposite direction from the way you viewed the sketch created in Task 3. To make the sketch orientation consistent with the previous sketch's orientation, select the **Reverse V** option, as shown in Figure 18–11.

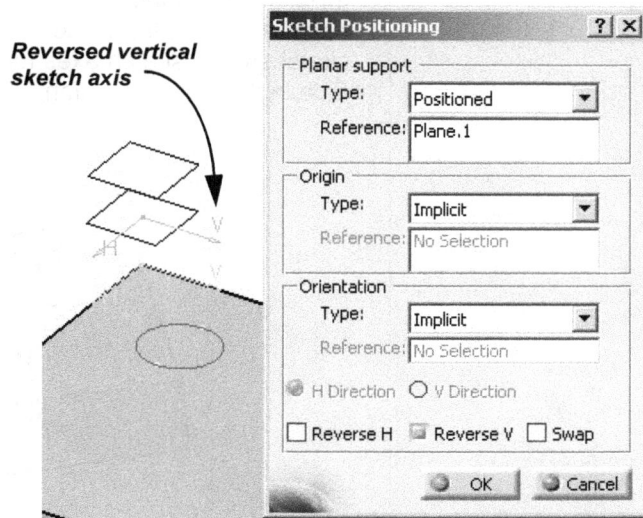

Reversed vertical sketch axis

Figure 18–11

4. Sketch a **19** diameter circle on the selected plane and dimension the circle, as shown in Figure 18–12.

5. Create another positioned sketch using the second reference plane (the one furthest from the base Pad feature). Ensure that the sketch orientation is the same as the first two sketches.

6. Create a **37.5** diameter circle and dimension the sketch as shown in Figure 18–13.

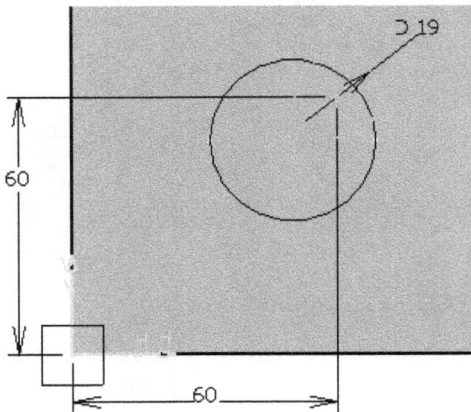

Figure 18–12

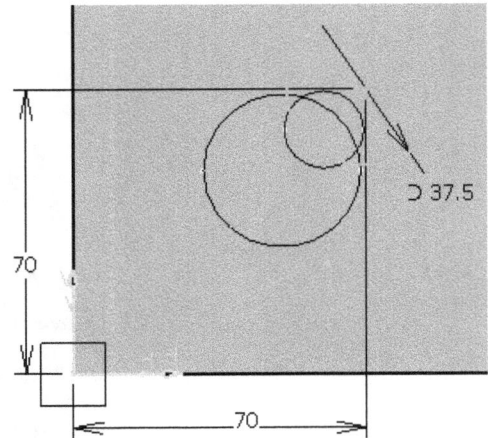

Figure 18–13

The model displays as shown in Figure 18–14. Note that in all three sketches the Horizontal and Vertical sketch axes face the same direction. If the sketches were not created as positioned sketches, the sketch axes for the three sketches would not all face in the same direction.

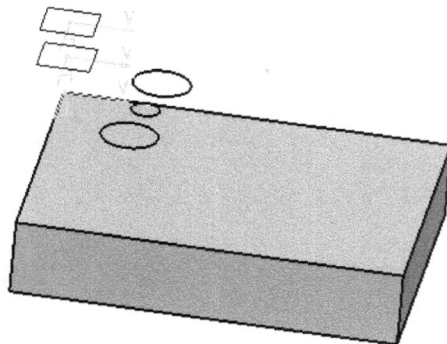

Figure 18–14

7. Save the part.

Task 4 - Create a Multi-sections Solid feature.

1. Click ![icon] (Multi-sections Solid) to create a Multi-sections Solid feature.

2. Select the three circular sections in the same sequence in which they were created to add them to the Multi-sections Solid Definition dialog box, as shown in Figure 18–15.

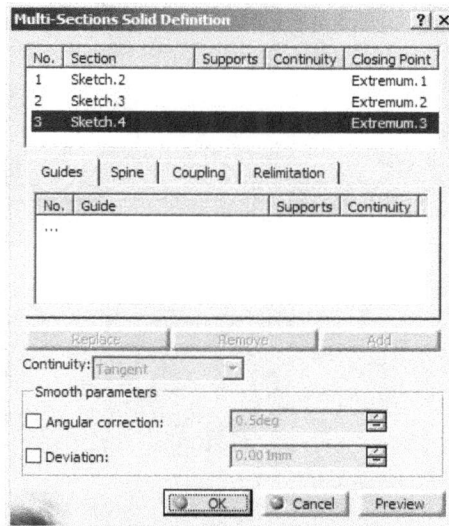

No.	Section	Supports	Continuity	Closing Point
1	Sketch.2			Extremum.1
2	Sketch.3			Extremum.2
3	Sketch.4			Extremum.3

Figure 18–15

3. Ensure that the three closing point arrows point in the same direction, as shown in Figure 18–16. Select the arrows to toggle the direction, as required.

4. Click **OK** to create the Multi-sections Solid feature. It displays as shown in Figure 18–17.

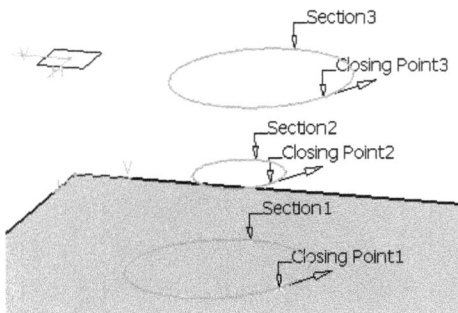

Figure 18–16

Figure 18–17

Task 5 - Create a Removed Multi-sections Solid feature.

Design Considerations

You will create two sketches, one on each of two opposing faces. These sketches will be used as the sections for the ends of the Removed Multi-sections Solid feature.

1. Create a sketch using the surface shown in Figure 18–18 as the sketching plane.

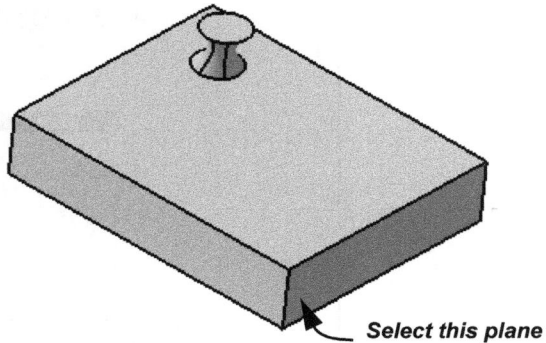

Select this plane

Figure 18–18

2. Sketch a **37.5 X 12.5** rectangle with constraints, as shown in Figure 18–19.

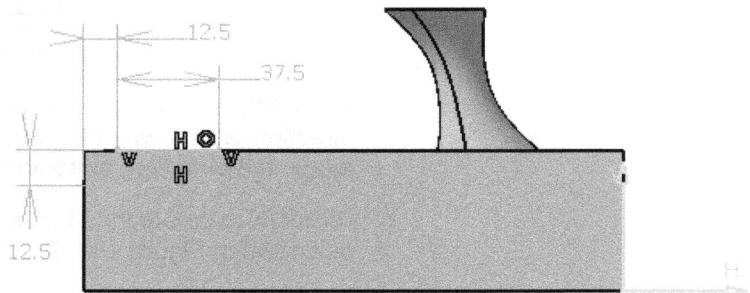

Figure 18–19

3. Click [icon] (Exit workbench) when the sketch profile is complete.

4. Create a sketch using the surface shown in Figure 18–20.

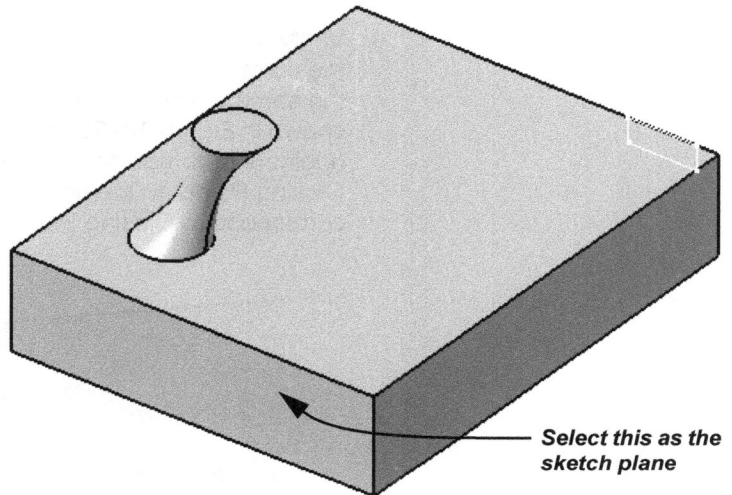

*Select this as the
sketch plane*

Figure 18–20

5. Sketch a **19** rectangle with constraints, as shown in
    Figure 18–21.

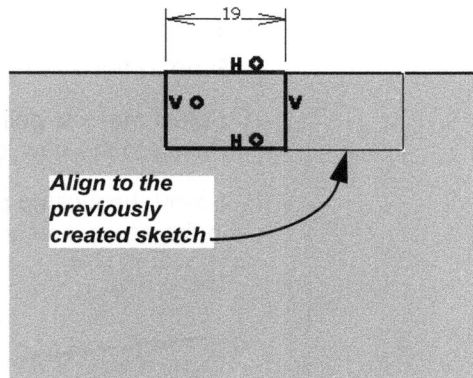

*Align to the
previously
created sketch*

Figure 18–21

6. Click (Exit workbench) when the sketch profile is
    complete.

7. Click (Removed Multi-sections Solid) to create a
    Removed Multi-sections Solid feature.

8. Select the two rectangular sections to add them to the Multi-sections Solid Definition dialog box.

9. Verify that the closing points on each section are located on the corresponding vertex to be connected and are pointing in the same direction. For example, the two closing points, shown in Figure 18–22 are pointing in opposite directions and originate from non-corresponding vertices. You must move Closing Point2 to the upper right vertex in this view to correspond to Closing Point1.

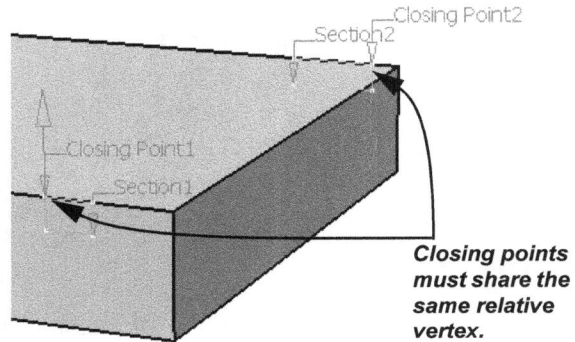

Closing points must share the same relative vertex.

Figure 18–22

10. To move the closing point, select the existing **Closing Point2**, right-click, and select **Replace**.

11. Select the new point vertex location. This moves Closing Point2 to the new location.

12. Select the closing point direction arrow until the arrows point in the same direction, as shown in Figure 18–23.

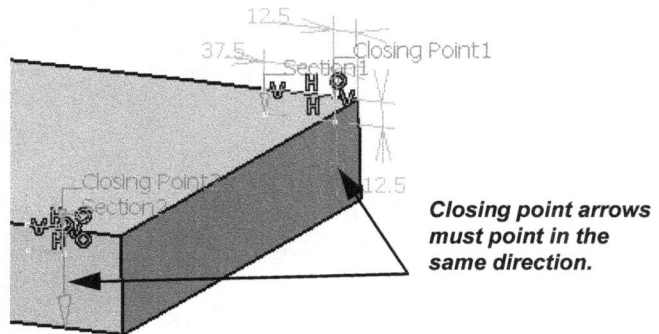

Closing point arrows must point in the same direction.

Figure 18–23

13. Click **OK** to create the Removed Multi-sections Solid feature. The model displays as shown in Figure 18–24.

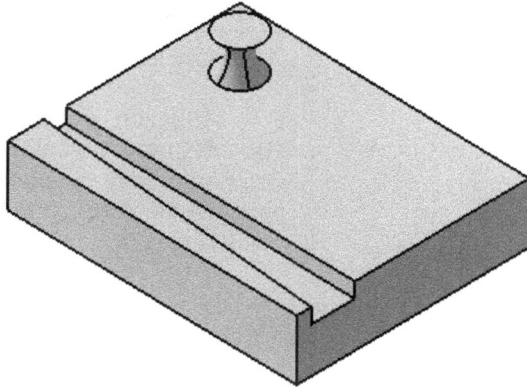

Figure 18–24

Task 6 - Save the part and close the window.

1. Click [Save icon] (Save).

2. Select **File>Close**.

Practice 18b

Transition Tube

Practice Objective

- Create a Multi-sections Solid feature.

In this practice, you will create the model shown in Figure 18–25. You will create one sketch and copy it into different planes. You will then modify the copied sketches to use them as the sections for the tube. After completing the Multi-sections Solid feature, you will shell it.

Figure 18–25

Task 1 - Create three reference planes.

Design Considerations

You will create three reference planes to use as sketching planes for profiles. These profiles will be used as some of the sections for a multi-sections solid.

1. Create a new part called **TransitionTube.CATPart**.

2. Verify that the units are set to millimeters (mm).

3. Create a reference plane offset **100** from the ZX plane. The reference plane displays as shown in Figure 18–26.

Figure 18–26

4. Create a second plane offset **175** from the ZX plane.

5. Create a third plane offset **250** from the ZX plane. The three reference planes are shown in Figure 18–27.

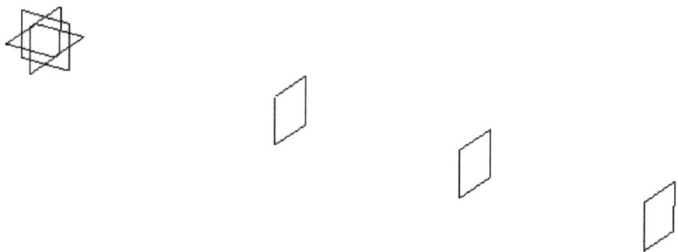

Figure 18–27

Task 2 - Create sketches to be used for a Multi-sections Solid feature.

1. If required, activate the PartBody.

2. Create a sketch on the ZX plane, as shown in Figure 18–28.

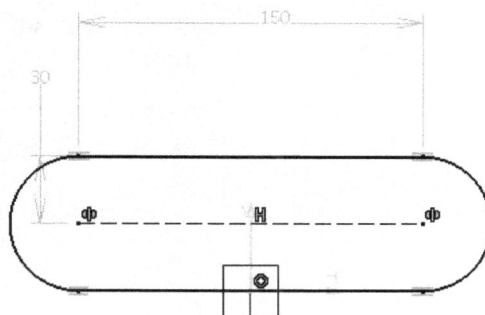

Figure 18–28

3. Copy **Sketch.1** from the specification tree and paste it onto Plane.1 (your first reference plane).

4. Modify **Sketch.2** and change the **150** dimension to **120**.

5. Paste **Sketch.1** again on **Plane.2** (your second reference plane).

6. Modify **Sketch.3** and change the *150* length dimension to **5** and the *30* dimension to **50**.

7. Copy **Sketch.3** onto **Plane.3**. The model is shown in Figure 18–29.

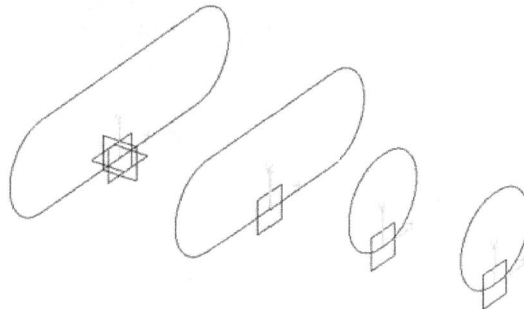

Figure 18–29

Task 3 - Reposition the sketches in the specification tree.

When pasting the sketches onto the three reference planes, the software places the sketch into the geometrical set. You must use the Change Geometrical Set operation to position them in the PartBody.

1. Select **Sketch.2**, **Sketch.3**, and **Sketch.4** using <Ctrl>, right-click, and select **Selected Objects>Change Geometrical Set**.

2. The Change geometrical set dialog box opens. Set *Destination* to **PartBody**, as shown in Figure 18–30.

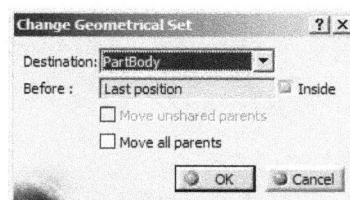

Figure 18–30

3. Click **OK** to complete the operation. The specification tree is shown in Figure 18–31.

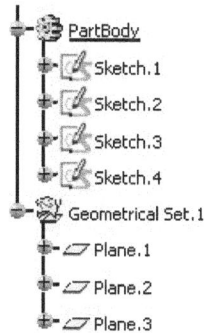

Figure 18–31

Task 4 - Create the Multi-sections Solid feature.

---

1. Click (Multi-sections Solid) to create a Multi-sections Solid feature.

2. Select the four sketched sections in the order in which they were created to add them to the Multi-sections Solid Definition dialog box.

3. Verify that the four closing point arrows point in the same direction and are located at the same vertices in each section. Select the arrows to toggle the direction, as required. The model displays as shown in Figure 18–32.

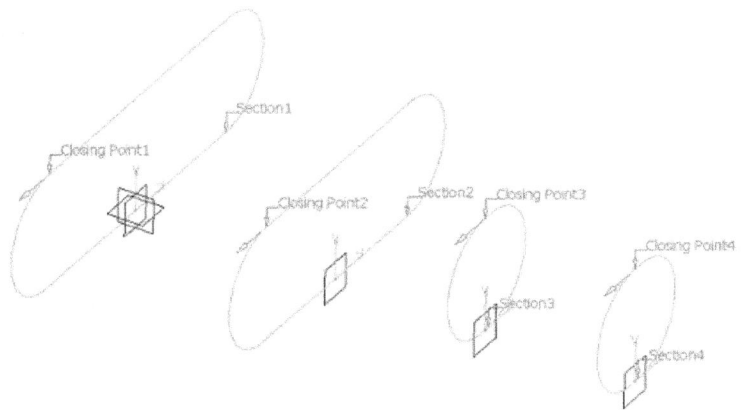

Figure 18–32

4. Click **OK** to create the Multi-sections Solid feature.

5. Hide all planes in the model. The model is shown in Figure 18–33.

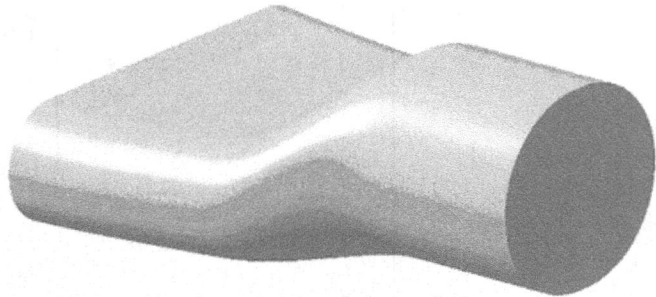

Figure 18–33

Task 5 - Shell the part.

1. Create a **4** inside thickness Shell feature and remove the two end faces of the model. The model displays as shown in Figure 18–34.

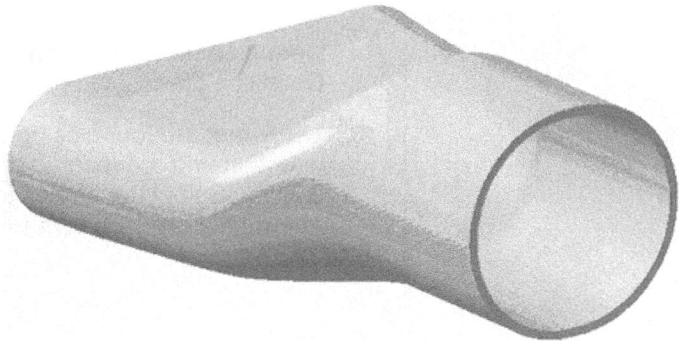

Figure 18–34

2. Click (Save).

3. Click **File>Close**.

Practice 18c | (Optional) Screwdriver

Practice Objective

- Create a Multi-sections Solid feature.

In this practice, you will finish modeling the screwdriver by creating a multi-section solid. Sketches and points have been provided for you. To successfully complete the feature, the multi-section solid will use a **Coupling** option. Coupling enables more control over how the multi-section solid blends from one section to the next. The completed model is shown in Figure 18–35.

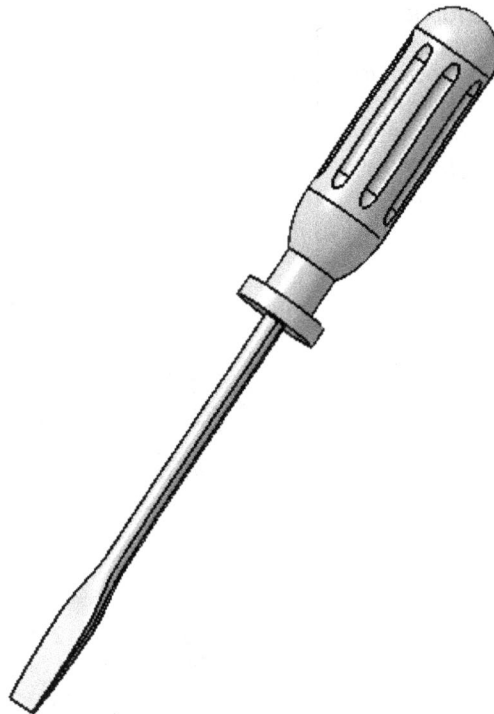

Figure 18–35

Task 1 - Create a multi-sections solid.

1. Open **Screwdriver.CATPart**.

2. Expand the specification tree to examine the provided elements.

3. Click [icon] (Multi-sections Solid) to create a Multi-sections Solid feature.

4. Select **Sketch1** as the first section. Verify that the closing point is located on **Point.1**, as shown in Figure 18–36. If required, select **Point.1** to set it as the Closing Point.

To change the location of a closing point, right-click on the point in the model and select **Replace***. Select a new location for the point by clicking directly in the model.*

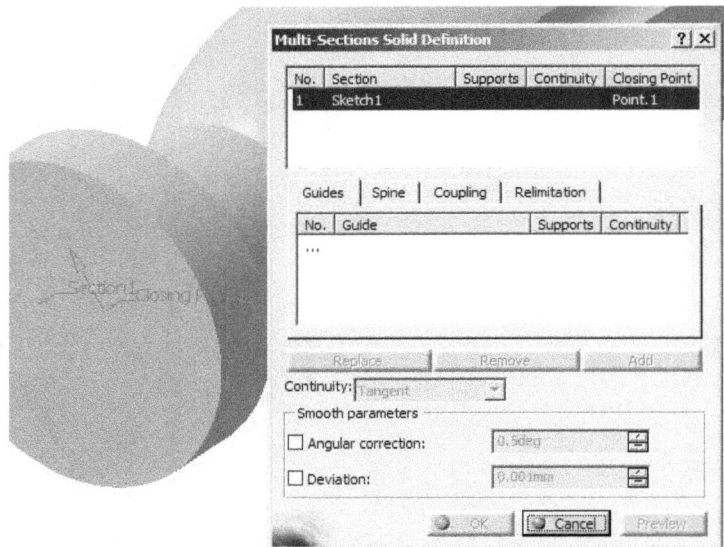

Figure 18–36

5. Select **Sketch2** as the next section. Verify that the closing point is located on **Point.6** as shown in Figure 18–37. Select **Point.6**, if required. If the closing point was changed in Step 4, you might not be able to select the next section. To select the section, right-click on the section window on the Multi-sections Solid Definition dialog box and select **Add**.

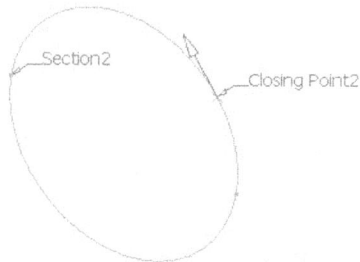

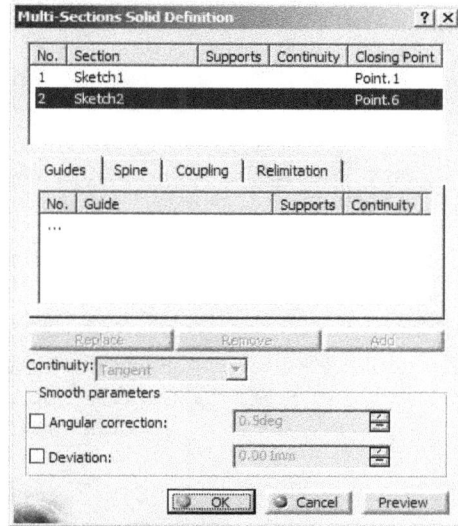

Figure 18–37

6. Select the rest of the sketches, as shown in Figure 18–38. Verify that the closing points of the two rectangular sections are pointing in the required direction.

The two rectangular sections use their vertices as closing points.

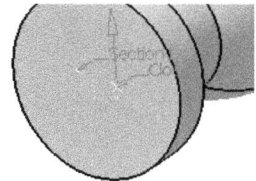

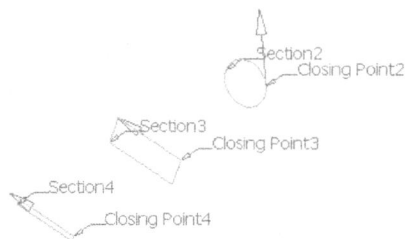

Figure 18–38

7. Click **Preview**. An error message displays, as shown in Figure 18–39. Click **OK**.

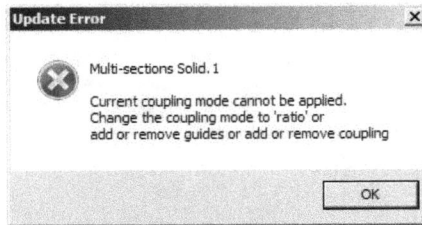

Figure 18–39

8. In the Multi-sections Solid Definition dialog box, select the *Coupling* tab as shown in Figure 18–40. Set *Sections coupling* to **Ratio**.

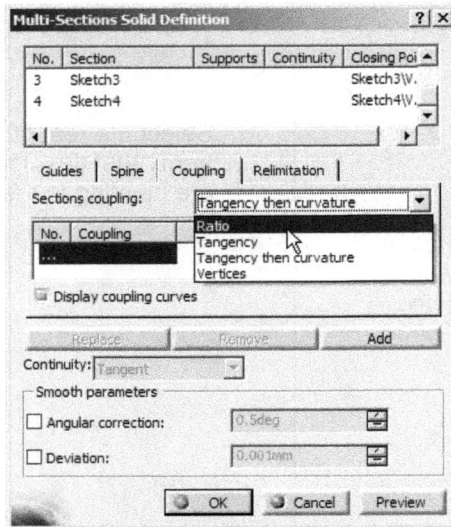

Figure 18–40

9. Click **Preview** again. This time, no error messages display. However, the tip of the screwdriver is twisted, as shown in Figure 18–41.

10. Click **OK**.

The tip is twisted

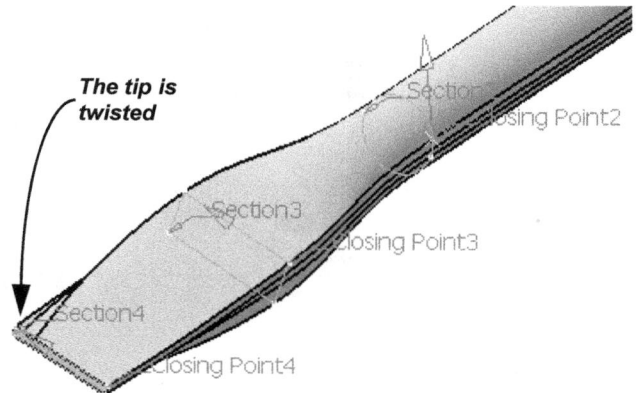

Figure 18–41

Task 2 - Create coupling curves.

1. Expand **Geometrical Set.1** and show all of the points, as shown in Figure 18–42.

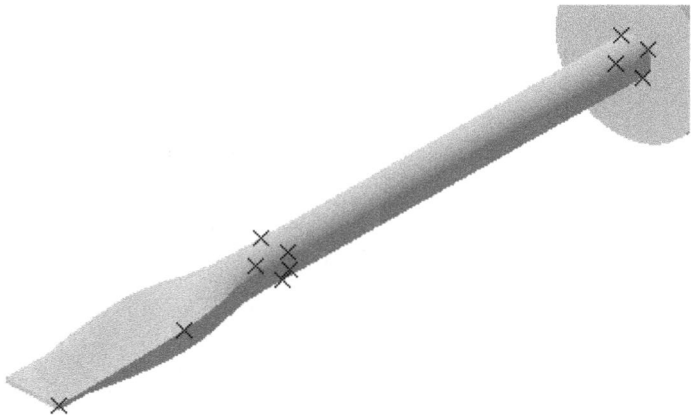

Figure 18–42

2. In the specification tree, double-click on multi-sections solid.

3. Select the *Coupling* tab and make the *Coupling* field active, as shown in Figure 18–43.

4. Click **Add**. The Coupling dialog box opens as shown in Figure 18–44.

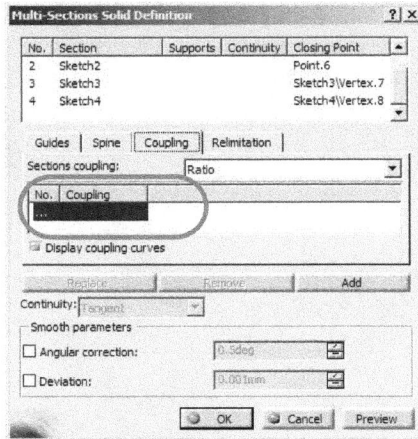

Figure 18–43

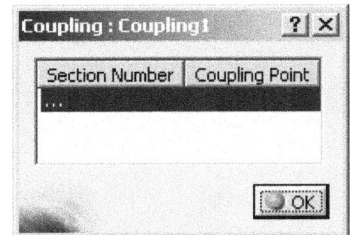

Figure 18–44

5. In the specification tree, select **Point.1**, **Point.6**, **Point.10**, and **Point.11**. The mode is shown in Figure 18–45. The first coupling curve consists of four points that are located at the four closing points of the multi-section solid.

Figure 18–45

6. For the second coupling curve, select the points in the order shown in Figure 18–46.

*Display **Sketch3** and **Sketch4** located under the Multi-sections **Solid.1** branch in the specification tree.*

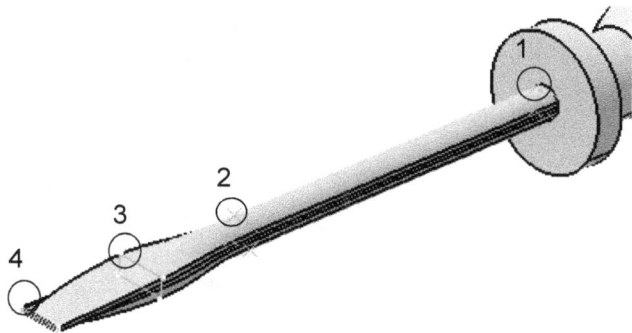

Figure 18–46

7. Repeat the previous step to add two more coupling curves using the remaining points. Click **OK**. The twist in the tip is now repaired, as shown in Figure 18–47.

Figure 18–47

8. Click ⊟.

9. Select **File>Close**.

Chapter Review Questions

1. Which of the following statements regarding Multi-sections Solids is true?

   a. A Multi-sections Solid creates a single feature where the geometry is blended between multiple sections.

   b. A Multi-sections Solid can only be added to the model after the base feature has been created.

   c. The profiles for the Multi-sections Solid can only be sketched.

   d. The Multi-sections Solid creates a single feature whose geometry is swept along a defined path.

2. Sections must be selected in the required creation order.

   a. True

   b. False

3. What is the minimum number of sections that must exist in a Multi-sections Solid feature?

   a. 0

   b. 1

   c. 2

   d. 4

4. What is the maximum number of sections that can exist in a Multi-sections Solid feature?

   a. 2

   b. 4

   c. 36

   d. Unlimited

5. A Multi-sections Solid adds material and a Removed Multi-section Solid removes material.

   a. True

   b. False

6. You have accidentally created a Multi-sections Solid instead of a Removed Multi-sections Solid. To correct this, right-click on the feature, select Multi-sections Solid.object>Definition and select Removed Multi-sections Solid.

   a. True

   b. False

7. The twist shown in Figure 18–48 is not the design intent. The best way to correct the twist is to redefine the closing points and ensure they are all aligned and pointing in the same direction.

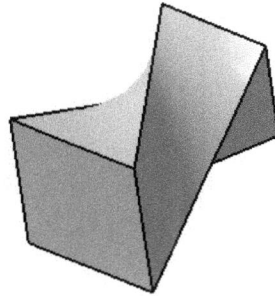

Figure 18–48

   a. True

   b. False

Answers: 1.a, 2.a, 3.c, 4.d, 5.a, 6.b, 7.a

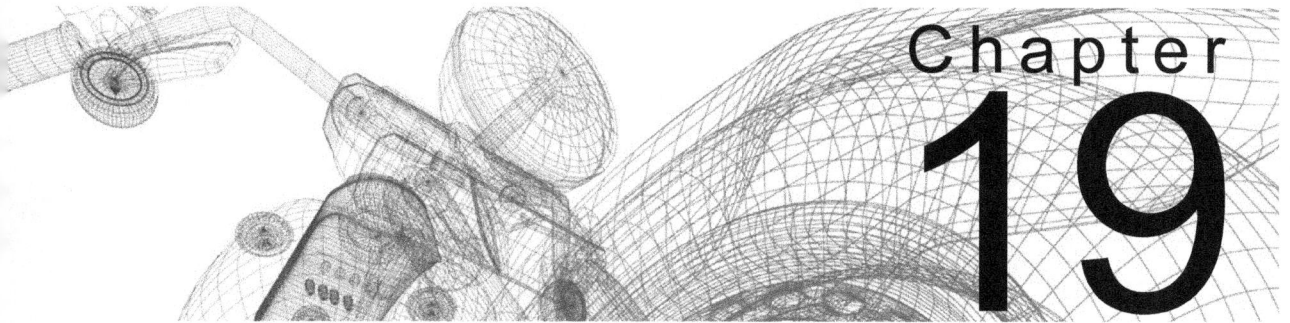

Working With Multi-Body Models

Working with the complex and highly structured models that you encounter while using CATIA within your work environment.

Learning Objectives in this Chapter

- Learn how part bodies are organized.
- Insert additional bodies and a geometrical set.
- Understand Boolean operations for combining bodies.
- Understand the options available for feature visualization.
- Review several best practices for reviewing or modifying multi-body parts.

19.1 Body Organization

Typically, all features you create are added to the PartBody in the specification tree. This linear tree structure is acceptable for models with a low feature count or simple geometry. CATIA enables you to create multiple bodies in a single CATPart model and to structure your model based on your design intent.

When planning the creation of a part, such as a car rim, the designer might break the model into three functional areas: base, spokes, and air chamber, as shown in Figure 19–1.

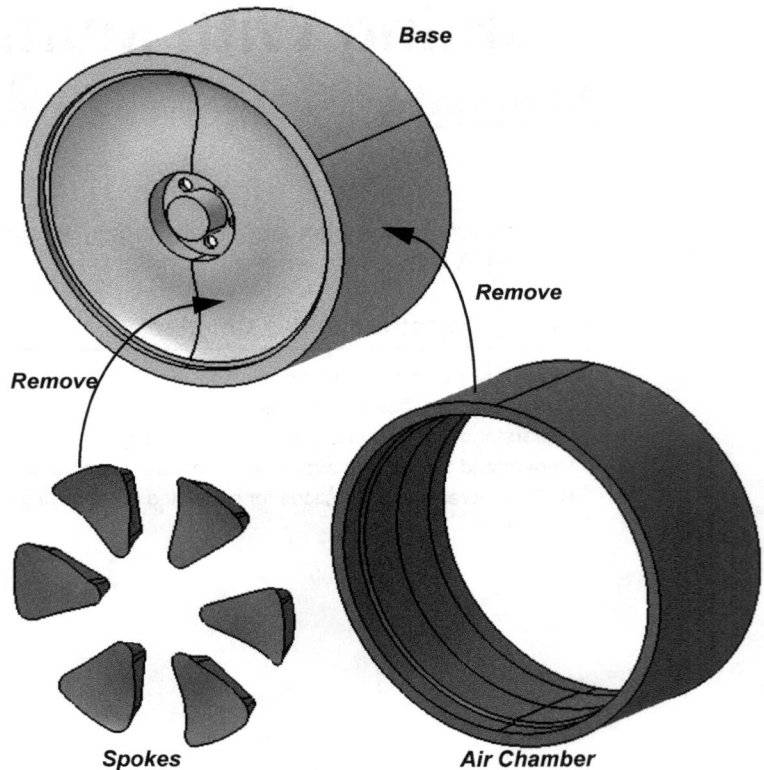

Figure 19–1

These bodies can then be combined using boolean operations to create the model shown in Figure 19–2.

Figure 19–2

Using boolean operations to create a model provides the following advantages:

• Update times are reduced, since a multi-body approach provides a more organized specification tree. For example, the six cutouts from the Spoke body are removed from the base geometry in a single step. If a standard modeling approach were used, each cutout would be developed and then removed individually, requiring extra update time.

• Features are grouped by function or area. By naming bodies after their group of features, the model structure is easier to interpret.

• Visualization tools are available which leverage the multi-body approach. For example, **Hide/Show** can be used to hide the geometry from the base and air chamber bodies. This enables the designer to simplify the model display while working on the spoke geometry. With a standard modeling approach, solid features cannot be independently hidden and must be deactivated to remove them from the display.

• The creation of the part model becomes easier when the model is divided into smaller, functional areas. A complex model becomes more manageable when the designer can focus on a smaller area of geometry to develop.

• Features such as a Shell or Fillet can be restricted to a finite area of the model. For example, if a specific area of the model requires a constant wall thickness, a Shell feature can be applied to only this area by breaking it out into a separate body.

Some disadvantages of using boolean operations include the following:

- Developing the model is time consuming, since the creation of a multi-body part requires planning of body organization and feature placement. In addition, you might need to frequently switch between bodies to position features correctly.

- Designers who are not familiar with the multi-body approach and boolean operations find interpreting and modifying these parts difficult.

- It is important to consider the complexity, feature count, and amount of possible downstream modification beforehand. Although this technique yields performance gains with big models, the development and planning required might be overkill for smaller models.

Inserting a Body

To add a body to a part model, select **Insert>Body**. The body is added after the active body in the specification tree with the name Body.#, where # is a sequential number, as shown in Figure 19–3.

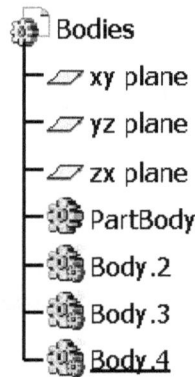

Bodies
- xy plane
- yz plane
- zx plane
- PartBody
- Body.2
- Body.3
- Body.4

Figure 19–3

- To activate a body, right-click and select **Define In Work Object**. The body is underlined to indicate it as the body to which new features are to be added.

Inserting a Geometrical Set

A geometrical set is a container for any reference planes, lines, or points that have been created while developing the part geometry. To organize a multi-body part, geometrical sets are typically placed beneath the body to which they are referenced. If the geometrical set already exists, it can be placed beneath a body by right-clicking on it, selecting **Geometrical Set.# object> Change Geometrical Set**, and then selecting the body in the Change geometrical set dialog box, as shown in Figure 19–4.

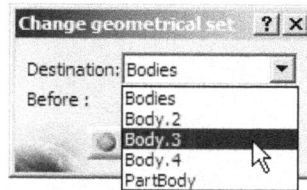

Figure 19–4

19.2 Boolean Operations

Bodies are combined using boolean operations. There are various boolean features feature types that can be used in some of the complex models that you might need to review or modify in your work environment. Figure 19–5 shows the Boolean Operations toolbar and its functionality.

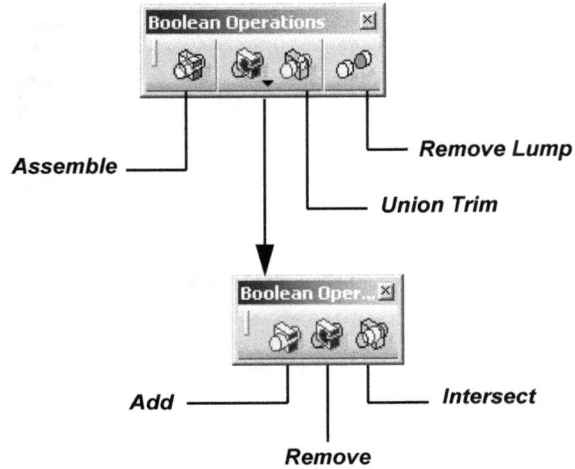

Figure 19–5

The boolean operation types and results are described as follows:

Operation	Result
(Assemble)	Pocket = Pocket Pad = Pad
(Add)	Pocket = Pad Pad = Pad
(Remove)	Pocket = Pocket Pad = Pocket
(Intersect)	Shared volume
(Union Trim)	Select faces to keep and/or remove (adds part of selected body)
(Remove Lump)	Reshape a body by selecting faces to remove and/or faces to keep

When a boolean operation is performed, the source body is connected to the target body through the boolean feature. For example, when a Core (source) body is removed from the Cavity (target) body, the specification tree displays as shown in Figure 19–6.

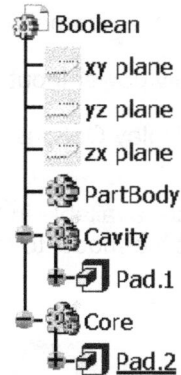

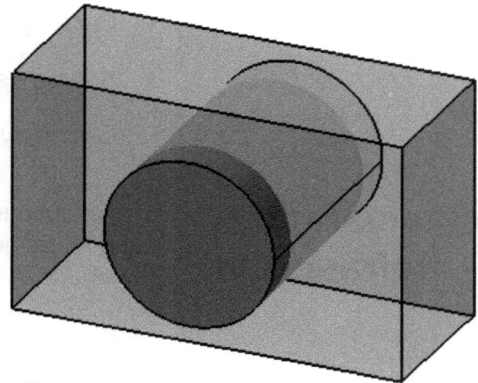

Before boolean operation

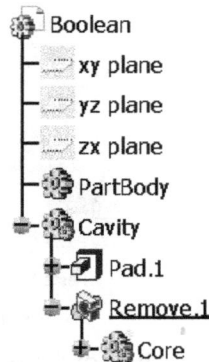

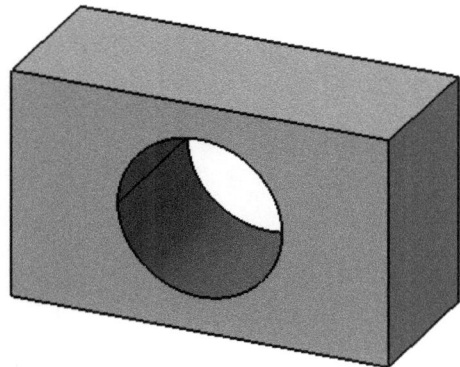

After boolean operation

Figure 19–6

19.3 Feature Visualization

When modifying multi-body parts, it can be difficult to locate a feature due to the multi-level structure of the part. The following techniques can be used to locate a feature for modification:

- Center graph & Reframe On

- Search - show power input

- Geometry Display Options

Center Graph & Reframe On

These options are available in the shortcut menu and can be used to connect the model to the specification tree, as shown in Figure 19–7.

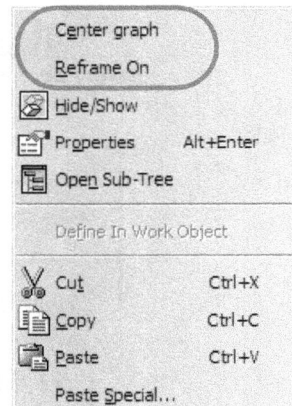

Figure 19–7

- To locate a feature of the model in the specification tree, right-click on the feature in the model display and select **Center Graph**. The software expands the specification tree, highlights the selected feature, and places it at the vertical center of the window.

- To locate a feature from the specification tree on the model, right-click on the feature name and select **Reframe On**. The software zooms into the model to display the selected feature.

Search

The **Search** tool can be used to locate features by name, type, or color. As an alternative to the Search dialog box, the *Power Input* field in the bottom right corner of the CATIA window can be used.

Use the following syntax to search and select features:

Name	n:<feature name> locates a feature by name. For example, entering **n:sketch*** selects all features whose names start with sketch.
Type	t:<feature type> locates a feature by type. For example, entering **t:point** selects all points in the model.
Color	col:<color> locates a feature by color. For example, entering **col:red** selects all features that have been assigned the color red.
Visibility	vis:<hidden/shown> locates a feature by its display status. For example, entering **vis:hidden** selects all hidden features.

Geometry Display Options

You can control the display of the model based on the active body or geometrical set. These tools are useful in organizing the display of a complex, multi-body part, because they enable the designer to focus on the geometry of the active body or geometrical set. These options can be accessed by opening the Options dialog box (select **Tools>Options**). Expand **Infrastructure>Part Infrastructure** and then select the *Display* tab, as shown in Figure 19–8.

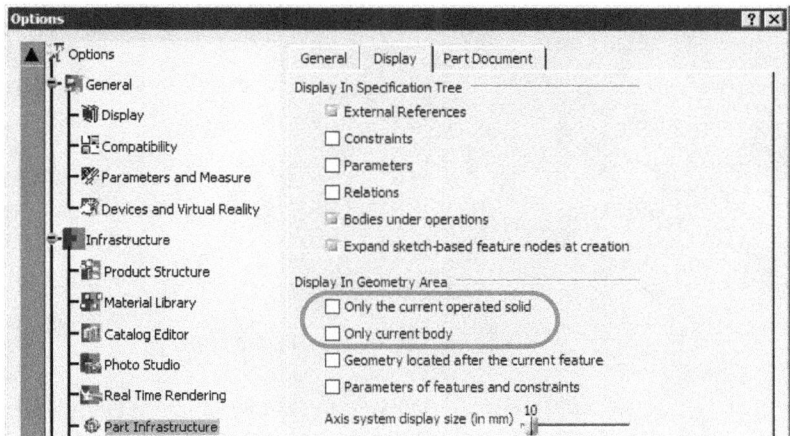

Figure 19–8

The options are also located in the Tools toolbar, as shown in Figure 19–9.

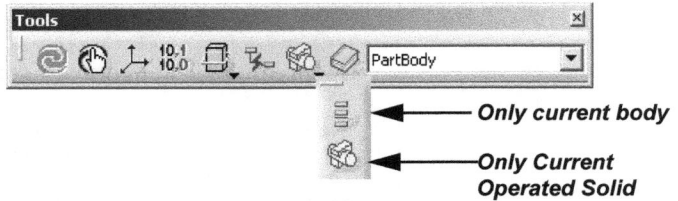

Only current body

Only Current Operated Solid

Figure 19–9

Only Current Operated Solid

When (Only Current Operated Solid) is selected, all bodies and geometrical sets display, except for any parent bodies. Figure 19–10 shows a scenario where **Body.3** is activated but all features in the parent **Body.2** are not displayed. However, all features of **Body.3**, **Body.4**, **Geometrical Set.1**, and **Body.5** display.

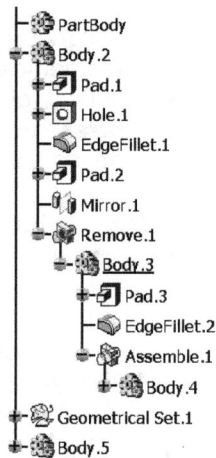

Figure 19–10

Only Current Body

When (Only Current Body) is clicked, only the geometry of the active geometrical set or solid body displays. Bodies located beneath the active body (through a Boolean operation) are also displayed. Figure 19–10 shows a scenario where only the geometry of **Body.3** and **Body.4** display. Since **Geometrical Set.1** and **Body.5** do not belong to **Body.3**, they are hidden.

19.4 Tips and Techniques

Use the following tips when reviewing or modifying multi-body parts:

- Use the **Edit>Scan or Define In Work Object** tool with the **Update** option selected to review the creation of the model. When working with someone else's data, it is recommended to become familiar with their design intent and model creation techniques.

- Use the **Tools>Parents/Children** tool to review the parents and children of a feature to be modified. To understand the modification process, it is recommended to investigate the children of this feature and the relationship that has been developed.

- Review any parameters and formulas that have been created. Often, designers drive frequently modified dimensions by parameters easily accessed in the specification tree. You might not need to drill deep into a model to make a common modification.

- To help you interpret the model when adding new geometry to the model, name the features as they are created. To develop a consistent model, try to match the original design intent.

- Place features in the body to which they apply, as shown in Figure 19–11. For example, Fillet features should be added to the body that contains their reference geometry. If the Fillet references an edge created by a boolean operation, the Fillet must be placed in the body that contains the boolean Add feature. This is because the lower-level body does not contain the required reference.

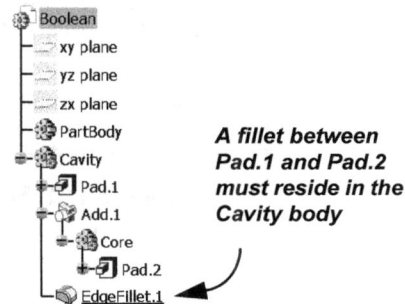

A fillet between Pad.1 and Pad.2 must reside in the Cavity body

Figure 19–11

Practice 19a	# Working with Multi-Body Models

Practice Objectives

- Locate and display features in a multi-body model.
- Perform modifications to complex models.
- Create additional features in a complex model.

In this practice, you will investigate and modify a multi-body model. Assume that this model has been created by another designer in your company and you have been asked to perform modifications in their absence. The model displays as shown in Figure 19–12.

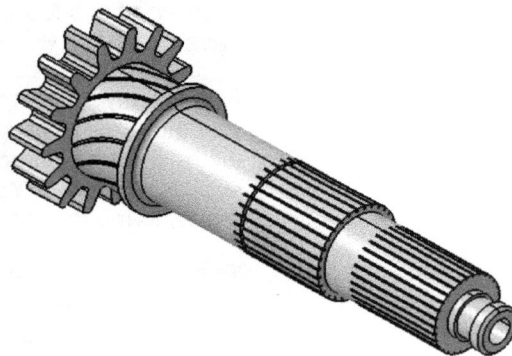

Figure 19–12

The modifications you must complete are:

- Modify the number of grooves in the spline shaft.

- Change the shape of the gear teeth.

- Add Fillet and Chamfer features.

A variety of display and feature management tools and techniques will be used to accomplish these tasks.

Task 1 - Open Shaft_Multi_Body.CATPart and scan the model

---

1. Open **Shaft_Multi_Body.CATPart**.

2. Expand the Shaft body in the specification tree. The Shaft body has been created using multiple bodies connected with boolean operations, as shown in Figure 19–13.

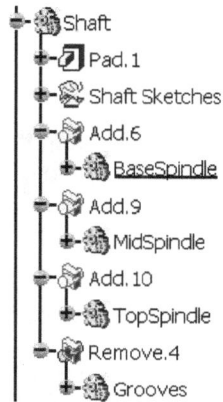

Figure 19–13

3. Select **Edit>Scan or Define In Work Object** and click

 to rewind the model to the beginning.

Design Considerations

Scanning a multi-body model using the **Structure** option might add clutter to the part visualization. The software considers each boolean operation as a feature and therefore only displays the features that are currently active. However, bodies beneath the features are still visible. For this reason, any geometry that has been modeled as a positive volume and removed from the part with a boolean operation now displays as a positive solid, as shown in Figure 19–14.

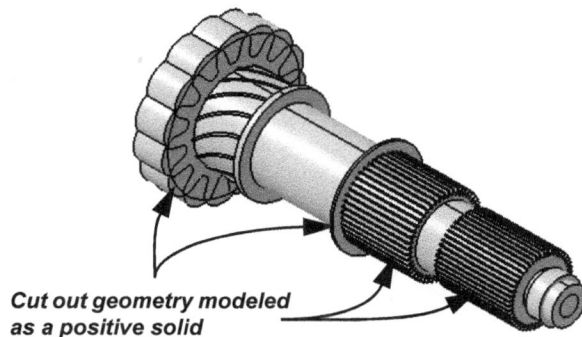

Cut out geometry modeled as a positive solid

Figure 19–14

*Use the **Update** option to scan the model. This will step through the model displaying the features as they are updated by CATIA.*

4. Select **Update** in the drop-down list, as shown in Figure 19–15.

Figure 19–15

5. Step through the update of the model. As each feature is highlighted on the model, track its location in the specification tree. This will help you determine the body location of geometry in the model.

6. Once you have finished scanning the model, close the Scan dialog box.

7. If required, activate the Shaft body so that all model geometry displays. To do so, right-click on the visible **Sketch.16** and select **Hide/Show**, as shown in Figure 19–16.

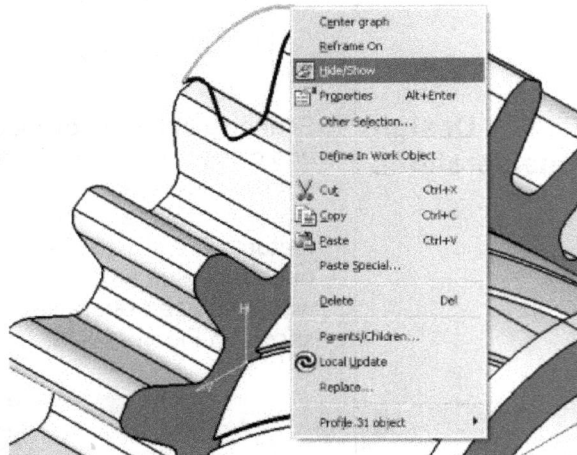

Figure 19–16

Task 2 - Create an Additional Part Body.

1. Select **Insert>Body** to insert a new body. The new body is placed beneath the Geometrical Set.

2. In the specification tree, select **Shaft_Multi_Body**, right-click and select **Shaft_Multi_Body object>Reorder Children**.

3. In the Reorder Children dialog box, select **Body.1** and click the up arrow until it displays below **Shaft**, as shown in Figure 19–17.

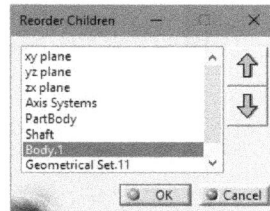

Figure 19–17

4. Click **OK** in the Reorder Children dialog box.

5. Rename the new body as **Support**, as shown in Figure 19–18.

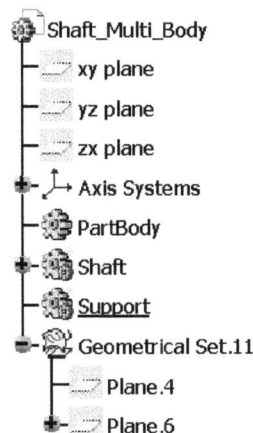

Figure 19–18

6. If required, activate the Support body.

7. Show **Plane.6** from **Geometrical Set.11**.

8. Create a Positioned sketch on **Plane.6.** In the Positioned Sketch dialog box, Reverse H might need to be selected to obtain the orientation, as shown in Figure 19–19.

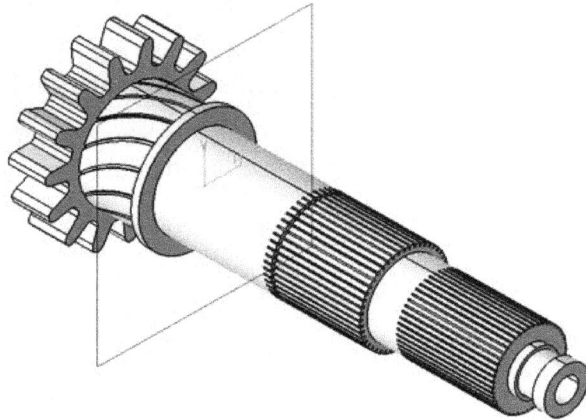

Figure 19–19

9. Click (Cut Part by Sketch Plane) in the Visualization toolbar. The geometry in front of the sketch plane is now cut away, as shown in Figure 19–20.

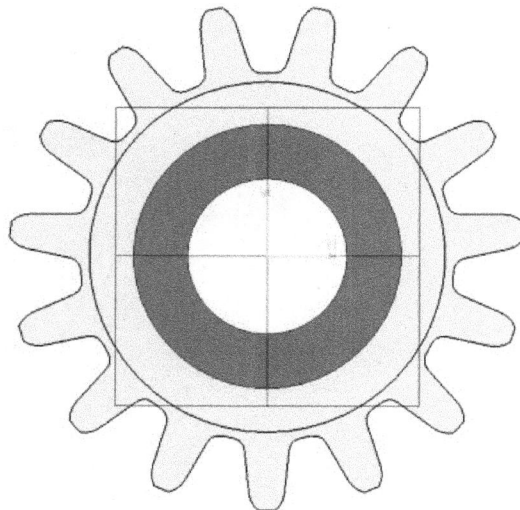

Figure 19–20

10. Click (No 3D Background).

11. Sketch the profile shown in Figure 19–21. Ensure the profile is symmetrical about the vertical sketch axis.

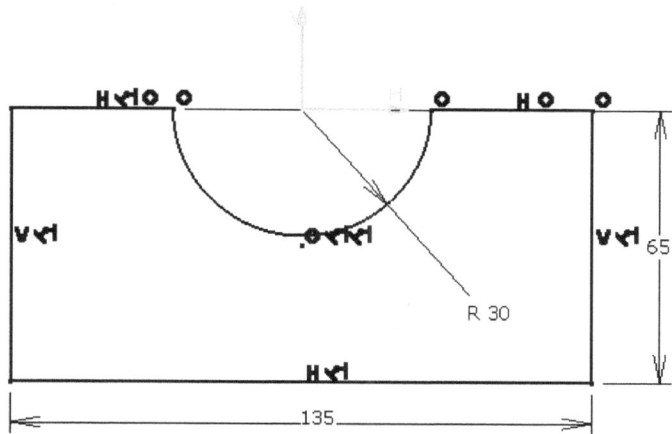

Figure 19–21

12. Exit the Sketcher workbench.

13. Create a Pad feature using the profile you just created. Enter a length of **70mm (2.756 in)** so that the resulting feature displays as shown in Figure 19–22.

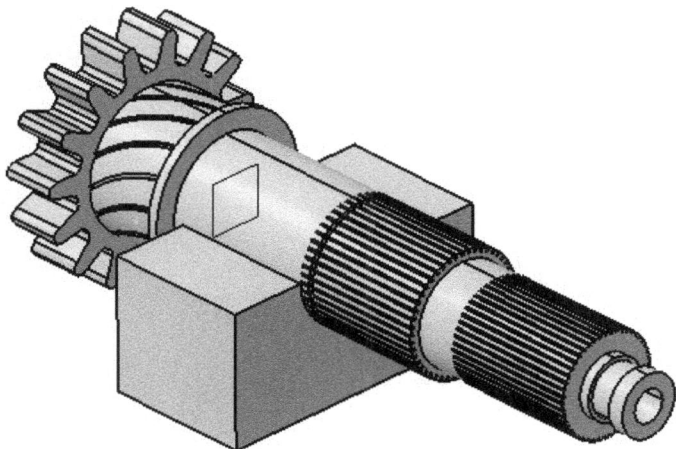

Figure 19–22

14. Hide the Support body.

Task 3 - Use the Only Current Body option.

In this task, you will explore the impact of the **Only Current Body** option. This option is found in the Tools toolbar and can be toggled on and off by clicking the icon.

1. Expand **Shaft>Add.10**.

2. Right-click on the TopSpindle body and select **Define In Work Object**, as shown in Figure 19–23.

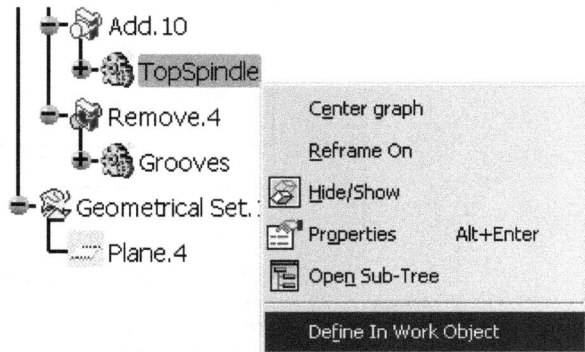

Figure 19–23

Design Consideration

With TopSpindle activated, the software displays all features from the beginning of the model to those contained within TopSpindle. Note that the **Remove.4** feature is not active, but the Grooves body beneath it displays. Therefore, a Remove feature displays as a negative volume.

3. Click ⬚ (Only Current Body) in the Tools toolbar. Clicking the icon once will enable the option. The model now displays only features that belong to TopSpindle, as shown in Figure 19–24.

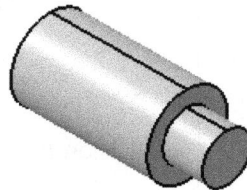

Figure 19–24

4. Experiment with this option by activating other bodies in the model.

5. Disable the **Only Current Body** option by clicking the icon in the toolbar.

6. Activate and show the Shaft body.

Task 4 - Use the Only the current operated solid option.

In this task, you will experiment with the **Only the current operated solid** option. To demonstrate its impact, you will first show the contents of a geometrical set.

1. Expand **Shaft>Add.10>TopSpindle>Add.8>SpindleTip** in the specification tree.

2. Right-click on SpindleTip Sketches and select **SpindleTip Sketches object>Show Components** to display all contents of this geometrical set. A sketch and a point element display on the model.

3. Activate the SpindleTip body.

4. Activate ▤ (Only Current Body) in the Tools toolbar. Note that although the SpindleTip Sketches geometrical set is beneath TopSpindle, the sketch and point are not displayed. This option does not display any geometrical sets in the active body.

5. Activate the TopSpindle body.

6. Activate the MidSpindle body.

7. Disable ▤ (Only Current Body).

8. Activate 🗗 (Only Current Operated Solid) in the Tools toolbar (beneath the **Only Current Body** icon). With this tool, the MidSpindle and Support bodies display. **Plane. 6** from **Geometrical Set.11** is also displayed.

9. Activate the TopSpindle body. Note that the TopSpindle, SpindleTip, and Support bodies are all displayed. **Plane.6** is also displayed from **Geometrical Set.11**.

10. Activate the SpindleTip body.

11. Disable 🗗 (Only Current Operated Solid).

---

12. Activate the Shaft body.

Task 5 - Run a search from the Power Input field.

In this task, you will use a search to locate and select the SpindleTip Sketches geometrical set. You will do this by searching for all geometrical sets. This can also be accomplished by selecting **Tools>Hide>All Geometrical Sets**.

1. Enter the following syntax into the *Power Input* field at the bottom right corner of the CATIA window: **t:geometrical set**.

2. Press <Enter>. The software will run a search for all elements that have the type *geometrical set*.

3. Click [icon] (Hide/Show) to hide all geometrical sets.

4. Hide the Support body and **Plane.6**.

Task 6 - Modify the number of pattern instances.

In this task, you will change the number of grooves of the spline shaft. To locate the pattern feature that defines the grooves, you will use the **Center Graph** option. This option is useful when a feature needs to be located in the specification tree.

1. Zoom in on the grooved end of the model so that you can select an interior surface of a groove.

2. Right-click on the face shown in Figure 19–25 and select **Center Graph**.

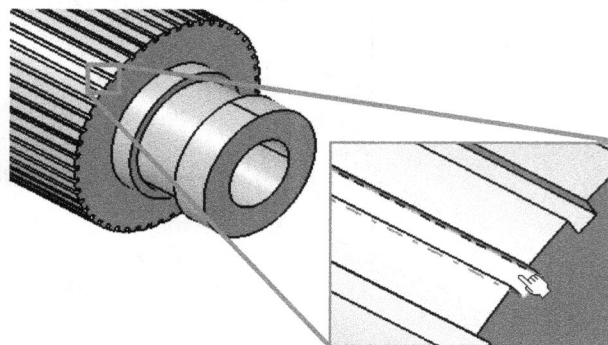

Figure 19–25

3. The software will expand the specification tree and highlight **CircPattern.10**.

4. Modify the **CircPattern.10** feature. Change the number of instances from *49* to **30** and complete the modification. The model displays as shown in Figure 19–26.

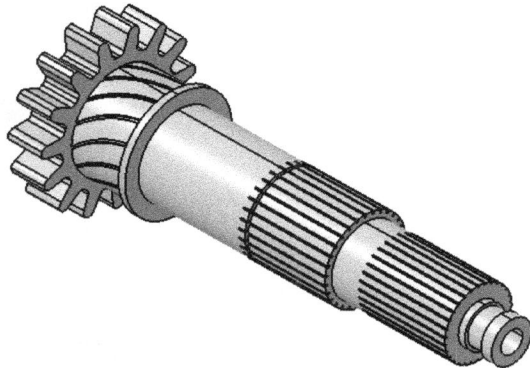

Figure 19–26

Task 7 - Modify the dimension of the gear teeth.

In this task, you will modify the radius of the inner corner on the gear teeth. To locate the feature to modify, you will use the **Parents/Children** tool.

1. Right-click on the face shown in Figure 19–27 and select **Parents/Children**.

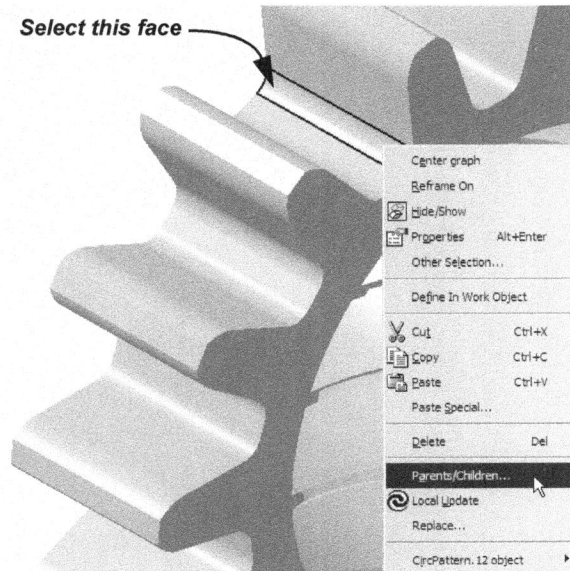

Select this face

Center graph	
Reframe On	
Hide/Show	
Properties	Alt+Enter
Other Selection...	
Define In Work Object	
Cut	Ctrl+X
Copy	Ctrl+C
Paste	Ctrl+V
Paste Special...	
Delete	Del
Parents/Children...	
Local Update	
Replace...	
CircPattern.12 object	▶

Figure 19–27

2. The Parents and Children dialog box opens as shown in Figure 19–28. It indicates that **Pad.19** was patterned to create the gear teeth.

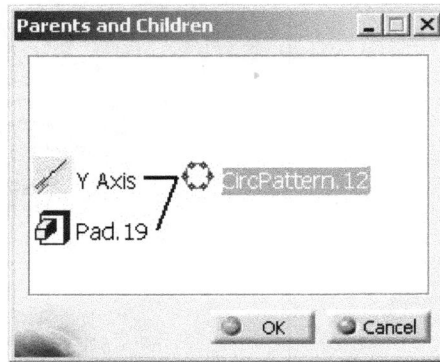

Figure 19–28

3. Double-click on **Pad.19** to display parent information. The dialog box updates to show that **Sketch.40** was used to define the profile of the gear teeth.

4. Right-click on **Sketch.40** in the Parents and Children dialog box and select **Edit**. The sketch displays as shown in Figure 19–29.

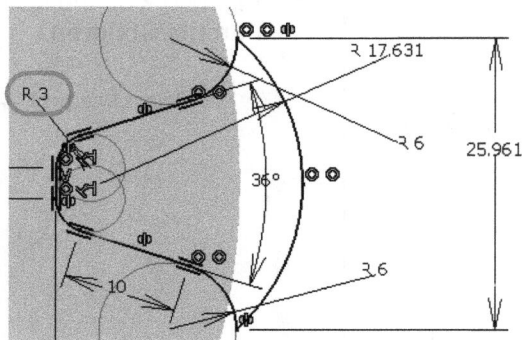

Figure 19–29

5. Change the *radius* value from *3* (0.118 in) to **4 (0.157 in)** and exit Sketcher. The model displays as shown in Figure 19–30.

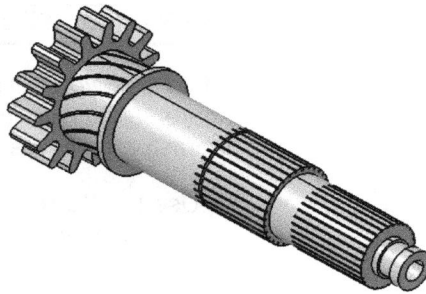

Figure 19–30

Task 8 - Add a chamfer to the model.

In this task, you will add a Chamfer feature to the end of the Shaft. When adding geometry to the model, carefully consider the body location that you will use. The feature should be added to the body that contains the geometry being referenced; in this case, the edge reference shown in Figure 19–32. The body that contains this geometry must be located.

1. Use the **Center Graph** tool to locate the body that contains the geometry shown in Figure 19–31.

2. The feature is **Pad.6** and belongs to SpindleTip. Activate SpindleTip.

3. Create a **2mm (0.079 in) by 45 degree** chamfer on the outer edge of the model.

4. Select the **Only Current Body** option.

5. Activate the Shaft body. The model displays as shown in Figure 19–32.

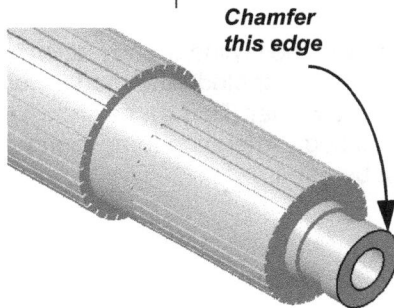

Chamfer this edge

Figure 19–31

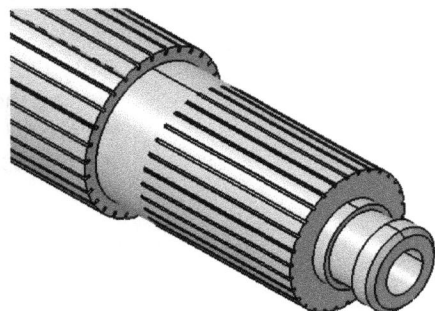

Figure 19–32

Task 9 - Add a Fillet feature to the model.

In this task, you will add a Fillet feature to the edge as shown in Figure 19–33. Again, you will investigate the surrounding geometry to ensure that the feature is placed in the correct body.

1. Use the **Center Graph** tool to locate the features for the two faces shown in Figure 19–34.

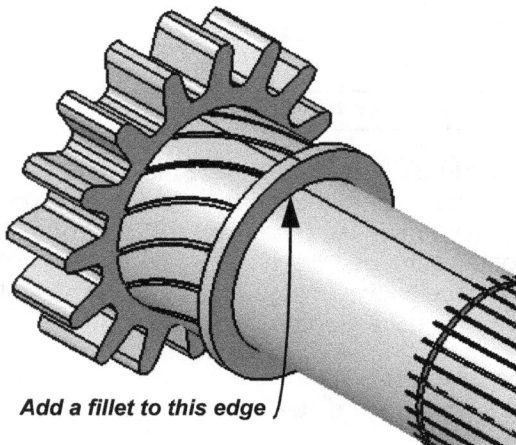

Add a fillet to this edge

Figure 19–33

Identify these two features

Figure 19–34

The two features are **Pad.3** from MidSpindle and **Pad.4** from Cylinder.

Design Considerations

When adding a Fillet on an edge that is created by the joining of two bodies, always add the Fillet to the higher-level body; in this case MidSpindle. This body contains the Add feature that connects the Cylinder geometry and creates the edge reference of the fillet.

This is very apparent with the Cylinder body activated and the **Only Current Body** option enabled. The model would only display the contents of Cylinder (**Pad.4**), as shown in Figure 19–35. With no edge reference to be found in Cylinder, the MidSpindle must be used.

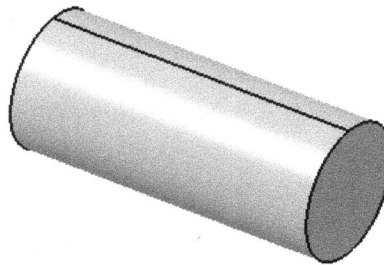

Figure 19–35

2. Activate the MidSpindle body.

3. Activate the **Only Current Body** option.

4. Create a **3.5mm (0.138 in)** Edge Fillet on the edge shown in Figure 19–36.

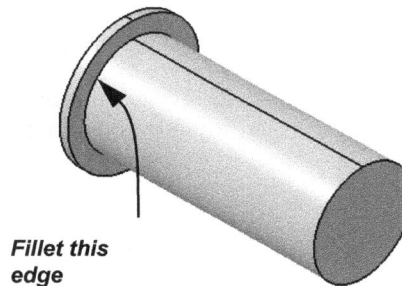

Fillet this edge

Figure 19–36

5. Complete the feature and activate the Shaft body.

6. Disable the **Only Current Body** option.

7. Show the Support body. The model displays as shown in Figure 19–37.

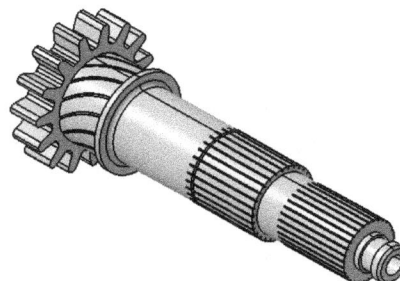

Figure 19–37

8. Save model and close the window.

Chapter Review Questions

1. Multiple bodies are combined using _____ operations.

   a. Combine

   b. Boolean

   c. Merge

   d. None of the above.

2. Advantages of using boolean operations include:

   a. The creation of the part model becomes easier when the model is divided into smaller, functional areas.

   b. Features can be grouped by function or area, making the model structure easy to interpret.

   c. Update times are reduced.

   d. All of the above.

3. One of the advantages of using the multi-body approach is that you can hide geometry in specific bodies while viewing others.

   a. True

   b. False

4. To locate a feature in the specification tree, right-click on the feature in the model display and select which of the following options?

   a. Search

   b. Center graph

   c. Reframe on

   d. Name

5. Looking at Figure 19–38, if (Only Current Operated Solid) were clicked, **Pad.1**, **Multi-pad.1**, and **Edgefillet.1** would display.

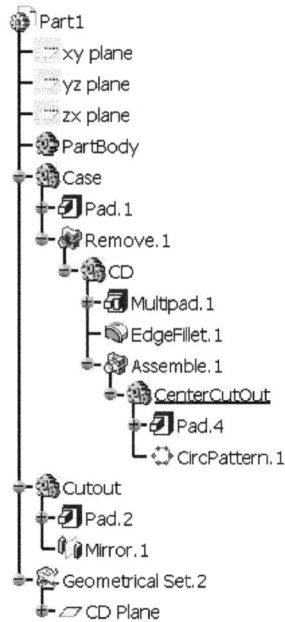

Part1
├─ xy plane
├─ yz plane
├─ zx plane
├─ PartBody
├─ Case
│   ├─ Pad.1
│   ├─ Remove.1
│   │   └─ CD
│   │   ├─ Multipad.1
│   │   ├─ EdgeFillet.1
│   │   └─ Assemble.1
│   │   └─ CenterCutOut
│   │   ├─ Pad.4
│   │   └─ CircPattern.1
├─ Cutout
│   ├─ Pad.2
│   └─ Mirror.1
├─ Geometrical Set.2
└─ CD Plane

Figure 19–38

    a. True

    b. False

6. Looking at Figure 19–38, if (Only Current body) were selected, only features in the Center CutOut body would display.

    a. True

    b. False

Answers: 1.b, 2.d, 3.a, 4.b, 5.b, 6.a

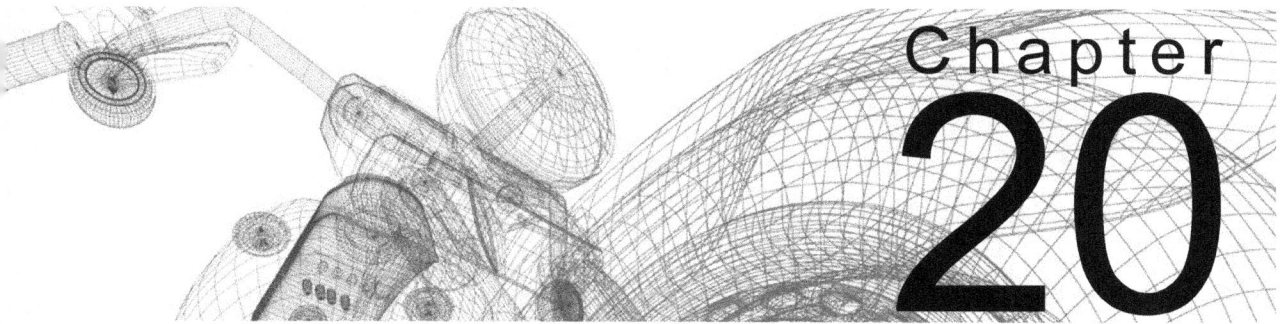

Assembly Design

This chapter covers how to activate the Assembly workbench and access assembly-specific toolbars. This chapter also guides you through the process of creating an assembly and describes the available assembly constraints.

Learning Objectives in this Chapter

- Learn about the Assembly Workbench interface.
- Create an assembly and add components to it.
- Understand product properties and assembly product structure.
- Use the compass to move components.
- Automatically snap objects to the compass.
- Understand the various constraints available for parametrically locating components.
- Understand what PDM systems are and their benefits.

20.1 Assembly Workbench

*The terms **Product** and **Assembly** can be used interchangeably.*

In the Part workbench, features are created in the model to build the final part. In the Assembly workbench, components can be added to a product file to create an assembly. To activate the Assembly workbench, use one of the following methods:

- Select **Start>Mechanical Design>Assembly Design**.

- Click [icon] (Assembly Design) in the Workbench toolbar.

- Select **File>New>Product**.

A CATIA V5 assembly file is identified with the .CATProduct file extension. Assembly-specific toolbars become available once the Product workbench is enabled.

Commonly Used Toolbars

The Assembly Workbench contains various toolbars. These are described as follows:

- The Product Structure toolbar controls how new components are added to the assembly. This toolbar is shown in Figure 20–1.

- The Constraints toolbar controls the relative position of components in the assembly. This toolbar is shown in Figure 20–2.

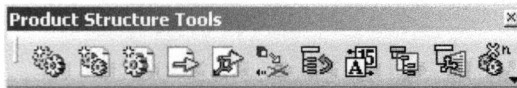

Figure 20–1

Figure 20–2

- The **Update All** option in the Update toolbar updates the position of components as assembly constraints are applied or if constraints have been modified. The options is shown in Figure 20–3.

- The Measure toolbar enables you to perform various analyses within the assembly. This toolbar is shown in Figure 20–4.

Figure 20–3

Figure 20–4

20.2 Create an Assembly

How To: Create a New Assembly

1. Create a new product file by activating the Assembly Design workbench.
2. Modify any product properties (i.e., defining part numbers).
3. Add components to the assembly using the Product Structure Tools.
4. Position components using the compass and/or using parametric constraints.
5. Add assembly features to the model or modify parts within the context of the assembly.
6. Analyze and extract any critical information from the assembly.
7. Prepare the assembly for drawing creation.
8. Create the drawing showing the assembly.

Product Properties

When a new product file is created, the software assigns a default filename and part number. The filename takes the form of Product#, where # is the number of new Product in session.

The filename is also the default part number. To change the part number, select **Edit>Properties**. The Properties dialog box opens as shown in Figure 20–5.

You can also change the part number using the shortcut menu.

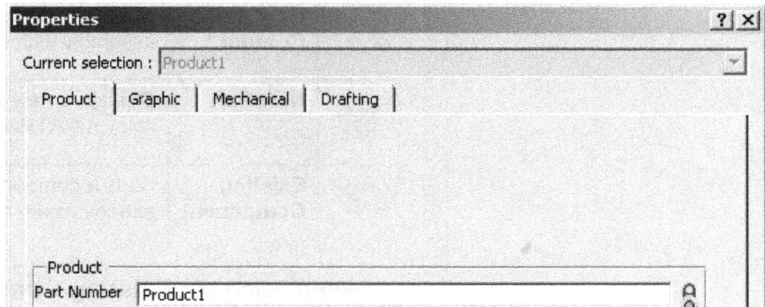

Figure 20–5

Adding Components

A component is an object that is added to an assembly. The following components can be added to a *.CATProduct assembly.

- *.CATPart

- *.CATProduct

- *.model (V4)

- *.iges

Components can be added to the assembly in the following ways:

- Select the assembly in the specification tree and use the shortcut menu.

- Use the icons in the Product Structure Tools toolbar.

- Use the **Insert** menu in the menu bar.

The following icons are found in the Product Structure toolbar.

Icon	Option	Description
	New Component	Creates a new component that has no file associated with it.
	New Product	Creates a new subassembly in the top-level assembly with its own CATProduct file.
	New Part	Creates a new part in the top-level assembly with its own CATPart file.
	Existing Component	Adds a component to the assembly whose file already exists at the operating system level.

- When using the **Existing Component** option, multiple objects can be added to the assembly at the same time by pressing <Ctrl> or <Shift> while selecting objects.

Product Structure

The product structure of an assembly consists of the top level assembly (.CATProduct), components (.CATParts), and subassemblies (.CATProducts) as shown in Figure 20–6.

- The active level in the product structure is highlighted in blue in the specification tree. When performing actions on a top level or subassembly (such as Inserting Components), the active level of the product structure is affected by the actions performed.

- To activate a subassembly, double-click on the subassembly from the specification tree.

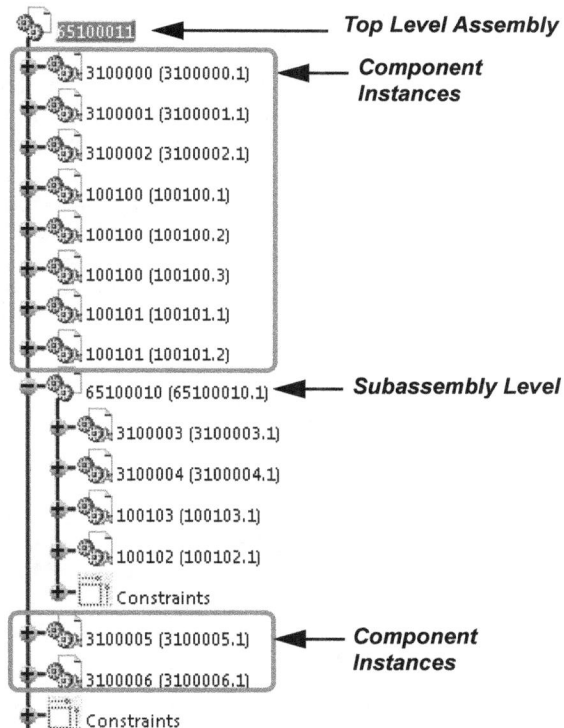

Figure 20–6

- Once components are added to the assembly, they display in the specification tree. The part number and the instance name in parenthesis is listed, as shown in Figure 20–7.

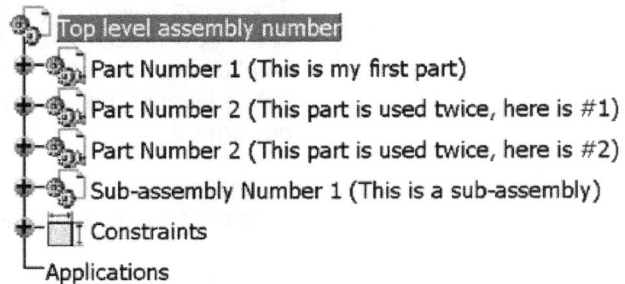

Top level assembly number
Part Number 1 (This is my first part)
Part Number 2 (This part is used twice, here is #1)
Part Number 2 (This part is used twice, here is #2)
Sub-assembly Number 1 (This is a sub-assembly)
Constraints
Applications

Figure 20–7

- In this example, Part Number 2 is used twice in the assembly. The instance name in parenthesis is the unique identifier for each time the part number is used in the assembly.

- Both the part number and the instance name can be modified by right-clicking and selecting **Properties**.

- If you need to investigate the CATPart specification tree, expand the specification tree for the component.

20.3 Use the Compass

Once existing components are added to the assembly, the components display in a default position and orientation. The compass is used to move components in the main window.

General Steps

Use the following general steps to move selected components with the compass:

1. Activate a component to move.
2. Move the component.
3. Complete the movement.

Step 1 - Activate a component to move.

Hover the cursor over the red dot in the compass until the cursor changes to a move symbol, as shown in Figure 20–8. Once the move symbol displays, press the left mouse button to move the compass.

Once the move symbol displays, press the left mouse button to move the compass.

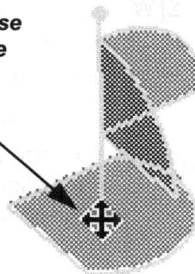

Figure 20–8

Drag the compass to the component to be moved. The compass will snap and reorient to geometry belonging to the component, as shown in Figure 20–9. Once the orientation is correct, release the left mouse button to place the compass.

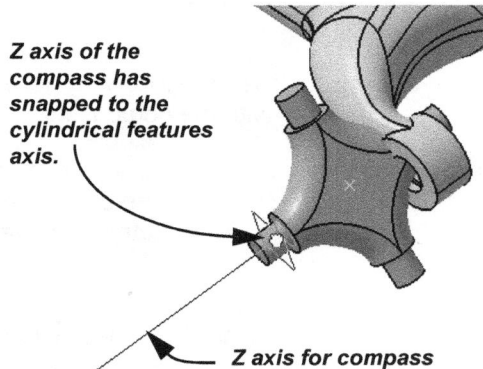

Z axis of the compass has snapped to the cylindrical features axis.

Z axis for compass

Figure 20–9

Once the compass has snapped to a component, the compass turns green. If the compass does not turn green, verify that the active model in the specification tree is an assembly. Then, select the component from the model or specification tree to activate movement of the selected component. You can activate any component for movement; it does not need to be the component the compass is snapped to.

You can also activate multiple components by selecting them while pressing <Ctrl>.

Automatic Snap

You can automatically snap the compass to a selected object by right-clicking and selecting **Snap Automatically to Selected Object**, as shown in Figure 20–10.

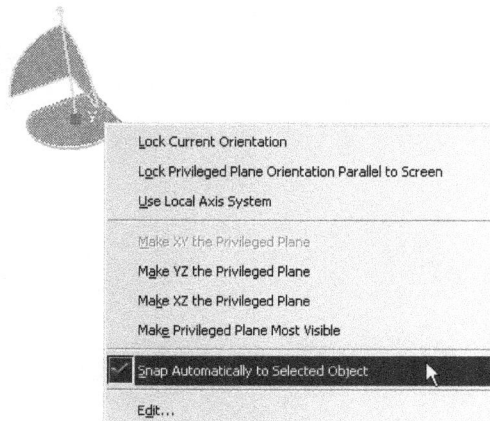

Ensure that this option is toggled off once you have finished moving components.

Lock Current Orientation

Lock Privileged Plane Orientation Parallel to Screen

Use Local Axis System

Make XY the Privileged Plane

Make YZ the Privileged Plane

Make XZ the Privileged Plane

Make Privileged Plane Most Visible

Snap Automatically to Selected Object

Edit...

Figure 20–10

The software automatically selects the orientation of the compass based on the origin of the selected component.

Once the option is activated, select from the model or component you want to move. The compass automatically snaps to the selected component, as shown in Figure 20–11.

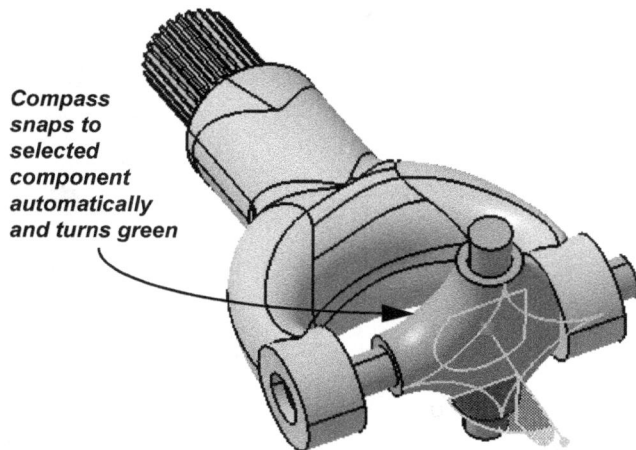

Compass snaps to selected component automatically and turns green

Figure 20–11

Step 2 - Move the component.

Once the compass is activated on the component, only compass movements control the selected component(s). To move components while accounting for the placement constraints, hold <Shift> while pressing the left mouse button. Note that more than one component might move, depending on how the constraints are defined.

*It is recommended to restore any changed values to 0 once you have completed the **Move** operation. This ensures that further operations do not snap to the previous increment values.*

More precise movements of a component can be achieved by right-clicking on the compass and selecting **Edit**. The Parameters for Compass Manipulation dialog box, shown in Figure 20–12, enables you to enter exact translation or rotational increment values for precise movements.

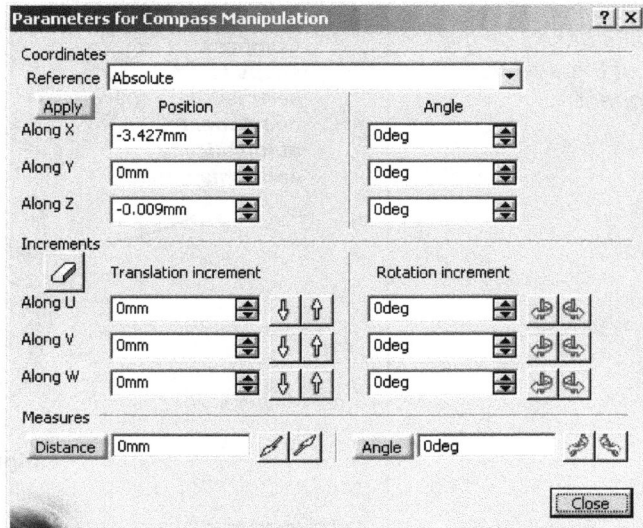

Figure 20–12

Step 3 - Complete the movement.

Once the component has been moved to the correct location, complete the movement by selecting another component to move or clicking anywhere on the screen to deactivate the compass control. The compass returns to its default color and controls the entire assembly. To return the compass to its default position, select **View>Reset Compass**, or drag the compass off the model and move it anywhere in the background of the screen.

20.4 Constraints

Constraints are specified to locate components parametrically with respect to existing components. Any references made to other components when constraining creates parent/child relationships. The available constraints are described as follows:

Icon	Name	Description
	Coincidence	Aligns axes, planes, or points.
	Contact	Mates two planar surfaces. Can also force curved surfaces to touch. Note that reference planes cannot be used as a contact surface.
	Offset	Specifies an offset distance between two planar elements.
	Angle	Permits a typed in value between planar selections. Parallel and perpendicular can also be specified.
	Fix	Fastens a component in the assembly space. It has no other constraints to components.
	Fix Together	*Welds* components together.
	Quick Constraint	Enables the software to automatically select which constraint to use based on your selection. This constraint can be changed later.

Coincidence

Once additional components are added to the assembly, how they are constrained is dependent on their geometry. Coincidence can be used to align axes and planes. Figure 20–13 shows a T-brace positioned over the mounting block by using the coincidence constraint and selecting the axis of the holes. The T-brace can be further constrained by using the coincidence constraint and selecting planar surfaces, as shown in Figure 20–14.

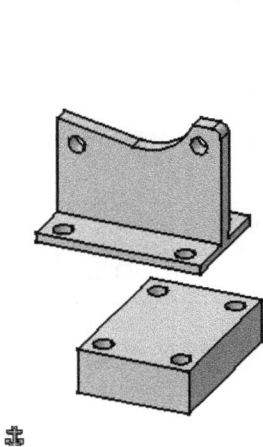

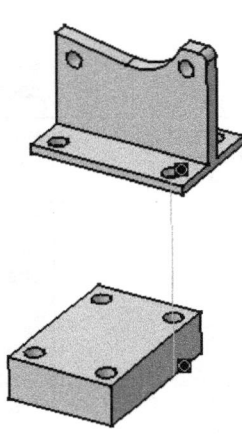

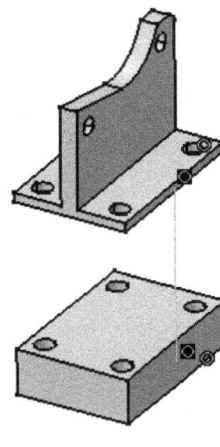

Figure 20–13   **Figure 20–14**

When specifying the coincidence constraint with planar surfaces, you can change the orientation of the surfaces, as shown in Figure 20–15.

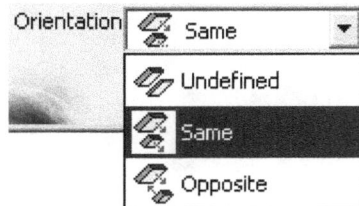

Figure 20–15

Contact

Contact mates two surfaces. Figure 20–16 shows a T-brace fully constrained after mating the top surface of the mounting block with the underside surface of the T-brace.

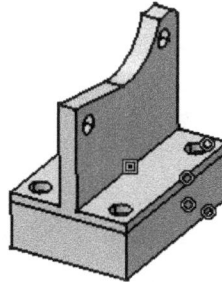

Figure 20–16

Offset

Offset behaves like contact or align with planar surfaces, without the selections being coplanar. The selections are parallel with a specified offset distance. Figure 20–17 shows a bolt offset from the T-brace to permit space for future washer placement. Similar to coincidence, the direction of orientation can be specified.

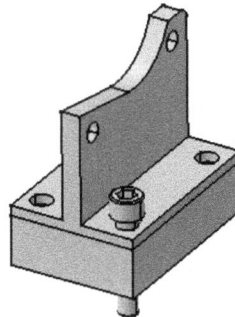

Figure 20–17

Angle

Figure 20–18 shows an example of a finger that is assembled with a coincidence constraint. Note the intersecting geometry.

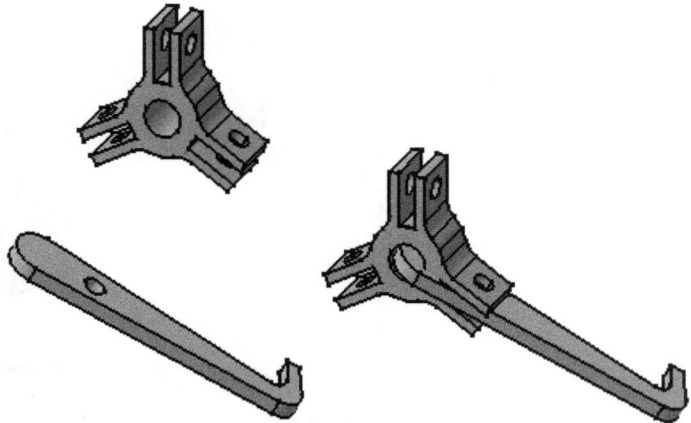

Figure 20–18

The angle constraint is used to show the correct orientation of components. Figure 20–19 shows an example where interference exists. The finger component is under-constrained; therefore, a parallel or angle constraint must be added. The parallel and angle options are shown in Figure 20–19.

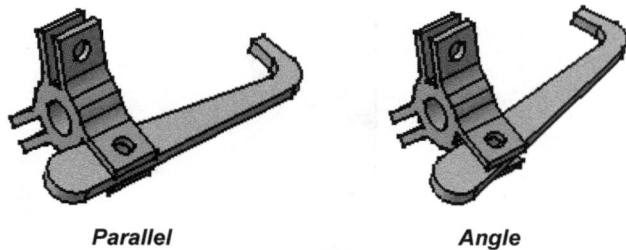

Parallel   *Angle*

Figure 20–19

Fix Component

In CATIA, the base component is usually constrained to be fixed. This essentially creates a zero position of reference. Once constrained to be fixed, the *Constraints* area displays in the specification tree, as shown in Figure 20–20, and ⚓ displays.

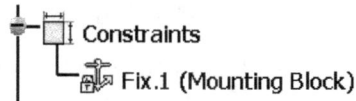

Figure 20–20

Fix Together

Fix together is normally used to fix any remaining degrees of freedom from an under-constrained component. The components behave as a single body in space.

When moving components assembled with a fix together constraint, press <Shift> while using the compass. This forces CATIA to obey the assembly constraints during the move. If a component is moved without pressing <Shift>, the fix together constraint updates based on the new locations.

Quick Constraint

Quick constraint enables the software to decide which constraint to use on a component. If planar surfaces are selected, CATIA might select a coincidence, offset, or contact constraint. If the required constraint is not selected, you can click 🔄 (Change Constraint) in the toolbar and select the correct constraint in the Possible Constraints dialog box, as shown in Figure 20–21.

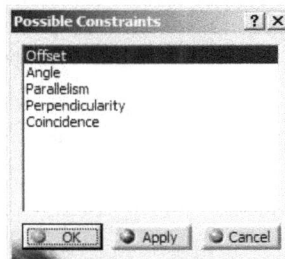

Figure 20–21

Assembly Considerations

When modeling parts, consider what feature form best captures the design intent of the base feature. When working with assemblies, consider which component is best suited for use as the base component.

Additionally, consider the active level of the product structure. If the top level of the structure is active (highlighted in blue), then the constraint you are creating will be grouped with the top level assembly constraints.

If you want to create a constraint specific to the components in a subassembly, double-click on the subassembly level in the specification tree to activate it. When you create the constraint, it is grouped with the subassembly constraints. The product structure, top level assembly constraints, and subassembly constraints are shown in Figure 20–22.

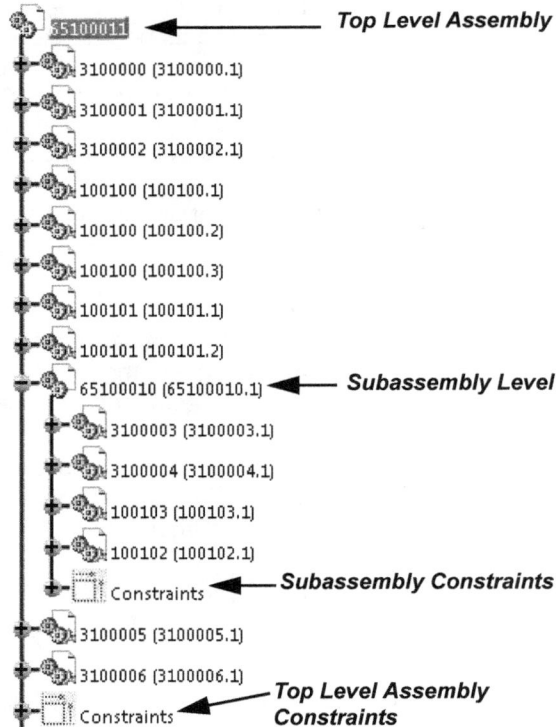

Figure 20–22

20.5 Product Data Management

What is PDM?

Product Data Management (PDM) is a type of software that organizes and manages files in a database. Files in a PDM system are related to the development of a product. While most of these files are engineering-related, it is not limited to managing engineering data.

Types of files that a PDM system can organize depend on the specific PDM software being used. Some examples include:

- Parts
- Assemblies
- Drawings
- Metadata
- Spreadsheets
- Word processing documents

These files are stored on a server commonly referred to as the vault. From here, you open files and save them back to the server. The PDM system keeps track and controls all file operations. Multiple users can view the file at the same time, but only one person can work on it.

Common capabilities of a PDM system include:

- Track revisions of a document.
- Advanced tools to search documents in the database.
- Viewing file information.
- Managing change orders.
- Managing bill of materials.
- Permissions control over files.

Some of the benefits of implementing a PDM system include:

- Vital data is kept organized.
- You can work with the most up-to-date information and concurrent engineering is promoted.
- Productivity is increased through a controlled design collaboration environment where the modification and status of a file is communicated by the PDM system.

PDM Considerations

Some PDM systems manage assemblies and their related data differently. It is important to understand the capabilities of the PDM system because this might impact the way that you build your assemblies. Your company might have corporate standards for assemblies and their use in a PDM system.

Some PDM systems might delete the constraints that have been created to define the relative position of components when the assembly is checked in. In this case, the company might enforce a design standard that in-place modeling techniques are required.

- In-place modeling positions components relative to a central axis system so that no constraints are required.

- It is recommended that you speak to your CAD administrator regarding the presence of a PDM system. Additionally, you should be aware of any company standards or assembly design procedures that need to be followed to maximize the benefits of the PDM system. This could affect how you use the Assembly Design workbench.

Creating Assemblies I

Learning Objectives

- Change product properties.
- Move components with the compass.
- Apply assembly constraints.

In this practice, you will create a new ball mount assembly, as shown in Figure 20–23. You will use constraints to assemble the four components of the assembly. The ball mount assembly that you create is a subassembly of a larger assembly.

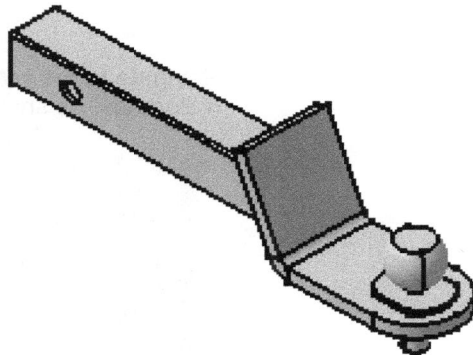

Figure 20–23

Task 1 - Assign properties for the product.

You should be in the Assembly Design workbench. This workbench is indicated

by [icon] *in the Workbench toolbar.*

1. Select **File>New** and select the **Product** option in the *Type* area.

2. Save the file as **Ball_Mount**. Verify that it is saved in the *Hitch* folder.

3. Select **Product1** in the specification tree. Note that the default part number is applied. Right-click and select **Properties**.

4. Select the *Product* tab. Change the *part number* to **65000010**.

5. Click **OK** to confirm the change.

Task 2 - Assemble the first component and fix it.

1. Right-click on the top level assembly (**65000010**) in the
   specification tree and select **Components>Existing
   Component**, as shown in Figure 20–24.

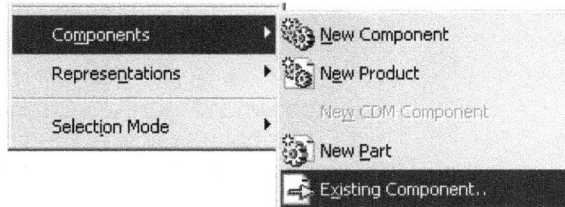

Figure 20–24

2. Navigate to the *Hitch* folder and select the **Slide** part in the
   dialog box, as shown in Figure 20–25.

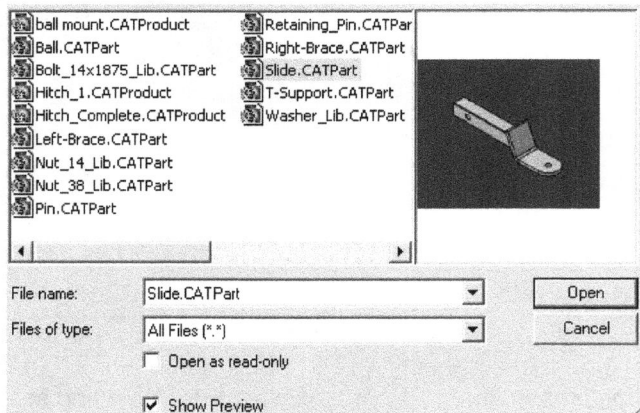

Figure 20–25

3. Click **Open**. The **Slide** part is brought into the assembly.

4. The Slide is the base component that is referenced by
   subsequent components. The component should be fixed.

   Click [icon] (Fix Component) in the Constraints toolbar.

5. Select the part from the display area. This component is now fixed. Note the *Constraints* area in the specification tree, as shown in Figure 20–26.

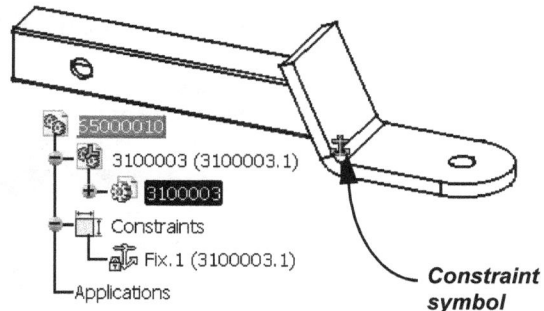

Figure 20–26

Task 3 - Add the second component in a free position.

---

1. Bring another component into the assembly by selecting **65000010** in the specification tree. Right-click and select **Components>Existing Component**.

2. Select **Ball** as the component to assemble and click **Open**. Note that the part is placed in the default position and intersects the Slide component.

3. To view the **Ball** geometry, the part needs to be moved away from the fixed assembly. Drag the compass onto the Slide part. Once positioned, the compass color changes to green.

4. Select the **Ball** part and use the compass to position the **Ball** in a similar position to the one shown in Figure 20–27. In this position, you can more easily apply assembly constraints.

*To reset the compass, select **View>Reset Compass**.*

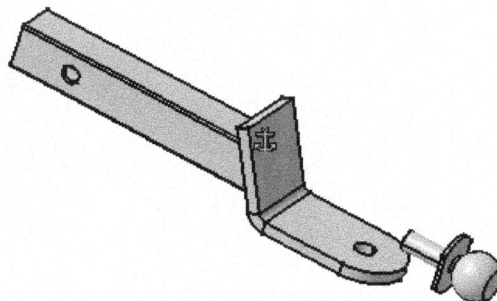

Figure 20–27

Task 4 - Constrain the Ball part.

1. Create a coincidence constraint by clicking

   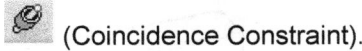 (Coincidence Constraint).

2. If the dialog box shown in Figure 20–28 opens, select the **Do not prompt in the future** option and close the window.

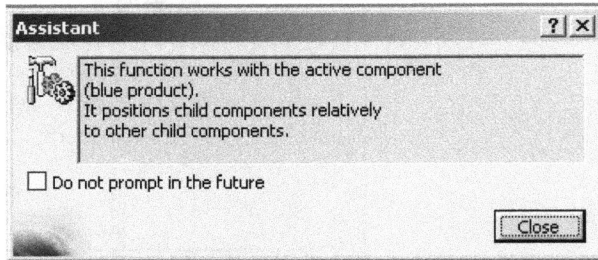

Figure 20–28

3. Select the axis of the **Ball** stem by selecting the cylindrical surface, as shown in Figure 20–29. You might need to zoom into the part.

4. Select the axis on the **Slide** by selecting the inner cylindrical surface of the hole, as shown in Figure 20–30.

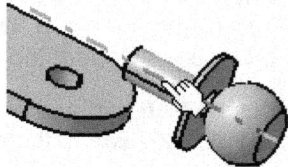   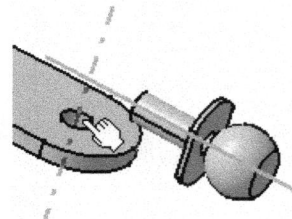

Figure 20–29   **Figure 20–30**

5. The **Ball** is now partially constrained. Show the position of

   Ball by clicking 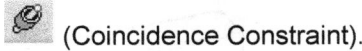 (Update All). The assembly updates the position of all components. The assembly displays similar to that shown in Figure 20–31.

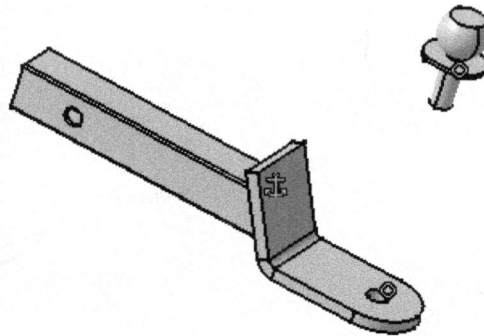

Figure 20–31

Design Considerations

The **Ball** is only constrained along its axis. Therefore, it can still be translated and rotated on its axis.

6. To position the **Ball** along the coincident axis, use a contact constraint. Click 🔳 (Contact Constraint).

7. Select the mating surface of the **Slide**, as shown in Figure 20–32.

8. Select the underside surface of the **Ball**, as shown in Figure 20–33.

9. Update the position of the components. The assembly displays as shown in Figure 20–34.

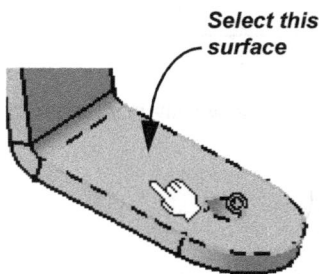

Select this surface

Figure 20–32

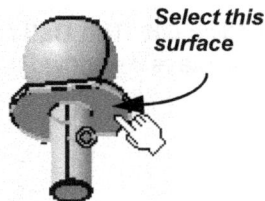

Select this surface

Figure 20–33

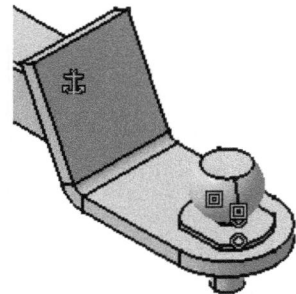

Figure 20–34

10. The **Ball** can still rotate about the coincident axis. Add an angle constraint to fully constrain the ball by clicking 📐 (Angle Constraint).

11. Select the two surfaces shown in Figure 20–35.

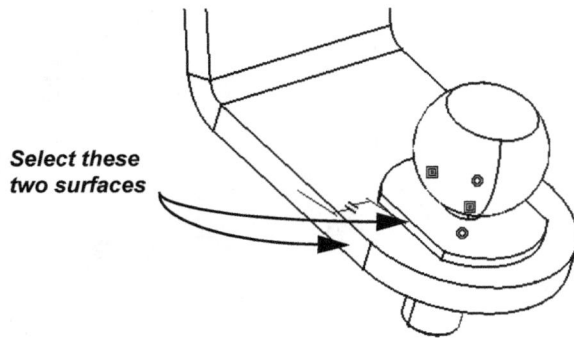

Figure 20–35

12. Select the following options when the Constraint Properties dialog box opens, as shown in Figure 20–36:

- Select **Parallelism**.
- *Orientation:* **Same**

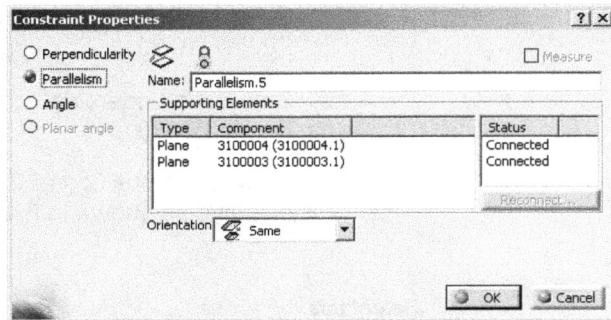

Figure 20–36

13. Click **OK**. The **Ball** component is now fully constrained and displays as shown in Figure 20–37.

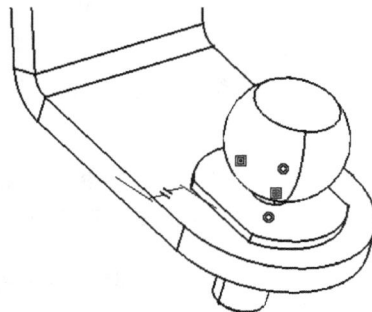

Figure 20–37

Task 5 - Hide the constraints.

1. Note that the constraint symbols display. To remove these symbols from the display, right-click on constraints in the specification tree and select **Hide/Show**.

Task 6 - Assemble the washer.

1. Insert **Washer_Lib into 65000010** by right-clicking on **65000010** and selecting **Components>Existing Component**.

2. Part number 100103 displays in the specification tree, but the washer is not visible. Position the cursor over the red square of the compass so that the cursor turns to four arrows, as shown in Figure 20–38.

Figure 20–38

3. Right-click and select **Snap Automatically to Selected Object**.

4. Select **100103** in the specification tree. The compass snaps to the washer component. Drag the washer using the compass to the position shown in Figure 20–39. Then, drag the compass off the washer.

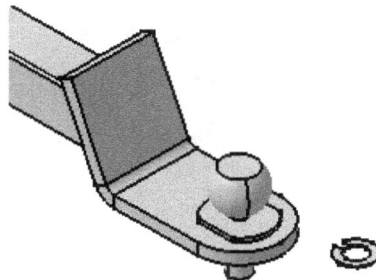

Figure 20–39

5. Create a coincidence constraint by clicking

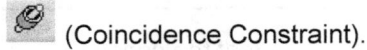

   ![Coincidence Constraint icon] (Coincidence Constraint).

6. Select the axis of the washer and the axis of the ball (zoom in to select the washer axis).

7. Create a contact constraint by clicking ![Contact Constraint icon] (Contact Constraint).

8. Select the surface of the washer and the underside surface of the slide, as shown in Figure 20–40.

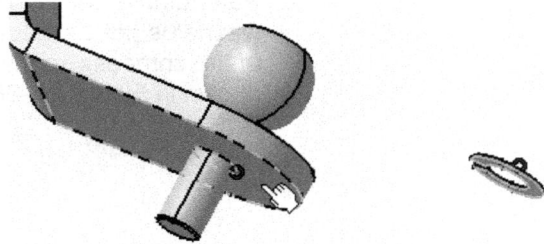

Figure 20–40

9. To update the position of the components, expand the *Constraints* area of the specification tree.

10. Select the two newly created constraints, right-click and select **Update**.

11. The washer still has a degree of freedom to rotate about the coincident axis. Click ![Fix Together icon] (Fix Together) and select both the washer and the ball parts to fix them together.

12. Click **OK**.

13. Update the assembly, if required.

14. Toggle the visibility setting of the constraints so that all constraints are hidden.

Task 7 - Add the nut component.

1. Insert the **Nut_38_Lib** component into the assembly.

2. The nut is not displayed. Drag the compass onto the Slide part.

3. Select **100102** in the specification tree. Using the compass, drag the nut to the position shown in Figure 20–41.

4. Create a coincident constraint by clicking (Coincidence Constraint). Select the axis of the nut and the axis of the ball, as shown in Figure 20–42.

5. Create a contact constraint by clicking (Contact Constraint). Select the surface of the nut and the surface of the washer, as shown in Figure 20–43.

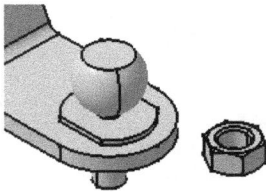

Figure 20–41

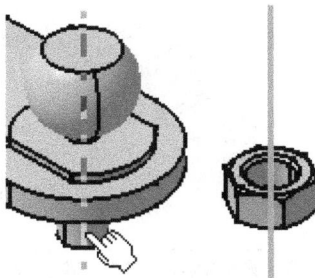

Figure 20–42

Figure 20–43

6. Update the assembly.

7. Create a (Fix Together) constraint between the nut and the washer.

8. Save the file and close the assembly.

Practice 20b | Creating Assemblies II

Practice Objectives

- Apply constraints.
- Insert a subassembly.

In this practice, you will create the assembly shown in Figure 20–44. This assembly will consist of various parts and the subassembly that you created in a previous practice.

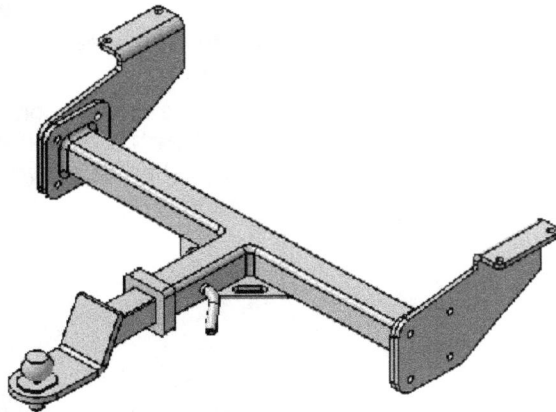

Figure 20–44

Task 1 - Assign product properties.

1. Select **File>New** and select the **Product** option in the *Type* area.

2. Save the file as **Hitch** in the *Hitch* folder.

3. Select **Product1** in the specification tree. The default part number is applied. Right-click and select **Properties**.

4. Select the *Product* tab and change the *part number* to **65000011**.

5. Click **OK** to confirm the change.

Task 2 - Assemble the first component and fix it.

1. Right-click on the top level assembly (**65000011**) in the specification tree and select **Components>Existing Component**.

2. Select the part called **T-Support** in the *Hitch* folder and click **Open**.

3. The **T-Support** is the base component that is referenced by subsequent components. The component needs to be fixed.

   Click ⚓ (Fix Component) in the toolbar.

4. Select the part in the display area. This component is now fixed. Note the *Constraints* area in the specification tree.

Task 3 - Assemble the braces.

1. Insert the **Left-Brace** component into **65000011** using the same method as in Task 3.

2. Create a 🌐 (Coincidence) constraint between the axes, as shown in Figure 20–45.

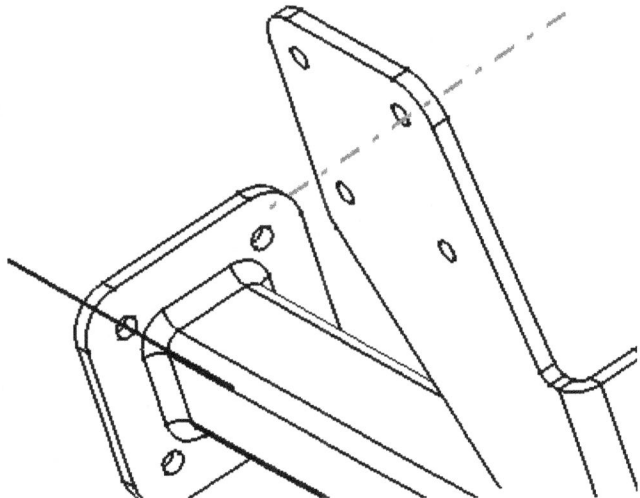

Figure 20–45

3. Create a 🔲 (Contact) constraint between the surfaces shown in Figure 20–46. Update the assembly.

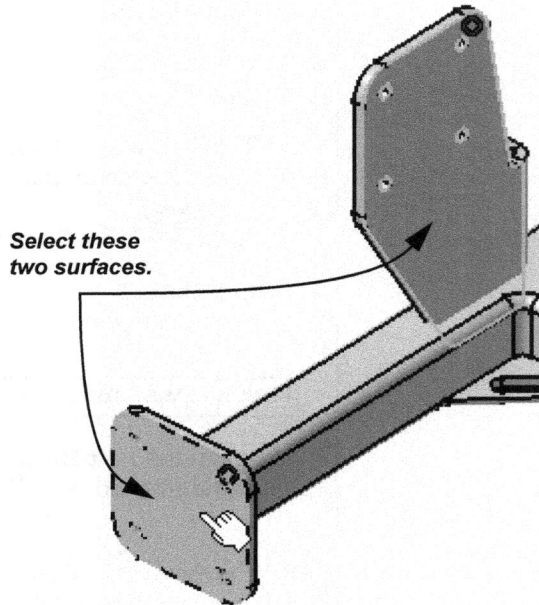

Select these two surfaces.

Figure 20–46

4. Using 📐 (Angle Constraint), apply a parallelism constraint between the surfaces shown in Figure 20–47. Update the assembly.

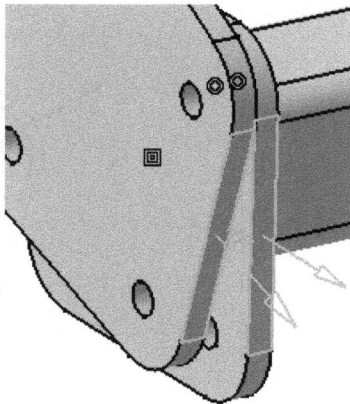

Figure 20–47

5. Assemble the **Right-Brace** using the same steps described in this task. The assembly displays as shown in Figure 20–48.

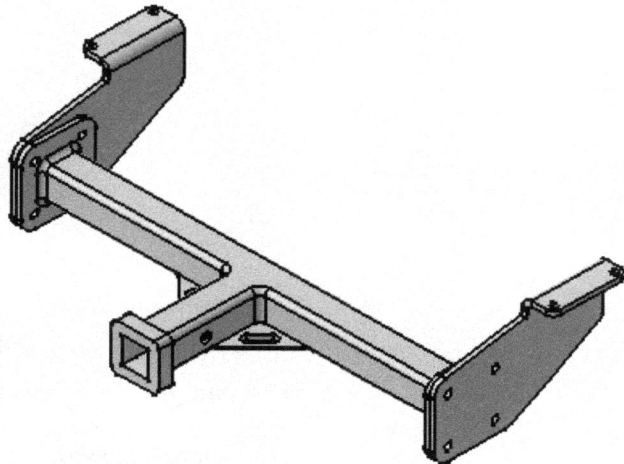

Figure 20–48

Task 4 - Assemble the Ball_Mount subassembly.

1. Insert the **Ball_Mount_Complete** assembly into **65000011** by right-clicking and selecting **Components>Existing Component**.

2. Place the compass on the **T-Support** and drag the **Ball_Mount** assembly away from the model, as shown in Figure 20–49.

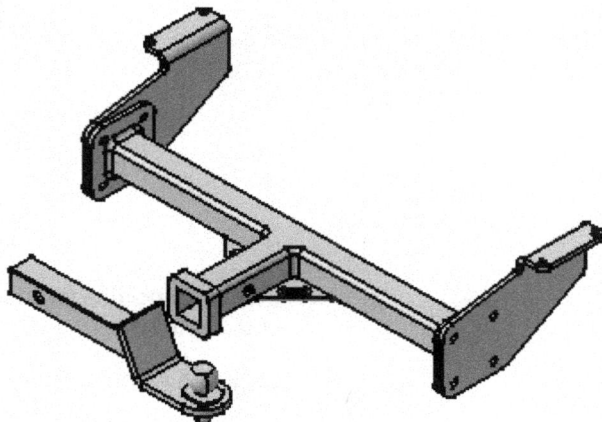

Figure 20–49

3. Create a ⌕ (Coincidence) constraint between the axes shown in Figure 20–50.

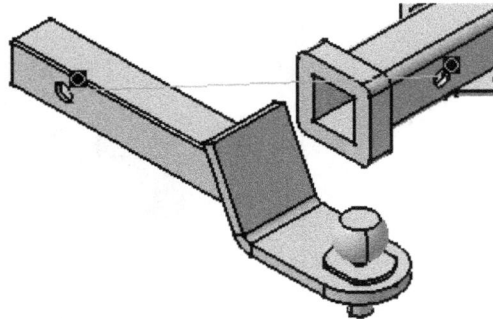

Figure 20–50

4. The **Ball_Mount** is now partially constrained. Use the

   ⌕ (Offset) constraint to position along the axis by offsetting two surfaces.

5. Select the surface on the Slide and on the **T-Support,** as shown in Figure 20–51. The Constraint Definition dialog box opens.

Select these two surfaces.

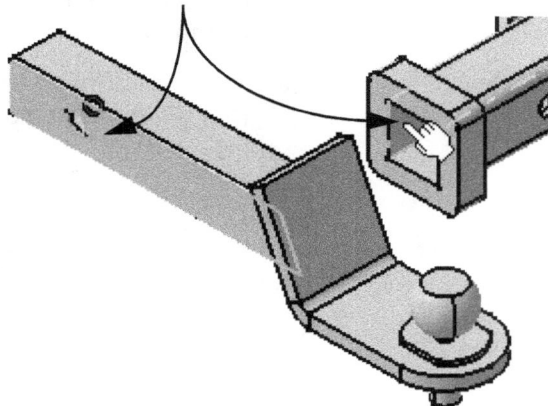

Figure 20–51

6. Select **Opposite** for the orientation and enter an *offset value* of **0.4 (0.016 in)**.

7. Click **OK** when finished.

8. Using ⛋ (Angle Constraint), apply a parallelism constraint between the surfaces shown in Figure 20–52.

Select these two surfaces.

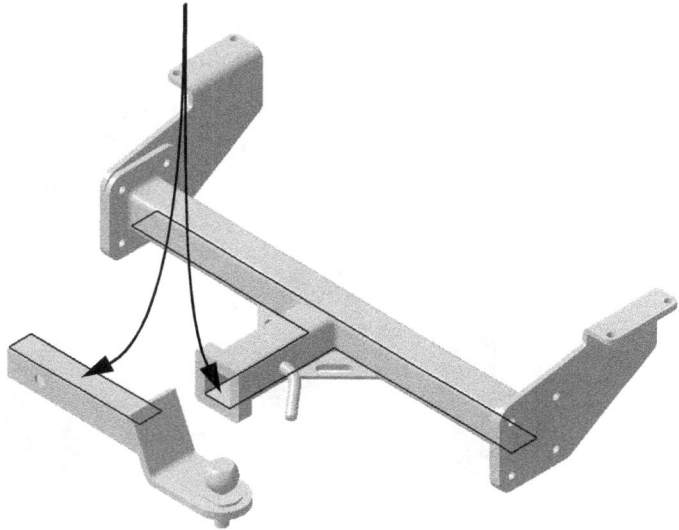

Figure 20–52

9. Update the assembly. The model displays as shown in Figure 20–53.

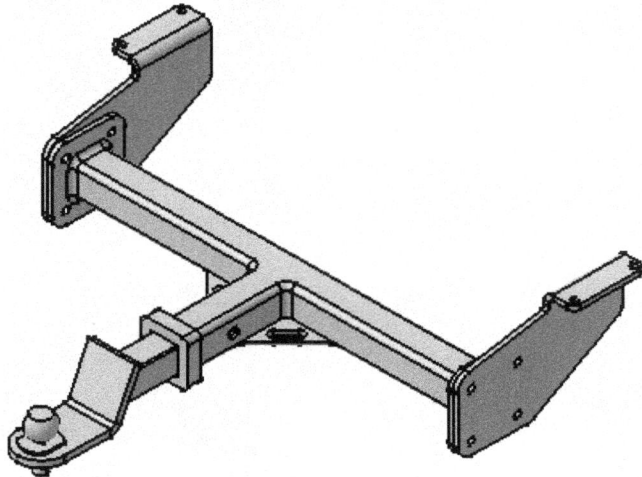

Figure 20–53

Task 5 - Assemble the pin.

1. Insert **Pin** into **65000011** by right-clicking and selecting **Components>Existing Component**.

2. Place the compass on the **T-Support**, and drag part **3100005** away from the model.

3. Create a coincidence constraint between the hole of the **T-Support** and the axis of the **Pin**, as shown in Figure 20–54.

4. Create an offset constraint and select the face of the **Pin** shown in Figure 20–55.

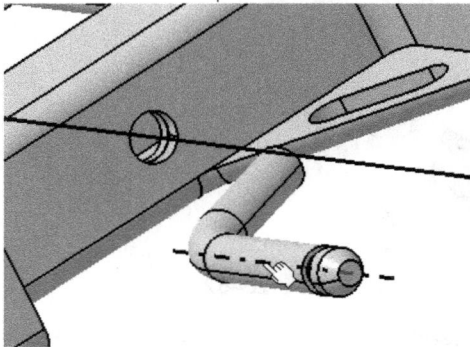

Figure 20–54

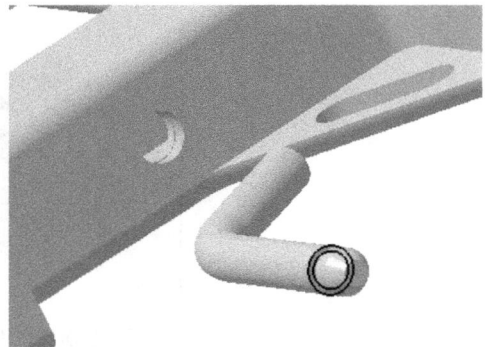

Figure 20–55

5. Select the face of **T-Support** shown in Figure 20–56. Set the following:

   • *Orientation*: **Same**
   • *Offset value*: **0**

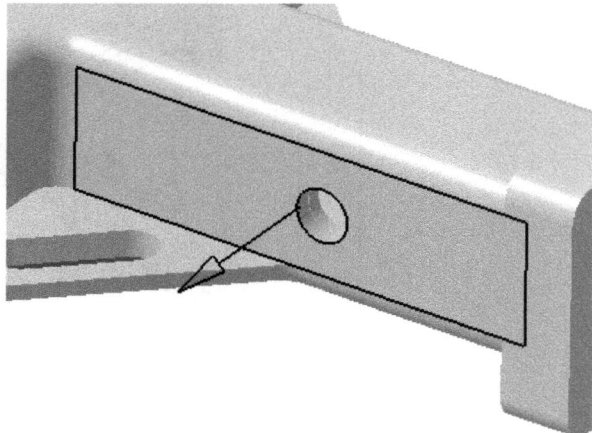

Figure 20–56

6. Update the assembly. The model displays as shown in Figure 20–57.

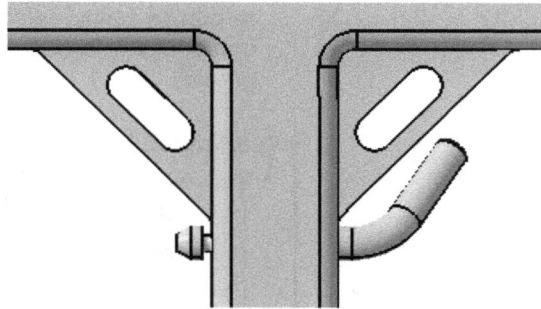

Figure 20–57

Task 1 - Assemble the Retaining_Pin.

In this task, you will position the **Retaining_Pin** model in the assembly and then constrain its location by fixing it to the Pin model.

1. Insert **Retaining_Pin** into **65000011** by right-clicking and selecting **Components>Existing Component**.

2. Using the compass, reposition **Retaining_Pin** to a location near the slotted end of Pin, as shown in Figure 20–58.

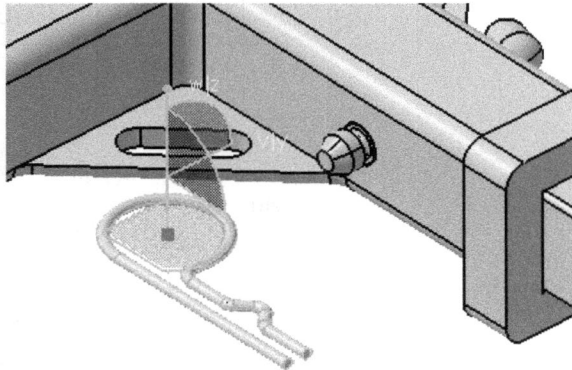

Figure 20–58

Design Considerations

Note the curved geometry of the **Retaining_Pin**. Few references can be selected from the model to position it relative to the **T-Support** and **Pin**. For this reason, reference elements have been added to the model that will assist during constraint creation.

3. Show the RefGeom geometrical set under **Retaining_Pin** (**3100006**) and **Pin** (**3100005**) in the specification tree. The **Retaining_Pin** model contains two reference planes and a reference point, as shown in Figure 20–59. The **Pin** model contains a reference plane located at the center of the groove.

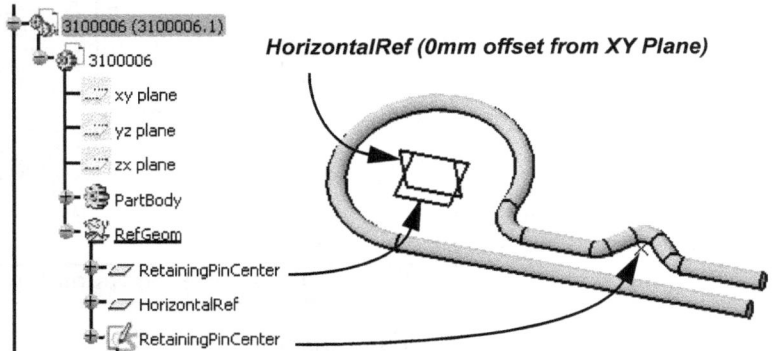

HorizontalRef (0mm offset from XY Plane)

Figure 20–59

4. Create the constraints using Figure 20–60 as a guide.

No.	Constraint	Reference 1	Reference 2
1	Coincident	Axis of Pin	RetainingPinCenter (sketched point) of Retaining Pin
2	Offset (0mm)	GrooveCenter (plane) of Pin	RetainingPinCenter (plane) of Retaining Pin
3	Parallelism	Face of T-Support	HorizontalRef (plane) of Retaining Pin

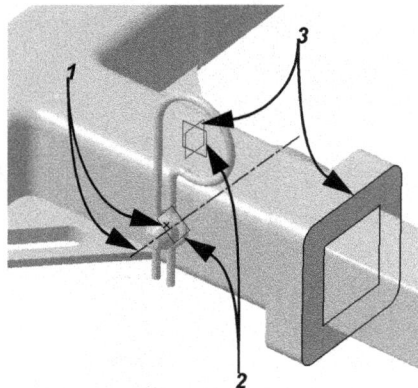

Figure 20–60

5. Update the assembly and hide **RefGeom** from **Retaining_Pin**. The completed model displays as shown in Figure 20–61.

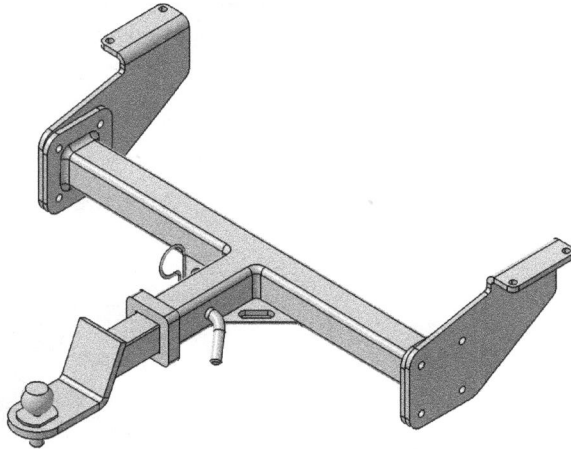

Figure 20–61

6. Save the file and close the assembly.

Practice 20c | Creating Assemblies III

Practice Objectives

- Create a new product.
- Apply constraints.

In this practice, you will create the assembly shown in Figure 20–62.

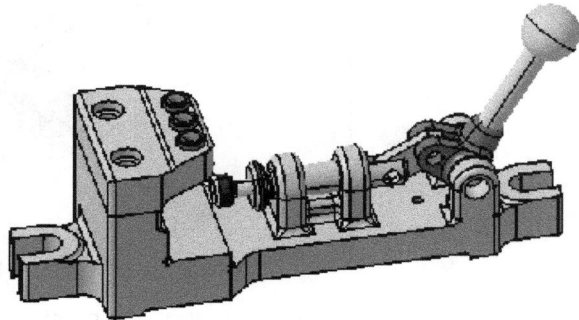

Figure 20–62

Task 1 - Create a new product file and assign properties.

1. Select **File>New** and select the **Product** option in the *Type* area.

2. Change the *part number* to **65200000**.

3. Save the file as **Bore-Device** in the *Bore_Fixture* folder.

4. Ensure that the units are set to millimeters.

Task 2 - Create the product structure.

1. Insert all ten parts contained in the *Bore_Fixture* folder into this assembly.

   Do not select **Bore-Device-Assembled.CATProduct**.

2. Place the compass onto the parts and drag the components so they can be easily seen, as shown in Figure 20–63.

Use <Ctrl> to select multiple files at once.

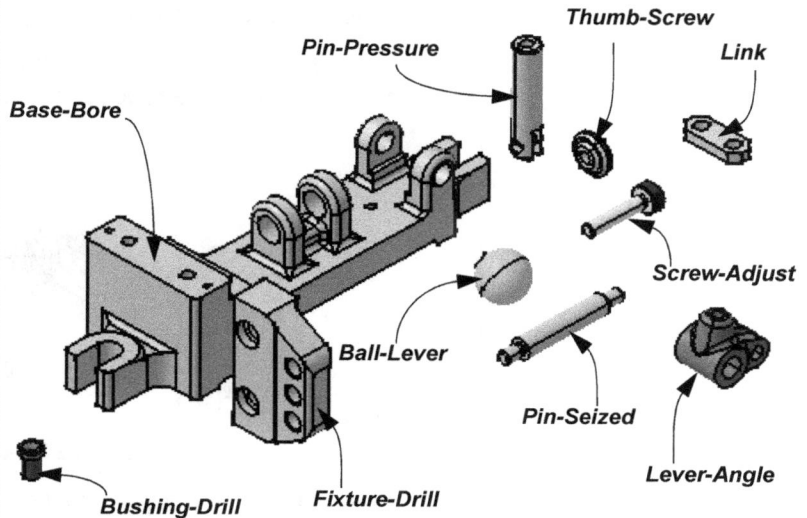

Figure 20–63

3. Create two new instances of the drill bushing (**3200003**) in the assembly.

4. Move the copies of the bushing so they can be easily seen in the display.

Task 3 - Assemble the components.

---

1. Fix the **Base-Bore** part (**3200000**).

2. Assemble the **Drill Fixture (3200001)** to the base shown in Figure 20–64. Use the coincidence, contact, and angle constraints.

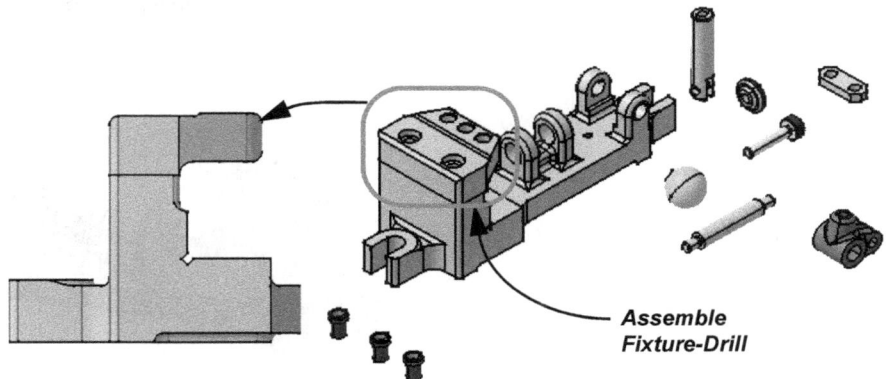

Figure 20–64

3. Assemble the three drill bushings into the drill fixture.

4. Assemble the **Ball-Lever 3200005**, **Pin-Seized 3200004**, and **Lever-Angle 3200002**, as shown in Figure 20–65.

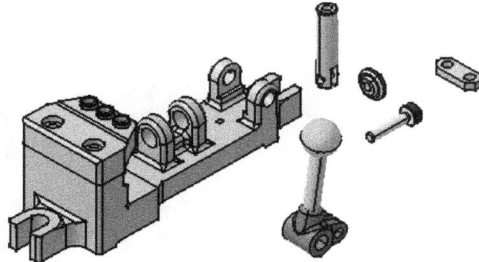

Figure 20–65

5. Assemble **Lever-Angle-3200002**, **Link-3200007**, and **Pin-Pressure 3200006,** as shown in Figure 20–66.

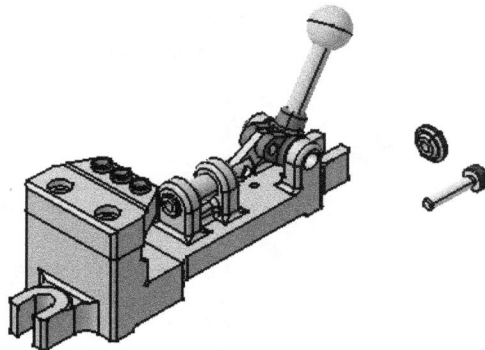

Figure 20–66

6. Assemble the remaining components, as shown in Figure 20–67.

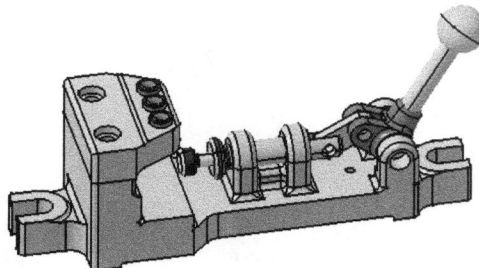

Figure 20–67

7. Save the file and close the assembly.

Practice 20d | (Optional) Motor Assembly

Practice Objective

- Create an assembly without instructions.

1. Insert the **Cylinder_Block**, **Crankshaft**, **Connecting_Rod**, and **Piston** part models. If you have not completed these parts, you can access completed models in the *Completed* folder.

2. Create a new assembly called **Motor**. Assemble the components to create the assembly shown in Figure 20–68.

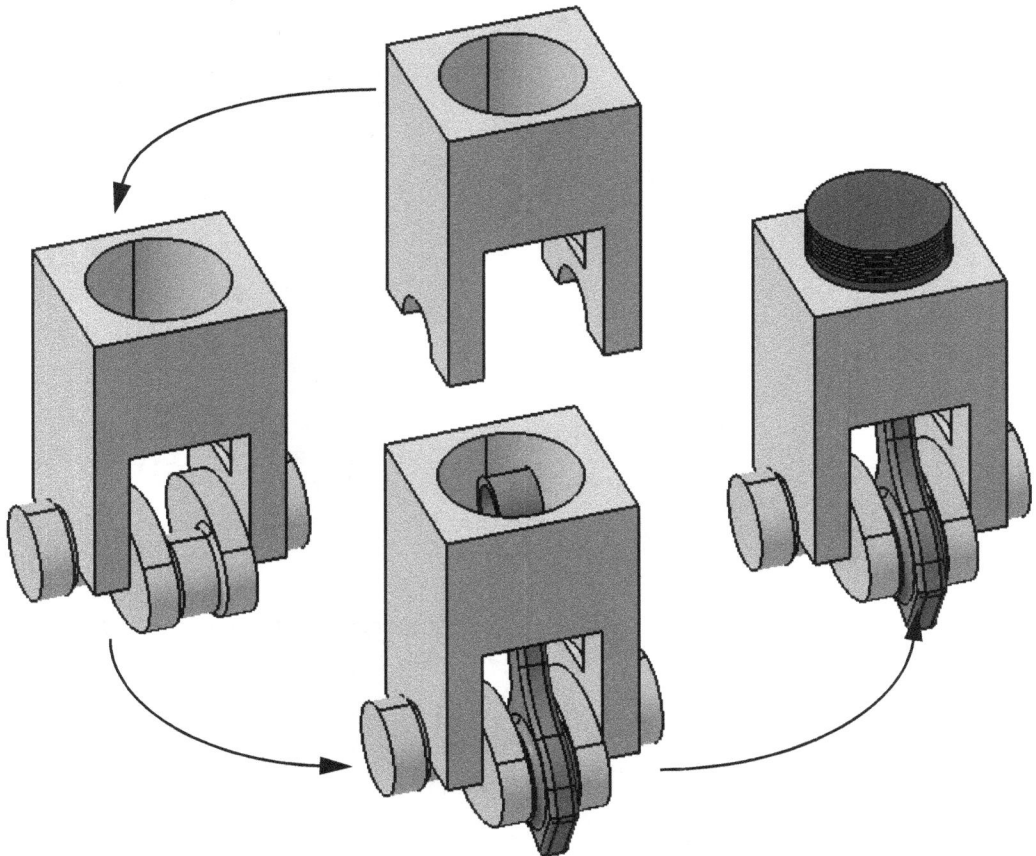

Figure 20–68

Chapter Review Questions

1. Which assembly constraint should be applied to the base component of a product?

    a.

    b.

    c.

    d.

2. What type of constraint would you use to define perpendicularity between components?

    a.

    b.

    c.

    d.

3. Parent/child relationships cannot exist between the components in an assembly.

    a. True

    b. False

4. What types of components can be added to a product? (Select all that apply.)

    a. *.CATPart

    b. *.CATProduct

    c. *.CATDrawing

    d. *.model

5. Multiple components can be added to an assembly at the same time.

    a. True

    b. False

6. Which constraint can be used to constrain a component so that two surfaces are mated but you maintain the flexibility of entering an offset value if the design intent changes?

    a. Contact

    b. Offset

    c. Coincidence

    d. Angle

7. Which of the assemblies shown in Figure 20–69 could have used the coincidence constraint to constrain surfaces C and 2 and surfaces A and 3? (Select all that apply.)

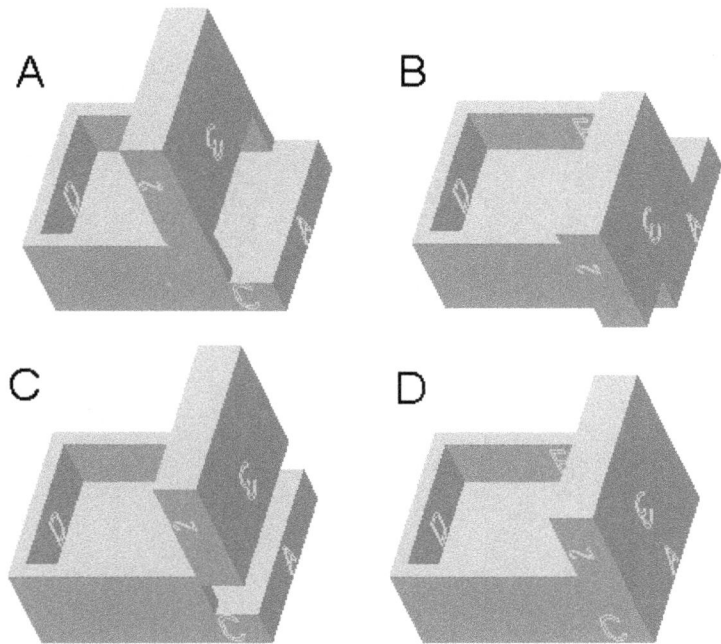

Figure 20–69

    a. A

    b. B

    c. C

    d. D

8. Once a constraint is created, the only way to change it to another type is to delete it and recreate it.

    a. True

    b. False

9. How can you force CATIA to obey the assembly constraints while moving components using the compass?

   a. Press and hold <Ctrl> while using the compass.

   b. Press and hold the middle mouse button while using the compass.

   c. Press and hold <Shift> while using the compass.

   d. Constraints cannot be obeyed when using the compass to move components.

Answers: 1.a, 2.d, 3.b, 4.abd, 5.a, 6.b, 7.cd, 8.b, 9.c

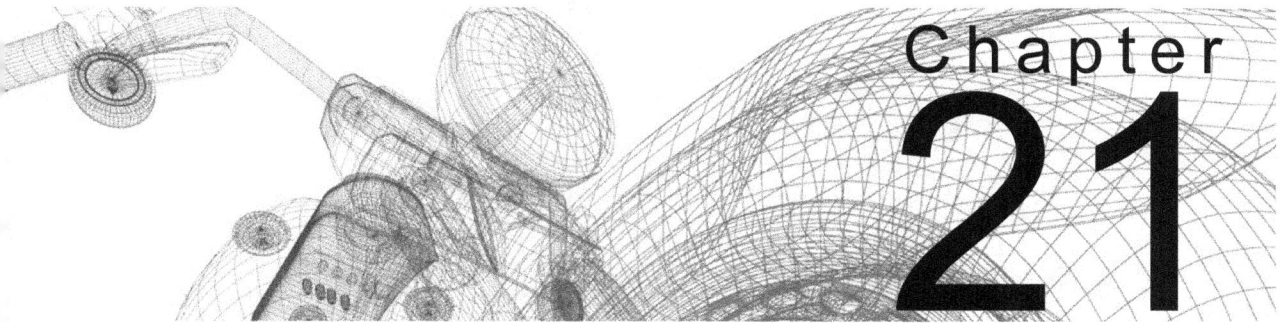

Assembly Techniques

Knowledge on additional assembly techniques, as well as how to design in context enables designers to work with greater efficiency. Additionally, designing in the context of an assembly simulates a top-down design philosophy.

Learning Objectives in this Chapter

- Place components using the Copy and Paste commands.
- Place multiple components using the same constraint command.
- Apply the Reuse Pattern command to quickly assemble components by referencing patterns.
- Use external references.

21.1 Additional Placement Options

If a component is used more than once in an assembly, you can add the components and position them accordingly using the Copy/Paste or Multi-constraint mode method.

Copy and Paste

Copy and Paste is an easy way to duplicate a component in an assembly. Select the required component from the specification tree, right-click and select **Copy**. Select the assembly that you want to copy into, right-click and select **Paste**. A duplicate instance of the component now exists. The instance name changes and can be modified, as shown in Figure 21–1.

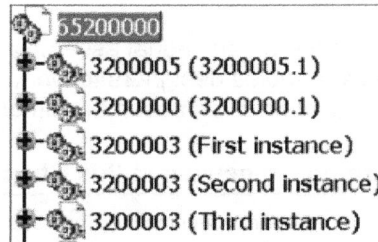

```
65200000
  3200005 (3200005.1)
  3200000 (3200000.1)
  3200003 (First instance)
  3200003 (Second instance)
  3200003 (Third instance)
```

Figure 21–1

- Copied components display directly *on top of* the original component in the assembly display. A copy (instance) must then be moved using the compass. Once moved, constraints can then be applied to position the copied component.

Multi-Constraint

Multi-constraint enables you to position many components using the same constraint command. To activate Multi-constraint mode, select the required mode in the Constraint Creation toolbar shown in Figure 21–2. Then, double-click on the required assembly constraint. Once constraints are applied, select the constraint to deactivate it.

Figure 21–2

Default Mode

Click ⬚ (Default Mode) to activate Default mode. The constraint that is selected can be applied between any references. Once the elements are selected, the constraint can be applied to the next set. Figure 21–3 shows an example of a model where the Default mode might be used. Each bolt axis must be specified along with the axis of the corresponding hole.

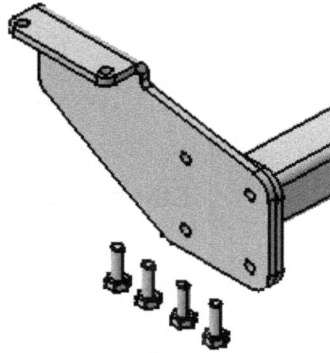

Figure 21–3

Chain Mode

Click ⬚ (Chain Mode) to activate Chain mode. Chain mode is useful when numerous components are offset incrementally from one another. Select the surfaces shown in Figure 21–4 as references and enter a value.

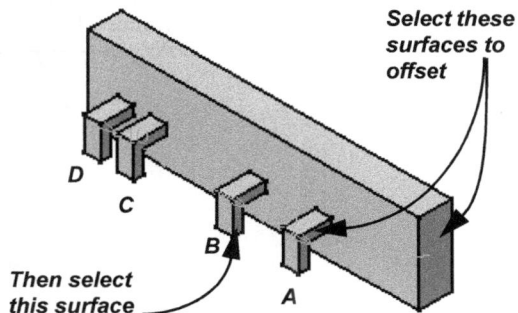

Select these surfaces to offset

Then select this surface

Figure 21–4

Select a reference surface on B part and enter an offset value in the Constraints Properties dialog box, as shown in Figure 21–5.

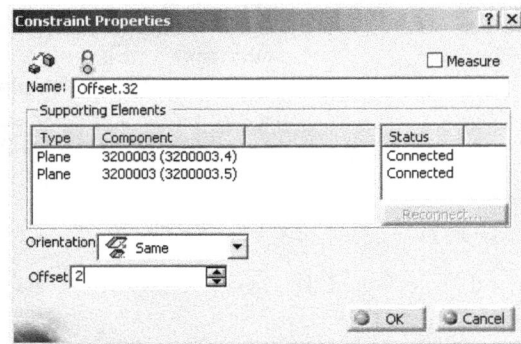

Figure 21–5

Stack Mode

Click ![icon] (Stack Mode) to activate Stack mode. Stack mode is used when a shared reference exists between parts. Figure 21–6 shows an example of a common reference as the surface of the plate. The underside surfaces of the bolts are then selected consecutively and the constraints are applied to the plate.

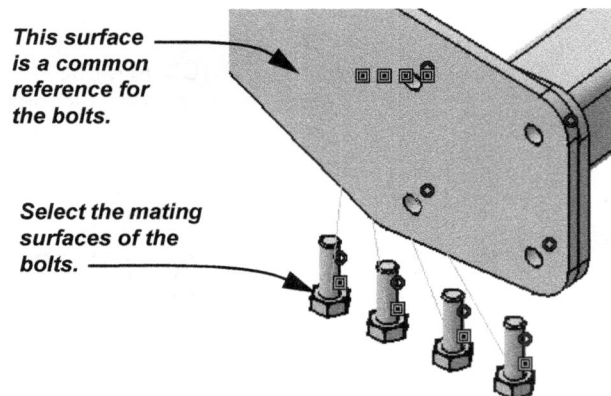

This surface is a common reference for the bolts.

Select the mating surfaces of the bolts.

Figure 21–6

Reuse Patterns

If a component is assembled by referencing the initial feature of a pattern, that pattern can be reused to quickly assemble more components. For example, the bolt shown in Figure 21–7 is assembled to the hole in the plate. This hole is the original hole that was patterned.

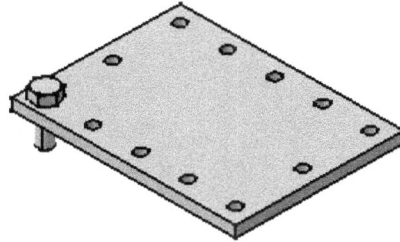

Figure 21–7

Click (Reuse Pattern). The Instantiation on a pattern dialog box opens as shown in Figure 21–8.

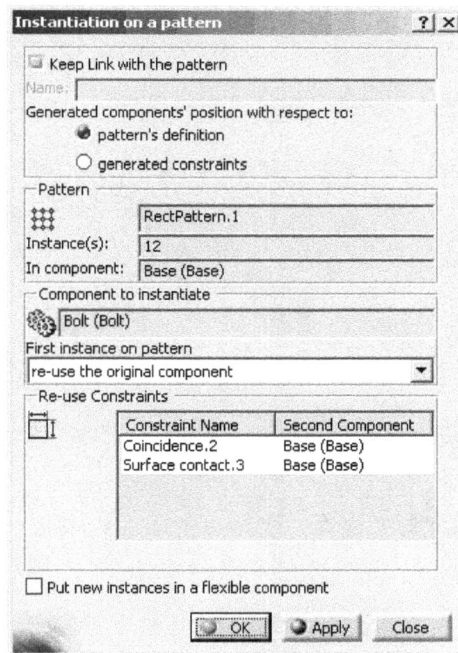

Figure 21–8

Select the corresponding pattern to place a bolt at each hole, as shown in Figure 21–9. The bolt can remain linked to the pattern, or the placement can be independent of the pattern.

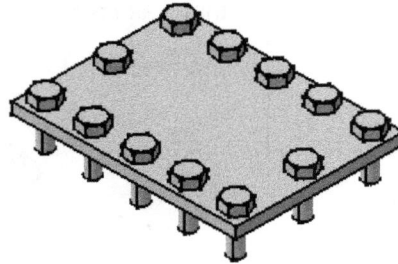

Figure 21–9

21.2 Designing in Context

CATIA has the ability to design in the context of an assembly. Parts and subassemblies can be created or modified in the presence of other components. Working in the context of the assembly is often referred to as *top-down design*.

While creating and/or editing components in the context of an assembly, external references can be created automatically. When creating external references, carefully consider the selection of the following items:

- Selection of sketching planes

- Dimensional references

- Constraints

- Depth option

External References

External references come from another part or product file. When designing in the context of the assembly, you can create external references depending on a configuration setting. If the reference changes position or shape, the feature making the reference associatively updates. To toggle on external references, select **Tools>Options>Infrastructure>Part Infrastructure**. Select the **Keep link with selected object** option to enable external references, as shown in Figure 21–10.

Discuss the recommended setting of this option with your system administrator.

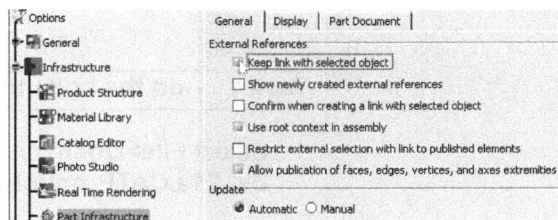

Figure 21–10

- If external references are not enabled, any references that result in external references are copied to the part as a geometrical set, and do not associatively update with changes.

- To edit a part in the context of the assembly, select the part in the specification tree and make it the active object (blue). Once active, the Part Design workbench is loaded. All other assembly components will still be visible and available for reference selection (provided external references have been enabled).

Practice 21a	# Repeating Component Placement

Practice Objectives

- Use the Multi-constraint tool.
- Reuse an existing pattern.

In this practice, you will complete the Hitch assembly by adding the remaining hardware. The completed assembly displays as shown in Figure 21–11. You will use the **Multi-constraint** tool and reuse existing patterns to efficiently constrain a number of small identical parts.

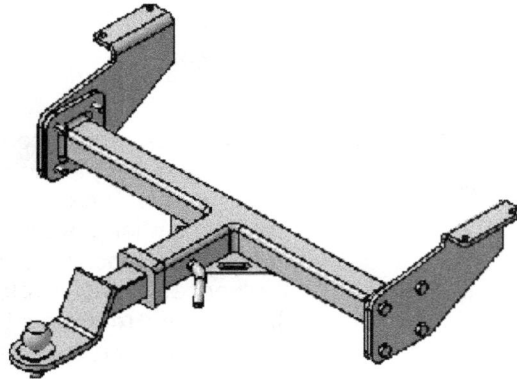

Figure 21–11

Task 1 - Add the bolts to the left side.

1. Select **File>Open**, and select the **Hitch_Complete_ Ex_21a.CATProduct** assembly from the *Hitch* folder.

   If you completed practice 20b, you will continue working with **Hitch.CATProduct** instead.

2. Add the existing **Bolt_14x1875_Lib,**component to the top-level assembly. The part displays as part number 100100 in the specification tree.

3. Move the compass onto the assembly and drag the bolt to the position shown in Figure 21–12.

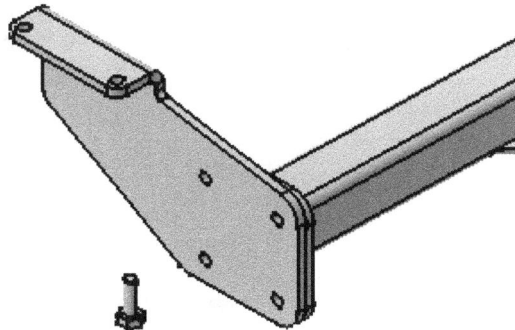

Figure 21–12

4. Three more bolts are required. Select **100100** in the specification tree and select **Edit>Copy**.

5. Select the top level assembly (**65000011**) in the specification tree and select **Edit>Paste**. Another instance displays in the assembly.

6. Repeat the previous step two more times. The copied instances are placed above the original.

7. Move the copies to the positions shown in Figure 21–13.

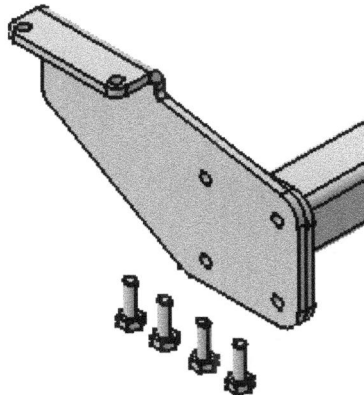

Figure 21–13

Design Considerations

Task 2 - Constrain the bolts using the Multi-constraint tool.

Constraining large numbers of identical parts using identical constraints can be time-consuming. The **Multi-constraint** tool enables you to reduce the number of required selections.

1. Click ⊞ (Default Mode) in the Constraint Creation toolbar.

2. Double-click on ⌾ (Coincidence Constraint). Apply this constraint to the axis of the bolt and the axis of the hole for each instance.

3. Click ⌾ (Coincidence Constraint) to deactivate it.

4. Click ↥↦ (Stack Mode) to change the Multi-constraint to Stack mode.

5. Double-click on ▦ (Contact Constraint). The first selection is shared by all instances.

6. Select the mounting surface of the **Left-Brace** and the bottom surfaces of the bolt heads, as shown in Figure 21–14.

Figure 21–14

7. Click ⬚ (Contact Constraint) to deactivate it.

8. Update the assembly. The bolts move into position, as shown in Figure 21–15.

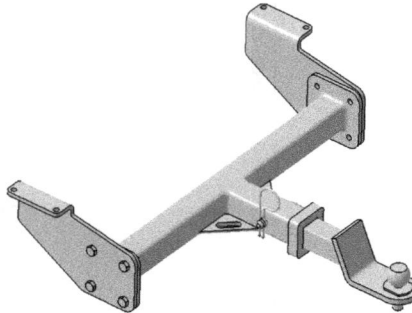

Figure 21–15

Task 3 - Add the bolts for the right side using the Reuse Pattern tool.

In this task, you will reuse a pattern developed in a part model to position bolts in the assembly. Before you begin to assemble the bolts, you will first investigate the pattern.

1. Expand **3100002** in the specification tree to view the features in the **PartBody**, as shown in Figure 21–16.

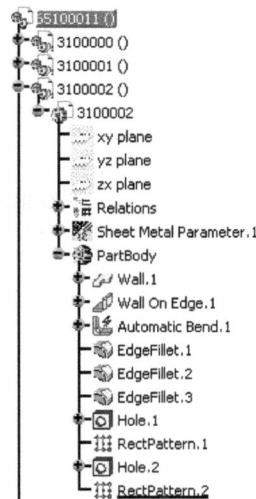

Figure 21–16

2. Select **Hole.1** in the specification tree and note the Hole feature that highlights on the model, as shown in Figure 21–17. This feature is termed the lead pattern feature, because it is the feature that was patterned.

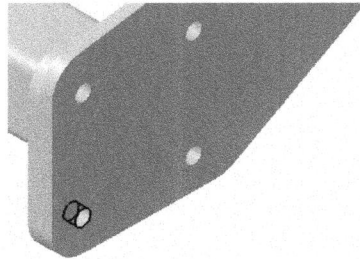

Figure 21–17

3. Highlight **RectPattern.1** and note that the remaining three holes are highlighted on the model.

4. Select any instance of the bolt in the specification tree and copy it to the top-level assembly.

5. Drag the copied bolt to the position shown in Figure 21–18.

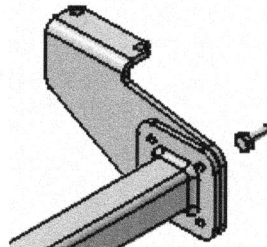

Figure 21–18

6. Use the coincidence and contact constraints to assemble the bolt to the **Lead Pattern** feature in **3100002**, as shown in Figure 21–19. Ensure that all assembly references point to the **3100002** component.

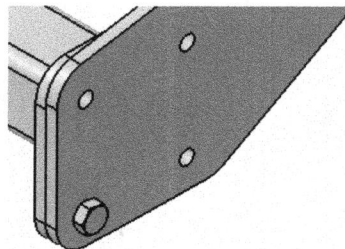

Figure 21–19

7. Select the newly constrained bolt.

8. Click ![icon](Reuse Pattern) in the Constraints toolbar.

9. Select **RectPattern.1** under **3100002**.

10. Click **OK** to accept the selection. The model displays as shown in Figure 21–20.

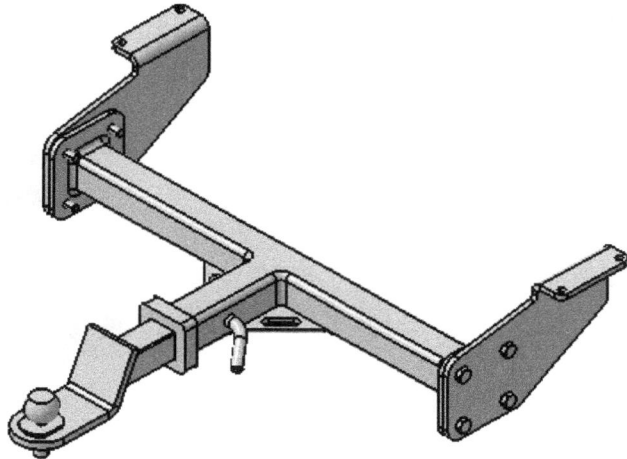

Figure 21–20

Task 4 - Assemble the remaining hardware.

1. Using **Nut_14_Lib**, repeat Tasks 1 to 3 to practice with Multi-constraint mode and use the **Reuse Pattern** tool to finish the Hitch assembly.

2. Save the assembly and close the window.

Practice 21b	# Designing in Context

Practice Objective

- Modify parts in assemblies.

In this practice, you will modify the **Bore-Device** assembly by adding holes at the part level, as shown in Figure 21–21. By creating the holes at the assembly level, all parts affected by the hole creation are automatically updated to reflect the creation of the holes.

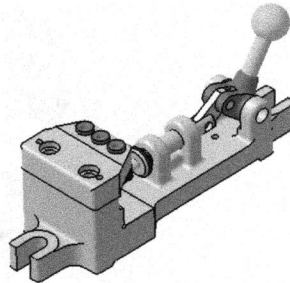

Figure 21–21

Task 1 - Open the Bore-Device assembly and activate Part Design workbench and create holes.

---

*If you completed practice 20c, you can continue working with the **Bore-Device** assembly instead.*

1. Select **File>Open**, and select **Bore-Device-Assembled** from the *Bore_Fixture* folder.

   The **Base-Bore** has two smaller holes that are not present in the Fixture-Drill part, as shown in Figure 21–22.

Two hole features

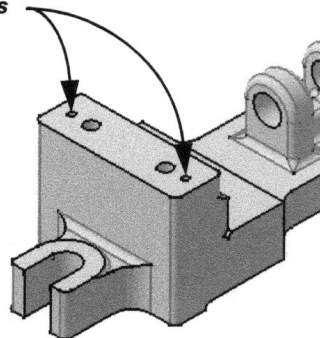

Figure 21–22

---

2. Change external reference settings by selecting **Tools> Options>Infrastructure>Part Infrastructure** and selecting the **Keep link with selected object** option, as shown in Figure 21–23.

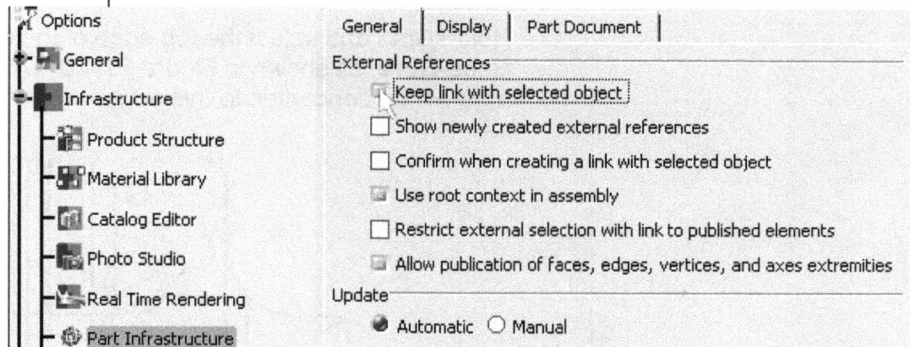

Figure 21–23

3. Activate the **Fixture-Drill** part by double-clicking on part **3200001** in the specification tree, as shown in Figure 21–24. The Part Design workbench is now activated. Note the change in icons.

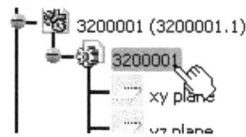

Figure 21–24

4. Select the surface of the drill fixture, as shown in Figure 21–25.

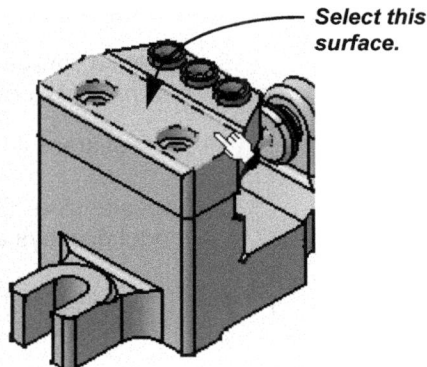

Select this surface.

Figure 21–25

5. Change the *Display mode* to **wireframe** by clicking

   ⊞ (Wireframe (NHR)).

6. Change the *orientation* to **Front View**.

7. Hold <Ctrl> and select the top edge of the existing hole in the **Base-Bore**, as shown in Figure 21–26. This ensures the new hole will be concentric to this edge.

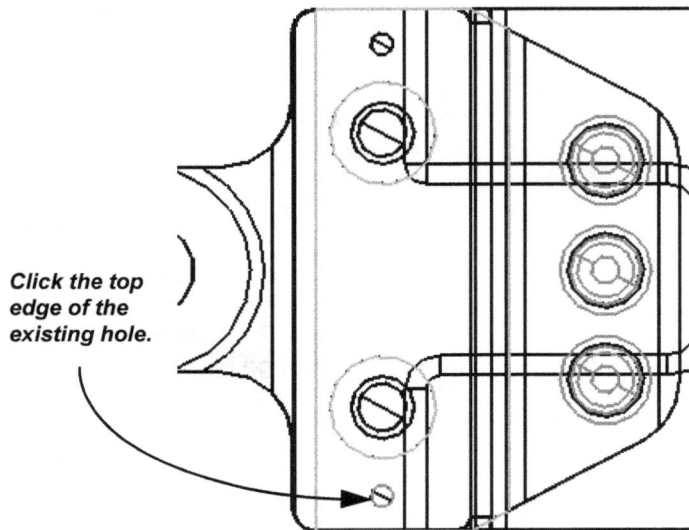

Click the top edge of the existing hole.

Figure 21–26

8. Click ◉ (Hole) to create a Hole feature. The Hole Definition dialog box opens.

9. Create a simple type Hole with a *diameter* of **5 (0.197 in)** and a *depth* of **Up to Last**.

10. Repeat steps 4., 7., 8., and 9. to create a second Hole on the opposite side. Click ▥ (Shading With Edges) and the model displays as shown in Figure 21–27.

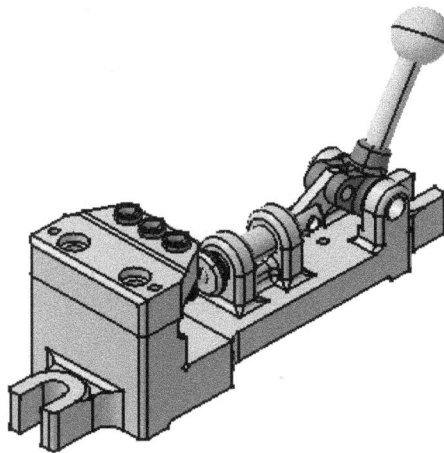

Figure 21–27

Task 2 - Incorporate design changes.

1. A design change requires that the position of the referenced hole feature be modified. Activate **Base-Bore** (**3200000**) from the specification tree.

2. Modify **Sketch.23** of **Hole.4**. Change the *5 (0.197 in)* *dimension* to **7.5 (0.295 in)**, as shown in Figure 21–28. Exit the sketch.

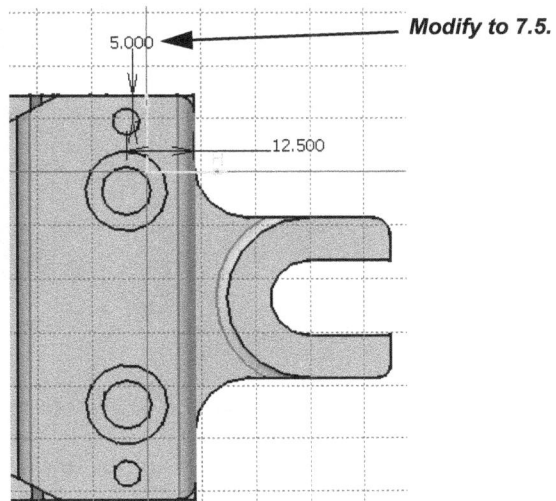

Figure 21–28

3. The model turns red as it automatically updates. Note that the **Fixture-Drill** (**3200001**) part has not been updated. Perform a local update on this part by right-clicking and selecting **Local Update**, as shown in Figure 21–29.

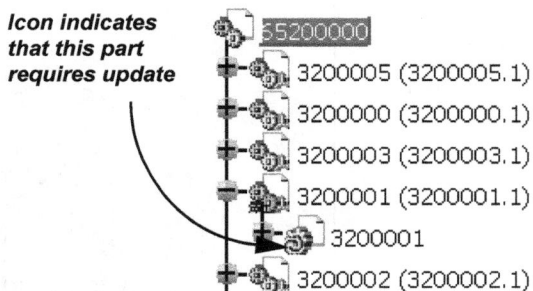

*Icon indicates
that this part
requires update*

55200000

3200005 (3200005.1)

3200000 (3200000.1)

3200003 (3200003.1)

3200001 (3200001.1)

3200001

3200002 (3200002.1)

Figure 21–29

4. The assembly displays as shown in Figure 21–30. View the assembly and note the updated position of the holes.

Figure 21–30

5. Save the assembly and close the window.

Chapter Review Questions

1. What tool can be used to assemble multiple components to the same shared reference?

    a.

    b.

    c.

2. To use the **Reuse Pattern** tool, the component to be patterned must be constrained relative to the initial feature of the pattern.

    a. True

    b. False

3. Where is a copied component placed into the assembly?

    a. At the origin of the assembly.

    b. On top of the original component.

    c. There is no way of knowing, it is random.

    d. In the same location as it would be if it was inserted into the assembly using the **Insert>Existing component** tool.

4. What does the **Keep link with selected object** option do? The option is located in **Tool>Options>Infrastructure>Part Infrastructure**.

    a. Enables external references.

    b. Disables external references.

    c. Creates a report of external references.

    d. None of the above.

5. Working in the context of an assembly is often referred to as_____.

    a. Bottom up approach.

    b. Top down approach.

    c. Multi-body approach.

    d. None of the above.

6. Parent/child relationships are created between components when creating external references.

   a. True

   b. False

7. How do you edit a part in the context of the assembly? (Select all that apply.)

   a. Double-click on the part in the specification tree.

   b. Right-click on the part in the specification tree and select **x object>Edit**.

   c. Click .

   d. You cannot edit a part within the context of the assembly.

Answers: 1.b, 2.a, 3.b, 4.a, 5.b, 6.a, 7.ab

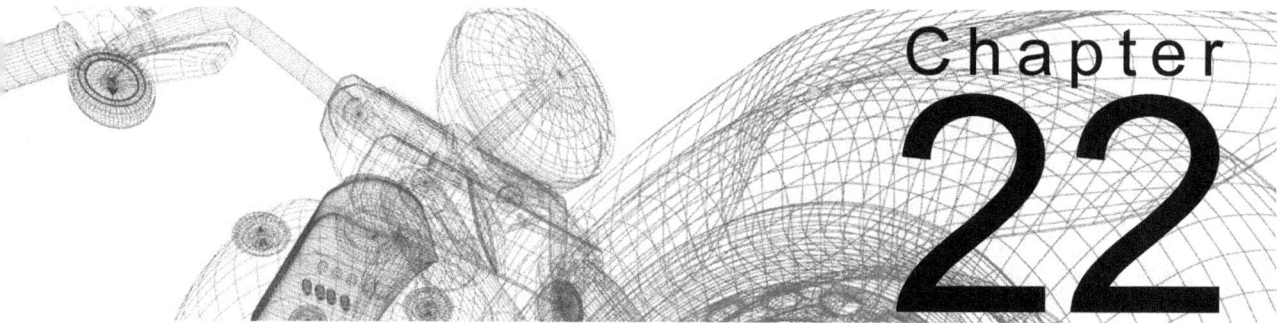

Assembly Information

This chapter covers the techniques that you can use to obtain information about an assembly. The Measure toolbar enables you to take measurements of the assembly in the same way that you take measurements of parts. The Clash and Clearance Analysis tool enables you to determine whether any interference is present in the assembly. Additionally, the bill of materials enables you to generate a list of the components that are used in the assembly.

Learning Objectives in this Chapter

- Use the measurement toolbar options for assembly components.
- Apply materials to components.
- Determine whether interference exists in an assembly.
- Create a Bill of Material report.

22.1 Measurements

CATIA provides tools to extract important information from your assembly model. The Measurements toolbar enables you to perform the following functions:

- Measure the distance between items on different parts.

- Measure the distance between items on a single part.

- Measure the mass properties of the assembly.

These functions can be accessed using the **Analyze** menu in the menu bar or the Measure toolbar, as shown in Figure 22–1.

Figure 22–1

Component Materials

Materials can be applied to the components of an assembly in the Part Design or Assembly Design workbench. Using the Assembly Design workbench, this can be accomplished by selecting the specific component(s) in the specification tree before applying the material. When finished, the system considers each component's material property when performing measure inertia calculations.

- If the entire assembly is to be manufactured from the same material, it is faster to apply this material to the assembly and not to the components. This is done by selecting the assembly from the tree when applying the material.

22.2 Clash and Clearance

When creating an assembly, the software permits interference between components. The clash functionality must be used to determine whether interference exists. A clash analysis also calculates the degree of interference.

*This analysis can also be run from the **Analyze** menu.*

To run a clash analysis, click ![icon] (Clash) in the Space Analysis toolbar. In the Check Clash dialog box, select **Contact + Clash** from the Type drop-down list. The scope of products to include in the calculation must then be selected from the drop-down list below the Type drop-down list. To see the results of this analysis, click **Apply**. The results display as shown in Figure 22–2. If any conflicts occur, you can select and preview the result.

Note that the dialog boxes in this chapter may vary slightly depending on the license you have.

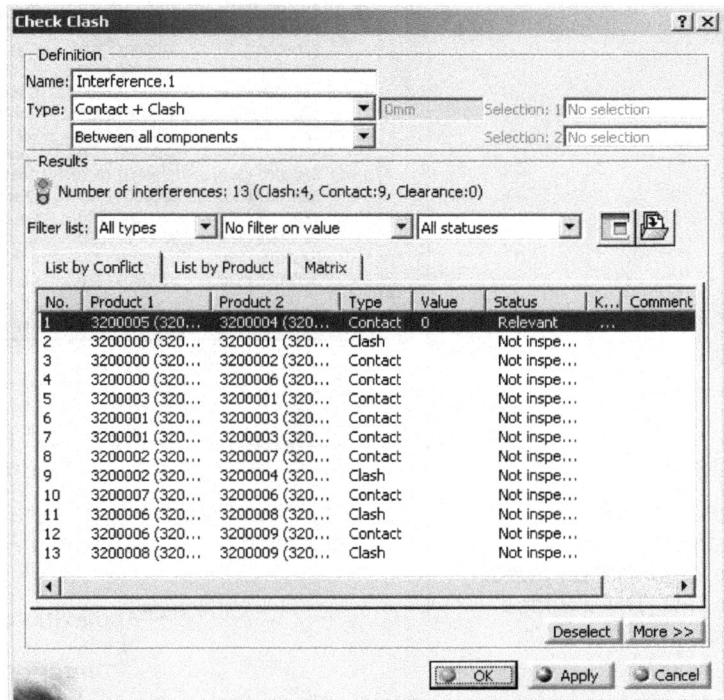

Figure 22–2

To check the minimum amount of clearance between components, select **Clearance + Contact + Clash** in the Type drop-down list. Set the scope of components to include in the analysis and click **Apply**. The results display as shown in Figure 22–3.

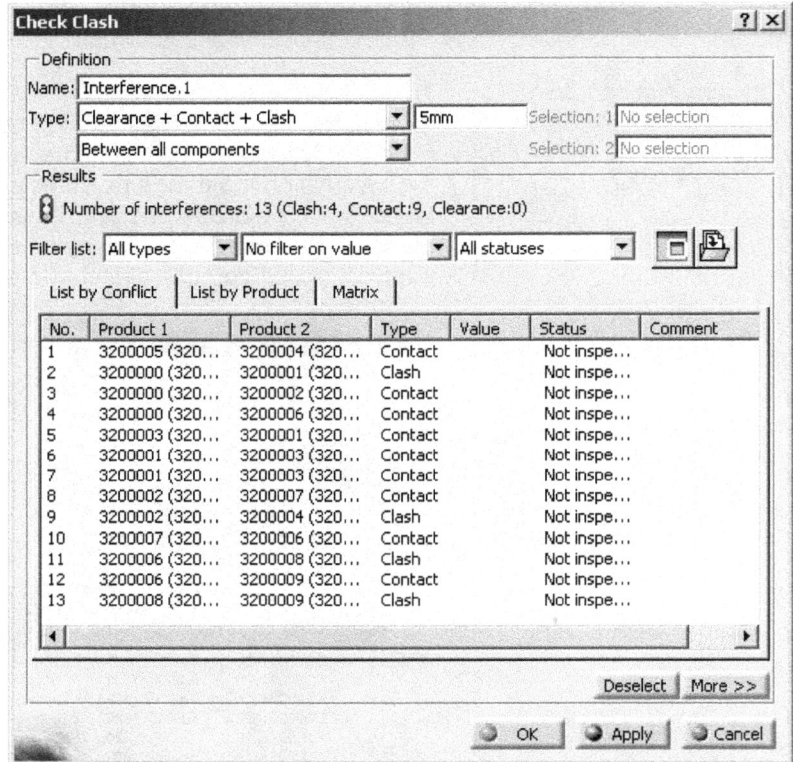

Figure 22–3

The interference analysis is only added to the specification tree if an SPA (DMU Space Analysis) license is obtained.

The results of both analyses are stored under Applications in the specification tree, as shown in Figure 22–4.

Figure 22–4

22.3 Creating Bill of Material Report

The Bill of Material (BOM) report is used to examine which components are used in the assembly and the numbers of each component present in the assembly.

How To: Create a Bill of Material Report

1. Activate the assembly by double-clicking on its name in the specification tree.
2. Select **Analyze>Bill of Material...**, as shown in Figure 22–5.

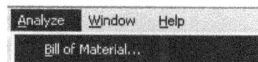

Figure 22–5

3. A Bill of Material report is generated. Two tabs of information display. The *Bill Of Material* tab shows the BOM, as shown in Figure 22–6. The report shows the top level BOM for the assembly and the BOM for each subassembly. The *Recapitulation* area shows all individual parts that are required to construct the top level assembly.

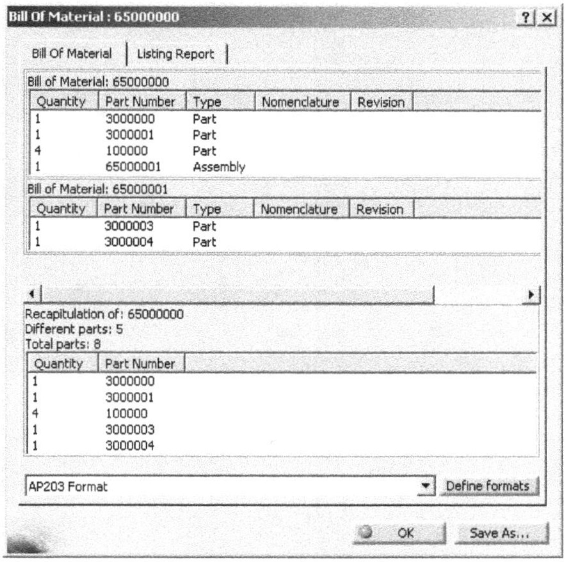

Figure 22–6

The *Listing Report* tab provides additional information about the components. The instance name and product description are added as additional displayed properties, as shown in Figure 22–7.

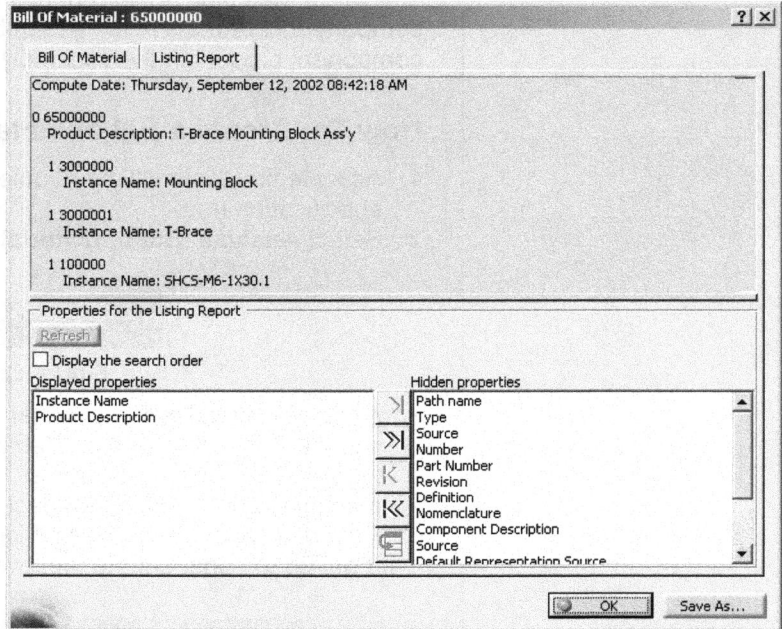

Figure 22–7

The BOM report can be exported out of CATIA by clicking **Save As**. The file can be stored as a text, HTML, or Excel file. However, the listing report can only be exported as a text file.

Practice 22a

Assembly Information

Practice Objectives

- Extract measurements from the assembly.
- Create a BOM.
- Calculate interference.

Task 1 - Open the Hitch assembly.

1. Select **File>Open** and select the **Hitch_Complete** assembly from the *Hitch* folder.

2. Fit the model to the display area and activate the isometric view. The assembly displays as shown in Figure 22–8.

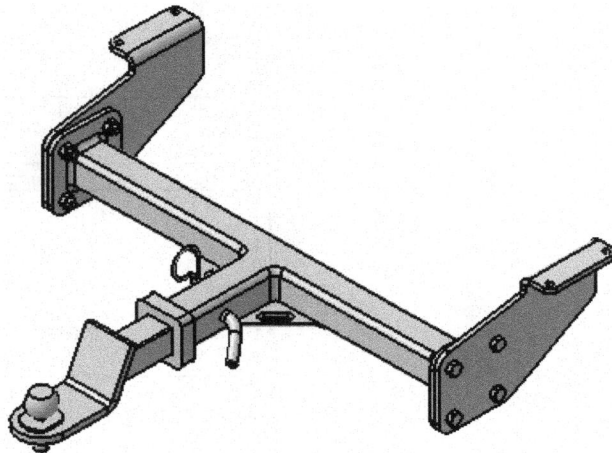

Figure 22–8

3. Ensure that the top level assembly is the active object.

*If you completed Practice 21a, you can continue working with **Hitch.CATProduct** instead.*

4. Select **Analyze>Bill of Material**. The Bill Of Material dialog box opens, as shown in Figure 22–9.

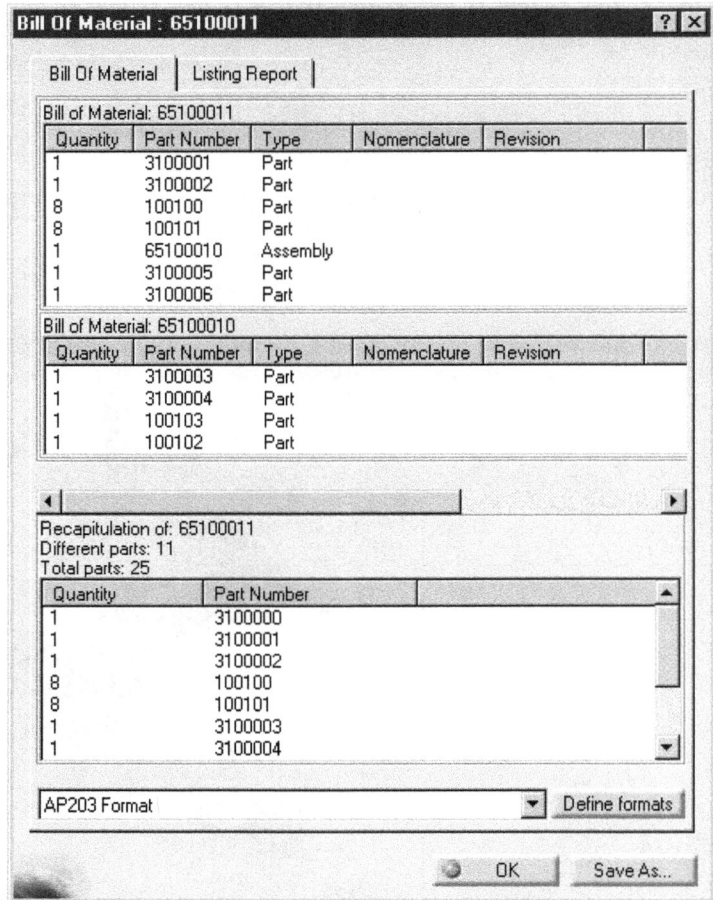

Figure 22–9

Note the structure of the report. Since a subassembly (**65100010**) is in the top level, its bill of materials is also reported.

5. Click **Save As**.

6. Save the BOM as a text file called **hitch-tla**.

7. Repeat the previous step for an Excel spreadsheet and for an HTML document.

8. Click **OK** when finished with the report.

9. Use Windows Explorer to browse to the *Hitch* folder, as shown in Figure 22–10.

ball mount.CATProduct	32 KB	CATIA Product
Ball.CATPart	121 KB	CATIA Part
Bolt_14x1875_Lib.CATPart	79 KB	CATIA Part
Hitch_1.CATProduct	34 KB	CATIA Product
Hitch_Complete.CATProduct	96 KB	CATIA Product
hitch-tla.html	3 KB	HTML Document
hitch-tla.txt	4 KB	Text Document
hitch-tla.xls	3 KB	Microsoft Excel Worksheet
Left-Brace.CATPart	281 KB	CATIA Part
Nut_14_Lib.CATPart	86 KB	CATIA Part
Nut_38_Lib.CATPart	87 KB	CATIA Part
Pin.CATPart	106 KB	CATIA Part
Retaining_Pin.CATPart	97 KB	CATIA Part
Right-Brace.CATPart	283 KB	CATIA Part
Slide.CATPart	323 KB	CATIA Part
T-Support.CATPart	597 KB	CATIA Part
Washer_Lib.CATPart	61 KB	CATIA Part

Figure 22–10

10. Open the saved BOM files to view the format of the three BOM files.

Task 2 - Check for interference.

---

1. Select **Analyze>Clash** in the menu bar. The Check Clash dialog box opens.

2. Set the following, as shown in Figure 22–11:

   - *Type:* **Contact + Clash**
   - *Type (second drop-down):* **Between all components**

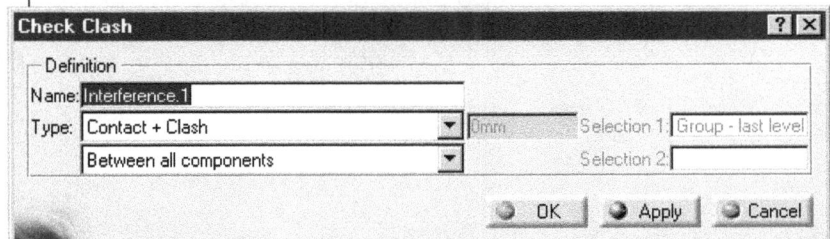

Figure 22–11

3. Click **Apply**. The results of the clash check are shown in Figure 22–12.

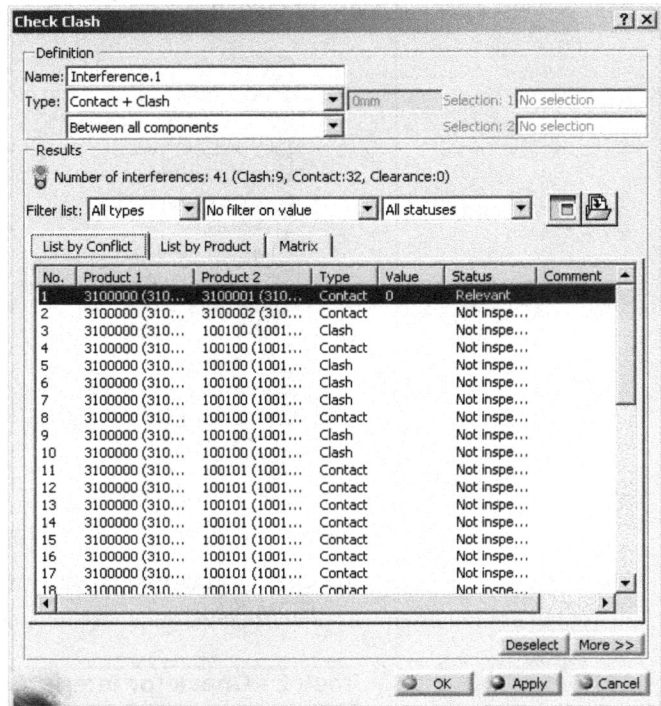

Figure 22–12

4. Note the detected clash conditions listed in the *Type* column.

5. Select the first row where clash is indicated. A preview window displays that shows the place of clash on the model. The clash is between the **T-Support** and the **Bolt**.

6. Continue to review the other clashes in the model. There is problem with the placement of some of the bolts, and possibly the retaining pin, and the **Ball_Mount** assembly.

7. Click **OK** to close the window.

Task 3 - Investigate the cause of the clash with measurements.

1. Click ⬛ (Measure Item) to investigate.

2. Select the edge of the support as shown in Figure 22–13. Its value is **89.2mm (3.512 in)**.

3. Select the edge shown in Figure 22–14. Its value is also **89.2mm (3.512 in).** These dimensions are used for the increment of the hole pattern.

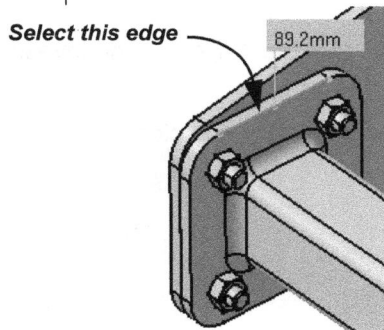

Figure 22–13

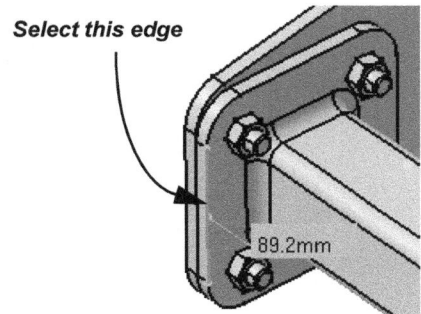

Figure 22–14

You might have to close the Measure Item dialog box to verify the dimensional increment of RectPattern.

4. Verify that the dimensional increment of **RectPattern.1** and **RectPattern.2** for part **3100000** is 89.2mm (3.512 in) in both directions.

5. Click ↔ (Measure Between) in the Measure dialog box.

6. Measure between the spacing of the holes in the brace, as shown in Figure 22–15.

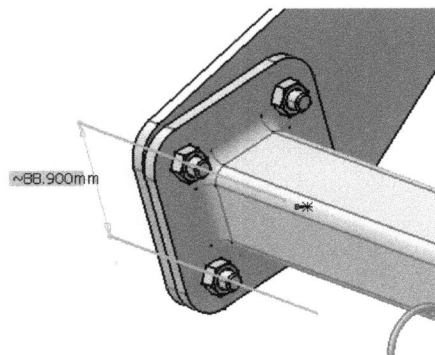

Figure 22–15

7. Note that the hole spacing for this pattern is **88.9 (3.5 in)** and not 89.2 (3.512 in), which is the dimension used by the pattern.

8. Modify the spacing of **RectPattern.1** in both the **3100001** and **3100002** parts to **89.2 (3.512 in)**.

9. Update the assembly. Ensure that the top-level assembly is active by double-clicking on **65100011** in the specification tree.

10. Check for clash again. There should not be any clash involving the bolts.

11. Click (Measure Inertia) and investigate the mass properties.

12. Save the assembly and close the window.

Chapter Review Questions

1. You must be in the Part Design workbench to apply material to a component.
   a. True
   b. False

2. Mass Properties of an assembly can be calculated using which of the following tools?

   a.

   b.

   c.

   d.

3. Material can be applied to the entire assembly or individual components, if required.
   a. True
   b. False

4. In the Check Clash dialog box, clicking **OK** runs the analysis and closes the dialog box while clicking **Apply** keeps the dialog box open, enabling you to review the results of the analysis.
   a. True
   b. False

5. What types of analysis can be reviewed in the Check Clash dialog box? (Select all that apply.)
   a. Clash
   b. Contact
   c. Clearance

6. A Bill of Material report can be exported out of CATIA to either an HTML or an Excel file.
   a. True
   b. False

7. A bill of material is generated for an assembly where the current active model is a part in a subassembly. Which of the following options is correct as shown in Figure 22–16?

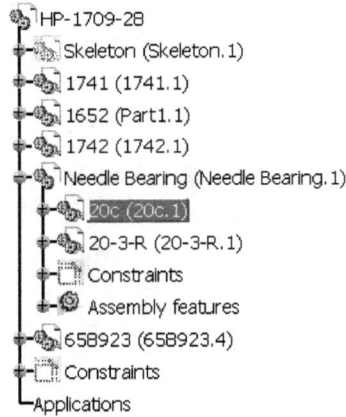

Figure 22–16

   a. The Bill of Material always reports the top-level assembly.

   b. The Bill of Material reports all components in the subassembly that the active part is in.

   c. The Bill of Material reports only the active part.

   d. The Bill of Material fails.

8. In the Check Clash dialog box, a negative number in the *Value* column indicates _____.

   a. Contact

   b. Clearance

   c. Clash.

   d. None of the above.

Answers: 1.a, 2.b, 3.a, 4.a, 5.abc, 6.a, 7.c, 8.c

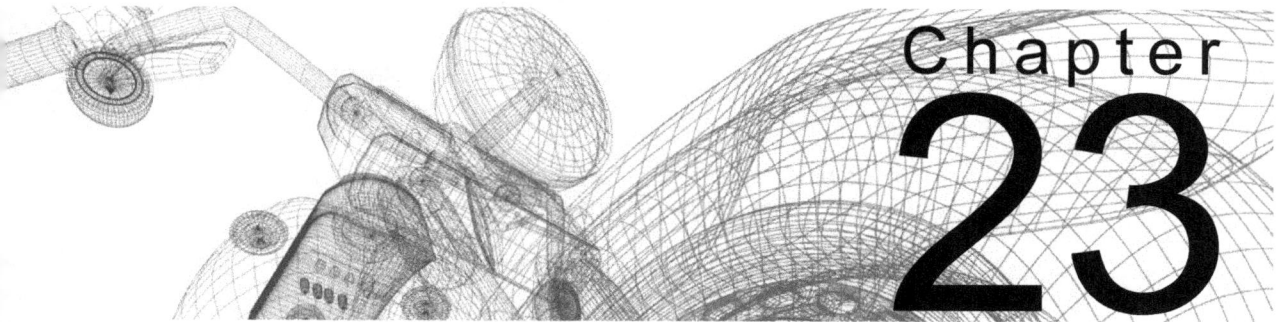

Catalogs and Save Management

This chapter discusses how to use catalog parts and save management. The catalog enables you to browse through CATIA's library of industry standard fasteners and common parts. Save management enables you to save modifications made to a component by saving the part with a new name.

Learning Objectives in this Chapter

- Access and use the default library of fasteners and components.
- Learn how to replace components using Save Management.

23.1 Catalog Parts

CATIA V5 contains a library of industry-standard fasteners and common parts. These parts are stored in a catalog. In the catalog, click ⬦ (Catalog Browser). The Catalog Browser dialog box opens, as shown in Figure 23–1.

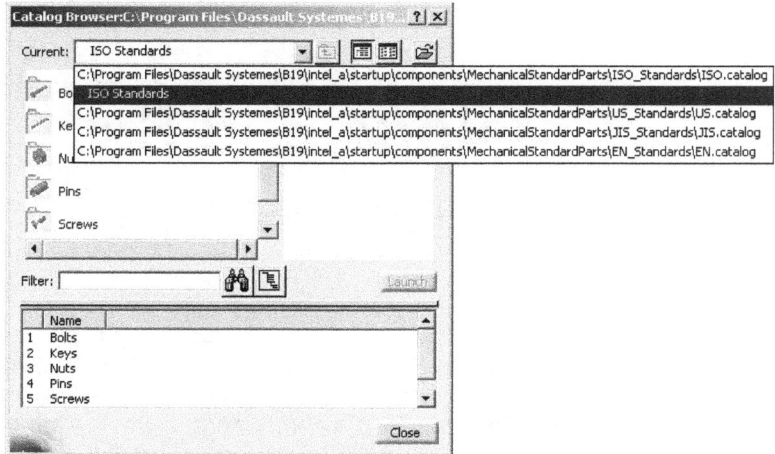

Figure 23–1

Default standards include the following:
- ISO
- EN
- JIS
- US

Groups of standard fasteners include the following:
- Screws
- Bolts
- Nuts
- Washers
- Pins
- Keys

You can select a standard fastener from the Catalog Browser dialog box, as shown in Figure 23–2.

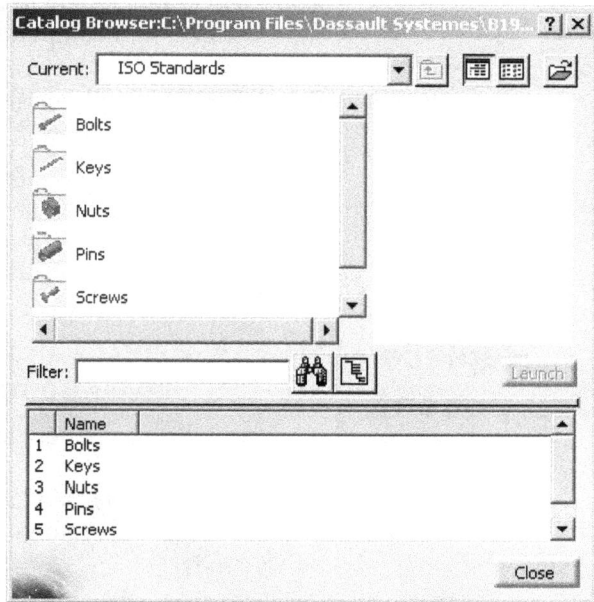

Figure 23–2

Once selected, a catalog part is opened into the CATProduct file and can be assembled into an assembly file.

23.2 Using Save Management

The Save Management functionality enables you to make modifications to a component in an assembly and save the changes to a part file with a different name. To enable the rapid modification of components and creation of similar part files, activate the Part Design workbench for a specific part while working in an assembly.

Once variations of a particular part have been created and saved, **Replace Component** can be used to quickly explore various design alternatives.

Replace Component

How To: Replace an Assembled Component with a Similar Component

1. Select the component to be replaced.

2. Click (Replace Component).
3. Select the replacement component from the working directory.

You can only replace components that have been modified from an existing component, and saved with a different name using **Save Management**. The software updates the assembly once a component has been replaced.

Assembly constraints do not have to be redefined when replacing a component that has been created using **Save Management**. Any child components of the replaced component automatically reference the replacement components.

Save Management combined with **Replace Component** enables efficient design changes and exploration of the *what if* scenarios typical of an early prototype environment.

Practice 23a | Catalog Parts

Practice Objectives

- Open and use catalog parts.
- Use Save management.

In this practice, you will modify an assembly so that it displays as shown in Figure 23–3. You will assemble catalog parts into the assembly and use **Save Management** to save a modified version of a component. You will then replace the modified component with the original component.

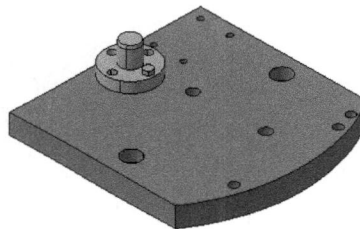

Figure 23–3

Task 1 - Open the Fixture assembly.

1. Open **Fixture.CATProduct** from the *Assembly_Jig* folder. Verify that the units are set to millimeters.

2. Measure the distance between the surfaces of the two parts, as shown in Figure 23–4.

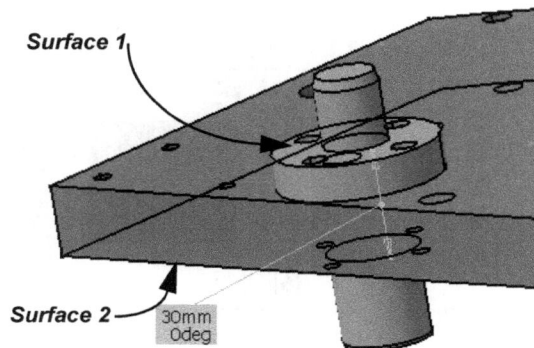

Figure 23–4

The distance is 30 mm (1.181 in). In the following task, you will assemble a catalog bolt with a length of 30 mm (1.181 in).

Task 2 - Assemble a part from the standard catalog.

*You can also open the Catalog Browser dialog box by selecting **Tools> Catalog Browser**.*

1. Click 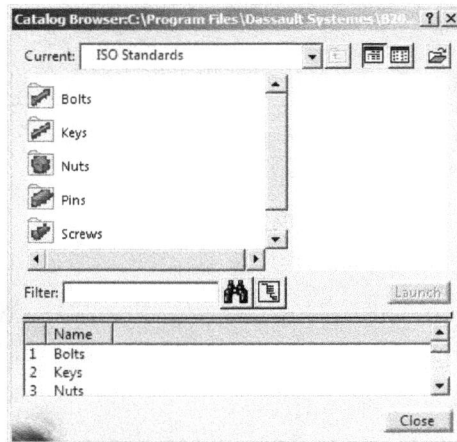 (Catalog Browser). The Catalog Browser dialog box opens as shown in Figure 23–5.

Figure 23–5

2. Select the **ISO Standards** option in the Current drop-down list.

3. Double-click on **Bolts** in the displayed list.

4. Double-click on **ISO_4016_GRADE_C_HEXAGON_ HEAD_BOLT**, as shown in Figure 23–6.

5. Double-click on **ISO 4016 BOLT M6x30 STEEL GRADE**, as shown in Figure 23–7.

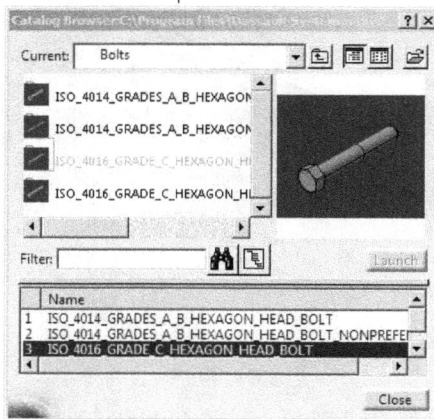

Figure 23–6

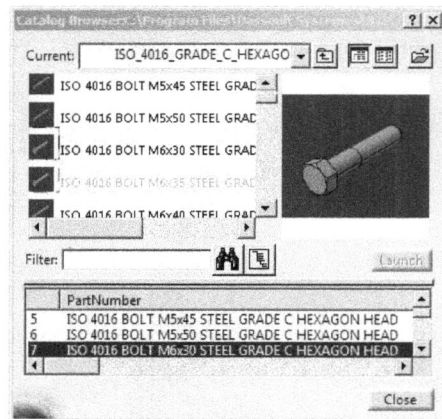

Figure 23–7

The selected bolt displays in the Catalog dialog box, as shown in Figure 23–8.

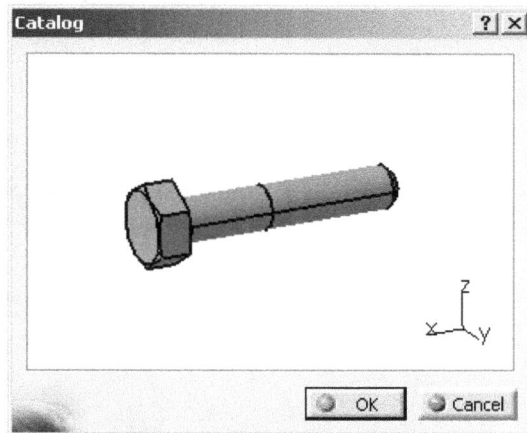

Figure 23–8

6. Click **OK** in the Catalog dialog box and click **Close** in the Catalog Browser dialog box. The selected catalog bolt displays, as shown in Figure 23–9.

7. Assemble the bolt, as shown in Figure 23–10.

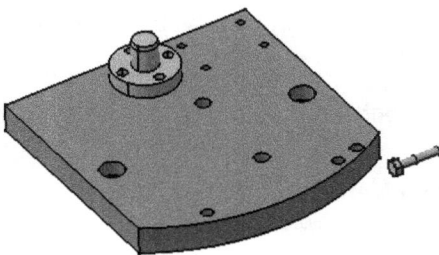

Figure 23–9

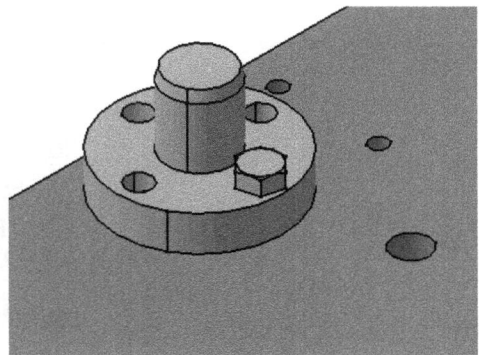

Figure 23–10

8. Rotate the assembly to view the bottom surface of the plate to ensure that the bolt is the correct length.

Task 3 - Modify a component.

1. Activate **Pivot_Shaft**. Ensure that the Part Design workbench is active.

2. Create a simple hole coincident with the center of the **Pivot_Shaft** with a *diameter* of **7 mm (0.276 in)** and a *blind depth* of **50 mm (1.969 in)**.

3. Activate the top level assembly. The **Pivot_Shaft** displays as shown in Figure 23–11.

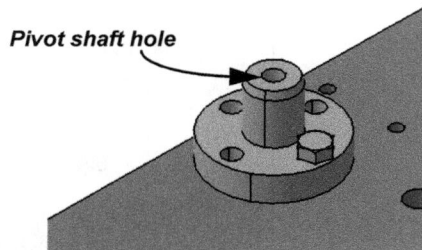

Figure 23–11

4. Right-click on **Pivot_Shaft** and select **Properties**.

5. Select the *Product* tab and rename the *Part Number* as **Shaft_Center_Hole**.

Task 4 - Use save management to save a variation of a component.

1. Close any document windows not used with the current practice.

2. Select **File>Save Management**. The Save Management dialog box opens as shown in Figure 23–12.

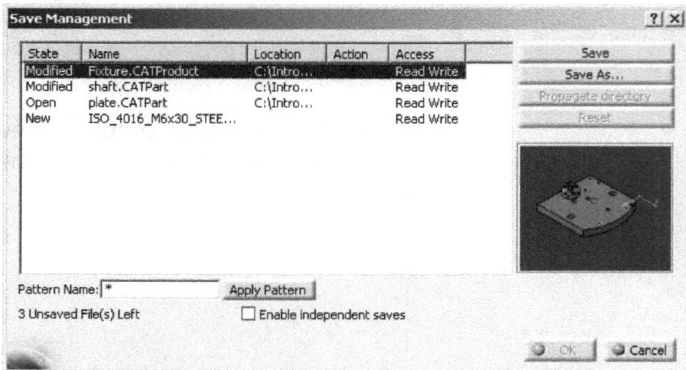

Figure 23–12

3. Note the modified state of the **Fixture.CATProduct** and **shaft.CATPart** files. Also note the state of the catalog bolt part.

4. Select **shaft.CATPart** in the Save Management dialog box and click **Save As**.

5. Enter **shaft_center_hole** as the name of the new shaft component and save the change. The new part, **shaft_center_hole.CATPart**, is now listed in the Save Management dialog box. The **shaft_center_hole.CATPart** model in now being referenced in the assembly in place of the **shaft.CATPart** model.

6. Select the catalog bolt part in the Save Management dialog box and click **Save As**. Save the model in the *Assembly_Jig* folder with the default name. Note the actions listed in the action column in the Save Management dialog box.

7. Click **OK** in the Save Management dialog box.

Task 5 - Replace a component.

1. With the top-level assembly active, select **Shaft_Center_Hole** and click ⬚ (Replace Component). You will place the **shaft.CATPart** model back into the assembly in place of **shaft_center_hole.CATPart**.

2. Double-click on **shaft.CATPart** to select it in the list.

3. Click **OK** in the Impacts on Replace dialog box. The model displays as shown in Figure 23–13.

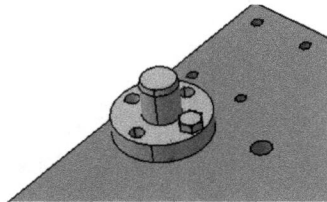

Figure 23–13

4. If time permits, assemble three more bolts using various techniques and replace the pivot shaft part with the **Shaft_Center_Hole** part.

5. Save the assembly and close the file.

Chapter Review Questions

1. You can replace a component with any other component using the Replace Component tool.

    a. True

    b. False

2. When you replace a component you must recreate all the constraints applied to that component.

    a. True

    b. False

3. A library of common parts can be stored in a _____.

    a. Spreadsheet

    b. Catalog

    c. Book

    d. None of the above.

Answers: 1.b, 2.b, 3.b

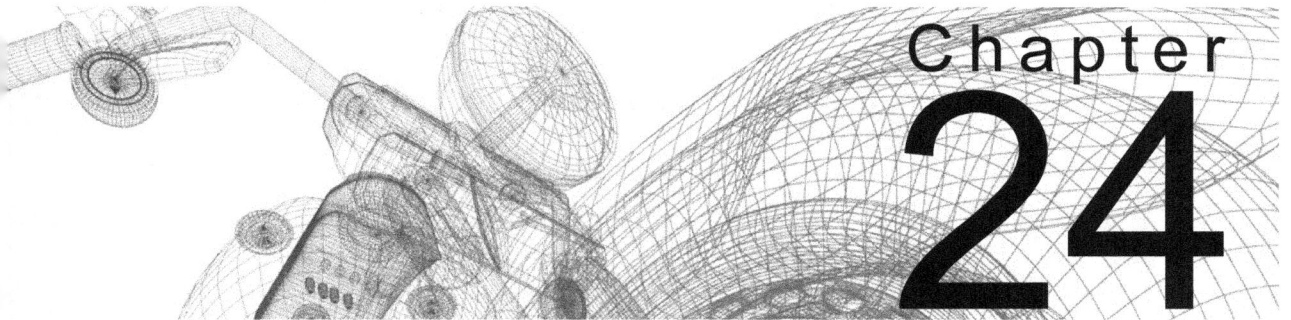

Generative Drafting

This chapter introduces the Generative Drafting workbench by outlining the drawing creation process. You learn how to create, modify, and manipulate drawing views. Once drawing views are placed on a drawing sheet, you must add dimensions and notes to communicate manufacturing information.

Learning Objectives in this Chapter

- Understand the steps required to create a drawing.
- Review the Drafting workbench interface.
- Add views and create a drawing frame and title block.
- Understand the view orientation compass.
- Review the available view properties.
- Learn how to manipulate views.
- Manually create dimensions and move dimensions.
- Learn how to update a drawing when geometry changes.

24.1 Creating a New Drawing

All view geometry and dimension information comes from the 3D model. The 3D model must be open to create a drawing.

How To: Create a New Drawing

1. Open the model that is included in the new drawing as shown in Figure 24–1.

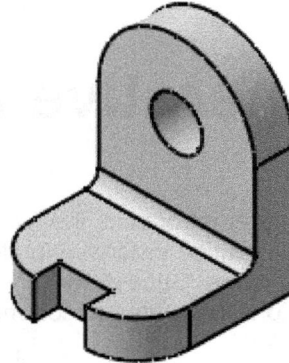

Figure 24–1

2. With the model active, enter the Drafting workbench by selecting **Start>Mechanical Design>Drafting**. The New Drawing Creation dialog box opens, as shown in Figure 24–2.

Begin with a blank sheet.

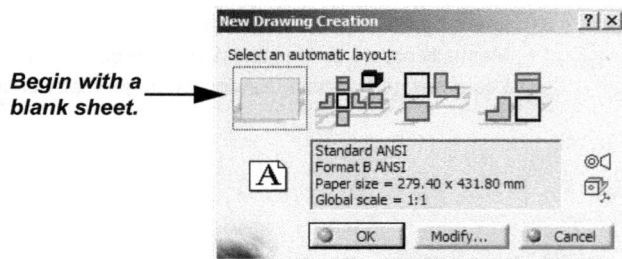

Figure 24–2

3. Click the **Blank Sheet** icon to begin with an empty drawing.
4. Click **Modify** to change the settings. The New Drawing dialog box opens, as shown in Figure 24–3.

Figure 24–3

5. Select the drawing standard (e.g., ANSI, ISO, JIS, etc.). Then select the drawing format and orientation, as required.
6. Click **OK** in the New Drawing dialog box and **OK** in the New Drawing Creation dialog box. A new drawing file opens in the Drafting workbench. Views can now be added to the drawing.

24.2 Drafting Workbench

The user interface of the Drafting workbench displays as shown in Figure 24–4.

Specification tree lists drawing views.

Use sheet tabs to toggle between sheets.

Drawing-specific icons

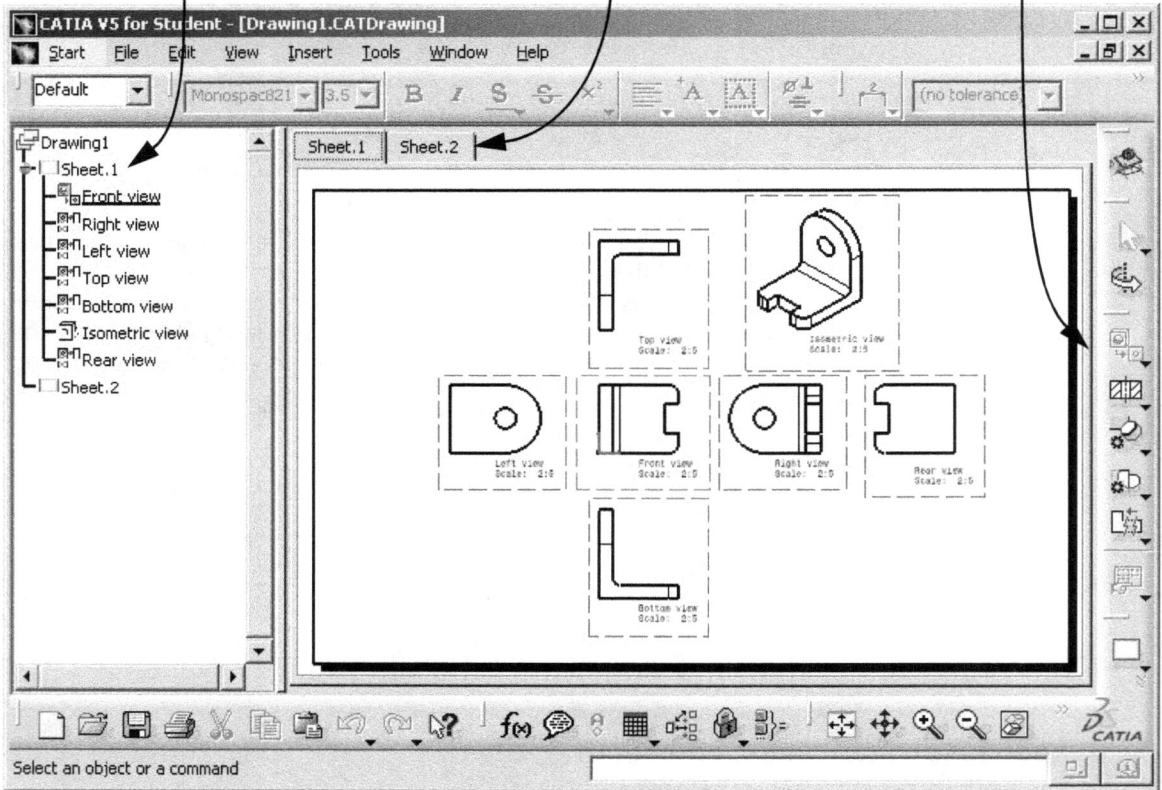

Figure 24–4

24.3 Creating Drawing Frame and Title Block

Title Block

You can assign titles to identify the drawings.

How To: Insert a Title Block

1. Select **Edit>Sheet Background** to set the Drawing mode to Background mode. Note that the background of the drawing changes to blue to indicate that you are in the background.

2. Select **Insert>Drawing>Frame and Title Block**, or click

   (Frame Creation). The Insert Frame and Title Block dialog box opens as shown in Figure 24–5, where you can select the required title block.

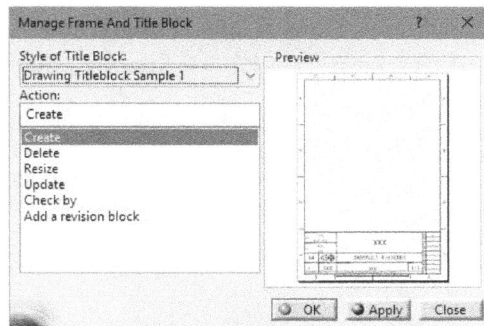

*You can also use this process to delete, resize, and update a title block, as well as to add **CheckedBy** and revision information.*

Figure 24–5

3. Select **Edit>Working views** to exit Background mode.

24.4 Adding Views

Generative views are added to the drawing using the icons in the Views toolbar, as shown in Figure 24–6.

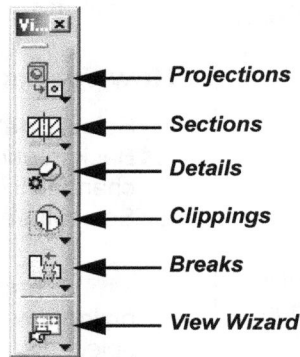

Figure 24–6

General Steps

Use the following general steps to add views to a drawing:

1. Arrange the model and drawing windows (optional).
2. Initiate view creation.
3. Select an orientation reference.
4. Place the view.
5. Add additional views, as required.

Step 1 - Arrange the model and drawing windows (optional).

The placement and orientation of the first drawing view requires the selection of a reference from the 3D model. To facilitate this selection, tile the two windows (recommended) so that you can access them simultaneously.

Select **Window>Tile Horizontally**. The drawing and model windows display as shown in Figure 24–7.

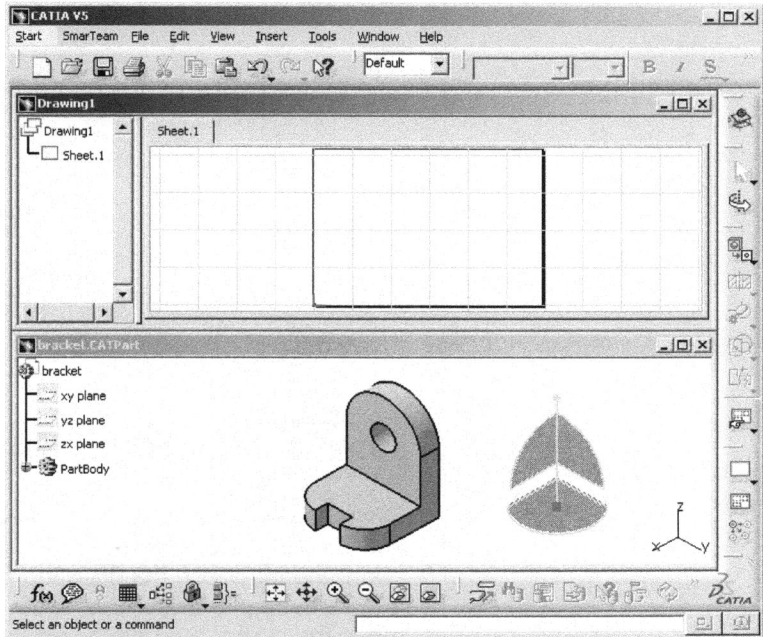

Figure 24–7

Step 2 - Initiate view creation.

The first drawing view can be one of the view types listed below. Select the appropriate icon in the Projections toolbar to initiate the creation of the first view.

View Type	Description
(Front View)	The front view is also known as the main view. You can use the view compass to orient it. Front view Scale: 1:2

| (Isometric View) | An isometric view is used as a reference view, and is typically set at a smaller scale. A reference surface must be selected from the 3D model. You can use the view compass to orient this view. |

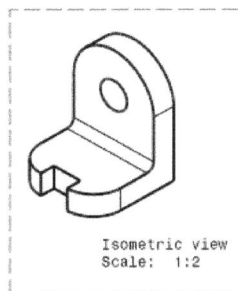

Isometric view
Scale: 1:2

Step 3 - Select an orientation reference.

Once a view icon has been clicked, the software prompts you to select a reference plane on the 3D geometry so that you can orient the model on the drawing. Switch to the model window and select a planar surface, face, or reference plane. As you move the cursor over each surface, a preview displays to help you select the correct surface, as shown in Figure 24–8.

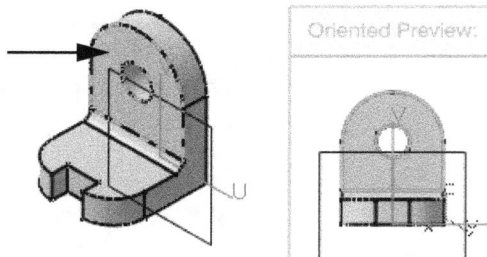

Oriented Preview:

Figure 24–8

Step 4 - Place the view.

Once a reference surface is selected on the 3D model, the view orientation compass displays in the top right corner of the interface, as shown in Figure 24–9.

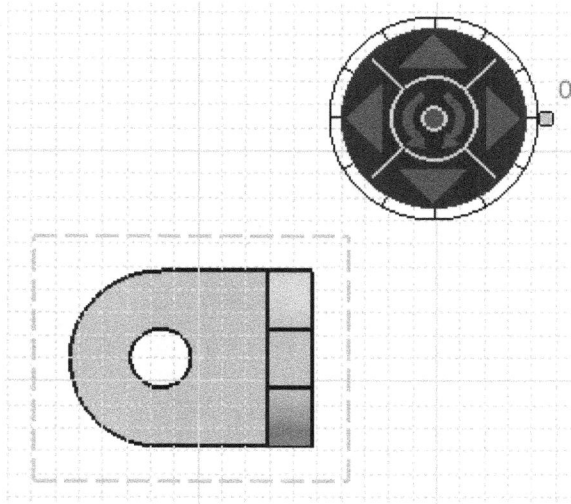

Figure 24–9

View Orientation Compass

The view orientation compass enables you to rotate and flip the front view until you achieve the required orientation. The view compass functionality is shown in Figure 24–10.

Use the shortcut menu to change the compass properties, as shown in Figure 24–11 (right-click over the green rotate handle).

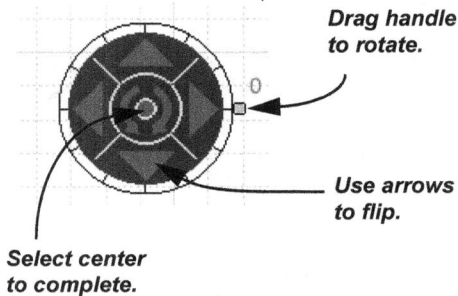

Drag handle to rotate.

Use arrows to flip.

Select center to complete.

Figure 24–10

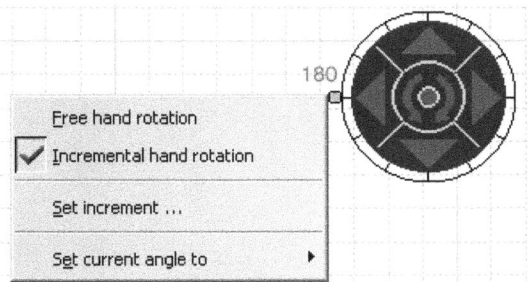

Free hand rotation

✓ Incremental hand rotation

Set increment ...

Set current angle to ▶

Figure 24–11

When you reach the required view orientation, select the center of the compass or select the active view to complete the view definition. The completed view definition is shown in Figure 24–12.

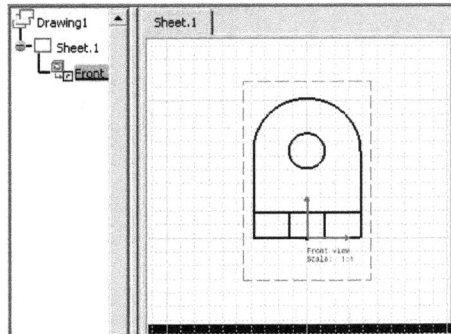

Figure 24–12

The view is added to the sheet in the drawing specification tree. The view displays on the drawing with a red border, indicating that it is the active view. When more than one view is present, a view can be activated by double-clicking on its border.

Step 5 - Add additional views, as required.

A variety of view types can be added to complete the drawing. Three of these view types are as follows:

View Type	Description
(Projection View)	The projection view projects a view from the front view. This creates views such as top, right, left, and bottom. It is placed by selecting a location on the screen. The software applies the correct label (name) based on its position relative to the front view. A projection view maintains the same scale value as its parent view.

 (Detail View)	The detail view creates a scaled view focusing on a specific area of an existing view. The detailed view is created by sketching a circle on an existing, active view that encloses the geometry to be represented. To complete the view, assign a name, boundary type, and note location. The software automatically assigns a label identifying the scale value and view name of the detailed view. Orientation of this view corresponds to its parent view. 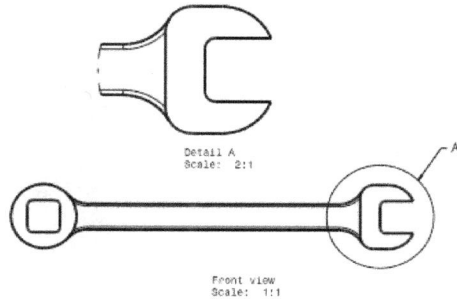 Detail A Scale: 2:1 Front view Scale: 1:1
 (Offset Section View)	The offset section view creates a section that displays all edges that are behind the cutting plane. You can create this view as planar, or as a sketched cutting plane. 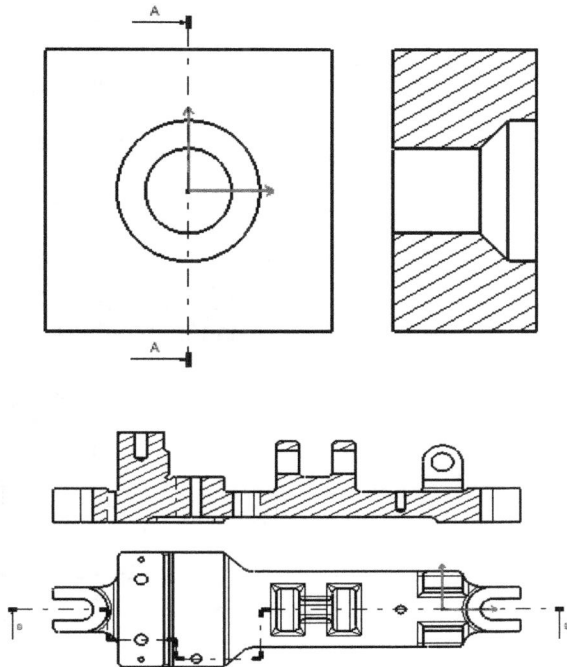

24.5 View Properties

View properties include scale and orientation, view name, frame display, hidden line display, and fillet display. The Properties dialog box is shown in Figure 24–13.

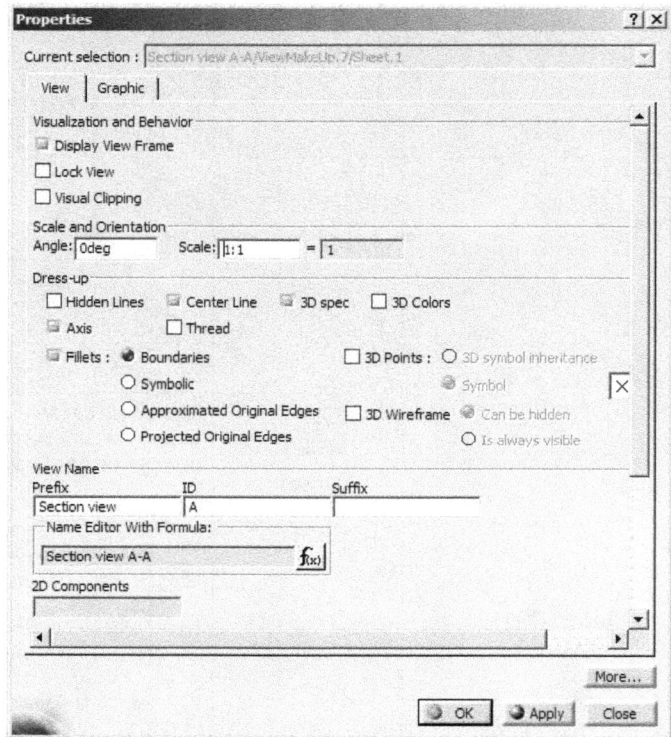

Figure 24–13

You can select to display your views in various ways, as shown in Figure 24–14.

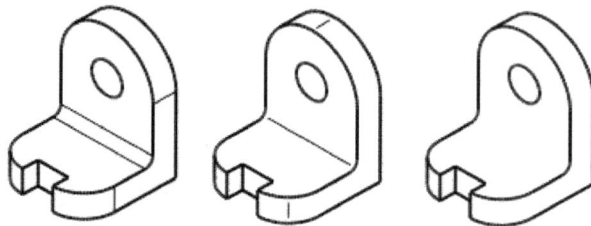

Figure 24–14

Moving Views

You can move a view to another sheet or in the same sheet by selecting the dashed line frame of the view and draging it to the required location.

- Standard windows shortcut keys can also be used: Cut (<Ctrl>+<X>) and Paste (<Ctrl>+<V>)

To move a view to another sheet, cut and paste it from the display or in the specification tree.

Delete View

To delete a view, select the view from the display or in the specification tree, right-click and select **Delete**.

Hide/Show

You can hide a view to simplify the sheet. To hide a view, select the view from the display or specification tree, right-click and select **Hide/Show**.

Section Arrow Properties

To modify section arrows, select the arrows, right-click and select **Properties**.

Hatching

To modify section hatching, select the section view from the display, right-click and select **Properties**.

24.6 Manually Creating Dimensions

Use the Dimensions flyout in the Dimensioning toolbar, as shown in Figure 24–15, to manually create dimensions.

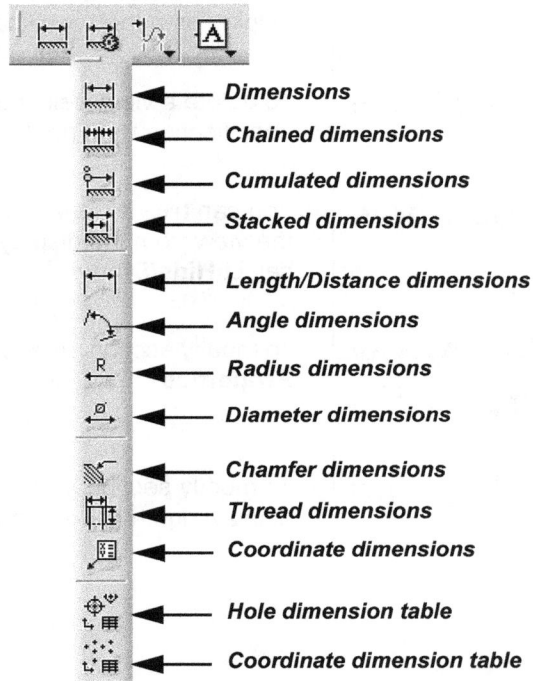

◄— Dimensions
◄— Chained dimensions
◄— Cumulated dimensions
◄— Stacked dimensions

◄— Length/Distance dimensions
◄— Angle dimensions
◄— Radius dimensions
◄— Diameter dimensions

◄— Chamfer dimensions
◄— Thread dimensions
◄— Coordinate dimensions

◄— Hole dimension table
◄— Coordinate dimension table

Figure 24–15

How To: Manually Create a Dimension

1. Click the icon that resembles the required dimension type.
2. Select entities as dimension references, as shown in Figure 24–16.

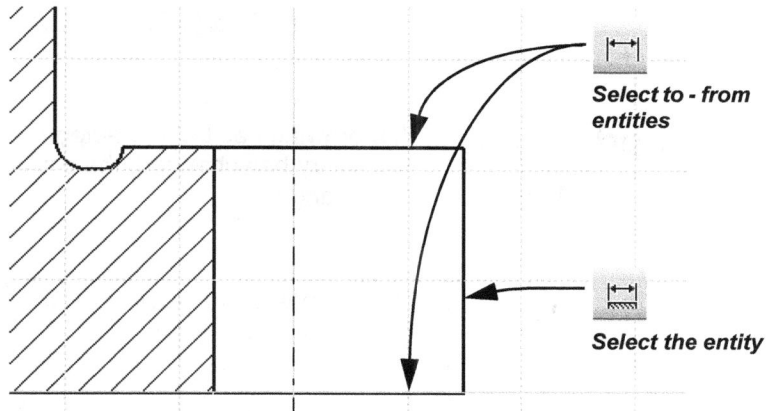

Select to - from entities

Select the entity

Figure 24–16

3. Place the dimension, as shown in Figure 24–17.

2 2

Figure 24–17

Moving Dimensions

To clean up the display move dimensions using one of the following methods:

- Click and drag on a handle to move both witness lines.

- Click and drag on a dimension to move it left, right, up, or down.

- Click on an arrow head to *flip* it.

These methods are shown in Figure 24–18.

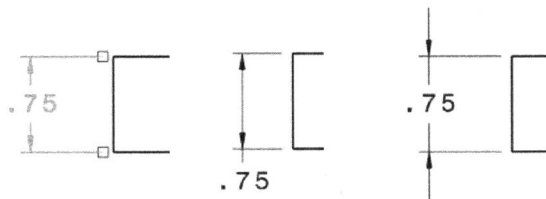

. 7 5

. 7 5

. 7 5

Figure 24–18

24.7 Changed Geometry

Updating a Drawing

If a drawing has been created from a 3D model and the model geometry has changed, the drawing must be updated to reflect the changes.

- To update the drawing, click (Update current sheet) or press <Ctrl>+<U>.

- A grayed out indicates that the 3D model has not changed, and that the model does not need to be updated.

Links to 3D Models

The drawing cannot update if a drawing is open but the 3D model it references is not. To open the referenced model, select **Edit>Links>**_Pointed Documents_ tab.

The software displays the file path to the referenced 3D model. Click **Open** to bring the model in session.

Practice 24a | Create a Drawing

Practice Objectives

- Create a new drawing.
- Place views using the View Wizard.
- Manipulate the views in various ways.

In this practice, you will use a part to create a new drawing. The drawing will consist of two sheets and multiple views. One of the sheets displays as shown in Figure 24–19. You will use the View Wizard to place and modify the views.

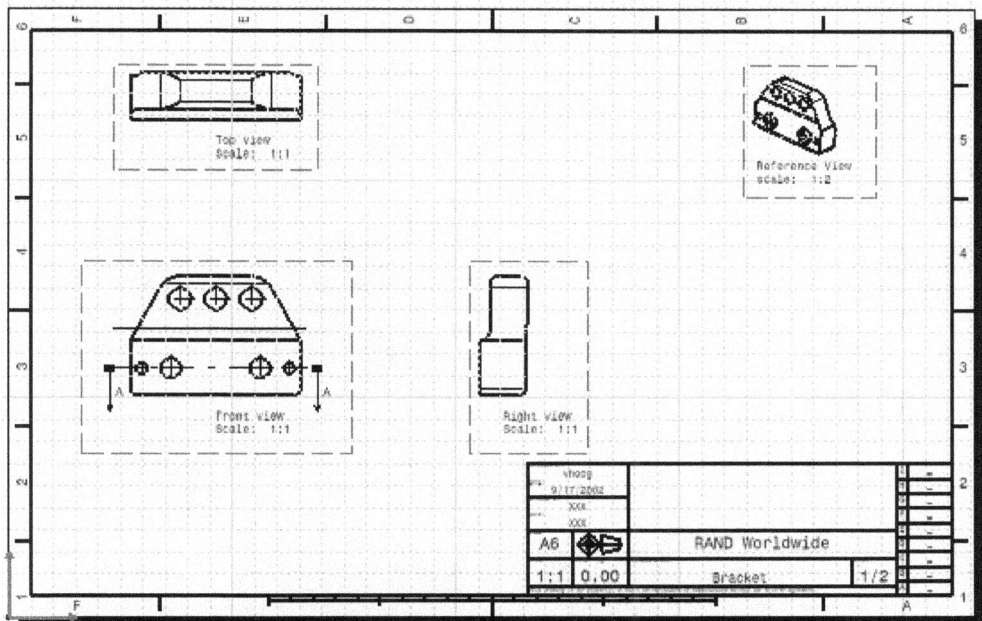

Figure 24–19

Task 1 - Create a blank drawing.

1. Select **File>Open** and select **Bracket.CATPart**.

2. Select **Start>Mechanical Design>Drafting**. The New Drawing Creation dialog box opens.

3. Click the **Blank Sheet** icon, as shown in Figure 24–20.

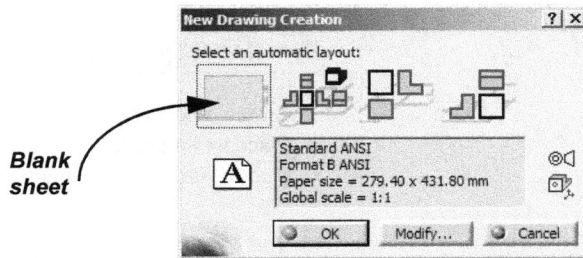

Figure 24–20

4. Click **Modify**. In the New Drawing dialog box that opens, select the following options, as shown in Figure 24–21:

- *Standard:* **ANSI**
- *Format:* **B ANSI**
- *Orientation:* **Landscape**

Figure 24–21

5. Click **OK** twice to create an empty drawing.

Task 2 - Create a front view.

1. Arrange the windows by selecting **Window>Tile Horizontally**. This enables you to select from the drawing or model without having to switch windows.

2. Click (Front View) in the Views toolbar.

3. You must now orient the view by selecting a face from the model. Select anywhere in the **Bracket.CATPart** window and hover over the faces of the model. An Orientation Preview window displays the resulting view orientation.

4. Select the face shown in Figure 24–22. This surface is selected to face the front of the screen in the front view.

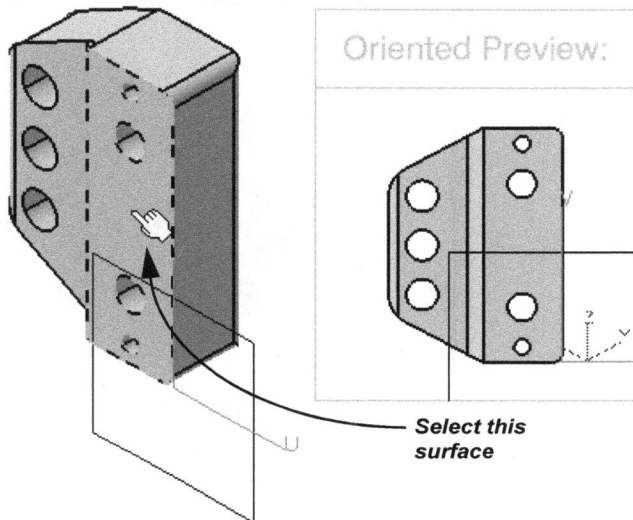

Figure 24–22

5. The display automatically toggles back to the drawing sheet. A compass displays in the top right corner of the interface. Use the cursor to drag the green handle to the 270° location. The front view is oriented as shown in Figure 24–23.

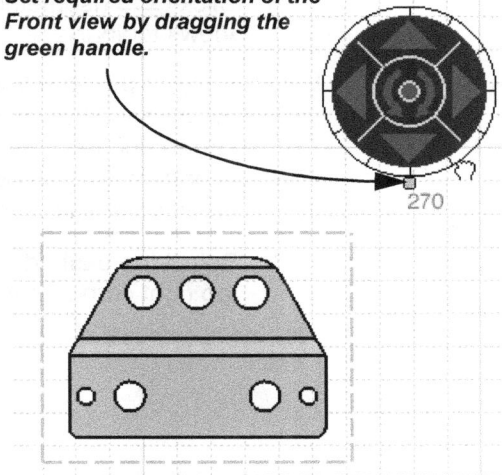

Figure 24–23

6. Select the center of the compass to complete the orientation. The drawing sheet is shown in Figure 24–24.

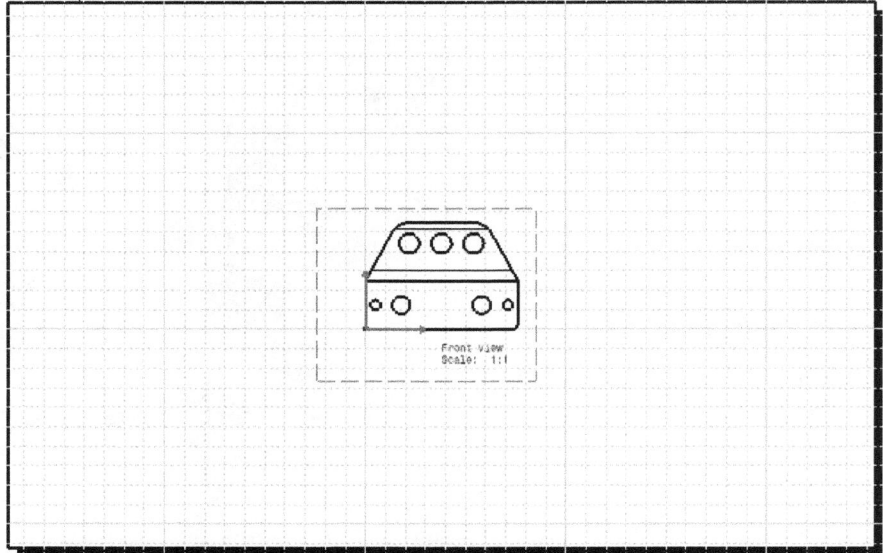

Figure 24–24

Task 3 - Create an isometric view.

1. Click ▣ (Isometric View) in the Projections flyout in the Views toolbar.

2. Activate the **Bracket.CATPart** window and select a face on the model. The software orients the isometric view using the current model orientation. Therefore, the face selected is not important. The software places the view on the drawing and the orientation compass displays.

3. Select the dashed green border of the view and drag it to the top right corner of the drawing, as shown in Figure 24–25.

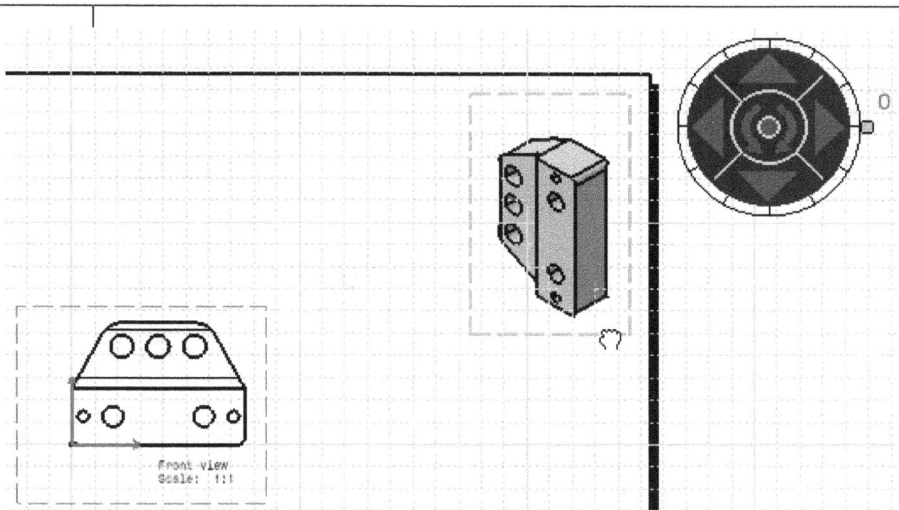

Figure 24–25

4. Select anywhere on the drawing to complete the creation of the view.

Design Considerations

The border of the front view is currently red, while the border of the isometric view is blue. The red border indicates that this is the active view. Any view operations are always performed on the active view. As well, the creation of a section or projection view will reference the active view. Double-click on the view border to activate a view.

Task 4 - Create a projection view.

In this task, you will project a view from the front view. The front view must be active.

1. Ensure that the front view is active.

2. Click (Projection View).

3. Position the cursor around the front view. Four possible projections can be created, as shown in Figure 24–26.

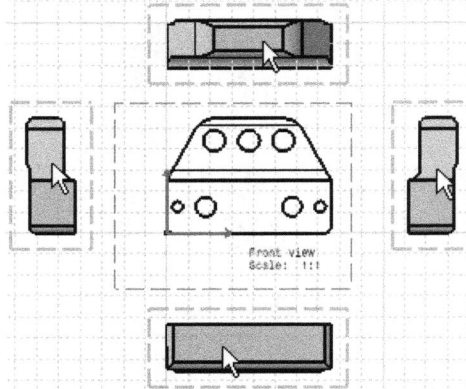

Figure 24–26

4. Create the projection to the right of the front view. The drawing displays as shown in Figure 24–27.

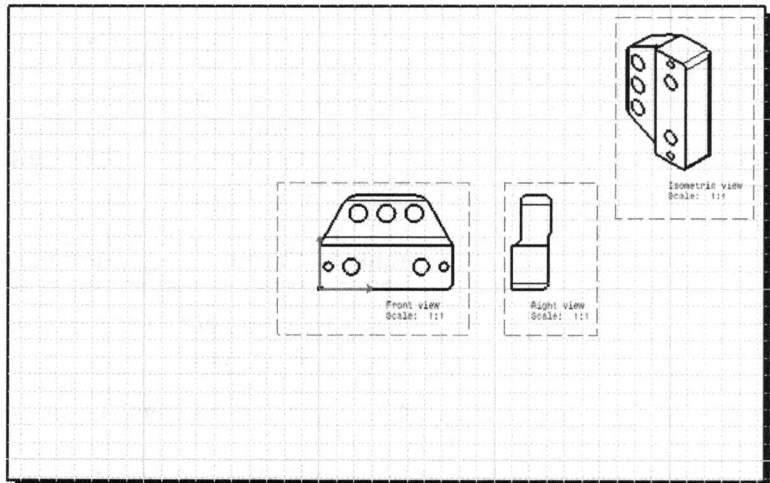

Figure 24–27

Task 5 - Move the views.

1. Select the dashed view frame of the front view and drag it to the bottom left corner of the sheet.

2. Experiment by moving the right view. Move the isometric view as well and note the differences between the linked and unlinked views.

Design Considerations

The projected right view is a child of the front view, so it maintains an aligned position with it. The isometric view can be moved independent of the front view.

Task 6 - Change the properties of a view

1. Right-click on the Front view in the specification tree and select **Properties**.

2. Select **Center Line** and **Axis** in the *Dress-up* area in the *View* tab of the Properties dialog box, as shown in Figure 24–28.

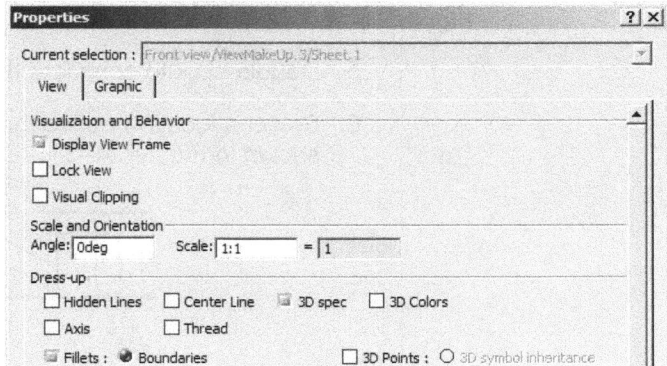

Figure 24–28

3. Click **OK**.

Task 7 - Create a section view.

1. Zoom in on the front view.

2. Click (Offset Section View) in the Views toolbar.

To align the start of the section line with the hole, try positioning the cursor over the hole to create a coincidence constraint before starting the creation of the line.

3. Sketch a line that starts approximately one grid square space to the left of the view, as shown in Figure 24–29. Enable the system to assume an alignment with the axis of the Hole feature.

4. Drag the line across the front view and select a location approximately one grid square space to the right of the view, as shown in Figure 24–30.

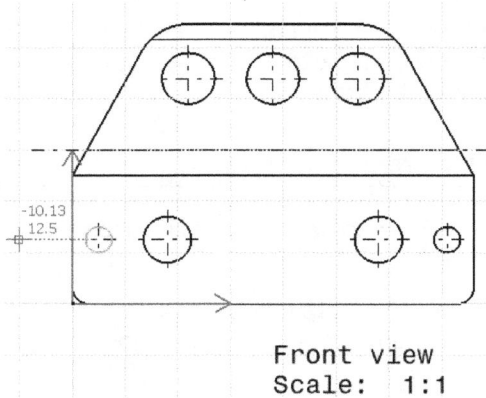

Figure 24–29

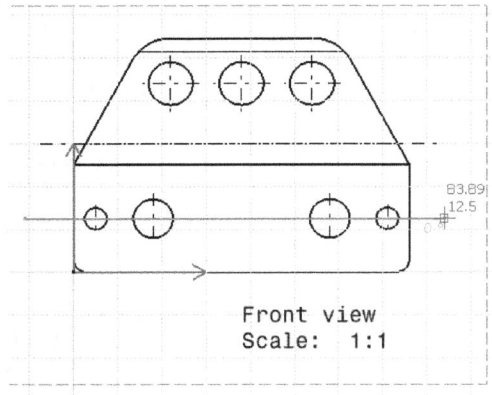

Figure 24–30

5. Double-click to complete the x-section definition.

6. Select a location above the front view. The view displays as shown in Figure 24–31.

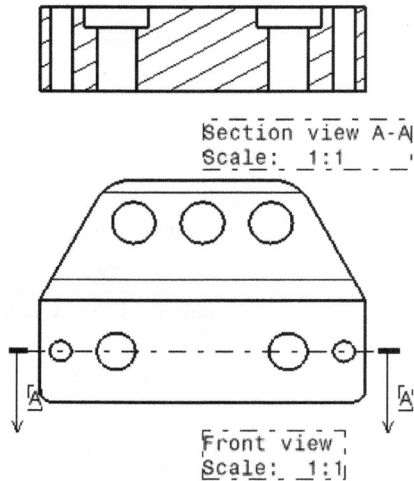

Figure 24–31

If the section view call out arrows are pointing in the wrong direction, right-click on the arrow. From the shortcut menu, select **Callout (Section View).x object>Definition** as shown in Figure 24–32.

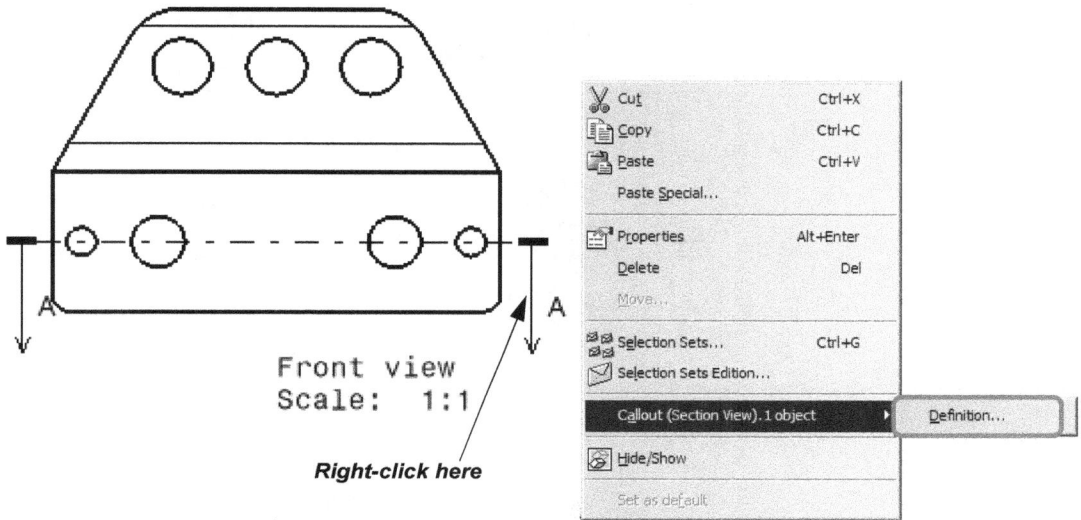

Figure 24–32

7. The Profile Edition mode displays. From the Edit/ Replace toolbar, click [icon] (Invert Profile Direction).

8. Click [icon] (End Profile Edition) to complete the action.

Task 8 - Add a detail view.

1. Zoom in on the section view.

2. Double-click on the dashed frame of the section view to make it active. The border turns red and the name of the view in the view tree is underlined, indicating that this view is the active view.

3. Click [icon] (Quick Detail View) in the Views toolbar.

4. Select a location on the right side of the counterbored hole feature and drag the cursor to create a circle callout, as shown in Figure 24–33.

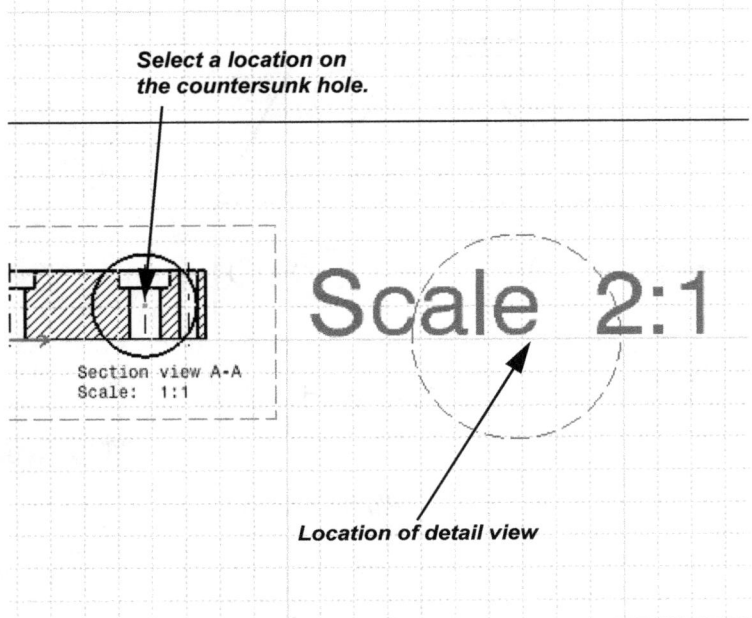

Select a location on the countersunk hole.

Scale 2:1

Section view A-A
Scale: 1:1

Location of detail view

Figure 24–33

*If the axis is not visible, right-click and select **Properties>Axis** in the View tab, in the Properties dialog box.*

5. Select a point to the right of the section view to define a location for the detail view. The complete detail view containing the callout is shown in Figure 24–34.

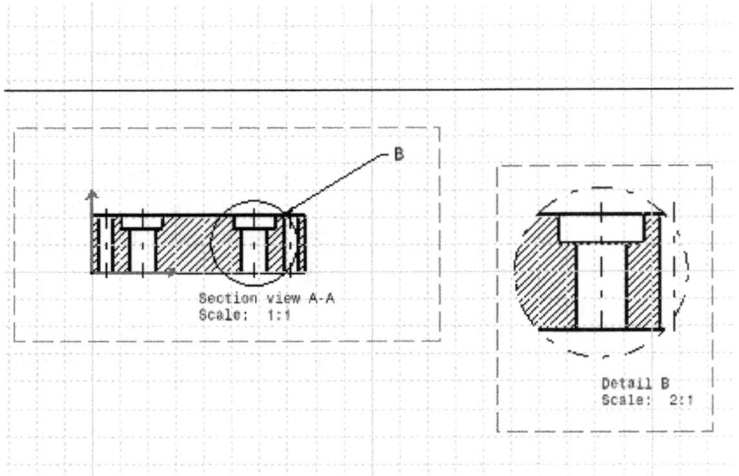

B

Section view A-A
Scale: 1:1

Detail B
Scale: 2:1

Figure 24–34

Task 9 - Insert a frame and title block.

1. You must change the mode for the drawing to enable editing of the background. Select **Edit>Sheet Background** to set the Drawing mode to Background mode.

2. Select **Insert>Drawing>Frame and Title Block**. The Insert Frame and Title Block dialog box opens.

3. Set *Style of Titleblock* to **Drawing_Titleblock_RAND**, as shown in Figure 24–35.

*If Drawing_Titleblock_ RAND is not available, select **Drawing Titleblock Sample 1**.*

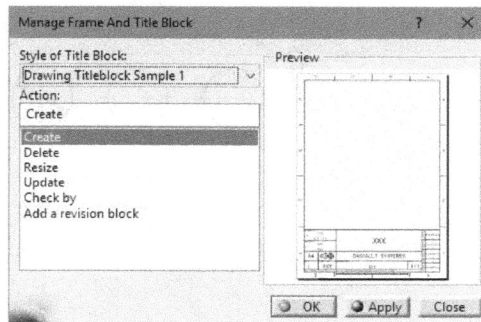

Figure 24–35

4. Click **Apply**. The frame and title block display. Close the Insert Frame and Title Block dialog box.

5. Select **Edit>Working Views** and reposition the drawing views as required.

6. Save the drawing as **Bracket.CATDrawing**.

7. Do not close the file. It is used in the next practice.

Practice 24b | Annotate a Drawing

Practice Objective

• Create and manipulate dimensions.

In this practice, you will add dimensions to a drawing. You will modify these dimensions and explore their various properties. The end result is shown in Figure 24–36.

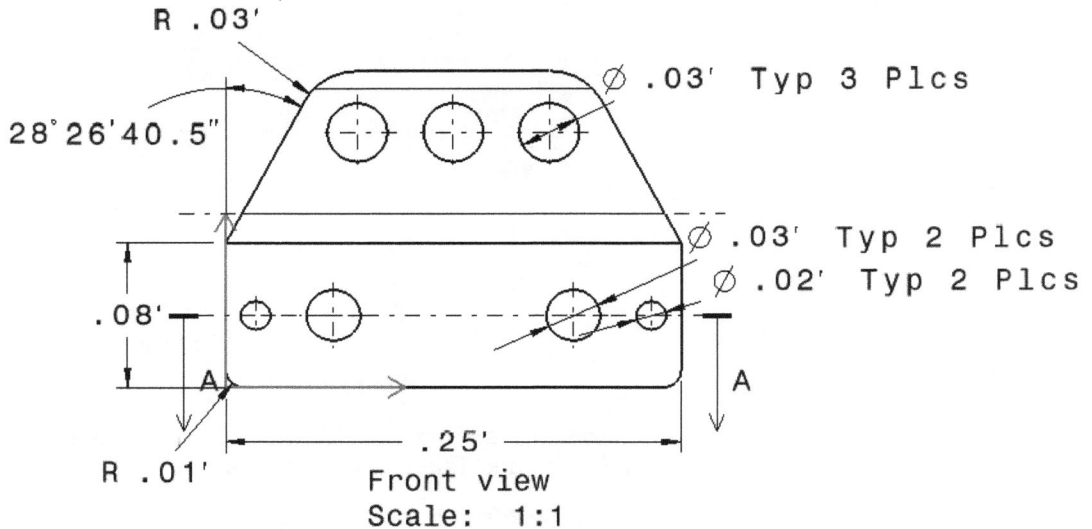

R .03'

28°26'40.5"

Ø .03' Typ 3 Plcs

Ø .03' Typ 2 Plcs

Ø .02' Typ 2 Plcs

.08'

.25'

A

A

R .01'

Front view
Scale: 1:1

Figure 24–36

Task 1 - Generate manual dimensions.

1. Open **Bracket_Views.CATDrawing**.

2. Activate the front view.

3. Hide all views except the front view.

*If you completed the last practice you can continue to use **Bracket.CATDrawing** instead.*

4. Zoom in on the front view and click ⊞ (Dimensions).

5. Select the edge shown in Figure 24–37. The software creates a linear dimension for the edge.

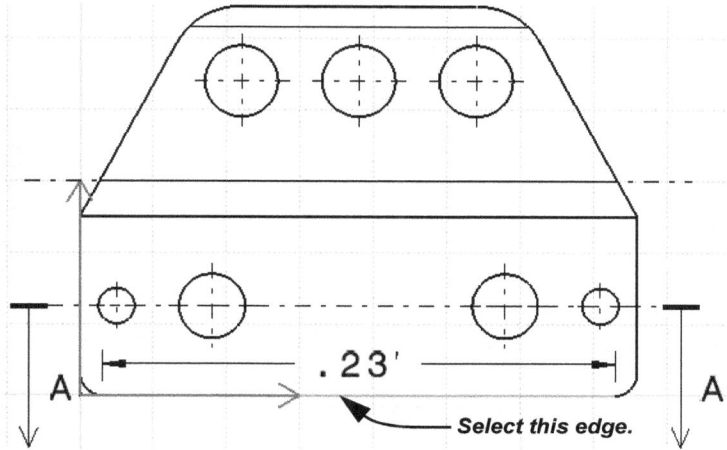

Figure 24–37

6. Select a second reference for the dimension, as shown in Figure 24–38. The software displays a length dimension between the two references.

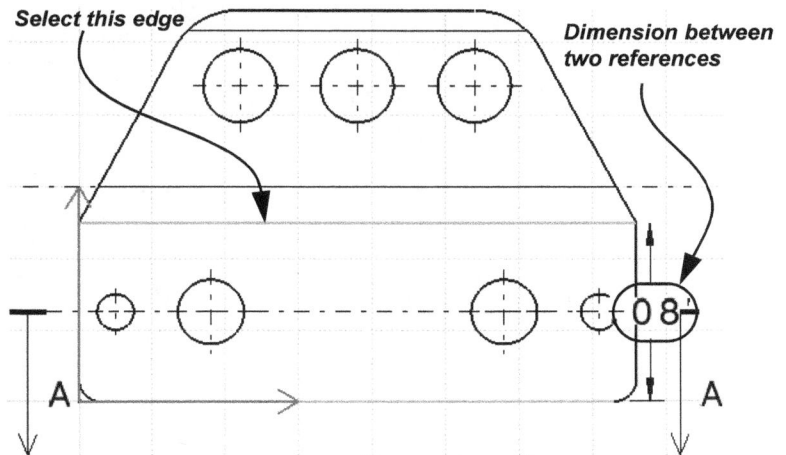

Figure 24–38

7. Press the left mouse button to complete the reference selection and place the dimension. The dimension highlights in orange and can now be moved.

8. Move the dimension to the side, as shown in Figure 24–39.

9. Create the horizontal dimension shown in Figure 24–40.

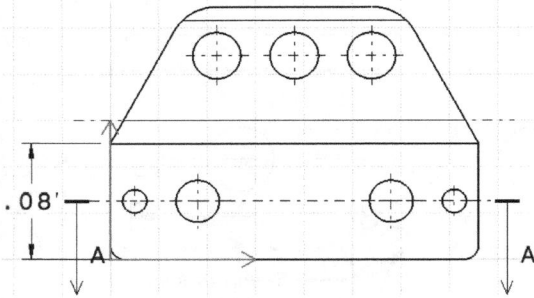

Figure 24–39

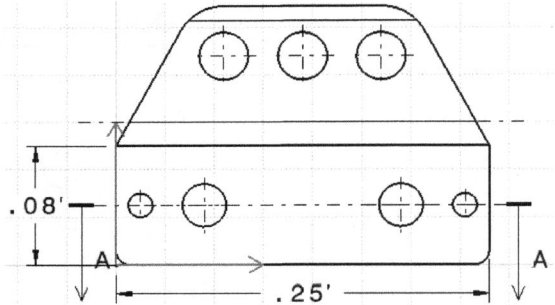

Figure 24–40

10. Click (Diameter Dimensions) in the Dimensions toolbar.

11. Select the circle as shown in Figure 24–41, and place the diameter dimension.

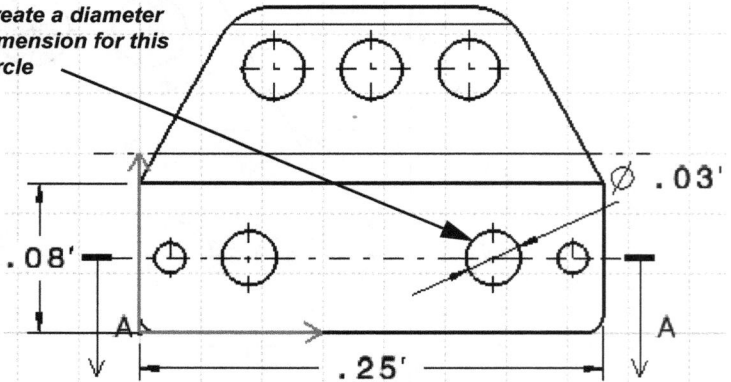

Figure 24–41

12. Use ⌀↔ (Diameter Dimensions) and R↔ (Radius Dimensions) to create the four other dimensions as shown in Figure 24–42.

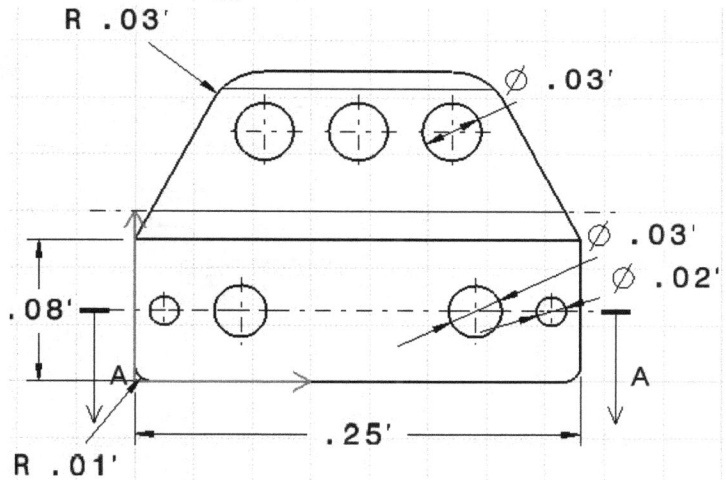

Figure 24–42

Task 2 - Manipulate dimensions.

1. Select the **.03'** diameter dimension on the right Hole feature, as shown in Figure 24–43.

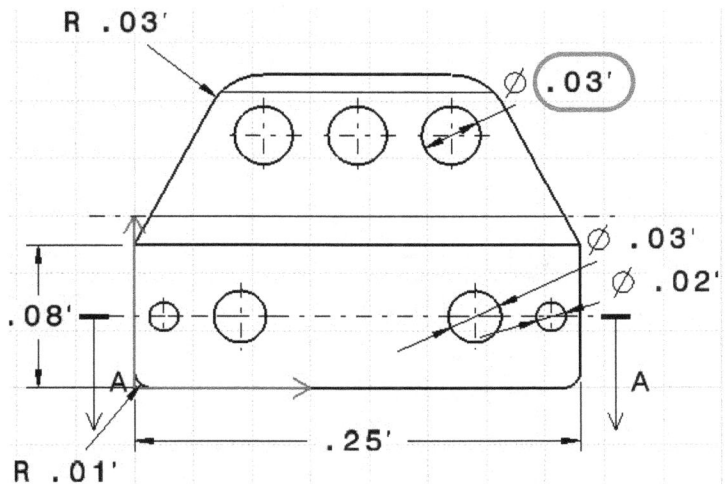

Figure 24–43

2. Right-click and select **Properties**.

3. Select the *Dimension Texts* tab in the Properties dialog box.

4. Enter **Typ 3 Plcs** in the suffix text field, as shown in Figure 24–44.

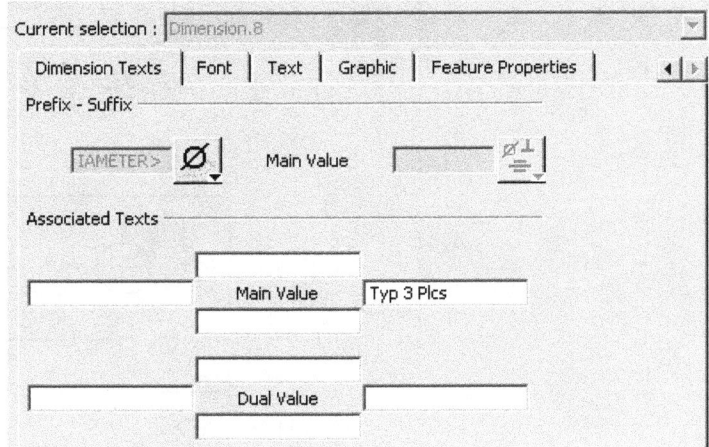

Figure 24–44

5. Click **Apply** and **OK**. The dimension updates with the changes, as shown in Figure 24–45.

6. Select the **.03'** and **.02'** diameter dimensions (hold <Ctrl> to select both) and add the suffix dimension text, as shown in Figure 24–46.

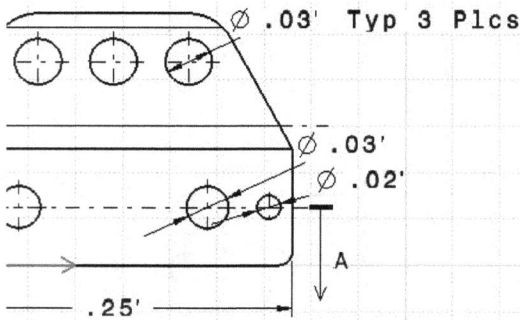

Figure 24–45

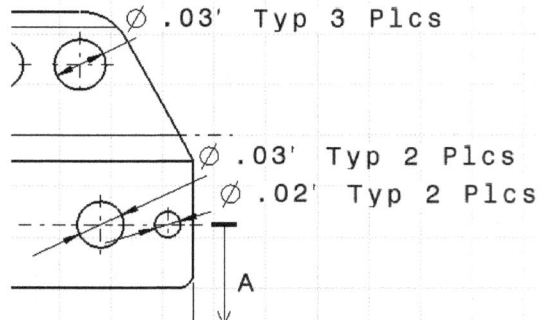

Figure 24–46

Task 3 - Create an angle dimension on the Front view.

1. Click ![icon] (Angle Dimensions) (click the flyout arrow if not visible) and select the two entities shown in Figure 24–47.

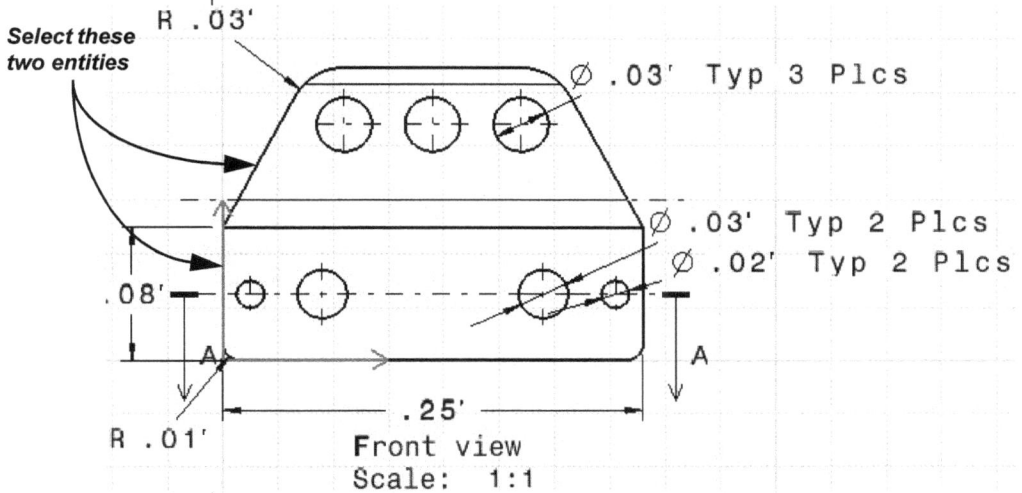

Figure 24–47

2. Define how the angled dimension is generated. While moving the dimension into position, right-click and select **Angle Sector>Sector 2**, as shown in Figure 24–48.

Depending on where the cursor is located, you might need to select a different angle sector to get the result shown in Figure 24–49.

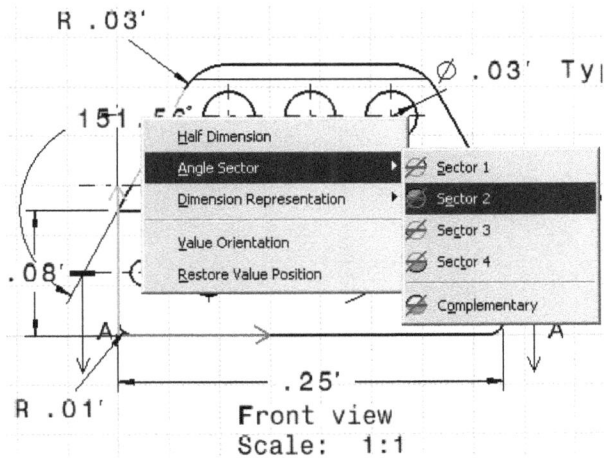

Figure 24–48

3. Place the dimension with the left mouse button. The dimension displays as shown in Figure 24–49.

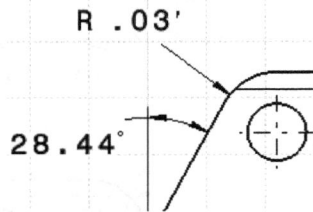

R .03'

28.44°

Figure 24–49

4. Modify the format of the angle dimension by right-clicking it and selecting **Properties**.

5. Select the *Value* tab in the Properties dialog box. Modify the value in the *Display* field to **3 factors** and the value in the *Precision* field to **0.1** as shown in Figure 24–50.

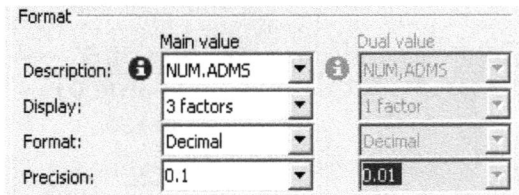

Format	Main value		Dual value	
Description:	NUM.ADMS	▼	NUM.ADMS	▼
Display:	3 factors	▼	1 Factor	▼
Format:	Decimal	▼	Decimal	▼
Precision:	0.1	▼	0.01	▼

Figure 24–50

6. Apply the changes and close the Properties dialog box. The dimension displays as shown in Figure 24–51.

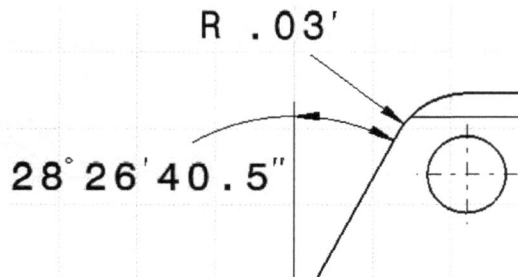

R .03'

28°26'40.5"

Figure 24–51

7. The completed drawing is shown in Figure 24–52. Save the drawing and close the window.

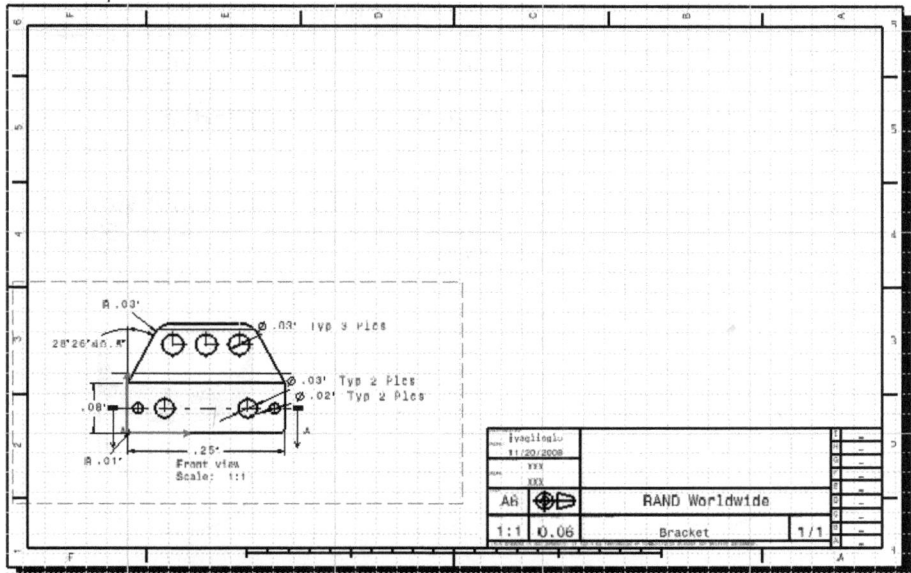

Figure 24–52

Practice 24c | (Optional) Piston Drawing

Practice Objective

- Create a drawing without instruction.

1. Finish the **Piston.CATPart** model if it has not been completed.

2. Create a new drawing called **Piston**. Add views and detailing, as shown in Figure 24–53.

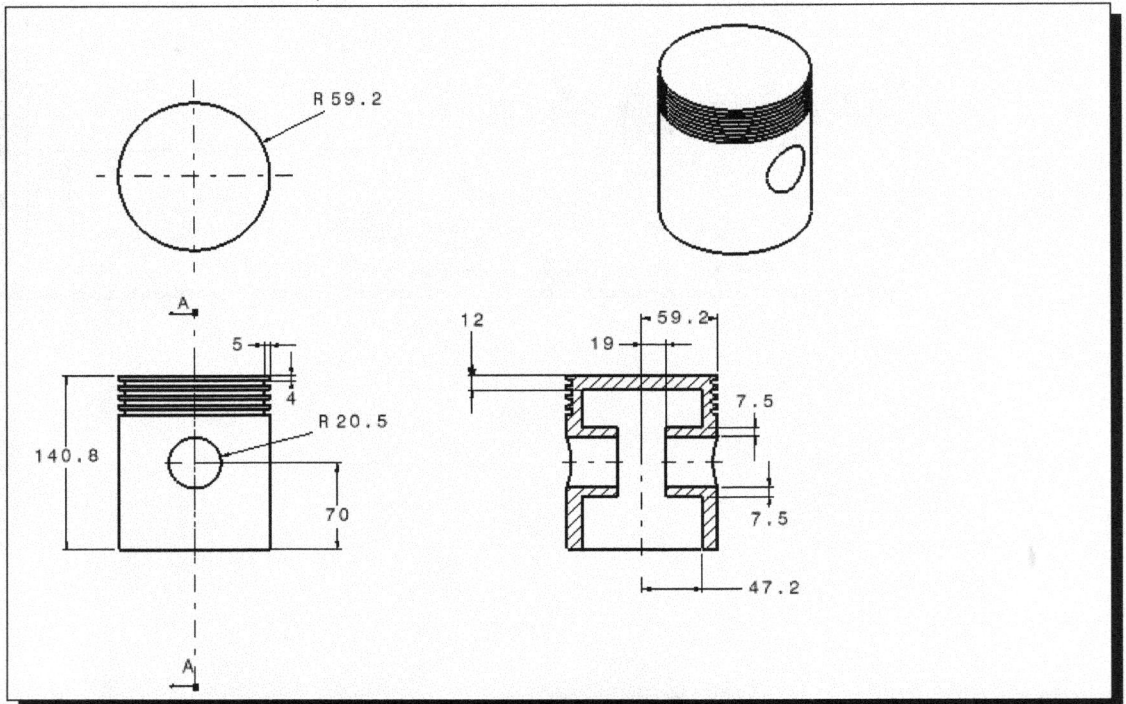

Figure 24–53

Practice 24d | (Optional) Flange Drawing

Practice Objective

- Create a drawing without instruction.

1. Finish the **Flange.CATPart** model if it has not been completed.

2. Create a new drawing called **Flange**. Add views and detailing, as shown in Figure 24–54.

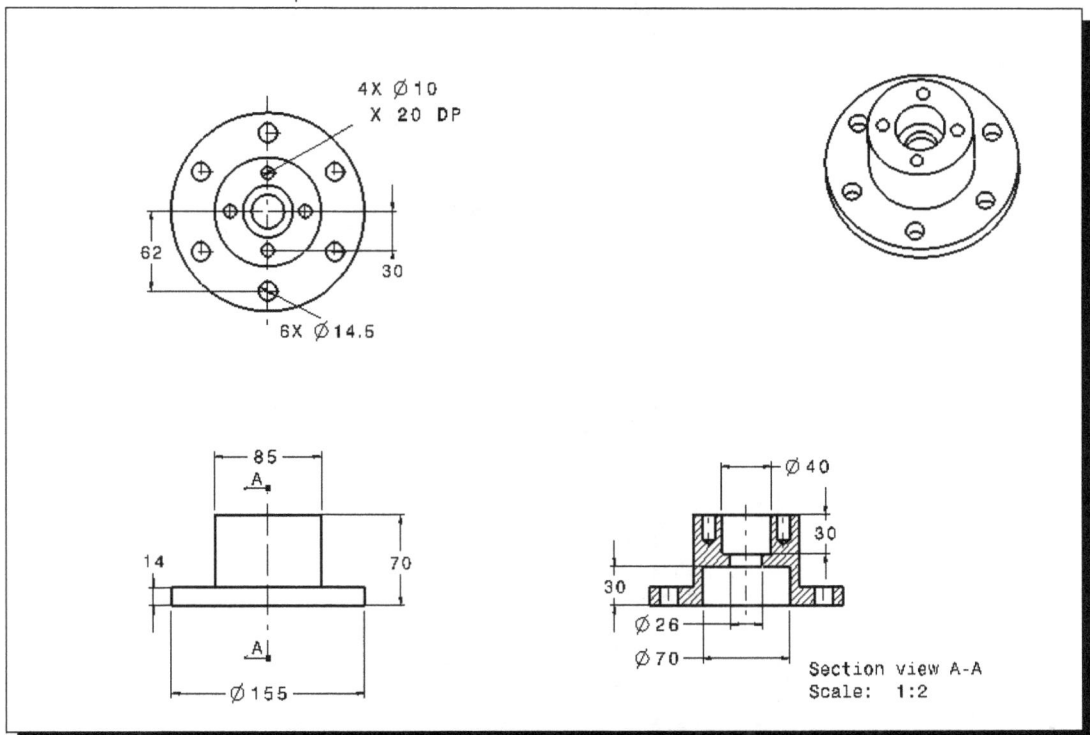

4X Ø10
X 20 DP

62

30

6X Ø14.5

85
A

14

70

A

Ø155

Ø40

30

30

Ø26

Ø70

Section view A-A
Scale: 1:2

Figure 24–54

Chapter Review Questions

1. Which of the following view types can be the first view in a drawing?

   a. Offset Section view

   b. Projection view

   c. Front view

   d. Detail view

2. When you delete a parent view, dependent views are automatically deleted.

   a. True

   b. False

3. An isometric view is placed in the drawing at the same orientation as in the model. This orientation can be changed inside the drawing using the compass before the view has been placed.

   a. True

   b. False

4. The only way to tell which view on a drawing is active is that is has a red border.

   a. True

   b. False

5. Dimensions created in a drawing update when changes are made to the model.

   a. True

   b. False

6. You cannot hide a drawing view.

   a. True

   b. False

7. Changes in the 3D model automatically display in the drawing.

   a. True

   b. False

Answers: 1.c, 2.b, 3.a, 4.b, 5.b, 6.a, 7.b

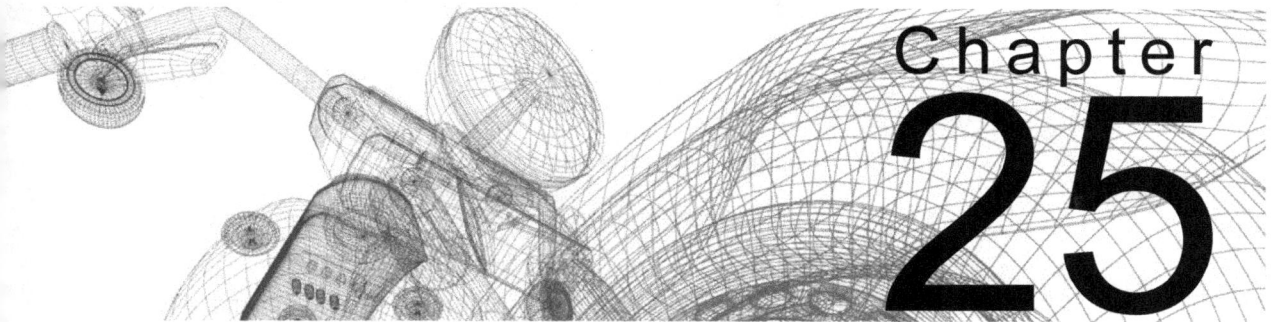

Chapter
25

Effective Modeling

This chapter discusses some important design considerations which ensures that your model captures the design intent more effectively. You also learn some tips and techniques that improve the creation of your model.

Learning Objectives in this Chapter

- Review the design considerations for creating models.
- Review various modeling best practices.
- Review various tools for investigating models.
- Create a model on your own that meets the defined design criteria.

25.1 Design Considerations

A designer strives to create models that meet the following criteria:

- Communicates the design's intent.

- Can be prototyped to generate a model that meets design goals.

- Is flexible, so future design changes require minimal effort.

- Can be used to generate design documentation (drawings).

Before creating any model (part or assembly), consider its design intent. This helps to select the most appropriate options that maximize design flexibility. Considering *what if* scenarios that might be introduced into the model in the future helps to create a robust model that requires minimal effort when being modified.

Part Design Considerations

Consider the following:

- What is the best choice for the base feature?

- Which parent/child relationships are required?

- Which parent/child relationships should be avoided?

- Which dimensions are required to drive the design?

- Which dimensions on the part might change?

- How should the part react to dimension changes?

- Should relations be added to capture design intent?

- What feature order best captures the design intent?

Assembly Design Considerations

Consider the following:

- What is the best choice for the base component?

- Which assembly constraints capture the design intent?

- Which parent/child relationships are required?

- Which parent/child relationships should be avoided?

- Should the offset constraint be used, rather than contact? Will motion be simulated in the design?

- Should subassembly components be incorporated into the design?

- Should assembly relations be added to capture design intent?

- What component order best captures the design intent?

- What parts should display an assembly feature?

External References

Ensure that the use of external references complies with company standards. Keep this functionality in the experience level of the users in your company.

25.2 Modeling Tips and Techniques

Planning ahead helps you better understand the design intent that you want to achieve, resulting in a more robust model.

As you acquire new modeling tips and techniques, you should consider them all during the design stage. In addition, many companies have their own design requirements or best practice recommendations. A summary of some of the key items includes the following:

Features

Features either add or remove material from the model to create the final design. Consider the following tips when adding features to the model:

- It is recommended to select a stable base feature that requires few changes. The base feature is used as a parent for additional features.

- Use feature types (dress-up or sketched) that best capture the design intent.

- Select references that correctly reflect the intent of the design. Any reference selected while creating a new feature establishes a dependency between the new feature and the reference.

- Carefully consider which sketching tools should be used to capture the design intent (3D projection).

- Use depth options (**Up to Next**, **Up to Last**, **Up To Surface**, etc.) to capture the design intent. Also, consider whether an **Offset** option is required.

- Create features in the order that best captures the design intent.

- Apply names to features so they can be easily identified in the specification tree.

Drafts and Fillets

Review company standards when considering whether to add drafts to accurately represent your model. Some companies prefer not to add drafts to models, while others insist on it. Some considerations include the following:

• Does adding a draft increase model accuracy or does it adversely affect drawing creation?

• If a draft is not added to the model, how do you communicate this requirement to the manufacturer?

• Does the model need to undergo interference or analysis testing? If so, you might want to add the draft to ensure accurate results.

Fillets generally represent the finishing stages of the design. Similar to drafts, always consider company standards when deciding whether to add fillets to the model. Some considerations include the following:

• Is the model going to be used for FEA analysis? If so, fillets are generally removed before the analysis and are therefore not required.

• Depending on the type of fillets used in the model, the manufacturing department might remove fillets that are created at the end of the process. In this situation, you might want to add all fillets and only deactivate the ones that you do not need for generating the NC toolpaths.

• Variable fillets are difficult to manufacture. Consider the necessity of this feature as you create a model.

• Avoid using fillets as references, as they are often changed or completely removed in the design process. This could result in a major model failure.

The order of fillet and draft creation can affect the resulting geometry, and should be added as late as possible in the feature order. Always consider the order in which features are manufactured (for example, draft geometry should be added to the model before fillets). It is also recommended that you consider the order in which fillets are added to the model and how the order affects the geometry.

25.3 Model Investigation

It is not practical to assume that you might always be creating new models. In many situations, you are required to continue someone else's design or make modifications to a previously completed model. It is recommended to investigate the model to review it. Some reviewing techniques that can be used include the following:

- Scan the model

- Specification tree

- Parent/child relationships

Model Scan

The scan functionality reviews the construction history of a model, one feature at a time. This is especially useful when working with models that were created by others. The **Scan** tool can give you an idea of the modeler's design intent and modeling techniques by replaying and reviewing the design.

Specification Tree

The specification tree displays all features in the model and can be used to review the model. Consider renaming features to enable others to easily search for features. Display relations and parameters.

Parent/Child

The **Parent/Children** tool displays information on the parents and children of a selected feature. To activate the **Parent/Children** tool, select a feature in the specification tree or on the screen, right-click and select **Parent/Children**. Alternatively, you can select **Tools>Parent/Children** in the menu bar after selecting the feature.

25.4 Interactive Practice

The model shown in Figure 25–1 must be designed so that the changes shown in Figure 25–1 and Figure 25–2 are possible. Consider the following issues:

- Types of features to be used

- Best feature order

- Dimension scheme

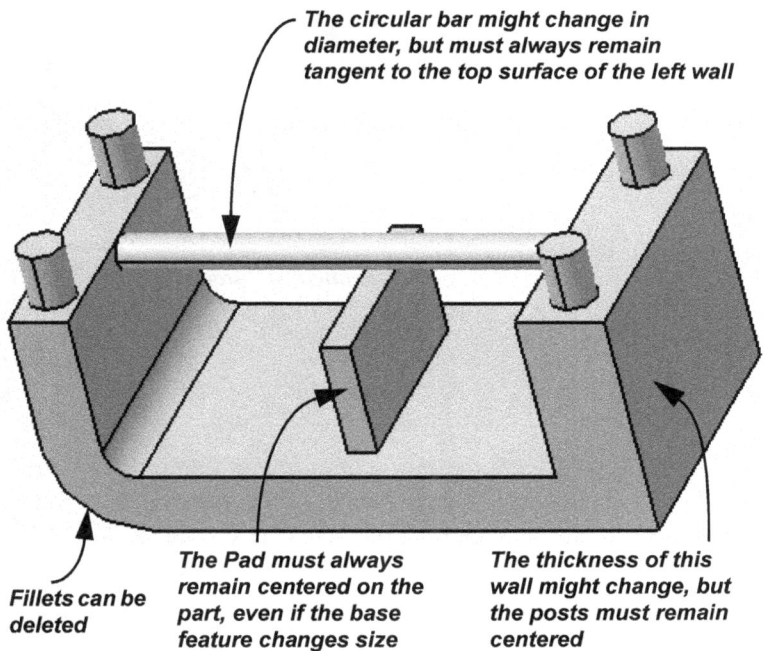

The circular bar might change in diameter, but must always remain tangent to the top surface of the left wall

Fillets can be deleted

The Pad must always remain centered on the part, even if the base feature changes size

The thickness of this wall might change, but the posts must remain centered

Figure 25–1

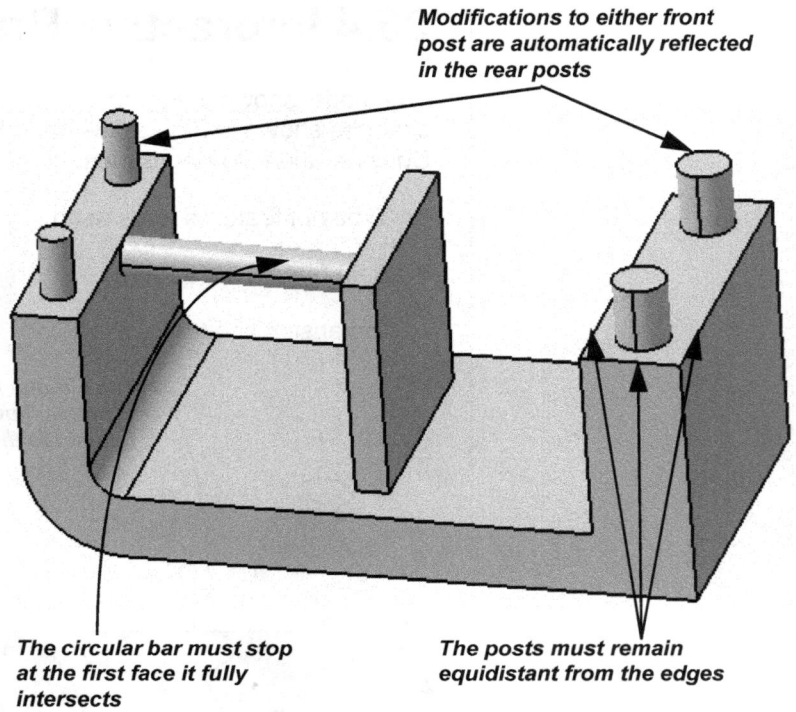

Modifications to either front post are automatically reflected in the rear posts

The circular bar must stop at the first face it fully intersects

The posts must remain equidistant from the edges

Figure 25–2